A Guide to Selected Federal Agency Programs and Publications for Librarians and Teachers

A Guide to
Selected Federal Agency Programs
and Publications for
Librarians and Teachers

Carol Smallwood

LIBRARIES UNLIMITED, INC.
Littleton, Colorado
1986

Copyright © 1986 Carol Smallwood
All Rights Reserved
Printed in the United States of America

No part of this publication may be reproduced, stored in a retrieval system, or transmitted, in any form or by any means, electronic, mechanical, photocopying, recording, or otherwise, without the prior written permission of the publisher.

LIBRARIES UNLIMITED, INC.
P.O. Box 263
Littleton, Colorado 80160-0263

Library of Congress Cataloging-in-Publication Data

Smallwood, Carol, 1939-
    A guide to selected federal agency programs and publications for librarians and teachers.

    Includes index.
    1. Acquisition of government publications.
2. United States--Government publications--Bibliography.
3. Libraries and state--United States--Directories.
4. Federal aid to libraries--United States--
Directories. 5. Education and state--United States--
Directories. 6. Federal aid to education--United
States--Directories. 7. Teaching--Aids and devices--
Catalogs. I. Title.
Z688.G6S53 1986   025.2'834   86-10561
ISBN 0-87287-528-8

Libraries Unlimited books are bound with Type II nonwoven material that meets and exceeds National Association of State Textbook Administrators' Type II nonwoven material specifications Class A through E.

To **MARTIN COHEN,** Professor Emeritus,
School of Librarianship, WMU

Contents

INTRODUCTION xv

ADMINISTRATIVE CONFERENCE OF THE UNITED STATES 1
ADMINISTRATIVE OFFICE OF THE UNITED STATES COURTS 1
AGENCY FOR INTERNATIONAL DEVELOPMENT 1
AGRICULTURAL COOPERATIVE SERVICE 2
AGRICULTURAL RESEARCH SERVICE 2
AGRICULTURAL STABILIZATION AND CONSERVATION SERVICE 3
AMERICAN FOLKLIFE CENTER 3
ANACOSTIA NEIGHBORHOOD MUSEUM 4
ANIMAL AND PLANT HEALTH INSPECTION SERVICE 4
ANTIETAM NATIONAL BATTLEFIELD 5
APPALACHIAN REGIONAL COMMISSION 5
ARCHITECT OF THE CAPITOL 6
ARCHITECTURAL AND TRANSPORTATION BARRIERS COMPLIANCE BOARD 6
BUREAU OF ALCOHOL, TOBACCO AND FIREARMS 7
BUREAU OF ECONOMIC ANALYSIS 9
BUREAU OF ENGRAVING AND PRINTING 9
BUREAU OF INDIAN AFFAIRS 9
BUREAU OF LABOR STATISTICS 11
BUREAU OF LAND MANAGEMENT 12
BUREAU OF MINES 14
BUREAU OF RECLAMATION 15
BUREAU OF THE CENSUS 16
BUREAU OF THE MINT 18
CARL SANDBURG HOME 19
CENTER FOR HEALTH PROMOTION AND EDUCATION 19
CENTER FOR PREVENTION SERVICES 20

CENTER FOR THE BOOK...20
CENTERS FOR DISEASE CONTROL..20
CENTRAL INTELLIGENCE AGENCY..25
CHILDREN'S LITERATURE CENTER..25
CLARA BARTON NATIONAL HISTORIC SITE..25
CLEARINGHOUSE ON CHILD ABUSE AND NEGLECT INFORMATION......26
CLEARINGHOUSE ON THE HANDICAPPED..27
COMMISSION OF FINE ARTS..27
COMMISSION ON CIVIL RIGHTS..28
COMPTROLLER OF THE CURRENCY..29
CONGRESSIONAL BUDGET OFFICE...30
CONSERVATION AND RENEWABLE ENERGY INQUIRY AND REFERRAL SERVICE.............30
CONSUMER PRODUCT SAFETY COMMISSION......................................31
COPYRIGHT OFFICE..32
COUNCIL ON ENVIRONMENTAL QUALITY...33
CROP REPORTING BOARD..33
DEATH VALLEY NATIONAL MONUMENT...36
DEPARTMENT OF AGRICULTURE...36
DEPARTMENT OF COMMERCE...36
DEPARTMENT OF EDUCATION...36
DEPARTMENT OF ENERGY...37
DEPARTMENT OF HOUSING AND URBAN DEVELOPMENT....................41
DEPARTMENT OF JUSTICE...42
DEPARTMENT OF LABOR...47
DEPARTMENT OF STATE..48
DEPARTMENT OF THE AIR FORCE...49
DEPARTMENT OF THE INTERIOR...49
DEPARTMENT OF THE NAVY..49
DEPARTMENT OF THE TREASURY...51
DEPARTMENT OF TRANSPORTATION..51
DEPOSITORY ADMINISTRATION BRANCH...52
DIVISION OF BIRTH DEFECTS AND DEVELOPMENTAL DISABILITIES......55
ECONOMIC DEVELOPMENT ADMINISTRATION.....................................56
ECONOMIC RESEARCH SERVICE...56
EDGAR ALLAN POE NATIONAL HISTORIC SITE....................................59
EMPLOYMENT STANDARDS ADMINISTRATION....................................59
ENERGY INFORMATION ADMINISTRATION...60
ENVIRONMENTAL PROTECTION AGENCY...65

EQUAL EMPLOYMENT OPPORTUNITY COMMISSION....................................67
ERIC PROCESSING AND REFERENCE FACILITY.....................................67
EXTENSION SERVICE...68
FEDERAL AVIATION ADMINISTRATION..73
FEDERAL BUREAU OF INVESTIGATION..75
FEDERAL BUREAU OF PRISONS..79
FEDERAL COMMUNICATIONS COMMISSION....................................80
FEDERAL CROP INSURANCE CORPORATION....................................81
FEDERAL DEPOSIT INSURANCE CORPORATION.................................82
FEDERAL ELECTION COMMISSION..83
FEDERAL EMERGENCY MANAGEMENT AGENCY..................................84
FEDERAL HALL NATIONAL MEMORIAL...93
FEDERAL HIGHWAY ADMINISTRATION..94
FEDERAL HOME LOAN BANK BOARD..94
FEDERAL LABOR RELATIONS AUTHORITY......................................95
FEDERAL MARITIME COMMISSION..97
FEDERAL MEDIATION AND CONCILIATION SERVICE...........................98
FEDERAL RESERVE SYSTEM..98
FEDERAL TRADE COMMISSION..100
FISH AND WILDLIFE SERVICE...102
FOOD AND DRUG ADMINISTRATION...103
FOOD AND NUTRITION INFORMATION CENTER................................105
FOOD AND NUTRITION SERVICE..106
FOREIGN AGRICULTURAL SERVICE..107
FOREIGN CLAIMS SETTLEMENT COMMISSION OF THE UNITED STATES.....................108
FOREST SERVICE...108
FREDERICK DOUGLASS HOME..109
GENERAL ACCOUNTING OFFICE DOCUMENT HANDLING AND INFORMATION
SERVICES FACILITY..109
GENERAL SERVICES ADMINISTRATION......................................110
GOVERNMENT PRINTING OFFICE...112
HEAD START BUREAU...114
HEALTH RESOURCE CENTER..115
HEALTH RESOURCES AND SERVICES ADMINISTRATION.......................117
HEMINGWAY MUSEUM..117
HIGH BLOOD PRESSURE INFORMATION CENTER..............................117
HUD USER...118
HUMAN NUTRITION INFORMATION SERVICE..................................119
IMMIGRATION AND NATURALIZATION SERVICE...............................119

x / Contents

INTERNAL REVENUE SERVICE	123
INTERNATIONAL TRADE ADMINISTRATION	128
INTERSTATE COMMERCE COMMISSION	131
JOHN F. KENNEDY CENTER FOR THE PERFORMING ARTS	132
LIBRARY OF CONGRESS GEOGRAPHY AND MAP DIVISION	133
LIBRARY OF CONGRESS INFORMATION OFFICE	133
LIBRARY OF CONGRESS LOAN DIVISION	133
LIBRARY OF CONGRESS MOTION PICTURE, BROADCASTING AND RECORDED SOUND DIVISION	133
LIBRARY OF CONGRESS SCIENCE REFERENCE SECTION	134
LIBRARY OF CONGRESS SERIAL AND GOVERNMENT PUBLICATIONS DIVISION	134
LIBRARY OF CONGRESS TOUR OFFICE	135
LONGFELLOW NATIONAL HISTORIC SITE	135
MARITIME ADMINISTRATION	135
MATERIALS AND TRANSPORTATION BUREAU	136
MINERALS MANAGEMENT SERVICE	137
MINORITY BUSINESS DEVELOPMENT AGENCY INFORMATION CLEARINGHOUSE	137
NATIONAL AERONAUTICS AND SPACE ADMINISTRATION	138
NATIONAL AGRICULTURAL LIBRARY	142
NATIONAL ARCHIVES AND RECORDS SERVICE	143
NATIONAL ARCHIVES TRUST FUND BOARD	145
NATIONAL AUDIOVISUAL CENTER	145
NATIONAL BUREAU OF STANDARDS	147
NATIONAL CANCER INSTITUTE	152
NATIONAL CAPITAL PARKS	152
NATIONAL CENTER FOR DEVICES AND RADIOLOGICAL HEALTH	153
NATIONAL CENTER FOR EDUCATION IN MATERNAL AND CHILD HEALTH	155
NATIONAL CENTER FOR EDUCATION STATISTICS	161
NATIONAL CENTER FOR PREVENTION AND CONTROL OF RAPE	161
NATIONAL CENTER FOR SERVICE LEARNING	162
NATIONAL CLEARINGHOUSE FOR ALCOHOL INFORMATION	162
NATIONAL CLEARINGHOUSE FOR BILINGUAL EDUCATION	168
NATIONAL CLEARINGHOUSE FOR DRUG ABUSE INFORMATION	168
NATIONAL COMMISSION ON LIBRARIES AND INFORMATION SCIENCE	170
NATIONAL COUNCIL ON THE HANDICAPPED	170
NATIONAL DIGESTIVE DISEASES EDUCATION AND INFORMATION CLEARINGHOUSE	170
NATIONAL ENDOWMENT FOR THE ARTS	171
NATIONAL ENDOWMENT FOR THE HUMANITIES	174
NATIONAL EYE INSTITUTE	178
NATIONAL GALLERY OF ART	178

NATIONAL HEALTH INFORMATION CLEARINGHOUSE..................................179
NATIONAL HEART, LUNG, AND BLOOD INSTITUTE.................................179
NATIONAL HIGHWAY TRAFFIC SAFETY ADMINISTRATION............................180
NATIONAL HISTORICAL PUBLICATIONS AND RECORDS COMMISSION...................184
NATIONAL INFORMATION CENTER FOR HANDICAPPED CHILDREN AND YOUTH............188
NATIONAL INJURY INFORMATION CLEARINGHOUSE.................................188
NATIONAL INSTITUTE OF ALLERGY AND INFECTIOUS DISEASES.....................189
NATIONAL INSTITUTE OF DENTAL RESEARCH.....................................190
NATIONAL INSTITUTE OF EDUCATION...190
NATIONAL INSTITUTE OF GENERAL MEDICAL SCIENCES............................193
NATIONAL INSTITUTE OF JUSTICE...193
NATIONAL INSTITUTE OF MENTAL HEALTH.......................................193
NATIONAL INSTITUTE OF NEUROLOGICAL AND COMMUNICATIVE DISORDERS
    AND STROKE...194
NATIONAL INSTITUTE ON AGING...195
NATIONAL INSTITUTES OF HEALTH...195
NATIONAL LABOR RELATIONS BOARD..196
NATIONAL LIBRARY OF MEDICINE..199
NATIONAL LIBRARY SERVICE FOR THE BLIND AND PHYSICALLY HANDICAPPED.........201
NATIONAL MARINE FISHERIES SERVICE...211
NATIONAL MEDIATION BOARD..211
NATIONAL MUSEUM OF AMERICAN ART...211
NATIONAL OCEAN SERVICE..212
NATIONAL OCEANIC AND ATMOSPHERIC ADMINISTRATION...........................213
NATIONAL PARK SERVICE...216
NATIONAL PARK SERVICE SCIENCE PUBLICATIONS OFFICE.........................217
NATIONAL PORTRAIT GALLERY...217
NATIONAL PRESERVATION PROGRAM OFFICE......................................218
NATIONAL REHABILITATION INFORMATION CENTER................................218
NATIONAL SCIENCE FOUNDATION...219
NATIONAL SUDDEN INFANT DEATH SYNDROME CLEARINGHOUSE.......................220
NATIONAL TECHNICAL INFORMATION SERVICE....................................220
NATIONAL TECHNICAL INSTITUTE FOR THE DEAF.................................222
NATIONAL TRANSPORTATION SAFETY BOARD......................................222
NATIONAL WEATHER SERVICE..223
NATIONAL WILDLIFE REFUGES...224
NUCLEAR REGULATORY COMMISSION...225
OCCUPATIONAL SAFETY AND HEALTH ADMINISTRATION.............................225
OCCUPATIONAL SAFETY AND HEALTH REVIEW COMMISSION..........................227

xii / Contents

OFFICE OF CLINICAL REPORTS AND INQUIRIES	228
OFFICE OF CONSUMER AFFAIRS	228
OFFICE OF ELEMENTARY AND SECONDARY EDUCATION	229
OFFICE OF FEDERAL PROCUREMENT POLICY	230
OFFICE OF HUMAN DEVELOPMENT SERVICES	230
OFFICE OF OCEAN AND COASTAL RESOURCE MANAGEMENT	231
OFFICE OF PRESIDENTIAL LIBRARIES	234
OFFICE OF SCIENTIFIC AND TECHNICAL INFORMATION	235
OFFICE OF STUDENT FINANCIAL ASSISTANCE	236
OFFICE OF TECHNOLOGY ASSESSMENT	236
OFFICE OF TERRITORIAL AND INTERNATIONAL AFFAIRS	237
OFFICE OF THE FEDERAL REGISTER	237
OFFICE OF THE LAW LIBRARIAN	238
OFFICE OF WOMEN IN DEVELOPMENT	238
OFFICE ON SMOKING AND HEALTH	239
PANAMA CANAL COMMISSION	239
PASSPORT SERVICES	239
PATENT AND TRADEMARK OFFICE	240
THE PRESIDENT'S COMMITTEE ON EMPLOYMENT OF THE HANDICAPPED	241
THE PRESIDENT'S COUNCIL ON PHYSICAL FITNESS AND SPORTS	244
SAINT LAWRENCE SEAWAY DEVELOPMENT CORPORATION	245
SALEM MARITIME NATIONAL HISTORIC SITE	245
SECURITIES AND EXCHANGE COMMISSION	245
SMALL BUSINESS ADMINISTRATION	247
SMITHSONIAN ENVIRONMENTAL RESEARCH CENTER	254
SMITHSONIAN INSTITUTION OFFICE OF ELEMENTARY AND SECONDARY EDUCATION	254
SMITHSONIAN INSTITUTION PRESS	255
SMITHSONIAN INSTITUTION TRAVELING EXHIBITION SERVICE	255
SMITHSONIAN INSTITUTION VISITOR INFORMATION AND ASSOCIATES' RECEPTION CENTER	256
SOCIAL SECURITY ADMINISTRATION	257
SOIL CONSERVATION SERVICE	258
TENNESSEE VALLEY AUTHORITY	262
U.S. ARMS CONTROL AND DISARMAMENT AGENCY	264
U.S. ARMY CORPS OF ENGINEERS	264
U.S. COAST GUARD	267
U.S. CUSTOMS SERVICE	268
U.S. GEOLOGICAL SURVEY	271
U.S. HOUSE OF REPRESENTATIVES	281

Contents / xiii

U.S. INFORMATION AGENCY..282
U.S. INTERNATIONAL TRADE COMMISSION..282
U.S. MISSION TO THE UNITED NATIONS...282
U.S. POSTAL SERVICE...282
U.S. SECRET SERVICE...284
URBAN MASS TRANSPORTATION ADMINISTRATION.......................................288
WATER RESOURCES SCIENTIFIC INFORMATION CENTER................................289
THE WHITE HOUSE OFFICE...290
WOMEN'S BUREAU...290
WOMEN'S RIGHTS NATIONAL HISTORICAL PARK..291

ACRONYMS AND ABBREVIATIONS..293
FEDERAL INFORMATION CENTERS...301
LAND GRANT UNIVERSITY FILM LIBRARIES..303
SEA GRANT PROGRAMS..307
SUBJECT BIBLIOGRAPHIES..309
SUBJECT INDEX..315

Introduction

A Guide to Selected Federal Agency Programs and Publications surveys federal agencies whose services and materials will benefit librarians and teachers. Federal agencies are considered to be those that are completely or partially funded by the federal government, that are established by congressional or presidential action, that are federally administered, or that are required by statute to publish certain information on their programs and activities in the *Federal Register.*

Federal agency publications and other materials offer diverse, current, objective information, and in many cases are the only source for certain kinds of data. Services provided by federal agencies include printed material and audiovisuals, both suited to the needs of librarians and teachers. What is more, those materials and services are often free—or available at very low cost.

Unfortunately, locating federal resources often proves difficult. This guide is designed to help. It provides information about 227 federal agencies and the materials and services they offer. A complete list of the agencies included may be found in the table of contents. Appendices provide information on federal information centers, land grant university film libraries, and sea grant programs as well as a list of subject bibliographies available from the Superintendent of Documents. For the sake of practicality, inclusion has had to be highly selective, but the selection is based on years of library and classroom experience. Exclusion of any agency does not mean that it offers nothing to the educator.

Arrangement is alphabetical by agency. For each agency the following information is given as available and, in the case of publications and services, as pertinent to the purpose of this guide:

Agency name, address, and phone number.

Date established.

Objectives of the agency.

Curriculum (suggested area of application).

Subjects (suggested vertical file headings based on *Sears*).

Locations (state and regional addresses giving additional access).

Publications.

Bibliographies, sales catalogs, publications lists, etc. (with title, frequency of publication, number of pages, place and publisher if not agency, date, price, identifying numbers, and annotation).

Serials, subscription publications, etc. (with title, annual domestic and foreign subscription price, and annotation).

Selected list of books and pamphlets (with title, place and publisher if not agency, date, pages, price, identifying numbers, and annotation).

Audiovisuals.

Filmographies, sales lists, etc. (with title, place and publisher if not agency, date, pages, price, identifying numbers, and annotation).

Individual audiovisuals (with title, producer, date, running time, format, color or B&W, price, purchase or rental, free loan, identification number, and annotation, including distributor if necessary for ordering).

Library (location, services).

Special services (mailing lists, databases, tours, speakers, and other special services).

xvi / Introduction

The information given in this guide mirrors that given in the sources. Differences in form and degree of information have necessarily resulted, but we preferred such variation to a parallelism imposed at the expense of accuracy.

Materials may be easily accessed through the subject index that begins on page 315. A list of acronyms and abbreviations may be found beginning on page 293.

Unless otherwise indicated all materials listed may be ordered through the producing agency. Government material may also be ordered through such agencies as the Government Printing Office, the National Audiovisual Center, and the National Technical Information Service. Entries for these appear within.

If the agency indicates that materials are free, order only single copies as multiple copies are often accompanied by charges. When ordering include any unique number which appears after the price notation. And remember that prices are subject to change.

I do wish to thank Heather Cameron and Hannah L. Kelminson of Libraries Unlimited for their guidance and suggestions, and Jill Cohoe of Northern Michigan University for proofreading.

Directory

ADMINISTRATIVE CONFERENCE OF THE UNITED STATES
Information Officer
2120 L St., NW
Washington, DC 20037
(202) 254-7020

Date Established: 1964

Objectives of the Agency: Develop improvements in the procedures by which federal agencies administer regulatory, benefit, and other government programs.

Curriculum: Government

Subjects: Public Administration

Publications: Bibliography. Reports. Books.

Bibliographies, Sales Catalogs, Publications Lists, etc.

"Administrative Conference of the United States: A Bibliography 1968-1983." 1984. 25p. free.

Lists 162 entries to acquaint the user with the work of the Administrative Conference and to help locate reports. Materials may be obtained directly from their source. Index assists one in finding reports on topics of special interest.

Selected List of Books and Pamphlets

Annual Report. Current. 143p. free.

Describes organization, activities, and actions of the assembly and the committees. Provides biographical information. Includes the Administrative Conference Act and the bylaws of the Administrative Conference. Photographs.

ADMINISTRATIVE OFFICE OF THE UNITED STATES COURTS
811 Vermont Ave., NW
Washington, DC 20544
(202) 633-6097

Date Established: 1939

Objectives of the Agency: Supervise administrative matters relating to the offices of clerks and others; examine the state of the dockets of the courts; secure information about the courts' need of assistance; prepare and transmit statistical data and reports; prepare a budget; perform other related duties. The Supreme Court is not under this administrative office.

Curriculum: Government

Subjects: Courts—U.S.

Publications: Reports. Statistics. Volumes on judicial statistics.

Selected List of Books and Pamphlets

"Federal Judicial Statistics." 13p. free.

Describes early history, the Division of Procedural Studies and Statistics, the Statistical Analysis and Reports Division, the case reporting systems, the judicial statistical process cycle, and adaptive judicial statistics. Includes a 5 page matrix on SARD (Statistical Analysis and Reports Division) statistical reporting requirements.

Special Services: Computer tapes of Administrative Office statistical data are available. For information about computer tapes, write:
Chief, Statistical Analyses and Reports Division
Administrative Office of the United States Courts
Washington, DC 20544
(202) 633-6094

AGENCY FOR INTERNATIONAL DEVELOPMENT
Office of Public Inquiries
Bureau of External Affairs
320 Twenty-First St., NW
Washington, DC 20523
(202) 632-1850

Date Established: 1961

Objectives of the Agency: Coordinate U.S. foreign assistance efforts.

Curriculum: Current issues

Subjects: U.S. — foreign relations

Publications: Pamphlets. Fact sheets. On the agency's functions and accomplishments.

Selected List of Books and Pamphlets

"A.I.D. Policy Paper: Basic Education and Technical Training." 1982. 13p. free.

Discusses education and economic development, education problems in the 1980s, and implementation issues and constraints.

"A.I.D. Education Sector Strategy." 1983. 7p. free.

Explains the sector strategy and program implementation.

"Facts about A.I.D.." n.d. 2p. free.

Describes its functions. Gives statistics about less developed countries. Offers summary of major economic assistance program.

Audiovisuals:

Filmographies, Sales Lists, etc.

"Film List." 1981. 2p. free.

Lists films available from the National Audio Visual Center. Request from:
The National Audio Visual Center
Information Service
Washington, DC 20409
(202) 763-1896
Includes such countries as Haiti, Nicaragua, and Bangladesh.

AGRICULTURAL COOPERATIVE SERVICE
U.S. Department of Agriculture
14th St. and Independence Ave., SW
Washington, DC 20250
(202) 447-8870

Date Established: 1926

Objectives of the Agency: Promote the knowledge of cooperative principles and practices; and work in promoting such knowledge, with educational and marketing agencies, cooperative associations, and others.

Curriculum: Agriculture

Subjects: Agriculture — economic aspects

Publications: Reports. Magazine.

Bibliographies, Sales Catalogs, Publications Lists, etc.

"Farmer Cooperative Publications." Rev. 1985. 70p. free. Cooperative Information Report No. 4.

Reports on history and statistics, organization, operations, marketing/bargaining, member and public relations, purchasing, rural development, and transportation and distribution. Includes publication number, title, date published, number of pages, and summary of contents.

AGRICULTURAL RESEARCH SERVICE
Department of Agriculture
Information Staff
Fourteenth St. and Independence Ave., SW
Washington, DC 20250
(202) 447-3656

Date Established: 1938 (centers)

Objectives of the Agency: Administer a basic, applied, and developmental research program in animal and plant protection and production; in the advancement of soil, water, and air; in processing, storage, and distribution of farm products; and in human nutrition.

Curriculum: Agriculture

Subjects: Agriculture — research

Locations:

CT, DC, DE, MA, MD, ME, NH, NJ, NY, PA, RI, VT, WV

Agricultural Research Service
Northeastern Regional Office
Bldg. 003, Room 333
Agricultural Research Center, West
Beltsville, MD 20705
(301) 344-3418

IA, IL, IN, KS, MI, MN, MO, NE, ND, OH, SD, WI

Agricultural Research Service
North Central Regional Office
1815 N. University St.
Peoria, IL 61604-3999
(309) 671-7176

AL, AR, FL, GA, KY, LA, MS, NC, OK, PR, SC, TN, TX, VA, VI

Agricultural Research Service
Southern Regional Office
701 Loyola Ave.
P.O. Box 53326
New Orleans, LA 70153
(504) 589-6753

AK, AZ, CA, CO, HI, ID, MT, NM, NV, OR, UT, WA, WY

Agricultural Research Service
Western Regional Office
1333 Broadway
Suite 400
Oakland, CA 94612
(415) 273-4191

Regional Centers

Eastern Regional Research Center
600 E. Mermaid Lane
Philadelphia, PA 19118

Specializes in animal products (milk, meats, animal fats and hides) and plant products (eastern fruits, vegetables, and forage).

Northern Regional Research Center
1815 N. University St.
Peoria, IL 61604

Specializes in corn, wheat, grain, sorghum, oats, soybeans, horticultural and special crops. Location of northern agricultural energy center.

Southern Regional Research Center
P.O. Box 19687
New Orleans, LA 70179

Specializes in cotton and cottonseed, rice, grain, sorghum, peanuts, cane sugar, and aquaculture.

Western Regional Research Center
800 Buchanan St.
Berkeley, CA 94710

Specializes in western fruits and vegetables, eggs, forage crops, wheat, barley, rice, dry beans and peas, and toxicology.

Publications: Lists. Articles.

Bibliographies, Sales Catalogs, Publications Lists, etc.

"Publications and Patents." Annual. 50p. free.
Lists publications. Subject and author indexes.

AGRICULTURAL STABILIZATION AND CONSERVATION SERVICE
Department of Agriculture
Information Division
Room 24-W
P.O. Box 2415
Washington, DC 20013
(202) 447-4122

Date Established: 1961

Objectives of the Agency: Administer commodity and related land use programs designed for voluntary production adjustment, resource protection, and stabilization in price, market, and farm income.

Curriculum: Agriculture

Subjects: Agriculture

Publications: Pamphlets on ASCS programs and activities. Annual reports. Summaries. Handbooks. Fact sheets.

Bibliographies, Sales Catalogs, Publications Lists, etc.

"ACSC Publications." n.d. 6p. free.
Lists what is available in free materials. Arranges information by format, such as "Commodity Fact Sheets."

Selected List of Books and Pamphlets

"ASCS Aerial Photography." 1983. 8p. free.
Contains the history and types of aerial photography, ASCS products and services, and how to obtain them.

"Agricultural Stabilization and Conservation Service." 1978. 7p. free.
Explains the functions, responsibilities, and organization of the Service. Map.

"The Commodity Credit Corporation and Its Activities." 1980. 6p. free.
Describes the responsibilities and organization of the Corporation, and its domestic and export programs.

"Commodity Programs and Related Legislation through the Years." 1976. 21p. free.
Chronicles early programs beginning in 1933 and various others, such as the Upland Cotton Program of 1973, or the Rice Program of 1975.

"Farmer Committee Administration of Agricultural Programs." 1978. 3p. free.
Relates when the committees were established and what they do.

"Production Adjustment Programs." 1977. 3p. free.
Explains what these programs to adjust production and marketing do.

AMERICAN FOLKLIFE CENTER
The Library of Congress
10 First St., SE
Washington, DC 20540
(202) 287-5510

Date Established: 1976

Objectives of the Agency: Support, preserve, and present American folklife through collections, maintenance of archives, research, and other activities. The Archive of Folk Culture maintains and administers a collection of folk music.

Curriculum: Art, History, Sociology

Subjects: Folk Art, American

Publications: Pamphlets. Bibliographies. Guides on American folklore.

Bibliographies, Sales Catalogs, Publications Lists, etc.

"American Folk Architecture: A Selected Bibliography." (No. 8.) 1981. 92p. free.
Divides materials into theory and general works, antecedents to American building, regional works, museums and historic preservation, and field documentation.

4 / American Folklife Center

"An Inventory of the Bibliographies and Other Reference and Finding Aids Prepared by the Archive of Folk Culture." 1984. 10p. free.

Underlines subjects. Arranges titles alphabetically within each group. Includes name, date, and number of pages.

"Traditional Crafts and Craftsmanship in America." (No. 11.) 1983. 84p. free.

Lists about 1,000 references drawn from books, catalogs, abstracts, magazines, newsletters, and journals, both published items and some unpublished dissertations and theses. Index.

Serials, Subscription Publications, etc.

"Folklife Center News." Current. 16p. free.

Covers in a newsletter the recent developments, publications, recordings, and other items for sale from the American Folklife Center.

Selected List of Books and Pamphlets

"American Folklife Center." 1984. 8p. free.

Includes the activities and purpose of the center, its holdings and publications.

"The Archive of Folk Culture." 1985. 8p. free.

Details the history, collections, services, publications and other activities of the Archive of Folk Culture.

"A Guide to the Collections of Recorded Folk Music and Folklore in the Library of Congress." Current. 6p. free.

Contains indexes to the collection. Explains access to finding aids, obtaining copies, restrictions on use of library's recorded collections, obtaining letters of permission, listening facilities, etc.

Audiovisuals:

Individual Films

"Folk Recordings." 1983. 37p. free.

Includes Anglo-ballads, cowboy songs, folk music of Mexico, songs of war, music of the American Indian, Afro-American folk music, railroad songs, religious music, and other types. Includes prices and order blank.

ANACOSTIA NEIGHBORHOOD MUSEUM
Smithsonian Institution
1901 Fort Place, SE
Washington, DC 20020
(202) 287-3306

Date Established: 1967

Objectives of the Agency: Provide an exhibition hall and cultural center; support exhibit design and educational programs; and conduct independent studies in Afro-American history, minority and ethnic studies, and the history of Anacostia and Washington, DC.

Curriculum: Black studies

Subjects: Blacks—race identity

Publications: Curriculum materials. Pamphlets. Kits. On black achievement.

Selected List of Books and Pamphlets

"Black Contributors to Science and Energy Technology." 1979. 26p. free. DOE/OPA-0035(79).

Contains biographical sketches and drawings of some of the blacks that have contributed to American science and technology.

"Black Women: Achievements Against the Odds." n.d. 23p. free.

Teacher's resource booklet on varied achievements of black women. Selected film and print bibliography.

"Explore Your Heritage at the Smithsonian!" n.d. 6p. free.

Tells what of the black experience the various museums offer.

"Frederick Douglass." 1979. 22p. free.

Chronicles the life and struggles of the statesman, civil rights advocate, orator, author, journalist, husband, and father.

"Here, Look at Mine!." n.d. kit. free.

A teacher's resource packet on the selected art works by black artists John N. Robinson and Larry Francis Lebby. Lists galleries and similar organizations in the Washington, DC, area that promote black art. Glossary of selected art terms.

"How and Why African People Came to North America." 1979. 33p. free.

An introductory flannelboard activity on black history for the pre-school and primary teacher.

"The Kwanza Kit." n.d. 25p. free.

Explains what *Kwanza* means. Provides ideas for teachers in a kit that can be used with all age levels.

"A Woman of Courage." n.d. 48p. free.

Tells of the life of Anna J. Cooper, a slave born in 1858, in a resource unit for grades 6-8.

ANIMAL AND PLANT HEALTH INSPECTION SERVICE
United States Department of Agriculture
Federal Center Bldg.
Room 700
Hyattsville, MD 20782
(202) 447-3977

Date Established: 1977

Objectives of the Agency: Conduct regulatory programs to protect and improve animal and plant health; administer, in cooperation with state governments, federal laws and regulations on animal and plant health and quarantine, humane treatment of animals, and control and eradication of pests and diseases.

Curriculum: Agriculture

Subjects: Agriculture, animals — treatment

Publications: Pamphlets on animal and plant health.

Selected List of Books and Pamphlets

"APHIS Facts." 1985. 4p. free.
Tells the damage that gypsy moths can cause, how to inspect for the moths, and their life stages. Includes a check list, map, and suggestions for more information.

"Careers for Veterinarians." 1979. 12p. free.
Lists benefits and jobs available in the U.S. Department of Agriculture.

"One Hundreds of Animal Health." 1984. 11p. free.
Covers development from 1884 to 1984, with information such as the fact that the bacteria salmonella was named after the Bureau of Animal Industry's first director.

"Plant Protection and Quarantine." 1983. 16p. free.
Describes pest exclusion, survey and detection, eradication, management, etc.

"Travelers' Tips." 1980. 17p. free.
Gives information about bringing food and plant and animal products into the United States.

"Veterinary Services: Protecting America's Animal Health." 1982. 34p. free.
Describes domestic programs and international operations of veterinary services.

ANTIETAM NATIONAL BATTLEFIELD
U.S. Department of the Interior
National Park Service
National Capital Region
P.O. Box 158
Sharpsburg, MD 21782-0158

Date Established: 1890

Objectives of the Agency: Present information through exhibits, film programs, and tour stops, about the Battle of Antietam (or Sharpsburg) on September 17, 1862, which climaxed the first of General Robert E. Lee's two attempts to carry the war into the north.

Curriculum: History

Subjects: U.S. — history

Publications: Fact sheets. Bibliographies. On the Battle of Antietam.

Bibliographies, Sales Catalogs, Publications Lists, etc.

"Bibliography of Women in the Civil War." n.d. 1p. free.
Gives bibliographical citations (title, author, publisher, date) for books about women in the Civil War.

"Civil War Bibliography — Antietam." n.d. 2p. free.
Gives bibliographical citations (title, author, place of publication, date) for books about the battle.

Selected List of Books and Pamphlets

"Antietam: The Bloodiest Day in the Civil War." n.d. 2p. free.
Provides information about the war and about visiting the battlefield. Maps. Photographs.

"Antietam National Battlefield Chronology." n.d. 2p. free.
Gives events at the battlefield. Begins in the 1830s and ends in the 1960s, when the visitor center was completed. Page 2 gives statistics on such things as the miles of fencing, the number of cast iron tablets, the number of graves in the national cemetery, and the depth of Antietam Creek.

"Summary of Civil War Weapons and Tactics at Antietam Battlefield for West Point History Teachers Tour." 1983. 1p. free.
Provides information about the infantry, artillery, and cavalry by an interpretive specialist.

APPALACHIAN REGIONAL COMMISSION
1666 Connecticut Ave., NW
Washington, DC 20235
(202) 673-7835

Date Established: 1965

Objectives of the Agency: Improve the economic, physical, and social development of the 13-state Appalachian region.

Curriculum: Social studies

Subjects: Appalachian mountains

Publications: Pamphlets on commission accomplishments in Appalachian progress.

Selected List of Books and Pamphlets

Appalachia. (Vol. 18, No. 3.) 1985. 108p. free.
Chronicles the history of Appalachia, its decades of change, and its future. Examines changes made since 1965 on: highways; rail, air, and water transportation; education; health; child development; community building; and other changes. Tables. Graphs. Photographs.

6 / Architect of the Capitol

ARCHITECT OF THE CAPITOL
U.S. Capitol Building
Washington, DC 20515
(202) 225-1200

Date Established: 1793

Objectives of the Agency: Care for and maintain the Capitol and its grounds, and additional buildings.

Curriculum: Social studies

Subjects: Washington, DC—buildings

Publications: Fact sheets. Flyers. Books. On the U.S. Capitol and grounds.

Selected List of Books and Pamphlets

"Architects of the Capitol." 1974. 5p. free.
 Contains biographical sketches, construction contributions of architects of the Capitol, from 1793 to the present. Drawings.

Art in the United States Capitol. $21.00. #052-071-00564-3.
 Published by the Architect of the Capitol office, the book is available from: Superintendent of Documents, U.S. Government Printing Office, Washington, DC 20402.

"Capitol Building and Grounds, United States Capitol." 1975. 7p. free.
 Describes location, purchase, plans, building, and extension of the Capitol and its grounds.

Report to the Congress of the United States for the Master Plan for Future Development of the Capitol Grounds and Related Areas. $11.00. #052-071-006397.
 Published by the Architect of the Capitol office, the book is available from: Superintendent of Documents, U.S. Government Printing Office, Washington, DC 20402.

"United States Botanic Garden Conservatory." n.d. 4-fold. free.
 Provides diagram, photographs, and information arranged for "a self-guided tour." Includes interesting history and characteristics of the various plant collections.

"The United States Botanic Gardens." 1982. 2p. free.
 Details the founding and development of the United States Botanic Garden, the permanent and major collections, and its services.

Special Services: For hours, tours, and other U.S. Botanic Garden visitor information, write:
Botanic Garden
First St. and Maryland Ave., SW
Washington, DC 20024
(202) 225-7099

ARCHITECTURAL AND TRANSPORTATION BARRIERS COMPLIANCE BOARD
Public Information Office
330 C St., SW
Washington, DC 20202
(202) 245-1591

Date Established: 1973

Objectives of the Agency: Ensure that certain facilities designed, constructed, or altered with federal funds since September 1969 are accessible to and usable by disabled persons; provide technical help on the removal of barriers; and provide information on architectural, transportation, communication, and attitudinal barriers affecting physically handicapped persons.

Curriculum: Education, special education

Subjects: Architecture and the handicapped
 Handicapped

Publications: Pamphlets. Lists. Reports. Guides.

Bibliographies, Sales Catalogs, Publications Lists, etc.

"Publications Check List." Current. 2p. free.
 Includes order form for free publications about barriers.

Selected List of Books and Pamphlets

"About Barriers." 1982. 20p. free.
 Describes what barriers are, whom they affect, what they cost, what is being done about them, what you can do. Sources. Resources.

"Access America: The Architectural Barriers Act and You." 1982. 1p. free.
 Tells what the act is, what it means to you whether or not you are handicapped. Explains what authority the Architectural and Transportation Barriers Compliance Board has. Complaint form.

"Access America: Laws Concerning the Federal Architectural and Transportation Barriers Compliance Board." 1984. 6p. free.
 Prints the Architectural Barriers Act of 1968 as amended through 1984 (Public Law 90-480; 42 U.S.C. 4151 et. seq.) and the Rehabilitation Act of 1973 (P.L. 93-112) as amended through 1984 (sections 502, 506, 507; U.S.C. 792, 794(B) and 794(C)).

"Telecommunications Devices for the Deaf: A Guide to Selection, Ordering and Installation." n.d. 5-fold. free.
 Describes what a TDD (telecommunications device for the deaf) is, who uses them, how is it used, what are its features, cost and installation, and selection guidelines. Includes a chart of TDD features by price range and addresses of sources of further information.

Special Services: If you wish to be added to the mailing list, just indicate that wish on the order form in "Publications Check List," described above.

BUREAU OF ALCOHOL, TOBACCO AND FIREARMS
Department of the Treasury
ATF Distribution Center
7943 Angus Court
Springfield, VA 22153
(202) 566-7777

Date Established: 1972

Objectives of the Agency: Enforce and administer firearms and explosives laws, and laws covering production, use, and distribution of alcohol and tobacco. The compliance operations activity determines and ensures full collection of revenue due from legal alcohol and tobacco industries, helps in consumer deception, deals in licenses and storage, and assists other agencies.

Curriculum: Government

Subjects: Alcohol
Firearms
Tobacco

Locations:

Compliance Operations Regional Offices

IA, IL, IN, KS, KY, MI, MN, MO, NE, ND, OH, SD, WI, WV

Bureau of Alcohol, Tobacco and Firearms
Department of the Treasury
Compliance Operations Regional Office
230 S. Dearborn St.
Chicago, IL 60604

CT, DC, DE, MA, MD, ME, NH, NJ, NY, PA, PR, RI, VA, VI, VT

Bureau of Alcohol, Tobacco and Firearms
Department of the Treasury
Compliance Operations Regional Office
6 World Trade Center
New York, NY 10048

AL, FL, GA, MS, NC, SC, TN

Bureau of Alcohol, Tobacco and Firearms
Department of the Treasury
Compliance Operations Regional Office
3835 Northeast Expressway
Atlanta, GA 30340

AR, CO, LA, NM, OK, TX, WY

Bureau of Alcohol, Tobacco and Firearms
Department of the Treasury
Compliance Operations Regional Office
1114 Commerce St.
Dallas, TX 75242

AK, AZ, CA, GU, HI, ID, MT, NV, OR, UT, WA

Bureau of Alcohol, Tobacco and Firearms
Department of the Treasury
Compliance Operations Regional Office
525 Market Street
San Francisco, CA 94105

District Law Enforcement Offices

Bureau of Alcohol, Tobacco and Firearms
Department of the Treasury
District Law Enforcement Office
44 Broad St.
Suite 302
Atlanta, GA 30303

Bureau of Alcohol, Tobacco and Firearms
Department of the Treasury
District Law Enforcement Office
2121 Eighth Ave., NW
Birmingham, AL 35203

Bureau of Alcohol, Tobacco and Firearms
Department of the Treasury
District Law Enforcement Office
JFK Federal Bldg.
Government Center
Boston, MA 02203

Bureau of Alcohol, Tobacco and Firearms
Department of the Treasury
District Law Enforcement Office
222 S. Church St.
Suite 404
Charlotte, NC 28202

Bureau of Alcohol, Tobacco and Firearms
Department of the Treasury
District Law Enforcement Office
55 Erie View Plaza
Suite 500
Cleveland, OH 44114

Bureau of Alcohol, Tobacco and Firearms
Department of the Treasury
District Law Enforcement Office
1114 Commerce St.
Dallas, TX 75242

Bureau of Alcohol, Tobacco and Firearms
Department of the Treasury
District Law Enforcement Office
231 W. Lafayette St.
Room 533
Detroit, MI 48226

Bureau of Alcohol, Tobacco and Firearms
Department of the Treasury
District Law Enforcement Office
701 W. Broad St.
Second Floor
Falls Church, VA 22046

Bureau of Alcohol, Tobacco and Firearms
Department of the Treasury
District Law Enforcement Office
16630 Imperial Valley Dr.
Suite 263
Houston, TX 77060

Bureau of Alcohol, Tobacco and Firearms
Department of the Treasury
District Law Enforcement Office
1150 Grand Ave.
Room 200
Kansas City, MO 64106

Bureau of Alcohol, Tobacco and Firearms
Department of the Treasury
District Law Enforcement Office
300 N. Los Angeles St.
Room 4354
Los Angeles, CA 90012

Bureau of Alcohol, Tobacco and Firearms
Department of the Treasury
District Law Enforcement Office
600 Federal Pl.
Room 8720
Louisville, KY 40202

Bureau of Alcohol, Tobacco and Firearms
Department of the Treasury
District Law Enforcement Office
5205 N.W. 84th Ave.
Suite 108
Miami, FL 33166

Bureau of Alcohol, Tobacco and Firearms
Department of the Treasury
District Law Enforcement Office
4404 Hillsboro Rd.
Room 210
Nashville, TN 37215

Bureau of Alcohol, Tobacco and Firearms
Department of the Treasury
District Law Enforcement Office
500 Camp St.
Room 330
New Orleans, LA 70130

Bureau of Alcohol, Tobacco and Firearms
Department of the Treasury
District Law Enforcement Office
90 Church St.
New York, NY 10008

Bureau of Alcohol, Tobacco and Firearms
Department of the Treasury
District Law Enforcement Office
2115 Butterfield Rd.
Suite 300
Oakbrook, IL 60521

Bureau of Alcohol, Tobacco and Firearms
Department of the Treasury
District Law Enforcement Office
Second and Chestnut Sts.
Philadelphia, PA 19106

Bureau of Alcohol, Tobacco and Firearms
Department of the Treasury
District Law Enforcement Office
525 Market St.
Twenty-fifth Floor
San Francisco, CA 94105

Bureau of Alcohol, Tobacco and Firearms
Department of the Treasury
District Law Enforcement Office
915 Second Ave.
Room 806
Seattle, WA 98174

Bureau of Alcohol, Tobacco and Firearms
Department of the Treasury
District Law Enforcement Office
1114 Market St.
Room 611
St. Louis, MO 63101

Bureau of Alcohol, Tobacco and Firearms
Department of the Treasury
District Law Enforcement Office
316 N. Robert St.
Room 156
St. Paul, MN 55101

Publications: Statistics and regulations about alcohol, tobacco, and firearms use. Governmental structure, organization, and application.

Bibliographies, Sales Catalogs, Publications Lists, etc.

"ATF Publications." 1984. 13p. free. ATF P 1321.2.
 Lists of publications, including titles that have replaced obsolete publications. Publications are coded if they are not for general public issue.

"Directives and Publications Subject Index." Current. 50p. free. ATF P 1321.1.
 Lists ATF directives and publications by subject. Includes brief description and publication number. Includes subjects from *accidents* to *wineries*.

Selected List of Books and Pamphlets

"District Offices." 1984. 1p. free. ATF P 1100.4.

Prints a map of the United States showing district offices and district boundaries of the Office of Law Enforcement's district offices of the Bureau of Alcohol, Tobacco and Firearms.

"Excerpt—(General Information) from (Your Guide to) Federal Firearms Regulation." 1984. 33p. free. ATF P 5300.4E.

Contains subject index to rulings, procedures, and industry circulars, questions and answers, and general information.

"State Laws and Published Ordinances—Firearms." Current. 231p. free. ATF P 5300.5.

Lists state attorneys general and regulations of each state. Includes a table of common elements in state laws.

BUREAU OF ECONOMIC ANALYSIS
Public Information Office
U.S. Department of Commerce
1401 K St., NW
Washington, DC 20230
(202) 523-0777

Date Established: 1953

Objectives of the Agency: Measure and analyze U.S. economic activity; be involved in the development, preparation, and interpretation of the economic accounts of the country.

Curriculum: Economics

Subjects: U.S.—economic conditions

Publications: Periodicals. Staff papers. Working papers. Handbooks. Books. Catalog. Computer tapes. On economics and statistical analysis.

Bibliographies, Sales Catalogs, Publications Lists, etc.

"Catalog of Publications & Computer Tapes." Current. 59p. free.

Describes and gives ordering information and order forms for publications and computer tapes. Computer tapes' recording mode is odd parity, 9 track, and either 800 or 1600 BPI density. The standard output tape is the ASCII character set with ANSI standard labels. Publications are for sale from the Superintendent of Documents, the National Technical Information Service, and the Economics and Statistical Analysis of the Bureau of Economic Analysis.

BUREAU OF ENGRAVING AND PRINTING
Department of the Treasury
Public Affairs Section
Room 602-11A
Fourteenth and C Sts., SW
Washington, DC 20228
(202) 447-1391

Date Established: 1862

Objectives of the Agency: Design, engrave, and print U.S. currency, postage stamps, treasury obligation bills, and other U.S. securities; advise federal agencies in design and production of other government documents.

Curriculum: Government

Subjects: Government publications
Money

Publications: Pamphlets. Notes. Cards. Seals. Prints.

Bibliographies, Sales Catalogs, Publications Lists, etc.

"Cards and Prints." Current. 3p. free.

Gives types of souvenir cards and series prints for sale. Order form.

"Engraved and Lithographed Printings." Current. 5p. free.

Tells what portraits, vignettes, seals, and other materials are for sale.

"News." Current. 2p. free.

Tells what is being offered for sale.

Selected List of Books and Pamphlets

"Production of Government Securities." n.d. 8p. free.

Gives facts and miscellaneous information about the various ways of engraving and printing.

BUREAU OF INDIAN AFFAIRS
Department of the Interior
Public Information Staff
Main Interior Bldg.
Washington, DC 20240
(202) 343-7445

Date Established: 1824

Objectives of the Agency: Encourage and train Indian and Alaskan—native people to manage their own affairs under the trust relationship with the federal government; help develop human and natural resources; mobilize public and private aid for their use.

Curriculum: Native American Studies

Subjects: Indians of North America

Locations: (arranged alphabetically by city)

Bureau of Indian Affairs Area Office
115 Fourth Ave., SE
Aberdeen, SD 57401

Bureau of Indian Affairs Area Office
5301 Central Ave., NE
Albuquerque, NM 87108

10 / Bureau of Indian Affairs

Bureau of Indian Affairs Area Office
P.O. Box 368
Anadarko, OK 73005

Bureau of Indian Affairs Area Office
316 N. Twenty-Sixth St.
Billings, MT 59101

Bureau of Indian Affairs Area Office
Box 3-8000
Juneau, AK 99802

Bureau of Indian Affairs Area Office
15 S. Fifth St.
Minneapolis, MN 55402

Bureau of Indian Affairs Area Office
Federal Bldg.
Muskogee, OK 74401

Bureau of Indian Affairs Area Office
P.O. Box 7007
3030 N. Central
Phoenix, AZ 85011

Bureau of Indian Affairs Area Office
P.O. Box 3785
1425 N.E. Irving St.
Portland, OR 97208

Bureau of Indian Affairs Area Office
2800 Cottage Way
Sacramento, CA 95825

Bureau of Indian Affairs Area Office
Eastern Area
1951 Constitution Ave., NW
Washington, DC 20245

Bureau of Indian Affairs Area Office
Navajo Area
Window Rock, AZ 86515

Publications: Pamphlets. Fact sheets.

Selected List of Books and Pamphlets

"American Indians." 1984. 46p. free.
  Contains information about U.S. Indian policy, tribes and reservations, functions of the Bureau of Indian Affairs, and Indian economic development. Many photographs.

"Indian and Eskimo Children." 1969. 50p. free.
  A picture story book for children to help them understand Indians and Eskimos.

"Indians: The Shoshoni." 1972. 3p. free.
  Where the Shoshoni lived, what the origin of their name was, and how they lived. Suggested reading list.

"Information about American Indians and Alaskan Natives." 1985. 3p. free.
  Contains facts about population, reservations, trust lands, Indian tribes, and related topics.

"Information about the Indian People." 1981. 6p. free.
  Explains who an Indian is, what an Indian tribe is, how many Indians there are in the United States, what their legal status is, and other information.

"The Law and the Indian." 1978. 4p. free.
  Tells where to find information about the legal status of the Indian.

Audiovisuals:

Filmographies, Sales Lists, etc.

"The American Indian in Films." 1977. 7p. free.
  Describes content of films, where they can be obtained, and under what conditions. Inquire if a film is free loan, for purchase or rental.

Individual Films

"American Indian Influence on the United States." n.d. 20 minutes. color.
  Explains different ways U.S. life has been influenced by the contributions of Native Americans. Order from: Donars Productions, P.O. Box 24, Loveland, CO 80537.

"American Indian Speaks." n.d. 23 minutes. 16mm. color.
  Relates visits with Muskogee Creek, Sioux, and Nisqually Indians to show picture of life on reservations of today. Order from: Encyclopedia Brittanica Educational Corp., 425 N. Michigan Ave., Chicago, IL 60611.

"Annie and the Old One." n.d. 14½ minutes. 16mm. color.
  Shows the passing of wisdom from a grandmother to a Navajo girl. The grandmother helps Annie to understand life's cycle. Order from: Bailey Film Association, 2211 Michigan Ave., Box 1795, Santa Monica, CA 90408.

"I Will Fight No More Forever: The Story of Chief Joseph." n.d. 106 minutes. 16mm. color.
  Relates Chief Joseph's attempts to escape into Canada and his surrender. Order from: Macmillan Films, Inc., 34 Macquestern Pkwy. South, Mt. Vernon, NY 10550.

Library: Reading room has extensive collection of materials on Indians, Indian tribes, and their relationship to the U.S. government. Visit:
National Resources Library
Main Interior Building
Washington, DC 20240
(202) 343-5815

BUREAU OF LABOR STATISTICS
U.S. Department of Labor
441 G St., NW
Washington, DC 20212
(202) 523-1221

Date Established: 1913

Objectives of the Agency: Collect, process, analyze, and disseminate data relating to employment, unemployment, and other characteristics of the labor force; worker compensation, prices and family spending, and related labor concerns.

Curriculum: Consumer education, economics, guidance

Subjects: Employment
　　　　　　Labor and laboring classes

Locations:

CT, MA, ME, NH, RI, VT

Bureau of Labor Statistics
Regional Office
1603 JFK Federal Building
Government Center
Boston, MA 02203
(617) 223-6727

CZ, NJ, NY, PR, VI

Bureau of Labor Statistics
Regional Office
1515 Broadway
Suite 3400
New York, NY 10036
(212) 944-3121

DC, DE, MD, PA, VA, WV

Bureau of Labor Statistics
Regional Office
3535 Market St.
P.O. Box 13309
Philadelphia, PA 19101
(215) 596-1154

AL, FL, GA, KY, MS, NC, SC, TN

Bureau of Labor Statistics
Regional Office
1371 Peachtree St., NE
Atlanta, GA 30367
(404) 881-4418

IL, IN, MI, MN, OH, WI

Bureau of Labor Statistics
Regional Office
Federal Office Bldg.
230 S. Dearborn St.
Ninth Floor
Chicago, IL 60604
(312) 353-1880

AR, LA, NM, OK, TX

Bureau of Labor Statistics
Regional Office
Federal Bldg.
525 Griffin St.
Room 221
Dallas, TX 75202
(214) 767-6971

CO, IA, KS, MO, MT, ND, NE, SD, UT, WY

Bureau of Labor Statistics
Regional Office
911 Walnut St.
Kansas City, MO 64106
(816) 374-2481

*AK, AS, AZ, CA, GU, HI, ID, NV, OR,
Trust Territory of the Pacific Islands, WA*

Bureau of Labor Statistics
Regional Office
450 Golden Gate Ave.
P.O. Box 36017
San Francisco, CA 94102
(415) 556-4678

Publications: Periodicals. General publications. Projections in economic growth and employment, employment and unemployment statistics, occupational safety and health statistics, prices and living conditions, productivity and technology, wages and industrial relations. Those in guidance would find occupational information particularly useful.

Bibliographies, Sales Catalogs, Publications Lists, etc.

"Current BLS Publications." 1985. 15p. free.
　　Gives annotations of selected publications and how to order them. Prices quoted apply to the United States. Order form is on the back cover.

"Data Files on Tape." n.d. 4p. free.
　　Tells what is available on magnetic tape. Standard format is 9-track, 6,250 BPI. Also available are some micro data tapes and customized data files on a cost-for-service basis. Order form to obtain cost information.

"Information in Print." n.d. 1p. free.
　　Gives annotation, price, and order form for one quarterly and five monthly periodicals that report on employment, unemployment, prices, wages, productivity, and related economic indicators.

"Just Published." Monthly. 2p. free. #321.
　　Describes what is new, for sale, and for free. Tells what is available in data services such as mailgram, tape, microfiche, telephone and how to obtain services.

12 / Bureau of Labor Statistics

"Mailing Lists for News Releases and Announcements." n.d. 1p. free.
Lists what is available and provides boxes to check to indicate if you would like a sample or wish to have material sent regularly. Categories include labor force, prices, productivity, wages, collective bargaining, etc.

"Occupational Outlook Publications." Current. 1p. free.
Describes handbook's contents and prices.

"Telephone Contacts for Data Users." Current. 4p. free.
Lists title, name, and phone number for information services, employment and unemployment statistics, economic growth and employment projections, occupational safety and health statistics, prices and living conditions, productivity and technology, wages and industrial relations, publications, and Bureau of Labor Statistics regional offices.

Serials, Subscription Publications, etc.

Area Wage Surveys. Individual bulletins. $88.00/yr.
Surveys wages for office, professional, technical, maintenance, custodial, and material movement occupations. Order from: Superintendent of Documents, U.S. Government Printing Office, Washington, DC 20402.

Monthly Labor Review. Monthly. $24.00/yr.
Contains employment, wages, prices, productivity, industrial relations, book reviews, current labor statistics. Order from: Superintendent of Documents, U.S. Government Printing Office, Washington, DC 20402.

Occupational Outlook Quarterly. Quarterly. $11.00/yr.
Supplements information in the *Occupational Outlook Handbook.* Gives information on careers of particular interest to vocational counselors. Order from: Superintendent of Documents, U.S. Government Printing Office, Washington, DC 20402.

U.S. Department of State Indexes of Living Costs Abroad. Quarterly. $10.00/yr. domestic, $12.00/yr. foreign.
Reports indexes based on the difference between living costs in Washington, DC, and each of more than 160 foreign cities. Order from: Superintendent of Documents, U.S. Government Printing Office, Washington, DC 20402.

Selected List of Books and Pamphlets

"Employment in Perspective: Working Women." Quarterly. 4p. free.
Reports on various aspects of women in the labor force.

"How To Get Information from the Bureau of Labor Statistics." 1984. 12p. free.
Tells what information is produced, where to find it, and how to get in touch with the Bureau of Labor Statistics.

"Important Events in American Labor History 1778-1978." 40p. free.
Summarizes major steps, beginning with the journeymen printers of New York City combining to demand an increase in wages in 1778.

"Major Programs, Bureau of Labor Statistics." 1985. n.p. free. Report 718.
Examines the scope of the bureau's major statistical programs, data, form of publications, and data uses. Describes other services the bureau offers.

"Our Changing Economy: A BLS Centennial Chartbook." 1984. $2.75. Bulletin 2211.
Covers 100 years of statistics, giving a graphic picture of changes in the American economy. Order from: Superintendent of Documents, U.S. Government Printing Office, Washington, DC 20402.

Library:
Department of Labor Library
Frances Perkins Bldg.
200 Constitution Ave., NW
Room N2439
Washington, DC 20210
(202) 523-6992
Provides reading rooms.

Special Services: Major data series are available online such as: The Consumer Price Index, The Producer Price Index, The Employment Situation, Commissioner's Statement on the Employment Situation, Major Collective Bargaining Settlements, Productivity and Costs, State and Metropolitan Area Employment and Unemployment, Employment Cost Index, U.S. Import and Export Prices Indexes, Real Earnings, Earnings of Workers and Their Families. The cost of online access, from $10.00 to $30.00 per release, depends on length and transmission speed. Inquire about one-time service fees. Request "Information Online" form from the Department of Labor Library at the address given above.

BUREAU OF LAND MANAGEMENT
United States Department of the Interior
Office of Public Affairs
Washington, DC 20240
(202) 343-9435

Date Established: 1946

Objectives of the Agency: Manage under multiple-use principles the federal public lands located mostly in western states with some scattered lands in the east.

Curriculum: Geography

Subjects: U.S. — public lands
U.S. — geography

Locations:

AK

Bureau of Land Management
State Office
701 C St.
P.O. Box 13
Anchorage, AK 99513
(907) 271-5555

AZ

Bureau of Land Management
State Office
3707 N. Seventh St.
P.O. Box 16563
Phoenix, AZ 85011
(602) 241-5504

CA

Bureau of Land Management
State Office
2800 Cottage Way
Sacramento, CA 95825
(916) 484-4724

CO, KS

Bureau of Land Management
State Office
2020 Arapahoe St.
Denver, CO 80205
(303) 294-7092

ID

Bureau of Land Management
State Office
3380 Americana Terrace
Boise, ID 83706
(208) 334-1770

Eastern States (All states bordering on and east of the Mississippi River)

Bureau of Land Management
Eastern States Office
350 S. Pickett St.
Alexandria, VA 22304
(703) 274-0190

MT, ND, SD

Bureau of Land Management
State Office
222 N. Thirty-Second St.
P.O. Box 36800
Billings, MT 59107
(407) 657-6561

NV

Bureau of Land Management
State Office
300 Booth St.
P.O. Box 12000
Reno, NV 89520
(702) 784-5311

NM, OK, TX

Bureau of Land Management
State Office
Joseph M. Montoya Federal Bldg.
South Federal Place
P.O. Box 1449
Santa Fe, NM 87504-1449
(505) 988-6316

OR, WA

Bureau of Land Management
State Office
825 N.E. Multonomah St.
P.O. Box 2965
Portland, OR 97208
(503) 231-6274

UT

Bureau of Land Management
State Office
324 S. State St.
Salt Lake City, UT 84111-2303
(801) 524-5311

NE, WY

Bureau of Land Management
State Office
2515 Warren Ave.
P.O. Box 1828
Cheyenne, WY 82003
(307) 772-2111

Publications: Pamphlets. Magazine. On public lands.

Serials, Subscription Publications, etc.

"Your Public Lands." Issued spring, summer, autumn, winter. 24p. $11.90/yr.

Official publication of the Bureau of Land Management. Contains news highlights and articles. Order from: Superintendent of Documents, U.S. Government Printing Office, Washington, DC 20402.

Selected List of Books and Pamphlets

"BLM in the East." 1985. 3p. free.

Introduces responsibilities, programs, and accomplishments carried on in states bordering on and east of the Mississippi River.

14 / Bureau of Land Management

"Camping on the Public Lands." n.d. folded map. free.

Describes what various western states have to offer in camping services, such as boat ramps, picnicking, hiking, snowmobiling, etc.

"Managing the Nation's Public Lands." Current. 63p. free.

Covers in a progress report energy and mineral programs, land programs, renewable resource programs, support services, financial management, and the future. Organizational chart. Map.

"Promise of the Land." n.d. 40p. free.

Gives background of the land management agency. Defines the public lands. Proposes to acquaint the general public with the bountiful assets of public lands.

BUREAU OF MINES
U.S. Department of the Interior
Office of Technical Information
2401 E St., NW
Washington, DC 20241
(202) 634-4704

Date Established: 1910

Objectives of the Agency: Provide research, statistics, operations, safety and health issues in mines and minerals.

Curriculum: Geography

Subjects: Mines and mineral resources

Publications: Bulletins. Yearbooks. Reports of investigations. Information circulars. Technical progress reports. Mineral commodity profiles. Mineral issues. Handbooks. Surveys. Perspectives.

Bibliographies, Sales Catalogs, Publications Lists, etc.

"Bureau of Mines Commodity Reports." n.d. 1p. free.

Describes how to obtain free copies of mineral industry surveys and other reports. Includes list of subjects to request. Indicates frequency of publication.

"Bureau Publications." n.d. 2p. free.

Describes publications available as well as associated documents.

"Indexed List of Publications and Articles." n.d. 1p. free.

Lists books that comprise a complete, indexed list of Bureau of Mines publications and articles. Includes microfiche price. Makes yearly lists of publications and articles available from 1975. Before 1975 lists are cumulative.

"List of Journal Articles by Bureau of Mines Authors Published July 1, 1910 to January 1, 1960." 295p. $17.00. Item no. PB295432/AS. $3.50 on microfiche.

Order from: National Technical Information Service, 5285 Port Royal Rd., Springfield, VA 22161.

"List of Publications Issued by the Bureau of Mines from July 1, 1910, to January 1, 1960." 826p. $38.00. Item no. PB295062/AS. $3.50 on microfiche. Order from: National Technical Information Service, 5285 Port Royal Rd., Springfield, VA 22161.

"New Publications." Monthly. 10p. free. Monthly List 839.

Describes new publications, both free and for sale, with instructions for ordering.

"Reports of Investigations and Information Circulars." 2p. free.

Describes how to obtain free copies of bureau publications. Includes list of subjects to be requested.

Serials, Subscription Publications, etc.

Minerals Yearbook. 3 vol./year. Vol. 1, *Metals and Minerals;* vol. 2, *Area Reports: Domestic;* vol. 3, *Area Reports; International.*

Order from: Superintendent of Documents, U.S. Government Printing Office, Washington, DC 20402.

Vol. 1. 1984. 961p. $16.00. 024-004-92124-1.

Contains 73 chapters covering metals and minerals; commodity or commodity group chapters with mineral data; mining and quarrying trends with a statistical summary.

Vol. 2. 1984. 601p. $14.00. 024-004-02132-2.

Contains 52 chapters: mineral industry of each of the 50 states, the U.S. island possessions in the Pacific Ocean, the Caribbean, and Puerto Rico. Statistical summary.

Vol. 3. 1984. 1239p. $20.00. 024-004-02129-2.

Contains 90 chapters: latest mineral data on over 130 foreign countries and the importance of those minerals in the economies of those countries. Reviews international minerals industry as a whole.

Selected List of Books and Pamphlets

"Bureau of Mines Research 1984." Annual. 138p. free.

Summarizes significant results in mineral technology and economics. Includes selected bibliography of publications and patents issued during the past three years.

Audiovisuals:

Filmographies, Sales, Lists, etc.

"Films." current. 29p. free.

Describes films and ordering information. Most

of the films depict mining and metallurgical operations and related manufacturing processes. Some show where minerals are found and how they are extracted from the earth and turned into useful products. Others deal with mineral and other natural resources as an important asset. Borrower only pays return postage for the film when from the central Pittsburgh library. Catalog lists distribution centers located in various states and indicates restrictions. Films are grouped under such curriculum areas as physics, industrial arts, general sciences, etc. to aid the educator. Include identification number and order from: Motion Pictures, Bureau of Mines, 4800 Forbes Ave., Pittsburgh, PA 15213.

Individual Audiovisuals

"Copper." n.d. 27½ minutes. 16mm. color. free loan. ID #256.

Explains the past and present importance of copper from scenes of an ancient tomb painting to modern cities. Shows metal's atomic and molecular structures. Describes how this oldest of modern metals may be recycled.

"Lead in Motion." Made in cooperation with Lead Industries Association. n.d. 20 minutes. 16mm. color. free loan. ID #277.

Shows how the diverse properties of lead are linked through the common denominator of the universe, energy. Also shows how ore minerals are extracted from the earth, the process of smelting and refining, commercial uses, and recycling.

"The Minerals Challenge." Made in cooperation with the Natural Resources Division of the Union Pacific Railroad Company. n.d. 27 minutes. 16mm. color. free loan. ID #271.

Relates how the country's ever-increasing need for fuels, metals, and other mineral materials is being met by technological advances. Shows key role of minerals in society and how low-grade ores present challenges and opportunities for American youth.

"Pennsylvania and Its Natural Resources." Made in cooperation with Atlantic Richfield Corporation. n.d. 28 minutes. 16mm. color. free loan. ID #272.

Describes how the state conserves its natural resources to assure a heritage for coming generations. Includes modern lumbering and reforestation efforts along with various mineral resources. Covers research in coal and making municipal refuse into energy.

"Silver." Made in cooperation with the Silver Institute. n.d. 28 minutes. 16mm. color. free loan. ID #265.

Relates story of silver mining, the formation of silver-bearing ores millions of years ago, and the importance of silver in the development of the American west. Covers metallurgical processes necessary today along with waste disposal, land reclamation, and air pollution. Shows properties of silver in animation.

"Wealth out of Waste." n.d. 27 minutes. 16mm. color. free loan. ID #274.

Explains recycling and waste utilization research aimed at turning rubbish heaps into valuable resources for supplementing the nation's declining mineral reserves. Shows testing of experimental waste-processing techniques in pilot plants and what is produced.

Special Services: If you wish to receive "press notices" on Bureau of Mines activities, obtain a list of 12 subjects, such as environmental information and science engineering features, to request.

BUREAU OF RECLAMATION
Office of Public Affairs
Department of the Interior
Eighteenth and C Sts., NW
Washington, DC 20240
(202) 343-4662

Date Established: 1902

Objectives of the Agency: Locate, build, and maintain works for the storage, diversion, and development of waters for arid and semiarid lands in the West; aid states, local governments, and other federal agencies to stabilize and stimulate local and regional economies, and to enhance and protect the environment.

Curriculum: Environmental studies, geography

Subjects: Environment
U.S. – geography

Locations:

Bureau of Reclamation Commissioner's Office
Department of the Interior
Eighteenth and C Sts., NW
Room 7654
Washington, DC 20240
(202) 343-4157

Bureau of Reclamation Engineering and Research
 Center
Bldg. 67
P.O. Box 25007
Denver, CO 80225
(303) 234-2041

Bureau of Reclamation Pacific Northwest Region
550 W. Fort St.
P.O. Box 043
Boise, ID 83724
(208) 334-1938

16 / Bureau of Reclamation

Bureau of Reclamation Mid-Pacific Region
2800 Cottage Way
Sacramento, CA 95825
(916) 484-4647

Bureau of Reclamation Lower Colorado Region
Nevada Hwy. and Park St.
P.O. Box 427
Boulder City, NV 89005
(702) 293-8000, ext. 419

Bureau of Reclamation Southwest Region
715 S. Tyler
Suite 201
Amarillo, TX 79101
(806) 378-5400, ext. 437

Bureau of Reclamation Upper Missouri Region
316 N. Twenty-Sixth St.
P.O. Box 2553
Billings, MT 59103
(406) 657-6218

Bureau of Reclamation Lower Missouri Region
Denver Federal Center
P.O. Box 25247
Building 20
Denver, CO 80225
(303) 234-4257

Publications: Pamphlets. Maps. Posters. On water uses and history of water development.

Selected List of Books and Pamphlets

"Conservation and Full Utilization of Water." 1975. over-size poster. free.
  Illustrates various uses of water.

"Historical Site: Boise Diversion Dam." 1978. 12p. free.
  Describes the history and development of the dam that is on the National Register of Historic Places.

"Historical Site: Minidoka Powerplant." 1978. 12p. free.
  Describes the history and development of the Snake River Dam, which was added to the National Register of Historical Places in 1974.

"Map 1." n.d. folded map. free.
  Shows the recreation areas of Idaho, Oregon, and Washington. Includes a chart of facilities, activities, and visitor aids.

"Map 2." n.d. folded map. free.
  Shows the recreation areas of Montana, Nebraska, North Dakota, South Dakota, and Wyoming. Includes a chart of facilities, activities, and visitor aids.

"Map 3." n.d. folded map. free.
  Shows the recreation areas of Arizona, California, Nevada, and Utah. Includes a chart of facilities, activities, and visitor aids.

"Map 4." n.d. folded map. free.
  Shows the recreation areas of Colorado, Kansas, Oklahoma, New Mexico, and Texas. Includes a chart of facilities, activities, and visitor aids.

Audiovisuals:

Filmographies, Sales Lists, etc.

"Bureau of Reclamation 16mm Films." n.d. 1p. free.
  Describes free loan films and where to request them.

BUREAU OF THE CENSUS
Public Information Office
Department of Commerce
Washington, DC 20233
(301) 763-4051

Date Established: 1902

Objectives of the Agency: Collect, tabulate, publish statistical data about the people and economy of the country.

Curriculum: Government, social studies, sociology

Subjects: Census
  U.S. — census
  U.S. — population

Locations:

AL, FL, GA (all counties except Richmond), TN (all counties except Dyer, Lake, Obion, Shelby)

Bureau of the Census Regional Office
1365 Peachtree St., NE
Room 645
Atlanta, GA 30309
(404) 881-2274

CT, MA, ME, NH, NY (counties of Albany, Allegany, Broome, Cattaraugus, Cayuga, Chatauqua, Cnemung, Chenango, Clinton, Courtland, Erie, Essex, Franklin, Fulton, Genesee, Hamilton, Herkimer, Jefferson, Lewis, Livingston, Madison, Monroe, Montgomery, Niagara, Oneida, Onandaga, Ontario, Orleans, Oswego, Otsego, Rensselaer, St. Lawrence, Saratoga, Schenectady, Schoharie, Schuyler, Seneca, Steuben, Tioga, Tompkins, Warren, Washington, Wayine, Wyoming, Yeates), PA (Susquehanna County), RI, VT

Bureau of the Census Regional Office
441 Stuart St.
Tenth Floor
Boston, MA 02116
(617) 223-0226

DC, GA (Richmond County), IN (counties of Clark and Floyd), KY (all counties except Boone, Campbell, Henderson, Kenton), MD (counties of Calvert, Charles, Montgomery, Prince Georges, St. Mary's), NC, OH (Lawrence County), SC, VA, WV (counties of Boone, Cabell, Lincoln, Logan, McDowell, Mercer, Mingo, Wayne, Wyoming)

Bureau of the Census Regional Office
230 S. Tryon St.
Suite 800
Charlotte, NC 28202
(704) 371-6144

IL (all counties except Madison and St. Clair), IN (all counties except Clark, Dearborn, De Kalb, Floyd, Steuben), IA (Scott County), KY (Henderson County)

Bureau of the Census Regional Office
55 E. Jackson Blvd.
Suite 1304
Chicago, IL 60604
(312) 353-0980

AR, LA, MS, NM, OK (counties of Le Flore, McCurtain, Sequoyah), TN (Shelby County), TX

Bureau of the Census Regional Office
1100 Commerce St.
Room 3E27
Dallas, TX 75242
(214) 767-0625

AZ, CO IA (Pottawattamie County), KS (all counties except Bourbon, Crawford, Douglas, Franklin, Jefferson, Johnson, Leavenworth, Linn, Miami, Neosho, Osage, Shawnee, Wyandotte), MT (all counties except Lincoln), NE, ND (all counties except Cass), OK (all counties except Le Flore, McCurtain, Sequoyah), SD, UT, WY

Bureau of the Census Regional Office
7655 W. Mississippi Ave.
P.O. Box 26750
Denver, CO 80226
(303) 236-2200

IN (counties of Dearborn, De Kalk, Steuben), KY (counties of Boone, Campbell, Kenton), MI, OH (all counties except Lawrence), PA (Mercer County), WV (counties of Brooke, Hancock, Marshall, Ohio)

Bureau of the Census Regional Office
Federal Bldg. and U.S. Courthouse
231 W. Lafayette St.
Room 565
Detroit, MI 48226

IA (all counties except Pottawattamie and Scott), IL (counties of Madison and St. Clair), KS (counties of Bourbon, Crawford, Douglas, Franklin, Jefferson, Johnson, Leavenworth, Linn, Miami, Neosho, Osage, Shawnee, Wyandotte), MN, MO, ND (Cass County), TN (counties of Dyer, Lake, Obion), WI

Bureau of the Census Regional Office
1 Gateway Center
Fourth and State Sts.
Kansas City, KS 66101
(913) 236-3731

CA (counties of Fresno, Imperial, Inyo, Kern, Kings, Los Angeles, Madera, Mariposa, Merced, Monterey, Orange, Riverside, San Benito, San Bernardino, San Diego, San Luis Obispo, Santa Barbara, Santa Cruz, Tulare, Ventura), HI, NV (Clark County)

Bureau of the Census Regional Office
11777 San Vicente Blvd.
Room 810
Los Angeles, CA 90049
(213) 209-6612

NJ (counties of Bergen, Essex, Hudson, Middlesex, Morris, Passaic, Somerset, Union), NY (counties of Bronx, Columbia, Delaware, Dutches, Greene, Kings, Nassau, New York, Orange, Putnam, Queens, Richmond, Rockland, Suffolk, Sullivan, Ulster, Westchester)

Bureau of the Census Regional Office
26 Federal Plaza
Room 37-130
New York, NY 10273

DE, MD (counties of Allegany, Anne Arundel, Baltimore, Baltimore City, Caroline, Carroll, Cecil, Dorchester, Frederick, Garrett, Harford, Howard, Kent, Queen Annes, Somerset, Talbot, Washington, Wicomico, Worcester), NJ (counties of Atlantic, Burlington, Camden, Cape May, Cumberland, Gloucester, Hunterdon, Mercer, Monmouth, Ocean, Salem, Sussex, Warren), PA (all counties except Mercer and Susquehanna), WV (all counties except Boone, Brooke, Cabell, Hancock, Lincoln, Logan, Marshall, McDowell, Mercer, Mingo, Ohio, Wayne, Wyoming)

Bureau of the Census Regional Office
William J. Green Jr. Federal Bldg.
600 Arch St.
Room 9244
Philadelphia, PA 19106

AK, CA (counties of Alameda, Alpine, Amador, Butte, Calevaras, Colusa, Contra Costa, Del Norte, El Dorado, Glenn, Humboldt, Lake, Lassen, Marin, Mendocino, Modoc, Mono, Napa, Nevada, Placer, Plumas, Sacramento, San Francisco, San Joaquin, San Mateo, Santa Clara, Shasta, Sierra, Siskiyou, Solano, Sonoma, Stanislaus, Sutter, Tehama, Trinity, Tuolumne, Yolo, Yuba), ID, MT (Lincoln County), NV (all counties except Clark), OR, WA

Bureau of the Census District Office
Lake Union Bldg.
1700 Westlake Ave., N
Seattle, WA 98109
(206) 442-7080

Specialized Offices

Data Preparation Division
1201 E. Tenth St.
Jeffersonville, IN 47132

Personal Census Service Branch
Walnut and Pine Sts.
Pittsburg, KS 66762

Publications: Reports. Tapes. Statistics. Catalogs. Guides. Directories. Microfiche. Include data on agriculture, manufacturing, construction, population, foreign trade, housing, transportation, etc.

Bibliographies, Sales Catalogs, Publications Lists, etc.

Bureau of the Census Catalog. Current. c.270p. $7.00. S/N 003-024-05668-2.
   Includes index and subject guide. Data products, data subjects, data services, reference for census data. Order from: Superintendent of Documents, U.S. Government Printing Office, Washington, DC 20402.

"Monthly Product Announcement." Monthly. 12p. free.
   Describes publications, microfiche, what is becoming available, and other current news. Order from: Data User Services Division, Customer Services (Publications), Bureau of the Census, Washington, DC 20233.

Special Services: Cendata, the Census Bureau's on-line data service, may be accessed by subscribing to Dialog Information Services: (800) 227-1927; or in California: (800) 982-5838.

Inquire about the "Factfinder for the Nation" series (CFFI-22). Dates and pages vary. $.25 per copy. Each of the 22 pamphlets deals with some census material, such as "Agricultural Statistics" (Feb. 1983, 4p.) and "Data for Small Communities" (Sept. 1981, 12 p.).

For a fee, searches are made of decennial census records, and certificates issued to individuals for use as evidence of age, relationship, or place of birth.

BUREAU OF THE MINT
Department of the Treasury
501 Thirteenth St., NW
Washington, DC 20220
(202) 376-0477

Date Established: 1792

Objectives of the Agency: Manufacture coins for the United States; distribute coins through Federal Reserve Banks; produce foreign coins; oversee the custody, processing, and movement of treasury bullion; and manufacture national medals and numismatic items for sale.

Curriculum: Social studies

Subjects: Coinage
             Mints

Locations:

United States Mint
The Department of the Treasury
Philadelphia, PA 19106

United States Mint
The Department of the Treasury
Denver, CO 80204

United States Assay Office
The Department of the Treasury
San Francisco, CA 94102

United States Bullion Depository
The Department of the Treasury
Fort Knox, KY 40121

United States Bullion Depository
The Department of the Treasury
West Point, NY 10996

Publications: Catalogs. Fact sheets. Pamphlets. On coins, medals, coin tours, and coinage.

Bibliographies, Sales Catalogs, Publications Lists, etc.

"Books of Interest to Coin Collectors." n.d. 1p. free.
   Tells name and price of various books, and how to order.

"Catalogue of Official Coins and Medals." Current. 13p. free.
   Describes coins, medals and medallions. Order form.

Selected List of Books and Pamphlets

"Financial Tour." n.d. 4-fold. free.
   Gives locations and descriptions of six financial institutions, such as Carpenter's Hall and the First

Bank of the United States. Acquaints visitors with the development of the U.S. banking system and the men who built it.

"How To Make a Penny at the Philadelphia Mint." 1975. 4p. free.

Describes step-by-step the way that pennies are made. Gives history of the United States Mint. Illustrations.

"Mint Marks." 1984. 2p. free.

Gives the history, function, and use of mint marks. Includes tables of current mint marks and special coins and sets.

"Mint Tour Data." 1982. 4p. free.

Gives locations and visitor information of the Bureau of Mint headquarters, Denver Mint, San Francisco Old Mint, Philadelphia Mint.

"Percentage of Composition of Metallic Elements in Current United States Coins." 1982. 2p. free.

Discusses composition of various coins and the Coinage Act of 1965.

"The United States Mint." 1983. 1p. free.

Describes the history and activities of the mint, a bureau of the Department of the Treasury.

Special Services: If interested in being on the mailing list, request the form "Please Add My Name to the Bureau of the Mint Mailing List."

CARL SANDBURG HOME
National Historic Site
P.O. Box 395
Flat Rock, NC 28731

Date Established: 1968

Curriculum: English

Subjects: American literature
Poets, American

Publications: Fact sheet.

Selected List of Books and Pamphlets

"Carl Sandburg Home." 1984. 2p. free.

Provides biographical information about Carl Sandburg and briefing about the Connemara home. Map for touring the grounds. Photographs.

CENTER FOR HEALTH PROMOTION AND EDUCATION
Centers for Disease Control
Department of Health and Human Services
CHPE-ER
Building 1 South
1600 Clifton Rd., NE
Room SSB 249
Atlanta, GA 30333
(404) 329-3492

Date Established: 1979

Objectives of the Agency: Offer technical help primarily to state and local health agencies, schools, and health care delivery settings in the areas of health education, health promotion, nutrition, reproductive health, violence, and epidemiology; address risks from smoking, obesity, and hypertension; and provide programmatic interventions in the case of these risks.

Curriculum: Health

Subjects: Health education

Publications: Fact sheets. Serials. Catalogs.

Bibliographies, Sales Catalogs, Publications Lists, etc.

"Community Health Education Resources." Current. 20p. free.

Provides order number, price, and title of material for sale from the National Technical Information Service.

"Health Education Materials and the Organizations That Offer Them." Prepared by the Health Insurance Institute. n.d. 25p. free.

Provides information on disease prevention and health education. Indicates whether materials are provided for small fee or free. Lists such categories as: *accident prevention, aging, alcoholism, allergies,* etc.

"Staying Healthy: A Bibliography of Health Promotion Materials." 2d ed. 42p. free.

Provides a guide to current information on health promotion and disease prevention topics. Arranged by subject and followed by a general resource section giving an overview of health information services within the Department of Health and Human Services. Order from: NHIC, Dept. FPS, P.O. Box 1133, Washington, DC 20013-1133. Enclose a self-addressed mailing label.

Serials, Subscription Publications, etc.

"Current Awareness in Health Education." Monthly. 63p. $34.00/yr. domestic, $42.50/yr. foreign.

Disseminates the growing body of information about health education. Includes citations and abstracts of current journal articles, monographs, conference proceedings, reports, nonpublished documents, and descriptions of programs. Order from: Superintendent of Documents, U.S. Government Printing Office, Washington, DC 20402.

"Focal Points." Bimonthly. 12p. $8.50/yr. domestic, $10.65/yr. foreign.

Provides articles and news on health education, and information on schools, grants, and teaching module programs.

Selected List of Books and Pamphlets

"Source Book for Health Education Materials and Community Resources." 1982. 92p. $5.50. S/N 017-023-00144-2.

Describes materials in state or federal sources, nonprofit or for profit sources, directories and catalogs, newsletters and periodicals.

CENTER FOR PREVENTION SERVICES
Centers for Disease Control
Department of Health and Human Services
Public Health Service
Atlanta, GA 30333
(404) 329-3286

Date Established: 1973

Objectives of the Agency: Promote immunization.

Curriculum: Health

Subjects: Vaccination

Publications: Pamphlets. Lists on immunization.

Selected List of Books and Pamphlets

"The Immunization Division at DCD." 1983. 16p. free.

Explains the development and progress of immunization. Organization chart.

Audiovisuals:

Filmographies, Sales Lists, etc.

"Films and Tapes on Immunization." 1982. 4p. free.

Describes audiovisuals, including suggested audience theme, where to obtain them, and the cost.

CENTER FOR THE BOOK
The Library of Congress
Washington, DC 20540
(202) 287-5221

Date Established: 1977

Objectives of the Agency: Investigate the transmission of human knowledge and heighten public interest in the role that books and printing play in the spread of knowledge.

Curriculum: Library

Subjects: Library science

Publications: Books. Pamphlets.

Bibliographies, Sales Catalogs, Publications Lists, etc.

"The Center for the Book." 1985. 7p. free.

Lists publications in 2p. Includes title, date, pages, price, and addresses for ordering the publications, some of which are free. Also reports news about books.

Selected List of Books and Pamphlets

"The Center for the Book: Seeking Outreach." 1985. 7p. free.

Provides the Library of Congress and Daniel Boorstin's proposal for the Center for the Book. Explains present and future scope of the center. Gives information on publications sponsored by the center.

CENTERS FOR DISEASE CONTROL
Public Inquiries
Building 1
1600 Clifton Rd., NE
Room B-63
Atlanta, GA 30333
(404) 329-3286

Date Established: 1973

Objectives of the Agency: Protect public health by providing leadership and direction in the prevention and control of diseases and other preventable conditions and by responding to public health emergencies. Its major operating parts are: Epidemiology Program Office, International Health Program Office, Laboratory Program Office, Center for Prevention Services, Center for Environmental Health, National Institute for Occupational Safety and Health, Center for Health Promotion and Education, Center for Professional Development and Training, and Center for Infectious Diseases.

Curriculum: Health

Subjects: Communicable diseases—prevention

Locations:

HHS Regional Offices

CT, MA, ME, NH, RI, VT

HHS Region 1 Office
Division of Preventive Health Services
John Fitzgerald Kennedy Bldg.
Boston, MA 02203
(617) 223-4045

NJ, NY, PR, VI

HHS Region 2 Office
Division of Preventive Health Services
Federal Bldg.
26 Federal Plaza
Room 3337
New York, NY 10278
(212) 264-2441

DC, DE, MD, PA, VA, WV

HHS Region 3 Office
Division of Preventive Health Services
Gateway Bldg. #1
3521-35 Market St.
Philadelphia, PA 19101
(215) 596-6650

AL, FL, GA, KY, MS, NC, SC, TN

HHS Region 4 Office
Division of Preventive Health Services
101 Marietta Tower
Suite 1007
Atlanta, GA 30323
(404) 221-2313

IL, IN, MI, MN, OH, WI

HHS Region 5 Office
Division of Preventive Health Services
300 S. Wacker Dr.
Thirty-Third Floor
Chicago, IL 60606
(312) 886-3652

AR, LA, NM, OK, TX

HHS Region 6 Office
Division of Preventive Health Services
1200 Main Tower Bldg.
Room 1835
Dallas, TX 75202
(214) 767-3916

IA, KS, MO, NE

HHS Region 7 Office
Division of Preventive Health Services
601 E. Twelfth St.
Kansas City, MO 64106
(816) 374-3491

CO, MT, ND, SD, UT, WY

HHS Region 8 Office
Division of Preventive Health Services
1185 Federal Bldg.
1961 Stout St.
Denver, CO 80294
(303) 844-6163, ext. 16

AS, AZ, CA, GU, HI, NV, Trust Territory of the Pacific Islands, Commonwealth of Northern Mariana Islands

HHS Region 9 Office
Division of Preventive Health Services
50 United Nations Plaza
San Francisco, CA 94102
(415) 556-2219

AK, ID, OR, WA

HHS Region 10 Office
Division of Preventive Health Services
2901 Third Ave.
M.S. 402
Seattle, WA 98121
(206) 442-0502

State and Territorial Health Departments

AK

Alaska Department of Health and Social Services
Alaska Office Bldg.
Pouch H06
Juneau, AK 99811
(907) 465-3090

AL

Alabama State Department of Public Health
381 State Office Bldg.
Montgomery, AL 36130-1701
(205) 261-5052

AS

Government of American Samoa
LBJ Tropical Medical Center
Pago Pago, AS 96799
Overseas: 011-684-633-4590

AR

Arkansas Department of Health
4815 W. Markham St.
Little Rock, AR 72201
(501) 661-2111

AZ

Arizona Department of Health Services
1740 W. Adams St.
Phoenix, AZ 85007
(602) 255-1024

CA

Department of Health Services
714 P St.
Room 1253
Sacramento, CA 95814
(916) 445-1248

CO

Colorado Department of Health
4210 E. Eleventh Ave.
Denver, CO 80220
(303) 320-8333, ext. 6315

CT

Connecticut State Department of Health Services
150 Washington St.
Hartford, CT 06106
(203) 566-2279

DC

Department of Human Services
801 N. Capitol St., NE
Seventh Floor
Washington, DC 20002
(202) 727-0518

DE
Department of Health and Social Services
Jesse Cooper Bldg.
Capitol Square
Dover, DE 19901
(302) 736-4701

FL
Department of Health and Rehabilitative Services
Building 1
1323 Winewood Blvd.
Room 115
Tallahassee, FL 32301
(904) 487-2705

GA
Georgia Department of Human Resources
Division of Public Health
47 Trinity Ave., SW
Room 522H
Atlanta, GA 30334
(404) 656-4655

GU
Department of Public Health and Social Services
Government of Guam
P.O. Box 2816
Agana, GU 96910
Overseas: 011-671-734-2944

HI
Hawaii Department of Health
P.O. Box 3378
Honolulu, HI 96801
(808) 548-6505

IA
State Department of Health
Lucas State Office Bldg.
Des Moines, IA 50319
(515) 281-5605

ID
Department of Health and Welfare
Division of Health
Statehouse
Boise, ID 83720
(208) 334-4283

IL
Illinois Department of Public Health
535 W. Jefferson St.
Springfield, IL 62761
(217) 782-4977

IN
Indiana State Board of Health
1330 W. Michigan St.
P.O. Box 1964
Indianapolis, IN 46206-1964
(317) 633-8400

KS
Kansas Department of Health and Environment
Forbes Field
Topeka, KS 66620
(913) 862-9360, ext. 522

KY
Cabinet for Human Resources
Department of Health Services
275 E. Main St.
Frankfort, KY 40601
(502) 564-3970

LA
Office of Health Services and Environmental Quality
Department of Health and Human Resources
325 Loyola Ave.
P.O. Box 60630
New Orleans, LA 70160
(504) 568-5052

MA
Massachusetts Department of Public Health
150 Tremont St.
Boston, MA 02111
(617) 727-2700

Mariana Islands
Department of Health Services
Commonwealth of the Northern Mariana Islands
Office of the Governor
Saipan, Mariana Islands 96950
Overseas: 011-670-6111
011-670-6112

MD
Maryland State Department of Health and Mental Hygiene
201 W. Preston St.
Baltimore, MD 21201
(301) 383-6195

ME
Maine Department of Human Services
Bureau of Health
Statehouse Station 11
Augusta, ME 04333
(207) 289-3201

MI

Michigan Department of Public Health
3500 N. Logan St.
P.O. Box 30035
Lansing, MI 48909
(517) 373-1320

MN

Minnesota Department of Health
717 Delaware St., SE
Minneapolis, MN 55440
(612) 623-5100

MO

Missouri Department of Social Services
Division of Health
Broadway State Office Bldg.
P.O. Box 570
Jefferson City, MO 65102
(314) 751-4330

MS

State Department of Health
Felix J. Underwood Building
2423 N. State St.
P.O. Box 1700
Jackson, MS 39215-1700
(601) 354-6646

MT

State Department of Health and Environmental Sciences
Cogswell Building
Helena, MT 59620
(406) 444-2544

NE

State Department of Health
301 Centennial Mall, S
P.O. Box 95007
Lincoln, NE 68509
(402) 471-2133

NC

Division of Health Services
Department of Human Resources
225 N. McDowell St.
P.O. Box 2091
Raleigh, NC 27602
(919) 733-3446

ND

State Department of Health
State Capitol Bldg.
Bismarck, ND 58505
(701) 224-2372

NH

Division of Public Health Services
State Department of Health and Welfare
Health and Welfare Bldg.
Hazen Drive
Concord, NH 03301
(603) 271-4501

NJ

State Department of Health
C N 360
Trenton, NJ 08625
(609) 292-7837

NM

Health Services Division
New Mexico Health and Environment Department
725 St. Michael's Dr.
P.O. Box 968
Santa Fe, NM 87504
(505) 984-0030

NV

State Department of Human Resources
Division of Health
505 E. King St.
Room 201
Carson City, NV 89710
(702) 885-4740

NY

State Department of Health
Empire State Plaza
Tower Building
Fourteenth Floor
Albany, NY 12237
(518) 474-2011

OH

Ohio Department of Health
246 N. High St.
P.O. Box 118
Columbus, OH 43216
(614) 466-2253

OK

State Department of Health
1000 N.E. Tenth
P.O. Box 53551
Oklahoma City, OK 73152
(405) 271-4200

OR

State Health Division
Department of Human Resources
1400 S.W. Fifth Avenue
Portland, OR 97201
(503) 229-5032

PA

Pennsylvania Department of Health
P.O. Box 90
Harrisburg, PA 17108
(717) 783-8770

PR

Puerto Rico Department of Health
Edificio a Hospital de Psiquiatria
Rio Piedras, PR 00936
(809) 765-5165

RI

Rhode Island Department of Health
75 Davis St.
Room 401
Providence, RI 02908
(401) 277-2231

SC

South Carolina Department of Health and
    Environmental Control
2600 Bull St.
Columbia, SC 29201
(803) 758-5445

SD

State Department of Health
Joe Foss Building
Pierre, SD 57501
(605) 773-3361

TN

Tennessee Department of Health and Environment
Cordell Hull Building
Room 344
Fifth Ave., North
Nashville, TN 37219
(615) 741-3111

Trust Territory of the Pacific Islands

Bureau of Health Services
Office of the High Commissioner
Trust Territory of the Pacific Islands
Saipan, Mariana Islands 96950
Overseas: 011-670-9854

TX

Texas Department of Health
1100 W. Forty-Ninth St.
Austin, TX 78756
(512) 458-7375

UT

Utah Department of Health
150 W. North Temple
Salt Lake City, UT 84110
(801) 533-6111

VA

State Department of Health
The James Madison Bldg.
109 Governor St.
Richmond, VA 23219
(804) 786-3561

VI

Virgin Islands Department of Health
P.O. Box 7309
St. Thomas, VI 00801
(809) 774-6097

VT

Vermont Department of Health
60 Main St.
Burlington, VT 05401
(802) 863-7200

WA

Division of Health
Department of Social and Health Services
Mail Stop ET-21
Olympia, WA 98504
(206) 753-5871

WI

Division of Health
Department of Health and Social Services
One W. Wilson St.
Room 234
P.O. Box 309
Madison, WI 53702
(608) 266-1511

WV

West Virginia Department of Health
1800 E. Washington St.
Room 206
Charleston, WV 25305
(304) 348-2971

WY

Division of Health and Medical Services
Wyoming Department of Health and Social Services
Hathaway Bldg.
Cheyenne, WY 82002
(307) 777-7121

Publications: If you wish information on a specific disease or condition, the center will try to send an appropriate brochure or reprint. It does not have a list of publications or keep a mailing list.

Selected List of Books and Pamphlets

"Centers for Disease Control Communications Directory." n.d. 99p. free.

Provides alphabetical listing, organizational listing, regional and state addresses, committees, telecommunications information, telephone dialing information, and office services guide.

CENTRAL INTELLIGENCE AGENCY
Public Affairs
Washington, DC 20505
(703) 351-7676
(703) 351-2053

Date Established: 1947

Objectives of the Agency: Advise the National Security Council and President on all matters of foreign intelligence related to the national security.

Curriculum: Government

Subjects: U.S.—national security

Publications: Maps. Atlases. Pamphlets. Documents. On functions, background information, and accomplishments.

Serials, Subscription Publications, etc.

To subscribe to all CIA publications at an annual subscription fee of $300.00 domestic, $325.00 foreign surface mail, $375.00 foreign air mail, write:
Document Expediting Project (DOCEX)
Exchange and Gifts Division
Library of Congress
Washington, DC 20540
(202) 287-9527

Selected List of Books and Pamphlets

"Fact Book on Intelligence." 1985. 31p. free.
Explains Central Intelligence Agency chronology, history, organization chart, biographies of directors, duties of various directors, the intelligence cycle, the president's intelligence organization, CIA medals, and agency credo. Photographs.

"Intelligence: The Acme of Skill." n.d. 29p. free.
Answers basic questions about the Central Intelligence Agency such as: who watches the Central Intelligence Agency? What kind of people work in the Central Intelligence Agency? What is the intelligence cycle? What is the president's intelligence organization? What are seal, medals, and headquarters building of the agency? Chronology. History. Photographs.

Special Services: Microfiche or microfilm service is available from the National Technical Information Service and the Library of Congress.

To obtain publications and selected maps, full or tailored subscriptions for documents published after February 1, 1979, write:
National Technical Information Service
U.S. Department of Commerce
5285 Port Royal Rd.
Springfield, VA 22161
NTIS order desk: (703) 487-4650
Subscription desk: (703) 487-4630

To obtain individual current publications as well as those published before February 1979, write:
Library of Congress
Photoduplication Service
Washington, DC 20540
(202) 287-5650

To subscribe to all CIA publications for $225.00 per year, write:
Document Expediting Project (DOCEX)
Exchange and Gifts Division
Library of Congress
Washington, DC 20540
(202) 287-5253

CHILDREN'S LITERATURE CENTER
Public Inquiries
Library of Congress
10 First St., SE
Washington, DC 20540
(202) 287-5535

Date Established: 1963

Objectives of the Agency: Provide reference and bibliographic assistance on all aspects of the study of children's literature, including critical reviews.

Curriculum: English, Library

Subjects: Children's literature
Library science

Publications: Bibliographies. Pamphlets. News sheets. Catalogs. Books. Lectures about books for children.

Bibliographies, Sales Catalogs, Publications Lists, etc.

"Publications." n.d. 2p. free.
Lists books and pamphlets for sale or free from the Library of Congress or Superintendent of Documents.

Selected List of Books and Pamphlets

"The Children's Literature Center." 1984. 2p. free.
Summarizes what the center does and what it has to offer.

"Dare to Be Creative!" 1984. 30p. free.
Reprints a lecture about writing for children presented at the Library of Congress by Madeleine L'Engle.

CLARA BARTON NATIONAL HISTORIC SITE
National Park Service
5801 Oxford Rd.
Glen Echo, MD 20768
(301) 492-6245

Date Established: 1974

Objectives of the Agency: Preserve the home of the founder of the American Red Cross, which was used for seven years as the organization's headquarters.

26 / Clara Barton National Historic Site

Curriculum: History, women's studies

Subjects: America—history
Women—U.S.

Publications: Books. Postcards. Posters. Souvenirs. On Clara Barton, the Civil War, and Victorian times.

Bibliographies, Sales Catalogs, Publications Lists, etc.

"Parks & History Association Price List." 1p. free.
Gives title, category (book, souvenir, postcard, or poster), and price.

Selected List of Books and Pamphlets

"Clara Barton National Historic Site." n.d. 2p. free.
Provides background information about the site and Clara Barton's work.

"Clara Barton Site Brochure." 1983. 4-fold. free.
Chronicles the life of Clara Barton and the American Red Cross. Chronology. Map. Photographs.

"Directions to Clara Barton National Historic Site." n.d. 1p. free.
Provides map with information on roads and visitor parking.

Audiovisuals:

Filmographies, Sales Lists, etc.

"Programs Available for Off-Site and On-Site Presentation." n.d. 1p. free.
Gives titles of slide programs and films. For reservations and further information, please call the telephone number cited above.

CLEARINGHOUSE ON CHILD ABUSE AND NEGLECT INFORMATION
P.O. Box 1182
Washington, DC 20013
(301) 251-5157

Date Established: 1974

Objectives of the Agency: Provide focal point for federal activities related to child abuse and neglect; conduct research into causes, prevention, treatment; support demonstration projects; publish annual directories of programs and research; give technical aid; and provide state grants.

Curriculum: Child care, guidance

Subjects: Child abuse

Publications: Bibliographies. Directories. Reviews. Data tapes. Catalogs. Pamphlets. Manuals. Guidelines. Posters. Studies. Material aimed at general public, parents, educators, and professionals.

Bibliographies, Sales Catalogs, Publications Lists, etc.

"Catalog of Materials." 1986. 3p. free. 20-1017.
Describes what is available, both for sale and free. You are requested to circle the order number, price, and code for the materials you wish to order and send the entire catalog along with any necessary payment.

Selected List of Books and Pamphlets

"The Educator's Role in the Prevention and Treatment of Child Abuse and Neglect." 1984. 73p. free. 84-30172 code 12A.
Describes roles of teachers, administrators, staff, and others in identification, treatment, and prevention.

"Everything You Always Wanted to Know About Child Abuse and Neglect." 1984. 23p. free. 20-01016 code 16A.
Gives types and signs of child abuse and neglect, profiles of victims and families, causes, treatment, and reporting laws.

"National Study of the Incidence and Severity of Child Abuse and Neglect: Executive Summary." 1981. 17p. free. 81-30329 code 15D.
Covers data analysis of reported and estimated cases of child abuse and neglect, incidence rates, numbers of major forms of child maltreatment, age and sex of victims.

Selected Readings on Adolescent Maltreatment. 1981. 118p. $11.80. 81-30301 code 11D.
Gives incidence of teenage abuse and neglect, adolescent sexual mistreatment, and physical abuse. Describes intervention and service.

Audiovisuals:

Filmographies, Sales Lists, etc.

"Audiovisual Materials." n.d. 7p. free.
Includes title, date of issue, running time, format, and ordering information for each entry. Includes purchase or rental of films, video, and VHS from various distributors.

"Parenting and Parent Education: Audiovisual Materials." n.d. 13p. free.
Provides materials on prevention, discipline, child behavior, conferences, social problems, parenting, and related topics. Includes videocassettes, audiocassettes, and films, from individual distributors or producers.

Individual Audiovisuals

"Battered Teens." 1982. 31 minutes. 16mm or video. color. $495.00 (16mm). $370.00 (video).
Pictures the efforts of a 16-year-old girl and her family to stop the cycle of abuse. Discusses Parents

Anonymous and a teen self-help group. Order from: Films Incorporated, 1213 Wilmette Ave., Wilmette, IL 60091. (312) 256-3200 or (800) 323-4222.

"Better Safe than Sorry." 1985. 19 minutes. 16mm or video. color. $395.00. (16mm or video).

Teaches adolescents how to avoid sexually abusive situations. Order from: Filmfair Communications, 10900 Ventura Blvd., Studio City, CA 91604. (818) 985-0244.

"Breaking Silence." 1984. 58 minutes. 16mm or video. color. $800.00 (16mm). $250.00 (video). Rentals: $100.00 for group of 40 or fewer; $150.00-$300.00 for community/campus wide; $20.00 for preview, public libraries only.

Documentary about incest and child sexual abuse. First person accounts from adults who were sexually abused as children. Order from: Film Distribution Center, 1028 Industry Dr., Seattle, WA 98188. (206) 575-1575.

"Finding Out: Incest and Family Sexual Abuse." 1984. 25 minutes. 16mm or video. color. $550.00/$75.00 (16mm). $495.00/$75.00 (video).

Portrays the role played by the victim's mother in a case of father-daughter sexual abuse and the devastating emotional effects of incest experienced by a young girl. Order from: Kinetic Films, 255 Delaware Ave., Suite 340, Buffalo, NY 14202. (716) 856-7631.

"Touch." 1983. 32 minutes. 16mm or video. color. $495.00/$80.00 (16mm). $395.00/$80.00 (video).

Teaches children the difference between good and bad touching. Presents their right to say "no." Order from: Simon and Schuster Communications, MTI Teleprograms, Inc., 108 Wilmot Rd., Deerfield, IL 60015. (312) 940-1260. (800) 621-7870.

Special Services: Publicly searchable database, DIALOG FILE 64, contains several types of information such as court case decisions, abstracts of journal articles, and state laws relating to child abuse and neglect.

The "Child Abuse and Neglect Searching Service" replies to telephone and written requests for information from the Clearinghouse on Child Abuse and Neglect Information.

CLEARINGHOUSE ON THE HANDICAPPED
Office of Special Education and Rehabilitative Services
U.S. Department of Education
Switzer Bldg.
Room 3132
Washington, DC 20202
(202) 732-1241
(202) 732-1245
(202) 732-1250

Date Established: 1973

Objectives of the Agency: Provide special education programs and services to meet the needs and develop the potential of handicapped children; design programs to reduce human dependency and use capabilities of all handicapped persons; train personnel; give grants, financial aid, and media services.

Curriculum: Special education

Subjects: Handicapped

Publications: Guides. Newsletter. Reports. Directories. Magazines. Digests.

Bibliographies, Sales Catalogs, Publications Lists, etc.

"Publication List." n.d. 2p. free.

Lists publications available from various sources. Includes annotations.

Selected List of Books and Pamphlets

Digest of Data on Persons with Disabilities. 1984. 177p. free.

Compiles statistical data on persons with disabilities and includes such topics as *impairments, work disabilities, limitation of activity, employment,* etc. Interprets the data through highlights and explanatory notes. Tables. Charts.

Directory of National Information Sources on Handicapping Conditions and Related Services. 1985. 263p. $7.50. ID #E-85-2207. S/N 065-000-00219-1.

Describes 363 organizations and federal operations. For information and service providers, order from: Superintendent of Documents, U.S. Government Printing Office, Washington, DC 20402.

COMMISSION OF FINE ARTS
708 Jackson Place, NW
Washington, DC 20006
(202) 566-1066

Date Established: 1910

Objectives of the Agency: Give artistic advice regarding the appearance of Washington, DC; review plans for public buildings, parks, and other architectural elements in the capital.

Curriculum: Art

Subjects: Washington, DC—buildings

Publications: Books about Washington, D.C., architecture and commission functions.

Selected List of Books and Pamphlets

The Commission of Fine Arts: A Brief History. 1985. 166p. free.

Relates the development of such Washington attractions as the Jefferson Memorial, the Kennedy Center, and recent projects.

COMMISSION ON CIVIL RIGHTS
Office of Congressional and Public Affairs
1121 Vermont Ave., NW
Washington, DC 20425
(202) 376-8307

Date Established: 1957

Objectives of the Agency: Collect, study, and hold public hearings on information about discrimination or denials of equal protection of the laws because of race, color, religion, sex, age, handicap, national origin, or in the administration of justice.

Curriculum: Government

Subjects: Civil rights

Locations:

CT, MA, ME, NH, RI, VT
U.S. Commission on Civil Rights
New England Regional Office
55 Summer St.
Eighth Floor
Boston, MA 02110
(617) 223-4671

NJ, NY
U.S. Commission on Civil Rights
Eastern Regional Office
26 Federal Plaza
Room 1639
New York, NY 10007
(212) 264-0400

DC, DE, MD, PA, VA, WV
U.S. Commission on Civil Rights
Mid-Atlantic Regional Office
2120 L St., NW
Room 510
Washington, DC 20037
(202) 254-6717

AL, FL, GA, KY, MS, NC, SC, TN
U.S. Commission on Civil Rights
Southern Regional Office
75 Piedmont Ave., NE
Room 362
Atlanta, GA 30303
(404) 221-4391

IL, IN, MI, MN, OH, WI
U.S. Commission on Civil Rights
Midwestern Regional Office
230 S. Dearborn St.
Thirty-Second Floor
Chicago, IL 60604
(312) 353-7371

AR, LA, NM, OK, TX
U.S. Commission on Civil Rights
Southwestern Regional Office
418 South Main
First Floor
San Antonio, TX 78204
(512) 229-5570

IA, KS, MO, NE
U.S. Commission on Civil Rights
Central States Regional Office
911 Walnut St.
Room 3103
Kansas City, MO 64106
(816) 374-2454

CO, ND, MT, SD, UT, WY
U.S. Commission on Civil Rights
Rocky Mountain Regional Office
1020 Fifteenth St.
Suite 2235
Denver, CO 80202
(303) 837-2211

AZ, CA, HI, NV
U.S. Commission on Civil Rights
Western Regional Office
3660 Wilshire Blvd.
Suite 810
Los Angeles, CA 90010
(213) 688-3437

AK, ID, OR, WA
U.S. Commission on Civil Rights
Northwestern Regional Office
915 Second Ave.
Room 2852
Seattle, WA 98174
(206) 442-1246

Publications: Directories. Catalogs. Hearings. Conferences. Reports. Guides. Pamphlets. Studies. On voting rights, enforcement of federal civil rights laws, equality of opportunity in education, employment, status of women, housing, etc.

Bibliographies, Sales Catalogs, Publications Lists, etc.

"Catalog of Publications." Current. 26p. free.
  Describes what is available. Includes what is available from each state in Advisory Committee reports. Some material in Spanish.

Serials, Subscription Publications, etc.

"Civil Rights Update." Current. 6p. free.
  Gives news about issues and personnel.

Selected List of Books and Pamphlets

"Civil Rights Directory." Rev. ed. 549p. free.

Lists federal government agencies, state and local government agencies, private organizations, women's organizations, research organizations, and others. Includes name, address, telephone number, director, area served, and functions.

"Fair Textbooks: A Resource Guide." 1979. 430p. free. Clearinghouse Publication 61.

Covers material resources, procedural resources, directories, and organizational resources. Includes codes for minorities, grade levels, and subjects.

"Getting Uncle Sam To Enforce Your Civil Rights." 1980. 59p. free. Clearinghouse Publication 59.

Explains how to file a complaint about discrimination because of race, color, sex, religion, national origin, etc. Includes agency regional and local offices. Also available in Spanish.

New Perspectives. Quarterly. 42p. free.

Contains current issues and book reviews. Order from: Superintendent of Documents, Government Printing Office, Washington, DC 20401.

"United States Commission on Civil Rights." n.d. 16p. free.

Describes duties, powers, organization, offices, and other information on the commission.

"Women Still in Poverty." 1979. 50p. free. Clearinghouse Publication 60.

Describes women on welfare, job training, employment, and child care. Statistics.

Audiovisuals:

Filmographies, Sales Lists, etc.

"Catalog of Publications." Current. 26p. free.

Lists what free loan films are available and where to request them.

Individual Audiovisuals

"A Woman, A Spaniel, and a Walnut Tree." Colorado Advisory Committee and the Denver Human Relations Commission. n.d. 13 minutes. 16mm. free loan.

Examines the crime of battering women. Request from: Community Relations Division, U.S. Commission on Civil Rights, Washington, DC 20425. (202) 376-8318.

Library: Clearinghouse of Civil Rights Information has reference works, journals, periodicals, newspapers, microfilm/fiche, and other materials. It has OCLC and DIALOG. Write:
Robert S. Rankin Civil Rights Memorial Library
1121 Vermont Ave., NW
Washington, DC 20425
(202) 376-8110

COMPTROLLER OF THE CURRENCY
Communications Division
Department of the Treasury
490 L'Enfant Plaza, SW
Washington, DC 20219
(202) 447-1800

Date Established: 1863

Objectives of the Agency: Approve or deny applications for new charters, branches, capital or other changes in corporate or banking structure; examine the banks; take various supervisory actions against banks which do not conform to laws and regulations or engage in unsound banking practices; and issue rules and regulations concerning banking practices.

Curriculum: Business

Subjects: Banks and banking

Locations:

Northeastern District
CT, DE, MA, MD, ME, NH, NJ, NY, PA, PR, RI, VI, VT
New York District Office
1211 Avenue of the Americas
Suite 4250
New York, NY 10036
(212) 944-3495

Southeastern District
AL, FL, GA, MS, NC, SC, TN, VA, WV
Atlanta District Office
Peachtree Cain Tower
229 Peachtree St., NE
Suite 2700
Atlanta, GA 30303
(404) 221-4926

Central District
IL, IN, KY, MI, OH, WI
Chicago District Office
Sears Tower
233 S. Wacker Dr.
Suite 5750
Chicago, IL 60606
(312) 353-0300

Midwestern District
IA, KS, MN, MO, ND, NE, SD
Kansas City District Office
2345 Grand Ave.
Suite 700
Kansas City, MO 64108
(816) 556-1800

Southwestern District
AR, LA, NM, OK, TX
Dallas District Office
1201 Elm St.
Suite 3800
Dallas, TX 75270
(214) 767-4400

Western District
AK, AZ, CA, CO, GU, HI, ID, MT,
NV, OR, UT, WA, WY
San Francisco District Office
50 Fremont St.
Suite 3900
San Francisco, CA 94105
(415) 545-5900

Publications: Pamphlets.

Selected List of Books and Pamphlets

"Comptroller of the Currency." n.d. 36p. free.

Explains the duties of the comptroller of the currency, the opportunities in various banking positions, and continuing education programs. Photographs.

CONGRESSIONAL BUDGET OFFICE
U.S. Congress
Second and D Sts., SW
Washington, DC 20515
(202) 226-2621

Date Established: 1974

Objectives of the Agency: Furnish Congress key information relating to the U.S. economy, the federal budget and federal programs; in capacity of a nonpartisan agency, help Congress analyze the interaction between the federal budget and the nation's economy, and assess the fiscal and budgetary results of legislation.

Curriculum: Government

Subjects: U.S. — economic policy

Publications: Pamphlets. Catalogs. Reports. Papers. On U.S. economy and fiscal policy, tax expenditures and receipts, federal budget, aid to states and localities, etc.

Bibliographies, Sales Catalogs, Publications Lists, etc.

"List of Publications." Rev. 1984. 93p. free.

Lists publications by subject area: *U.S. Economy and Fiscal Policy, Federal Budget, Commerce, Industry and Trade, Social Programs, National Security,* and *Government Operations*. Also has a chronological listing.

Selected List of Books and Pamphlets

"Responsibilities and Organization." 1984. 13p. free.

Examines the services, structure, and economic advisers of the Congressional Budget Office. Organization chart. Appendix.

CONSERVATION AND RENEWABLE ENERGY INQUIRY AND REFERRAL SERVICE
P.O. Box 8900
Silver Spring, MD 20907
U.S. Including VI, PR: (800) 523-2929
PA: (800) 462-4983
AK, HI: (800) 233-3071

Date Established: 1976

Objectives of the Agency: Provide information on renewable technologies and energy conservation; maintain contact with a nationwide network of public and private organizations specializing in highly technical or regionally-specific information in the areas of solar, wind, and hydroelectric power, photovoltaics, and geothermal energy, bioconversion, and energy conservation.

Curriculum: Environmental studies

Subjects: Energy conservation

Publications: Posters. Bibliographies. Fact sheets. Pamphlets.

Bibliographies, Sales Catalogs, Publications Lists, etc.

"Renewable Energy Reading List for Young Adults." 1984. 2p. free. DOE/CE-0066.

Lists books for grades 6-12. Includes title, author, pages, price, grade suggestion, publisher, publisher's address, and annotation.

"Solar Greenhouse Bibliography and List of Plans." 1983. 3p. free. DOE/CE-0064.

Lists a variety of solar greenhouse publications, on such topics as greenhouse plans, reports, papers, bibliographies, proceedings, books, and pamphlets.

Selected List of Books and Pamphlets

"Learning about Renewable Energy." 1985. 4p. free. FS 189.

Explains producing electricity from sunlight, wind power, hydroelectric power, geothermal energy, and biomass. Questions. Research topics.

"Solar Electricity from Photovoltaic Conversion." n.d. 10p. free. DOE/PA 0011 (1-80).

Solar cells, solar modules, power systems, economics.

"Solar Energy and Your Home: Questions and Answers." 1985. 5p. free. FS 176.

Answers to such questions as: What are the various kinds of solar energy systems? Where can you find more information on solar energy? Lists books and periodicals with annotations.

"Solar Factsheet." 1980. 6p. free. FS 115.

Explains how solar heat is stored in various kinds of systems. Sketches.

"U.S. Direct Normal Solar Radiation." Poster. free. SERI/SP-633-1042.

Shows the amount of direct normal solar radiation on a color-coded map of the 50 states. Legend.

CONSUMER PRODUCT SAFETY COMMISSION
1111 Eighteenth St., NW
Washington, DC 20207
(800)638-2772
MD: (800) 492-8104

Date Established: 1972

Objectives of the Agency: Protect the public against the unreasonable risks of injury or death associated with consumer products.

Curriculum: Consumer education, safety

Subjects: Consumer protection

Locations:

AL, FL, GA, KY, MS, NC, SC, TN

Southeastern Regional Office
Consumer Product Safety Commission
800 Peachtree St., NE
Suite 210
Atlanta, GA 30308
(404) 881-2231

CT, MA, ME, NH, RI, VT

Boston Regional Office
Consumer Product Safety Commission
100 Summer St.
Room 1607
Boston, MA 02110
(617) 223-5576

IL, IN, MN, WI

Midwestern Regional Office
Consumer Product Safety Commission
230 S. Dearborn St.
Room 2945
Chicago, IL 60604
(312) 353-8260

Twin Cities District Office
Consumer Product Safety Commission
Metro Square
Seventh and Robert Sts.
Suite 580
St. Paul, MN 55101
(612) 725-7781

MI, OH

Cleveland Regional Office
Consumer Product Safety Commission
1404 E. Ninth St.
Bancohio Bldg.
Sixth Floor
Cleveland, OH 44114
(216) 522-3886

AR, LA, NM, OK, TX

Southwestern Regional Office
Consumer Product Safety Commission
1100 Commerce St.
Room 1C10
Dallas, TX 75242
(214) 767-0841

IA, CO, KS, MO, MT, ND, NE, SD, UT, WY

Kansas City Regional Office
Consumer Product Safety Commission
Midland Bldg.
1221 Baltimore Ave.
Suite 1000
Kansas City, MO 64105
(816) 374-2034

Denver District Office
Consumer Product Safety Commission
Guaranty Bank Bldg.
817 Seventeenth St.
Suite 938
Denver, CO 80202
(303) 837-2904

AZ, Southern California

Los Angeles Regional Office
Consumer Product Safety Commission
3660 Wilshire Blvd.
Suite 1100
Los Angeles, CA 90010
(213) 688-7272

NJ, NY, PR, VI

Northeastern Regional Office
Consumer Product Safety Commission
6 World Trade Center
Vesey St.
Sixth Floor
New York, NY 10048
(212) 264-1125

DC, DE, MD, PA, VA, WV

Philadelphia Regional Office
Consumer Product Safety Commission
400 Market St.
Tenth Floor
Philadelphia, PA 19106
(215) 597-9105

AK, HI, ID, Northern California, NV, OR, WA

Western Regional Office
Consumer Product Safety Commission
U.S. Customs House
555 Battery St.
Room 416
San Francisco, CA 94111
(415) 556-1816

Seattle District Office
Consumer Product Safety Commission
3240 Federal Bldg.
915 Second Ave.
Seattle, WA 98174
(206) 442-5276

Publications: Pamphlets. Reports. Fact sheets. Curriculum material. Catalogs.

Bibliographies, Sales Catalogs, Publications Lists, etc.

"Listing of Education Materials for Use by Schools." Current. 19p. free.

Lists curriculum materials on bicycle safety, child and infant safety, fire and burn prevention, kitchen safety, playground safety, and other topics.

"Publications List." n.d. 6p. free.

Lists what is available in safety publications. Arranges materials by topics such as *Christmas safety, fire safety, poison prevention,* etc. Some publications available in Spanish.

Selected List of Books and Pamphlets

Consumer's Resource Handbook. Revised regularly. 111p. free.

Gives sources of help, consumer assistance directory, selected federal agencies, and directions on how to write a complaint letter. Subject and organizational index.

"CPSC Guide to Electrical Safety." 1984. 12p. free.

Shows how to use electricity and electrical products more safely and avoid possible tragedy around the home.

"Flammable Fabrics." Revised 1981. 4p. free. Product Safety Fact Sheet No. 17.

Provides suggestions for the purchase, use, and laundering of flame-resistant fabrics and some first-aid suggestions for burns.

"From Our Desk to Yours . . . ." Current. 16p. free.

Describes over 200 federal consumer booklets, including those from the U.S. Consumer Product Safety Commission, that are available from the Consumer Information Center, Pueblo, CO 81002.

"How To Develop a Community Consumer Product Safety Program." n.d. 62p. free.

Provides notebook material in nine chapters on how to promote local product safety. Includes how to organize workshops and other programs.

"Kitchen Ranges." Rev. 1979. 3p. free. Product Safety Fact Sheet No. 9.

Details major accident patterns associated with kitchen ranges. Makes suggestions for the purchase, safe use, and maintenance of kitchen ranges.

"Locked Up Poisons Prevent Tragedy." Rev. 1982. 6p. free.

Gives tips on preventing accidental poisoning of children. Contains steps on poison-proofing the home.

"Safer Products, Safer People." 1984. 18p. free.

Tells what the Consumer Product Safety Commission does to help reduce injuries and save lives.

"Some Federal Consumer-Oriented Agencies." Rev. 1980. 4p. free. Product Safety Fact Sheet No. 52.

Provides address, telephone, and summary of services of 24 federal agencies which deal most frequently with consumer inquiries. Also gives their location and telephone number.

"The Super Sitter." Rev. 1983. 15p. free.

Gives guidelines for the baby sitter to follow. Tells what is expected of the baby sitter and what to expect from the parents. Also gives tips on necessary telephone numbers, toys, playing outdoors, cribs, poisons, and other things.

"U.S. Consumer Product Safety Commission Home Electrical Safety Audit Room-by-Room Checklist." 1984. 11p. free.

Gives checklist to help find any electrical problems that may be in various rooms of the home and around the home.

"U.S. Consumer Product Safety Commission Poison Lookout Checklist." 1984. 2p. free.

Gives checklist to help isolate poisons found in the kitchen, bathroom, garage, or storage area.

"What You Should Know about Smoke Detectors." 1985. 4p. free.

Tells why have them, how they work, what kind to get, and how to install and care for them.

COPYRIGHT OFFICE
Publications Section, LM-455
Library of Congress
Washington, DC 20559
(202) 287-9100

Date Established: 1870

Objectives of the Agency: Be responsible for a form of protection provided by law to the authors of original works of authorship such as literary, dramatic, musical, artistic, and certain other intellectual works. It is available to both published and unpublished works.

Curriculum: Library

Subjects: Copyright

Publications: Circulars. Reports. Catalogs. Books. Forms. Fact sheets.

Bibliographies, Sales Catalogs, Publications Lists, etc.

"Publications on Copyright." Current. 12p. free.

Groups publications according to the source: the Copyright Office, National Technical Information Service, the Library of Congress Photoduplication Service, or the Superintendent of Documents. Ordering information. Prices. Order form.

Selected List of Books and Pamphlets

"Circular R1: Copyright Basics." 1983. 12p. free.

Tells what copyright is, who can claim copyright, what works are protected, how long protection endures, gives application forms, fees, and related information.

"New Hotline Established at the Copyright Office." 1985. 2p. free.

Tells what the hotline is and what forms are necessary to apply for registration of a claim to copyright for various works, for example, Form TX for nondramatic literary works.

Special Services: 24-hour hotline, (202) 287-9100, to speed up service to callers who know what application forms they need.

COUNCIL ON ENVIRONMENTAL QUALITY
Executive Office of the President
722 Jackson Place, NW
Washington, DC 20006
(202) 395-5700

Date Established: 1969

Objectives of the Agency: Formulate and recommend national policies to promote the improvement of the quality of the environment.

Curriculum: Environmental studies

Subjects: Environment

Publications: Reports. Lists. Studies. Summaries. Proceedings. Indexes. Directories.

Bibliographies, Sales Catalogs, Publications Lists, etc.

"Publications List." Current. 33p. free.

Groups publications in such categories as: *Air, Coastal Zone, Data and Monitoring, Economics, Energy, Wildlife,* etc. Ordering instructions. Publications are free and for sale. Materials are from the Council on Environmental Quality, Government Printing Office, and National Technical Information Service.

Selected List of Books and Pamphlets

Annual Report of the Council on Environmental Quality. Current. approximately 330p. $8.00.

Chapters on such topics as natural resource management, environmental conditions and trends, and environmental economics. Tables. Figures. Appendices. Order from: Superintendent of Documents, U.S. Government Printing Office.

CROP REPORTING BOARD
Statistical Reporting Service
U.S. Department of Agriculture
Room 5829 South
Washington, DC 20250
(202) 447-4230

Date Established: 1863

Objectives of the Agency: Issue state and national estimates of crops, livestock, poultry, dairy, prices, labor, and related agricultural items to maintain an orderly association among the output, supply, and marketing elements in agriculture.

Curriculum: Agriculture

Subjects: Agriculture—statistics

Locations:

AK

Crop Reporting Office
Box 799
Palmer, AK 99645

AL

Crop Reporting Office
Box 1071
Montgomery, AL 36192

AR

Crop Reporting Office
Box 1417
Little Rock, AR 72203

AZ

Crop Reporting Office
3001 Federal Bldg.
Phoenix, AZ 85025

CA

Crop Reporting Office
Box 1258
Sacramento, CA 95806

CO

Crop Reporting Office
Box 17066
Denver, CO 80217

CT

See New England.

DE

See MD.

FL
Crop Reporting Office
1222 Woodward St.
Orlando, FL 32803

GA
Crop Reporting Office
Stephens Federal Bldg.
Suite 320
Athens, GA 30613

HI
Crop Reporting Office
Box 22159
Honolulu, HI 96822

IA
Crop Reporting Office
210 Walnut St.
Des Moines, IA 50309

ID
Crop Reporting Office
Box 1699
Boise, ID 83701

IL
Crop Reporting Office
Box 429
Springfield, IL 62705

IN
Crop Reporting Office
Purdue University
West Lafayette, IN 47907

KS
Crop Reporting Office
444 S.E. Quincy St.
Room 290
Topeka, KS 66683

KY
Crop Reporting Office
Box 1120
Louisville, KY 40201

LA
Crop Reporting Office
Box 5524
Alexandria, LA 71301

MA
See New England.

MD, DE
Crop Reporting Office
Box AG
College Park, MD 20740

ME
See New England.

MI
Crop Reporting Office
Box 20008
Lansing, MI 48901

MN
Crop Reporting Office
P.O. Box 70068
St. Paul, MN 55107

MO
Crop Reporting Office
Box L
Columbia, MO 65201

MS
Crop Reporting Office
Box 980
Jackson, MS 39205

MT
Crop Reporting Office
Box 4369
Helena, MT 59604

NC
Crop Reporting Office
Box 27767
Raleigh, NC 27611

ND
Crop Reporting Office
Box 3166
Fargo, ND 58102

NE
Crop Reporting Office
Box 81069
Lincoln, NE 68501

New England: ME, NH, VT, CT, RI, MA
Crop Reporting Office
Box 1444
Concord, NH 03301

NH
See New England.

NJ

Crop Reporting Office
Health and Agriculture Bldg.
CN-330 New Warren St.
Room 204
Trenton, NJ 08625

NM

Crop Reporting Office
Box 1809
Las Cruces, NM 88004

NV

Crop Reporting Office
Box 8888
Reno, NV 89507

NY

Crop Reporting Office
State Campus
Building 8
Albany, NY 12235

OH

Crop Reporting Office
New Federal Bldg.
200 N. High St.
Room 608
Columbus, OH 43215

OK

Crop Reporting Office
Box 1095
Oklahoma City, OK 73101

OR

Crop Reporting Office
1220 S.W. Third Ave.
Portland, OR 97204

PA

Crop Reporting Service
2301 N. Cameron St.
Harrisburg, PA 17110

RI

See New England.

SC

Crop Reporting Office
Box 1911
Columbia, SC 29202

SD

Crop Reporting Office
Box V
Sioux Falls, SD 57117

TN

Crop Reporting Office
Box 1250
Nashville, TN 37202

TX

Crop Reporting Office
Box 70
Austin, TX 78767

UT

Crop Reporting Office
Box 11486
Salt Lake City, UT 84147

VA

Crop Reporting Office
Box 1659
Richmond, VA 23213

VT

See New England.

WA

Crop Reporting Office
909 First Ave.
Seattle, WA 98174

WI

Crop Reporting Office
Box 9160
Madison, WI 53715

WV

Crop Reporting Office
State Department of Agriculture
Charleston, WV 25305

WY

Crop Reporting Office
Box 1148
Cheyenne, WY 82001

Publications: Pamphlets. Calendars.

Selected List of Books and Pamphlets

"Crop Reporting Board Calendar." Current. 1p. free.

Shows when in the 12 months of the current year various reports are issued on such items as celery, milk, catfish, poultry, eggs, and peanuts.

"Preparing Crop and Livestock Estimates." Rev. 1981. 16p. free.

Explains who uses the estimates, types of surveys, farm labor and wages, and the composition of the Crop Reporting Board.

DEATH VALLEY NATIONAL MONUMENT
National Park Service
Death Valley, CA 92328

Date Established: 1933

Objectives of the Agency: Preserve the desert area, surrounded by high mountains, containing the lowest point in the western hemisphere.

Curriculum: Geography

Subjects: National parks and reserves

Publications: Pamphlets. Fact sheets.

Selected List of Books and Pamphlets

"Death Valley." 1985. 12-fold flyer. free.
  Gives a map on one side, photographs, charts, information about features, and visitor tips on the other side.

"Death Valley National Monument." 1984. 4p. free.
  Reports information on plants, animals, history, attractions, and tours.

"Death Valley Weather Data." 1984. 2p. free.
  Provides temperature and precipitation records.

DEPARTMENT OF AGRICULTURE
Fourteenth St. and Independence Ave., SW
Washington, DC 20250
(202) 447-2791

Date Established: 1862

Objectives of the Agency: Improve and maintain farm income; develop markets abroad; help to cure hunger and malnutrition; protect soil, water, forests, and natural resources; oversee rural development, credit, and conservation programs; and provide inspection and grading services.

Curriculum: Agriculture, home economics

Subjects: Agriculture
         Home economics

Publications: Bulletins. Handbooks. Reports. Pamphlets. Manuals. Catalogs. Yearbooks. Guides.

Selected List of Books and Pamphlets.

"How To Get Information from the United States Department of Agriculture." Current. 14p. free.
  Lists sources of information and agencies of the U.S. Department of Agriculture. Also lists names of the various Freedom of Information Act officers.

"Services Available through the U.S. Department of Agriculture." 23p. free. Program Aid No. 1336.
  Groups agencies under areas of service. Includes what services, who may apply, and where to apply.

"Your United States Department of Agriculture." Rev. 32p. free.
  Explains how the USDA started, its reponsibilities, activities, organization, and relationship to land-grant colleges.

DEPARTMENT OF COMMERCE
Office of the Secretary
Fourteenth St. and Constitution Ave., NW
Washington, DC 20230
(202) 377-2000

Date Established: 1913

Objectives of the Agency: Promote the nation's international trade, economic growth, and technological advancement; increase exports; provide statistics for business and government; grant patents and trademarks; study the earth's physical environment; promote travel; and assist minority businesses.

Curriculum: Economics

Subjects: Economic policy

Audiovisuals:

Filmographies, Sales Lists, etc.

"Film Inventory of the Department of Commerce." n.d. 8p. free.
  Lists annotated films available from various departments of the Commerce Department, with addresses of where to obtain them on loan, purchase, or rent. Inventory includes: National Bureau of Standards, the National Oceanic and Atmospheric Administration, U.S. Patent and Trademark Office, and the International Trade Administration.

Special Services: The Department of Commerce telephone directory is available for sale from:
Superintendent of Documents
Government Printing Office
Washington, DC 20402
(202) 783-3238

DEPARTMENT OF EDUCATION
Information Center
400 Maryland Ave., SW
Washington, DC 20202
(202) 245-3192

Date Established: 1979

Objectives of the Agency: Be the information source of the Department of Education

Curriculum: Education

Subjects: Education—U.S.

Locations:

CT, MA, ME, NH, RI, VT

Secretary's Regional Representative
John W. McCormack Post Office and Courthouse
Boston, MA 02109
(617) 223-7500

NJ, NY, PR, VI

Secretary's Regional Representative
26 Federal Plaza
Room 3954
New York, NY 10278
(212) 264-7005

DC, DE, MD, PA, VA, WV

Secretary's Regional Representative
3535 Market St.
Room 16350
Philadelphia, PA 19101
(215) 596-1001

AL, FL, GA, KY, MS, NC, SC, TN

Secretary's Regional Representative
101 Marietta Tower
Suite 2221
Atlanta, GA 30323
(404) 221-2502

IL, IN, MI, MN, OH, WI

Secretary's Regional Representative
300 S. Wacker Dr.
Sixteenth Floor
Chicago, IL 60606
(312) 353-5215

AR, LA, NM, OK, TX

Secretary's Regional Representative
1200 Main Tower
Room 1460
Dallas, TX 75202
(214) 767-3626

IA, KS, MO, NE

Secretary's Regional Representative
324 E. Eleventh St.
Ninth Floor
Kansas City, MO 64106
(816) 374-2276

CO, MT, ND, SD, UT, WY

Secretary's Regional Representative
1961 Stout St.
Room 380
Denver, CO 80294
(303) 837-3544

AS, AZ, CA, GU, HI, NV, Trust Territory of the Pacific Islands

Secretary's Regional Representative
50 United National Plaza
Room 205
San Francisco, CA 94102
(415) 556-4920

AK, ID, OR, WA

Secretary's Regional Representative
2901 Third Ave.
First Floor
Room 108
Seattle, WA 98121
(206) 442-0460

Publications: Catalogs. Lists of publications.

Bibliographies, Sales Catalogs, Publications Lists, etc.

"Publications of the U.S. Department of Education." Current. 14p. free.

Lists available materials under such headings as: *civil rights, Indian education, postsecondary education, special education,* and others. Free and for sale. Information on how to order. If not from the Superintendent of Documents, gives the address of the source.

Selected List of Books and Pamphlets

"Education and Title VI." n.d. 8p. free.

Tells what the act says, what the Office for Civil Rights does, how to file a discrimination complaint, and where to request additional information or file a complaint. Lists regional civil rights offices.

"Pocket Guide to Federal Help for the Disabled Person." 1983. 23p. free. Publication No. E-83-22002.

Explains developmental disabilities, vocational rehabilitation, civil rights, financial assistance and other benefits applicable to blind, deaf, and developmentally disabled persons.

"Sexual Harassment: It's Not Academic." 1984. 13p. free.

Contains questions and answers about sexual harassment of students. Title IX. Gives addresses for information and/or materials.

"Title IX and Sex Discrimination." n.d. 8p. free.

Tells what Title IX says, what education programs and activities it covers, what the Office for Civil Rights does, how to file a discrimination complaint, and where to request additional information or file a complaint.

DEPARTMENT OF ENERGY
Office of Public Affairs
1000 Independence Ave., SW
Washington, DC 20585
(202) 252-5575

Date Established: 1977

Objectives of the Agency: Coordinate and administer the energy functions of the federal government, the research and development of energy technology, the marketing and conservation of power, the nuclear weapons program, the energy regulatory programs, and energy data collection and analysis.

Curriculum: Consumer education

Subjects: Energy conservation

38 / Department of Energy

Locations:

AK

Alaska Energy Office
Division of Energy and Power Development
McKay Bldg.
338 Denali St.
Seventh Floor
Anchorage, AK 99501
(907) 276-0508

AL

Alabama Department of Energy
3734 Atlanta Hwy.
Montgomery, AL 36130
(205) 832-5010

AR

Arkansas Department of Energy
3000 Kavanaugh
Little Rock, AR 72205
(501) 371-1370

AS

Office of the Governor Territorial Energy Office
Pago Pago, AS 96799
(Overseas operator) 633-1306

AZ

Arizona Energy Programs
Capitol Tower
1700 W. Washington Street
Room 504
Phoenix, AZ 85007
(602) 255-4955

CA

California Energy Commission
1111 Howe Ave.
Sacramento, CA 95825
(916) 920-6811

CO

Colorado Office of Energy Conservation
1600 Downing St.
Second Floor
Denver, CO 80218
(303) 839-2507

CT

Office of Energy Policy and Management
80 Washington St.
Hartford, CT 06115
(203) 566-2800

DC

Energy Unit of Planning and Development
1420 New York Ave., NW
Washington, DC 20004
(202) 727-1800

DE

Governor's Energy Advisor
P.O. Box 1401
56 The Green
Dover, DE 19901
(302) 678-5644

FL

Governor's Energy Office
301 Bryant Bldg.
Tallahassee, FL 32304
(904) 488-6764

GA

Office of Energy Resources
270 Washington St., SW
Atlanta, GA 30334
(404) 656-5176

GU

Guam Energy Office
P.O. Box 2950
Agana, GU 96910
(Overseas operator) 477-9526 or 477-9445

HI

Department of Planning and Economic Development
1164 Bishop St.
Suite 1515
Honolulu, HI 96813
(808) 548-3033

IA

Iowa Energy Policy Council
Capitol Complex
Lucas Bldg.
Sixth Floor
Des Moines, IA 50319
(505) 281-4420

ID

Idaho Office of Energy
State House
Boise, ID 83720
(208) 384-2559

IL

Institute of Natural Resources
325 W. Adams St.
Springfield, IL 62706
(217) 785-2800

IN

Department of Commerce Energy Group
440 N. Meridan St.
Indianapolis, IN 46204
(317) 236-8940

KS

Kansas Energy Office
214 W. Sixth St.
Topeka, KS 66603
(913) 296-2496

KY

Kentucky Department of Energy
Capitol Plaza Tower
Twelfth Floor
Frankfort, KY 40601
(502) 564-7416

LA

Louisiana Department of Natural Resources
P.O. Box 44156
Baton Rouge, LA 70804
(504) 342-4500

MA

Executive Office of Energy Resources
73 Tremont St.
Room 701
Boston, MA 02108
(617) 727-4732

MD

Maryland Energy Office
State Department of Natural Resources
301 W. Preston St.
Suite 1302
Baltimore, MD 21201
(301) 383-6810

ME

Office of Energy Resources
55 Capitol St.
Augusta, ME 04330
(207) 289-3811

MI

Michigan Energy Administration
Michigan Department of Commerce
P.O. Box 30228
Lansing, MI 48901
(517) 374-9090

MN

Minnesota Energy Agency
980 American Center Bldg.
150 E. Kellogg Blvd.
St. Paul, MN 55101
(612) 296-6424

MO

Missouri Energy Programs
Department of Natural Resources
1014 Madison
P.O. Box 176
Jefferson City, MO 65101
(314) 751-4000

MS

Department of Transportation and Energy
1504 Walter Sillers Bldg.
Jackson, MS 39201
(601) 354-7018

MT

Energy Division
Department of Natural Resources and Conservation
32 S. Ewing St.
Helena, MT 59601
(406) 449-3773

NC

Energy Division
North Carolina Department of Commerce
P.O. Box 25249
Raleigh, NC 27611
(919) 733-2230

ND

North Dakota Energy Management and
  Conservation
1533 N. Twelfth St.
Bismarck, ND 58501
(701) 224-2250

NE

Nebraska State Energy Office
P.O. Box 95085
301 S. Centennial Mall
Fourth Floor
Lincoln, NE 68509
(402) 471-2867

NH

Governor's Council on Energy
2½ Beacon St.
Concord, NH 03301
(603) 842-2121

NJ

New Jersey Department of Energy
101 Commerce St.
Newark, NJ 07102
(201) 648-2744

NM

Department of Energy and Minerals
P.O. Box 2770
Santa Fe, NM 87501
(505) 827-2471

NV

Nevada Department of Energy
1050 E. William St.
Suite 405
Carson City, NV 89710
(702) 885-5157

NY

New York State Energy Office
Agency Building No. 2
Rockefeller Plaza
Albany, NY 12223
(518) 474-8181

OH

Ohio Department of Energy
State Office Tower
30 E. Broad St.
Thirty-Fourth Floor
Columbus, OH 43215
(616) 466-3465

OK

Oklahoma Department of Energy
4400 N. Lincoln Blvd.
Oklahoma City, OK 73105
(405) 521-3941

OR

Oregon Department of Energy
528 Cottage St., NE
Salem, OR 97310
(503) 378-4040

PA

Governor's Energy Council
1625 N. Front St.
Harrisburg, PA 17102
(717) 783-8610

PR

Office of Energy
Minillas Station
P.O. Box 41089
Santurce, PR 00940
(809) 726-4740
(809) 726-3636

RI

Energy Office
80 Dean St.
Providence, RI 02903
(401) 277-3374

SC

Governor's Division of Energy Resources
S.C.N. Center
1122 Lady St.
Suite 1130
Columbia, SC 29201
(803) 758-7502

SD

Office of Energy Policy
Capitol Plaza
Pierre, SD 57501
(606) 224-3603

TN

Tennessee Energy Authority
226 Capitol Blvd.
Suite 707
Nashville, TN 37219
(615) 741-1772

TX

Texas Energy and Natural Resources Advisory Council
800 Executive Office Bldg.
411 W. Thirteenth St.
Austin, TX 78701
(512) 475-5491

UT

Utah Energy Office
221 East, 400 South
Suite 101
Salt Lake City, UT 84111
(801) 533-5424

VA

Office of Emergency and Energy Services
310 Turner Rd.
Richmond, VA 23225
(804) 745-3305

VI

U.S. Virgin Islands Energy Office
P.O. Box 2996
St. Thomas, VI 00801
(890) 774-0001

VT

Vermont State Energy Office
State Office Bldg.
Montpelier, VT 06602
(802) 828-2393

WA
Washington State Energy Office
400 E. Union Ave.
First Floor
Olympia, WA 98504
(206) 754-1351

WI
Wisconsin Department of Energy
101 S. Webster
Eighth Floor
Madison, WI 53702
(608) 266-1741

WV
Fuel and Energy Division
Governor's Office of Economic and Community
    Development
Charleston, WV 25305
(304) 348-8860

WY
Wyoming Governor's Office
State Capitol
2320 Capitol Ave.
Cheyenne, WY 82002
(307) 777-7574

Publications: Pamphlets. Fact sheets. Reports.

Selected List of Books and Pamphlets

"Energy Facts." Current. 52p. free.
    Organized by energy source. Gives quick reference to a broad range of domestic and international energy data. Graphs portray various energy sources and uses.

"Tips for an Energy Efficient Apartment." 1985. 22p. free.
    Provides consumer information on heating, air conditioning, lighting, water, and various appliances.

"Tips for Energy Savers." 1983. 30p. free.
    Provides help on insulating, hot water savers, car maintenance, and other energy consumer aids.

"Your Keys to Energy Efficiency." 1985. 21p. free.
    Gives keys to saving energy at home, with your car, appliances, and other tips. Includes information and resource directory to obtain additional help.

DEPARTMENT OF HOUSING AND URBAN DEVELOPMENT
Office of Administrative and Management Services
451 Seventh St., SW
Washington, DC 20419
(202) 655-4000

Date Established: 1965

Objectives of the Agency: Administer the programs which provide aid for housing and the development of communities, fair housing opportunities, and administer mortgage insurance programs, rental subsidy programs, and neighborhood rehabilitation.

Curriculum: Government

Subjects: Housing

Locations:

U.S. Department of Housing and Urban
    Development
Region 1 Boston Office
John F. Kennedy Federal Bldg.
Room 800
Boston, MA 02203-0801
(617) 223-4066
or
Bulfinch Bldg.
15 New Chardon St.
Boston, MA 02114-2598
(617) 223-4100

U.S. Department of Housing and Urban
    Development
Region 2 New York Office
26 Federal Plaza
New York, NY 10278-0068
(212) 264-8053

U.S. Department of Housing and Urban
    Development
Region 3 Philadelphia Office
Liberty Square Bldg.
105 S. Seventh St.
Philadelphia, PA 19106-3392
(215) 597-2560

U.S. Department of Housing and Urban
    Development
Region 4 Atlanta Office
Richard B. Russell Federal Bldg.
75 Spring St., SW
Atlanta, GA 30303-3109
(404) 221-5136

U.S. Department of Housing and Urban
    Development
Region 5 Chicago Office
300 S. Wacker Dr.
Chicago, IL 60606-6765
(312) 353-5680
or
547 W. Jackson Blvd.
Chicago, IL 60606-5760
(312) 353-7660

42 / Department of Housing and Urban Development

U.S. Department of Housing and Urban
    Development
Region 6 Fort Worth Office
221 W. Lancaster
P.O. Box 2905
Fort Worth, TX 76113-2905
(817) 870-5401

U.S. Department of Housing and Urban
    Development
Region 7 Kansas City Office
Professional Bldg.
1103 Grand Ave.
Kansas City, MO 64106-2496
(816) 374-2661

U.S. Department of Housing and Urban
    Development
Region 8 Denver Office
Executive Tower Bldg.
1405 Curtis St.
Denver, CO 80202-2349
(303) 844-4513

U.S. Department of Housing and Urban
    Development
Region 9 San Francisco Office
Phillip Burton Federal Building and U.S.
    Courthouse
450 Golden Gate Ave.
P.O. Box 36003
San Francisco, CA 94102-3448
(415) 556-4752

U.S. Department of Housing and Urban
    Development
Region 10 Seattle Office
Arcade Plaza Bldg.
1321 Second Ave.
Seattle, WA 98101-2054
(206) 442-5414

Publications: Pamphlets. Transmittals.

Selected List of Books and Pamphlets

Programs of HUD. Current. 116p. free.
    Explains community planning and development, housing, public and Indian housing, fair housing and equal opportunity, policy development and research, access to housing for the handicapped, and other programs.

"U.S. Department of Housing and Urban Development Regional and Field Office Locations and Jurisdictions." Current. 4p. free.
    Gives map of regional and various other field offices. Includes addresses and telephone numbers of offices.

DEPARTMENT OF JUSTICE
Constitution Ave. and Tenth St., NW
Washington, DC 20530
(202) 633-2000

Date Established: 1870

Objectives of the Agency: Enforce the law in the public interest; protect against criminals and subversion; ensure healthy competition in business; and enforce drug, immigration, and naturalization laws.

Curriculum: Government

Subjects: Law—U.S.

Locations:

AK

U.S. Attorney District Office
C-252 Federal Bldg. and U.S. Courthouse
701 C St.
Mail Box 9
Anchorage, AK 99513

AL

U.S. Attorney Northern District Office
200 Federal Bldg.
1800 Fifth Ave., N.
Birmingham, AL 35203

U.S. Attorney Middle District Office
P.O. Box 197
Montgomery, AL 36101

U.S. Attorney Southern District Office
P.O. Drawer E
Mobile, AL 36601

AR

U.S. Attorney Eastern District Office
P.O. Box 1229
Little Rock, AR 72203

U.S. Attorney Western District Office
P.O. Box 1524
Fort Smith, AR 72901

AZ

U.S. Attorney District Office
4000 U.S. Courthouse
230 N. First Ave.
Phoenix, AZ 85025

CA

U.S. Attorney Northern District Office
450 Golden Gate Ave.
San Francisco, CA 94102

U.S. Attorney Eastern District Office
3305 Federal Bldg.
650 Capitol Mall
Sacramento, CA 95814

U.S. Attorney Central District Office
312 N. Spring St.
Los Angeles, CA 90012

U.S. Attorney Southern District Office
5-N-19 U.S. Courthouse
940 Front St.
San Diego, CA 92189

CO

U.S. Attorney Office
Federal Bldg.
1961 Stout St.
Suite 1200
Drawer 3615
Denver, CO 80294

CT

U.S. Attorney Office
P.O. Box 1824
New Haven, CT 06508

DC

U.S. Attorney Office
U.S. Courthouse
Third St. and Constitution Ave., NW
Room 2800
Washington, DC 20001

DE

U.S. Attorney Office
5001 New Federal Bldg.
844 King St.
Wilmington, DE 19801

FL

U.S. Attorney Northern District Office
227 N. Bronough St.
Suite 4014
Tallahassee, FL 32301

U.S. Attorney Middle District Office
410 Robert Timberlake Bldg.
500 Zack St.
Tampa, FL 33602

U.S. Attorney Southern District Office
155 S. Miami Ave.
Miami, FL 33130

GA

U.S. Attorney Northern District Office
1800 Richard Russell Bldg.
75 Spring St., SW
Atlanta, GA 30335

U.S. Attorney Middle District Office
P.O. Box U
Macon, GA 31202

U.S. Attorney Southern District Office
P.O. Box 8999
Savannah, GA 31412

GU

U.S. Attorney Office
PDN Bldg.
238 O'Hara St.
Suite 502-A
Agana, GU 96910

HI

U.S. Attorney Office
300 Ala Moana Blvd.
Box 50183
Room C-242
Honolulu, HI 96850

IA

U.S. Attorney Northern District Office
P.O. Box 4710
Cedar Rapids, IA 52407

U.S. Attorney Southern District Office
115 U.S. Courthouse
E. First and Walnut Sts.
Des Moines, IA 50309

ID

U.S. Attorney Office
693 Federal Bldg.
550 W. Fort St.
Box 037
Boise, ID 83724

IL

U.S. Attorney Northern District Office
1500 S. Everett McKinley Dirksen Bldg.
219 S. Dearborn St.
Room 1500
Chicago, IL 60604

U.S. Attorney Central District Office
P.O. Box 375
Springfield, IL 62705

U.S. Attorney Southern District Office
750 Missouri Ave.
Room 330
East St. Louis, IL 62202

IN

U.S. Attorney Northern District Office
312 Federal Bldg.
507 State St.
Hammond, IN 46320

U.S. Attorney Southern District Office
274 U.S. Courthouse
46 E. Ohio St.
Indianapolis, IN 46204

KS

U.S. Attorney Office
444 Quincy St.
Topeka, KS 66683

KY

U.S. Attorney Eastern District Office
P.O. Box 1490
Lexington, KY 40591

U.S. Attorney Western District Office
211 USPO and Courthouse Bldg.
601 W. Broadway
Louisville, KY 40202

LA

U.S. Attorney Eastern District Office
Hale Boggs Federal Bldg.
500 Camp St.
New Orleans, LA 70130

U.S. Attorney Middle District Office
352 Florida St.
Baton Rouge, LA 70801

U.S. Attorney Western District Office
12 Federal Bldg.
Room 3B
Shreveport, LA 71101

MA

U.S. Attorney Office
1107 John W. McCormack Federal Bldg.
USPO and Courthouse
Boston, MA 02109

MD

U.S. Attorney Office
U.S. Courthouse
101 W. Lombard St.
Eighth Floor
Baltimore, MD 21201

ME

U.S. Attorney Office
P.O. Box 1588
Portland, ME 04104

MI

U.S. Attorney Eastern District Office
817 Federal Bldg.
231 W. Lafayette
Detroit, MI 48226

U.S. Attorney Western District Office
399 Federal Bldg. and U.S. Courthouse
110 Michigan Ave., NW
Grand Rapids, MI 49503

MN

U.S. Attorney Office
234 U.S. Courthouse
110 S. Fourth St.
Minneapolis, MN 55401

MO

U.S. Attorney Eastern District Office
414 U.S. Court and Custom House
1114 Market St.
St. Louis, MO 63101

U.S. Western District Office
549 U.S. Courthouse
811 Grand Ave.
Kansas City, MO 64106

MS

U.S. Attorney Northern District Office
P.O. Drawer 886
Oxford, MS 38655

U.S. Attorney Southern District Office
P.O. Box 2091
Jackson, MS 39205

MT

U.S. Attorney Office
P.O. Box 1478
Billings, MT 59103

NC

U.S. Attorney Eastern District Office
P.O. Box 26897
Raleigh, NC 27611

U.S. Attorney Middle District Office
P.O. Box 1858
Greensboro, NC 27402

U.S. Attorney Western District Office
P.O. Box 132
Asheville, NC 28802

ND

U.S. Attorney Office
P.O. Box 2505
Fargo, ND 58108

NE

U.S. Attorney Office
P.O. Box 1228, DTS
Omaha, NE 68101

NH

U.S. Attorney Office
James Cleveland Federal Bldg. and Courthouse
55 Pleasant St.
Fourth Floor
Concord, NH 03301

NJ

U.S. Attorney Office
502 Federal Bldg.
970 Broad St.
Newark, NJ 07102

NM

U.S. Attorney Office
P.O. Box 607
Albuquerque, NM 87103

North Mariana Islands

U.S. Attorney Office
PDN Bldg.
238 O'Hara St.
Suite 502-A
Agana, GU 96910

NV

U.S. Attorney Office
Box 16030
Las Vegas, NV 89101

NY

U.S. Attorney Northern District Office
369 Federal Bldg.
100 S. Clinton St.
Syracuse, NY 13260

U.S. Attorney Southern District Office
1 St. Andrews Plaza
New York, NY 10007

U.S. Attorney Eastern District Office
225 Cadman Plaza East
Brooklyn, NY 11201

U.S. Attorney Western District Office
502 U.S. Courthouse
Court and Franklin Sts.
Buffalo, NY 14202

OH

U.S. Attorney Northern District Office
1404 E. Ninth St.
Suite 500
Cleveland, OH 44144

U.S. Attorney Southern District Office
220 USPO and Courthouse
Fifth and Walnut Sts.
Cincinnati, OH 45202

OK

U.S. Attorney Northern District Office
460 U.S. Courthouse
333 W. Fourth St.
Tulsa, OK 74103

U.S. Attorney Eastern District Office
P.O. Box 1009
Muskogee, OK 74401

U.S. Attorney Western District Office
4434 U.S. Courthouse and Federal Office Bldg.
Oklahoma City, OK 73102

OR

U.S. Attorney Office
312 U.S. Courthouse
620 S.W. Main St.
Portland, OR 97205

PA

U.S. Attorney Eastern District Office
3310 U.S. Courthouse
Independence Mall West
601 Market St.
Philadelphia, PA 19106

U.S. Attorney Middle District Office
P.O. Box 309
Scranton, PA 18501

U.S. Attorney Western District Office
633 USPO and Courthouse
Seventh Ave. and Grant St.
Pittsburgh, PA 15219

PR

U.S. Attorney Office
101 Federal Bldg.
Carlos Chardon St.
Hato Rey, PR 00918

RI

U.S. Attorney Office
P.O. Box 1401
Providence, RI 02901

SC

U.S. Attorney Office
P.O. Box 2266
Columbia, SC 29202

SD

U.S. Attorney Office
135 Federal Bldg. and U.S. Courthouse
400 S. Phillips Ave.
Sioux Falls, SD 57102

TN

U.S. Attorney Eastern District Office
P.O. Box 872
Knoxville, TN 37901

U.S. Attorney Middle District Office
879 U.S. Courthouse
801 Broadway
Nashville, TN 37203

U.S. Attorney Western District Office
1026 Federal Office Bldg.
167 N. Main St.
Memphis, TN 38103

TX

U.S. Attorney Northern District Office
310 U.S. Courthouse
Tenth and Lamar Sts.
Ft. Worth, TX 76102

U.S. Attorney Southern District Office
P.O. Box 61129
Houston, TX 77208

U.S. Attorney Eastern District Office
P.O. Box 1510
Beaumont, TX 77704

U.S. Attorney Western District Office
John Wood, Jr. Federal Bldg.
655 E. Durango Blvd.
San Antonio, TX 78206

UT

U.S. Attorney Office
200 Post Office and Courthouse Bldg.
350 S. Main St.
Salt Lake City, UT 84101

VA

U.S. Attorney Eastern District Office
701 Prince St.
Second Floor
Alexandria, VA 22314

U.S. Attorney Western District Office
P.O. Box 1709
Roanoke, VA 24008

VI

U.S. Attorney Office
P.O. Box 1440
St. Thomas, VI 00801-1440

VT

U.S. Attorney Office
Federal Bldg.
P.O. Box 570
Burlington, VT 05402

WA

U.S. Attorney Eastern District Office
P.O. Box 1494
Spokane, WA 99210

U.S. Attorney Western District Office
3600 Seafirst Fifth Ave. Plaza
800 Fifth Ave.
Seattle, WA 98104

WI

U.S. Eastern District Office
330 Federal Bldg.
517 E. Wisconsin Ave.
Milwaukee, WI 53202

U.S. Western District Office
P.O. Box 112
Madison, WI 53701

WV

U.S. Attorney Northern District Office
P.O. Box 591
Wheeling, WV 26003

U.S. Southern District Office
P.O. Box 3234
Charleston, WV 25332

WY

U.S. Attorney Office
P.O. Box 668
Cheyenne, WY 82003

Publications: Pamphlets on justice activities.

Selected List of Books and Pamphlets

"Antitrust Enforcement and the Consumer." 1975. 9p. free.

Explains what the antitrust laws can do, what the consumer can do, and how the public can act in antitrust enforcement.

"United States Department of Justice Legal Activities." Current. 44p. free.

Summarizes various offices, divisions, commissions, and other departments. Designed for those interested in the legal employment opportunities offered by the Department of Justice.

DEPARTMENT OF LABOR
Office of Information and Public Affairs
200 Constitution Ave., NW
Washington, DC 20210
(202) 523-8165

Date Established: 1913

Objectives of the Agency: Foster, promote, and develop the welfare of American wage earners.

Curriculum: Economics, government

Subjects: Employment

Locations:

CT, MA, ME, NH, RI, VT

Department of Labor
Region 1 Information Office
John F. Kennedy Federal Bldg.
Government Center
Boston, MA 02203
(616) 223-4220

NJ, NY, PR, VI

Department of Labor
Region 2 Information Office
1515 Broadway
New York, NY 10036
(212) 944-3442

DC, DE, MD, PA, VA, WV

Department of Labor
Region 3 Information Office
3535 Market St.
Philadelphia, PA 19104
(215) 596-1116

AL, FL, GA, KY, MS, NC, SC, TN

Department of Labor
Region 4 Information Office
1371 Peachtree St., NE
Atlanta, GA 30367
(404) 881-4366

IL, IN, MI, MN, OH, WI

Department of Labor
Region 5 Information Office
230 S. Dearborn St.
Chicago, IL 60604
(312) 353-3703

AR, LA, NM, OK, TX

Department of Labor
Region 6 Information Office
555 Griffin Square Bldg.
Griffin and Young Sts.
Dallas, TX 75202
(214) 767-6807

CO, IA, KS, MO, ND, NE, SD

Department of Labor
Region 7 Information Office
911 Walnut St.
Kansas City, MO 64106
(816) 374-6371

AZ, CA, HI, NV, UT

Department of Labor
Region 8 Information Office
Federal Office Bldg.
450 Golden Gate Ave.
San Francisco, CA 94102
(415) 556-9326

AK, ID, MT, OR, WA, WY

Department of Labor
Region 9 Information Office
Federal Office Bldg.
909 First Ave.
Seattle, WA 98174
(206) 442-0574

Publications: Reports. Pamphlets. Catalogs. Fact sheets.

Bibliographies, Sales Catalogs, Publications Lists, etc.

"Publications of the U.S. Department of Labor." Current. 30p. free.

Lists department publications currently available from various places such as the department's individual agencies, the U.S. Government Printing Office, or the National Technical Information Service. Groups publications by topics such as *mine safety, wages, women,* etc.

Selected List of Books and Pamphlets

"Targeted Jobs Tax Credit." n.d. 2p. free. Fact Sheet No. ETA-82-6.

Explains how targeted tax credit works. Lists the ten target groups from which qualified employees may be drawn.

"Trade Act of 1974." n.d. 2p. free.

Explains what the Trade Act is and what it provides workers who believe they have lost employment as a result of increased imports.

United States Department of Labor Annual Report. Annual. 171p. free.

Summarizes the year according to developments of the various divisions of the department such as the Women's Bureau, Mine Safety and Health Administration, and Veterans' Employment and Training. Appendix. Tables.

48 / Department of Labor

Library:
Department of Labor Library
Frances Perkins Bldg.
200 Constitution Ave., NW
Room N2439
Washington, DC 20210
(202) 523-6992

Special Services: Inquire about materials specific to each region of the country.

DEPARTMENT OF STATE
Bureau of Public Affairs
Correspondence Management Division
2201 C St., NW
Room 5819
Washington, DC 20520
(202) 632-6575

Date Established: 1789

Objectives of the Agency: Advise the President in the formulation and execution of foreign policy; promote the long-range security and welfare of the country; negotiate treaties and agreements; speak for the country in the United Nations and other international organizations and conferences.

Curriculum: Current issues

Subjects: U.S.—Foreign relations

Publications: Fact sheets. Pamphlets. Lists. Policies. Serials. Reports. Books. Bulletins. Atlases.

Bibliographies, Sales Catalogs, Publications Lists, etc.

"Selected State Department Publications." Current. 7p. free. Lists selected publications recently released. Includes free and for sale material. Provides order form for obtaining materials from: Superintendent of Documents, Government Printing Office, Washington, DC 20402.

Serials, Subscription Publications, etc.

"Background Notes." $32.00/yr. domestic, $40.00/yr. foreign.
Gives brief, factual summaries of the people, history, government, economy and foreign relations of about 170 countries and selected international organizations.

"Current Policy." Issued as needed. 3-5p. free.
Reprints addresses and statements by officials like Secretary Shultz's "The U.S. and ASEAN: Partners for Peace and Development," an address at the postministerial consultations of the Association of South East Asian Nations.

Department of State Bulletin. Monthly. $25.00/yr. domestic, $31.25/yr. foreign, $1.50/single copy domestic, $1.90/single copy foreign. Subscription includes an annual index.
The official record of U.S. foreign policy. Includes major addresses, news conferences of the President and the secretary, statements before congressional committees, treaties, and other agreements to which this country is or may become a party, and other information.

Diplomatic List. Quarterly. $14.00/yr. domestic, $17.50/yr. foreign. $3.75/single copy domestic, $4.70/single copy foreign.
Lists foreign diplomatic representatives in Washington, DC, and their addresses.

"Gist." Issued various times monthly. 2p. free.
Gives brief summaries on such topics as the U.S. nuclear export and nonproliferation policy or U.S.-Mexican Relations. Designed to be "a quick reference aid on U.S. foreign relations."

NATO Review. Bimonthly. 34p. free.
Prints articles concerning the Atlantic Alliance involving such countries as Belgium, Canada, Denmark, France, Italy, U.S. and others. The *Review* is also published in French, German, Dutch, and other languages.

Selected List of Books and Pamphlets

Atlas of NATO. 1985. 24p. $1.75. GPO S/N 044-000-02039-4.
Relates information about the North Atlantic Treaty Organization. Illustrates membership, structure, military strength, members' roles and other information. Order from: Superintendent of Documents, U.S. Government Printing Office, Washington, D.C. 20402.

Department of State Telephone Directory. Current. 196p. $5.50. GPO S/N 044-000-02034-3.
Lists telephone numbers for the Department of State and related agencies. Order from: Superintendent of Documents, U.S. Government Printing Office, Washington, DC 20402.

"The Department of State Today." 1984. 12p. free.
Discusses foreign policy machinery, public services, general organization, bureaus and current news of the Department of State.

Special Services: Educators may be placed on the mailing list by writing:
Bureau of Public Affairs
Office of Opinion Analysis and Plans
Room 5815A, U.S. Department of State
Washington, DC 20520

For information on borrowing or purchasing films and videotapes, contact:
Bureau of Public Affairs
Special Projects Staff
Room 4827A
U.S. Department of State
Washington, DC 20520
(202) 632-2353

Speakers can be furnished for groups. Conferences and seminars can be arranged. Direct requests to:
Office of Public Programs
Bureau of Public Affairs
Department of State
Washington, DC 20520
(202) 632-2406

DEPARTMENT OF THE AIR FORCE
Air Force Office of Public Affairs—Magazines and Books
1221 S. Fern St.
Room D-159
Arlington, VA 22202-2889
(202) 695-5331

Date Established: 1947

Objectives of the Agency: Provide help to researchers about Air Force functions.

Curriculum: Guidance, library.

Subjects: U.S. Air Force

Publications: Magazines. Reports.

Serials, Subscription Publications, etc.

Air Force. Published by the Air Force Association. Monthly. 240p. $14.00/yr. (as part of the Air Force Association membership $18.00 application).
Contains news and articles of interest to those associated with the Air Force. Photographs.

"Profile." Monthly (November through April). 24p. free.
Informs young people and guidance personnel about benefits, opportunities, privileges and programs of military service. Photographs. Distribution is directly to junior and senior high schools, colleges, universities, libraries, career centers and ROTC units.

Selected List of Books and Pamphlets.

"Basic Facts Edition of Profile." Annual. 64p. free.
Provides a quick reference guide to various aspects of the military services. Includes a general section, and sections on the Air Force, Army, Marine Corps, Navy, and Coast Guard.

"USAF Report." Annual. 72p. free.
Summarizes Air Force resources, programs, installations, space activities, etc. Photographs. Tables. Graphs.

DEPARTMENT OF THE INTERIOR
Office of the Secretary
C St. between Eighteenth and Nineteenth Sts., NW
Washington, DC 20240
(202) 343-3171

Date Established: 1849

Objectives of the Agency: Administer federal land, Indian reservations, conserve and develop mineral and water resources, fish and wildlife; coordinate federal and state recreation programs; preserve and administer the country's scenic and historic areas; operate and coordinate youth training programs; reclaim arid lands and manage hydroelectric power systems; promote social and economic development of the territories of the United States and in the Trust Territory of the Pacific Islands; and administer programs to Indians and Alaska natives.

Curriculum: Environmental studies, social studies

Subjects: Environment
Geography
Science

Publications: List. Catalog.

Selected List of Books and Pamphlets

"United States Department of the Interior List of Department Names and Addresses." n.d. 1p. free.
Identifies the 10 departments within the Interior Department. Includes address and telephone number.

Audiovisuals:

Filmographies, Sales Lists, etc.

"Film Catalog." 1976. 22p. free.
Lists annotated films covering: parks and related activities, outdoor recreation, wildlife resources, earth sciences, water and power resources, saline water conversion, electric power in the Pacific Northwest and Pacific Southwest, public land resources, mineral resources, states and their natural resources. Films are from various sources and may be free loan, rental, or for purchase.

DEPARTMENT OF THE NAVY
Office of Information
The Pentagon
Washington, DC 20350
(202) 697-7391

Date Established: 1775

Objectives of the Agency: Protect the United States by the effective use of sea power including, with its Marine Corps component, the seizure or defense of naval bases; support the forces of all military departments; and maintain freedom of the seas.

Curriculum: Social studies

Subjects: Geography
History

Locations:

Local recruiting offices.

Department of the Navy

Publications:

Information on naval careers available from recruiting offices.

Audiovisuals:

Filmographies, Sales Lists, etc.

"U.S. Navy Films for the Public." 1974. 87p. free. NAVSO P-3549.

Lists films that are available on a free loan basis from five distribution centers. Annotations. Subjects include: *Acoustics, Aviation, Biological Sciences, Communications, Computers and Data Processing, Construction and Civil Engineering, Dentistry, Diving, Earth Sciences, Meteorology, Oceanography, Electricity and Magnetism, Engines and Hydraulics, Food Preparation and Preservation, Machines and Machine Shop and Tools, Management Engineering and Management, Medical, Navigation, Photography, Polar Regions and Cold Weather Operations, Recruiting and General Interest, Safety and Survival, Ships and Boats, Training,* and *Uniform Code of Military Justice and Drills.* Films are assigned one of nine different release codes. These range from "REL 01 Limited Exhibition — Professional Audiences Only," to "REL 10 Public Exhibition, Television, Domestic Sale & Theatre." Films are also available for sale or rental from the National Audiovisual Center. For a copy of their catalog, write: National Audiovisual Center, Washington, DC 20409.

Navy films may be obtained for a limited time on a free loan basis from the office serving individual states.

CT, MA, ME, NH, NJ, NY, RI, VT

Education and Training Support Center
Film Library
Federal Office Bldg.
Third Ave. and Twenty-Ninth St.
Fifth Floor
Brooklyn, NY 11232

CZ, DC, DE, KY, MD, OH, PA, PR, VA, WV

Education and Training Support Detachment
Film Library
Naval Base
Norfolk, VA 23511

AL, FL, GA, MS, NC, SC, TN

Education and Training Support Detachment
Film Library
Naval Base
Charleston, SC 29408

CO, IA, IL, IN, KS, MI, MN, MO, ND, NE, SD, WI, WY

Education and Training Support Detachment
Film Library
Great Lakes, IL 60088

AK, AR, AZ, CA, HI, ID, LA, MT, NM, NV, OK, OR, TX, UT, WA

Education and Training Support Center, Pacific
Film Library
Fleet Station Post Office Bldg.
San Diego, CA 92132

Individual Films

"Assault on the Unknown — Oceanographic Research Platform." 1972. 28½ minutes. 16mm. color. free loan. Film No. MN-10994.

Examines sophisticated research platform used to provide essential information for a better understanding of the oceans.

"Beyond Magellan." 1961. 28 minutes. 16mm. color. free loan. Film No. MC-9613

Describes a submerged trip around the world by the nuclear submarine, USS Triton.

"Biography of Admiral Nimitz." 1963. 28 minutes. 16mm. color. free loan. Film No. MC-9937.

Describes life of Fleet Admiral Chester W. Nimitz. Shows action footage from World War II.

"Charting the Oceans." 1972. 28 minutes. 16mm. color. free loan. Film No. MN-10993.

Explains the history of charts, how the Navy makes them, and the importance of charts to mariners.

"Flight to the South Pole." 1968. 29 minutes. 16mm. color. free loan. Film No. MN-10489.

Chronicles the challenge of Antarctic flying, from Byrd's first polar flight to Operation Deepfreeze, the C-130 Hercules aircraft operations in the Antarctic.

"Fury in the Pacific." 1945. 20 minutes. 16mm. B&W. free loan. Film No. MN-9045.

Chronicles the invasion of the Palau Islands, bombardment by the fleet, landing of the Marines, and the struggle against the Japanese. Described as "historical document."

"Gulf Stream." 1971. 28 minutes. 16mm. color. free loan. Film No. MN-10842.

Describes Gulf Stream research and investigations conducted by the Navy and Navy-sponsored oceanographers.

"Hurricane Hunters." 1970. 28½ minutes. 16mm. color. free loan. Film No. MN-10504.

Relates a mission of a squadron operating in Florida, Puerto Rico, and over the Atlantic Ocean during hurricane season. Shows an actual penetration flight into the eye of a hurricane.

"Law of the Sea." 1970. 28½ minutes. 16mm. color. free loan. Film No. MN-10496.

Illustrates various legal problems and solutions in a documentary form.

"Nature of Sea Water." 1967. 29 minutes. 16mm. color. free loan. Film No. MN-10317.

Shows physical and chemical properties of sea water. Explains how man's understanding of the sea is basic to making use of ocean resources.

"Ocean Desert." 1971. 28½ minutes. 16mm. color. free loan. Film No. MN-10844.

Chronicles oceanographic investigation of the Sargasso Sea by Navy scientists and private oceanographic institutions.

"Oceanography—Science for Survival." 1963. 42 minutes. 16mm. color. free loan. Film No. MN-9835.

Describes content, aims, importance, and progress of the National Oceanographic Program, its supporting research, surveys, and resources. Introduced by President John F. Kennedy.

"Sea Power—A Destiny upon the Waters." 1969. 28 minutes. 16mm. color. free loan. Film No. MN-10365A.

Shows the evolution of naval power from the Phoenicians to the mid-eighteenth century and its impact on the development of empires and the Age of Exploration.

"Seapower in the Pacific." 1946. 30 minutes. 16mm. B&W. free loan. Film No. MN-6124.

Chronicles American sea power in World War II, the loss of our ships at Pearl Harbor, the steady growth of the fleet, the widening of sea lanes, the fall of Manila, and final victory. Described as "historical document."

"A Tradition in Music." 1969. 28½ minutes. 16mm. color. free loan. Film No. MN-10697.

Shows the U.S. Navy Band in operation: rehearsals, recording sessions, and the work involved in keeping the band in shape.

"Victory at Sea—D-Day." 1953. 30 minutes. 16mm. B&W. free loan. Film No. MN-73080.

Show events in Sicily, Italy, and south of France during World War II. Described as "historical document."

"Victory at Sea—Guadalcanal." 1953. 30 minutes. 16mm. B&W. free loan. Film No. MN-7308F.

Chronicles Guadalcanal. Described as "historical document."

"Victory at Sea—The Pacific Boils Over." 1953. 30 minutes. 16mm. B&W. free loan. Film No. MN-7308B.

Chronicles Pearl Harbor. Described as "historical document."

"Water Masses of the Oceans." 1967. 45 minutes. 16mm. color. free loan. Film No. MN-10064.

Scientifically studies the locations and dynamic movements of the major water masses of the oceans.

Special Services: Information on speakers and exhibits can be obtained by writing to the address or calling the number given at the beginning of the entry.

DEPARTMENT OF THE TREASURY
Public Affairs
Fifteenth and Pennsylvania Ave., NW
Room 2315
Washington, DC 20220

Date Established: 1789

Objectives of the Agency: Formulate and recommend economic, financial, tax, and fiscal policies; serve as financial agent for the U.S. government; enforce the law; and manufacture coins and currency.

Curriculum: Economics

Subjects: Economic policy

Publications: Financial releases.

Selected List of Books and Pamphlets

"Treasury News." Released periodically. 2p. free.

Gives news about the Department of the Treasury activities. Inquire about being placed on mailing list.

DEPARTMENT OF TRANSPORTATION
400 Seventh St., SW
Washington, DC 20590
(202) 426-4000

Date Established: 1967

Objectives of the Agency: Administer transportation programs of the federal government and develop national transportation policies and programs.

Curriculum: Social studies

Subjects: Transportation

Locations:

Northeastern Region
(Includes Puerto Rico and Virgin Islands)
Department of Transportation
Regional Secretary
Suite 1000
434 Walnut St.
Philadelphia, PA 19106

Southeastern Region
Department of Transportation
Regional Secretary
1720 Peachtree St., NW
Suite 515
Atlanta, GA 30309

52 / Department of Transportation

Great Lakes Region

Department of Transportation
Regional Secretary
300 S. Wacker Dr.
Room 700
Chicago, IL 60606

Central South Region

Department of Transportation
Regional Secretary
819 Taylor St.
Room 7A29
Fort Worth, TX 76102

North Central Region

Department of Transportation
Regional Secretary
601 E. Twelfth St.
Room 634
Kansas City, MO 64106

Western Region
(Includes Hawaii and Alaska)

Department of Transportation
Regional Secretary
211 Main St.
Suite 1005
San Francisco, CA 94105

Selected List of Books and Pamphlets

Consumer's Resource Handbook. Current. 111p. free.
   Explains how to write a complaint letter and sources of help. Includes a Consumer Assistance Directory.

"Meeting America's Transportation Needs." n.d. 16p. free.
   Explains what the various departments, such as the Federal Highway Administration or the Federal Railroad Administration, do.

DEPOSITORY ADMINISTRATION BRANCH
Library Division
Library Programs Service
Information Dissemination/Superintendent of Documents
U.S. Government Printing Office
Washington, DC 20402
(202) 275-2051

Date Established: 1968

Curriculum: Library

Subjects: Library science

Designated regional depositories are required to receive and retain one copy of all government publications made available to depository libraries either in printed or microfacsimile form. To save space, depository libraries (numbering about 1,400) are not listed. For a complete listing, order "Government Depository Libraries," described under *Selected List of Books and Pamphlets.*

Locations:

Regional Depository Libraries

AK

None

AL

Auburn University at Montgomery Library
Documents Department
Montgomery, AL 36193
(205) 279-9110, ext. 253

University of Alabama Library
Reference Department/Documents
Box S
University, AL 35486
(205) 348-6046

AR

Arkansas State Library
Documents Service Section
1 Capitol Mall
Little Rock, AR 72201
(501) 371-2090

AZ

Department of Library Archives and Public Records
1700 W. Washington
Third Floor State Capitol
Phoenix, AZ 85007
(602) 255-4121

University of Arizona Library
Government Documents Department
Tucson, AZ 85721
(602) 621-4871

CA

California State Library
Government Publications Service
914 Capitol Mall
Sacramento, CA 95814
(916) 322-4572

CO

University of Colorado at Boulder
Norlin Library
Government Publications
Campus Box 184
Boulder, CO 80309
(303) 492-8834

Denver Public Library
Government Publications Department
1357 Broadway
Denver, CO 80203
(303) 571-2140

CT, RI

Connecticut State Library
231 Capitol Ave.
Hartford, CT 06106
(203) 566-4971

DC

See MD.

DE

None

FL, PR

University of Florida Libraries
Documents Department
Library West
Gainesville, FL 32611
(904) 392-0367

GA

University of Georgia Libraries
Government Documents Department
Athens, GA 30602
(404) 542-8949

HI

University of Hawaii
Hamilton Library
Government Documents Collection
2550 The Mall
Honolulu, HI 96822
(808) 948-8230

IA

University of Iowa Libraries
Government Publications Department
Iowa City, IA 52242
(319) 353-3318

ID

University of Idaho Library
Documents Section
Moscow, ID 83843
(208) 885-6344

IL

Illinois State Library
Government Documents
Centennial Bldg.
Springfield, IL 62756
(217) 782-5012

IN

Indiana State Library
Serials Section
140 N. Senate Ave.
Indianapolis, IN 46204
(317) 232-3686

KS

University of Kansas
Spencer Research Library
Documents Collection
Lawrence, KS 66045
(913) 864-4662

KY

University of Kentucky Libraries
Government Publications Department
Lexington, KY 40506
(606) 257-3139

LA, VI

Louisiana State University
Middleton Library
Government Documents Department
Baton Rouge, LA 70803
(504) 388-2570

Louisiana Technical University
Prescott Memorial Library
Documents Department
Ruston, LA 71272
(318) 257-4962

MA

Boston Public Library
Documents Receipts
666 Boylston St.
Boston, MA 02117
(617) 536-5400, ext. 226

MD, DC

University of Maryland
McKeldin Library
Documents Division
College Park, MD 20742
(301) 454-3034

ME, NH, VT

University of Maine
Raymond H. Fogler Library
Tri-State Regional Documents Depository
Orono, ME 04469
(207) 581-1680

MI

Detroit Public Library
5201 Woodward Ave.
Detroit, MI 48202
(313) 833-1409

Library of Michigan
Government Documents
P.O. Box 30007
735 E. Michigan Ave.
Lansing, MI 48909
(517) 373-1593

MN

University of Minnesota
Wilson Library
Government Publications
309 Nineteenth Ave. South
Minneapolis, MN 55455
(612) 373-7813

MO

None

MS

University of Mississippi
J. D. Williams Library
Documents Department
University, MS 38677
(601) 232-5857

MT

University of Montana
Maurene and Mike Mansfield Library
Documents Division
Missoula, MT 59812
(406) 243-6700

NC

University of North Carolina at Chapel Hill
Davis Library
080ABA/SS Division Documents
Chapel Hill, NC 27514
(919) 962-1151

ND

North Dakota State University Library
Government Documents Department
Fargo, ND 58105
(701) 237-8886

NE

University of Nebraska-Lincoln
D. L. Love Memorial Library
Documents Dept.
Lincoln, NE 68588
(402) 472-2562

NH

See ME.

NJ

Newark Public Library
U.S. Documents Division
5 Washington St.
P.O. Box 630
Newark, NJ 07101
(201) 733-7782

NM

University of New Mexico
General Library
Government Publications and Maps Dept.
Albuquerque, NM 87131
(505) 277-5441

New Mexico State Library
325 Don Gaspar Ave.
Santa Fe, NM 87501
(505) 827-3823

NV

University of Nevada-Reno Library
Government Publications Dept.
Reno, NV 89557
(702) 784-6579

NY

New York State Library
Documents Control
Cultural Education Center
Sixth Floor
Empire State Plaza
Albany, NY 12230
(518) 474-7646

OH

State Library of Ohio
Documents Section
65 S. Front St.
Columbus, OH 43266
(614) 462-7051

OK

Oklahoma Department of Libraries
Government Documents
200 N.E. Eighteenth St.
Oklahoma City, OK 73105
(405) 521-2502 Ext. 252

Oklahoma State University Library
Documents Department
Stillwater, OK 74078
(405) 624-6546

OR

Portland State University
Millar Library
934 S.W. Harrison
Portland, OR 97207
(503) 229-3673

PA

State Library of Pennsylvania
Government Publications Section
Walnut St. and Commonwealth Ave.
Box 1601
Harrisburg, PA 17105
(717) 787-3752

RI

See CT.

SC, SD, TN

None

TX

Texas State Library
Public Services Department
1201 Brazos
P.O. Box 12927
Austin, TX 78711
(512) 463-5455

Texas Tech University Library
Documents Department
Lubbock, TX 79409
(806) 742-2268

UT

Utah State University
Merrill Library and Learning Resources Center
UMC-30
Documents Department
Logan, UT 84322
(801) 750-2682

VA

University of Virginia
Alderman Library
Government Documents
Charlottesville, VA 22903
(804) 924-3133

VI

See LA.

VT

See ME.

WA

Washington State Library
Documents Section
Olympia, WA 98504
(206) 753-4027

WV

West Virginia University Library
Government Documents Section
P.O. Box 6069
Morgantown, WV 26506
(304) 293-3640

WI

State Historical Society of Wisconsin Library
Government Publications Section
816 State St.
Madison, WI 53706
(608) 262-4347

Milwaukee Public Library
Documents Division
814 W. Wisconsin Ave.
Milwaukee, WI 53233
(414) 278-3017

WY

Wyoming State Library
Supreme Court and Library Bldg.
Cheyenne, WY 82002
(307) 777-5919

Publications: Guides. Laws. Guidelines for depository libraries.

Selected List of Books and Pamphlets

"Depository Libraries: Your Source for Government Information." n.d. 4p. free.
   Tells what is available at depository libraries.

"Guidelines for the Depository Library System." n.d. 11p. free.
   Reprints guidelines adopted in 1977. Includes minimum standards for the depository library system adopted in 1976.

Government Depository Libraries. 1984. 148p. free.
   Explains current law governing designated depository libraries. Lists libraries by state with addresses, telephone numbers, and what year they were designated depositories.

List of Classes of United States Government Publications Available for Selection by Depository Libraries. 1984. 147p. free.
   Lists class titles and depository item numbers of various departments.

**DIVISION OF BIRTH DEFECTS AND
   DEVELOPMENTAL DISABILITIES**
Centers for Disease Control
Center for Environmental Health
Chamblee-5
1600 Clifton Rd., NE
Atlanta, GA 30333
(404) 452-4084

56 / Division of Birth Defects and Developmental Disabilities

Date Established: 1985

Objectives of the Agency: Conduct and disseminate findings of epidemiologic research, investigations, demonstrations, and programs directed toward determining the environmental causes of selected adverse reproductive outcomes and perinatal and childhood diseases, including developmental disabilities.

Curriculum: Child care, health

Subjects: Child development
Prenatal care

Publications: Bibliography.

Bibliographies, Sales Catalogs, Publications Lists, etc.

"Bibliography, 1975-1985." 1985. 13p. free.
Groups 160 entries by year. Underlines entries written by Division of Birth Defects and Developmental Disabilities staff. References to professional journals predominate.

ECONOMIC DEVELOPMENT ADMINISTRATION
Department of Commerce
Assistant for Public Affairs
Washington, DC 20230
(202) 377-5113

Date Established: 1965

Objectives of the Agency: Facilitate long-range economic development of areas with severe unemployment and low family income problems; and aid in the development of public facilities and private enterprise to create jobs.

Curriculum: Government

Subjects: U.S. — Economic policy

Locations:

Regional Offices

CT, DC, DE, MA, MD, ME, NH, NJ, NY, PA, PR, RI, VA, VI, VT, WV

Economic Development Administration
Regional Office
325 Chestnut St.
Fourth Floor
Philadelphia, PA 19106

AL, FL, GA, KY, MS, NC, SC, TN

Economic Development Administration
Regional Office
1365 Peachtree St., NE
Suite 750
Atlanta, GA 30309

IL, IN, MI, MN, OH, WI

Economic Development Administration
Regional Office
175 W. Jackson Blvd.
Suite A-1630
Chicago, IL 60604

CO, IA, KS, MO, MT, ND, NE, SD, UT, WY

Economic Development Administration
Regional Office
333 W. Colfax Ave.
Denver, CO 80204

AR, LA, NM, OK, TX

Economic Development Administration
Regional Office
221 W. Sixth St.
Austin, TX 78701

AK, AS, AZ, CA, GU, HI, ID, NV, OR, WA

Economic Development Administration
Regional Office
1700 Westlake Ave. North
Seattle, WA 98109

Publications: Handbooks. Manuals. Reports on activities. Guidelines on economic conditions in various locations.

Bibliographies, Sales Catalogs, Publications Lists, etc.

Summary Description of Recent Studies and Publications. Current. 130p. free.
Tells what is available and how to obtain recent publications.

ECONOMIC RESEARCH SERVICE
United States Department of Agriculture
1301 New York Ave., NW
Room 1208
Washington, DC 20005-4788
(202) 447-4230

Date Established: 1961

Objectives of the Agency: Provide economic information to aid public policy officials and program managers in developing and administering agricultural and rural policies and programs.

Curriculum: Agriculture

Subjects: Agriculture — economic aspects

Locations:

AK

Statistician in Charge
P.O. Box 799
Palmer, AK 99645
(907) 745-4272

AL

Statistician in Charge
P.O. Box 1071
Montgomery, AL 36192

AR

Statistician in Charge
P.O. Box 1417
Little Rock, AR 72203

AZ

USDA-ERS-ECON
Department of Agricultural Economics
Economics Bldg.
University of Arizona
Room 419
Tucson, AZ 85721

CA

Statistician in Charge
P.O. Box 1258
Sacramento, CA 95806

CO

Statistician in Charge
P.O. Box 17066
Denver, CO 80217

CT, DC, DE

None

FL

Statistician in Charge
1222 Woodard St.
Orlando, FL 32803

GA

Statistician in Charge
Stephens Federal Bldg.
Suite 320
Athens, GA 30613

HI

Statistician in Charge
P.O. Box 22159
Honolulu, HI 96822
(808) 546-5527

IA

Statistician in Charge
833 Federal Bldg.
210 Walnut St.
Des Moines, IA 50309

ID

Statistician in Charge
P.O. Box 1699
Boise, ID 83701

IL

Statistician in Charge
P.O. Box 429
Springfield, IL 62705

IN

Statistician in Charge
Agricultural Administration Bldg.
Purdue University
West Lafayette, IN 47907

KS

Statistician in Charge
444 S.E. Quincy St.
Room 290
Topeka, KS 66683

KY

Statistician in Charge
P.O. Box 1120
Louisville, KY 40201

LA

Statistician in Charge
P.O. Box 5524
Alexandria, LA 71301

MA

None

MD

Statistician in Charge
50 Harry S. Truman Pkwy.
Annapolis, MD 21401
(301) 841-5740

ME

None

MI

Statistician in Charge
P.O. Box 20008
Lansing, MI 48901

MN

Statistician in Charge
P.O. Box 7068
St. Paul, MN 55107

MO

Statistician in Charge
P.O. Box L
Columbia, MO 65205

MS

Statistician in Charge
P.O. Box 980
Jackson, MS 39205

MT
Statistician in Charge
P.O. Box 4369
Helena, MT 59604

NC
Statistician in Charge
P.O. Box 27767
Raleigh, NC 27611

ND
Statistician in Charge
P.O. Box 3166
Fargo, ND 58102

NE
Statistician in Charge
P.O. Box 81069
Lincoln, NE 68501

NH
Statistician in Charge
P.O. Box 1444
Concord, NH 03301

NJ
Statistician in Charge
Health and Agriculture Bldg.
CN-330 New Warren St.
Room 204
Trenton, NJ 08625
(609) 291-6385

NM
Statistician in Charge
P.O. Box 1809
Las Cruces, NM 88004

NV
Statistician in Charge
P.O. Box 8888
Reno, NV 89507

NY
Statistician in Charge
Department of Agriculture and Markets
1 Winners Circle
Albany, NY 12235

OH
Statistician in Charge
New Federal Bldg.
200 N. High St.
Room 608
Columbus, OH 43215

OK
None

OR
Statistician in Charge
1735 Federal Bldg.
1220 S.W. Third Ave.
Portland, OR 97204

PA
Statistician in Charge
2301 N. Cameron St.
Room G-19
Harrisburg, PA 17110

SC
Statistician in Charge
P.O. Box 1911
Columbia, SC 29202

SD
Statistician in Charge
P.O. Box V
Sioux Falls, SD 57117

TN
Statistician in Charge
P.O. Box 41505
Nashville, TN 37204

TX
Statistician in Charge
P.O. Box 70
Austin, TX 78767

UT
Statistician in Charge
P.O. Box 25007
Salt Lake City, UT 84125

VA
Statistician in Charge
P.O. Box 1659
Richmond, VA 23213

WA
Statistician in Charge
P.O. Box 609
Olympia, WA 98507

WI
Statistician in Charge
P.O. Box 9160
Madison, WI 53715

WV

Statistician in Charge
State Department of Agriculture
Charleston, WV 25312

WY

Statistician in Charge
P.O. Box 1148
Cheyenne, WY 82003

Publications: Reports. Serials. Pamphlets. Background papers.

Bibliographies, Sales Catalogs, Publications Lists, etc.

"Reports." Quarterly. 12p. free.
Describes publication reports issued by the U.S. Department of Agriculture's Economic Research Service. Includes photographs of report covers. Provides GPO order form to order the inexpensive reports.

Selected List of Books and Pamphlets

"Food Cost Review." Current. 56p. $2.00. S/N 001-019-00411-8.
Shows how much of the retail food price the farm value represents, how recent developments affected food industry costs, and how much Americans spent for farm-produced foods during the last year. Order from: "Reports," USDA-EMS Information, 1301 New York Ave., NW, Room 237, Washington, DC 20005-4788.

"History of Agricultural Price-Support and Adjustment Programs, 1933-84." 1984. 52p. free. Agriculture Information Bulletin No. 485.
Reviews the history of how congressional legislation and programs have been modified for changing economic situations. Begins with the origin of adjustment programs and ends with recent legislation. Summarizes major agricultural legislation. Table. Chart. Index.

Special Services: To be placed on the mailing list to receive "Reports" regularly, write: "Reports," USDA-EMS Information, 1301 New York Avenue, NW, Room 237, Washington, DC 20005-4788.

EDGAR ALLAN POE NATIONAL HISTORIC SITE
Independence National Historical Park
313 Walnut St.
Philadelphia, PA 19106
(215) 597-8780

Date Established: 1980

Objectives of the Agency: Portray the life and work of Poe at 532 N. Seventh Street where he lived from 1843-1844.

Curriculum: English

Subjects: American literature

Publications: Flyer about Poe and the site.

Selected List of Books and Pamphlets

"Edgar Allan Poe." n.d. 4-fold flyer. free.
Gives biographical sketch and photographs of Poe. Includes photographs and information about other sites honoring Poe.

EMPLOYMENT STANDARDS ADMINISTRATION
U.S. Department of Labor
200 Constitution Ave., NW
Washington, DC 20210
(202) 523-8305

Date Established: 1971

Objectives of the Agency: Administer and direct employment standards programs dealing with minimum wage, overtime, and registration of farm labor contractors; determine prevailing wage rates to be paid on government contracts and subcontracts; support nondiscrimination, affirmative action, and workers' compensation programs.

Curriculum: Consumer education

Subjects: Employment

Locations:

CT, MA, ME, NH, RI, VT

Employment Standards Administration Field Office
JFK Federal Bldg.
Room 1612-C
Boston, MA 02203

CZ, NJ, NY, PR, VI

Employment Standards Administration Field Office
1515 Broadway
Room 3300
New York, NY 10036

DC, DE, MD, PA, VA, WV

Employment Standards Administration Field Office
Gateway Bldg.
3535 Market St.
Fifteenth Floor
Philadelphia, PA 19104

AL, FL, GA, KY, MS, NC, SC, TN

Employment Standards Administration Field Office
1371 Peachtree St., NE
Room 305
Atlanta, GA 30309

IL, IN, MI, MN, OH, WI

Employment Standards Administration Field Office
230 S. Dearborn St.
Eighth Floor
Chicago, IL 60604

AR, LA, NM, OK, TX

Employment Standards Administration Field Office
555 Griffin Square Bldg.
Young and Griffin Sts.
Dallas, TX 75202

IA, KS, MO, NE

Employment Standards Administration Field Office
Federal Office Bldg.
911 Walnut St.
Room 2000
Kansas City, MO 64106

CO, MT, ND, SD, UT, WY

Employment Standards Administration Field Office
Federal Office Bldg.
1961 Stout St.
Room 15412
Denver, CO 80202

AZ, CA, HI, NV

Employment Standards Administration Field Office
450 Golden Gate Ave.
Room 10353
San Francisco, CA 94102

AK, ID, OR, WA

Employment Standards Administration Field Office
Federal Office Bldg.
909 First Ave.
Room 4141
Seattle, WA 98104

Publications: Pamphlets. Guides. Acts on employment.

Selected List of Books and Pamphlets

"All About the Employment Standards Administration." 1978. 12p. free. PAM ESA-1.
  Describes its component offices: the Office of Federal Contract Compliance Programs, the Office of Workers' Compensation Programs, and the Wage and Hour Division.

"Contract Work Hours and Safety Standards Act, As Amended." Rev. 9p. free. WH Publication 1432.
  Reprints objectives of the act, and the act itself.

"Executive, Administrative, Professional and Outside Sales Exemptions Under the Fair Labor Standards Act." 1983. 10p. free. WH Publication 1363.
  Tells what the act covers and does not cover.

"Handy Reference Guide to the Fair Labor Standards Act." 1983. 4p. free.
  Tells what the act establishes, who is covered, what terms are used, how it is enforced, and how to recover back wages.

Special Services: For information about exhibits, slide shows, and films on programs, write: ESA Office of Information and Consumer Affairs
NDOL
200 Constitution Ave., NW
Room C4331
Washington, DC 20210

ENERGY INFORMATION ADMINISTRATION
National Energy Information Center
Forrestal Bldg., IF-048
1000 Independence Ave., SW
Washington, DC 20585
(202) 252-8800

Date Established: 1977

Objectives of the Agency: Collect, evaluate, analyze, and disseminate energy data.

Curriculum: Environmental studies

Subjects: Energy conservation

Locations:

The National Energy Extension Service is a federal/state arrangement to give aid to energy users on energy conservation and the use of renewable and abundant resources.

AK

Energy Extension Service
Division of Community Development
Department of Community and Regional Affairs
949 E. Thirty-Sixth Ave.
Suite 400
Anchorage, AK 99508
(907) 563-1955

AL

Energy Extension Service
Department of Economic and Community Affairs
Energy Division
3465 Norman Bridge Rd.
P.O. Box 2939
Montgomery, AL 36105
(205) 284-8936

AS

Territorial Energy Office
Office of the Governor
Pago Pago, AS 96799
(684) 699-1101

AR
Energy Extension Service
Arkansas Energy Office
No. 1 State Capitol Mall
Little Rock, AR 72201
(501) 371-1370

AZ
Energy Office
1700 W. Washington
Fifth Floor
Phoenix, AZ 85007
(602) 255-3632

CA
California Energy Extension Service
Governor's Office of Planning and Research
1400 Tenth St.
Sacramento, CA 95814
(916) 323-4388

CO
Colorado Energy Extension Service
Colorado Office of Energy Conservation
112 E. Fourteenth Ave.
Denver, CO 80203
(303) 866-2507

CT
Energy Division
80 Washington St.
Hartford, CT 06106
(203) 566-2800

DC
DC Energy Office
420 Seventh St., NW
Room 500
Washington, DC 20004
(202) 727-1800

DE
Energy Office
Oneill Bldg.
Federal St.
P.O. Box 1401
Dover, DE 19903
DE only: (800) 282-8616
(302) 736-5644

FL
Governor's Energy Office
301 Bryant Bldg.
Tallahassee, FL 32301-8047
(904) 488-2475

GA
Office of Energy Resources
270 Washington St., SW
Room 615
Atlanta, GA 30334
(404) 656-5176

GU
Guam Energy Office
P.O. Box 2950
Agana, GU 96910
Direct dial: (671) 734-4452
Overseas operator: (671) 734-4452
                   (671) 734-4530

HI
Department of Planning and Economic Development
P.O. Box 2359
Honolulu, HI 96804
(808) 548-6914

IA
Energy Conservation Division
Iowa Energy Policy Council
Lucas State Office Bldg.
Des Moines, IA 50319
(515) 281-4308

ID
Energy Resources Bureau
State House Mall
450 W. State St.
Boise, ID 83720
(208) 334-3406

IL
Department of Energy and Natural Resources
325 W. Adams
Room 300
Springfield, IL 62706
(217) 785-2800

IN
Energy Extension Service
Indiana Commerce Center
One N. Capitol
Suite 700
Indianapolis, IN 46204-2288
(317) 232-8995

KS
Energy Extension Service
Kansas State University
Ward Hall
Manhattan, KS 66506
(913) 532-6026

KY

Division of Conservation
Kentucky Energy Cabinet
P.O. Box 11888
Lexington, KY 40578-1916
(606) 252-5535

LA

Energy Extension Service Program
Energy Research and Planning Division
Department of Natural Resources
P.O. Box 44156
Baton Rouge, LA 70804
(504) 342-2133

MA

Energy Extension Service
Executive Office of Energy Resources
100 Cambridge St.
Room 1303
Boston, MA 02202
(617) 727-6964

MD

Energy Extension Service
Maryland Energy Office
301 W. Preston St.
Suite 903
Baltimore, MD 21201-9943
Maryland only: (800) 492-5903
(301) 225-1810

ME

Energy Extension Service
Maine Office of Energy Resources
State House
Station No. 53
Augusta, ME 04333
(207) 289-3811

MI

Energy Administration
Michigan Department of Commerce
North Ottawa Tower
611 W. Ottawa St.
P.O. Box 30228
Lansing, MI 48909
(517) 373-0480

MN

Department of Energy and Economic Development
Energy Development
Energy Division
900 American Center Bldg.
150 E. Kellogg Blvd.
St. Paul, MN 55101
(612) 297-1965

MO

Division of Energy Programs
P.O. Box 176
Jefferson City, MO 65102
(314) 751-4000

MS

Extension Service Program
Mississippi State University
Box 5406
Mississippi State, MS 39762
(601) 325-3152

MT

Department of Natural Resources and Conservation
Energy Bureau
Energy Division
1520 E. Sixth Ave.
Helena, MT 59620
(406) 444-6696

NC

North Carolina Department of Commerce
Energy Division
P.O. Box 25249
Raleigh, NC 27611
(919) 733-2230

ND

EES Coordinator
Office of Intergovernmental Assistance
State Capitol
Fourteenth Floor
Bismarck, ND 58505
(701) 224-2676

NE

Nebraska State Energy Office
P.O. Box 95085
Ninth Floor
State Capitol Bldg.
Lincoln, NE 68509
(402) 471-2867

NH

Energy Extension Services
Governor's Energy Office
2½ Beacon St.
Second Floor
Concord, NH 03301
(603) 271-2711

NJ

Energy Information Service
New Jersey Department of Energy
101 Commerce St.
Newark, NJ 07102
NJ only: (800) 492-4242
(201) 648-3185

NM

New Mexico Energy and Minerals Department
525 Camino De Los Marquez
Santa Fe, NM 87501
NM only: (800) 432-6782
(505) 827-5900

Northern Mariana Islands

Office of Energy and Environment
P.O. Box 340
Saipan, Mariana Islands 96950
(670) 322-9229
(670) 322-9236

NV

Governors Office of Community Services
1100 E. Williams
Suite 117
Carson City, NV 89710
(702) 885-4420

NY

New York State Energy Office
2 Rockefeller Plaza
Tenth Floor
Albany, NY 12223
NY only: (800) 342-3722
(518) 473-4375

OH

Energy Extension Service
Office of Energy Conservation
30 E. Broad St.
Twenty-Fourth Floor
Columbus, OH 43215
(614) 466-6797

OK

Energy Information Center
Oklahoma Energy Conservation
Services Department
Oklahoma Corporation Commission
17 N.E. Twenty-Eighth St.
Oklahoma City, OK 73105
(405) 521-3941

OR

Energy Extension Service
303 Batcheller
Oregon State University
Corvallis, OR 97331
(503) 754-3004

PA

Governor's Energy Council
P.O. Box 8010
Harrisburg, PA 17105
(717) 783-0225

PR

Energy Extension Service
Office of Energy
Minillas Station
P.O. Box 41089
Santurce, PR 00940
(809) 721-3860

RI

Governor's Energy Office
72 Orange St.
Providence, RI 02903
(401) 277-3370

SC

State Energy Office
Bankers Trust Tower
Box 11405
Suite 1118
Columbia, SC 29211
(803) 758-8405

SD

Energy Extension Service
Energy Office
217½ W. Missouri
Pierre, SD 57501-4516
(605) 773-3603

TN

Office of Energy Conservation
Energy Division
Department of Economic and Community
  Development
320 Sixth Ave., N.
Sixth Floor
Nashville, TN 37219-5308
(615) 741-6671

Trust Territory of the Pacific Islands

Office of Planning and Statistics
Office of the High Commissioner
Trust Territory of the Pacific Islands
Saipan, Mariana Islands 96950
(885) 099-9333
(670) 322-9333

TX

Energy Efficiency Division
Public Utility Commission
800 Shoal Creek Blvd.
Suite 400 North
Austin, TX 78757
(512) 458-0301

UT

Energy Extension Service
Utah Energy Office
355 N.W. Temple
3 Triad Center
Suite 450
Salt Lake City, UT 84180-1204
UT only (800) 662-3633
(801) 538-5428

VA

Energy Division
Department of Mines, Minerals, and Energy
2201 W. Broad St.
Richmond, VA 23220
VA only: (800) 552-3831
(804) 257-1639

VI

Virgin Islands Energy Office
P.O. Box 2996
St. Thomas, VI 00801
(809) 774-6726

Virgin Islands Energy Office
Building 3
Room 233
Lagoon Complex
Frederiksted
St. Croix, VI 00840
(809) 772-2616

VT

Energy Program Coordinator
Cooperative Extension Service
University of Vermont
Vo-Tech Dept.
Agricultural Engineering Bldg.
Burlington, VT 05405
(802) 656-2001

WA

Conservation Division
Washington State Energy Office
400 E. Union St.
First Floor
Olympia, WA 98504
(206) 786-5089

WI

Wisconsin Division of State Energy
Department of Administration
P.O. Box 7868
Madison, WI 53707
(608) 266-6850

WV

EES Coordinator
West Virginia Fuel and Energy Office
1426 Kanawaha Blvd. East
Charleston, WV 25301
(304) 348-8860

WY

Wyoming Energy Extension Service
Casper College
Warner Tech Bldg.
125 College Dr.
Casper, WY 82601
(307) 266-4904

Publications: Reports. Guides. Machine-readable data. Catalogs. Bibliographies. Indexes. Surveys. Regulations. Directories. Serials. Newsletters. Handbooks. Pamphlets. Microfiche. Monographs. Forecasts.

Bibliographies, Sales Catalogs, Publications Lists, etc.

EIA Publications Directory: A User's Guide. 1985. 115p. free. DOE/EIA-0149(84).

Provides a subject index, title index, and a report number listing for recent EIA publications and information on how to order. The abstracts of the publications are arranged by broad subject categories such as *Coal, Petroleum,* or *Natural Gas.* Free and for sale. Provides order forms for distributing agencies, such as the Government Printing Office.

"EIA Publications: New Releases." Bimonthly. 40p. free. DOE/EIA-0204(85/03).

Materials arranged under: *Special Interest, New Reports, Periodicals, Data Files and Data Models,* and *Ordering Information and Order Forms.* Furnishes new materials each issue in a "Highlights" category. Lists periodical reports and one-time reports by subject (*Coal, Electricity,* etc.) in chart arrangement.

Serials, Subscription Publications, etc.

Monthly Energy Review. Monthly. 112p. $42.00/yr. domestic, $52.00/yr. foreign; $3.75 single domestic copy, $4.69 single foreign copy. DOE/EIA-0035.

Gives overview of the nation's energy picture and data on petroleum, natural gas, coal, electricity, nuclear energy, oil and gas resource development, prices, and the international energy situation. Order from: Superintendent of Documents, Government

Printing Office, Mail List Branch (STOP: SSOM), Washington, DC 20402.

Selected List of Books and Pamphlets

"Energy Data Contacts Finder." Current. 4p. free. DOE/EIA-0259.

Lists position, name, and telephone number for people in information services, data programs, forecasting and analysis, and conservation and consumption.

"Energy Information Directory." Semiannually. 73p. free. DOE/EIA-0205.

Lists government offices involved in energy, classified according to their specialties. Includes name of person in charge, address, telephone number and summary of functions. Name and subject indexes.

ENVIRONMENTAL PROTECTION AGENCY
Office of Public Affairs (A 107)
401 M St., SW
Washington, DC 20460
(202) 382-4361

Date Established: 1970

Objectives of the Agency: Protect and enhance our current and future environment by pollution abatement of water, air, solid waste, pesticides, radiation, and toxic substances.

Curriculum: Environmental studies, health

Subjects: Environment
Pesticides

Locations:

CT, MA, ME, NH, RI, VT

Environmental Protection Agency
Region 1 Office
Public Information Office
JFK Federal Bldg.
Boston, MA 02203
(617) 223-7210

NJ, NY, PR, VI

Environmental Protection Agency
Region 2 Office
26 Federal Plaza
New York, NY 10007
(212) 261-2525

Environmental Protection Agency
Region 2
Field Component
Public Information Office
Caribbean Field Office
P.O. Box 792
San Juan, PR 00902
(809) 725-7825

DC, DE, MD, PA, VA, WV

Environmental Protection Agency
Region 3 Office
Public Information Office
Sixth and Walnut Sts.
Philadelphia, PA 19106
(215) 597-9800

AL, FL, GA, KY, MS, NC, SC, TN

Environmental Protection Agency
Region 4 Office
Public Information Service
345 Courtland St., NE
Atlanta, GA 30365
(404) 881-4727

IL, IN, MI, MN, OH, WI

Environmental Protection Agency
Region 5 Office
Public Information Office
230 S. Dearborn St.
Chicago, IL 60604
(312) 353-2000

Environmental Protection Agency
Field Component
Eastern District Office
Public Information Office
25089 Center Ridge Rd.
West Lake, OH 44145
(216) 835-5200

AR, LA, NM, OK, TX

Environmental Protection Agency
Region 6 Office
Public Information Office
1201 Elm St.
Dallas, TX 75270
(214) 767-2600

IA, KS, MO, NE

Environmental Protection Agency
Region 7 Office
Public Information Office
726 Minnesota Ave.
Kansas City, KS 66101
(913) 236-2800

CO, MT, ND, SD, UT, WY

Environmental Protection Agency
Region 8 Office
Public Information Office
1860 Lincoln St.
Denver, CO 80295
(303) 837-3895

AS, AZ, CA, GU, HI, NV, Trust Territories of the Pacific

Environmental Protection Agency
Region 9 Office
Public Information Office
215 Freemont St.
San Francisco, CA 94105
(415) 974-8153

Environmental Protection Agency
Field Component
Pacific Islands Office
Public Information Office
300 Ala Moana Blvd.
Room 1302
P.O. Box 50003
Honolulu, HI 96850

AK, ID, OR, WA

Environmental Protection Agency
Region 10 Office
Public Information Office
1200 Sixth Ave.
Seattle, WA 98101
(206) 442-5810

Environmental Protection Agency
Alaska Operations Office
Public Information Office
Federal Bldg.
701 C St.
Room E556
Anchorage, AK 99513
(907) 271-5083

Environmental Protection Agency
Alaska Operations Office
Public Information Office
3200 Hospital Dr.
Juneau, AK 99801
(907) 586-7619

Environmental Protection Agency
Idaho Operations Office
Public Information Office
422 W. Washington St.
Boise, ID 83702
(208) 334-1450

Environmental Protection Agency
Oregon Operations Office
Public Information Office
522 S.W. Fifth Ave.
Yeon Bldg.
Second Floor
Portland, OR 97204
(503) 221-3250

Environmental Protection Agency
Washington Operations Office
c/o Washington Department of Ecology
Public Information Office
Mailstop PV 11
Olympia, WA 98504
(206) 753-9437

Publications: Pamphlets. Addresses. Flyers. Serials. Posters. General and technical materials. Safety guidelines. Educational material for children.

Serials, Subscription Publications, etc.

EPA Journal. Monthly. $20.00/yr. domestic, $25.00/yr. foreign; $2.00 single domestic copy, $2.50 single foreign copy.

Gives trends, concerns, people involved in protecting the environment. B&W photographs. Charts. Order from: Superintendent of Documents, Government Printing Office, Washington DC 20402.

Selected List of Books and Pamphlets

"Assessing and Managing Risks in the Real World." 1985. 8p. free.

Reprints an address by an EPA administrator before the National Petroleum Refiners Association. Tells of philosophical concerns in successfully meeting environmental challenges.

"Is Your Drinking Water Safe." 1985. 10p. free.

Describes the Safe Drinking Water Act of 1974, how the law works, and what progress has been made.

"Kids: Don't Touch Pesticides." 1977. 6p. free.

Outlines safety guides for children's protection from pesticides in an illustrated flyer. Includes tips for parents.

"The Next Four Years: An Agenda for Environmental Results." 1985. 9p. free.

Reprints the address of an EPA administrator at the National Press Club. Explains a four-point environmental management plan.

"Six Steps to Safer Use of Pesticides." n.d. 1p. free.

Gives tips to follow and an address to obtain more information about the use and regulation of pesticides.

"Superfund's Remedial Response Program." 1984. 18p. free.

Explains how the law, the Comprehensive Environmental Response, Compensation, and Liability Act of 1980 (commonly called the Superfund Law) works, summarizes field accomplishments. On-site photographs across the country.

"Trends in the Quality of the Nation's Air." 1985. 19p. free.
  Explains how air quality is determined, summary, and the background of air pollution. Shows trends in lead, carbon monoxide, particulates, ozone, and other pollutants. Chart.

"Water: A Resource You Can Help Restore." n.d. 4-fold poster. free.
  Gives tips on how to make life more fun through clean water management. Lists addresses of state offices that deal with water quality programs.

"What You Should Know about Your Auto Emissions Warranty." 1979. 8p. free.
  Gives questions and answers.

"Your Guide to the United States Environmental Protection Agency." 1984. 25p. free.
  Relates the history, organization, and services of the agency.

Audiovisuals:

Request a list of available audiovisuals from your region.

Special Services: For more information on pesticide safety, write: Pesticides
EPA
Public Information Center (PM-215)
401 M St., SW
Washington, DC 20460

A telephone directory is available. For ordering information, write:
Superintendent of Documents
Government Printing Office
Washington, DC 20402

Freedom of Information Officer: (202) 382-4048.

Ask about reports just concerning your region.

EQUAL EMPLOYMENT OPPORTUNITY COMMISSION
2401 E St., NW
Washington, DC 20507
(202) 634-6922

Date Established: 1964

Objectives of the Agency: Eliminate discrimination based on race, color, religion, sex, national origin, or age in hiring, promoting, firing, wages, testing, training, apprenticeship, and other employment conditions. The commission promotes voluntary action programs by employers, unions, and community organizations to make equal employment opportunity effective.

Curriculum: Guidance

Subjects: Employment

Publications: Fact sheets. Pamphlets. Guidelines on what the commission covers.

Selected List of Books and Pamphlets

"Age Discrimination Is against the Law." 1985. 1p. free.
  Tells what the law covers, what its exceptions are, and how and where to file a suit or charge.

"Backgrounder/The Equal Employment Opportunity Commission." n.d. 1p. free.
  Gives history, organization, and list of chairmen of the commission.

"Equal Employment Opportunity." 1979. 10p. free.
  Reprints questions and answers on guidelines on sex discrimination from the *Federal Register*.

"Federal Agency Equal Employment Opportunity Public Information Materials." 1981. 31p. free.
  Provides an annotated bibliography from the Office of Interagency Coordination of the Equal Employment Opportunity Commission. Lists equal employment information materials available from various federal agencies.

"Title VII." n.d. 1p. free.
  Explains what is covered under Title VII of the Civil Rights Act of 1964.

"Women and Men Equal Work Equal Pay." n.d. 1p. free.
  Tells what the Equal Pay Act does, what it covers, what the exceptions are, and where to file a complaint.

Special Services: Obtain further information from an Equal Employment Opportunity Commission office that may be listed in your telephone directory under *U.S. Government, Equal Employment Opportunity Commission.*

ERIC PROCESSING AND REFERENCE FACILITY
4833 Rugby Ave.
Suite 301
Bethesda, MD 20814-3073
(301) 656-9723

Date Established: 1966

Objectives: Facilitate user awareness and access to information through the Educational Resources Information Center Processing and Reference Facility.

Curriculum: Library

Subjects: Library science

Publications: Pamphlets. Directories. Serials. ERIC-tapes.

68 / ERIC Processing and Reference Facility

Bibliographies, Sales Catalogs, Publications Lists, etc.

"A Bibliography of Publications about the Educational Resources Information Center." 1978. 15p. free.

Lists materials alphabetically by personal author or corporate author or title. Includes 269 entries that may be used to answer questions on ERIC.

Selected List of Books and Pamphlets

"All about ERIC." 1982. 31p. free.

Explains what ERIC is and who can use ERIC. Tells about the ERIC network, reference tools, and the ERIC database, and information about other ERIC products. Order forms provided from ERIC Processing and Reference Facility, ERIC Document Reproduction Service, Oryx Press, Superintendent of Documents, and the National Audiovisual Center.

"Directory of ERIC Microfiche Collections." 1983. 69p. free.

Attempts to list every organization with a sizeable collection of ERIC microfiche whether or not that collection is currently being kept up-to-date by a subscription. Designed to help users of ERIC microfiche find the collection closest to them which answers their particular information needs. Covers telephone numbers, information contacts, equipment available, access hours, years covered and services offered. Indicates organizations that provide computer search services. Arranged alphabetically by state and by cities within each state.

"Directory of ERIC Search Services." 1981. 83p. free.

Describes organizations which are currently providing computerized searches of the ERIC database. Groups the 457 entries by state and within state by city with foreign entries appearing at the end.

"Submitting Documents to ERIC." n.d. 8p. free.

Describes the ERIC system, the advantages of having a document accepted by ERIC, the kinds of documents ERIC is seeking, the selection criteria, and where to send the documents.

EXTENSION SERVICE
United States Department of Agriculture
Information and Communications
Fourteenth St. and Independence Ave., SW
Washington, DC 20250
(202) 447-3029

Date Established: 1914

Objectives of the Agency: Provide an educational agency for the Department of Agriculture.

Curriculum: Agriculture, home economics

Subjects: Agriculture
Child development
Food

Locations:

AK
Cooperative Extension
University of Alaska
Fairbanks, AK 99701
(907) 474-7246

AL
Cooperative Extension Service
Auburn University
Auburn, AL 36849
(205) 826-4444

1890 Extension Service
Tuskegee Institute
Tuskegee, AL 36088
(205) 727-8808

Associate Dean for Extension Service
Alabama A&M University
Normal, AL 35762
(205) 859-7342

AR
Cooperative Extension Service
University of Arkansas
P.O. Box 391
Little Rock, AR 72203
(501) 373-2575

1890 Agricultural Programs
University of Arkansas
Box 82
Pine Bluff, AR 71601
(501) 541-6868

AS
Land Grant Programs
American Samoa Community College
Pago Pago, AS 96799

AZ
Cooperative Extension Service
University of Arizona
Tucson, AZ 85721
(602) 621-7209

CA
Cooperative Extension Service
University of California
Berkeley, CA 94720
(415) 644-4306

CO
Cooperative Extension Service
Colorado State University
Administration Bldg.
Fort Collins, CO 80523
(303) 491-6281

CT

Cooperative Extension Service
University of Connecticut
1376 Storrs Rd.
Box U-66
Storrs, CT 06268
(203) 486-2917

Cooperative Extension Service
College of Agriculture and Natural Resources
University of Connecticut
1376 Storrs Rd.
Box U-36
Storrs, CT 06268
(203) 486-4125

DC

Cooperative Extension Service
University of the District of Columbia
4200 Connecticut Ave., NW
Washington, DC 20008
(202) 576-6993

DE

Cooperative Extension Service
University of Delaware
Newark, DE 19717-1303
(302) 451-2504

1890 Extension Program
Delaware State College
Dover, DE 19901
(302) 736-4929

FL

Agricultural Affairs
Institute of Food and Agriculture
University of Florida
1038 McCarty Hall
Gainesville, FL 32611
(904) 392-1971

Dean for Extension Service
University of Florida
1038 McCarty Hall
Gainesville, FL 32611
(904) 392-1761

1890 Extension Program
Florida A&M University
Box 320
Tallahassee, FL 32307
(904) 599-3561

GA

Cooperative Extension Service
University of Georgia
Athens, GA 30602
(404) 542-3824

1890 Extension Program
The Fort Valley State College
Fort Valley, GA 31030
(912) 825-6296

GU

Cooperative Extension Service
University of Guam
UOG Station
Mangiloa, GU 96913
(671) 734-9162

HI

Extension Service
University of Hawaii
Honolulu, HI 96822
(808) 948-8234

Extension Service
University of Hawaii
3050 Maile Way
Gilmore 202
Honolulu, HI 96822
(808) 948-8131

IA

Cooperative Extension Service
Iowa State University
110 Curtiss Hall
Ames, IA 50011
(515) 294-4576

ID

Cooperative Extension Service
Agricultural Extension Bldg.
University of Idaho
Moscow, ID 83843
(208) 885-6639

IL

Cooperative Extension Service
University of Illinois
Mumford Hall
Urbana, IL 61801
(217) 333-2661

IN

Cooperative Extension Service
Purdue University
Agricultural Administration Bldg.
West Lafayette, IN 47907
(317) 494-8489

KS

Cooperative Extension Service
Kansas State University
Manhattan, KS 66506
(913) 532-5820

KY

Cooperative Extension Service
University of Kentucky
AG Science Bldg. North
Lexington, KY 40546
(606) 257-4772
(606) 257-3333

1890 Extension Program
Kentucky State University
Frankfort, KY 40601
(502) 564-6152

LA

Cooperative Extension Service
Louisiana State University
Baton Rouge, LA 70803
(504) 388-6083

1890 Extension Program
Southern University and A&M College
Baton Rouge, LA 70813
(504) 771-2242

MA

Extension Service
University of Massachusetts
Amherst, MA 01003
(413) 545-2766

MD

Cooperative Extension Service
University of Maryland
College Park, MD 20742
(301) 454-3742

1890 Extension Programs
University of Maryland
Eastern Shore
Princess Anne, MD 21853
(301) 651-2229

ME

Cooperative Extension Service
University of Maine
Orono, ME 04473
(207) 581-3188

MI

Cooperative Extension Service
Michigan State University
East Lansing, MI 48824
(517) 355-2308

Micronesia

Land Grant Office
College of Micronesia
Drawer F
Ponape, E.C.I. 96941

MN

Cooperative Extension Service
University of Minnesota
St. Paul, MN 55108
(612) 373-1223

MO

Cooperative Extension Service
University of Missouri
309 University Hall
Columbia, MO 65211
(314) 882-7754

Cooperative Extension Service
Lincoln University
Jefferson City, MO 65101
(314) 751-3797

MS

Cooperative Extension Service
Mississippi State University
Box 5446
Mississippi State, MS 39762
(601) 325-3036

1890 Extension Programs
Alcorn State University
Lorman, MS 39096
(601) 877-2916

MT

Cooperative Extension Service
Montana State University
Bozeman, MT 59715
(406) 994-3402

NC

Cooperative Extension Service
North Carolina State University
Box 7602
Raleigh, NC 27695-7602
(919) 737-2811

1890 Extension Programs
North Carolina A&T State University
Box 21928
Greensboro, NC 27420
(919) 379-7691

ND

Cooperative Extension Service
North Dakota State University
Fargo, ND 58105
(701) 237-8944

NE

Cooperative Extension Office
University of Nebraska
Lincoln, NE 68583-0703
(402) 472-2966

NH

Cooperative Extension Office
University of New Hampshire
Durham, NH 03824
(603) 862-1520

NJ

Cooperative Extension Service
Rutgers State University
Box 231
Cook Campus
New Brunswick, NJ 08903
(201) 932-9306

NM

Cooperative Extension Service
New Mexico State University
Las Cruces, NM 88003
(505) 646-3015

Northern Marianas

Cooperative Extension Service
Department of Natural Resources
Saipan, CNMI 96950

NV

College of Agriculture
University of Nevada
Reno, NV 89557
(702) 784-6611

Cooperative Extension Office
University of Nevada
Reno, NV 89557
(702) 784-1619

NY

Cooperative Extension Service
New York State Colleges of Agriculture and Life
   Sciences and Human Ecology
103 Roberts Hall
Ithaca, NY 14853
(607) 256-2117

OH

Cooperative Extension Service
Ohio State University
2120 Fyffe Rd.
Columbus, OH 43210
(614) 422-4067

OK

Cooperative Extension Service
Oklahoma State University
Stillwater, OK 74078
(405) 624-5400

Cooperative Extension Service
Oklahoma State University
Ag. Hall
Stillwater, OK 74078
(405) 624-5400

1890 Extension
Langston University
Langston, OK 73050
(405) 466-2231

OR

Cooperative Extension Service
Oregon State University
Corvallis, OR 97331
(503) 754-2713

PA

Cooperative Extension Service
The Pennsylvania State University
323 Agricultural Administration Bldg.
University Park, PA 16802
(814) 863-3438

PR

Cooperative Extension Service
University of Puerto Rico
College Station
Mayaguez, PR 00708
(809) 834-4040

RI

Agricultural Extension Service
University of Rhode Island
Kingston, RI 02881
(401) 792-2474

SC

Cooperative Extension Service
Clemson University
Clemson, SC 29631
(803) 656-3382

Vice President for Research and Extension
South Carolina State College
Box 1765
Orangeburg, SC 29117
(803) 534-6916

SD

Cooperative Extension Service
South Dakota State University
Brookings, SD 57006
(605) 688-4147

72 / Extension Service

TN

Agricultural Extension Service
University of Tennessee
Box 1071
Knoxville, TN 37901
(615) 974-7114

1890 Extension Program
Tennessee State University
Nashville, TN 37203
(615) 320-3650

TX

Cooperative Extension Service
Texas A&M University
College Station, TX 77843
(409) 845-7967

1890 Extension Program
Prairie View A&M University
Prairie View, TX 77445
(409) 857-2023

UT

Cooperative Extension Service
Utah State University
Logan, UT 84321
(801) 750-2200

VA

Cooperative Extension Service
Virginia Polytechnic Institute and State University
Blacksburg, VA 24061
(703) 961-6705

1890 Extension Program
Virginia State University
Petersburg, VA 23803
(804) 520-6421

VI

Cooperative Extension Service
College of the Virgin Islands
Box L
Kingshill
St. Croix, VI 00850
(809) 778-0246

VT

Cooperative Extension Service
University of Vermont
Morrill Hall
Burlington, VT 05401
(802) 656-2990

WA

Cooperative Extension Service
Washington State University
Ag. Sciences Bldg.
Pullman, WA 99164-6230
(509) 335-2933

WI

Cooperative Extension Service
University of Wisconsin
432 N. Lake St.
Room 527
Madison, WI 53706
(608) 262-3786

Cooperative Extension Service
University of Wisconsin
432 N. Lake St.
Room 601
Madison, WI 53706
(608) 263-2775

WV

Cooperative Extension Service
West Virginia University
817 Knapp Hall
Morgantown, WV 26507
(304) 293-2431

WY

Cooperative Extension Service
University of Wyoming
Ag. Bldg.
Room 155
Box 3354
Laramie, WY 82071
(307) 766-5124

Publications: Catalogs. Pamphlets. Handbooks. Directories.

Selected List of Books and Pamphlets

"Directory—Extension Service, USDA Administration Council, State Extension Service Directors and Administrators, 1890 and Tuskegee Extension Programs." Current. 14p. free.

Lists names, titles, addresses, and telephones of the various offices.

Directory of Professional Workers in State Agricultural Experiment Stations and Other Cooperating State Institutions. Current. 236p. free. Agriculture Handbook No. 306.

Gives information arranged by state and grouped by divisions such as: *Agronomy and Soils, Animal and Dairy Sciences Animal Health Research, Botany Plant Pathology and Microbiology, Forestry, Veterinary Medicine.* Index. Map.

Special Services: Inquire about a catalog of publications issued by each state.

FEDERAL AVIATION ADMINISTRATION
U.S. Department of Transportation
Public Information Center, APA-430
Office of Public Affairs, FAA
800 Independence Ave., SW
Washington, DC 20591
(202) 426-8058

Date Established: 1958

Objectives of the Agency: Regulate air commerce and promote development and safety.

Curriculum: Guidance, social studies

Subjects: Flight
Occupations

Locations:

AK

Federal Aviation Administration Regional Office
Alaskan Region, AAL-5
701 C St.
Box 14
Anchorage, AK 99513
(907) 271-5296

IA, KS, MO, NE

Federal Aviation Administration Regional Office
Central Region, ACE-5
601 E. Twelfth St.
Kansas City, MO 64106
(816) 374-5449

DC, DE, MD, NJ, NY, PA, VA, WV

Federal Aviation Administration Regional Office
Eastern Region, AEA-R
Fitzgerald Federal Bldg.
JFK International Airport
Jamaica, NY 11430
(212) 917-1023

Europe, Africa, Middle East

Federal Aviation Administration Regional Office
Europe, Africa, and Middle East Region, AEU-1
FAA, 15 Rue de la Loi
1040 Brussels, Belgium
513.38.30, ext. 2700

U.S. Mailing Address:
American Embassy—FAA
APO, NY 09667

IL, IN, MI, MN, ND, OH, SD, WI

Federal Aviation Administration Regional Office
Great Lakes Region, AGL-5
2300 E. Devon Ave.
Des Plaines, IL 60018
(312) 694-7427

CT, MA, ME, NH, RI, VT

Federal Aviation Administration Regional Office
New England Region, ANE-5
Box 510
12 New England Executive Park
Burlington, MA 01803
(617) 273-7391

CO, ID, MT, OR, UT, WA, WY

Federal Aviation Administration Regional Office
Northwest Mountain Region, ANM-5
17900 Pacific Hwy. South
C-68966
Seattle, WA 98168
(206) 431-2005

AL, FL, GA, KY, MS, NC, SC, TN, PR, VI

Federal Aviation Administration Regional Office
Southern Region, ASO-5
P.O. Box 20636
Atlanta, GA 30320
(404) 763-7201

AZ, CA, NV, HI, Pacific/Asia

Federal Aviation Administration Regional Office
Western-Pacific Region, AWP-5
Worldway Postal Center
P.O. Box 92007
Los Angeles, CA 90009
(213) 536-6431

AR, LA, NM, OK, TX

Federal Aviation Administration Regional Office
Southwest Region, ASW-IC
4400 Blue Mound Rd.
P.O. Box 1689
Fort Worth, TX 76101
(817) 877-2020

Publications: Booklets. Reports. Monographs. Magazines. Curriculum material. Career outlines. Air regulation material. Material reflects FAA's mission of aviation safety, safety standards, technical and regulatory advisory duties.

Bibliographies, Sales Catalogs, Publications Lists, etc.

"Guide to Federal Aviation Administration Publications." Annually in June. 64p. free. FAA-APA-PG-7.

Describes how materials are distributed. Categorizes. Tells where and how to get publications. Provides order blanks for those materials that come from: National Technical Information Service, Superintendent of Documents, Department of Transportation. When ordering the educational and career material, use the special blank provided.

"Teachers' Guide to Aviation Education." n.d. n.p. free. GA 300-135.

Provides a variety of enrichment activities for grades 2-6. To order, use form in "Guide to Federal Aviation Administration Publications."

Serials, Subcription Publications, etc.

FAA Directory. $14.00/yr.

Gives the address, telephone number, and chief's name for each FAA facility, the offices in Washington headquarters, the two centers, and the nine regions. Order from: Superintendent of Documents, U.S. Government Printing Office, Washington, DC 20402.

FAA General Aviation News. Bimonthly. 16-24p. $14.00 domestic, $17.50 foreign. 050-007-8000-1.

Covers flying concerns and safety problems of such craft as helicopters, gliders. Order from: Superintendent of Documents, U.S. Government Printing Office, Washington, DC 20402.

Selected List of Books and Pamphlets

"The Airport—Its Influence on the Community Economy." n.d. 79p. free. APA-430.

Explains how an airport contributes to the economy of a community.

"August Martin Activities Book." n.d. n.p. free. GA 300-143A.

Provides learning activities based on a biography of the world's first black airline pilot. Use order blank provided in "Guide to Federal Aviation Administration Publications."

"Aviation Careers: Airline Careers." n.d. 17p. free. GA 300-126.

Duties and requirements for a career with the airlines. Use order blank provided in "Guide to Federal Aviation Administration Publications."

"Aviation Careers: Airport Careers." n.d. 8p. free. GA 300-124.

Describes job opportunities. Use order blank provided in "Guide to Federal Aviation Administration Publications."

"Aviation Careers: Government Careers." n.d. 32p. free. GA 300-128.

Describes different aviation careers. Use order blank provided in "Guide to Federal Aviation Administration Publications."

"Aviation Science Activities for Elementary Grades." n.d. n.p. free. GA 20-30.

Contains science demonstrations pertaining to physical properties of air. Experiments use simple equipment.

Bonfires to Beacons: Federal Civil Aviation Policy Under the Air Commerce Act, 1926-1938. n.d. 454p. $16.00. 050-007-00419-2.

Examines the background to the passage of the first federal civil aviation regulatory statute in 1926. Describes the evolution of federal civil aviation policy. Ends with the enactment of the Civil Aeronautics Act. Order from: Superintendent of Documents, U.S. Government Printing Office, Washington, DC 20402.

"Federal Aviation Administration." n.d. 20p. free. APA-420.

Explains the responsibilities and programs of the FAA.

"How We Made the First Flight." n.d. 8p. free. GA 20-62.

Describes the flight of Orville and Wilbur Wright. Use order blank provided in "Guide to Federal Aviation Administration Publications." Available in Spanish (GA 20-625).

"A Model Aerospace Curriculum." n.d. n.p. free. GA 300-143B.

Describes the aerospace thematic program of August Martin High School. Use order blank provided in "Guide to Federal Aviation Administration Publications."

"A Trip to the Airport." n.d. n.p. free. GA 300-120.

Provides English-Spanish bilingual teaching material for elementary grades. Use order blank provided in "Guide to Federal Aviation Administration Publications."

"Women in Aviation and Space." n.d. n.p. free. GA 300-144.

Gives personality profiles of some successful women in these careers. Use order blank provided in "Guide to Federal Administration Publications."

Audiovisuals:

Filmographies, Sales Lists, etc.

"FAA Film Catalog." n.d. 14p. free.

Describes 37 16mm color motion pictures available for audience viewing and how to obtain them. Gives tips on making the showing most effective. Films may be purchased or are available for free loan. Films are cleared for use on television.

Individual Films

"Airports Mean Business." n.d. 28 minutes. 16mm. color. free loan. #11111.

Illustrates the economic benefits that an airport brings to a community, primarily to medium-sized ones. Shows how airports attract new industry, provide new jobs, generate additional revenue, strengthen the tax base, etc.

"How Airplanes Fly." n.d. 18 minutes. 16mm. color. free loan. #11131.

Shows what makes an airplane get off the ground and stay flying. Explains basic aerodynamics in animated and live sequences. Shows forces of lift, weight, thrust and drag in relation to flight.

"In Celebration of Flight." n.d. 28½ minutes. 16mm. color. free loan. #11134.

Pays tribute to individuals and institutions that have made American aviation what it is today. Shows how men and women contributed their special knowledge and skills to aviation.

"Looking Up to Your Aviation Career." n.d. 14 minutes. 16mm. color. free loan. #10314.

Shows how careers in aviation present wide-ranging opportunity: for every pilot there are 1,500 other aviation professionals supporting air operations on the ground and in over 60 different career specialties.

"Put Wings on Your Career." n.d. 15 minutes. 16mm. color. free loan. #11144.

Shows how the diversity of jobs in aircraft maintenance, both in government and private industry, can be rewarding. Outlines the basic technical requirements. Directs interested people to specific career information.

"These Special People." n.d. 14 minutes. 16mm. color. free loan. #10315.

Gives a behind-the-scenes look at how electronics technicians install, operate, and maintain the complex airway facilities network supporting the national aviation system.

Library: For information about reading rooms, call (202) 426-4723.

Most of the FAA publications are available for examination in:
The Department of Transportation Library
10A Services Section
80 Independence Ave., SW
Room 930
Washington, DC 20591

The Federal Depository Library program provides government publications to designated libraries. The regional depository libraries receive and retain at least one copy of nearly every federal government publication, either in printed or microfilm form for use by the general public. These libraries provide reference services and interlibrary loans. A list of these DOT/federal depository libraries can be found in "Guide to Federal Aviation Administration Publications," which is the first of the publications described.

FEDERAL BUREAU OF INVESTIGATION
Ninth St. and Pennsylvania Ave., NW
Washington, DC 20535
(202) 324-3444

Date Established: 1908

Objectives of the Agency: Gather and report facts; locate witnesses; compile evidence in matters in which the federal government is or may be a part, including such areas as: espionage, sabotage, kidnapping, extortion, bank robbery, interstate transportation of stolen property, civil rights matters, interstate gambling violations, narcotics violations, fraud against the government, assaulting or killing the president or a federal officer; provide services including fingerprint identification, laboratory services, police training, and the National Crime Information Center.

Curriculum: Government

Subjects: Crime—U.S.
Occupations

Locations:

AK

Federal Bureau of Investigation
Field Division
Federal Office Bldg.
701 C St.
Room E-222
Anchorage, AK 99513
(907) 276-4441

AL

Federal Bureau of Investigation
Field Division
2121 Bldg.
Room 1400
Birmingham, AL 35203
(205) 252-7705

Federal Bureau of Investigation
Field Division
U.S. Courthouse
113 Saint Joseph St.
Mobile, AL 36602
(205) 438-3674

AR

Federal Bureau of Investigation
Field Division
215 U.S. Post Office Bldg.
Little Rock, AR 72201
(501) 372-7211

AZ

Federal Bureau of Investigation
Field Division
2721 N. Central Ave.
Phoenix, AZ 85004
(602) 279-5511

CA

Federal Bureau of Investigation
Field Division
Federal Office Bldg.
11000 Wilshire Blvd.
Los Angeles, CA 90024
(213) 477-6565

Federal Bureau of Investigation
Field Division
Federal Office Bldg.
2800 Cottage Way
Sacramento, CA 95825
(916) 481-9110

Federal Bureau of Investigation
Field Division
Federal Office Bldg.
880 Front St.
Room 6S31
San Diego, CA 92188
(619) 231-1122

Federal Bureau of Investigation
Field Division
450 Golden Gate Ave.
San Francisco, CA 94102
(415) 552-2155

CO

Federal Bureau of Investigation
Field Division
Federal Office Bldg.
Room 1823
Denver, CO 80202
(303) 629-7171

CT

Federal Bureau of Investigation
Field Division
Federal Office Bldg.
150 Court St.
New Haven, CT 06510
(203) 777-6311

DC

Federal Bureau of Investigation
Field Division
1900 Hall St., SW
Washington, DC 20535
(202) 324-3000

Federal Bureau of Investigation
Field Division
Tenth St. and Pennsylvania Ave., NW
Room 1028
Washington, DC 20535
(202) 324-3000

FL

Federal Bureau of Investigation
Field Division
7820 Arlington Expy.
Fourth Floor Oaks V
Jacksonville, FL 32211
(904) 721-1211

Federal Bureau of Investigation
Field Division
3801 Biscayne Blvd.
Miami, FL 33137
(305) 573-3333

Federal Bureau of Investigation
Field Division
Federal Office Bldg.
500 Zack St.
Room 610
Tampa, FL 33602
(813) 228-7661

GA

Federal Bureau of Investigation
Field Division
Federal Office Bldg.
275 Peachtree St., NW
Tenth Floor
Atlanta, GA 30302
(404) 521-3900

Federal Bureau of Investigation
Field Division
5401 Paulsen St.
Savannah, GA 31405
(912) 354-9911

HI

Federal Bureau of Investigation
Field Division
Kalanianaole Federal Office Bldg.
300 Ala Moana Blvd.
Room 4307
Honolulu, HI 96850
(808) 521-1411

IL

Federal Bureau of Investigation
Field Division
Everett McKinley Dirksen Federal Office Bldg.
219 S. Dearborn St.
Chicago, IL 60604
(312) 431-1333

Federal Bureau of Investigation
Field Division
535 W. Jefferson St.
Springfield, IL 62702
(217) 522-9675

IN

Federal Bureau of Investigation
Field Division
Federal Office Bldg.
575 North Pennsylvania St.
Room 679
Indianapolis, IN 46204
(317) 639-3301

KY

Federal Bureau of Investigation
Field Division
Federal Office Bldg.
600 Federal Plaza
Room 502
Louisville, KY 40202
(502) 583-3941

LA

Federal Bureau of Investigation
Field Division
701 Loyola Ave.
New Orleans, LA 70113
(504) 522-4670

MA

Federal Bureau of Investigation
Field Division
John F. Kennedy Federal Office Bldg.
Boston, MA 02203
(617) 742-5533

MD

Federal Bureau of Investigation
Field Division
7142 Ambassador Rd.
Baltimore, MD 21207
(301) 265-8080

MI

Federal Bureau of Investigation
Field Division
Patrick V. McNamara Federal Office Bldg.
477 Michigan Ave.
Detroit, MI 48226
(313) 965-2323

MN

Federal Bureau of Investigation
Field Division
392 Federal Office Bldg.
Minneapolis, MN 55401
(612) 339-7861

MO

Federal Bureau of Investigation
Field Division
U.S. Courthouse
Room 300
Kansas City, MO 64106
(816) 221-6100

Federal Bureau of Investigation
Field Division
Federal Office Bldg.
1520 Market St.
Room 2704
St. Louis, MO 63103
(314) 241-5357

MS

Federal Bureau of Investigation
Field Division
Federal Office Bldg.
100 W. Capitol St.
Suite 1553
Jackson, MS 39269
(601) 948-5000

MT

Federal Bureau of Investigation
Field Division
U.S. Courthouse and Federal Office Bldg.
Butte, MT 59702
(406) 792-2304

NC

Federal Bureau of Investigation
Field Division
307 S. Tryon St.
Room 1120
Charlotte, NC 28202

NE

Federal Bureau of Investigation
Field Division
Federal Office Bldg. and U.S. Post Office and
    Courthouse
215 N. Seventeenth St.
Room 7401
Omaha, NE 68102
(402) 348-1210

NJ

Federal Bureau of Investigation
Field Division
Gateway 1
Market St.
Newark, NJ 07102
(201) 622-5613

NM

Federal Bureau of Investigation
Field Division
301 Grand Ave., NE
Albuquerque, NM 87102
(505) 247-1555

NV

Federal Bureau of Investigation
Field Division
Federal Office Bldg.
Las Vegas Blvd.
Room 219
Las Vegas, NV 89101
(702) 385-1281

NY

Federal Bureau of Investigation
Field Division
U.S. Post Office and Court House
Room 502
Albany, NY 12207
(518) 465-7551

Federal Bureau of Investigation
Field Division
Federal Office Bldg.
111 W. Huron St.
Room 1400
Buffalo, NY 14202
(716) 856-7800

Federal Bureau of Investigation
Field Division
26 Federal Plaza
New York, NY 10278
(212) 553-2700

OH

Federal Bureau of Investigation
Field Division
Federal Office Bldg.
550 Main St.
Room 9023
Cincinnati, OH 45202
(513) 421-4310

Federal Bureau of Investigation
Field Division
Federal Office Bldg.
1240 E. Ninth St.
Room 3005
Cleveland, OH 44199
(216) 522-1400

OK

Federal Bureau of Investigation
Field Division
50 Penn Place
Suite 1600
Oklahoma City, OK 73118
(405) 842-7471

OR

Federal Bureau of Investigation
Field Division
Crown Plaza Bldg.
1500 S.W. First Ave.
Portland, OR 97201
(503) 224-4181

PA

Federal Bureau of Investigation
Field Division
William J. Green, Jr. Federal Office Bldg.
600 Arch St.
Philadelphia, PA 19106
(215) 629-0800

Federal Bureau of Investigation
Field Division
Federal Office Bldg.
1000 Liberty Ave.
Room 1300
Pittsburgh, PA 15222
(412) 471-2000

PR

Federal Bureau of Investigation
Field Division
U.S. Courthouse and Federal Office Bldg.
Room 526
San Juan, PR 00918
(809) 754-6000

SC

Federal Bureau of Investigation
Field Division
1529 Hampton St.
Columbia, SC 29201
(803) 254-3011

TN

Federal Bureau of Investigation
Field Division
1111 Northshore Dr.
Room 800
Knoxville, TN 37919
(615) 588-8571

Federal Bureau of Investigation
Field Division
Clifford Davis Federal Office Bldg.
Room 841
Memphis, TN 38103
(901) 525-7373

TX

Federal Bureau of Investigation
Field Division
1801 N. Lamar
Suite 300
Dallas, TX 75202
(214) 741-1851

Federal Bureau of Investigation
Field Division
202 U.S. Courthouse
El Paso, TX 79901
(915) 533-7451

Federal Bureau of Investigation
Field Division
Federal Office Bldg. and U.S. Courthouse
515 Rusk Ave.
Room 6015
Houston, TX 77002
(713) 224-1511

Federal Bureau of Investigation
Field Division
Old Post Office Bldg.
615 E. Houston
Room 433
San Antonio, TX 78205
(512) 225-6741

UT

Federal Bureau of Investigation
Field Division
Federal Office Bldg.
125 S. State St.
Room 3203
Salt Lake City, UT 84138
(801) 355-8584

VA

Federal Bureau of Investigation
Field Division
300 N. Lee St.
Room 500
Alexandria, VA 22314
(703) 683-2680

Federal Bureau of Investigation
Field Division
200 Granby Mall
Room 839
Norfolk, VA 23510
(804) 623-3111

Federal Bureau of Investigation
Field Division
200 W. Grace St.
Richmond, VA 23220
(804) 644-2631

WA

Federal Bureau of Investigation
Field Division
Federal Office Bldg.
915 Second Ave.
Room 710
Seattle, WA 98174
(206) 622-0460

WI

Federal Bureau of Investigation
Field Division
Federal Office Bldg. and U.S. Court House
517 E. Wisconsin Ave.
Milwaukee, WI 53202
(414) 276-4684

DE, IA, ID, KS, ME, ND, NH, SD, VT, WV, WY

See the Washington, D.C., office listed at the beginning of the chapter.

Publications: Pamphlets. Kits. On functions, careers, history.

Selected List of Books and Pamphlets

"Career Opportunities." n.d. 32p. kit. free.
Provides fact sheets and information on application and types of jobs. Includes questions and answers.

"FBI Laboratory." 1982. 39p. free.
Gives history, services, and operating techniques of the laboratory. Photographs.

"The FBI: The First 75 Years." 1983. 29p. free.
Chronicles development from 1908 to 1983.

"99 Facts about the FBI: Questions and Answers." 1984. 8th ed. 30p. free.
Gives answers to such questions as: When was the FBI founded? Who is the head of the FBI?

FEDERAL BUREAU OF PRISONS
U.S. Department of Justice
320 First St., NW
Washington, DC 20534
(202) 724-3198

Date Established: 1930

Objectives of the Agency: Operate a nationwide system of maximum, medium, and minimum security prisons and community program offices.

Curriculum: Government

80 / Federal Bureau of Prisons

Subjects: Prisons—U.S.

Locations:

South Central Region

Bureau of Prisons
Regional Office
1607 Main
Suite 700
Dallas, TX 75201
(214) 767-0012

Southeast Region

Bureau of Prisons
Regional Office
5213 McDonough Blvd., SE
Atlanta, GA 30315
(404) 624-5202

North Central Region

Bureau of Prisons
Regional Office
Airworld Center
10920 Ambassador Dr.
Kansas City, MO 64154
(816) 891-7007

Northeast Region

Bureau of Prisons
Regional Office
U.S. Customs House
Second and Chestnut St.
Seventh Floor
Philadelphia, PA 19106
(215) 597-6317

Western Region

Bureau of Prisons
Regional Office
330 Primrose Rd.
Fifth Floor
Burlingame, CA 94010
(415) 347-0721

Publications: Reports about prisons and management of facilities.

Selected List of Books and Pamphlets

Facilities. Current. 112p. free.
 Gives survey of institutions including name, location, telephone, history, type of security level, map, photograph and description of activities. Includes organization chart of the bureau and a map of bureau facilities.

"Federal Bureau of Prisons." Current. 16p. free.
 Tells about history, organization and administration, and inmate care. Includes graphs showing percentage of population confined to institutions by offense, directory of regions and centers, and a map of the federal correctional system.

FEDERAL COMMUNICATIONS COMMISSION
1919 M St., NW
Washington, DC 20554
(202) 632-7260

Date Established: 1934

Objectives of the Agency: Regulate interstate and foreign communications by radio, television, wire and cable; foster efficient nationwide and worldwide telephone and telegraph services, and the safety of life and property through radio; and strengthen national defense through radio and television.

Curriculum: Government

Subjects: Communication

Locations:

Federal Communications Commission
 Regional Office
1365 Peachtree St., NE
Room 433
Atlanta, GA 30309

Federal Communications Commission
 Regional Office
1500 Customhouse
165 State St.
Boston, MA 02109

Federal Communications Commission
 Regional Office
1550 Northwest Hwy.
Room 306
Park Ridge, IL 60068

Federal Communications Commission
 Regional Office
8800 E. Sixty-Third St.
Room 320
Kansas City, MO 64133

Federal Communications Commission
 Regional Office
211 Main St.
Room 537
San Francisco, CA 94106

Federal Communications Commission
 Regional Office
915 Second Ave.
Room 3244
Seattle, WA 98174

Publications: Fact sheets. Pamphlets. On regulations, progress, and functions of the commission.

Selected List of Books and Pamphlets

"EEO Fact Sheet." Current. 3p. free.
 Relates highlights of equal opportunity history at the commission.

"The FCC in Brief." 1985. 6p. free.
    Gives overview of functions, staff, and publications.

"Information Seeker's Guide." 1985. 16p. free.
    Shows how to find information at the Federal Communications Commission. Organization charts.

"Memo to All Young People Interested in Radio." 1978. 3p. free.
    Provides information of interest to youth about the Amateur Radio Service and publication on career guidance.

FEDERAL CROP INSURANCE CORPORATION
Department of Agriculture
Fourteenth St. and Independence Ave., SW
Washington, DC 20250
(202) 447-3287

Date Established: 1938

Objectives of the Agency: Improve the economic stability of agriculture through a sound system of crop insurance.

Curriculum: Agriculture

Subjects: Insurance, crop

Locations:

AL, AR, LA, MS
Field Crop Insurance Corporation
Field Crop Operations Office
100 W. Capital
Suite 1201
Jackson, MS 39201
(601) 960-4328

AZ, CA, NV
Federal Crop Insurance Corporation
Field Operations Office
133 D St.
Suite A
Davis, CA 95616
(916) 753-7880

CO, KS
Field Crop Insurance Corporation
Field Crop Operations Office
2601 Anderson Ave.
Manhattan, KS 66502
(913) 537-4980

CT, DE, MA, ME, MD, NH, NJ, NY, PA, RI, VT
Field Crop Insurance Corporation
Field Operations Office
3555 N. Progress Ave.
Harrisburg, PA 17110
(717) 782-4803

FL, GA, SC
Federal Crop Insurance Corporation
Field Operations Office
1835 Assembly St.
Room 1065
Columbia, SC 29201
(803) 765-5766

IA
Federal Crop Insurance Corporation
Field Operations Office
210 Walnut St.
Room 509
Des Moines, IA 50309
(515) 284-4316

ID, OR, UT, WA
Field Crop Insurance Corporation
Field Operations Office
West 920 Riverside Ave.
Room 294
Spokane, WA 99201
(509) 456-3763

IL
Field Crop Insurance Corporation
Field Operations Office
320 W. Washington St.
Room 607
Springfield, IL 62701
(217) 492-4280

IN, MI, OH
Field Crop Insurance Corporation
Field Crop Operations Office
5610 Crawfordsville Rd.
Suite 1501
Indianapolis, IN 46224
(317) 248-4141

KY, TN
Field Crop Insurance Corporation
Field Operations Office
U.S. Courthouse
Room 508
Nashville, TN 37203
(615) 251-5591

MN, WI
Field Crop Insurance Corporation
Field Operations Office
316 Robert St.
Room 222
St. Paul, MN 55101
(612) 725-5871

MO

Federal Crop Insurance Corporation
Field Operations Office
700 E. Cherry
Room 201
Columbia, MO 65201
(314) 875-5287

MT, WY

Federal Crop Insurance Corporation
Field Operations Office
2401 Grand Ave.
Fourth Floor
Billings, MT 59102
(406) 657-6196

NC, VA, WV

Field Crop Insurance Corporation
Field Operations Office
310 New Bern Ave.
Room 608
Raleigh, NC 27601
(919) 755-4470

ND

Federal Crop Insurance Corporation
Field Operations Office
230 E. Rosser Ave.
Room 234
Bismarck, ND 58501
(701) 255-4011

NE

Field Crop Insurance Corporation
Field Crop Operations Office
100 Centennial Mall
Room 443
Lincoln, NE 68508
(402) 471-5531

NM, OK, TX

Federal Crop Insurance Corporation
Field Operations Office
USDA Bldg.
College Station, TX 77840
(713) 846-8821

SD

Field Crop Insurance Corporation
Field Operations Office
200 Fourth St., SW
Room 210
Huron, SD 57350
(605) 352-8651, ext. 385

Selected List of Books and Pamphlets

"Actual Production History (APH) Program." n.d. 1p. free.
   Covers some features of the new program such as records, guarantees, units, premium adjustment table, and offers.

"Fact Sheet: Crop Insurance." Current. 2p. free.
   Tells what the current, improved Crop Insurance Program has to offer. Lists insurable crops.

"Federal Crop Insurance Questions & Answers." Rev. 1983. 16p. free.
   Gives answers to such questions as: Who can purchase federal crop insurance? Historically, what have been the major causes of insured crop loss?

"Federal Crop Insurance Corporation." 1983. 2p. free.
   Gives programs, responsibilities, organization, information contacts, statistics and other current information about the Federal Crop Insurance Corporation.

"Individual Yield Coverage: For Crop Insurance Protection As Good As You Are." 1983. 4-fold. free.
   Gives answers to such questions as: What is the purpose of the IYC program? How is the yield history determined for the IYC program?

FEDERAL DEPOSIT INSURANCE CORPORATION

Information Office
550 Seventeenth St., NW
Washington, DC 20429
(202) 389-4221

Date Established: 1933

Objectives of the Agency: Promote and preserve public confidence in banks; and protect the money supply through provision of insurance coverage for bank deposits and examinations.

Curriculum: Consumer education, economics

Subjects: Banks and banking

Locations:

AK, AZ, CA, GU, HI, ID, NV, OR, UT, WA

Federal Deposit Insurance Corporation
Regional Office
25 Ecker St.
Suite 2300
San Francisco, CA 94105
(415) 546-0160

AL, FL, GA, NC, SC

Federal Deposit Insurance Corporation
Regional Office
233 Peachtree St., NE
Atlanta, GA 30303
(404) 221-6631

AR, LA, MS, TN
Federal Deposit Insurance Corporation
Regional Office
1 Commerce Square
Memphis, TN 38103
(901) 521-3872

CO, NM, OK, TX
Federal Deposit Insurance Corporation
Regional Office
350 N. Saint Paul St.
Dallas, TX 75201
(214) 767-5501

CT, MA, ME, NH, RI, VT
Federal Deposit Insurance Corporation
Regional Office
60 State St.
Boston, MA 02109
(617) 223-6420

DE, MD, PA, VA
Federal Deposit Insurance Corporation
Regional Office
1900 Market St.
Philadelphia, PA 19103
(215) 597-2295

IA, NE
Federal Deposit Insurance Corporation
Regional Office
1700 Farnam St.
Omaha, NE 68102
(402) 221-3366

IL, IN, WI
Federal Deposit Insurance Corporation
Regional Office
233 S. Wacker Dr.
Chicago, IL 60606
(312) 353-2600

KS, MO
Federal Deposit Insurance Corporation
Regional Office
2345 Grand Ave.
Kansas City, MO 64108
(816) 374-2851

KY, MI, OH, WV
Federal Deposit Insurance Corporation
Regional Office
1 Nationwide Plaza
Columbus, OH 43215
(614) 469-7301

MN, MT, ND, SD, WY
Federal Deposit Insurance Corporation
Regional Office
730 Second Ave. South
Minneapolis, MN 55402
(612) 340-0746

NJ, NY, PR, VI
Federal Deposit Insurance Corporation
Regional Office
452 Fifth Ave.
New York, NY 10018
(212) 704-1200

Publications: Pamphlets on business topics in consumer education.

Selected List of Books and Pamphlets

"The Community Reinvestment Act." n.d. 16p. free.
Tells what the act is, requirements, community input. Includes Spanish version.

"Consumer Information." 1981. 8p. free.
Describes 10 consumer and civil rights laws and regulations protecting bank customers. Form to send for a complaint, a question, or a suggestion about banks. Spanish version available.

"Equal Credit Opportunity and Women." n.d. 6p. free.
Explains how a credit history is established, how an individual is rated as a credit risk, and what questions you may not be asked.

"Fair Credit Billing." n.d. 6p. free.
Describes how to resolve a billing dispute and protect a credit rating.

"Truth in Lending." n.d. 6p. free.
Explains the cost of credit, credit cards, advertising, cancellations and other provisions.

FEDERAL ELECTION COMMISSION
1325 K St., NW
Washington, DC 20463
In Washington: 523-4068
Toll free: (800) 424-9530

Date Established: 1975

Objectives of the Agency: Administer, formulate, seek compliance with the campaign financing provisions of the Federal Election Campaign Act of 1971, as amended, and Title 26 of the U.S. Code.

84 / *Federal Election Commission*

Curriculum: Government

Subjects: Elections—U.S.

Publications: Guides. Pamphlets. Manuals. Reports. Regulations and Laws. Newsletters.

Bibliographies, Sales Catalogs, Publications Lists, etc.

"Free Publications." Current. 6p. free.
 Annotates available materials. Order blank.

Serials, Subscription Publications, etc.

The FEC Record. Monthly. Binder insert. free.
 Summarizes advisory opinions.

Selected List of Books and Pamphlets

"The FEC and the Federal Campaign Finance Law." n.d. 14p. free.
 Tells the history of campaign finance laws, highlights of the current law, and how to get additional information.

Library: Open to the public on weekdays. Includes basic legal research resources with an emphasis on political campaign financing, corporate and labor political activity, and election campaign reform.

Special Services: If interested in being placed on the mailing list, contact the public communications office.

FEDERAL EMERGENCY MANAGEMENT AGENCY
Office of Public Affairs
500 C St., SW
Washington, DC 20472
(202) 646-3631

Date Established: 1978

Objectives of the Agency: Develop, coordinate, and execute plans and programs to give continuity to and maintain effective operation of the federal government during a national emergency; and handle emergency management information processing.

Curriculum: Geography, safety

Subjects: Disaster relief

Locations:

CT, ME, VT, MA, NH, RI

Federal Emergency Management Agency
Region 1 Office
J. W. McCormack Post Office and Court House
Room 442
Boston, MA 02109
(617) 223-4741

NJ, NY, PR, VI

Federal Emergency Management Agency
Region 2 Office
26 Federal Plaza
Room 1349
New York, NY 10278
(212) 264-8980

DC, DE, MD, PA, VA, WV

Federal Emergency Management Agency
Region 3 Office
105 S. Seventh St.
Second Floor
Philadelphia, PA 19106
(215) 597-9419

AL, FL, GA, KY, MS, NC, SC, TN

Federal Emergency Management Agency
Region 4 Office
1371 Peachtree St., NE
Atlanta, GA 30309
(404) 881-2400

IL, IN, MI, MN, OH, WI

Federal Emergency Management Agency
Region 5 Office
300 S. Wacker Dr.
Chicago, IL 60606
(312) 886-3671

AR, LA, TX, NM, OK

Federal Emergency Management Agency
Region 6 Office
Federal Regional Center
800 N. Loop 288
Room 206
Denton, TX 76201
(817) 387-5811

IA, KS, NE, MO

Federal Emergency Management Agency
Region 7 Office
911 Walnut St.
Room 300
Kansas City, MO 64106
(816) 374-5912

CO, MT, ND, SD, UT, WY

Federal Emergency Management Agency
Region 8 Office
Denver Federal Center
Building 710
Box 25267
Denver, CO 80225-0267
(303) 235-4811

AZ, CA, HI, NV, Pacific Commonwealths and Territories

Federal Emergency Management Agency
Region 9 Office
Presidio of San Francisco
Building 105
San Francisco, CA 94129
(415) 556-8794

AK, ID, OR, WA

Federal Emergency Management Agency
Region 10 Office
Federal Regional Center
130 Two-Hundred-Twenty-Eighth St., SW
Bothell, WA 98021-9796

State Emergency Directors

AK

Director
Division of Emergency Services
Department of Military Veterans Affairs
P.O. Box 2267
Palmer, AK 99645
(907) 376-3061

AL

State Emergency Director
Alabama Emergency Management Agency
220 N. Hull St.
Montgomery, AL 36130
(205) 261-3519

AR

Director
Office of Emergency Services
P.O. Box 758
Conway, AR 72032
(501) 329-5601
Little Rock: (501) 374-1201

AS

Director
Office of Territorial Emergency Management
  Coordination
Office of the Governor
P.O. Box 3296
Pago Pago, AS 96799
(011) 684-633-2331

AZ

Director
Arizona Division of Emergency Services
National Guard Bldg.
5636 E. McDowell Rd.
Phoenix, AZ 85008
(602) 244-0504

CA

Director
Office of Emergency Services
State of California
P.O. Box 9577
Sacramento, CA 95823
(916) 427-4201

CO

Director
Disaster Emergency Services
DOC, Camp George West
Golden, CO 80401
(303) 273-1624

CT

State Director
Office of Civil Preparedness
Department of Public Safety
360 Broad St.
Hartford, CT 06105
(203) 566-3180/4338

DC

Director
Office of Emergency Preparedness
Municipal Center
300 Indiana Ave., NW
Room 5009
Washington, DC 20001
(202) 727-6161

DE

Director
Division of Emergency Planning and Operations
P.O. Box C
Delaware City, DE 19706
(302) 834-4531

FL

Director
Division of Emergency Management
1720 S. Gadsden St.
Tallahassee, FL 32301
(904) 488-1900

GA

Deputy Director
Georgia Emergency Management Agency
P.O. Box 18055
Atlanta, GA 30316
(404) 656-5500

GU

Director
Civil Defense
Guam Emergency Services
Territory of Guam
P.O. Box 2877
Agana, GU 96910
(011) 671-477-9841

HI

Vice-Director of Civil Defense
Department of Defense
3949 Diamond Head Rd.
Honolulu, HI 86816
(808) 734-2161

IA

Director
Office of Disaster Services
Hoover State Office Bldg.
Level A, Room 29
Des Moines, IA 50319
(515) 281-3231

ID

Coordinator
Bureau of Disaster Services
Military Division
650 W. State St.
Boise, ID 83720
(208) 334-3460

IL

Director
Illinois Emergency Services and Disaster Agency
110 E. Adams St.
Springfield, IL 62706
(217) 782-2700

IN

Director
Indiana Department of Civil Defense and Emergency Management
State Office Bldg., B-90
100 N. Senate Ave.
Indianapolis, IN 46204
(317) 232-3830

KS

Deputy Director
Division of Emergency Preparedness
P.O. Box C-300
Topeka, KS 66601
(913) 233-9253, ext. 301

KY

Executive Director
Kentucky Disaster and Emergency Services
Boone Center
Parkside Dr.
Frankfort, KY 40601
(502) 564-8680

LA

Assistant Secretary
Office of Emergency Preparedness
Department of Public Safety
Audubon Station
P.O. Box 66536
Baton Rouge, LA 70896
(505) 342-5470

MA

Director
Massachusetts Civil Defense Agency and Office of Emergency Preparedness
400 Worcester Rd.
P.O. Box 1496
Framingham, MA 01701
(617) 237-0200
(617) 875-1381

MD

Director
Maryland Emergency Management and Civil Defense Agency
Reisterstown Road and Sudbrook Lane
Pikesville, MD 21208
(301) 486-4422

ME

Director
Bureau of Civil Emergency Preparedness
Department of Defense and Veterans Services
State Office Bldg.
Station 72
Augusta, ME 04333
(207) 622-6201
(207) 289-3211

MI

Deputy Director
State Division of Emergency Services
Department of State Police
11 S. Capitol Ave.
Lower Level
Lansing, MI 48913
(517) 373-0617
(517) 337-6100

MN

Director
Division of Emergency Services
Department of Public Safety
State Capitol, B-5
St. Paul, MN 55155
(612) 296-2233

MO

Acting Director
State Emergency Management Agency
P.O. Box 116
Jefferson City, MO 65102
(314) 751-2321, ext. 379

MS

Director
Emergency Management Agency
Fondren Station
P.O. Box 4501
Jackson, MS 39216
(601) 353-9100

MT

Administrator
Disaster and Emergency Services Division
Department of Military Affairs
P.O. Box 4789
Helena, MT 59604
(406) 444-6911

NC

Director
North Carolina Division of Emergency Management
Administration Bldg.
116 W. Jones St.
Raleigh, NC 27611
(919) 733-3867

ND

Director
Disaster Emergency Services
P.O. Box 1817
Bismarck, ND 58505
(701) 224-2111

NE

Assistant Director
Nebraska Civil Defense Agency
Military Dept.
1300 Military Rd.
Lincoln, NE 68508
(402) 473-1410

NH

Director
New Hampshire Civil Defense Agency
State Office Park South
107 Pleasant St.
Concord, NH 03301
(603) 271-2231

NJ

Deputy Director
Office of Emergency Management
New Jersey State Police
P.O. Box 7068
West Trenton, NJ 08625
(609) 882-2000

NM

Deputy Director
Civil Emergency Preparedness Division
P.O. Box 4277
Santa Fe, NM 87501
(505) 473-2476

Northern Mariana Islands

Director of Civil Defense
Office of the Governor
Commonwealth of the Northern Mariana Islands
Saipan, Mariana Islands 96950
(011) 670-9274

NV

Director
Nevada Division of Emergency Services
Military Dept.
Capitol Complex
2525 S. Carson St.
Carson City, NV 89710
(702) 885-4240

NY

Director
State Emergency Management Office
Division of Military and Naval Affairs
Public Security Bldg.
State Campus
Albany, NY 12226
(518) 454-2159

OH

Deputy Director
Ohio Disaster Services Agency
2825 W. Granville Rd.
Worthington, OH 43085
(614) 889-7150

OK

Director
Oklahoma Civil Defense Agency
P.O. Box 53365
Oklahoma City, OK 73152
(405) 521-2481

OR

Administrator
Emergency Management Division
Oregon State Executive Department
43 State Capitol Bldg.
Salem, OR 97310
(503) 378-4124
(800) 452-0311

PA

Director
Pennsylvania Emergency Management Agency
Transportation and Safety Bldg., B-151
Harrisburg, PA 17120
(717) 783-8150

PR

Director
State Civil Defense Agency
P.O. Box 5127
San Juan, PR 00906
(809) 724-0124

RI

Executive Director
Rhode Island Emergency Management Agency
State House
Providence, RI 02903
(401) 421-7333

SC

Director
South Carolina Emergency Preparedness Division
Office of the Adjutant General
1429 Senate St.
Columbia, SC 29201
(803) 758-2826

SD

Director
Division of Emergency and Disaster Services
Department of Military Affairs
EOC—State Capitol
Pierre, SD 57501
(605) 773-3231

TN

Director
Tennessee Emergency Management Agency
3041 Sidco Dr.
Nashville, TN 37204
(615) 252-3300

Trust Territory of the Pacific

Chief
Office of Planning and Statistics
Office of the High Commissioner
Trust Territory Headquarters
Saipan, Mariana Islands 96950
(011) 670-9333

TX

Chief
Division of Disaster Emergency Services
Texas Department of Public Safety
N. Austin Station
Box 4087
Austin, TX 78773
(512) 465-2000, ext. 3700

UT

Director
Division of Comprehensive Emergency Management
Department of Public Safety
1543 Sunnyside Ave.
Salt Lake City, UT 84108
(801) 533-5271

VA

Acting State Coordinator
Office of Emergency and Energy Services
310 Turner Rd.
Richmond, VA 23225
(804) 323-2899

VI

Director
Civil Defense and Emergency Services
P.O. Box 1208
Charlotte Amalie
St. Thomas, VI 00801
(809) 774-2244

VT

Deputy Director
Office of Civil Defense
Department of Public Safety
Waterbury State Complex
102 S. Main St.
Waterbury, VT 05676
(802) 244-8721

WA

Director
Department of Emergency Management
4220 E. Martin Way
Olympia, WA 98504
(206) 459-9191

WI
Deputy Administrator
Division of Emergency Government
Dept. of Administration
P.O. Box 7865
Madison, WI 53707
(608) 266-3232

WV
Director
West Virginia Office of Emergency Services
State Capitol Complex, EB 80
Charleston, WV 25305
(304) 348-5380

WY
Coordinator
Wyoming Disaster and Civil Defense
P.O. Box 1709
Cheyenne, WY 82001
(307) 777-7566

Publications: General and technical guides. Leaflets. Manuals. Memorandums. Handbooks. Reports. Circulars. On natural disasters (hurricanes, floods, etc.) and nuclear attack emergencies.

Bibliographies, Sales Catalogs, Publications Lists, etc.

"FEMA Publications Catalog." 1984. 62p. free. FEMA-20.

Lists annotated publications on topics such as: earthquakes, floods, hurricanes, tornadoes, fire, nuclear accidents, acts of terrorism, dam safety, and hazardous materials.

Selected List of Books and Pamphlets

"Disaster Driving." 1981. 8p. free.

Gives safety tips for motorists in emergencies such as earthquakes, hurricanes, and blizzards.

"Earthquake Safety Checklist." 1983. 8p. free.

Explains supplies, home preparedness, drills, and other aids to help prepare against earthquakes.

The Effects of Nuclear Weapons. 3d ed. 653p. free.

Gives elementary information in the first part of most chapters, and more technical and mathematical information in the second. Glossary. Index. Photographs.

"Emergency Preparedness Coloring Book." 1984. 14p. free.

Features various tips on safety for young children, such as staying in the car.

"Environmental Realities." 1972. game. free.

Includes game directions with different age levels and variations for playing. Aims at developing an awareness of the city. For children and adults.

"Owlie Skywarn's Weather Book." 1984. 28p. free.

Explains what to do if in a hurricane, tornado, or other disaster. Designed and illustrated for children.

"What You Should Know about Nuclear Preparedness." 1983. 14p. free.

Answers commonly asked questions about nuclear attack.

Audiovisuals:

"FEMA Motion Picture Catalog." 1980. 33p. free. FEMA-2 (6/80).

Lists public information films cleared for television use and public nonprofit exhibition. Films may be free loan or purchased. A few are available for purchase on ¾" videocassette. For free loan requests write to the support center serving each area.

Major Army Training and Audiovisual Support Centers

AK
Training Aids Services Office
ATTN: AFZT-PTS-TA
Building 978
Fort Richardson, AK 99505

AL
Director (North)
Army Training & Audiovisual Support Center
Fort McClellan, AL 36205

Commander (Central)
ATZB-DPT-TASO-AVSC
Fort Benning, GA 31905

Director (South)
Army Training & Audiovisual Support Center
Building 9313
U.S.A. Aviation Center & Fort Rucker
Fort Rucker, AL 36362

AR
Director
Army Training & Audiovisual Support Center
Building 756
Fort Sill, OK 73503

AZ
Commander
Hq., Fort Huachuca
CCH-PTS-VA
Building 22328
Fort Huachuca, AZ 85613

CA

Director
Army Training & Audiovisual Support Center
ATTN: AFZW-DC-TA
Fort Ord, CA 93941

CO

Director
Army Training Aids & Audiovisual Support Center
Building 6103
Fort Carson, CO 80913

CT

Director
Army Training & Audiovisual Support Center
Fort Devens, MA 01433

DC

Director
U.S. Army Audiovisual Center
ATTN: MOAV—SC
Building 201
Fort Myer
Arlington, VA 22211

DE

Director
Army Training & Audiovisual Support Center
Building T-544
Fort George G. Meade, MD 20755

FL

Director (South)
Army Training & Audiovisual Support Center
Fort Stewart, GA 31313

Commander
U.S. Army Infantry Center
ATTN: ATZB-DPT-TASO-TASC
Fort Benning, GA 31905

GA

Commander (North)
U.S. Army Signal Center & Fort Gordon
ATTN: ATZHDT-C-A
Fort Gordon, GA 30905

Director (Southwest)
U.S. Army Infantry Center
ATTN: ATZB-DPT-TASO-AVSC
Fort Benning, GA 31905

Director (Southeast)
Army Training & Audiovisual Support Center
Fort Stewart, GA 31313

GU

Commander
U.S.A. SPT SMD-Hawaii
ATTN: APZ-RI-AV
Schofield Barracks, HI 96857

HI

Director
Audiovisual Unit
TASO, Training Division
DPTINT, USASCH
Fort Shafter, HI 96858

IA

Director
Hq. Fort McCoy
Army Training & Audiovisual Support Center
Sparta, WI 54656

ID

Director
Training & Audiovisual Support Center
ATTN: AFZH-DPTACS
Building 9641, Logistics Center
Fort Lewis, WA 98433

IL

Director (Chicago and 7 surrounding counties)
Army Training & Audiovisual Support Center
Building 440E
Fort Sheridan, IL 60037

Director (South)
Army Training & Audiovisual Support Center
Fort Leonard Wood, MO 65473

Director (North)
Hq. Fort McCoy
Army Training & Audiovisual Support Center
Sparta, WI 54656

IN

Director
Army Training & Audiovisual Support Center
Building 479
Fort Benjamin Harrison, IN 46216

KS

Director
TASO/AVSC
ATTN: AFZN-CE-T
Building 54
Fort Riley, KS 66442

KY

Director (Bowling Green, and North)
Army Training & Audiovisual Support Center
Building 2317
Fort Knox, KY 40121

Commander (South of Bowling Green)
Hq. Fifth INF DIV (M) & Fort Polk
ATTN: AFZX-DPT-GSM
Fort Polk, LA 74159

LA

Commander
Hq. Fifth INF DIV (M) & Fort Polk
ATTN: AFZX-DPT-GSM
Fort Polk, LA 74159

MA

Director
Army Training & Audiovisual Support Center
Fort Devens, MA 01433

MD

Director
Army Training & Audiovisual Support Center
Building T-544
Fort George G. Meade, MD 20755

ME

Director
Army Training & Audiovisual Support Center
Fort Devens, MA 01433

MI

Director (Upper Peninsula)
Hq. Fort McCoy
Army Training & Audiovisual Support Center
Sparta, WI 54656

Director (Lower Peninsula)
Army Training & Audiovisual Support Center
Building 479
Fort Benjamin Harrison, IN 46216

MN

Director
Hq. Fort McCoy
Army Training & Audiovisual Support Center
Sparta, WI 54656

MO

Director
Army Training & Audiovisual Support Center
Fort Leonard Wood, MO 65473

MS

Director (South)
Army Training & Audiovisual Support Center
Building 9313
U.S.A. Aviation Center & Fort Rucker
Fort Rucker, AL 36362

Director (North)
Army Training & Audiovisual Support Center
Fort McClellan, AL 36205

MT

Director
Army Training Aids & Audiovisual Support Center
Building 6103
Fort Carson, CO 80913

NC

Director
XVII Airborne Corps & Fort Bragg
Training Aids Service Office
ATTN: Audiovisual Support Center
Fort Bragg, NC 28307

ND

Director
TASO/AVSC
ATTN: AFZN-CE-T
Building 54
Fort Riley, KS 66442

NE

Director
TASO/AVSC
ATTN: AFZN-CE-T
Building 54
Fort Riley, KS 66442

NH

Director
Army Training & Audiovisual Support Center
Fort Devens, MA 04133

NJ

Director
Army Training & Audiovisual Support Center
Customer Service
Building 5713
Fort Dix, NJ 08640

NV

Director
Army Training & Audiovisual Support Center
ATTN: AFZW-DC-TA
Fort Ord, CA 93941

NY

Director (New York City)
Army Training & Audiovisual Support Center
Customer Service
Building 5713
Fort Dix, NJ 08640

Director (New York State)
Army Training & Audiovisual Support Center
Building T-1030
Fort Drum
Watertown, NY 13601

OH
Director
Army Training & Audiovisual Support Center
Building 2317
Fort Knox, KY 40121

OK
Director
Army Training & Audiovisual Support Center
Building 756
Fort Sill, OK 73503

OR
Director
Army Training & Audiovisual Support Center
ATTN: AFZH-DPTACS
Building 9641
Logistics Center
Fort Lewis, WA 98433

PA
Director
Army Training & Audiovisual Support Center
U.S. Army Garrison
Fort Indiantown Gap
Annville, PA 17003

PR
Director
Army Training & Audiovisual Support Center
U.S. Army Garrison
Fort Buchanan, PR 00934

RI
Director
Army Training & Audiovisual Support Center
Fort Jackson, SC 29207

SC
Director
Army Training & Audiovisual Support Center
ATTN: ATZJ-PTSA
Building 10−110
Fort Jackson, SC 29207

SD
Director
TASO/AVSC
ATTN: AFZN-CE-T
Building 54
Fort Riley, KS 66442

TN
Director
Army Training & Audiovisual Support Center
Building T−849
Fort Campbell, KY 42223

TX
Director (South)
Army Training & Audiovisual Support Center
ATTN: DPTSEC
Building 2016
Fort Sam Houston, TX 78234

Director (Central and North)
Army Training & Audiovisual Support Center
G3/DPT TASO
Bldg. 2219
Headquarters Ave.
Fort Hood, TX 76544

Director (El Paso area)
Army Training & Audiovisual Support Center
P.O. Box 8031
Fort Bliss, TX 79918

UT
Director
Army Training Aids & Audiovisual Support Center
Bldg. 6103
Ford Carson, CO 80913

VA
Director (Southeast)
Army Training & Audiovisual Support Center
Fort Eustis, VA 23064

Director (South and Central)
Army Training & Audiovisual Support Center
Building P−8045
Fort Lee, VA 23801

VI
Commander
Army Training & Audiovisual Support Center
Fort Clayton
APO Miami, FL 34004

VT
Director
Army Training & Audiovisual Support Center
Fort Devens, MA 01433

WA
Director
Army Training & Audiovisual Support Center
ATTN: AFZW-DPTACS
Building 9641
Logistics Center
Fort Lewis, WA 98433

WI
Director (Counties surrounding Milwaukee)
Army Training & Audiovisual Support Center
Building 440E
Fort Sheridan, IL 60037

Director (Outside of Milwaukee and environs)
Hq. Fort McCoy
Army Training & Audiovisual Support Center
Sparta, WI 54656

WV

Director
Army Training & Audiovisual Support Center
U.S. Army Garrison
Fort Indiantown Gap
Annville, PA 17003

WY

Director
Army Training Aids Office & Audiovisual Support
  Center
Bldg. 6103
Fort Carson, CO 80913

Individual Films

"About Fallout." 1963. 24 minutes. 16mm. color. free loan. DDCP 3-220. (Condensed version. 8¼ minutes. DDCP 3-256.)

Designed to dispel many commonly held wrong conceptions. Uses animation and live action to show the nature of fallout radiation, its effect on cells, what it would do to food and water after a nuclear attack, and what steps to take.

"Conflagration." 1975. 28 minutes. 16mm. color. free loan. DDCP 20-288.

Tells the story of the fire of October, 1973 that consumed 18 city blocks in Chelsea, MA. Tells how 700 firemen from 69 surrounding communities joined in the fight, battling 40 mile-per-hour winds and a fire that destroyed one-fourth of the city.

"Day of the Killer Tornadoes." 1978. 27 minutes. 16mm. color. free loan. DDCP 20-290. (Condensed version. 14 minutes. DDCP 20-294.)

Tells the story of many twisters sweeping through the South and Midwest, killing 315 people and turning 11 states into major disaster areas. Includes footage of the tornadoes hitting cities in Ohio and Kentucky.

"Earthquake!" 1972. 28½ minutes. 16mm. color. free loan. DDCP 20-278. (Condensed version. 13 minutes. DDCP 20-280.)

Chronicles the quake that shook most of southern California leaving fire and destruction.

"Environment for Education." 1973. 19 minutes. 16mm. color. free loan. DDCP 5-272.

Shows by example that well-designed school buildings can provide protection against vandalism, noise pollution, natural disaster hazards, and radioactive fallout.

"One Week in October." 1964. 29 minutes. 16mm. B&W. free loan. DDCP 20-223.

Tells the story of the Cuban missile crisis. Includes aerial reconnaissance photographs of Cuba and news coverage film during those critical weeks.

"Our Active Earth." 1972. 28½ minutes. 16mm. color. free loan. From regional offices or may be purchased for $90.00 from: Hollywood Film Enterprises, Inc., 6060 Sunset Blvd., Hollywood, CA 90028.

Shows preparatory and survival techniques for earthquakes, fires, and floods.

"Protection in the Nuclear Age." 1978. 23 minutes. 16mm. color. free loan. DDCP 3-291.

Explains the effects of blast, heat, radiation, and radioactive fallout. Includes information on protective measures, shelters, and relocations. Features color animation with special captions for the deaf. English language version is available from Army Training & Audiovisual Support Centers, Spanish version from Federal Emergency Management Regional Offices.

"Survival in the Winter Storm." 1974. 27 minutes. 16mm. color. free loan. DDCP 20-286.

Shows how to prepare for dangers of severe weather in the home and on the highway. Includes tips for those living in winter storm areas and those in warm areas who only infrequently experience storms.

"Though the Earth Be Moved." 1965. 45 minutes. 16mm. B&W. free loan. DDCP 20-238.

Chronicles the Good Friday earthquake of 1964 in Alaska that took 115 lives and left thousands homeless after fire, shock, and seismic sea wave. (Requires a 1,600-foot takeup reel.)

Special Services: For information on publications, films, freedom of information, contact: (202) 287-0313.

FEDERAL HALL NATIONAL MEMORIAL
Manhattan Sites
National Park Service
26 Wall St.
New York, NY 10005

Date Established: 1955

Objectives of the Agency: Preserve the site of John Peter Zenger's trial involving freedom of the press, the Stamp Act Congress, the adoption of the Bill of Rights, the first capitol, and other historical events.

Curriculum: History

Subjects: U.S.—history

Publications: Pamphlet.

94 / Federal Hall National Memorial

Selected List of Books and Pamphlets

"Federal Hall." n.d. 8-fold. free.
 Describes how the Federal Hall was used as a city hall, as the site of Washington's inauguration as the first U.S. President, and other historical uses and notes.

FEDERAL HIGHWAY ADMINISTRATION
U.S. Department of Transportation
Office of Management Systems
400 Seventh St., SW
Washington, DC 20590
(202) 426-0630

Date Established: 1966

Objectives of the Agency: Control the total operation and environment of the highway systems, with emphasis on improvement of highway-oriented highway safety; administer a federal aid program with the states; and regulate and enforce federal requirements for the safety of those engaged in interstate or foreign commerce.

Curriculum: Driver education, environmental studies

Subjects: Transportation, highway

Locations:

CT, MA, ME, NH, NJ, NY, PR, RI, VT

Federal Highway Administration Regional Office
Leo W. O'Brien Federal Bldg.
Clinton Ave. and N. Pearl St.
Room 729
Albany, NY 12270

DC, DE, MD, PA, VA, WV

Federal Highway Administration Regional Office
31 Hopkins Plaza
Room 1633
Baltimore, MD 21201

AL, FL, GA, KY, MS, NC, SC, TN

Federal Highway Administration Regional Office
1720 Peachtree Rd., NW
Suite 200
Atlanta, GA 30309

IL, IN, MI, MN, OH, WI

Federal Highway Administration Regional Office
18209 Dixie Hwy.
Homewood, IL 60430

AR, LA, NM, OK, TX

Federal Highway Administration Regional Office
819 Taylor St.
Fort Worth, TX 76102

IA, KS, MO, NE

Federal Highway Administration Regional Office
6301 Rockhill Rd.
Kansas City, MO 64131

CO, MT, ND, SD, UT, WY

Federal Highway Administration Regional Office
555 Zang St.
P.O. 25246
Denver, CO 80225

AZ, CA, HI, NV

Federal Highway Administration Regional Office
211 Main St.
Room 1100
San Francisco, CA 94105

AK, ID, OR, WA

Federal Highway Administration Regional Office
708 S.W. Third St.
Room 412
Portland, OR 97204

Publications: Reports. Reviews. Statistics. Proceedings. Manuals. Guides. On research, technology, safety, and environmental concerns of highways.

Bibliographies, Sales Catalogs, Publications Lists, etc.

FHWA Publications. Current. 217p. free.
 Lists what is available from various sources. Includes some audiovisuals.

Selected List of Books and Pamphlets

"Federal Highway Administration." n.d. 1p. free.
 Explains concerns, functions, and the organization of the administration.

FEDERAL HOME LOAN BANK BOARD
1700 G St., NW
Washington, DC 20552
(202) 377-6323

Date Established: 1932

Objectives of the Agency: Provide a nationwide structure to regulate and service local home financing institutions.

Curriculum: Consumer education

Subjects: Home finance
 Insurance, home

Locations:

CT, MA, ME, NH, RI, VT

Federal Home Loan Bank of Boston
One Federal St.
Thirtieth Floor
P.O. Box 2196
Boston, MA 02106

NJ, NY, PR, VI

Federal Home Loan Bank of New York
1 World Trade Center
Floor 103
New York, NY 10048

DE, PA, WV

Federal Home Loan Bank of Pittsburgh
Gateway Center
Fourth Floor
Pittsburgh, PA 15222

AL, DC, FL, GA, MD, NC, SC, VA

Federal Home Loan Bank of Atlanta
Peachtree Center Station
P.O. Box 56527
Atlanta, GA 30343

KY, OH, TN

Federal Home Loan Bank of Cincinnati
P.O. Box 598
Cincinnati, OH 45201

IN, MI

Federal Home Loan Bank of Indianapolis
1350 Merchants Plaza
South Tower
115 W. Washington St.
P.O. Box 60
Indianapolis, IN 46206

IL, WI

Federal Home Loan Bank of Chicago
111 E. Wacher Dr.
Suite 800
Chicago, IL 60601

IA, MN, MO, ND, SD

Federal Home Loan Bank of Des Moines
907 Walnut St.
Des Moines, IA 50309

AR, LA, MS, NM, TX

Federal Home Loan Bank of Little Rock
1400 Tower Bldg.
Little Rock, AR 72201

CO, KS, NE, OK

Federal Home Loan Bank of Topeka
P.O. Box 176
Topeka, KS 66601

AZ, CA, NV

Federal Home Loan Bank of San Francisco
600 California St.
P.O. Box 7948
San Francisco, CA 94120

AK, GU, HI, ID, MT, OR, UT, WA, WY

Federal Home Loan Bank of Seattle
600 Stewart St.
Seattle, WA 98101

Publications: Pamphlets. Lists. Reports. Statistical releases. Bulletins. Serials.

Bibliographies, Sales Catalogs, Publications Lists, etc.

"Publications List." Current. 3p. free.
Lists publications, for sale and free, available upon written request.

Selected List of Books and Pamphlets

"Deposit Insurance Coverage for Family Savings." n.d. 3-fold. free.
Explains the maximum deposit insurance coverage for savings for a family of two, three, and four.

"Equally Safe." 1982. 20p. free.
Provides seven major facts about savings accounts and their insurance in banks and savings and loan associations.

"How the FSLIC Insurance Pays Out." n.d. 3-fold. free.
How the law reads and what it means.

"Questions and Answers Concerning Your Insured Savings." Rev. 1982. 14p. free.
Gives examples of insurance coverage under the Federal Savings and Loan Insurance Corporation rules on the types of ownership of funds most frequently deposited in insured institutions.

FEDERAL LABOR RELATIONS AUTHORITY
500 C St., SW
Washington, DC 20424
(202) 382-0777

Date Established: 1978

Objectives of the Agency: Oversee the Federal Service Labor—Management Relations program; administer the law that protects the right of employees of the federal government to organize, bargain collectively, and participate through labor organizations of their choosing; and insure compliance with statutory rights and obligations of federal employees and the labor organizations representing them in their dealings with federal agencies.

Curriculum: Government

Subjects: Labor unions

Locations:

CT, NH, MA, ME, RI, VT, all land and water areas east of the continents of North and South America to long. 90¼E (except VI), Panama (limited jurisdiction), PR and coastal islands

Federal Labor Relations Authority
Boston Regional Office
441 Stuart St.
Ninth Floor
Boston, MA 02116
(617) 223-0920

DE, NJ, NY (counties of Ulster, Sullivan, Greene, Columbia and all counties south; all counties in northern NY are in the jurisdiction of Boston), PA, PR, VI

Federal Labor Relations Authority
New York Regional Office
26 Federal Plaza
Room 24-102
New York, NY 10278
(212) 264-4934

Federal Labor Relations Authority
Philadelphia Sub-Regional Office
Mall Bldg.
325 Chestnut St.
Room 500
Philadelphia, PA 19106
(212) 597-1527

DC, MD, VA (counties of Arlington, Alexandria, Fairfax, Fauquier, Loudon and Prince William; all counties in southern VA are in the jurisdiction of Atlanta), WV

Federal Labor Relations Authority
Washington Regional Office
1111 Eighteenth St., NW
Room 700
P.O. Box 33758
Washington, DC 20033-0758
(202) 653-8456

AL, FL, GA, KY, MS, NC, SC, TN, VA (southern counties)

Federal Labor Relations Authority
Atlanta Regional Office
1776 Peachtree St., NW
Suite 501
North Wing
Atlanta, GA 30309
(404) 881-2324
(404) 881-2325

IL, IN, MI, MN, OH, WI

Federal Labor Relations Authority
Chicago Regional Office
175 W. Jackson Blvd.
Suite 1359-A
Chicago, IL 60604
(312) 353-6306

Federal Labor Relations Authority
Cleveland Sub-Regional Office
1301 Superior Ave.
Suite 230
Cleveland, OH 44114
(216) 522-2114

AR, LA, NM, OK, Panama (limited jurisdiction), TX

Federal Labor Relations Authority
Dallas Regional Office
Downtown Post Office Station
Bryan and Ervay St.
P.O. Box 2640
Dallas, TX 75221
(214) 767-4996

CO, IA, KS, MO, MT, ND, NE, SD, UT, WY

Federal Labor Relations Authority
Denver Regional Office
1531 Stout St.
Suite 301
Denver, CO 80202
(303) 837-5224

AZ, CA (southern counties), HI, all land and water areas west of the continents of North and South America to long. 90¼E (except coastal islands)

Federal Labor Relations Authority
Los Angeles Regional Office
World Trade Center
350 S. Figueroa St.
Tenth Floor
Los Angeles, CA 90071
(213) 688-3805

Federal Labor Relations Authority
Honolulu Sub-Regional Office
Room 3206
300 Ala Moana Blvd.
Honolulu, HI 96850
(808) 546-8355

AK, CA (Monterey, Kings, Tulare, Inyo, and all counties to the north; all counties in southern California are within the Los Angeles jurisdiction), ID, NV, OR, WA

Federal Labor Relations Authority
San Francisco Regional Office
530 Bush St.
Suite 542
San Francisco, CA 94108
(415) 556-8105

Publications: Pamphlets. Guides. On rules, regulations, and statutes.

Selected List of Books and Pamphlets

"Chapter XIV—Federal Labor Relations Authority, General Counsel of the Federal Labor Relations Authority and Federal Service Impasses Panel." Rev. 1984. 80p. free.
   Covers such topics as transition rules and regulations, availability of official information, and the purpose and scope of the Federal Labor Relations Authority and its General Counsel.

"The Federal Service Labor—Management Relations Statute." 1980. 60p. free. FLRA Doc. 1071.
   Covers chapter 71 of Title 5 of the U.S. Code and related amendments to 5 USC 5596(b), the Back Pay Act.

"Guide to the Federal Service Labor—Management Relations Statute." 1984. 54p. free. FLRA Doc. 1213.
   Designed to help employees, labor organizations, and agencies which are subject to the statute to better understand their responsibilities and rights under its provisions. Includes a nontechnical, detailed summary of the statute. Explains the structure of the Federal Labor Relations Authority and refers to the specific statutory or regulatory section for more information.

FEDERAL MARITIME COMMISSION
Office of the Chairman
1100 L St., NW
Washington, DC 10573
(202) 523-5911

Date Established: 1961

Objectives of the Agency: Approve or disapprove agreements between common carriers, terminal operators, freight forwarders and others subject to the shipping act of 1916; and monitor activities under approved agreements for compliance with the provisions of law and its rules, orders, and regulations.

Curriculum: Government

Subjects: Shipping—U.S.

Locations:

Federal Maritime Commission
Atlantic District Office
6 World Trade Center
Suite 614
New York, NY 10048-0949

Federal Maritime Commission
Gulf District Office
600 South St.
Room 1035
P.O. Box 30550
New Orleans, LA 70190-0550

Federal Maritime Commission
Miami Office
1001 North America Way
Room 102
Miami, FL 33132

Federal Maritime Commission
Pacific District Office
525 Market St.
Twenty-Fifth Floor
San Francisco, CA 94105

Federal Maritime Commission
Los Angeles Office
Terminal Island Sta.
300 S. Ferry St.
Room 2040-A
P.O. Box 3184
San Pedro, CA 90731

Federal Maritime Commission
Puerto Rico District Office
Room 762
U.S. District Courthouse
Carlos Chardon St.
Hato Rey, PR 00918-2254

Federal Maritime Commission
Great Lakes District Office
610 Canal St.
Chicago, IL 60607

Publications: Reports. Act. Subscriptions.

Bibliographies, Sales Catalogs, Publications Lists, etc.

"Summary of Publications." 3p. free.
   Tells what is available to order materials.

Serials, Subscription Publications, etc.

Subscription No. 2. $120.00/yr.
   Prints final decisions issued by the commission in all formal docketed proceedings. For calendar year January through December.

98 / Federal Maritime Commission

Selected List of Books and Pamphlets

Annual Report of the Federal Maritime Commission. Annual. 129p. free.

Reviews history, the function of the commission, and significant activities of the year.

FEDERAL MEDIATION AND CONCILIATION SERVICE
2100 K St., NW
Washington, DC 20427
(202) 653-5280

Date Established: 1947

Objectives of the Agency: Promote the development of sound labor-management relationships; assist in settling disputes through mediation; and foster constructive joint relationships of labor and management.

Curriculum: Social studies

Subjects: Labor disputes

Locations:

Federal Mediation and Conciliation Service
Region 1 Office
2937 Federal Bldg.
26 Federal Plaza
New York, NY 10007
(212) 264-1000

Federal Mediation and Conciliation Service
Region 2 Office
401 Mall Bldg.
Fourth and Chestnut St.
Philadelphia, PA 19106
(215) 597-7680

Federal Mediation and Conciliation Service
Region 3 Office
1422 W. Peachtree St., NW
Atlanta, GA 30309
(404) 881-2473

Federal Mediation and Conciliation Service
Region 4 Office
508 Mall Bldg.
118 St. Clair Ave., NE
Cleveland, OH 44114
(216) 522-4800

Federal Mediation and Conciliation Service
Region 5 Office
175 W. Jackson St.
Chicago, IL 60604
(312) 353-7350

Federal Mediation and Conciliation Service
Region 6 Office
12140 Wooderest Executive Dr.
Suite 325
St. Louis, MO 63141
(314) 425-3291

Federal Mediation and Conciliation Service
Region 7 Office
50 Francisco St.
Suite 235
San Francisco, CA 94133
(415) 556-4670

Federal Mediation and Conciliation Service
Region 8 Office
Fourth and Vine Bldg.
2615 Fourth Ave.
Seattle, WA 98121
(206) 442-5800

Publications: Pamphlets.

Selected List of Books and Pamphlets

"Arbitration." n.d. 12p. free.

Defines arbitration and its procedures. Lists office locations of the Federal Mediation and Conciliation Service.

"Labor—Management Committee: Planning for Progress." 1981. 20p. free.

Explains the process of determining need, obtaining agreement and commitment, and problems inherent in joint committees. Gives sample formats of bylaws for joint committees and sample format of contract language.

"Securing Labor—Management Peace through Mediation." 1978. 6p. free.

Tells what the Federal Mediation and Conciliation Service is, who the mediators are, how the mediators work, and how to locate them.

FEDERAL RESERVE SYSTEM
Board of Governors of the Federal Reserve System
Twentieth St. and Constitution Ave., NW
Washington, DC 20551
(202) 452-3000

Date Established: 1913

Objectives of the Agency: Administer and make policy for the nation's credit and monetary affairs; and, through supervisory and regulatory banking functions, help to keep the banking industry sound.

Curriculum: Business, consumer education

Subjects: Banks and banking

Locations:

Federal Reserve Bank of Atlanta
Research Department, Publications Unit
P.O. Box 1731
Atlanta, GA 30301
(404) 521-8500

Federal Reserve Bank of Boston
Bank and Public Services Department
Boston, MA 02106
(617) 973-3459

Federal Reserve Bank of Chicago
Public Information Center
230 S. La Salle St.
Box 834
Chicago, IL 60690-0834
(312) 322-5112

Federal Reserve Bank of Cleveland
Public Information Center
P.O. Box 6387
Cleveland, OH 44101
(216) 579-2048

Federal Reserve Bank of Dallas
Public Affairs Department
Station K
Dallas, TX 75222
(214) 651-6289
(214) 651-6266

Federal Reserve Bank of Kansas City
Public Affairs Department
925 Grand Ave.
Kansas City, MO 64198
(816) 881-2402

Federal Reserve Bank of Minneapolis
Office of Public Information
250 Marquette Ave.
Minneapolis, MN 55480
(612) 340-2446

Federal Reserve Bank of New York
Public Information Department
33 Liberty St.
New York, NY 10045
(212) 791-6134

Federal Reserve Bank of Philadelphia
Public Information Department
P.O. Box 66
Philadelphia, PA 19105
(215) 574-6115

Federal Reserve Bank of Richmond
Public Services Department
P.O. Box 27622
Richmond, VA 23261
(804) 643-1250

Federal Reserve Bank of St. Louis
Bank Relations and Public Information Department
P.O. Box 442
St. Louis, MO 63166
(314) 444-8421

Federal Reserve Bank of San Francisco
Public Information Department
P.O. Box 7702
San Francisco, CA 94120
(415) 974-3234

Publications: Pamphlets. Periodicals. Statistical data guides. Curriculum materials. Reports. Reviews. Newsletters.

Bibliographies, Sales Catalogs, Publications Lists, etc.

"Federal Reserve Board Publications." Current. 6p. free.
    Tells what is available, free and for sale. Includes handbooks, catalogs, and pamphlets, both technical and general.

"Federal Reserve System Public Information Materials." Current. 41p. free.
    Provides a guide to what is available. Designed for educators, bankers, economists, and the public. Arranged by subject with indications of intended audiences. Lists free and for sale material from various reserve banks. Order from: Federal Reserve Bank of New York, Public Information Department, 33 Liberty St., New York, NY 10045.

"Instructional Materials." Current. 16p. free.
    Lists material by intended audience level (elementary, high school and college). Includes teaching packages, audiovisual materials, and resource materials.

Serials, Subscription Publications, etc.

"Economic Commentary." Current. 4p. free.
    Biweekly periodical for bankers, economists, business people, college students or teachers. Tables. Charts. Order from: Federal Reserve Bank of Cleveland, Public Information Center, P.O. Box 6387, Cleveland, OH 44101.

"On Reserve." Current. 4p. free.
    Trends, happenings in economics. Includes regional news of economic education programs and activities. Order from: "On Reserve," Federal Reserve Bank of Chicago, Public Information Center, Box 834, Chicago, IL 60690. (312) 322-5112. Ask to be placed on the mailing list.

Selected List of Books and Pamphlets

"ABC's of Figuring Interest." 1984. 10p. free.
    Explains simple interest, add-on interest, compound interest and other information. Uses graphs and 13 examples. Order from: Federal Reserve Bank of Chicago, Public Information Center, Box 834, Chicago, IL 60690. (312) 322-5112.

100 / Federal Reserve System

"Business Forecasts." Current. 67p. free.

Gathers excerpts from econometric and judgmental forecasts for the year as a reference file of representative opinions. Order from: Federal Reserve Bank of Richmond, Public Services Dept., P.O. Box 27622, Richmond, VA 23261.

"Counterfeit." n.d. 8p. free.

Tells what to look for in a counterfeit bill and what to do if you receive one. Illustrated. Order from: Federal Reserve Bank of Chicago, Public Information Center, Box 835, Chicago, IL 60690.

"Credit Guide." 1982. 12p. free.

Gives tips on using credit and addresses for sources of additional information. Order from: Federal Reserve Bank of Chicago, Public Information Center, Box 834, Chicago, IL 60690.

"A Day at the Fed." 1983. 32p. free.

Describes the New York Federal Reserve Bank's operations and its role in the system and the economy. Photographs. Order from: Federal Reserve Bank of New York, Public Information Dept., 33 Liberty St., New York, NY 10045.

"Federal Reserve Glossary." 1985. 33p. free.

Defines many terms used in monetary policy, international transactions, the payments mechanism, and consumer credit. Order from: Board of Governors of the Federal Reserve System, Publications Services, Twentieth & C Sts., NW, Washington, DC 20551.

The Federal Reserve System: Purposes and Functions. 1984. 120p. free.

Supplements high school and college classroom texts on the role of the Federal Reserve in government and monetary policy responsibilities. Order from: Federal Reserve Bank of Philadelphia, Public Services Dept., P.O. Box 66, Philadelphia, PA 19105.

"I Bet You Thought . . . ." 1984. 33p. free.

Relates misconceptions and economic myths people follow. Order from: Federal Reserve Bank of New York, Public Information Dept., 33 Liberty St., New York, NY 10045.

"Making Money in Middlevillage." 1981. kit. free.

Describes the money creation process through a four-page teacher's guide, student activity sheets, and poster. For secondary use. Order from: Federal Reserve Bank of New York, Public Information Dept., 33 Liberty St., New York, NY 10045.

"Modern Money Mechanics." 1982. 31p. free.

A workbook on deposits, currency, and bank reserves. Describes the mechanical process of money creation. Order from: Federal Reserve Bank of Chicago, Public Information Center, Box 834, Chicago, IL 60690.

"Two Faces of Debt." 4th rev. 23p. free.

Explains debt in the American economy, its composition and distribution between debtors and creditors, and the vital role debt plays in channeling savings into productive investment. Order from: Federal Reserve Bank of Chicago, Public Information Center, Box 834, Chicago, IL 60690.

Audiovisuals:

Filmographies, Sales Lists, etc.

"Federal Reserve System Public Information Materials." Current. 41p. free.

Lists films, filmstrips, and videotapes. Gives annotations and recommended audience. Indicates which audiovisuals are free loan or for sale, which include teaching guides and student activity materials. Order from: Federal Reserve Bank of New York, Public Information Dept., 33 Liberty St., New York, NY 10045.

"Instructional Materials." Current. 16p. free.

Tells what is available for elementary, high school, and college students in filmstrips, cassettes, films, and video cassettes.

Individual Audiovisuals

"Money: Summing It Up." 1982. 23 minutes. 16mm. free loan.

Explains the development of money and banking from barter to checks. Includes events in American history that led to the Federal Reserve System. Suitable for high school students and general public. Order from: Chicago, Cleveland, Dallas, Kansas City, Richmond or St. Louis reserve banks at addresses previously listed.

"Truth in Lending—Regulation Z (Consumer)." n.d. 18 minutes. filmstrip with records. free loan.

Explains the provisions of the Truth in Lending Law and how to shop wisely for credit. Order from: Chicago or Dallas at addresses previously listed. Cassettes also available from Chicago.

FEDERAL TRADE COMMISSION
Office of Public Affairs
Pennsylvania Ave. at Sixth St., NW
Washington, DC 20580
(202) 523-3598

Date Established: 1914

Objectives of the Agency: Prevent the free enterprise system from being weakened by monopoly or restraints on trade or by unfair or deceptive trade practices.

Curriculum: Business, consumer education

Subjects: Business, consumer protection

Locations:

AL, FL, GA, MS, NC, SC, TN, VA

Federal Trade Commission
Atlanta Regional Office
1718 Peachtree St., NW
Atlanta, GA 30367
(404) 881-4836

CT, MA, ME, NH, RI, VT

Federal Trade Commission
Boston Regional Office
150 Causeway St.
Boston, MA 02114
(617) 223-6621

IA, IL, IN, KY, MN, MO, WI

Federal Trade Commission
Chicago Regional Office
55 E. Monroe St.
Chicago, IL 60603
(312) 353-4423

DE, MD, MI, NY (Western), OH, PA, WV

Federal Trade Commission
Cleveland Regional Office
118 St. Clair Ave.
Cleveland, OH 44114
(216) 522-4207

AR, LA, NM, OK, TX

Federal Trade Commission
Dallas Regional Office
8303 Elmbrook Dr.
Dallas, TX 75247
(214) 767-7050

CO, KS, MT, ND, NE, SD, UT, WY

Federal Trade Commission
Denver Regional Office
1405 Curtis St.
Denver, CO 80202
(303) 844-2271

AZ, CA (Southern)

Federal Trade Commission
Los Angeles Regional Office
11000 Wilshire Blvd.
Los Angeles, CA 90024
(213) 209-7575

NJ, NY (Eastern)

Federal Trade Commission
New York Regional Office
26 Federal Plaza
New York, NY 10278
(212) 264-1207

CA (Northern), HI, NV

Federal Trade Commission
San Francisco Regional Office
450 Golden Gate Ave.
San Francisco, CA 94102
(415) 556-1270

AK, ID, OR, WA

Federal Trade Commission
Seattle Regional Office
915 Second Ave.
Seattle, WA 98174
(206) 442-4656

Publications: Pamphlets. Notices. Lists. For both the general consumer and for business people.

Bibliographies, Sales Catalogs, Publications Lists, etc.

"FTC 'Best Sellers'." Current. 4p. free.
   Tells what is available in general information, energy, buying at home, credit, professional services, sales practices, and business publications. Some publications in Spanish. Free and for sale.

Serials, Subscription Publications, etc.

"FTC News Notes." Current. 4p. free.
   Provides briefs on recent happenings and commission rulings.

"Weekly Calendar and Notice of 'Sunshine' Meetings." 2p. free.
   Gives notices of commission meetings, hearings, speeches and other events.

Selected List of Books and Pamphlets

"Equal Credit Opportunity." 1982. 4p. free.
   Explains what a creditor may not do when you apply for credit, what to do if you suspect discrimination, and where to send complaints and questions.

"Facts for Consumers: Solving Credit Problems." 1984. 4p. free.
   Explains why your credit rating is important, how to deal with debts, and where to obtain more information and help.

"Fair Credit Billing." 1982. 4p. free.
   Explains how to use the Fair Credit Billing Act to help resolve disputes with creditors to ensure fair handling of credit accounts. Includes addresses and telephone numbers to report violations.

"What Truth in Lending Means to You." 1981. 8p. free.
   Gives tips on credit cards, advertising, cancellations, and other financial information. Includes addresses of federal enforcement agencies.

"Women and Credit Histories." 1982. 4p. free.
Tells what the law says, how to build your credit file, and other tips. Includes addresses and telephone numbers to obtain more information.

Special Services: To find out the latest news, updated daily, call the FTC Newsphone: (202) 523-3540.

FISH AND WILDLIFE SERVICE
Department of the Interior
Main Interior Bldg.
Washington, DC 20240
(202) 343-5634

Date Established: 1956

Objectives of the Agency: Conserve, protect, and enhance fish and wildlife for the continuing benefit of the country.

Curriculum: Social studies

Subjects: Wildlife — conservation

Locations:

AZ, NM, OK, TX

U.S. Fish and Wildlife Service
Regional Office
P.O. Box 329
Albuquerque, NM 87103
(505) 766-2091

AK

U.S. Fish and Wildlife Service
Regional Office
P.O. Box 4-2597
Anchorage, AK 99509
(907) 263-3330

AL, AR, FL, GA, KY, LA, MS, NC, PR, SC, TN, VI

U.S. Fish and Wildlife Service
Regional Office
Richard B. Russell Federal Bldg.
P.O. Box 4839
Atlanta, GA 30303
(404) 221-5872

CT, DE, MA, MD, ME, NH, NJ, NY, PA, RI, VA, VT, WV

U.S. Fish and Wildlife Service
Regional Office
1 Gateway Center
Room 400E
Newton Corner, MA 02158
(617) 965-2298

CO, KS, MT, NE, ND, SD, UT, WY

U.S. Fish and Wildlife Service
Regional Office
P.O. Box 25486
Denver Federal Center
Denver, CO 80225
(303) 234-4612

HI, ID, NV, OR, WA

U.S. Fish and Wildlife Service
Regional Office
Lloyd 500 Bldg.
500 N.E. Multnamah St.
Suite 1490
Portland, OR 97232
(503) 231-6125

IA, IL, IN, MI, MN, MO, OH, WI

U.S. Fish and Wildlife Service
Regional Office
Federal Bldg.
P.O. Box 45
Fort Snelling
Twin Cities, MN 55111
(612) 725-3530

Publications: Pamphlets. On laws, animals, fish, and lands.

Bibliographies, Sales Catalogs, Publications Lists, etc.

"Publications of the Fish and Wildlife Service." Rev. 4p. free.
Gives publications available and ordering instructions.

Selected List of Books and Pamphlets

"The American Bald Eagle." 1984. 19p. free.
Explains the eagle's importance, history, and the efforts to save it.

"Facts about Federal Wildlife Laws." 1982. 14p. free.
Explains the laws governing the import, export, trade, and sale of wildlife.

"Fish, Wildlife and People." 1984. 26p. free.
Relates functions and services of the fish and wildlife service that help both wildlife and people.

"Wetlands Values and Management." 1981. 25p. free.
Gives information on such wetlands as marshes and bogs. Tells the services they perform and how they should be protected and managed.

Special Services: Check with the appropriate regional office for a film catalog and regional news. The Twin Cities Regional Office, for example, has a 21-page free loan film catalog and news releases.

FOOD AND DRUG ADMINISTRATION
U.S. Department of Health and Human Services
Public Health Service
5600 Fishers Lane
Rockville, MD 20857
(301) 443-3380

Date Established: 1931

Objectives of the Agency: Protect the health of the country against impure and unsafe foods, drugs, and cosmetics, as well as other potential hazards.

Curriculum: Health, Safety

Subjects: Health education

Locations:

Region 1

FDA (HFR-1145)
585 Commercial St.
Boston, MA 02109
(617) 223-5857

Region 2

FDA (HFR-2145)
850 Third Ave.
Brooklyn, NY 11232
(718) 965-5043

FDA (HFR-2245)
599 Delaware Ave.
Buffalo, NY 14202
(716) 846-4483

FDA (HFR-2345)
20 Evergreen Place
East Orange, NJ 07018
(201) 645-3265

FDA (HFR-2420)
P.O. Box S4427
Old San Juan Station
San Juan, PR 00905
(809) 753-4264

Region 3

FDA (HFR-3145)
Second and Chestnut Sts.
Room 900 U.S. Customhouse
Philadelphia, PA 19106
(215) 597-0837

FDA (HFR-3245)
900 Madison Ave.
Baltimore, MD 21201
(301) 962-3731

FDA (HFR-3535)
1000 N. Glebe Rd.
Room 743
Arlington, VA 22201
(703) 285-2578

Region 4

FDA (HFR-4120)
1010 W. Peachtree St., NW
Atlanta, GA 30309
(404) 881-7355

FDA (HFR-4220)
7200 Lake Ellenor Dr.
Suite 120
Orlando, FL 32803
(305) 855-0900

FDA (HFR-4320)
297 Plus Park Blvd.
Nashville, TN 37217
(615) 251-5208

FDA (HFR-4575)
6501 N.W. Thirty-Sixth St.
Suite 200
Miami, FL 33166
(305) 526-2919

Region 5

FDA (HFR-5120)
1222 Main Post Office Bldg.
433 W. Van Buren St.
Chicago, IL 60607
(312) 353-7126

FDA (HFR-5525)
601 Rockwell Ave.
Room 464
Cleveland, OH 44114
(216) 522-4844

FDA (HFR-5245)
1141 Central Pkwy.
Cincinnati, OH 45202
(513) 684-3501

FDA (HFR-5345)
1560 E. Jefferson Ave.
Detroit, MI 48207
(313) 266-6273

FDA (HFR-5560)
575 N. Pennsylvania
Room 693
Indianapolis, IN 46204
(317) 269-6500

FDA (HFR-5445)
240 Hennepin Ave.
Minneapolis, MN 55401
(612) 349-3906

Region 6

FDA (HFR-6145)
1200 Main Tower Bldg.
Room 15-45
Dallas, TX 75202
(214) 767-5433

104 / Food and Drug Administration

FDA (HFR-6245)
4298 Elysian Fields Ave.
New Orleans, LA 70122
(504) 589-2420

FDA (HFR-6345)
Houston Station
1440 N. Loop
Suite 250
Houston, TX 77009
(713) 229-3550

FDA (HFR-6540)
727 E. Durango
Room B-406
San Antonio, TX 78206
(512) 229-6737

Region 7

FDA (HFR-7145)
1009 Cherry St.
Kansas City, MO 64106
(816) 374-3817

FDA (HFR-7245)
Laclede's Landing
808 N. Collins
St. Louis, MO 63102
(314) 425-5021

FDA (HFR-7515)
Brandeis Bldg.
200 S. Sixteenth St.
Suite 430
Omaha, NE 68102
(402) 221-4675

Region 8

FDA (HFR-8145)
500 U.S. Customhouse
Nineteenth and California St.
Denver, CO 80202
(303) 844-4915

Region 9

FDA (HFR-9145)
50 United Nations Plaza
Room 524
San Francisco, CA 94102
(415) 556-2682

FDA (HFR-9245)
1521 W. Pico Blvd.
Los Angeles, CA 90015
(213) 688-4395

Region 10

FDA (HFR-0145)
Federal Office Bldg.
909 First Ave.
#5009
Seattle, WA 98174
(206) 442-5258

Publications: Catalogs. Fact sheets. Article reprints. Pamphlets.

Bibliographies, Sales Catalogs, Publications Lists, etc.

"FDA Information for Consumers." Current. 22p. free. HHS Publication No. (FDA) 85-1108.
  Tells what is available in free publications for the general public. Some in Spanish.

Serials, Subscription Publications, etc.

FDA Consumer. $17.00/yr. domestic, $21.25/yr. foreign (10 issues).
  Prints articles about foods, vitamins, prescription and over-the-counter medicines, vaccines, cosmetics, medical equipment and devices, and radiation.

Selected List of Books and Pamphlets

"Here Are Some Things You Should Know about Prescription Drugs." 1982. 4p. free. HHS Publication No. (FDA) 82-3124.
  Explains adverse reactions, drug interactions, generic products, etc. Includes questions to ask.

"Hunger Is More than an Empty Stomach." 1984. 4p. free. HHS Publication No. (FDA) 84-2182.
  Explains how the appetite works, studies and research, and weight control.

"Keeping Your Pet Healthy." 1979. 4p. free. HEW Publication No. (FDA) 79-6034.
  Discusses responsible ownership, vet care, first aid, and feeding of your cat or dog.

"Milestones in U.S. Food and Drug Law History." 1979. 4p. free. HHS Publication No. (FDA) 79-1063.
  Chronicles the progress, beginning with 1784 when Massachusetts enacted the first general food law in the country.

"Nutrition Labels and U.S. RDA." 1981. 2p. free. HHS Publication No. (FDA) 81-2146.
  Gives consumer information on United States Recommended Daily Allowances, or guides to amounts of vitamins and minerals a person needs daily to stay healthy.

"On Making Food Labels Truthful." 1984. 4p. free. HHS Publication No. (FDA) 84-2181.
  Discusses types of food adulterations, regulatory devices, and the work of the FDA.

"Please Pass That Woman More Calcium and Iron." 1984. 6p. free. HHS Publication No. (FDA) 85-2198.

Explains the need of women in various stages of life for iron and calcium. Includes tables showing calcium and iron contents of various foods.

"Poison Safety Game." 1983. 4p. free. HHS Publication No. (FDA) 83-1099.

Contains a game designed for older elementary children and teenagers to reduce the toxic substance exposures that occur when children put something into their mouths that they shouldn't.

"Requirements of Laws and Regulations Enforced by the U.S. Food and Drug Administration." 1984. 77p. free. HHS Publication No. (FDA) 85-1115.

Summarizes the main requirements of laws and regulations enforced by the Food and Drug Administration. Covers such categories as *Foods, Cosmetics, Animal Products, Medical Devices,* etc.

"The U.S. Food and Drug Law: How It Came, How It Works." 1979. 8p. free. HEW Publication No. (FDA) 79-1054.

Gives history, progress of food and drug laws, the 1938 Federal Food, Drug and Cosmetic Act, and changes in the law.

"Who, Why, When and Where of Food Poisons (and What To Do about Them)." 1982. 4p. free. HHS Publication No. (FDA) 82-2167.

Provides a table of the diseases and organisms that cause food poisons, the sources of illness, symptoms, and prevention methods.

"A Word of Caution about Treating Flu or Chicken Pox." 6p. free. HHS Publication No. (FDA) 84-3132.

Questions and Answers about Reyes Syndrome.

Audiovisuals:

Request a listing of titles from the nearest district office. For example, the Detroit district has a 3-p. audiovisual list and a 2-p. videotape list. A list of slide shows and films also appears in "FDA Information for Consumers" described under "Bibliographies, Sales Catalogs, Publications Lists, etc."

Individual Audiovisuals

"The Big Quack Attack." n.d. 15 minutes. slide show. color. $62.00 purchase price. GSA-A02593.

Explains fraudulent medical devices, what to look for in ads for quack products, and what to do. Also available in Spanish. Order from: National Audiovisual Center, Washington, DC 20409. (301) 763-1896.

"Pioneers in Consumer Protection." 20 minutes. 16mm. color. $126.00 purchase price.

Provides a documentary about laws and the history of FDA. Order from: Byron Motion Pictures, 65 K St., NW, Washington, DC 20002.

Special Services: Check with the nearest district office for a list of publications. The Detroit office, for example, has a 6-page list.

The electronic bulletin board offers various services for a fee. Access to the most up-to-date FDA news through communicating word processors is available. For more information contact: (301) 443-3285.

FOOD AND NUTRITION INFORMATION CENTER
NAL Building
10301 Baltimore Blvd.
Room 304
Beltsville, MD 20705
(301) 344-3719

Date Established: 1971

Objectives of the Agency: Lend books and audiovisual materials; provide photocopies of journal articles as permitted by copyright law, title 17, U.S. code; and provide reference services and computer searches.

Curriculum: Health, home economics

Subjects: Food
Nutrition

Publications: Bibliographies. Indexes. Directories. Guides. Pamphlets.

Bibliographies, Sales Catalogs, Publications Lists, etc.

"Food and Nutrition Bibliography." n.d. 1p. free.

Gives description and order form for various volumes of *Food and Nutrition Bibliography*. The bibliographies are annotated indexes to materials in food, human nutrition, and food service management compiled from cataloging records prepared by the USDA's Food and Nutrition Information Center. Volume 11, for example, contains annotations for 3,566 records in 568p. Order from: Oryx Press, 2214 N. Central at Encanto, Phoenix, AZ 85004-1483. 1-800-457-ORYX. $40.00/volume.

"Nutrition and the Elderly: A Selected Annotated Bibliography for Nutrition and Health Professionals." 1985. $6.00. S/N 001-024-00218-6.

Provides a listing of resources that would be helpful to nutrition professionals, health care providers, and organizations involved with individuals over 60 years of age.

"Promoting Nutrition Through Education: A Resource Guide to the Nutrition Education and Training Program (NET)." 1985. $7.50. S/N 001-000-04436-2.

Includes information on 445 of the resources

developed under NET and a section on literature selected from articles, books, and private industry publications about the NET program. Each resource entry provides an abstract, descriptors, title, author, source, format, and FNIC shelf number. Order from: Superintendent of Documents, U.S. Government Printing Office, Washington, DC 20402.

"Pathfinder Topics." 1985. 1p. free.

Describes consumer, educator, and professional user levels. Lists pathfinders such as *Sports Nutrition* and *Anorexia Nervosa and Bulimia*. Pathfinders were designed to give guidance during the initial stages of information searches. Resources include print and audiovisual materials as well as contacts for assistance.

"Publications List." Current. 2p. free.

Lists series number, title, number of pages, date or revised publication, stock number, price. Ordering information. Publications (except one available from Consumer Information Center) are available from the Superintendent of Documents. Publications are grouped: *for consumers; for research workers, teachers, and leaders;* and *reports from nationwide food consumption surveys.*

Serials, Subscription Publications, etc.

Food and Nutrition Quarterly Index. Quarterly. 208p. $95.00/yr. plus postage and handling.

Contains indexes and abstracts of print and nonprint materials in food, human nutrition, and food service management acquired by the USDA's Food and Nutrition Information Center. Covers materials from children's materials through professional information. Order from: Oryx Press, 2214 N. Central at Encanto, Phoenix, AZ 85004-1483. 1-800-457-ORYX.

Selected List of Books and Pamphlets

Directory of Food and Nutrition Information Services and Resources. 1984. 296p. $74.50 plus postage and handling. ISBN 0-89774-078-5.

Provides a key to databases, microcomputer software, periodicals, indexes, organizations and other appropriate sources of food and nutrition information. Four indexes: by subject, by geographic location, by type of organization, and by approved American Dietetic Association training programs. Order from: Oryx Press, 2214 N. Central at Encanto, Phoenix, AZ 85004-1483. 1-800-457-ORYX.

"Food and Nutrition Information Center." 4p. free.

Gives information on what the center is, its collections, services provided, and lending policy.

Audiovisuals:

Filmographies, Sales Lists, etc.

Audiovisual Resources in Food and Nutrition, Vol. 2. 1984. 134p. $42.50 plus postage and handling. ISBN 0-89774-105-6.

Lists currently available audiovisual materials compiled by the U.S. Department of Agriculture's Food and Nutrition Information Center for the National Agricultural Library's AGRICOLA database. Includes motion pictures, film strips, slides, transparencies, records and audiotapes, kits and models, and charts and posters. From children's materials through professional information. Order from: Oryx Press, 2214 N. Central at Encanto, Phoenix, AZ 85004-1483. 1-800-457-ORYX.

Special Services: The Food and Nutrition Information Center functions as a demonstration center for nutrition software programs. Use of the software/hardware is by appointment, Monday through Friday, 8:00 A.M. to 4:30 P.M. A list of current holdings is available.

FOOD AND NUTRITION SERVICE
U.S. Department of Agriculture
Public Information Staff
3101 Park Center Dr.
Alexandria, VA 22302
(703) 756-3276

Date Established: 1969

Objectives of the Agency: Make food assistance available to those in need in cooperation with state and local governments.

Curriculum: Health, home economics

Subjects: Nutrition

Locations:

Northeast Region
U.S. Department of Agriculture
Food and Nutrition Service
33 North Avenue
Burlington, MA 08103

Southeast Region
U.S. Department of Agriculture
Food and Nutrition Service
1100 Spring St., N.W.
Atlanta, GA 30367

Southwest Region
U.S. Department of Agriculture
Food and Nutrition Service
1100 Commerce St.
Room 55-D-22
Dallas, TX 75242

Western Region
U.S. Department of Agriculture
Food and Nutrition Service
550 Kearny St.
San Francisco, CA 94108

Mid-Atlantic Region
U.S. Department of Agriculture
Food and Nutrition Service
Mercer Corporate Park
Corporate Boulevard CN 02150
Trenton, NJ 08650

Midwest Region
U.S. Department of Agriculture
Food and Nutrition Service
50 E. Washington St.
Chicago, IL 60602

Mountain Plains Region
U.S. Department of Agriculture
Food and Nutrition Service
2420 W. Twenty-Sixth Ave.
Suite 415-D
Denver, CO 80211

Publications: Pamphlets. Bibliographies. Publications List. Periodicals. Curriculum materials.

Bibliographies, Sales Catalogs, Publications Lists, etc.

"Nutrition and Fitness Materials." n.d. 15p. free.
Lists what is available from various state NET programs. Materials cited emphasize nutrition, exercise, and fitness. Print and audiovisual teaching aids for sale and free. Includes grade levels.

"Publications." Current. 9p. free.
Tells what is available and where to obtain publications.

"Publications List." Current. 2p. free.
Lists available items to be ordered from: the Superintendent of Documents, U.S. Government Printing Office, Washington, DC 20502.

Serials, Subscription Publications, etc.

"Food and Nutrition." Quarterly. 20p. $11.00/yr. domestic, $13.75/yr. foreign.
Prints articles on family food assistance and child nutrition programs administered by USDA's Food and Nutrition Service.

Selected List of Books and Pamphlets

"Building a Better Diet." 1979. 16p. free. Program Aid No. 1241.
Describes four food groups and how they help us maintain health. Color photographs.

"Eating for Better Health." 1981. 28p. free.
Gives breakfast, lunch, dinner, and snack recipes that are low-calorie, inexpensive, and easy to prepare.

"Food and Nutrition Information and Educational Materials Center." 1973. 4p. free.
Describes the center, its services, and its clients.

"The Nation's Largest Industry." 1983. 11p. free.
Gives information about the nation's agriculture and its impacts here and abroad.

"Nutrition Education for Preschoolers." 1983. 47p. free. FNS-241.
Provides a resource guide for use in the Child Care Food Program. Includes lesson plans, audiovisuals, and descriptions of nutrition education programs. Programs free loan or for purchase. Some materials are available in Spanish, Laotian, Vietnamese, and other languages.

"The Safe Food Book: Your Kitchen Guide." 1984. 32p. Home & Garden Bulletin No. 241.
Describes how food spoils, the kinds of food poisoners, and what to do when your freezer fails. Gives sources of more information.

"Sodium: Think about It. . . ." 1982. 8p. free. HHS Publication No. (FDA) 82-2164.
Tells where sodium is found, what the health considerations are, and how to use less.

"U.S. Department of Agriculture's Food Distribution Program." 1981. 12p. free. Program Aid No. 1291.
Tells what the program is, who benefits, and what types of food are available.

Special Services: Check with regional office serving each state for publications. The midwest region, for example, has a list of leaders in *Nutritional Education Training* for each midwest state along with other regional information.

FOREIGN AGRICULTURAL SERVICE
United States Department of Agriculture
AIMS
Room 4645 So. Bldg.
Washington, DC 20250
(202) 447-7103

Date Established: 1953

Objectives of the Agency: Stimulate overseas markets for U.S. agricultural products.

Curriculum: Agriculture

Subjects: Farm produce—marketing

Publications: Packet. Flyers. Bulletins. Notices. Profiles. Lists. Briefs.

Bibliographies, Sales Catalogs, Publications Lists, etc.

"Buyer Alert Program Flyer." 1985. 1p. free.
Explains what this service does as it links buyer and seller through an international trade network.

108 / Foreign Agricultural Service

"Executive Export Service Flyer." 1985. 1p. free.
Tells what three annual subscriptions are included in this service and what they each offer.

"Foreign Importer Listings Flyer." 1985. 1p. free.
Tells what the listings are and an example of how one might be used.

"International Marketing Profiles Flyer." 1985. 1p. free.
Explains what the profiles do: examine market performance of specific agricultural products or the agricultural trade activity in particular countries. Custom marketing profiles also can be produced.

"Product Publicity—Contacts Flyer." 1985. 1p. free.
Tells what the monthly newsletter does. Includes a sample listing of an entry.

"Trade Leads Flyer." 1985. 1p. free.
Describes a worldwide trade network that brings information on overseas sales opportunities.

"Trade Leads Order Booklet." 1985. 12p. free.
Gives ordering instructions and commodity code list. Grouped by such commodities as: oilseeds, tree nuts, grains, wines, and canned fruits.

"The USDA/FAS Agricultural Information and Marketing Services (AIMS) Packet." Current. 7p. free.
Gives information, price, and order forms for: trade leads service, export briefs, executive export service, product marketing profiles, country marketing profiles, AIMS foreign importer listing request, AIMS international marketing profile request, AIMS buyer alert notice, and contacts.

Selected List of Books and Pamphlets

"Agricultural Information and Marketing Service." n.d. 1p. free.
Tells what the service is and what it has to offer.

FOREIGN CLAIMS SETTLEMENT COMMISSION OF THE UNITED STATES
U.S. Department of Justice
1111 Twentieth St., NW
Washington, DC 20579
(202) 653-5883

Date Established: 1954

Objectives of the Agency: Determine claims of U.S. nationals for loss of property in specific foreign countries as a result of nationalization of property because of military operations during World War II and the claims of U.S. military personnel and civilians who have been held in a captured status during World War II and the Korean and Vietnam conflicts.

Curriculum: Current issues

Subjects: War

Publications: Reports of commission activities.

Selected List of Books and Pamphlets

"Foreign Claims Settlement Commission of the United States Annual Report." Current. 60p. free.
Covers the activities of the commission during the past year. Includes summary of past programs, future programs, claims under the War Claims Act of 1948, International Claims Settlement Act of 1949, and others. Tables. List of commissioner's terms.

FOREST SERVICE
Department of Agriculture
Information Office
P.O. Box 2417
Twelfth St. and Independence Ave., SW
Washington, DC 20013
(202) 447-3760

Date Established: 1905

Objectives of the Agency: Provide national leadership in the management, protection, and use of the nation's forests and rangelands; be dedicated to multiple-use land management of water, forage, wildlife, wood, and recreation.

Curriculum: Environmental studies, geography

Subjects: Environment
Forests and forestry—U.S.

Locations:

Forest Service, USDA
Northern Region Field Office
Federal Bldg.
P.O. Box 7669
Missoula, MT 59807

Forest Service, USDA
Rocky Mountain Region Field Office
11177 W. Eighth Ave.
P.O. Box 25127
Lakewood, CO 80225

Forest Service, USDA
Southwestern Region Field Office
517 Gold Ave., SW
Albuquerque, NM 87102

Forest Service, USDA
Intermountain Region Field Office
324 Twenty-Fifth St.
Ogden, UT 84401

Forest Service, USDA
Pacific Southwest Region Field Office
630 Sansome St.
San Francisco, CA 94111

Forest Service, USDA
Pacific Northwest Region Field Office
319 S.W. Pine St.
P.O. Box 3623
Portland, OR 97208

Forest Service, USDA
Southern Region Field Office
1720 Peachtree Rd., NW
Atlanta, GA 30367

Forest Service, USDA
Eastern Region Field Office
310 W. Wisconsin Ave.
Milwaukee, WI 53203

Forest Service, USDA
Alaska Region Field Office
Federal Office Bldg.
P.O. Box 1628
Juneau, AK 99802

Publications: Curriculum materials. Bibliographies. Pamphlets. Catalogs.

Bibliographies, Sales Catalogs, Publications Lists, etc.

"Trees, Forest Products, and Forest Management." 1984. 12p. free. SB-086.
   Provides subject bibliography of materials available. From the Superintendent of Documents. Gives title, date, annotation, stock number, and other information. Order from: Superintendent of Documents, U.S. Government Printing Office, Washington, DC 20402.

Selected List of Books and Pamphlets

Investigating Your Environment: Teaching Materials for Environmental Education." 1980. kit. free. FS-349.
   Provides lesson plans such as: *Forest Investigation, Animals and Their Environment, Land Use,* and *Water Investigation*. Includes tasks and topics designed to be adaptable to teacher's objectives and time constraints.

"What the Forest Service Does." Rev. 1983. 35p. free. FS-20.
   Gives responsibilities, history, and management of the Forest Service. Maps.

"Woodsy Owl's Campaign Catalog." Current. 18p. free.
   Lists balloons, pencils, posters, stickers, rulers, bookmarks, and other items for sale.

Audiovisuals:

Filmographies, Sales Lists, etc.

"Forest Service Audiovisual Aids." 1981. 32p. free.
   Lists addresses of free loan audiovisuals. Includes annotations with suggested audience. Slides. Subject and title indexes. Request catalog from your regional field office.

FREDERICK DOUGLASS HOME
National Park Service
1411 W St., SE
Washington, DC 20020
(202) 426-5961
(202) 472-9227

Date Established: 1962

Objectives of the Agency: Commemorate Douglass' leadership for oppressed black and white people and women's rights.

Curriculum: History, minority studies

Subjects: Slavery in the United States

Publications: Flyers. Bibliographies.

Bibliographies, Sales Catalogs, Publications Lists, etc.

"Reading about Frederick Douglass, a Selection." n.d. 1p. free.
   Provides materials grouped according to his own works, books about him, and books for children. Includes the author, title, place of publication, and date. Includes recommended grades if the book is for children. Books should be found in local libraries.

Selected List of Books and Pamphlets

"Frederick Douglass Home." 1984. 4-fold. free.
   Chronicles Douglass's life and his home. Photographs.

Audiovisuals:

Filmographies, Sales Lists, etc.

"Order Form for *American Chronicle*." n.d. 1p. free.
   Available in 16mm for purchase, preview, or rental and in videocassette for purchase. Order from: The National Audiovisual Center
Customer Services Section EB
8700 Edgeworth Dr.
Capitol Heights, MD 20743-3701
(301) 763-1896
Credit card orders only: (800) 638-1300

GENERAL ACCOUNTING OFFICE DOCUMENT HANDLING AND INFORMATION SERVICES FACILITY
P.O. Box 6015
Gaithersburg, MD 20760
(202) 275-6241

Date Established: 1921

110 / General Accounting Office

Objectives of the Agency: Help Congress carry out legislative and administrative responsibilities; carry out legal, accounting, auditing, and claims settlement duties; and make recommendations designed to provide for better government operations.

Curriculum: Government

Subjects: Government publications

Publications: Reports. Testimony. Decisions and opinions. Bibliographies.

Bibliographies, Sales Catalogs, Publications Lists, etc.

"General Accounting Office Publications." Semiannual. 61p. free.

Prints reports, testimony, and other material.

"Monthly List of GAO Reports." Monthly. 11p. free.

Summarizes reports in a newsletter. You may request to receive these regularly.

Selected List of Books and Pamphlets

"Additional Actions Taken To Control Marijuana Cultivation and Other Crimes on Federal Lands." 1984. 67p. free. GAO/RCED-85-18.

Prints a report to the chairman, Subcommittee on Public Lands and National Parks, Committee on Interior and Insular Affairs, House of Representatives.

"An Analysis of Issues Concerning Acid Rain." 1984. 185p. free.

Prints a report to Congress by the Comptroller General. Examines the implications of current knowledge for policy decisions and offering observations. Tables. Appendices.

"Better Federal Program Administration Can Contribute to Improving State Foster Care Programs." 1984. 80p. free. GAO/HRD-84-2.

Prints a report by the Comptroller General of recommendations dealing with the Adoption Assistance and Child Welfare Act of 1980.

"Better Monitoring and Recordkeeping Systems Needed to Accurately Account for Juvenile Justice Practices." 1984. 22p. free. GAO/GGD-84-85.

Prints a report to the chairman, Subcommittee on Human Resources, Committee on Education and Labor, House of Representatives. Testimony about state monitoring efforts and progress made under the Juvenile Justice and Delinquency Prevention Act of 1974.

"Education Block Grant Alters State Role and Provides Greater Local Discretion." 1984. 78p. free. GAO/HRD-85-18.

Prints a report to Congress by the Comptroller General. Results of the Omnibus Budget Reconciliation Act of 1981 consolidating numerous federal programs into the Education Block Grant, shifting primary administrative responsibility to states.

Federal Information Sources and Systems. 1984. 1041p. $24.00 (free to academic libraries). GAO Report No. AFMD-85-3.

Describes 2500 federal information sources and systems. Introduction and user's guide provides aid in using this report which is one in the Congressional Sourcebook series. Compiled through government-wide inventories. Includes citation and index sections.

"Further Actions Needed To Improve Emergency Preparedness Around Nuclear Powerplants." 1984. 135p. free. GAO/RCED-84-43.

Prints a report to Congress by the Comptroller General. Includes recommendations to improve preparedness for a nuclear powerplant accident and the coordination of the federal response.

"Information on Aliens Admitted into the United States as Nonmigrant Workers." 1984. 16p. free. GAO/GGD-85-27.

Prints a report to the chairman, Committee on the Judiciary, House of Representatives. Tables. Appendices.

"Regional Information Sharing Systems." 1984. 45p. free. GAO/GGD-85-17.

Prints a report to the chairman, Subcommittee on Commerce, Justice, State, and the Judiciary Committee on Appropriations, Senate. Reviews some projects of the Sharing System funded by the Department of Justice to encourage the coordination of criminal investigations across political jurisdictions.

"Status of Bonneville Power Administration's Efforts To Improve Its Oversight of Three Nuclear Power Projects." 1984. 53p. free. GAO/RCED-84-27.

Prints a report by the Comptroller General. Recommendations such as policies and defining responsibilities.

GENERAL SERVICES ADMINISTRATION
General Services Bldg.
Eighteenth and F Streets, NW
Washington, DC 20405
(202) 655-4000

Date Established: 1949

Objectives of the Agency: Establish policy and provide for the government an economical, efficient system for the management of its property and records, construction and operations of buildings, procurement and distribution of supplies, utilization and disposal of property, transportation, traffic and communications management, stockpiling of strategic materials, and management of automatic data processing resources program. Functions are carried out at the central office, the regional office, and in field activities.

Curriculum: Library

Subjects: Library science

Locations:

CT, MA, ME, NH, RI, VT

General Services Administration
Region 1 Office
John W. McCormick Post Office and Courthouse
Boston, MA 02109
(617) 223-2100

NJ, NY

General Services Administration
Region 2 Office
26 Federal Plaza
New York, NY 10278
(212) 264-3311

DC, DE, MD, PA, VA, WV

General Services Administration
Region 3 Office
Ninth and Market Sts.
Philadelphia, PA 19107
(215) 597-3311

AL, FL, GA, KY, MS, NC, TN, SC

General Services Administration
Region 4 Office
75 Spring St., SW
Atlanta, GA 30303
(404) 221-3110

IL, IN, MI, MN, OH, WI

General Services Administration
Region 5 Office
230 S. Dearborn St.
Chicago, IL 60604
(312) 353-4401

IA, KS, NE, MO

General Services Administration
Region 6 Office
1500 E. Bannister Rd.
Kansas City, MO 64131
(816) 374-3024

AR, LA, OK, NM, TX

General Services Administration
Region 7 Office
819 Taylor St.
Ft. Worth, TX 76102
(817) 334-3011

CO, MT, ND, SD, UT, WY

General Services Administration
Region 8 Office
Denver Federal Center
Denver, CO 80225
(303) 234-3131

AZ, CA, HI, NV

General Services Administration
Region 9 Office
525 Market St.
San Francisco, CA 94105
(415) 556-9000

AK, ID, OR, WA

General Services Administration
Region 10 Office
GSA Center
Auburn, WA 98002
(206) 442-4898

National Capital Region

General Services Administration
Seventh and D Sts., SW
Washington, DC 20407
(202) 655-4000

Publications: Catalogs. Directories. Leaflets. Many publications available for sale through Government Printing Office bookstores; others may be obtained free or at production cost from a federal information center. Directories for the various regions provide addresses and telephone numbers.

Bibliographies, Sales Catalogs, Publications Lists, etc.

"Consumer Information Catalog." Quarterly. 16p. free.

Consumer Information Center was established to help federal agencies promote and distribute consumer information. Includes categories like: careers & education, children, federal benefits, financial planning, food, gardening, health, housing, small business, travel & hobbies, cars, and miscellaneous. Booklets are free or for sale. When more than one free booklet is ordered, there is a $1.00 fee.

Selected List of Books and Pamphlets

"How Can GSA Help You?" n.d. 2p. free.

Tells what GSA has for business people, for consumers, for everybody.

"GSA Facts." 2p. 1985. free.

Gives scope, personnel, space, sales and related statistics, and other information.

"Library Services." Current. 16p. free.
Gives the services available and a list of new books.

"Telephone Directory." Current. pages vary. free.
Lists government agencies. Order from the region serving your state.

Library: Offers full reference services during business hours. Online search services include: ELECTRONIC MAIL, DIALOG, NEXIS/INFOBANK, WESTLAW, AUTO-CITE. General reference and loan is room 1033, ext. 535-7788. Library hours are 9:00 A.M. to 4:00 P.M., Monday-Friday.

Special Services: The "Consumer Information Catalog" can be mailed on a regular basis to educators, libraries, consumer groups, and other nonprofit groups who distribute 25 or more copies quarterly.

GOVERNMENT PRINTING OFFICE
North Capitol and H Sts., NW
Washington, DC 20401
(202) 275-2051

Date Established: 1860

Objectives of the Agency: Execute orders for printing and binding placed by Congress, departments, and establishments of the federal government; furnish blank paper, inks, and similar supplies to all governmental activities on order; prepare catalogs; and distribute and sell government publications.

Curriculum: Library

Subjects: Government publications

Locations:

AL

Government Printing Office Bookstore
Roebuck Shopping City
9220-B Parkway East
Birmingham, AL 35206
(205) 254-1056

CA

Government Printing Office Bookstore
Arco Plaza, C-Level
505 S. Flower St.
Los Angeles, CA 90071
(213) 894-5841

Government Printing Office Bookstore
Federal Bldg.
450 Golden Gate Ave.
Room 1023
San Francisco, CA 94102
(415) 556-0643

CO

Government Printing Office Bookstore
Federal Bldg.
1961 Stout St.
Room 117
Denver, CO 80294
(303) 844-3964

Government Printing Office Bookstore
World Savings Bldg.
720 N. Main St.
Pueblo, CO 81003
(303) 544-3142

DC

Government Printing Office Bookstore
U.S. Government Printing Office
710 N. Capitol St., NW
Washington, DC 20402
(202) 275-2091

Government Printing Office Bookstore
Commerce Dept.
Fourteenth and E Sts., NW
Room 1604
First Floor
Washington, DC 20230
(202) 377-3527

Government Printing Office Bookstore
Farragut West
Matomic Bldg.
1717 H St., NW
Washington, DC 20036
(202) 653-5075

Government Printing Office Bookstore
Pentagon
Main Concourse, South End
Room 2E172
Washington, DC 20310
(703) 557-1821

FL

Government Printing Office Bookstore
Federal Bldg.
400 W. Bay St.
Room 158
Jacksonville, FL 32202
(904) 791-3801

GA

Government Printing Office Bookstore
Federal Bldg.
275 Peachtree St., NE
Room 100
P.O. Box 56445
Atlanta, GA 30343
(404) 221-6947

IL

Government Printing Office Bookstore
Federal Bldg.
219 S. Dearborn St.
Room 1365
Chicago, IL 60604
(312) 353-5133

MA

Government Printing Office Bookstore
Federal Bldg.
Sudbury St.
Room G25
Boston, MA 02203
(617) 223-6071

MI

Government Printing Office Bookstore
Federal Bldg.
Suite 160
Detroit, MI 48226
(313) 226-7816

MO

Government Printing Office Bookstore
120 Bannister Mall
5600 E. Bannister Rd.
Kansas City, MO 64137
(816) 765-2256

NY

26 Federal Plaza
Room 110
New York, NY 10278
(212) 264-3825

OH

Government Printing Office Bookstore
Federal Bldg.
1240 E. Ninth St.
First Floor
Cleveland, OH 44199
(216) 522-4922

Government Printing Office Bookstore
Federal Bldg.
200 N. High St.
Room 207
Columbus, OH 43215
(614) 469-6956

PA

Government Printing Office Bookstore
Federal Bldg.
600 Arch St.
Room 1214
Philadelphia, PA 19106
(215) 597-0677

Government Printing Office Bookstore
Federal Bldg.
1000 Liberty Ave.
Room 118
Pittsburgh, PA 15222
(412) 644-2721

TX

Government Printing Office Bookstore
Federal Bldg.
1100 Commerce St.
Room IC50
Dallas, TX 75242
(214) 767-0076

Government Printing Office Bookstore
45 College Center
9319 Gulf Freeway
Houston, TX 77017
(713) 229-3515

WA

Government Printing Office Bookstore
Federal Bldg.
915 Second Ave.
Room 194
Seattle, WA 98174
(206) 442-4270

WI

Government Printing Office Bookstore
Federal Bldg.
517 E. Wisconsin Ave.
Room 190
Milwaukee, WI 53202
(414) 291-1304

Retail Sales Outlet

Government Printing Office Retail Sales Outlet
8660 Cherry Lane
Laurel, MD 20707
(301) 953-7974
(301) 792-0262

Publications: Catalogs. Pamphlets. Handbooks. Books. Bibliographies. Reports. Manuals. Yearbooks. Directories. Guides. Bulletins. Curriculum materials. Surveys. Periodicals. Transmittal letters. Maps. Posters.

Bibliographies, Sales Catalogs, Publications Lists, etc.

"Government Periodicals and Subscription Services." Rev. quarterly. 80p. free. Price List 36.

Lists all government subscriptions sold by the Government Printing Office. Partially annotated.

"New Books." Current. 20p. free.

Lists titles that were recently placed for sale

114 / Government Printing Office

grouped by subjects such as: *Agriculture, Business and Labor, Census, Computers and Computer Science,* etc. Ordering information and ordering form.

"Order Form." 1984. original, carbon, carbon copy. free.

The back of the order form includes ordering information.

"Subject Bibliography Index." Current. 8p. free. SB-599.

Lists the free bibliographies of government publications available from the Government Printing Office. Order form.

"U.S. Government Books." Current. 62p. free.

Lists publications for sale by the U.S. Government Printing Office. Organized into subject categories such as: *Agriculture, Business and Industry, Careers, Children & Families,* etc. Provides order form and ordering information. Lists government bookstores.

Serials, Subscription Publications, etc.

"American Education." Monthly. $23.00/yr. domestic, $28.75/yr. foreign.

Covers preschool to adult education, new research and demonstration projects, legislation affecting education, grants, educational trends, and other information.

Monthly Catalog of U.S. Government Publications. Monthly. $217.00/yr. domestic, $271.25/yr. foreign.

Lists all publications of the government issued during each month, whether offered for sale or not.

Occupational Outlook Quarterly. Quarterly. $11.00/yr. domestic, $13.75/yr. foreign.

Contains articles on new occupations, training opportunities, salary trends, career counseling programs, and other information.

"PRF." $142.00/yr. domestic, $177.50/yr. foreign.

A subscription service which catalogs all publications and subscriptions currently offered for sale by the Superintendent of Documents. Available only in 48X microfiche. Provides bimonthly mailings of about 350 fiche and monthly mailings of a one fiche containing new publications. Use order form found in "U.S. Government Books" described above. Available online from: Dialog Information Service, Inc., 3460 Hillview Ave., Palo Alto, CA 94304.

"Resources in Education." Monthly. $56.00/yr. domestic, $70.00/yr. foreign.

Announces recent report literature related to education to keep educators and others abreast of current research, development, implementation, and trends in education.

Selected List of Books and Pamphlets

Animal Health—Livestock and Pets: 1984 Yearbook of Agriculture. 1984. 688p. $10.00. S/N 001-000-04434-6.

A comprehensive volume of 87 chapters and 10 sections. Covers most ailments and nutrition aids for poultry, pet birds, dairy and beef cattle, sheep, goats, fish, dogs, cats, rabbits, horses, etc. Thirty-two color pages.

"Fact Sheet." n.d. 2p. free.

Tells what the GPO does: facts, statistics, and interesting sidelights of printing.

"It's No Accident": A Consumer Product Safety Education Curriculum Resource Guide for Teachers of Grades 3 through 6. 1984. 119p. $4.50. S/N 052-011-00242-0.

Provides safety information that can be taught. Looseleaf. 3-hole punch.

"Perspectives on Child Maltreatment in the Mid '80's." 1984. 70p. $2.75. S/N 017-090-00076-3.

Prints papers on the various aspects of child abuse to promote public dialogue on the problems of sexual abuse, emotional abuse, the developmentally disabled, etc.

Women in Nontraditional Careers: Curriculum Guide. 1984. 652p. $19.00. S/N 029-002-00070-3.

Helps educators increase young women's knowledge of opportunities and aid them in making career plans.

Special Services: For information on standing orders (to allow you to place an order one time and then automatically receive all subsequent editions or issuances in the same series), write:
Standing Order Specialist
Publication Order Branch
Stop SSOP, U.S. Government Printing Office
Washington, DC 20402
(202) 275-3082

HEAD START BUREAU
Administration for Children, Youth, and Families
U.S. Department of Health and Human Services
P.O. Box 1182
Washington, DC 20013
(202) 755-7782

Date Established: 1965

Objectives of the Agency: Help communities overcome the handicaps of disadvantaged preschool children.

Curriculum: Education

Subjects: Education, preschool

Locations:

CT, MA, ME, NH, RI, VT

Administration for Children, Youth and Families
OHDS/DH & HS
Federal Bldg.
Government Center
Room 2000
Boston, MA 02203
(617) 233-6450

NJ, NY, PR, VI

Administration for Children, Youth and Families
OHDS/DH & HS
Federal Bldg.
26 Federal Plaza
Room 3900
New York, NY 10007
(212) 264-2974

DC, DE, MD, PA, VA, WV

Administration for Children, Youth and Families
OHDS/DH & HS
3535 Market St.
P.O. Box 13716
Philadelphia, PA 19101
(215) 596-6763

AL, FL, GA, KY, MS, NC, SC, TN

Administration for Children, Youth and Families
OHDS/DH & HS
Seventh Bldg.
50 Seventh St., NE
Room 358 Peachtree
Atlanta, GA 30323
(404) 221-2134

IL, IN, MI, MN, OH, WI

Administration for Children, Youth and Families
OHDS/DH & HS
300 S. Wacker Dr.
Fifteenth Floor
Chicago, IL 60606
(312) 353-1781

AR, LA, NM, OK, TX

Administration for Children, Youth and Families
OHDS/DH & HS
1200 Main Tower Bldg.
Twentieth Floor
Dallas, TX 75202
(214) 767-2976

IA, KS, MO, NE

Administration for Children, Youth and Families
OHDS/DH & HS
Federal Bldg.
601 E. Twelfth St.
Third Floor
Kansas City, MO 64106
(816) 374-5401

CO, MT, ND, SD, UT, WY

Administration for Children, Youth and Families
OHDS/DH & HS
1961 Stout St.
Room 7417
Denver, CO 80202

AZ, CA, HI, NV, Pacific Trust Territories

Administration for Children, Youth & Families
OHDS/DH & HS
Federal Bldg.
50 United Nations Plaza
Room 143
San Francisco, CA 94102
(415) 556-6153

AK, ID, OR, WA

Administration for Children, Youth and Families
OHDS/DH & HS
Third and Broad Bldg.
2901 Third Ave.
Seattle, WA 98121
(206) 442-0838

Indian and Migrant Programs

Head Start Bureau, SCYF
Department of Health and Human Services
Donohoe Bldg.
P.O. Box 1182
Room 5851
Washington, DC 20013
(202) 755-7715

Publications: Pamphlets. Fact sheets.

Selected List of Books and Pamphlets

"Head Start." 1983. 13p. free.
Tells what it is and how it works.

"Project Head Start Statistical Fact Sheet." Current. 4p. free.
Gives budget, enrollment, and other facts.

HEALTH RESOURCE CENTER
1 Dupont Circle, NW
Suite 670
Washington, DC 20036
(800) 544-3284
Washington, DC, area: (202) 939-9320

Date Established: 1918 (American Council on Education)

Objectives of the Agency: Operate the national clearinghouse on postsecondary education for handicapped individuals; and serve as an information exchange about educational support services, policies, procedures, adaptations, and opportunities.

Curriculum: Special education

Subjects: Handicapped

116 / *Health Resource Center*

Locations:

CT, MA, ME, NH, RI, VT

Regional Technical Assistance Staff
U.S. Department of Education
Region 1 Office for Civil Rights
John W. McCormack Post Office &
　Courthouse Bldg.
Room 222
Boston, MA 02109
(617) 223-5106

NJ, NY, PR, VI

Regional Technical Assistance Staff
U.S. Department of Education
Region 2 Office for Civil Rights
26 Federal Plaza
Room 33-130
New York, NY 10278
(212) 264-2906

DC, DE, MD, PA, VA, WV

Regional Technical Assistance Branch—
　Postsecondary Division
U.S. Department of Education
Region 3 Office for Civil Rights
Gateway Bldg.
Sixth Floor
3535 Market St.
Philadelphia, PA 19104
(215) 596-6091
(215) 596-6093
(215) 596-4231
(215) 596-6770

AL, FL, GA, KY, MS, NC, SC, TN

Regional Technical Assistance Staff
U.S. Department of Education
Region 4 Office of Civil Rights
101 Marietta Tower
Twenty-Seventh Floor
Atlanta, GA 30323
(404) 221-2806

IL, IN, MI, MN, OH, WI

Regional Technical Assistance Staff
U.S. Department of Education
Region 5 Office for Civil Rights
300 S. Wacker Dr.
Eighth Floor
Chicago, IL 60606
(312) 353-2520

AR, LA, NM, OK, TX

Regional Technical Assistance Staff—Postsecondary
　Division
U.S. Department of Education
Region 6 Office for Civil Rights
1200 Main Tower
Dallas, TX 75202
(214) 767-3985

IA, KS, MO, NE

Regional Technical Assistance Staff
U.S. Department of Education
Region 7 Office for Civil Rights
324 E. Eleventh St.
Twenty-Fourth Floor
Kansas City, MO 64106
(816) 374-7264

CO, MT, ND, UT, SD

Regional Technical Assistance Staff
U.S. Department of Education
Region 8 Office for Civil Rights
Federal Office Bldg.
1961 Stout St.
Third Floor
Denver, CO 80294
(303) 844-2991

AZ, CA, HI, NV, GU, Trust Territory of Pacific Islands, AS

Regional Technical Assistance Staff
U.S. Department of Education
Region 9 Office for Civil Rights
221 Main St.
Tenth Floor
San Francisco, CA 94105
(415) 227-8111

AK, ID, OR, WA

Regional Technical Assistance Staff
U.S. Department of Education
Region 10 Office for Civil Rights
2901 Third Ave.
MS 106
Seattle, WA 98121
(206) 442-1930

Publications: Directory. Bulletins. Fact sheets. Packets of materials.

Selected List of Books and Pamphlets

"Health Resource Center." n.d. 4-fold. free.
　Explains what the center is, who can use it, what is available, and how the center can be used. Includes list of free material.

"Resource Director." Current. 25p. free.
　Examines such subjects as architectural and program accessibility, legal resources, career preparation, directories. Provides addresses of sources that can answer questions and supply materials for helping the handicapped. Lists toll-free telephone numbers. Designed to help program administrators, instructors, counselors, vocational rehabilitation personnel, secondary teachers and counselors, service providers, and handicapped students and their parents.

Audiovisuals:

Filmographies, Sales Lists, etc.

"Audiovisual Materials." n.d. 5p. free.

Describes things to look for in media presentations on disability, selected audiovisual material resources. Lists films, with annotations, used at a national conference.

HEALTH RESOURCES AND SERVICES ADMINISTRATION
U.S. Department of Health and Human Services
Public Health Service
5600 Fishers Lane
Room 14-43
Rockville, MD 20857
(202) 443-2086

Date Established: 1982

Objectives of the Agency: Provide services for American Indians, Alaska Natives, and others; support states and communities in their efforts to help in providing health care; improve the nation's health personnel; administer the organ transplant program; provide technical help in modernizing or replacing health care facilities; improve use of health resources; and support efforts to integrate health services delivery programs with public and private health financing programs.

Curriculum: Health

Subjects: Health education

Publications: Catalogs. Pamphlets.

Bibliographies, Sales Catalogs, Publications Lists, etc.

"Current Publications." 1985. 24p. free.

Lists publications available from the Health Resources and Services Administration. Gives addresses where they may be obtained and price.

Selected List of Books and Pamphlets

"HRSA." 1985. 12p. free.

Explains the functions and formation of the Health Resources and Services Administration and its four bureaus: Bureau of Health Care Delivery and Assistance, Bureau of Health Maintenance Organizations and Resources Development, Bureau of Health Professions, and Indian Health Service. Organization charts.

HEMINGWAY MUSEUM
907 Whitehead St.
Key West, FL 33040
(813) 294-1575

Date Established: 1964

Curriculum: English

Subjects: American literature

Publications: Flyers.

Selected List of Books and Pamphlets

"Ernest Hemingway Home & Museum." n.d. 2p. free.

Explains how the home was granted National Historic Landmark status, the tour hours, and biographical highlights of Hemingway's life such as the books he wrote in Key West.

HIGH BLOOD PRESSURE INFORMATION CENTER
120/80 National Institutes of Health
Bethesda, MD 20205
(301) 496-1809

Date Established: 1972

Objectives of the Agency: Increase public and professional awareness about high blood pressure to reduce high blood pressure-related deaths and disability through improved detection and treatment efforts.

Curriculum: Health

Subjects: Blood pressure

Publications: Pamphlets. Catalogs. Posters. Reports. Handbooks. Newsletters. Article reprints. Books.

Bibliographies, Sales Catalogs, Publications Lists, etc.

"Behavioral Approaches to the Treatment of Hypertension: A Bibliography." Rev. 1980. 67p. free.

Includes sections on: *General References, Biofeedback, Relaxation, Psychotherapy, Environmental Modification, Placebo, Sleep, Exercise, Acupuncture, Etiological Mechanisms.* Appendix arranges materials by European regions.

"National High Blood Pressure Education Program Order Form." Current. 4p. free.

Lists free materials for patients and consumers. Includes posters, program planning resources, pamphlets, journal reprints, bibliographies, and other formats.

Printed Aids for High Blood Pressure Education. 1985. 124p. free. NIH Publication No. 85-1244.

Arranges for-sale and free materials alphabetically by title. Includes appendices on computer software for health education and assessment forms and worksheets. Lists by: producer, publication date, reproduction restrictions, format, content description, availability, readability rating, professional evaluation, and overall rating for each entry. Author, producer, distribution index.

Selected List of Books and Pamphlets

"High Blood Pressure & What You Can Do about It." Rev. 1985. 32p. free.

Explains the symptoms of hypertension, the definition of blood pressure, myths and facts about high blood pressure, causes of hypertension, and treatment.

"Questions about Weight, Salt, and High Blood Pressure." 1984. 12p. free. NIH Publication No. 84-1459.

Explains what high blood pressure is and the effects of weight and diet on it.

"What You Should Know about the National Program To Control High Blood Pressure." Rev. 1979. 8p. free. NIH Publication No. 80-632.

Examines the functions, supporting services, community organizations, and target groups of the program.

Audiovisuals:

Filmographies, Sales Lists, etc.

Audiovisual Aids for High Blood Pressure Education. 1979. 196p. free. NIH Publication No. 80-1663.

Lists audiocassettes, tapes, films, and filmstrips pertaining to high blood pressure, according to *public education, patient education,* and *professional education*. Includes title, producer, date produced, content, format, recommended audience, ordering information such as source, order number, cost, and availability for each entry. Lists entries alphabetically by title, by format, and by producer in appendices.

Special Services: Serves as a central national clearinghouse for information. Assists in locating sources of educational materials and audiovisual aids.

HUD USER
P.O. Box 280
Germantown, MD 20874
(301) 251-5154

Date Established: 1978

Objectives of the Agency: Provide programs of research, testing and demonstrations related to housing and community developments; be an information service operated by Aspen Systems for the office of the Assistant Secretary for Policy Development and Research, Department of Housing and Urban Development.

Curriculum: Industrial arts, social studies

Subjects: Housing

Locations:

Department of Housing and Urban Development
Region 1 Office
John F. Kennedy Federal Bldg.
Boston, MA 02203
(617) 223-4066

Department of Housing and Urban Development
Region 2 Office
26 Federal Plaza
New York, NY 10278
(212) 264-8068

Department of Housing and Urban Development
Region 3 Office
Sixth and Walnut Sts.
Philadelphia, PA 19106
(215) 597-2560

Department of Housing and Urban Development
Region 4 Office
75 Spring St., SW
Atlanta, GA 30303
(404) 221-5136

Department of Housing and Urban Development
Region 5 Office
300 S. Wacker Dr.
Chicago, IL 60606
(312) 353-5680

Department of Housing and Urban Development
Region 6 Office
221 W. Lancaster Ave.
Fort Worth, TX 76113
(817) 870-5431

Department of Housing and Urban Development
Region 7 Office
1103 Grand St.
Kansas City, MO 64106
(816) 374-2651

Department of Housing and Urban Development
Region 8 Office
1405 Curtis St.
Denver, Co 80202
(303) 837-4513

Department of Housing and Urban Development
Region 9 Office
450 Golden Gate Ave.
San Francisco, CA 94102
(415) 556-4752

Department of Housing and Urban Development
Region 10 Office
1321 Second Ave.
Seattle, WA 98101
(206) 442-5414

Publications: Catalogs. Case studies. Guidelines. Reports. Guides. Bibliographies. Kits.

Bibliographies, Sales Catalogs, Publications Lists, etc.

"HUD User Publications List and Order Form." n.d. 10p. free.

Groups publications into: *Individual Documents, Housing Rehabilitation, Community Development, Energy Efficiency, Neighborhood and City Development, Urban Planning, Housing Programs, Rental Housing, Fair Housing, Resource Guides, General, Special Kits,* and *Packages*. Order form.

Selected List of Books and Pamphlets

"HUD User: A Guide to Research Information Services." n.d. 4-fold. free.

Tells what types of services HUD User has to offer. Lists a sampling of subjects about which HUD User has current research information.

Special Services: Custom searches of the HUD User database are available for $50.00; standard searches for $10.00. A list of standard searches is available.

Photocopies of unpublished reports and out-of-print materials are available. Inquire about the charge per page.

Inquire about the mailing list and announcement bulletins.

HUMAN NUTRITION INFORMATION SERVICE
Department of Agriculture
Federal Bldg.
Hyattsville, MD 20782
(301) 436-8617
(301) 436-8474

Date Established: 1981

Objectives of the Agency: Do research in human nutrition to improve understanding of the nutritional adequacy of diets and food supplies as well as the nutritive value of food; and collect and disseminate technical, educational, and nonprint material and information on food use and food management.

Curriculum: Health, home economics

Subjects: Food
Nutrition

Publications: Pamphlets. Guides. Reports. General and technical health materials.

Bibliographies, Sales Catalogs, Publications Lists, etc.

"Machine-Readable Data Sets on Composition of Foods and Results from Food Consumption Surveys." 1985. 23p. free. Administrative Report No. 378.

Tells what is available in machine-readable form and how to obtain the data. Most of the data sets are available on 9-track, 1,600 or 6,250 BPI in EBCDIC or ASCII format. Some are available on 5¼-inch floppy disks.

"Publications List." Current. 3p. free.

Tells what is available from the Superintendent of Documents.

Selected List of Books and Pamphlets

Composition of Foods: Breakfast Cereals, Raw, Processed, Prepared. Rev. 1982. 160p. free.

Contains the detailed nutrient profile of one food item on each page of the looseleaf book.

"Composition of Foods: Sausages and Luncheon Meats, Raw, Processed, Prepared." Rev. 1980. 92p. free. Agriculture Handbook No. 8-7.

Contains a detailed nutrient profile of one food item on each page of the looseleaf handbook.

"Directory Human Nutrition Activities." Current. 21p. free.

Details the activities, research, and programs of various agencies such as the Agricultural Research Service. Prepared by the Subcommittee for Human Nutrition, Committee of Research and Education of the Secretary of Agriculture's Policy and Coordination Council.

"Human Nutrition Information Service." 1984. 2p. free.

Lists responsibilities, programs, organization, topics of current interest, and publications.

"Your Money's Worth in Foods." Rev. regularly. 39p. free. Home and Garden Bulletin No. 1830.

Explains meal planning and food shopping information to make food dollars count for good nutrition. Cost comparison tables. Bases information on research by the Human Nutrition Information Service.

IMMIGRATION AND NATURALIZATION SERVICE
Office of Information
Department of Justice
425 I St., NW
Washington, DC 20536
(202) 633-4316

Date Established: 1891

Objectives of the Agency: Administer immigration and naturalization laws relating to the admission, exclusion, deportation and naturalization of aliens; protect national borders against unlawful entry; helps stem the inflow of illegal drugs; and provide information to those seeking U.S. citizenship.

Curriculum: Government

Subjects: Citizenship

Locations:

CT, DE, MA, ME, MD, NH, NJ, NY, PA, PR, RI, VA, VT, WV

U.S. Immigration and Naturalization Service
Regional Office
Federal Bldg.
Burlington, VT 05401

AK, CO, IA, ID, IL, IN, KS, MI, MN, MO, MT, NE, ND, OH, OR, SD, UT, WA, WI, WY

U.S. Immigration and Naturalization Service
Regional Office
Federal Bldg.
Fort Snelling
Twin Cities, MN 55111

AL, AR, FL, GA, KY, LA, MS, NC, NM, OK, SC, TN, TX

U.S. Immigration and Naturalization Service
Regional Office
311 N. Stemmons Freeway
Dallas, TX 75207

AZ, CA, HI, NV

U.S. Immigration and Naturalization Service
Regional Office
Terminal Island
San Pedro, CA 90731

Domestic and Foreign Offices
(Arranged alphabetically by city)

U.S. Immigration and Naturalization Service
801 Pacific News Bldg.
238 O'Hara St.
Agana, GU 96910

U.S. Immigration and Naturalization Service
U.S. Post Office and Courthouse
445 Broadway
Room 220
Albany, NY 12207

U.S. Immigration and Naturalization Service
Federal Bldg.
U.S. Courthouse
701 C St.
Room D-229, Lock Box 16
Anchorage, AK 99513

U.S. Immigration and Naturalization Service
Athens, Greece
C/O American Embassy
APO New York, NY 09253

U.S. Immigration and Naturalization Service
Richard B. Russell Federal Office Bldg.
75 Spring St., SW
Room 1408
Atlanta, GA 30303

U.S. Immigration and Naturalization Service
E.A. Garmatz Federal Bldg.
101 W. Lombard St.
Baltimore, MD 21201

U.S. Immigration and Naturalization Service
John Fitzgerald Kennedy Federal Bldg.
Government Center
Boston, MA 02203

U.S. Immigration and Naturalization Service
68 Court St.
Buffalo, NY 14202

U.S. Immigration and Naturalization Service
1111 Hawthorne Lane
Charlotte, NC 28205

U.S. Immigration and Naturalization Service
Dirksen Federal Office Bldg.
219 S. Dearborn St.
Chicago, IL 60604

U.S. Immigration and Naturalization Service
U.S. Post Office and Courthouse
Fifth and Walnut Sts.
P.O. Box 537
Cincinnati, OH 45201

U.S. Immigration and Naturalization Service
Anthony J. Cebrezze Federal Office Bldg.
1240 E. Ninth St.
Room 1917
Cleveland, OH 44199

U.S. Immigration and Naturalization Service
Federal Bldg.
1100 Commerce St.
Room 6A21
Dallas, TX 75242

U.S. Immigration and Naturalization Service
1787 Federal Office Bldg.
1961 Stout St.
Denver, Co 80202

U.S. Immigration and Naturalization Service
Federal Bldg.
333 Mount Elliott St.
Detroit, MI 48207

U.S. Immigration and Naturalization Service
343 U.S. Courthouse
P.O. Box 9398
El Paso, TX 79984

U.S. Immigration and Naturalization Service
Frankfurt, Germany
C/O American Consulate General
APO NY 09757

U.S. Immigration and Naturalization Service
104 Federal Bldg.
507 State St.
Hammond, IN 46320

U.S. Immigration and Naturalization Service
2102 Teege Rd.
Harlingen, TX 78550

U.S. Immigration and Naturalization Service
Ribicoff Federal Bldg.
450 Main St.
Hartford, CT 06103-3060

U.S. Immigration and Naturalization Service
Federal Bldg.
301 S. Park
Room 512
Helena, MT 59601

U.S. Immigration and Naturalization Service
Hong Kong, British Crown Colony
C/O American Consulate General
Box 30
FPO San Francisco, CA 96659

U.S. Immigration and Naturalization Service
595 Ala Moana Blvd.
P.O. Box 461
Honolulu, HI 96809

U.S. Immigration and Naturalization Service
2627 Caroline St.
Houston, TX 77208

U.S. Immigration and Naturalization Service
324 E. Eleventh St.
Suite 1100
Kansas City, MO 64106

U.S. Immigration and Naturalization Service
Federal Bldg.
U.S. Courthouse
300 Las Vegas Blvd. South
Las Vegas, NV 89101

U.S. Immigration and Naturalization Service
300 N. Los Angeles St.
Los Angeles, CA 90012

U.S. Immigration and Naturalization Service
U.S. Courthouse Bldg.
W. Sixth and Broadway
Room 601
Louisville, KY 40202

U.S. Immigration and Naturalization Service
Manila, Philippine Islands
C/O American Embassy
1201 Roxas Blvd.
APO San Francisco, CA 96528

U.S. Immigration and Naturalization Service
814 Federal Bldg.
167 N. Main St.
Memphis, TN 38103

U.S. Immigration and Naturalization Service
Mexico City, Mexico
C/O American Embassy
Aparato Postal 88 BIS
Mexico, 5
D.F.

U.S. Immigration and Naturalization Service
155 S. Miami Ave.
Miami, FL 33130

U.S. Immigration and Naturalization Service
Federal Bldg.
517 E. Wisconsin Ave.
Room 186
Milwaukee, WI 53202

U.S. Immigration and Naturalization Service
Naples, Italy
C/O American Consulate General
Box 18
FPO New York, NY 09521

U.S. Immigration and Naturalization Service
Federal Bldg.
970 Broad St.
Newark, NJ 07102

U.S. Immigration and Naturalization Service
Postal Services Bldg.
701 Loyola Ave.
Room T-8005
New Orleans, LA 70113

U.S. Immigration and Naturalization Service
26 Federal Plaza
New York, NY 10007

U.S. Immigration and Naturalization Service
Norfolk Federal Bldg.
200 Granby Mall
Room 439
Norfolk, VA 23510

U.S. Immigration and Naturalization Service
Federal Bldg. and U.S. Courthouse
200 N.W. Fourth St.
Room 4423
Oklahoma City, OK 73102

U.S. Immigration and Naturalization Service
Federal Bldg.
106 S. Fifteenth St.
Room 1008
Omaha, NE 68102

U.S. Immigration and Naturalization Service
Palermo, Italy
C/O American Embassy
APO New York, NY 09794

U.S. Immigration and Naturalization Service
U.S. Courthouse Independence Mall West
601 Market St.
Room 1321
Philadelphia, PA 19106

U.S. Immigration and Naturalization Service
Federal Bldg.
230 N. First Ave.
Phoenix, AZ 85025

U.S. Immigration and Naturalization Service
2130 Federal Bldg.
1000 Liberty Ave.
Pittsburgh, PA 15222

U.S. Immigration and Naturalization Service
76 Pearl St.
Portland, ME 04112

U.S. Immigration and Naturalization Service
Federal Office Bldg.
511 N.W. Broadway
Portland, OR 97209

U.S. Immigration and Naturalization Service
Federal Bldg.
U.S. Post Office
Exchange Terrace
Providence, RI 02903

U.S. Immigration and Naturalization Service
350 S. Center St.
Suite 150
Reno, NV 89502

U.S. Immigration and Naturalization Service
Rome, Italy
C/O American Embassy
APO New York, NY 09794

U.S. Immigration and Naturalization Service
Federal Bldg.
P.O. Box 328
St. Albans, VT 05478

U.S. Immigration and Naturalization Service
210 N. Tucker Blvd.
Room 100
St. Louis, MO 63101

U.S. Immigration and Naturalization Service
932 New Post Office Bldg.
180 E. Kellogg Blvd.
St. Paul, MN 55101

U.S. Immigration and Naturalization Service
230 West, 400 South St.
Salt Lake City, UT 84101

U.S. Immigration and Naturalization Service
U.S. Federal Bldg.
727 E. Durango
Suite A301
San Antonio, TX 78206

U.S. Immigration and Naturalization Service
880 Front St.
San Diego, CA 92188

U.S. Immigration and Naturalization Service
Appraisers Bldg.
630 Sansome St.
San Francisco, CA 94111

U.S. Immigration and Naturalization Service
GPO Box 5068
San Juan, PR 00936

U.S. Immigration and Naturalization Service
815 Airport Way, South
Seattle, WA 98134

U.S. Immigration and Naturalization Service
Seoul, Korea
C/O American Embassy
APO San Francisco, CA 96301

U.S. Immigration and Naturalization Service
691 U.S. Courthouse Bldg.
Spokane, WA 99201

U.S. Immigration and Naturalization Service
Vienna, Austria
C/O American Embassy
1010 Vienna
Austria

U.S. Immigration and Naturalization Service
25 E St., NW
Washington, DC 20538

Publications: Fact sheets. Pamphlets. Reports. Applications. Guides. On U.S. immigration laws and naturalization procedures. Textbooks dealing with candidates for U.S. citizenship available for those in public schools.

Bibliographies, Sales Catalogs, Publications Lists, etc.

"Price List I&NS Forms and Publications." Current. 2p. free.
   Tells what is available for sale from: Superintendent of Documents, U.S. Government Printing Office, Washington, DC 20402.

"Requisition for Federal Textbooks on Citizenship." Current. 1p. free.
   Contains an order form for citizenship textbooks that are distributed free only to candidates for U.S. citizenship who are attending public school classes or classes under the supervision of the public schools. Includes books on citizenship about the constitution and government, and various home study courses.

Selected List of Books and Pamphlets

"Immigration & Naturalization Service Regional and District Areas." 1985. 2p. free.
   Identifies the areas on a map. Lists addresses on the other side.

"Information Concerning Citizenship Education To Meet Naturalization Requirements." 1983. 4p. free.
   Explains requirements and exceptions for those wishing to become citizens of the United States. Includes a list of citizenship text materials published by the Immigration and Naturalization Service.

"United States Immigration Laws." 1984. 24p. free.
   Provides information to help the problems most frequently met by aliens entering the United States.

Filmographies

"Availability of Citizenship Education Films." Current. 3p. free.
  Describes what films are available without charge. Educational organizations may show them free for citizenship educational purposes. Order from the nearest regional office.

Individual Films

"The American Flag." n.d. 14 minutes. 16mm. color. free loan.
  Dramatizes events in the history of our flag. Shows various flags and how the flag reflects the growth of the nation.

"The Jamestown Colony (1607 through 1620)." n.d. 16 minutes. 16mm. color. free loan.
  Shows the difficulties and triumphs of the early settlers in establishing the colony. Provides a representation of colonial life.

Special Services: Provides addresses of public educational institutions that have cooperated in setting up correspondence courses. Some charge a small fee for handling paper work but textbooks are free. Most states are represented.

INTERNAL REVENUE SERVICE
Department of the Treasury
1111 Constitution Ave., NW
Washington, DC 20224
(202) 566-5000

Date Established: 1862

Objectives of the Agency: Administer and enforce the internal revenue laws and statutes; encourage voluntary compliance with tax laws; advise the public of its rights and responsibilities; and collect taxes.

Curriculum: Business, consumer education

Subjects: Taxation—U.S.

Locations:

Regional Offices

IN, KY, MI, OH, WV

Internal Revenue Service Regional Office
550 Main St.
Cincinnati, OH 45202

DE, MD, NJ, PA, VA

Internal Revenue Service Regional Office
841 Chestnut St.
Philadelphia, PA 19107

IA, IL, MN, MO, ND, NE, SD, WI

Internal Revenue Service Regional Office
1 N. Wacker Dr.
Chicago, IL 60606

CT, MA, ME, NH, NY, RI, VT

Internal Revenue Service Regional Office
90 Church St.
New York, NY 10007

AL, GA, FL, MS, NC, SC, TN

Internal Revenue Service Regional Office
275 Peachtree St., NE
Atlanta, GA 30043

AR, CO, KS, LA, NM, OK, TX, WY

Internal Revenue Service Regional Office
LB-70
7839 Churchill Way
Dallas, TX 75251

AK, AZ, CA, HI, ID, MT, NV, OR, UT, WA

Internal Revenue Service Regional Office
525 Market St.
San Francisco, CA 94105

Internal Revenue District Offices

AK

Internal Revenue Service District Office
P.O. Box 1500
Anchorage, AK 99504
Anchorage: 276-1040
Elsewhere: ZENITH 3700

AL

Internal Revenue Service District Office
500 Twenty-Second St., South
Birmingham, AL 35233
(205) 254-0403
Toll free: (800) 424-1040

AR

Internal Revenue Service District Office
P.O. Box 3778
Little Rock, AR 72203
(501) 378-5685
Toll Free: (800) 424-1040

AZ

Internal Revenue Service District Office
2120 N. Central
Stop 470
Phoenix, AZ 85004
(602) 261-3861
Toll free: (800) 424-1040

CA

Internal Revenue Service District Office
Los Angeles
P.O. Box 3151
Los Angeles, CA 90053
(213) 688-4574
Toll free: (800) 424-1040

Internal Revenue Service District Office
San Francisco
450 Golden Gate Ave.
P.O. Box 36136, SF 13-6-02
San Francisco, CA 94102
(415) 556-0880
Toll free: (800) 424-1040

Internal Revenue Service District Office
Laguna Niguel
Chet Hollifield Federal Bldg.
2400 Avila Rd.
Laguna Niguel, CA 92677
(714) 831-4067
Toll free: (800) 424-1040

Internal Revenue Service District Office
Sacramento
801 One St.
SA 1607
Sacramento, CA 95814
(916) 440-2351
Toll free: (800) 424-1040

Internal Revenue Service District Office
San Jose
P.O. Box 100
San Jose, CA 95103
(408) 291-7114
Toll free: (800) 424-1040

CO

Internal Revenue Service District Office
1050 Seventeenth St.
Denver, CO 80265
(303) 825-7041
Toll free: (800) 424-1040

CT

Internal Revenue Service District Office
135 High St.
Stop 120
Hartford, CT 06103
(203) 244-3064

DC

Internal Revenue Service District Office
P.O. Box 1076
Baltimore, MD 21203
(202) 488-3100, ext. 2222

DE

Internal Revenue Service District Office
P.O. Box 28
Wilmington, DE 19899
(302) 573-6400
Toll free: (800) 424-1040

FL

Internal Revenue Service District Office
P.O. Box 35045
Stop 620.1
Jacksonville, FL 32202
(904) 791-2514
Toll free: (800) 424-1040

GA

Internal Revenue Service District Office
Federal Office Building
P.O. Box 1037
Room 512
ATTN: TPE Coordinator
Atlanta, GA 30370
(404) 221-6662
Toll free: (800) 424-1040

HI

Internal Revenue Service District Office
PJKK Federal Bldg.
300 Ala Moana Blvd.
#1002
Honolulu, HI 96850
Toll free: (800) 546-2803

IA

Internal Revenue Service District Office
P.O. Box 1337
Stop 28
Des Moines, IA 50305
(515) 284-4870
Toll free: (800) 424-1040

ID

Internal Revenue Service District Office
550 W. Fort
Box 041
Boise, ID 83724
(208) 336-1040
Toll free: (800) 424-1040

IL

Internal Revenue Service District Office
Chicago
P.O. Box 1193
Chicago, IL 60690
(312) 886-4669
Toll free: (800) 424-1040

Internal Revenue Service District Office
Springfield
P.O. Box 398
Springfield, IL 62705
(217) 492-4288
Toll free: (800) 424-1040

IN

Internal Revenue Service District Office
P.O. Box 44211
Indianapolis, IN 46244
(317) 269-6326
Toll free: (800) 424-1040

KS

Internal Revenue Service District Office
412 S. Main St.
Wichita, KS 67202
(316) 269-6112
Toll free: (800) 424-1040

KY

Internal Revenue Service District Office
P.O. Box 1216
Louisville, KY 40201
(502) 582-6259
Toll free: (800) 424-1040

LA

Internal Revenue Service District Office
500 Camp St.
Stop 21
New Orleans, LA 70130
(504) 589-2801
Toll free: (800) 424-1040

MA

Internal Revenue Service District Office
P.O. Box 9088
Boston, MA 02203
(617) 223-5177
Toll free: (800) 424-1040

MD

Internal Revenue Service District Office
P.O. Box 1076
Baltimore, MD 21203
(301) 962-2222
Toll free: (800) 424-1040

ME

Internal Revenue Service District Office
P.O. Box 1020
Augusta, ME 04330
(207) 622-8308
Toll free: (800) 424-1040

MI

Internal Revenue Service District Office
P.O. Box 32500
Room 2445
Detroit, MI 48232
(313) 226-3674
Toll free: (800) 424-1040

MN

Internal Revenue Service District Office
316 Robert St.
Stop 73
St. Paul, MN 55101
(612) 725-7320
Toll free: (800) 424-1040

MO

Internal Revenue Service District Office
P.O. Box 1147
H. W. Wheeler Station
St. Louis, MO 63188
(314) 425-5660
Toll free: (800) 424-1040

MS

Internal Revenue Service District Office
100 W. Capital St.
Suite 504
Jackson, MS 39269
(601) 960-4526
Toll free: (800) 424-1040

MT

Internal Revenue Service District Office
Federal Bldg.
301 S. Park
Drawer 10016
Helena, MT 59626
(406) 449-5392
Toll free: (800) 424-1040

NC

Internal Revenue Service District Office
320 Federal Place
Room 121
Greensboro, NC 27401
(919) 378-5620
Toll free: (800) 424-1040

NC

Internal Revenue Service District Office
P.O. Box 2461
Fargo, ND 58108
(701) 237-5771, ext. 5105
Toll free: (800) 424-1040

NE

Internal Revenue Service District Office
Fifteenth and Dodge
Stop 27
Omaha, NE 68102
(402) 221-3501
Toll free: (800) 424-1040

NH

Internal Revenue Service District Office
80 Daniel St.
Portsmouth, NH 03801
(603) 436-7720, ext. 772
Toll free: (800) 424-1040

NJ

Internal Revenue Service District Office
P.O. Box 476
Room 1103
Newark, NJ 07101
(201) 645-6478
Toll free: (800) 424-1040

NM

Internal Revenue Service District Office
517 Gold Ave., SW
P.O. Box 1967
Albuquerque, NM 87103
Toll free: (800) 424-1040

NV

Internal Revenue Service District Office
P.O. Box 16046
Las Vegas, NV 89101
Las Vegas: 385-6291
Reno: 784-5521
Toll free: (800) 424-1040

NY

Internal Revenue Service District Office
Manhattan
P.O. Box 3036
Church Street Station
New York, NY 10008
(212) 264-3310

Internal Revenue Service District Office
Brooklyn
P.O. Box 606
Brooklyn, NY 11202
(212) 330-7673

Internal Revenue Service District Office
Albany
O'Brien Federal Office Bldg.
Clinton and N. Pearl Sts.
Albany, NY 12207
(518) 472-3636

Internal Revenue Service District Office
Buffalo
P.O. Box 1040
Niagara Square Station
Buffalo, NY 14201
(716) 846-4007

OH

Internal Revenue Service District Office
Cincinnati
P.O. Box 3459
Cincinnati, OH 45201
(513) 684-2828
Toll free: (800) 424-1040

Internal Revenue Service District Office
Cleveland
P.O. Box 99184
Cleveland, OH 44199
(216) 522-3414
Toll free: (800) 424-1040

OK

Internal Revenue Service District Office
200 N.W. Fourth St.
ATTN: T:EC
Oklahoma City, OK 73102
(405) 272-9531
Tulsa: (918) 583-5121
Toll free: (800) 424-1040

OR

Internal Revenue Service District Office
1220 S.W. Third
Tenth Floor
Portland, OR 97204
(503) 221-3960
Toll free: (800) 424-1040

PA

Internal Revenue Service District Office
Philadelphia
P.O. Box 12080
ATTN: TPE Coordinator
Philadelphia, PA 19106
(215) 597-0512
Toll free: (800) 424-1040

Internal Revenue Service District Office
Pittsburgh
P.O. Box 2488
Room 1122
Pittsburgh, PA 15230
(412) 644-6504
Toll free: (800) 424-1040

PR

Internal Revenue Service District Office
Federal Courthouse Bldg.
Chardon St.
Room 300
Hato Rey, PR 00917
(809) 753-4646

RI
Internal Revenue Service District Office
P.O. Box 6627
Providence, RI 02940
(401) 528-4276

SC
Internal Revenue Service District Office
185 Assembly St.
Room 466
Columbia, SC 29201
(803) 765-5278
Toll free: (800) 424-1040

SD
Internal Revenue Service District Office
P.O. Box 370
Aberdeen, SD 57401
(605) 225-0250, ext. 262
Toll free: (800) 424-1040

TN
Internal Revenue Service District Office
P.O. Box 1107
Nashville, TN 37203
(615) 257-7291
Toll free: (800) 424-1040

TX
Internal Revenue Service District Office
Austin
300 E. Eighth St.
Stop 630
Austin, TX 78701
(512) 482-5314
Toll free: (800) 424-1040

Internal Revenue Service District Office
Houston
3223 Briarpark
Stop 6030BP
Houston, TX 77042
(713) 953-6432
Toll free: (800) 424-1040

Internal Revenue Service District Office
Dallas
1100 Commerce St.
Stop 410
Dallas, TX 75242
(214) 767-1428
Toll free: (800) 424-1040

UT
Internal Revenue Service District Office
465 South, Fourth East
Salt Lake City, UT 84111
(801) 524-4060
Toll free: (800) 424-1040

VA
Internal Revenue Service District Office
P.O. Box 10049
Richmond, VA 23240
(804) 771-2289
Toll free: (800) 424-1040

VT
Internal Revenue Service District Office
Federal Office Bldg.
11 Elmwood Ave.
Room 429
Burlington, VT 05401
(802) 951-6370

WA
Internal Revenue Service District Office
915 Second Ave.
Room 2356, MS-660
Seattle, WA 98174
(206) 442-5515
Toll free: (800) 424-1040

WI
Internal Revenue Service District Office
P.O. Box 493
Milwaukee, WI 53201
(414) 291-3302
Toll free: (800) 424-1040

WV
Internal Revenue Service District Office
P.O. Box 1666
Parkersburg, WV 26102
(304) 422-8551, ext. 1255
Toll free: (800) 424-1040

WY
Internal Revenue Service District Office
308 W. Twenty-First St.
Cheyenne, WY 82001
(307) 772-2162

Other Foreign Operations
Internal Revenue Service District Office
1325 K St., NW
Washington, DC 20225
(202) 566-6581

Publications: Catalogs. Guides. Pamphlets. Curriculum aids. Regulations. Magnetic media. Forms.

Bibliographies, Sales Catalogs, Publications Lists, etc.

"Publications Catalog." Current. 57p. free. Publication 897.
 Lists what is available in numerical, alphabetical, functional, and new/revised/obsolete categories.

Selected List of Books and Pamphlets

"IRS Community Outreach Tax Assistance." Current. 6p. free. Publication 1224.

Tells about what kinds of taxpayer assistance exist. Gives addresses and telephone numbers for IRS taxpayer education coordinators.

"Taxpayer's Guide to IRS Information, Assistance and Publications." Current. 27p. free. Publication 910.

Describes services available in preparing tax returns. Includes where to get help and what publications are available.

"Understanding Taxes." Current. 6p. free. Publication 488A.

Describes materials for educators.

"Understanding Taxes." Current. 8p. free. Publication 1185.

Provides ordering information and an order form for educational materials.

"Understanding Taxes." Current. 47p. free. Publication 21.

A student guide showing taxpayer's rights and responsibilities. Includes eight modules such as *History of Taxation* and *Glossary of Tax Terms*.

Audiovisuals:

Filmographies, Sales Lists, etc.

"Free Loan Films and Videocassettes." Current. 5p. free.

Tells what is available and how to obtain it.

Individual Audiovisuals

"The American Way of Taxing." n.d. 27½ minutes. 16mm. free loan.

Tells various services available to taxpayers through local IRS offices. Traces the history of the U.S. tax system.

"How To Fill out Form 1040 Schedules A and B Tax Returns." Updated yearly. 62 minutes. ¾" and ½" Beta and VHS. free loan.

Explains how to fill out Form 1040 and related schedules A and B.

"How To Fill out Form 1040A or 1040EZ Tax Returns." Updated yearly. 28 minutes. ¾" and ½" Beta and VHS. free loan.

Shows in a line-by-line guide how to fill out these tax returns.

"Money Talks." n.d. 27½ minutes. 16mm, ¾" and ½" Beta and VHS. free loan.

Shows taxes from colonial times to after World War II in the U.S.

"The Subject Was Taxes." n.d. 16½ minutes. 16mm, ¾" and ½" Beta and VHS. free loan.

Introduces taxes and managing personal finances. Shows high school students finding interesting things as they research.

"What Happened to My Paycheck?" n.d. 16½ minutes. 16mm, ¾" and ½" Beta and VHS. free loan.

Shows a high school student finding his paycheck is subject to various deductions. Illustrates tax Form 1040 and 1040A. Includes a tour through the IRS.

Special Services: For information on speakers, write to district offices.

Public reading rooms are located in the national office, and in regional office, and, in some cases, in a district office located in a regional office building.

Inquire about workshops to familiarize teachers with program materials and objectives.

INTERNATIONAL TRADE ADMINISTRATION
Department of Commerce
Fourteenth St. and Constitution Ave., NW
Washington, DC 20230
(202) 377-3808

Date Established: 1980

Objectives of the Agency: Promote world trade and strengthen the international trade and investment position of the United States.

Curriculum: Business

Subjects: U.S.—commerce

Locations:

(Alphabetically arranged by city)

International Trade Administration
District Office
505 Marquette Ave., NW
Suite 1015
Albuquerque, NM 87102
(506) 766-2386

International Trade Administration
District Office
701 C St.
P.O. Box 32
Anchorage, AK 99613
(907) 271-5041

International Trade Administration
District Office
1365 Peachtree St., NE
Suite 600
Atlanta, GA 30309
(404) 861-7000

International Trade Administration
District Office
415 U.S. Customhouse
Gay and Lombard Sts.
Baltimore, MD 21202
(301) 962-3560

International Trade Administration
District Office
908 S. Twentieth St.
Suite 200-201
Birmingham, AL 35205
(205) 254-1331

International Trade Administration
District Office
441 Stuart St.
Tenth Floor
Boston, MA 02116
(617) 223-2312

International Trade Administration
District Office
111 W. Huron St.
Room 1312
Buffalo, NY 14202
(716) 846-4191

International Trade Administration
District Office
500 Quarrier St.
Charleston, WV 25301
(304) 343-6181

International Trade Administration
District Office
1406 Mid-Continental Plaza Bldg.
55 E. Monroe St.
Chicago, IL 60603
(312) 353-4450

International Trade Administration
District Office
550 Main St.
Cincinnati, OH 45202
(513) 684-2944

International Trade Administration
District Office
666 Euclid Ave.
Room 600
Cleveland, OH 44114
(216) 522-4750

International Trade Administration
District Office
1835 Assembly St.
Suite 172
Columbia, SC 29201
(803) 765-5345

International Trade Administration
District Office
1100 Commerce St.
Room 7A5
Dallas, TX 75242
(214) 767-0542

International Trade Administration
District Office
721 Nineteenth St.
Room 119
Denver, CO 80202
(303) 837-3246

International Trade Administration
District Office
210 Walnut St.
Room 817
Des Moines, IA 50309
(515) 284-4222

International Trade Administration
District Office
231 W. Lafayette
Room 445
Detroit, MI 48226
(313) 226-3650

International Trade Administration
District Office
324 W. Market St.
P.O. Box 1950
Room 203
Greensboro, NC 27402
(919) 378-5345

International Trade Administration
District Office
450 Main St.
Room 610-B
Hartford, CT 06103
(203) 244-3530

International Trade Administration
District Office
300 Ala Moana Blvd.
P.O. Box 50026
Honolulu, HI 96850
(808) 546-8694

International Trade Administration
District Office
515 Rusk St.
Room 2625
Houston, TX 77002
(713) 229-2578

International Trade Administration
District Office
46 E. Ohio St.
Indianapolis, IN 46204
(317) 269-6214

International Trade Administration
District Office
300 Woodrow Wilson Blvd.
Suite 3230
Jackson, MS 39213
(601) 960-4388

International Trade Administration
District Office
601 E. Twelfth St.
Room 1840
Kansas City, MO 64106
(816) 374-3142

International Trade Administration
District Office
320 W. Capitol Ave.
Suite 635
Little Rock, AR 72201
(501) 378-5794

International Trade Administration
District Office
11777 San Vicente Blvd.
Room 800
Los Angeles, CA 90049
(213) 209-6707

International Trade Administration
District Office
U.S. Post Office and Courthouse Bldg.
Room 636B
Louisville, KY 40202
(502) 582-5066

International Trade Administration
District Office
51 S.W. First Ave.
Suite 224
Miami, FL 33130
(305) 350-5267

International Trade Administration
District Office
517 E. Wisconsin Ave.
Milwaukee, WI 53202
(414) 291-3473

International Trade Administration
District Office
110 S. Fourth St.
Room 218
Minneapolis, MN 55401
(612) 725-2133

International Trade Administration
District Office
1 Commerce Pl.
Suite 1427
Nashville, TN 37239
(615) 251-5161

International Trade Administration
District Office
2 Canal St.
432 International Trade Mart
New Orleans, LA 70130
(504) 589-6546

International Trade Administration
District Office
26 Federal Plaza
Room 3718
New York, NY 10278
(212) 264-0634

International Trade Administration
District Office
4024 Lincoln Blvd.
Oklahoma City, OK 73105
(405) 231-5302

International Trade Administration
District Office
300 S. Nineteenth St.
First Floor
Omaha, NE 68102
(402) 221-3664

International Trade Administration
District Office
600 Arch St.
Room 9448
Philadelphia, PA 19106
(215) 597-2866

International Trade Administration
District Office
201 N. Central Ave.
Suite 2950
Phoenix, AZ 85073
(602) 261-3285

International Trade Administration
District Office
1000 Liberty Ave.
Room 2002
Pittsburgh, PA 15222
(412) 644-2850

International Trade Administration
District Office
1220 S.W. Third Ave.
Room 618
Portland, OR 97204
(503) 221-3001

International Trade Administration
District Office
1755 E. Plumb Lane, No. 152
Reno, NV 89502
(702) 783-5203

International Trade Administration
District Office
400 N. Eighth St.
Room 8010
Richmond, VA 23240
(804) 771-2246

International Trade Administration
District Office
120 S. Central Ave.
St. Louis, MO 63105
(314) 425-3302
(314) 425-3304

International Trade Administration
District Office
350 S. Main St.
Room 340
Salt Lake City, UT 84101
(801) 524-5116

International Trade Administration
District Office
450 Golden Gate Ave.
Box 36013
San Francisco, CA 94102
(415) 556-5860

International Trade Administration
District Office
Federal Bldg.
Room 659
San Juan, PR (Hato Rey)
(809) 753-4555, ext. 555

International Trade Administration
District Office
27 E. Bay St.
P.O. Box 9746
Savannah, GA 31412
(912) 944-4204

International Trade Administration
District Office
1700 Westlake Ave. North
Room 706
Seattle, WA 98109
(206) 442-5616

International Trade Administration
District Office
240 W. State St.
Eighth Floor
Trenton, NJ 08608
(609) 989-2100

Publications: Surveys. Reports. Bulletins. Agreements. Statistics. Marketing trends for trade.

Bibliographies, Sales Catalogs, Publications Lists, etc.

"Export Licensing Information and Assistance." n.d. 3-fold. free.

Tells what the Office of Export Administration has to offer in information, telephone service, and publications. Provides addresses of both the Superintendent of Documents and the Exporter Assistance Division through which publications are sold.

"Let Commerce Daily . . . Tell You What Uncle Sam Is Buying, Selling, and Awarding in Contracts." 1984. 8p. free.

Describes the federal procurement publication charged by law with publicizing: all proposed procurements of $10,000 or more by civil and military agencies; all federal contract awards of $25,000 or more for the benefit of potential sub-contractors by civilian and military agencies; and foreign government procurements. For subscription information, call: (202) 783-3238. Also available online.

Selected List of Books and Pamphlets

"Enforcement of United States Trade Agreement Rights: A Descriptive Summary." 1980. 4p. free.

Summarizes issues that resulted from multilateral trade negotiations held under the general agreement on tariffs and trade.

"New Product Information Service." 1982. 10p. free.

Describes a service to promote new products overseas.

"How To Get the Most from Overseas Exhibitions." Rev. 26p. free.

Discusses whether to exhibit, considerations prior to the exhibition, actions during the exhibition, and follow-up after the exhibition.

INTERSTATE COMMERCE COMMISSION
Office of Public Affairs
Room 1211
Twelfth St. and Constitution Ave., NW
Washington, DC 20423
(202) 275-7252

Date Established: 1887

Objectives of the Agency: Regulate carriers engaged in surface transportation in interstate commerce and in foreign commerce taking place within the United States, including railroads, trucking companies, bus lines, freight forwarders, water carriers, etc.; settle controversies over rates and charges; and administer laws.

Curriculum: Consumer education, social studies

Subjects: Interstate commerce

Locations:

CT, MA, ME, NH, NJ, NY, RI, VT

Interstate Commerce Commission
Regional Office
150 Causeway St.
Boston, MA 02114

DC, DE, MD, OH, PA, VA, WV

Interstate Commerce Commission
Regional Office
101 N. Seventh St.
Philadelphia, PA 19106

AL, FL, GA, KY, MS, NC, SC, TN

Interstate Commerce Commission
Regional Office
1776 Peachtree St., NW
Atlanta, GA 30309

IL, IN, MI, MN, ND, SD, WI

Interstate Commerce Commission
Regional Office
219 S. Dearborn St.
Chicago, IL 60604

AR, IA, KS, LA, MO, NE, OK, TX

Interstate Commerce Commission
Regional Office
411 W. Seventh St.
Fort Worth, TX 76102

AK, AZ, CA, CO, HI, ID, MT, NM, NV, OR, UT, WA, WY

Interstate Commerce Commission
Regional Office
211 Main St.
San Francisco, CA 94105

Publications: Commission functions. Consumer moving rights. Reports. On governmental involvement and authority, general materials as well as technical and statistical items. Some may be purchased from the Government Printing Office, others free from various commission offices.

Bibliographies, Sales Catalogs, Publications Lists, etc.

"Interstate Commerce Commission Annual Report." Annual. 129p. free.
 Covers publications in an appendix. Tells where to obtain and gives annotations for various categories of publications. Provides addresses of different commission offices.

Selected List of Books and Pamphlets

"Household Goods Information." 1983. 22p. free. OCP-100.
 Explains consumer rights when moving household goods across state lines. Prepared by the commission's Office of Compliance and Consumer Assistance. Includes a service questionnaire.

"Interstate Commerce Commission Annual Report." Annually. 129p. free.
 Gives overview of the past year. Covers railroads, trucking, buses, water carriers, etc. Includes administration, legislation, economy, court actions events. Statistical data. Summarizes events for the year in a calendar.

"In the Public Interest." 1984. 24p. free.
 Tells what the commission does, its jurisdiction, history, staff organization, and policy. Gives chronology of major transportation legislation.

Library: Interstate Commerce Commission
Twelfth Street and Constitution Avenue NW
Room 3392
Washington, DC 20423
(202) 275-7428
 Open 8:30 A.M. to 5:00 P.M., Monday through Friday. Library and reading rooms available for record inspection and copying. Requests for access to public records should be made at the office of the secretary, room 2215 at the above address.

Special Services: For information about speakers, write:
Office of Public Affairs
Interstate Commerce Commission
Washington, DC 20423
 For information about current hearings before the commission contact the Office of Hearings: (202) 275-7501. Copies of recently issued (within 30 days) decisions may be obtained for a fee from:
T.S.I. Infosystems, Inc.
Room 2227
Interstate Commerce Commission Headquarters
Washington, DC 20423
(202) 275-4357

JOHN F. KENNEDY CENTER FOR THE PERFORMING ARTS

National Park Service
2700 F St., NW
Washington, DC 20566
(202) 254-3850

Date Established: 1971

Objectives of the Agency: Be a national culture center.

Curriculum: History, humanities

Subjects: Music
 Theater—U.S.
 Washington, DC—buildings

Publications: Flyers about the Kennedy Center and other Washington, DC attractions.

Selected List of Books and Pamphlets

"The John F. Kennedy Center for the Performing Arts." 1982. 4-fold. free.

Explains the center's history, development, and administration. Photographs.

"Welcome to Washington." 1982. 14-fold. free.

Gives description, hours, and telephone numbers of attractions such as the Washington Monument, Ford's Theatre, the Library of Congress, and others in the area. Maps. Photographs.

LIBRARY OF CONGRESS GEOGRAPHY AND MAP DIVISION
Library of Congress
101 Independence Ave., SE
Washington, DC 20540
(202) 287-MAPS

Date Established: 1897

Objectives of the Agency: Provide cartographic and geographic information for all parts of the world to the Congress, federal and local governments, scholars, and general public.

Curriculum: Geography, library

Subjects: Geography
Library science

Publications: Pamphlets. Monographs. Catalogs. Checklists. Lists. Reprints of articles. Map facsimiles. Microforms. Computer tapes. Bibliographies of maps. Charts. Atlases.

Bibliographies, Sales Catalogs, Publications Lists, etc.

"List of Publications." Current. 11p. free.

Lists free and for sale publications, with annotations, distributed by different agencies such as the Superintendent of Documents.

Selected List of Books and Pamphlets

"Geography and Map Division." Current. 8p. free.

Summarizes services, holdings, hours, and location. Photographs.

LIBRARY OF CONGRESS INFORMATION OFFICE
Library of Congress
10 First St., SE
Washington, DC 20540
(202) 287-5000

Date Established: 1942

Objectives of the Agency: Provide information about the Library of Congress.

Curriculum: Library

Subjects: Library science

Publications: Pamphlets. Catalogs. On services and available publications.

Bibliographies, Sales Catalogs, Publications Lists, etc.

"Publications in Print." Current. 93p. free.

Describes books, pamphlets, serials, bibliographies, recordings, and other material. Arranged in alphabetical order by title. Includes the LC call number or location. Index. Free and for sale. Certain materials free to libraries.

Selected List of Books and Pamphlets

"The Library of Congress." 1985. 34p. free.

Summarizes major activities for the fiscal year: additions to the collections, preserving and accessing the collections, automation, exhibits, publishing activities, etc.

LIBRARY OF CONGRESS LOAN DIVISION
Library of Congress
10 First St., SE
Washington, DC 20540
(202) 287-5444

Date Established: 1901

Objectives of the Agency: Lend materials to other libraries for the use of patrons engaged in research when the material is not available elsewhere; and help libraries find material not available from the Library of Congress.

Curriculum: Library

Subjects: Library science

Publications: Fact sheets. Pamphlets. On interlibrary loan services.

Selected List of Books and Pamphlets

"Interlibrary Loan Policy." Current. 1p. free.

Explains general policies, materials available, photoduplication service, verification of requests.

"Interlibrary Loan Services." 1983. 6p. free.

Explains what institutions are eligible for interlibrary loans, procedures for submitting a request, materials available for loan, and photoduplication service.

LIBRARY OF CONGRESS MOTION PICTURE, BROADCASTING AND RECORDED SOUND DIVISION
Public Services Coordinator
Library of Congress
10 First St., SE
Washington, DC 20540

Date Established: 1912

Objectives of the Agency: Acquire, preserve, and service for reference purposes the library's sound recordings, including recorded radio programs and musical recordings, in conjunction with the library's music division; and be responsible for the film and television collections.

Curriculum: History, library, music

Subjects: Folk Music
Motion Pictures
Music, American
Radio
Television

Publications: Pamphlets about the services of the motion picture broadcasting and recorded sound division. Lists of recordings.

Selected List of Books and Pamphlets

"Film and Television." 1983. 6p. free.

Explains the collections, research aids, related publications, preservation, and services of the film and television research collections.

"Sound Recordings." 1984. 8p. free.

Explains the collections, research aids, services, and preservation of the recorded sound collection of the Library of Congress.

Audiovisuals:

Filmographies, Sales Lists, etc.

"Folk Music in America." current. 18p. free.

Lists records for sale such as: *Songs of Childhood* and *Songs of War & History*. Also available on cassette. Includes ordering and price information.

"Folk Recordings." 1983. 38p. free.

Titles, ordering information. Grouped by type such as "Music of the American Indian."

"Our Musical Past." 1982. 4p. free.

Describes records containing a selection of band and vocal music popular in America during the 1850s and 1860s. Illustrated booklet accompanies each album. Includes order form and price.

"Spoken Recordings." 1983. 16p. free.

Gives titles and contents of literary recordings offered on cassette and record. Some in Spanish. Includes some poets: Robert Frost, E. E. Cummings, T. S. Eliot, Marianne Moore. Provides order form and prices.

LIBRARY OF CONGRESS SCIENCE REFERENCE SECTION
Science and Technology Division
10 First St., SE
Washington, DC 20540
(202) 287-5639

Date Established: 1949 (Tech 1952).

Objectives of the Agency: Provide reference and bibliographic services; and recommend acquisitions in science and technology.

Curriculum: Library

Subjects: Library science

Publications: Tracer bullets. Bibliographies. Books. Chronologies. Indexes.

Bibliographies, Sales Catalogs, Publications Lists, etc.

"LC Science Tracer Bullet." Current. 2p. free.

Lists TB number and title of guides. The bullets are designed to help readers begin to locate published materials on a subject about which they know little.

Selected List of Books and Pamphlets

"Computer Security." 1985. 10p. free. TB 85-4.

LC science tracer bullet guides the reader to materials dealing with computer security "on target."

"Endangered Species (Animals)." 1985. 11p. free. TB 85-3.

LC Science Tracer Bullet Literature Guide provides references to materials on animals that are endangered, threatened, or rare, excluding marine mammals.

"Science and Technology Division." 1982. 6p. free.

Surveys the division covering its mission, materials, services, hours, and telephone numbers.

Wilbur & Orville Wright: Pictorial Materials. 1982. 200p. free.

A documentary guide. Has index of persons, institutions, and geographic names. Photographs. (Four other bibliographies, chronologies, and studies on the Wright brothers are also available.)

LIBRARY OF CONGRESS SERIAL AND GOVERNMENT PUBLICATIONS DIVISION
Library of Congress
James Madison Bldg.
Between First and Second Sts. on
Independence Ave., SE
Room LM 133
Washington, DC 20540
(202) 287-5690

Date Established: 1895

Objectives of the Agency: Maintain an extensive collection of newspapers, current periodicals, and government publications for use.

Curriculum: Library

Subjects: Library of Congress

Publications: Bibliographies. Information circulars. Books. Guides. Pamphlets.

Bibliographies, Sales Catalogs, Publications Lists, etc.

"Newspapers and Current Periodical Room." 1985. 3-fold. free.

Gives general information on hours and services as well as bibliography of publications of the Serial and Government Publications Division and one of related publications prepared outside the Serial and Government Publications Division. The variety of publications are for sale or are free.

Selected List of Books and Pamphlets

"Information for Readers in the Library of Congress." Rev. 15p. free.

Provides information on reading rooms, reference services, collections, loans, special searches, employment, photographs, catalogs, and other visitor information.

"Newspaper and Current Periodical Room." 1985. 3-fold. free.

Tells about hours, collections, and services. Includes publications to aid the researcher and other readers.

LIBRARY OF CONGRESS TOUR OFFICE
10 First St., SE
Washington, DC 20540
(202) 287-5458

Date Established: 1963

Objectives of the Agency: Provide information on locations, hours, and services of the Library of Congress.

Curriculum: Library

Subjects: Library science

Publications: Calendars. Pamphlets. Catalogs.

Bibliographies, Sales Catalogs, Publications Lists, etc.

"The Library of Congress Card and Gift Catalog." Current. 31p. free.

Describes greeting cards, calendars, photographs, books, maps, posters, records, and assorted gift items, some with photographs. Includes order form.

Selected List of Books and Pamphlets

"Calendar of Events in the Library of Congress." Monthly. 2p. free.

Lists exhibits, concerts, and literary programs.

"Public Services in the Library of Congress: Locations and Hours of Opening." 1984. 6p. free.

Lists the hours, telephone numbers, and locations of various reading rooms such as the Law Library, Copyright Office, and Asian Reading Room. Gives information about orientation film, tours, sales, and holiday hours. Includes what is located in the Thomas Jefferson Building, the John Adams Building, and the James Madison Memorial Building.

"Services to the Nation." 1984. 16p. free.

Describes buildings, materials, services to libraries, and scholars, cultural programs, and history of the Library of Congress.

Special Services: "American's Library," an 18-minute slide/sound introduction, is shown regularly.

LONGFELLOW NATIONAL HISTORIC SITE
National Park Service
105 Brattle St.
Cambridge, MA 02138

Date Established: 1972

Objectives of the Agency: Preserve the home where the poet Henry Wadsworth Longfellow lived while teaching at Harvard.

Curriculum: English

Subjects: American literature
Poets, American

Publications: Flyer about Longfellow and the historic site.

Selected List of Books and Pamphlets

"Henry W. Longfellow." 1981. 6-fold. free.

Gives highlights about the life of Longfellow and his house. Photographs.

MARITIME ADMINISTRATION
Office of External Affairs
U.S. Department of Transportation
Room 7219
Washington, DC 20590
(202) 426-5807

Date Established: 1950

Objectives of the Agency: Administer programs to help the development, promotion, and operation of the U.S. Merchant Marine; organize and direct emergency merchant ship operations; and administer subsidy programs, financing guarantees, and capital fund agreements.

Curriculum: Social studies

Subjects: Merchant marine

Locations:

Eastern Region Office

Maritime Administration
Federal Bldg.
26 Federal Plaza
Thirty-Seventh Floor
New York, NY 10007
(212) 264-1320

Central Region Office

Maritime Administration
No. 2 Canal St.
I.T.M.
Suite 2830
New Orleans, LA 70130
(504) 589-6556

Western Region Office

Maritime Administration
211 Main St.
Room 112
San Francisco, CA 94105
(415) 974-7893

136 / Maritime Administration

Great Lakes Region Office

Maritime Administration
2300 E. Devon Ave.
Room 254
Des Plaines, IL 60018
(312) 298-4535

Ship Operations Office

Maritime Administration
666 Euclid Ave.
Room 324
Cleveland, OH 44114
(216) 522-3623

Publications: Books. Pamphlets. Catalogs. Reports. Pictures. Guides. Studies.

Bibliographies, Sales Catalogs, Publications Lists, etc.

"Marad Publications." Current. 65p. free.

Groups materials under such topics as: *Great Lakes, Fuels, Marine Pollution, Nuclear,* and *Trade.* Gives addresses and telephone numbers of sources. Includes materials for sale from the Superintendent of Documents and National Technical Information Service; free materials from the Office of External Affairs, Office of Port and Intermodal Development, Office of Trade Studies and Subsidy Contracts of the U.S. Department of Transportation.

Selected List of Books and Pamphlets.

"Introducing the Maritime Administration." 1980. 20p. free.

Describes the various activities of the Maritime Administration, including its history and development. Photographs. Organization chart.

MATERIALS AND TRANSPORTATION BUREAU
Research and Special Programs Administration
U.S. Department of Transportation
400 Seventh St., SW
Washington, DC 20590
(202) 755-9260

Date Established: 1975

Curriculum: Safety

Subjects: Transportation

Locations:

CT, DC, DE, MA, MD, ME, NH, NJ, NY, PA, PR, RI, VA, VT, WV

Materials Transportation Bureau
U.S. Department of Transportation
Room 8321
400 Seventh St., SW
Washington, DC 20590

AL, FL, GA, KY, MS, NC, SC, TN

Materials Transportation Bureau
U.S. Department of Transportation
Suite 505
1776 Peachtree Rd., NW
Atlanta, GA 30309

IA, IL, IN, KS, MI, MN, MO, NE, OH, WI

Materials Transportation Bureau
U.S. Department of Transportation
Room 1802
911 Walnut St.
Kansas City, MO 64106

AR, LA, NM, OK, TX

Materials Transportation Bureau
U.S. Department of Transportation
2320 Labranch
Houston, TX 77074

AK, AZ, CA, CO, HI, ID, MT, ND, NV, OR, SD, UT, WA, WY

Materials Transportation Bureau
U.S. Department of Transportation
555 Zang St.
Lakewood, CO 80228

Publications: Pamphlets. Guides. Kits. Fact sheets. On safe packaging and shipping of hazardous materials.

Bibliographies, Sales Catalogs, Publications Lists, etc.

"Information Concerning the Regulations." Rev. 1984. 2p. free.

Explains how to obtain the *Federal Register* and *Code of Federal Regulations*. Includes Superintendent of Documents order form and price information.

"Sources of Hazardous Materials Regulations and Other Publications." Rev. 1984. 2p. free.

Contains regulations and publications about the safe transportation of hazardous materials that are available for sale from various addresses. Includes international organizations.

Serials, Subscription Publications, etc.

"Hazardous Materials Newsletter." Current. 8p. free.

Provides news about recent events and publications.

Selected List of Books and Pamphlets

"A Guide to the Federal Hazardous Materials Transportation Regulatory Program." 1983. 53p. free. DOT-1-83-12.

Intended to promote awareness and understanding of the federal effort to improve the safety of hazardous materials transportation. Written for the general public. Includes general definitions of regulated materials, a history of the program, relationship with state, local and international community, and requirements imposed on shippers and carriers.

"Hazardous Materials Transportation." Current. kit. free.
   Contains various pamphlets, fact sheets, guides, emergency numbers, and current news in a folder.

"A Review of the Department of Transportation Regulations for Transportation of Radioactive Materials." Rev. 64p. free.
   Gives radioactive materials transportation regulations, summary of principal shipper's requirements in preparation and offering of radioactive materials for shipment, carrier requirements, and other information. Includes tables, illustrations, definitions, and references.

MINERALS MANAGEMENT SERVICE
Office of Public Affairs
U.S. Department of the Interior
Washington, DC 20240
(202) 343-3983

Date Established: 1982

Objectives of the Agency: Establish an effective means of collecting revenues generated from mineral leases offshore and on federal and Indian lands in the United States; and develop the country's offshore energy and mineral resources while safeguarding the environment.

Curriculum: Environmental studies, geography

Subjects: Environmental policy—U.S.
Mineralogy
Petroleum

Locations:

Field Offices
Mineral Management Service Field Office
Atlantic Region
Suite 601
1951 Kidwell Dr.
Vienna, VA 22180
(703) 285-2604
(703) 285-2168

Mineral Management Service Field Office
Gulf of Mexico Region
P.O. Box 7944
3301 N. Causeway Blvd.
Metairie, LA 70010
(504) 838-0589

Mineral Management Service Field Office
Pacific Region
1340 W. Sixth St.
Los Angeles, CA 90017
(213) 688-2050

Mineral Management Service Field Office
Alaska Region
P.O. Box 259
Anchorage, AK 99501
(907) 261-2307

Accounting and Service Centers
Mineral Management Accounting Center
P.O. Box 25165
Lakewood, CO 80225
(303) 231-3114

Mineral Management Administrative Center
Southern Service Center
P.O. Box 7944
3301 N. Causeway Blvd.
Metairie, LA 70010
(504) 837-9201

Mineral Management Administrative Service Center
Central Service Center
P.O. Box 25165
Lakewood, CO 80225
(303) 231-3730

Mineral Management Administrative Service Center
Alaska Service Center
800 A St.
Suite 201
Anchorage, AK 99501
(907) 271-4465

Publications: Reports. Studies. Maps. Monographs. Standards.

Bibliographies, Sales Catalogs, Publications Lists, etc.

"Offshore Scientific & Technical Publications Available to the Public." Current. 32p. free.
   Gives ordering information, including addresses of where to obtain publications. Lists new publications, offshore publications, available publications grouped by region. Indicates new publications with a special symbol. For sale and free.

**MINORITY BUSINESS DEVELOPMENT
   AGENCY INFORMATION
   CLEARINGHOUSE**
U.S. Department of Commerce
Fourteenth St. and Constitution Ave., NW
Washington, DC 20230
(202) 377-2414

Date Established: 1971

Objectives of the Agency: Collect and disseminate information that is of special importance to the successful establishment and operation of minority business for Blacks, Asian Americans, Spanish-speaking Americans, American Indians, Eskimos, and Aleuts.

Curriculum: Business, minority studies

Subjects: Business
Minorities

Locations:

AL, FL, GA, KY, MS, NC, SC, TN

Minority Business Development Agency
Atlanta Regional Office
1371 Peachtree St., NE
Suite 505
Atlanta, GA 30309
(404) 881-4091

IA, IL, IN, KS, MI, MN, MO, NE, OH, WI

Minority Business Development Agency
Chicago Regional Office
55 E. Monroe St.
Suite 1440
Chicago, IL 60603
(312) 353-0182

AR, CO, LA, MT, NM, ND, OK, SD, TX, UT, WY

Minority Business Development Agency
Dallas Regional Office
1100 Commerce St.
Room 7B19
Dallas, TX 75242
(214) 767-8001

CT, MA, ME, NH, NJ, NY, PR, RI, VI, VT

Minority Business Development Agency
New York Regional Office
26 Federal Plaza
Room 36-116
New York, NY 10278
(212) 264-3262

AK, AS, AZ, CA, HI, ID, NV, OR, WA

Minority Business Development Agency
San Francisco Regional Office
Federal Bldg.
Room 15043
P.O. 36114
450 Golden Gate Ave.
San Francisco, CA 94102
(415) 556-7234

DC, DE, MD, PA, VA, WV

Minority Business Development Agency
Washington Regional Office
1730 K St., NW
Suite 420
Washington, DC 20006

Publications: Lists. Flyers. Directories. Reports. Newsletters.

Bibliographies, Sales Catalogs, Publications Lists, etc.

"Publications List." Current. 1p. free.
   Lists what is available from the Minority Business Development Agency.

Selected List of Books and Pamphlets

"Closing the Information Gap." Rev. 3-fold. free.
   Describes Minority Business Development Agency's nationwide business information network and the data services it makes available to minority businesses.

"Directory of Regional & District Offices and Minority Business Development Centers." Current. 11p. free.
   Lists organizations funded by the Minority Business Development Agency to provide management and technical assistance to minority business owners.

"MBDA Minority Business Development Centers." n.d. 12p. free.
   Describes federal system for delivering business development services to minority Americans.

"MBDA—What You Need To Know." n.d. 3-fold. free.
   Describes programs and activities of the Minority Business Development Agency.

"Profile." 1984. 4-fold. free.
   Describes the Minority Business Development Agency locator system for minority vendors. Explains why minority-owned firms should be listed with "Profile" and how purchasers can obtain data on minority companies.

NATIONAL AERONAUTICS AND SPACE ADMINISTRATION
400 Maryland Ave., SW
Washington, DC 20546
(202) 453-1000

Date Established: 1958

Objectives of the Agency: Conduct research for the solution of flight problems; develop, construct, test, and operate aeronautical and space vehicles; conduct activities needed for space exploration; arrange for the best utilization of the scientific and engineering resources of this country with other nations; and provide information about activities.

Curriculum: Science

Subjects: Solar system
Space flight

Locations:

AK

Alaska State Library
Pouch G
Juneau, AK 99801

HI
The Department of Education
State of Hawaii
Office of Library Services
Support Services Branch
641 Eighteenth Ave.
Honolulu, HI 96816

CT, DC, DE, MA, MD, ME, NH, NJ, NY, PA, RI, VT
NASA Goddard Space Flight Center
Regional Office
Greenbelt, MD 20771
(301) 344-8101

AK, AZ, CA, HI, ID, MT, NV, OR, UT, WA, WY
NASA Ames Research Center
Regional Office
Moffett Field, CA 94035
(415) 965-6278

AL, AR, IA, LA, MO, MS, TN
NASA George C. Marshall Space Flight Center
Regional Office
Marshall Space Flight Center, AL 35812
(205) 453-0040

FL, GA, PR, VI
NASA John F. Kennedy Space Center
Regional Office
Kennedy Space Center, FL 32899
(305) 867-4444

KY, NC, SC, VA, WV
NASA Langley Research Center
Regional Library
Hampton, VA 23665
(804) 827-2634

IL, IN, MI, MN, OH, WI
NASA Lewis Research Center
Regional Office
21000 Brookpark Rd.
Cleveland, OH 44135
(216) 433-4000, ext. 708

CO, KS, ND, NE, NM, OK, SD, TX
NASA Lyndon B. Johnson Space Center
Regional Office
Houston, TX 77058
(713) 333-4980

Publications: Pamphlets. Posters. Lithographs. Serials. Workbooks. Bibliographies. Curriculum supplements. Guidebooks. Decals. Wallsheets. Teacher's guides. Catalogs. Chronologies. Handbooks. Tables and charts. Books. Data reports. Conference proceedings. Magnetic tapes. Indexes. Maps. Reviews.

Bibliographies, Sales Catalogs, Publication Lists, etc.

"Aerospace Bibliography." 1982. 140p. $6.00. EP-48. S/N 033-000-00866-0.

Lists government and nongovernment publications. Includes subject index, annotated bibliography, list of reference books, title index, and publisher's addresses.

"NASA Publications." 1984. 25p. free. PAM 101.

Includes subject index: *Aeronautics, Astronomy, Earth, Educational Publications, Miscellaneous, Rocketry, Satellites,* and *Technology Applications,* teacher resource materials. Annotations. Ordering information. Publications are for sale from the Superintendent of Documents. Make inquiries at regional offices.

"Records of Achievement: NASA Special Publications." 1983. 127p. free.

Annotates material whose scope outgrew customary research reports and articles. Traces NASA development since the early 1960s. Refers to past accomplishments on the occasion of NASA's 25th anniversary. Groups material in index into: *Aeronautics, Astronautics, Chemistry and Materials, Engineering, Geosciences, Life Sciences, Mathematical and Computer Sciences, Physics, Social Sciences,* and *Space Sciences.*

Serials, Subscription Publications, etc.

NASA Activities. Monthly. $20.00/yr. domestic, $25.00/yr. foreign. $2.00/single copy domestic, $2.50 foreign.

Contains significant space statements, legislative affairs about space, general NASA activities, new publications and films, and press releases. Order from: Superintendent of Documents, U.S. Government Printing Office, Washington, DC 20402.

Report to Educators. Quarterly. 8p. free.

Contains events, publications, and projects. Order from: Elementary and Secondary Programs Branch, Educational Affairs Division, NASA, Washington, DC 20546.

Selected List of Books and Pamphlets

All available from:
Superintendent of Documents
Government Printing Office
Washington, DC 20402
Prices subject to change. For current prices: (202) 783-3238 or (202) 783-3311.

"Activities in Planetary Geology for the Physical and Earth Sciences." 1982. 175p. $7.00. EP-179. S/N 033-000-00843-1.

Provides workbook of class exercises for high school science.

"Apollo." 1974. 64p. $4.75. EP-100 033-000-00553-9.

Summarizes the historic manned lunar landing. Photographs from each Apollo mission.

"Comparing the Planets." 1979. 32½"x15½". $3.50. NF-58. S/N 033-000-00744-2.

Gives sizes of planets, distances from the sun, composition, density, atmospheres, and geology. "Teacher's Guide for 'Comparing the Planets.'" (1980. 16p. $2.75. NF-109. S/N 033-000-00787-6.) Explains the wall chart and gives ideas for classroom use, a glossary, and data.

"Elementary School Aerospace Activities." 1977. 140p. $6.50. EP-147. S/N 033-000-00693-4.

Provides curriculum resource for teachers covering: *Earth Characteristics, Flight in the Atmosphere, Rockets, Technological Advances, Unmanned Earth Satellites, Unmanned Exploration of the Solar System, Life-Support Systems, Astronauts,* and *Projections.*

"Extragalactic Astronomy." 1977. 48p. $4.75. EP-131. S/N 033-000-00657-8.

Provides a curriculum for high school science teachers prepared by the American Astronomical Society. Examines the universe beyond our Milky Way.

"NASA 1958-1983: Remembered Images." 1983. 136p. $24.00. EP-200. S/N 033-000-901-1.

Shows NASA's first years in space in captioned photographs.

"The Next Step: Large Space Structures." 1982. 8p. $2.00. NF-129. S/N 033-000-0853-8.

Shows antennas and platforms in the coming decades. Includes suggestions for classroom activities.

"Planet Earth through the Eyes of Landsat 4." 1983. 12p. $2.25. NF-138. S/N 033-000-00875-9.

Contains Landsat photographs, captions, and text. Shows how pictures taken from orbit reveal surface features.

"Our Planets at a Glance." 1982. 16p. $2.75. NF-134. S/N 033-000-00859-7.

Provides a guide to current knowledge about the solar system based primarily on interplanetary explorations.

"Sixty Years of Aeronautical Research, 1917-1977." 1980. 96p. $5.50. EP-145. S/N 033-000-00 7736-1.

Explains the contributions of the Langley Research Center to air and space flight.

"The Solar System." 1979. 8"x10". $2.75. S/N 033-000-00760-4.

Shows solar system looking toward earth from the moon. Gives relative sizes of planets, sun, orbits. Prints facts on the reverse side.

"Sun, Earth, and Man." 1983. 77p. $5.50. EP-172. S/N 033-000-00848-1.

Explains space research into sun-earth relations.

"The Supernova." 1977. 48p. $4.75. EP-126. S/N 033-000-00654-3.

Contains one of four curriculum projects by the American Astronomical Society for secondary science teachers. Covers events that are believed to lead to neutron stars and black holes.

"This Is NASA." 1979. 52p. $4.75. EP-155. S/N 033-000-00773-6.

Gives history, programs, budgets, jobs, and how to obtain models and souvenirs.

"Voyage to Jupiter." 1980. 211p. $9.00. SP-439. S/N 033-000-00797-3.

Chronicles trips of Voyagers 1 and 2. Color photographs.

"Voyager Mission Pictures." 1977. 8 lithos, 8"x10". $4.50. S/N 033-000-00686-1.

Shows the Voyager spacecraft, Saturn, Jupiter, and giant satellites in a set of lithographs.

"The World of Tomorrow." 1979. 72p. $5.50. EP-144. S/N 033-000-00745-1.

Gives teachers of grades 2-4 and leaders of children's clubs suggestions for group activities.

Audiovisuals:

Filmographies, Sales Lists, etc.

"NASA Films." 32p. free.

Gives annotations of films: general interest, special interest, classroom use, life science, skylab science, space research, careers and others. Filmstrips and audiotapes only by purchase. Films are free loan or by purchase. For information about the purchase of films: National Audiovisual Center, National Archives and Records Service, General Services Administration, Order Section AP, Washington, DC 20409. (301) 763-1891. For free-loan film requests, contact your regional office and include the complete film title and the identifying number. Some NASA audio highlight tapes (cassette or reel-to-reel) are available for sale from Lion Recording Services, Inc., 1905 Fairview Ave., NE, Washington, DC 20002. (202) 832-7883. Includes a list of what is available and the price.

Individual Audiovisuals

"America's Wings." 1976. 28 minutes. 16mm. color. free loan. For purchase price, see notation under *Filmographies.* HQA 267.

Examines various people who contributed to the development of flying such as Igor Sikorsky, who invented the helicopter.

"Eagle Has Landed: The Flight of Apollo 11." 1969. 28½ minutes. 16mm. color. free loan. For purchase price, see notation under *Filmographies.* HQ 194.

Shows the first landing of men on the moon. Highlights events of the mission of astronauts through television, motion picture, and still photography.

"Earth-Sun Relationship." 1974. 6 minutes. 16mm. color. free loan. For purchase price, see notation under *Filmographies.* HQ 235.

Shows how our sun and planets were formed, how the earth is protected from solar wind and ion particles, and how a star dies. Animated.

"Geology from Space." 1967. 24 frames. filmstrip. color. For purchase only. FS-3.

Shows various geological features around the world.

"Land for People, Land for Bears." n.d. 14½ minutes. 16mm. color. free loan. For purchase price, see notation under *Filmographies.* HQ 279.

Shows animal biologists using Landsat satellite data to identify land for relocation of endangered animal species.

"Life?." 14½ minutes. 16mm. color. free loan. For purchase price, see notation under *Filmographies.* HQ 261.

Explores life and non-life characteristics, how life has adapted to earth, and the possibility of life on Mars.

"Jupiter Odyssey." 1974. 28 minutes. 16mm. color. free loan. For purchase price, see notation under *Filmographies.* HQA 243.

Chronicles the journey of Pioneer 10 to Jupiter, the first spacecraft to travel beyond Mars. Includes findings and questions raised from the 21-month trip.

"A Man's Reach Should Exceed His Grasp." 1972. 23½ minutes. 16mm. color. free loan. For purchase price, see notation under *Filmographies.* HQA 219.

Presents the story of flight from the Wright brothers to space missions. Includes statements by writers and philosophers about man's search for knowledge and the creative role of research.

"Mercury, Exploration of a Planet." 1976. 23½ minutes. 16mm. color. free loan. For purchase price, see notation under *Filmographies.* HQA 282.

Illustrates the flight of the Mariner 10 spacecraft to Venus and Mercury through animation and photography. Shows views of Mercury. Illustrates the origin of the solar system in animation.

"Our Solar System." 1973. 4½ minutes. 16mm. color. free loan. For purchase price, see notation under *Filmographies.* HQ 234.

Examines the names, arrangement, and characteristics of the planets.

"Planet Mars." 1979. 28½ minutes. 16mm. color. free loan. For purchase price, see notation under *Filmographies.* HQ 283.

Explores Mars from early investigation by telescope to the landing of the Viking robot lander.

"Pollution Solution?" 1976. 14½ minutes. 16mm. color. free loan. For purchase price, see notation under *Filmographies.* HQ 276.

Shows how Landsat's remote sensing capabilities can aid the environment.

"Reading the Moon's Secrets." 1976. 18 minutes. 16mm. color. free loan. For purchase price, see notation under *Filmographies.* HQA 275.

Designed as a teaching film for grades 7-12. Has accompanying teacher's guide.

"Space for Women." 1981. 27½ minutes. 16mm. color. free loan. For purchase price, see notation under *Filmographies.* HQ 301.

Interviews various NASA women.

"Space Shuttle: A Remarkable Flying Machine." 1981. 30 minutes. 16mm. color. free loan. For purchase price, see notation under *Filmographies.* HQ 318.

Shows the first flight of the space shuttle, Columbia. Includes lift-off, onboard activities, landing.

"Universe." 1976. 28 minutes. 16mm. color. free loan. For purchase price, see notation under *Filmographies.* HQ 220.

Illustrates the universe, from galaxies to subatomic particles, from cosmic events that occurred long ago to micro-cosmic present events. Winner of numerous awards.

"A View of the Sky." 1967. 27½ minutes. 16mm. color. free loan. For purchase price, see notation under *Filmographies.* HQ 163.

Examines various historical theories of the origin and order of the solar system from Copernicus through Einstein and space explorations.

"The Weather Watchers." 1977. 14½ minutes. 16mm. color. free loan. For purchase price, see notation under *Filmographies.* HQA 290.

Shows the use and importance of meteorological and related information obtained from NASA satellites as it relates to severe storms. Shows formation and action of a tornado.

"Who's Out There?" 1975. 26 minutes. 16mm. color. free loan. For purchase price, see notation under *Filmographies.* HQ 226.

Orson Welles explores science fiction and scientific fact about the new view of extraterrestrial life. Includes interstellar discoveries and findings about the nature of life.

142 / National Aeronautics and Space Administration

"The World Was There." 1975. 27½ minutes. 16mm. color. free loan. For purchase price, see notation under *Filmographies*. HQ 74.

Examines how the news media covered the manned space launches of NASA's Project Mercury. Shows Gordon Cooper's flight and recovery, John Glenn's orbits, Wally Schirra's launch, etc.

Library: NASA Headquarters Information Center
Federal Building 10-B (lobby)
Washington, DC 20546
(202) 453-1000

There are also special resource centers for educators at the Kennedy Space Center, Lewis Research Center, and Alabama Space and Rocket Center in Huntsville.

Special Services: There are educational services such as workshops available for teachers, demonstration-lecture assembly programs for students, and presentations for the general public. To request a program or learn more about the services, contact the education officer that serves your state. "NASA Aerospace Education Services Project" flyer outlines the aerospace education unit.

Request information about what your regional office has to offer. The Lewis Research Center, for example, has a speakers bureau, descriptive materials about the office, a teacher resource room, telelectures, and weekend programs.

NATIONAL AGRICULTURAL LIBRARY
United States Department of Agriculture
U.S. Route 1 and Interstate Route 495
Beltsville, MD 20705
(301) 344-3755

Date Established: 1862

Curriculum: Agriculture, library

Subjects: Agriculture—U.S.
Library science

Objectives of the Agency: Specialize in the collection of information on agriculture and subjects supporting agricultural research.

Locations:

AL

National Tillage Machinery Laboratory Library
ARS, USDA
P.O. Box 792
Auburn, AL 36831-0792
(205) 887-8596

CA

Pacific SW Forest and Range ES Library
FS, USDA
P.O. Box 245
Berkeley, CA 94701
(415) 486-3173

Western Regional Research Center Library
ARS, USDA
Berkeley, CA 94710
(415) 486-3351

CO

Rocky Mountain Forest and Range ES Library
FS, USDA
240 W. Prospect St.
Fort Collins, CO 80526
(303) 221-4390

DC

Office of General Counsel, Law Library
Other Agencies, USDA
South Bldg.
Room 1406
Washington, DC 20250
(202) 447-7751

National Arboretum Library
ARS, USDA
Twenty-Eighth and M Sts., NW
Washington, DC 20002
(202) 475-4828

GA

Russell Research Center
ARS, USDA
P.O. Box 5677
Athens, GA 30613
(404) 546-3314

IA

National Animal Disease Center Library
ARS, USDA
P.O. Box 70
Ames, IA 50010
(516) 232-0250

IL

Northern Regional Research Center Library
ARS, USDA
1851 N. University St.
Peoria, IL 61604
(309) 685-4011

LA

Southern Forest Experimentation Station Library
FS, USDA
USPS Bldg.
701 Loyola Ave.
Room T-10210
New Orleans, LA 70113
(504) 589-6798

Southern Regional Research Center Library
ARS, USDA
P.O. Box 19687
New Orleans, LA 70179
(504) 589-7072

MN

North Central Forest Experiment Station Library
FS, USDA
University of Minnesota
1992 Folwell Ave.
St. Paul, MN 55108
(612) 642-5257

MS

Sedimentation Laboratory Library
ARS, USDA
P.O. Box 1157
Oxford, MS 38655
(601) 234-4121, ext. 36

NY

Plum Island Animal Disease Center Library
ARS, USDA
P.O. Box 848
Greenport, L.I., NY 11944
(516) 323-2500

PA

Northeastern Forest ES Library
FS, USDA
370 Reed Rd.
Broomall, PA 19008
(215) 461-3105

Eastern Regional Research Center Library
ARS, USDA
600 E. Mermaid Lane
Philadelphia, PA 19118
(215) 232-6602

UT

Technical Information Officer
Intermountain Forest and Range ES Library
FS, USDA
507 Twenty-Fifth St.
Ogden, UT 84401
(801) 625-5444

WI

Forest Products Laboratory Library
FS, USDA
P.O. Box 5130
Madison, WI 53705
(608) 264-5711

Publications: Pamphlets. Fact sheets. Newsletters. On information resources in agriculture.

Serials, Subscription Publications, etc.

"Agricultural Libraries Information Notes." Monthly. 12p. free.
Provides news to technical information specialists, librarians, extension workers, researchers, and scientists on agricultural information activities in a newsletter.

Selected List of Books and Pamphlets

"AGRICOLA." Rev. 1984. 8p. free.
Describes the bibliographic database, subfiles, searching, access, and related information.

"Document Delivery Services Available to Libraries and Other Information Centers and Commercial Organizations." Current. 1p. free.
Summarizes services, such as photoduplication service rates and loan services.

"Document Delivery Services to Individuals." Current. 1p. free.
Explains loan service, photoduplication service, and request procedures.

"Food and Nutrition Information Center." 1984. 2-fold. free.
What the center is, collection, services, lending policy.

"Guide to Services." 1984. 12p. free.
Gives hours, telephone numbers, rooms, etc. Explains collections, bibliographic access, automated information retrieval services, tours, etc.

Special Services: For information on orientation and tours contact: (301) 344-3778; for interlibrary loans and copying services, contact: (301) 344-3776; for reference service, contact: (301) 344-3755.

NATIONAL ARCHIVES AND RECORDS SERVICE
Eighth St. and Pennsylvania Ave., NW
Washington, DC 20408
(202) 523-3134

Date Established: 1935

Objectives of the Agency: Preserve and make available for reference and research the permanently valuable records of the U.S. government; operate 15 records centers and 7 presidential libraries; and publish *Federal Register* and other major publications.

Curriculum: Government, library

Subjects: Government publications
Library science

Locations:

CT, ME, MA, NH, RI, VT

Regional Archivist
Federal Archives and Records Center
380 Trapelo Rd.
Waltham, MA 02154
(617) 647-8100

NJ, NY, PR, VI

Regional Archivist
Federal Archives and Records Center
Building 22
Military Ocean Terminal Bayonne
Bayonne, NJ 07002
(201) 823-7252

DE, MD, PA, VA, WV

Regional Archivist
Federal Archives and Records Center
Ninth and Market Sts.
Philadelphia, PA 19107
(215) 597-3000

IL, IN, MI, MN, OH, WI

Regional Archivist
Federal Archives and Records Center
7358 S. Pulaski Rd.
Chicago, IL 60629
(312) 581-7816

AL, FL, GA, KY, MS, NC, SC, TN

Regional Archivist
Federal Archives and Records Center
1557 St. Joseph Ave.
East Point, GA 30344
(404) 763-7477

IA, KS, MO, NE

Regional Archivist
Federal Archives and Records Center
2306 E. Bannister Rd.
Kansas City, MO 64131
(816) 926-7271

AR, LA, NM, OK, TX

Regional Archivist
Federal Archives and Records Center
501 W. Felix St.
P.O. Box 6216
Fort Worth, TX 76115
(817) 334-5525

CO, MT, ND, SD, UT, WY

Regional Archivist
Federal Archives and Records Center
Building 48
Denver Federal Center
Denver, CO 80225
(303) 236-0818

*CA (except southern California), HI,
NV (except Clark County), Pacific Ocean area*

Regional Archivist
Federal Archives and Records Center
1000 Commodore Dr.
San Bruno, CA 94066
(415) 876-9009

*AZ, CA (southern counties of Imperial, Inyo,
Kern, Los Angeles, Orange, Riverside,
San Bernardino, San Diego, San Luis Obispo,
Santa Barbara, Ventura),
NV (only Clark County)*

Regional Archivist
Federal Archives and Records Center
24000 Avila Rd.
Laguna Niguel, CA 92677
(714) 831-4220

AK, ID, OR, WA

Regional Archivist
Federal Archives and Records Center
6125 Sand Point Way, NE
Seattle, WA 98115

Publications: Pamphlets. Fact sheets. Catalogs. Lists. Guides. Inventories. Records. Conference papers. Serials.

Bibliographies, Sales Catalogs, Publications Lists

"Consumer Information Catalog." Current. 16p. free.

Lists publications available from the Consumer Information Center.

"Documentary Teaching Units for U.S. History and Social Studies Classes from the National Archives and Records Service." n.d. 4-fold. free.

Lists teaching units for use by U.S. history, government, and social issues classes at the secondary level. Each title is $30.00.

"Select List of Publications of the National Archives and Records Service." Revised. 67p. free.

Covers publications of the Office of the National Archives, Office of Presidential Libraries, Office of Federal Records Center, Office of the Federal Register, National Historical Publications and Records Commission, National Audiovisual Center, and conference papers of the National Archives. Also includes general information leaflets, catalogs, and documents from America's past.

Serials, Subscription Publications, etc.

Code of Federal Regulations. Rev. annually. $525.00/yr. domestic, $656.25/yr. foreign.

Codifies the administrative law from the *Federal Register.* Order from: Superintendent of Documents, Government Printing Office, Washington, DC 20402.

Federal Register. Daily since 1936. $75.00/yr. domestic, $145.00/yr. foreign. The index, published monthly, is available at the subscription price of $8.00 per year.

Contains all executive orders, proclamations,

and other edicts of the President, as well as the rules and regulations of the executive departments and agencies and the independent establishments. Order from: Superintendent of Documents, Government Printing Office, Washington, DC 20402.

Weekly Compilation of Presidential Documents. Weekly. $35.00/yr. domestic, $43.75/yr. foreign.

Prints the text of proclamations and executive orders, addresses and remarks, appointments, letters, nominations submitted to the Senate, acts of the President, checklists of White House press releases, messages to Congress, and announcements of resignations and retirements. Order from: Superintendent of Documents, Government Printing Office, Washington, DC 20402.

Selected List of Books and Pamphlets

"Magna Carta." 6p. free.

Examines the legacy and importance of the Magna Carta from Runnymede to Independence Hall. Display information. Selected bibliography.

"National Archives Expands Programs for Classroom Teachers." n.d. 1p. free.

Explains the learning materials available from services from the education branch.

"Some Facts about the National Archives." 1984. 3-fold. free. General information leaflet No. 18.

Explains what the National Archives does. Includes layout of the Exhibition Hall, information on the vault, and background on the Charters of Freedom.

Audiovisuals:

Filmographies, Sales Lists, etc.

"National Archives Microfilm Publications." Current. 173p. free.

Tells what is available in the many series of records of high research value. Provides order blanks to purchase rolls.

Special Services: The National Archives offers special programs for teachers. For more information write:
Academic, Professional and Public Programs
National Archives
Eighth St. and Pennsylvania Ave., NW
Washington, DC 20408

NATIONAL ARCHIVES TRUST FUND BOARD
National Archives Bldg.
Seventh St. and Pennsylvania Ave., NW
Washington, DC 20408
(202) 523-3047

Date Established: 1941

Objectives of the Agency: Receive and administer gifts or bequests of moneys, securities, or other personal property, for the benefit of or in connection with the National Archives, its collections, or its services.

Curriculum: History, library

Subjects: Government publications
Library science

Publications: Catalogs. Books. Pamphlets. On the resources and programs of the National Archives, the regional archives, and the presidential libraries.

Bibliographies, Sales Catalogs, Publications Lists, etc.

"Select List of Publications of the National Archives and Records Service." Rev. 67p. free.

Lists publications of the National Archives and Records Service that have not been superseded or discontinued. A list of all previous publications through 1968 is available in microfilm publication M248.

Serials, Subscription Publication, etc.

"Prologue." National Archives and Records Service. Quarterly. $12.00/yr. domestic, $15.00/yr. foreign.

Brings public attention to the resources and programs of the National Archives, the regional archives, and presidential libraries through our scholarly journal. Describes records not widely known but available for research. Order from: "Prologue," NEPS-RM-B-6, National Archives Trust Fund Board, Seventh St. and Pennsylvania Ave., NW, Washington, DC 20408.

Selected List of Books and Pamphlets

"Regional Branches of the National Archives." Rev. 1984. 6p. General Information Leaflet No. 22. free.

Tells what the National Archives is, what the 11 regional archives branches do, and what their record holdings are. Includes the branches' addresses, hours, and areas served.

NATIONAL AUDIOVISUAL CENTER
National Archives and Records Service
General Services Administration
Information Services/PC
Washington, DC 20409
(301) 763-1896

Date Established: 1969

Objectives of the Agency: Be a clearinghouse for over 13,000 audiovisuals produced by or for the U.S. government. Many programs are accompanied by printed materials to increase instructional value.

Curriculum: Library

Subjects: Audiovisual materials

Publications: Pamphlets. Catalogs. Fact sheets. Updates about services. Listings of materials are updated quarterly. Special catalogs for videotapes,

American history, quitting the smoking habit, award winning collections, black history, and other topics.

Bibliographies, Sales Catalogs, Publications Lists, etc.

"Facts about AIDS." n.d. 8p. free.
Lists general public, health professional, and patient materials for sale.

"Kits for Education." 1982. 18p. free.
Lists audiocassettes, texts, sound filmstrips, sound slide sets on guidance, foreign language study, health and safety, science and technology, inservice training/administrative issues, etc.

"A List of Audiovisual Materials Produced by the United States Government for Library and Information Science." 1983. 8p. free.
Covers computer subjects, library and archival science, online retrieval and other topics.

"Media for Black Studies." n.d. 8p. free.
Describes film, video, and sound/slide programs for black history. Ordering information.

"Media for Safety & Health." 1984. 40p. free.
Lists audiovisuals for first aid, alcohol and drug abuse, family planning, and related subjects.

"Quarterly Update." Quarterly. 31p. free.
Lists recent additions to the collection of videocassettes, films, slide/tape kits, filmstrips, and audiocassette programs.

"Science for the Classroom." n.d. 14p. free.
Describes 34 video, film, and sound/slide programs about earth sciences, space studies, geology, meteorology, lab safety, and environmental studies.

"Selected Audiovisual Materials on Consumer Education Produced by the United States Government." 1981. 57p. free.
Includes smoking, aging, alcohol, first aid, parenting, food and many other topics of consumer interest.

"Selected Audiovisual Materials Produced by the United States Government." Current. 200p. free.
Tells about subject, title lists, foreign language instruction courses. Includes information about purchase, rental, and free loan policies.

"The Videocatalog." Current. 34p. free.
Tells what is available in history, science, health and other subjects.

Selected List of Books and Pamphlets

"The Central Source." 6p. free.
Explains services available from the National Audiovisual Center.

Individual Audiovisuals

"Antietam Visit." 1982. 27 minutes. 16mm. color. $285.00. A01688/EB. Also available on ¾" video ($90.00. A07209/EB), VHS ($90.00. A07211/EB), and Beta 2 ($90.00. A07210/EB).
Reenacts the battle with period dress and music.

"Eagle Has Landed: The Flight of Apollo 11." National Aeronautics and Space Administration. 1969. 29 minutes. 16mm. color. $305.00. 283380/VT. Also available on ¾" video ($90.00. A00742/VT.), VHS ($90.00. A01547/VT.), and Beta 2 ($90.00. A01578/VT.).
Illustrates man's first moon landing in 1969. Shown through television, motion picture, and still photography.

"Jennifer: A Revealing Story about Genital Herpes." National Institute of Allergies and Infectious Diseases. n.d. 28 minutes. 16mm. color. $295.00. rental $30.00. A07521/SF. Also available in ¾" video ($90.00. A07522/SF.), VHS ($90.00. A07524/SF.), and Beta 2 ($90.00. A07523/SF.).
Shows Jennifer visiting a clinic to discuss the symptoms and psychosocial problems of this sexually transmitted disease.

"The Negro Soldier." U.S. War Dept. 1944. 42 minutes. 16mm. B&W. $260.00. Rental $30.00. 547275/JY. Also available in ¾" video ($115.00. 547275/JY.), VHS ($115.00. A05811/JY.), and Beta 2 ($115.00. A05812/JY.).
Traces the black soldier from the American revolution to World War II. Produced to demonstrate to black troops their stake in the fight against the Axis powers.

"A Place in History." Eisenhower Library. 1970. 28 minutes. 16mm. color. $295.00. Rental $30.00. 600375/VT. Also available in ¾" video ($90.00. A05149/VT.), VHS ($90.00. A05150/VT.), and Beta 2 ($90.00. A05151/VT.).
Shows the life of Dwight David Eisenhower from his boyhood to his White House years told through photographs, archival film clips, and original illustrations.

"Rethinking Tomorrow." Department of Energy. 1980. 28 minutes. 16mm. color. $265.00. A03832/GE. Also available in ¾" video ($80.00. A03833/GE.), VHS ($80.00. A06183/GE.), and Beta 2 (A06184/GE.).
Shows communities which have adopted conservation programs that have reduced energy consumption without giving up quality of life.

"Shelley & Pete . . . & Carol." Public Health Service. 1980. 23 minutes. 16mm. color. $245.00. Rental $30.00. A04050/SF. Also available in ¾" video ($90.00. A04051/SF.), VHS ($90.00. A05738/SF.), and Beta 2 ($90.00. A05739/SF.).
Shows a teenage boy and girl facing an unexpected pregnancy.

Special Services: Request by card to be placed on a mailing list to receive announcements of new materials in your interest area available from the National Audiovisual Center.

Free loan distribution of 16mm films is often available from commercial distributors and from regional federal agency offices. The center refers the user to the appropriate free loan distributor whenever possible.

NATIONAL BUREAU OF STANDARDS
Department of Commerce
Information Resources and Services Division
Washington, DC 20234
(301) 921-2318

Date Established: 1901

Objectives of the Agency: Strengthen the nation's science and technology and aid their effective application for public benefit; conduct research; provide a basis for the nation's physical measurement system; and perform scientific and technological services for industry and government.

Curriculum: Science

Subjects: Measurement

Locations:

Northeastern Region

U.S. Department of Commerce
Region 1 District Office
Federal Office Bldg.
450 Main St.
Room 610-B
Hartford, CT 06103
(203) 244-3530

U.S. Department of Commerce
Region 1 District Office
441 Stuart St.
Tenth Floor
Boston, MA 02116
(617) 223-2312

U.S. Department of Commerce
Region 1 District Office
Casco Bank Bldg.
1 Memorial Circle
Augusta, ME 04330
(207) 622-8249

NH serviced by Augusta office

U.S. Department of Commerce
Region 1 District Office
1312 Federal Bldg.
111 W. Huron St.
Buffalo, NY 14202
(716) 846-4191

U.S. Department of Commerce
Region 1 District Office
183 E. Main St.
Room 666
Rochester, NY 16404
(716) 263-6480

U.S. Department of Commerce
Region 1 District Office
Federal Office Bldg.
26 Federal Plaza
Foley Square
Room 3718
New York, NY 10278

U.S. Department of Commerce
Region 1 District Office
7 Jackson Walkway
Providence, RI 02903
(401) 277-2605, ext. 22

VT serviced by Boston district

Mid-Atlantic Region

DE serviced by Philadelphia office

DC serviced by Baltimore office

U.S. Department of Commerce
Region 2 District Office
415 U.S. Customhouse
Gay and Lombard Sts.
Baltimore, MD 21202
(301) 962-3560

U.S. Department of Commerce
Region 2 District Office
101 Monroe St.
Fifteenth Floor
Rockville, MD 20850
(301) 251-2345

U.S. Department of Commerce
Region 2 District Office
240 W. State St.
Capitol Plaza
Eighth Floor
Trenton, NJ 08608
(609) 989-2100

U.S. Department of Commerce
Region 2 District Office
9448 Federal Bldg.
600 Arch St.
Philadelphia, PA 19106
(215) 597 2866

U.S. Department of Commerce
Region 2 District Office
2002 Federal Bldg.
1000 Liberty Ave.
Pittsburgh, PA 15222
(412) 644-2850

148 / National Bureau of Standards

Appalachian Region

U.S. Department of Commerce
Region 3 District Office
U.S. Post Office and Courthouse Bldg.
Room 636B
Louisville, KY 40202
(502) 582-5066

U.S. Department of Commerce
Region 3 District Office
203 Federal Bldg.
West Market St.
P.O. Box 1950
Greensboro, NC 27402
(919) 378-5345

U.S. Department of Commerce
Region 3 District Office
430 N. Salisbury St.
Dobbs Bldg.
Room 294
Raleigh, NC 27611
(919) 755-4687

U.S. Department of Commerce
Region 3 District Office
Strom Thurmond Federal Bldg.
1835 Assembly St.
Suite 172
Columbia, SC 29201
(803) 765-5345

U.S. Department of Commerce
Region 3 District Office
505 Federal Bldg.
334 Meeting St.
Charleston, SC 29403
(803) 677-4361

U.S. Department of Commerce
Region 3 District Office
P.O. Box 5823
Station B
Greenville, SC 29606
(803) 235-5919

U.S. Department of Commerce
Region 3 District Office
1 Commerce Place
Suite 1427
Nashville, TN 37239
(615) 251-5161

U.S. Department of Commerce
Region 3 District Office
3693 Central Ave.
Memphis, TN 38111
(901) 521-4826

U.S. Department of Commerce
Region 3 District Office
8010 Federal Bldg.
400 N. Eighth St.
Richmond, VA 23240
(804) 771-2246

U.S. Department of Commerce
Region 3 District Office
3000 New Federal Bldg.
500 Quarrier St.
Charleston, WV 25301
(304) 343-6181, ext. 375

Southeastern Region

U.S. Department of Commerce
Region 4 District Office
908 S. Twentieth St.
Suite 200-201
Birmingham, AL 35205
(205) 254-1331

U.S. Department of Commerce
Region 4 District Office
51 S.W. First Ave.
Federal Bldg.
Suite 224
Miami, FL 33130
(305) 350-5267

U.S. Department of Commerce
Region 4 District Office
128 N. Osceola Ave.
Clearwater, FL 33515
(813) 461-0011

U.S. Department of Commerce
Region 4 District Office
3 Independent Dr.
Jacksonville, FL 32202
(904) 791-2796

U.S. Department of Commerce
Region 4 District Office
75 E. Ivanhoe Blvd.
Orlando, FL 32802
(305) 425-1247

U.S. Department of Commerce
Region 4 District Office
Collins Bldg.
Room G-20
Tallahassee, FL 32304
(904) 488-6469

U.S. Department of Commerce
Region 4 District Office
1365 Peachtree St., NE
Atlanta, GA 30309
(404) 881-7000

U.S. Department of Commerce
Region 4 District Office
27 E. Bay St.
P.O. Box 9746
Savannah, GA 31401
(912) 944-4204

U.S. Department of Commerce
Region 4 District Office
Jackson Mall Office Center
300 Woodrow Wilson Blvd.
Suite 3230
Jackson, MS 39213
(601) 960-4388

U.S. Department of Commerce
Region 4 District Office
Federal Bldg.
Room 659
San Juan, PR 00918
(809) 753-4555, ext. 555

Great Lakes Region

U.S. Department of Commerce
Region 5 District Office
1406 Mid Continental Plaza Bldg.
55 E. Monroe St.
Chicago, IL 60603
(312) 353-4450

U.S. Department of Commerce
Region 5 District Office
W.R. Harper College
Algonquin & Roselle Rd.
Palatine, IL 60603
(312) 397-3000

U.S. Department of Commerce
Region 5 District Office
357 U.S. Courthouse and Federal Office Bldg.
46 E. Ohio St.
Indianapolis, IN 46204
(317) 269-6214

U.S. Department of Commerce
Region 5 District Office
445 Federal Bldg.
231 W. Lafayette
Detroit, MI 48226
(313) 226-3650

U.S. Department of Commerce
Region 5 District Office
300 Monroe, NW
Room 409
Grand Rapids, MI 49503
(616) 456-2411

U.S. Department of Commerce
Region 5 District Office
108 Federal Bldg.
110 S. Fourth St.
Minneapolis, MN 55401
(612) 349-3338

U.S. Department of Commerce
Region 5 District Office
9504 Federal Office Bldg.
550 Main St.
Cincinnati, OH 45202
(513) 684-2944

U.S. Department of Commerce
Region 5 District Office
666 Euclid Ave.
Room 600
Cleveland, OH 44114
(216) 522-4750

U.S. Department of Commerce
Region 5 District Office
Federal Bldg.
U.S. Courthouse
517 E. Wisconsin Ave.
Milwaukee, WI 53202
(414) 291-3473

Plains Region

U.S. Department of Commerce
Region 6 District Office
817 Federal Bldg.
210 Walnut St.
Des Moines, IA 50309
(515) 284-4222

U.S. Department of Commerce
Region 6 District Office
P.O. Box 48
Wichita State University
Wichita, KS 67208
(316) 269-6160

U.S. Department of Commerce
Region 6 District Office
120 S. Central Ave.
St. Louis, MO 63105
(314) 425-3302

U.S. Department of Commerce
Region 6 District Office
601 E. Twelfth St.
Room 1840
Kansas City, MO 64106
(816) 374-3142

ND serviced by Omaha office

150 / *National Bureau of Standards*

U.S. Department of Commerce
Region 6 District Office
Empire State Bldg.
300 S. Nineteenth St.
First Floor
Omaha, NE 68102
(402) 221-3664

SD serviced by Omaha office

Central Region

U.S. Department of Commerce
Region 7 District Office
Savers Federal Bldg.
320 W. Capitol Ave.
Suite 635
Little Rock, AR 72201
(501) 378-5794

U.S. Department of Commerce
Region 7 District Office
432 International Trade Mart
No. 2 Canal St.
New Orleans, LA 70130
(504) 589-6546

U.S. Department of Commerce
Region 7 District Office
505 Marquette Ave., NW
Suite 1015
Albuquerque, NM 87102
(505) 766-2386

U.S. Department of Commerce
Region 7 District Office
4024 Lincoln Blvd.
Oklahoma City, OK 73105
(405) 231-5302

U.S. Department of Commerce
Region 7 District Office
440 S. Houston St.
Tulsa, OK 74127
(918) 581-7650

U.S. Department of Commerce
Region 7 District Office
1100 Commerce St.
Room 7A5
Dallas, TX 75242
(214) 767-0542

U.S. Department of Commerce
Region 7 District Office
2625 Federal Courthouse Bldg.
515 Rusk St.
Houston, TX 77002
(713) 229-2578

Rocky Mountain Region

U.S. Department of Commerce
Region 8 District Office
2750 Valley Bank Center
201 N. Central Ave.
Phoenix, AZ 85073
(602) 261-3285

U.S. Department of Commerce
Region 8 District Office
U.S. Customhouse
721 Nineteenth St.
Room 119
Denver, CO 80202
(303) 837-3246

U.S. Department of Commerce
Region 8 District Office
Statehouse
Boise, ID 83720
(208) 334-2470

MT serviced by Denver office

U.S. Department of Commerce
Region 8 District Office
17TT E. Plumb Lane, #152
Reno, NV 89502
(702) 784-5203

U.S. Department of Commerce
Region 8 District Office
U.S. Courthouse
350 S. Main St.
Salt Lake City, UT 84101
(801) 524-5115

WY serviced by Denver office

Pacific Region

U.S. Department of Commerce
Region 9 District Office
701 C St.
P.O. Box 32
Anchorage, AK 99513
(907) 271-5041

U.S. Department of Commerce
Region 9 District Office
11777 San Vicente Blvd.
Room 800
Los Angeles, CA 90049
(213) 209-6707

U.S. Department of Commerce
Region 9 District Office
Port Administration Bldg.
3165 Pacific Hwy.
Second Floor
San Diego, CA 92101
(619) 293-5395

U.S. Department of Commerce
Region 9 District Office
Federal Bldg.
450 Golden Gate Ave.
Box 36013
San Francisco, CA 36013
(415) 556-5860

U.S. Department of Commerce
Region 9 District Office
111 W. Saint John St.
Room 424
San Jose, CA 95113
(408) 275-7648

U.S. Department of Commerce
Region 9 District Office
4106 Federal Bldg.
300 Ala Moana Blvd.
P.O. Box 50026
Honolulu, HI 96850
(808) 546-8694

U.S. Department of Commerce
Region 9 District Office
1220 S.W. Third Ave.
Portland, OR 97204
(503) 221-3001

U.S. Department of Commerce
Region 9 District Office
Lake Union Bldg.
1700 Westlake Ave., North
Room 706
Seattle, WA 98109
(206) 442-5616

U.S. Department of Commerce
Region 9 District Office
P.O. Box 2170
Spokane, WA 99210
(509) 838-8202

Publications: Periodicals. Monographs. Handbooks. Proceedings. Statistics. Reports. Papers. Standards. Most publications may be purchased from the Superintendent of Documents or from Department of Commerce district offices. Papers include such subjects as acoustics, fire, lasers, nuclear physics, and thermodynamics.

Bibliographies, Sales Catalogs, Publications Lists, etc.

"NBS Publications Program: List of Publications." Rev. regularly. 70p. free. LP80.

Includes how to order materials, document availability, listing of NBS papers by major subject areas, list of U.S. Depository Libraries, and order blanks. Begins with *Acoustics and Sound* category and ends with *Thermodynamics and Chemical Kinetics.*"

The Bureau regularly announce their publications in:

Journal of Research of the National Bureau of Standards. Lists publications as issued. Description of this journal appears under *Serials* section.

Monthly Catalog of United States Government Publications. Issued by the Superintendent of Documents, U.S. Government Printing Office, Washington, DC 20402.

Catalog of all Publications. This list of almost 20,000 titles may be ordered from: Superintendent of Documents, U.S. Government Printing Office, Washington, DC 20402.

Commerce Publications Update. Biweekly annoucement of publications of the Department of Commerce. Lists titles and prices of National Bureau of Standards Publications, as well as other Department of Commerce offices. Write: Office of Information Services, U.S. Department of Commerce, Washington, DC 20230.

NBS Catalogs of NBS Publications. These catalogs list NBS publications through 1983 and are available from: Superintendent of Documents, U.S. Government Printing Office, Washington, DC 20402; or: National Technical Information Service, U.S. Department of Commerce, Springfield, VA 22161. A library which maintains sets of National Bureau of Standards Publications may be consulted.

Serials, Subscription Publications, etc.

Journal of Research of the National Bureau of Standards. Bimonthly. In paper covers, $18.00/yr. U.S. and its possessions, $22.00/yr. foreign. Bound volume (1 per year) price varies.

Reports NBS research and development in those areas of physical and engineering sciences such as physics, chemistry, engineering, mathematics, and computer sciences. Emphasizes measurement methodology and the basic technology underlying standardization.

Journal of Physical and Chemical Reference Data. Quarterly. American Chemical Society and American Institute of Physics. $199.00/yr. domestic, foreign rates vary.

Provides physical and chemical property data and critical reviews of measurement techniques. Its main source is the National Standard Reference Data System. Order from: American Chemical Society, Periodicals Marketing Department, 1155 Sixteenth St., NW, Washington, DC 20036. Members of ACS or of AIP or affiliated society should inquire about lower rates.

Selected List of Books and Pamphlets

"National Bureau of Standards." 1984. 48p. free. Publication 679.

Explains what the various centers, institutes,

152 / National Bureau of Standards

and offices do, for example, what services the center for basic standards performs. B&W photographs of on-site operations.

Special Services: Microfiche copies of all recent publications may be ordered from the National Technical Information Service, U.S. Department of Commerce, Springfield, VA 22161.

Copies of patents may be obtained for 50 cents each from:
U.S. Patent and Trademark Office
Washington, DC 20231

Photoduplicated copies of many publications may be purchased from the Library of Congress. For information, write:
Photoduplication Service
Library of Congress
Washington, DC 20540

You may have your name added to the announcement list of new publications as issued by the bureau. A form is provided (Notification Key N519) in "NBS Publications Program" (LP80), previously annotated. Publications may also be purchased directly from the Superintendent of Documents, Government Printing Office, Washington, DC 20402.

NATIONAL CANCER INSTITUTE
National Institutes of Health
Public Health Service
Public Inquiries Section
Office of Cancer Communications
Bethesda, MD 20205
(800) 4 CANCER
Oahu, HI: (808) 524-1234 (neighbor islands call collect)
Washington, DC and suburbs in MD and VA: (202) 636-5700
AK: (800) 638-6070
CA (area codes 213, 714, 619, 805), FL, GA, IL, TX, New York City, and northern New Jersey: Spanish-speaking staff members are available to callers during the daytime

Date Established: 1937

Objectives of the Agency: Expand existing scientific knowledge on cancer cause and prevention as well as on the diagnosis, treatment and rehabilitation of cancer patients.

Curriculum: Health

Subjects: Cancer

Publications: Pamphlets. Handbooks. Fact sheets. Books. Reports.

Bibliographies, Sales Catalogs, Publications Lists, etc.

"Publications List for the Public and Patients." Current. 10p. free.
Describes general and patient materials, which are all free. Order form.

Selected List of Books and Pamphlets

"Breast Cancer: We're Making Progress Every Day." 1983. 12p. free. NIH Publication No. 83-2409.
Describes risks, signs, self-examination, mammography, biopsy, and treatment options.

"Cancer Facts: For People over 50." 1984. 4p. free. NIH Publication No. 84-456.
Explains symptoms to watch for and what to do if you detect signs.

"Cancer Information Service Leaflet (1-800-4-CANCER)." 1984. 2p. free.
Explains the system of toll-free information lines.

"Cancer — What To Know — What To Do about It." 1983. 23p. free. NIH Publication No. 84-211.
Tells what cancer is, who gets it, and what to do about it. Glossary.

"Good News: Better News: Best News . . . Cancer Prevention." 1984. 16p. free.
Describes cancer risks and ways to reduce them. Gives information about tobacco, diet, alcohol, and sun exposure. Glossary.

"Medicine for the Layman." 1982. 32p. free.
Describes types of treatment for cancer and new directions. Includes a section of questions and answers.

"Why Do You Smoke?" 1980. 6p. free.
Administers a self-test to determine why you smoke. Provides alternatives and substitutes.

NATIONAL CAPITAL PARKS
U.S. Department of the Interior
National Park Service
1100 Ohio Dr., SW
Washington, DC 20242

Date Established: 1933

Objectives: Maintain a park system for the nation's capital.

Curriculum: Social studies

Subjects: Washington, DC — buildings

Publications: Pamphlets. On such attractions as the Washington Monument.

Selected List of Books and Pamphlets

"The Lincoln Memorial." 1982. 8p. free.
Describes building the memorial, architecture, murals, Lincoln's place as president, and statistics of the memorial. Photographs.

"Thomas Jefferson Memorial." 1980. 10p. free.
Describes Jefferson's accomplishments, the memorial site, the memorial building, and four panels. Includes portions of Jefferson's writings. Photographs.

"The Washington Monument." 1983. 8p. free.
Gives construction history, Washington's contributions, and statistics of the monument. Photographs.

"Welcome to Washington." 1982. 28p. free.
Lists attractions to visit. Includes hours, telephone numbers of various sites, and visitor information. Maps, photographs.

"The White House." 1985. 10p. free.
Gives history of the building; description, use, and location of various rooms; improvements and renovations; and visitor information.

NATIONAL CENTER FOR DEVICES AND RADIOLOGICAL HEALTH
U.S. Department of Health and Human Services
Public Health Service
Food and Drug Administration
Rockville, MD 20857
(301) 443-4690
(301) 427-7163

Date Established: 1982

Objectives of the Agency: Develop and implement national programs to protect the public health in the fields of medical devices and radiological health.

Curriculum: Health

Subjects: X-rays

Locations:

CT, MA, ME, NH, RI, VT

Regional Radiological Health Office
Food and Drug Administration
U.S. Department of Health and Human Services
585 Commercial St.
Boston, MA 12109
(617) 223-3178
(617) 223-5859

NJ, NY, PR, VI

Regional Radiological Health Office
Food and Drug Administration
U.S. Department of Health and Human Services
850 Third Ave.
Brooklyn, NY 11232
(212) 965-5052

DC, DE, MD, PA, VA, WV

Regional Radiological Health Office
Food and Drug Administration
U.S. Department of Health and Human Services
900 U.S. Customhouse
Second and Chestnut Sts.
Philadelphia, PA 19106
(215) 597-4506
(215) 597-9925

AL, FL, GA, KY, MS, NC, SC, TN

Regional Radiological Health Office
Food and Drug Administration
U.S. Department of Health and Human Services
880 W. Peachtree St., North
Atlanta, GA 30309
(404) 881-3576

IL, IN, MI, MN, OH, WI

Regional Radiological Health Office
Food and Drug Administration
U.S. Department of Health and Human Services
Room A 1945
175 W. Jackson Blvd.
Chicago, IL 60604
(312) 353-9408

AR, LA, NM, OK, TX

Regional Radiological Health Office
Food and Drug Administration
U.S. Department of Health and Human Services
3032 Bryan
Room 470B
Dallas, TX 75204
(214) 767-5431

IA, KS, MO, NE

Regional Radiological Health Office
Food and Drug Administration
U.S. Department of Health and Human Services
1009 Cherry St.
Kansas City, MO 64106
(816) 374-3817

CO, MT, ND, SD, UT, WY

Regional Radiological Health Office
Food and Drug Administration
U.S. Department of Health and Human Services
U.S. Customhouse
721 Nineteenth St.
Room 500
Denver, CO 80202
(303) 837-4917

AS, AZ, CA, GU, HI, NV

Regional Radiological Health Office
Food and Drug Administration
U.S. Department of Health and Human Services
Federal Office Bldg.
50 Fulton St.
San Francisco, CA 94102
(415) 556-2264

AK, ID, OR, WA

Regional Radiological Health Office
Food and Drug Administration
U.S. Department of Health and Human Services
Federal Office Bldg.
909 First Ave.
Room 5003
Seattle, WA 98174
(206) 442-7020

Publications: Reports. Handbooks. Guides. Catalogs. Bookmarks. Sourcebooks. Pamphlets. Cards. Posters.

Bibliographies, Sales Catalogs, Publications Lists, etc.

"Mini Communications Package." n.d. 12p. free.

Provides order form for free materials or for free negatives of the materials so you can print them yourself. Also gives announcements you can use in publications directed to health care professionals and one to consumers. Lists state coordinators to contact for help.

"Radiological Health Training Resources Catalog." Updated biennially. 52p. free.

Lists materials that are for sale from the Government Printing Office or the National Technical Information Service. Also lists materials that are available from the Office of Radiological Health.

"Sourcebook: Medical Radiation Material for Patients." n.d. 35p. free

Lists print and nonprint materials for sale and free on general radiation, diagnostic X-rays, dental X-rays, ultrasound, nuclear medicine, mammography, and other topics.

Selected List of Books and Pamphlets

"FDA and X-Ray Record Card." n.d. 3-fold. free. HHS Publication No. (FDA) 80-8024.

Gives consumer safety tips on X-rays and a record for an individual to keep of the date, type of exam, referring doctor, and address where X-ray is kept. Also available in Spanish: "FDA Tarjeta de Rayos X." (FDA) 80-8024S.

"Get the Picture on Dental X-Rays." 1982. 5-fold. free. HHS Publication No. (FDA) 80-811.

Answers the questions: How do X-rays work? What are they? Are dental X-ray examinations safe? Includes card on which to record X-ray examinations.

"Primer on Radiation." 1981. 8p. free. HHS Publication No. (FDA) 79-8099.

Reprints an article from "FDA Consumer." Photographs.

"X-Ray Scans: Getting a Clearer Picture." 1980. 8p. HHS Publication No. (FDA) 76-8062.

Reprints an article from "FDA Consumer." Photographs.

"X-Rays: Get the Picture on Protection." n.d. poster or table-top easel. free. HHS Publication No. (FDA) 78-1045.

Shows in illustration of a woman with the question: "Pregnant? Or think you might be . . . tell your doctor before getting an X-ray or prescription." Also available in Spanish. (FDA) 78-1045S.

"X-Rays: So You Want To Be in Pictures?" Bookmarks. free. HHS Publication No. (FDA) 80-8105.

Gives tips on X-ray safety. Also available in Spanish. (FDA) 80-8105S.

Audiovisuals

Filmographies, Sales Lists, etc.

"Radiological Health Training Resources Catalog." Updated biennially. 52p. free. HHS Publication No. (FDA) 83-8023.

Lists video programs, slide/sound programs. Includes titles of radiological health subjects ranging from basic fundamentals to historical perspectives and current state-of-the-art. Order forms.

"X-Rays: So You Want To Be in Pictures." Poster or table-top easel. free. HEW Publication No. (FDA) 80-8115.

Gives consumer tips on X-ray protection and ordering information on slide set package and filmstrip package programs for sale.

Special Services: Inquire about publications available in microfiche from:
National Technical Information Service
5285 Port Royal Rd.
Springfield, VA 22161

For a copy of the short courses announcements offered by universities, commercial companies, or agencies other than the center, write:
DTS, OTA, NCDRH, FHA (HFX-73)
5600 Fishers Lane
Rockville, MD 20857
(301) 443-4647

NATIONAL CENTER FOR EDUCATION IN MATERNAL AND CHILD HEALTH

3520 Prospect St., NW
Washington, DC 20057
(202) 625-8400

Date Established: 1982

Objectives of the Agency: Link between sources of information/services and the professional in areas of maternal and child health, including medical genetics; serve the lay public by providing specific information.

Curriculum: Child care

Subjects: Child development
Pregnancy

Locations:

AK
Family Health Section
State Department of Health and Social Services
Pouch H-06B
Juneau, AK 99801
(907) 465-3100

AL
Bureau of Maternal, Child Health, and Family Planning
State Department of Public Health
State Office Bldg.
Montgomery, AL 36130
(205) 832-6525

Division of Rehabilative and Crippled Children's Services
2129 E. South Blvd.
Montgomery, AL 36111
(205) 281-8780

AR
Division of Maternal and Child Health
State Health Department of Arkansas
4815 W. Markham
Little Rock, AR 72201
(501) 661-2242

Crippled Children's Section of Social Services
Department of Human Services
P.O. Box 1437
Little Rock, AR 72203
(501) 371-2277

AS
Chief of Maternal and Child Health Services
Division of Public Health
Department of Health
Pago Pago, AS 96799
011 (684) 633-5318

AZ
Bureau of Maternal and Child Health
Division of Family Health Services
State of Arizona Department of Health
200 N. Curry Rd.
Tempe, AZ 85281
(602) 968-6461

Bureau of Crippled Children's Services
State of Arizona Crippled Children's Services
200 N. Curry Rd.
Tempe, AZ 85281
(602) 968-6461

CA
Maternal and Child Health Branch
State Department of Health
741-744 P St.
Sacramento, CA 95814
(916) 322-2950

California Crippled Children's Services
State Department of Health
741-744 P St.
Sacramento, CA 95814
(916) 322-2090

CO
Medical Affairs and Special Programs
Colorado Department of Health
4210 E. Eleventh Ave.
Denver, CO 80220
(303) 320-6137

Family Health Services Division
Colorado Department of Health
4210 E. Eleventh Ave.
Denver, CO 80220
(303) 320-6137

CT
Chief, Maternal and Child Health Section
State Department of Health
79 Elm St.
Hartford, CT 06115
(203) 566-5425

Chief, Health Services for Handicapped Children's Section
State Department of Health
79 Elm St.
Hartford, CT 06115
(203) 566-2057

DC
D.C. Office of Maternal and Child Health
1875 Connecticut Ave., NW
Room 804D
Washington, DC 20009
(202) 673-6750

DE
Bureau of Personal Health Services
Division of Public Health
Jesse S. Cooper Memorial Bldg.
Capitol Square
Dover, DE 19901
(302) 736-4768

FL

Maternal and Child Health
Department of Health and Rehabilitative Services
1317 Winewood Blvd.
Building 1
Room 214
Tallahassee, FL 32301
(904) 487-1321

Children's Medical Services Program Office
Department of Health and Rehabilitative Services
1323 Winewood Blvd.
Building 5
Room 127
Tallahassee, FL 32301
(904) 487-2690

GA

Family Health, Division of Physical Health
Georgia Department of Human Resources
47 Trinity Ave., SW
Atlanta, GA 30334
(404) 656-4596

Children's Medical Services
Georgia Department of Human Resources
47 Trinity Ave., SW
Atlanta, GA 30334
(404) 656-4830

GU

Department of Public Health and Social Services
Government of Guam
P.O. Box 2816
Agana, GU 96910
Overseas Operator: 734-9918

HI

Maternal and Chief Health Branch
State of Hawaii Department of Health
741-A Sunset Ave.
Honolulu, HI 96816
(808) 548-6554

Crippled Children's Services Branch
State of Hawaii Department of Health
741 Sunset Ave.
Honolulu, HI 96816
(808) 732-3197

IA

Maternal and Child Health Section
State Department of Health
Lucas Office Bldg.
Third Floor
Des Moines, IA 50319
(515) 281-3732

Mobile and Regional Child Health Specialty Clinics and Related Programs
Specialized Child Health Services
The University of Iowa, Hospitals and Clinics
Iowa City, IA 52242
(319) 353-4250

ID

Bureau of Child Health and Crippled Children's Services
Idaho Department of Health and Welfare
450 W. State
Boise, ID 83720
(208) 334-4136

IL

Division of Family Health
Department of Public Health
535 W. Jefferson St.
Springfield, IL 62706
(217) 785-4899

Division of Services for Crippled Children
University of Illinois
540 Iles Park Place
Springfield, IL 62718
(217) 782-7001

IN

Maternal and Child Health Program
State Board of Health
1330 W. Michigan St.
Indianapolis, IN 46206
(317) 633-8449

Division of Services for Crippled Children
State Department of Public Welfare
100 N. Senate Ave.
Room 702
Indianapolis, IN 46204
(317) 232-4280

KS

Bureau of Maternal and Child Health
State Department of Health and Environment
Topeka, KS 66620
(913) 862-9360, ext. 437

Crippled Children's Services
State Department of Health and Environment
Topeka, KS 66620
(913) 862-9360, ext. 525

KY

Division of Maternal and Child Health
Bureau for Health Services
State Department of Human Resources
275 E. Main St.
Frankfort, KY 40601
(502) 564-4830

LA

Office of Health Services and Environmental
  Quality's Handicapped Children's Services
  Program
P.O. Box 60630
New Orleans, LA 70160
(504) 589-5055

MA

Division of Family Health Services
Massachusetts Department of Public Health
39 Boylston St.
Boston, MA 02116
(617) 727-3372

Services to Handicapped Children
Division of Family Health Services
Massachusetts Division of Family Health
39 Boylston St.
Boston, MA 02116
(617) 727-5812

Mariana Islands

Maternal and Child Health, Crippled Children's
  Services and Family Planning
Government of the Northern Mariana Islands
Saipan, Mariana Islands 96950

MD

Division of Infant, Child and Adolescent Preventive
  Medicine Administration
State Department of Health and Mental Hygiene
201 W. Preston St.
Fourth Floor
Baltimore, MD 21201
(301) 383-4797

Department of Maternal Health and Population
  Dynamics
201 W. Preston St.
Fourth Floor
Baltimore, MD 21201
(301) 383-6464

Division of Crippled Children's Services
Mental Retardation and Developmenal Disabilities
  Administration
State Department of Health and Mental Hygiene
201 W. Preston St.
Fourth Floor
Baltimore, MD 21201
(301) 383-2821

ME

Division of Child Health and Crippled Children's
  Services
Department of Human Services
157 Capital St.
Augusta, ME 04333
(207) 289-3311

MI

Health Promotion/Disease Prevention
  Administration
Department of Public Health
3500 N. Logan St.
P.O. Box 30035
Lansing, MI 48909
(517) 373-3650

MN

Maternal and Child Health Section
Department of Health
717 Delaware St., SE
Minneapolis, MN 55440
(612) 623-5539

Services for Children with Handicaps
Department of Health
717 Delaware St., SE
Minneapolis, MN 55440
(612) 623-5170

MO

Bureau of Maternal and Child Health
State Board of Health
705 S. Fifth St.
P.O. Box 570
Jefferson City, MO 65102
(314) 751-4667

Crippled Children's Services
Department of Social Services
Division of Health
207 Metro Dr.
Box 570
Jefferson City, MO 65102
(314) 751-2407

MS

Bureau of Personal Health Services
State Board of Health
P.O. Box 1700
Jackson, MS 39205
(601) 354-6680

MT

Maternal and Child Health Bureau
Health Services Division
Department of Health and Environmental Sciences
Cogswell Bldg.
Helena, MT 59601
(406) 449-2554

NC

Maternal and Child Health Branch
Division of Human Resources
P.O. Box 2091
Raleigh, NC 27602
(919) 733-7791

Maternal and Child Care Section
Division of Health Services
P.O. Box 2091
Raleigh, NC 27602
(919) 733-3816

Crippled Children's Program
Division of Health Services
P.O. Box 2091
Raleigh, NC 27602
(919) 733-7437

ND

Maternal and Child Health Program
State Capitol Bldg.
Bismarck, ND 58501
(701) 224-2493

Crippled Children's Program
State Capital
Bismarck, ND 58505
(701) 224-2436

NE

Maternal and Child Health Division
State Department of Health
301 Centennial Mall South
Third Floor
P.O. Box 95007
Lincoln, NE 68508
(402) 471-2907

Nebraska Services for Crippled Children
Department of Public Welfare
301 Centennial Mall South
Fifth Floor
Lincoln, NE 68508
(404) 471-3121, ext. 186

NH

Office of Family and Community Health
New Hampshire Division of Public Health Services
Hazen Dr.
Concord, NH 03301
(603) 271-4517

NJ

Maternal and Child Health Program
State Department of Health
CN 364
Trenton, NJ 08625
(609) 292-5616

Special Child Health Services
State Department of Health
CN 364
Trenton, NJ 08625
(609) 292-5676

NM

Children's Medical Services
Health and Environment Department
P.O. Box 968
Santa Fe, NM 87503
(505) 984-0030

Maternal and Child Health Bureau
Health and Environment Department
Maternal Health Section
P.O. Box 968
Santa Fe, NM 87503
(505) 984-0030

Health Services Division
Health and Environment Department
P.O. Box 968
Santa Fe, NM 87503
(505) 984-0030

NV

Bureau of Maternal, Child and School Health and
  Bureau of Crippled Children's Services
State Department of Human Resources
505 E. King St.
Carson City, NV 89710
(702) 885-4885

NY

Bureau of Maternal and Child Health
State Department of Health
Tower Bldg.
Empire State Plaza
Albany, NY 12237
(518) 474-3664

Special Children Services
Bureau of Maternal and Child Health
State Department of Health
Tower Bldg.
Empire State Plaza
Albany, NY 12237
(518) 474-1911

OH

Division of Maternal and Child Health
State Department of Health
P.O. Box 118
246 N. High St.
Columbus, OH 43215
(614) 466-3543

OK

MCH Medical Programs
Maternal and Child Health Services
State Department of Health
1000 N.W. Tenth St.
P.O. Box 53551
Oklahoma City, OK 73152
(405) 271-4476

Medical Services Administration
Department of Human Services
P.O. Box 25352
Oklahoma City, OK 73125
(405) 521-3902

OR

Maternal and Child Health Program
Oregon State Health Division
P.O. Box 231
Portland, OR 97207
(503) 229-5593

Crippled Children's Division
University of Oregon Medical School
3181 S.W. Sam Jackson Park Rd.
Portland, OR 97201
(503) 225-8362

PA

Division of Parent, Child, and School Health
Bureau of Professional Health Services
State Department of Health
P.O. Box 90
Harrisburg, PA 17120
(717) 787-7440

Children's Rehabilitative Services
Bureau of Professional Health Services
State Department of Health
P.O. Box 90
Harrisburg, PA 17120
(717) 783-5436

PR

Assistant Secretary for Health for Ambulatory Services
Box CH-11321
Caparra Heights Station
San Juan, PR 00922
(809) 783-5120

Maternal and Child Health
Commonwealth of Puerto Rico
Department of Health
Building A
Call Box 70184
San Juan, PR 00936
(809) 763-5120

RI

Division of Family Health
Department of Health
75 Davis St.
Room 302
Providence, RI 02908
(401) 277-2312

SC

Division of Maternal and Child Care
Department of Health and Environmental Control
J. Marion Sims Bldg.
2600 Bull St.
Columbia, SC 29201
(803) 758-8553

Commissioner for Health Protection
J. Marion Sims Bldg.
2600 Bull St.
Columbia, SC 29201
(803) 758-8553

Division of CC
Department of Health and Environmental Control
2600 Bull St.
Columbia, SC 29201
(803) 758-5491

SD

Division of Health Services
South Dakota State Department of Health
Joe Foss Bldg.
Room 313
Pierre, SD 57501
(605) 773-3737

TN

Maternal and Child Health
State Department of Public Health
R. S. Gass Bldg.
Ben Allen Rd.
Nashville, TN 37216
(615) 741-7335

Trust Territory of the Pacific

Maternal and Child Health and Crippled Children's Services
Department of Health Services
Office of the High Commissioner
Trust Territory of the Pacific Islands
Saipan, Mariana Islands 96950
9355 (through Overseas Operator 0-160691)

TX

Division of Maternal and Child Health
Texas Department of Health
1100 W. Forty-Ninth St.
Austin, TX 78756
(512) 458-7700

Crippled Children's Program
Texas Department of Health
1100 W. Forty-Ninth St.
Austin, TX 78756
(512) 458-7700

UT

Division of Family Health Services
Utah Department of Health
44 Medical Dr.
Salt Lake City, UT 84113
(801) 533-4217

Maternal and Child Health Bureau
Utah Department of Health
44 Medical Dr.
Salt Lake City, UT 84113
(801) 533-4217

Handicapped Children's Services Division
Utah Department of Health
2738 South, 2000 East
Salt Lake City, UT 84106
(801) 533-4173

VA

Bureau of Maternal and Child Health
State Department of Health
109 Governor St.
Richmond, VA 23219
(804) 786-7367

Bureau of Crippled Children's Services
State Department of Health
109 Governor St.
Richmond, VA 23219
(804) 786-7367

VI

Department of Health
P.O. Box 7309
Charlotte Amalie
St. Thomas, VI 00801
(809) 774-0117

VT

Medical Services Division
Vermont Department of Health
115 Colchester Ave.
Burlington, VT 05401
(802) 862-5701, ext. 365

WA

Maternal and Child Health
Office of Community Health
Division of Health Services
Airport Building 3
MS-LC-11A
Olympia, WA 98504
(206) 753-7520

Crippled Children's Services Section
Office of Community Health Services
Airport Building 3
MS-LC-12
Olympia, WA 98504
(206) 753-9619

WI

Bureau of Community Health and Prevention
Wisconsin Division of Health
P.O. Box 309
1 W. Wilson St.
Madison, WI 53701
(608) 266-2661

Bureau for Children with Physical Needs
P.O. Box 7841
Madison, WI 53707

WV

Division of Maternal and Child Care
State Department of Health
State Office Building No. 1
1800 Washington St., East
Charleston, WV 25305
(304) 348-2955

Division of Handicapped Children
West Virginia Department of Welfare
Morris Square
1212 Lewis St.
Charleston, WV 25301
(304) 348-3071

WY

Division of Health and Medical Services
State Department of Health and Social Services
Hathaway Office Bldg.
Cheyenne, WY 82002
(307) 777-7121

Publications: Pamphlets. Bibliographies. Newsletters. Directories. Workshop proceedings. Catalogs. Workbooks. Guides. On prenatal care and resources on child and maternal care.

Bibliographies, Sales Catalogs, Publications Lists, etc.

"Publications Catalog." Current. 14p. free.
    Lists materials on maternal and child health, genetic diseases, mental retardation, lead poisoning prevention, sickle cell, hemophilia, adolescent health, etc.

Selected List of Books and Pamphlets

"Food for the Teenager During and After Pregnancy." n.d. 32p. free. DHHS Publication No. (HRSA) 82-5106.
    Gives food guide to groups of foods, sample meals, general health tips.

"NCEMCH." n.d. 6p. free.
    Tells what the National Center for Education and Maternal and Child Health is, and what services it offers. Gives examples of publications.

"Prenatal Care." 1983. 98p. free.

Explains pregnancy signs, prenatal care, development of the baby, pregnant lifestyle, nutrition, common discomforts and problems, labor and delivery, hospital stay and recovery, the baby.

"Starting Early: A Guide to Federal Resources in Maternal and Child Health." 1984. 86p. free.

Provides a guide to help health professionals, educators, administrators and the general public to contact federal resources in maternal and child health. Divided into: *Maternal and Child Health; Infant, Child and Adolescent Health;* and *Appendix.* Each entry has: title, type of resource, length, date, publication number, audience level, availability and price, source, and annotation.

NATIONAL CENTER FOR EDUCATION STATISTICS
Department of Education
Statistical Information Office
400 Maryland Ave., SW
Brown Bldg.
Room 600
Washington, DC 20202
(301) 436-7900

Date Established: 1968

Objectives of the Agency: Collect and disseminate statistics and other data related to education in this country and in other countries.

Curriculum: Education

Subjects: Education—statistics

Publications: Bulletins. Releases. Reports. Microfiche. Data on educational topics.

Bibliographies, Sales Catalogs, Publications Lists, etc.

"Data Tape Available for the Fall 1982 Public School Universe, part I." 1985. 2p. free. NCES 85-101T.

Gives description of tape and ordering information. Includes name of school, mailing addresses, student enrollment, number of full-time teachers, code for type of school, code for type of agency that operates the school.

"High School and Beyond Data Files Now Include Pell Grant Data." 1985. 6p. free. NCES 85-204T.

Tells what the files contain. Gives ordering information.

"Selected Publications from NCES." Current. 16p. free.

Tells what is available and how to order. For sale and free publications from the National Center for Education Statistics, Superintendent of Documents, ERIC Document Reproduction Service, and National Technical Information Service.

Selected List of Books and Pamphlets

"More Coursework in the New Basics Is Needed To Meet Standards of National Commission on Excellence in Education." 1984. 10p. free.

Examines the distribution of courses taken in the new basics, with a look at the credits needed by some students to meet NCEE standards. Describes the number of credits earned by grade level. Compares credits earned among students with different backgrounds. Graphs. Tables. Analysis.

"Trends in Education 1972-73 to 1992-93." 1984. 4p. free.

Gives statistics for 50 states and DC for such categories as *Enrollment, Earned Degrees, Instructional Staff,* and others. Includes projected figures and percent change.

NATIONAL CENTER FOR PREVENTION AND CONTROL OF RAPE
National Institute of Mental Health
Parklawn Bldg.
5600 Fishers Lane
Room 6C-12
Rockville, MD 20857
(301) 443-1910

Date Established: 1975

Objectives of the Agency: Fund research projects and disseminate research findings in the area of rape and other forms of sexual abuse.

Curriculum: Guidance, women's studies

Subjects: Crime
Rape

Publications: Reports. Pamphlets. Directories. Bibliographies. On rape prevention, sexual abuse in the home, and activities of the center.

Bibliographies, Sales Catalogs, Publications Lists, etc.

"Bibliography on Sexual Abuse in the Home." 1982. 11p. free.

Gives author, title, publisher, date, and other information on material dealing with sexual abuse in the home.

"List of Publications." n.d. 2p. free.

Tells what is available from the National Center for the Prevention and Control of Rape.

Selected List of Books and Pamphlets

"Annual Report." Current. 20p. free.

Gives overview and conclusions, research program notices, and staffing information about the National Center for the Prevention and Control of Rape, the Emergency Research Program, the Crisis Counseling Program, and the Emergency Preparedness Program.

"Regional Directory: Rape Prevention and Treatment Resources." Current. approx. 47p. free.

Lists programs in each of the 10 Department of Health and Human Services regions. Organized alphabetically by state or territory within the region, by city or county, and by program title within each city or county.

"Surviving Sexual Assault." 1983. 13p. free.

Lists names, addresses, and telephone numbers of rape crisis service centers in the United States and Canada.

Audiovisuals:

Individual Audiovisuals

"Acquaintance Rape Prevention." n.d. 7 minutes. 16mm. color. free loan.

Designed to be used by junior and senior high schools. Encourages young people to think and act responsibly and to communicate honestly. Stresses mutual respect and understanding. Series of four films. Order from: Modern Talking Picture Service, 5000 Park St. North, St. Petersburg, FL 33709. (813) 541-6661.

"Rape: Victim or Victor." Los Angeles County Sheriff's Department. n.d. 17 minutes. 16mm. color. free loan and for sale.

Shows how to avoid potential situations and how to face a rape situation. Presents passive and active tactics. Order free loan from: Modern Talking Picture Service, 5000 Park St. North, St. Petersburg, FL 33709. (813) 541-6661. For sale from: MTI Teleprograms Inc., 3710 Commercial Ave., Northbrook, IL 60062. (800) 323-5343. In IL, AK, and HI call collect: (312) 291-9400.

NATIONAL CENTER FOR SERVICE LEARNING
806 Connecticut Ave., NW
Washington, DC 20525
(800) 922-5599

Date Established: 1969

Objectives of the Agency: Encourage and support students in secondary and post-secondary schools to participate in service-learning programs which address poverty-related human needs.

Curriculum: Education, guidance

Subjects: Student activities
  Volunteer workers

Publications: Fact sheets. Lists. Pamphlets. Guides. Manuals. On student volunteer programs.

Bibliographies, Sales Catalogs, Publications Lists, etc.

"NCSL Publication Request Form." n.d. 1p. free.
Describes free publications. Order form.

Selected List of Books and Pamphlets

"High School Student Volunteers." 1972. 60p. free.

Provides a manual for those desiring to learn more about the high school volunteer movement, as well as those who are already involved in coordinating student volunteer activities. Shows how to conceive and implement a program on a large or small scale.

"Marijuana and Driving." 1982. 5p. free.

Explains dangers of using marijuana alone or with alcohol.

"National Center for Service-Learning." n.d. 1p. free.

Explains its functions, aims, and activities. Tells what the concept of service-learning is.

"Planning by Objectives." 1980. 77p. free.

Provides a manual for student community service program coordinators. Glossary. Work sheets. Forms.

Service Learning: A Guide for College Students. n.d. 110p. free.

Designed for students interested in committing time to community service work as part of their education. Tabbed dividers. Index. Based on many college programs. Appendix contains resources for further reading and examples of service-learning projects relating to various fields of study.

NATIONAL CLEARINGHOUSE FOR ALCOHOL INFORMATION
P.O. Box 2345
Rockville, MD 20852
(301) 468-2600

Date Established: 1972

Objectives of the Agency: Distribute alcohol-related pamphlets, books, posters, and other materials published by the National Institute on Alcohol Abuse and Alcoholism.

Curriculum: Guidance, health

Subjects: Alcoholism

Locations:

AK

Department of Health and Social Services
Office of Alcoholism and Drug Abuse
Pouch H-05F
114 Second St.
Juneau, AK 99811
(907) 586-6201

AL

Department of Mental Health and Mental
  Retardation
200 Interstate Park Dr.
P.O. Box 3710
Montgomery, AL 36193
(205) 271-9209

AR

Arkansas Office on Alcohol and Drug Abuse
  Prevention
1515 W. Seventh Ave.
Suite 310
Little Rock, AR 72201
(501) 371-2603

AS

Human Services Clinic
Alcohol and Drug Program
LBJ Tropical Medical Center
Pago Pago, AS 96799
011-684-633-5139

AZ

Arizona Department of Health Services
Alcohol Abuse and Alcoholism Section
Office of Community Behavioral Health
1740 Adams
Room 001
Phoenix, AZ 85007
(602) 255-1152

CA

Department of Alcohol and Drug Programs
111 Capitol Mall
Suite 450
Sacramento, CA 95814
(916) 445-0834

CO

Alcohol and Drug Abuse Division
Colorado Department of Health
4210 E. Eleventh Ave.
Denver, CO 80220
(303) 331-8201

CT

Connecticut Alcohol and Drug Abuse Commission
999 Asylum Ave.
Third Floor
Hartford, CT 06105
(203) 566-4145

DC

Office of Health Planning and Development
1875 Connecticut Ave., NW
Suite 836A
Washington, DC 20009
(202) 673-7481

DE

Division of Alcoholism, Drug Abuse and
  Mental Health
Bureau of Alcoholism and Drug Abuse
1901 N. DuPont Hwy.
New Castle, DE 19720
(302) 421-6101

FL

Alcohol and Drug Abuse Program
Department of Health and Rehabilitation Services
1317 Winewood Blvd.
Room 157A
Tallahassee, FL 32301
(904) 488-0900

GA

Division of Mental Health
Mental Retardation and Substance Abuse
Georgia Department of Human Resources
878 Peachtree St., NE
Third Floor
Atlanta, GA 30309
(404) 894-6352

GU

Territory of Guam
Department of Mental Health and Substance Abuse
P.O. Box 8896
Tamuning, GU 96911
011-671-646-9260-9

HI

Alcohol and Drug Abuse Branch
Mental Health Division
Department of Health
P.O. Box 3378
Honolulu, HI 96801
(808) 548-4280

IA

Department of Substance Abuse
Colony Bldg.
507 Tenth St.
Suite 500
Des Moines, IA 50319

ID

Substance Abuse Section
Department of Health and Welfare
450 W. State St.
Fourth Floor
Boise, ID 83720
(208) 334-4368

IL

Department of Alcoholism and Substance Abuse
State of Illinois Center
100 W. Randolph St.
Suite 5-600
Chicago, IL 60610
(312) 917-3840

IN

Division of Addiction Services
Department of Mental Health
117 E. Washington St.
Indianapolis, IN 46204
(317) 232-7816

KS

Alcohol and Drug Abuse Services
Biddle Bldg.
2700 W. Sixth St.
Second Floor
Topeka, KS 66606
(913) 296-3925

KY

Cabinet for Human Resources
Division of Substance Abuse
Department for Mental Health and Mental
    Retardation
275 E. Main St.
Frankfort, KY 40621
(502) 564-2880

LA

Office of Prevention and Recovery from Alcohol
    and Drug Abuse
P.O. Box 53129
2744-B Wooddale Blvd.
Baton Rouge, LA 70892
(504) 922-0728

MA

Division of Alcoholism
150 Tremont St.
Boston, MA 02111
(617) 727-1960

MD

Alcoholism Control Administration
201 W. Preston St.
Fourth Floor
Baltimore, MD 21201
(301) 225-6541
(301) 225-6542

ME

Office of Alcoholism and Drug Abuse Prevention
State House Station #11
Augusta, ME 04333
(207) 289-2781

MI

Office of Substance Abuse Services
3500 N. Logan St.
P.O. Box 30035
Lansing, MI 48909
(517) 373-8603

MN

Chemical Dependency Program Division
Department of Human Services
Space Center
444 Lafayette Rd.
St. Paul, MN 55101
(612) 296-3991

MO

Division of Alcohol and Drug Abuse
2002 Missouri Blvd.
P.O. Box 687
Jefferson City, MO 65101
(314) 751-4942

MS

Division of Alcohol and Drug Abuse
1102 Robert E. Lee Office Bldg.
Jackson, MS 39201
(601) 359-1297

MT

Alcohol and Drug Abuse Division
State of Montana
Department of Institutions
1539 Eleventh Ave.
Helena, MT 59620
(406) 444-2827

NC

Division of Mental Health
Mental Retardation and Substance Abuse Services
Alcohol and Drug Abuse Section
325 N. Salisbury St.
Raleigh, NC 27611
(919) 733-4670

ND

State Department of Human Services
Division of Alcoholism and Drug Abuse
State Capitol
Bismarck, ND 58505
(701) 224-2769

NE

Division of Alcoholism and Drug Abuse
Box 94728
Lincoln, NE 68509
(402) 471-2851, ext. 5583

NH

Office of Alcohol and Drug Abuse Prevention
Health and Welfare Bldg.
Hazen Drive
Concord, NH 03301
(603) 271-4627
(603) 271-4630

NJ

Division of Alcoholism
New Jersey Department of Health
129 E. Hanover St.
Trenton, NJ 08608
(609) 292-8949

NM

Alcoholism Bureau
Behavioral Health Services Division
Crown Bldg.
P.O. Box 968
Santa Fe, NM 87504-0968
(505) 984-0020, ext. 493

Northern Mariana Islands

Dr. Torres Hospital
Saipan, Mariana Islands 96950
6112, 6222 (through International Operator 0-160691)

NV

Bureau of Alcohol and Drug Abuse
Department of Human Resources
505 E. King St.
Carson City, NV 89710
(702) 885-4790

NY

New York State Division of Alcoholism and Alcohol Abuse
194 Washington Ave.
Albany, NY 12210
(518) 474-5417

OH

Ohio Department of Health
Bureau of Alcohol Abuse and Alcoholism Recovery
170 North High St.
Third Floor
Columbus, OH 43215
(614) 466-3445

OK

Programs Division
P.O. Box 53277
Capitol Station
Oklahoma City, OK 73152
(405) 521-0044

OR

Program Office for Alcohol and Drug Abuse
Department of Human Resources
301 Public Service Bldg.
Salem, OR 97310
(503) 378-2163

PA

Office of Drug and Alcohol Programs
Department of Health
Health and Welfare Bldg
Eighth Floor
P.O. Box 90
Harrisburg, PA 17108
(717) 787-9857

PR

Puerto Rico Department of Addiction Control Services
P.O. Box 21414
Rio Piedras Station
Rio Piedras, PR 00928
(809) 763-5014
(809) 763-7575

RI

Department of Mental Health
Mental Retardation and Hospitals
Division of Substance Abuse
Substance Abuse Administration Bldg.
Cranston, RI 02920
(401) 464-2091

SC

South Carolina Commission on Alcohol and Drug Abuse
3700 Forest Dr.
Suite 300
Columbia, SC 29204
(803) 758-2521

SD

Division of Alcohol and Drug Abuse
Joe Foss Bldg.
523 E. Capitol
Pierre, SD 57501-3182
(605) 773-3123

TN

Tennessee Department of Mental Health and Mental Retardation
Division of Alcohol and Drug Abuse Services
James K. Polk Bldg.
505 Deaderick St.
Fourth Floor
Nashville, TN 37219
(615) 741-1921

Trust Territory of the Pacific Islands

Health Services
Trust Territory of the Pacific Islands
Office of the High Commissioner
Saipan, Mariana Islands 96950
9854, 9355 (through International Operator 0-160691)

TX

Texas Commission on Alcohol and Drug Abuse
1705 Guadalupe St.
Austin, TX 78701
(512) 475-2577

UT

Division of Alcoholism and Drugs
150 W. North Temple
P.O. Box 45500
Salt Lake City, UT 84145
(801) 533-6532

VA

Department of Mental Health/Mental Retardation
Office of Substance Abuse Services
109 Governor St.
P.O. Box 1797
Richmond, VA 23214
(804) 786-3906

VI

Division of Mental Health, Alcoholism and Drug
  Dependency Services
P.O. Box 7309
St. Thomas, VI 00801
(809) 774-4888

VT

Office of Alcohol and Drug Programs
Osgood Bldg.
103 S. Main St.
Waterbury, VT 05676
(802) 241-2170

WA

Bureau of Alcoholism and Substance Abuse
Mailstop, OB-44W
Olympia, WA 98504
(206) 753-5866

WI

Wisconsin Office of Alcohol and Other Drug Abuse
1 W. Wilson St.
Room 441
P.O. Box 7851
Madison, WI 53702
(608) 266-3443

WV

Division of Alcoholism and Drug Abuse
Office of Behavioral Health Services
State Capitol
1800 Washington St. East
Charleston, WV 25305
(304) 348-2276

WY

Division of Community Programs
Substance Abuse Program
Hathaway Bldg.
Third Floor
Cheyenne, WY 82002
(307) 777-7115, ext. 7118

Publications: Guidebooks. Conferences. Reports. Bibliographies. Curriculum material. Pamphlets. Periodicals. Posters. Lists. Fact sheets. On alcohol-related subjects. Some are available in Spanish. Some aimed at certain groups such as teenagers and youth, or pregnant women. Single copies free.

Bibliographies, Sales Catalogs, Publications Lists, etc.

"Alcohol Resources Update: Alcohol and Safety." 1985. 8p. free.

Abstracts resources to aid the professional and interested layperson. Includes a notation citing the availability and cost of each item.

"Alcohol Resource List Update: Prevention of Alcohol Problems." 1985. 13p. free.

Provides an annotated reading list on the subject of prevention of alcohol problems, selected to aid the professional as well as the layperson. Includes a notation giving the availability and cost of each item.

"Alcohol Resources Update: The Fetal Alcohol Syndrome." 1985. 5p. free.

Organizes entries into: *Publications* (professional and general); *Audiovisuals* (including films and posters); and *Organizations* (that offer services and additional information).

"Catalog of Alcohol Publications Available from the Government Printing Office. n.d. 6p. free.

Lists what is available for purchase. Bulk quantities.

"Publications Order Form." n.d. 2p. free.

Describes publications and posters on an order form.

"Publications Order Form: Youth." n.d. 2p. free.

Tells what is available on alcohol material related to young people.

"Publishers of Books on Alcohol Topics." 1985. 2p. free.

Lists names, addresses, and telephone numbers of those who can assist in the development of publications in the areas of alcohol abuse and alcoholism.

"Reading List: Alcohol Problems and Youth." Current. free. MS 229.

Gives annotated list of current publications and materials to aid the preteen and teenage reader.

"Updates, in Briefs and Research Reviews, Fact Sheets, Directories List." n.d. 1p. free.

Lists what is available in new single copies of resource materials with a check-off order form.

Serials, Subscription Publications, etc.

Alcohol Awareness Service. 6 issues/yr. $15.00/yr.

Gives annotated listings of the latest alcohol information with ordering information. Keeps readers on top of newly published literature and new audiovisuals. Prepared by and available from: National Clearinghouse for Alcohol Information, Department AAS, P.O. Box 2345, Rockville, MD 20852.

Alcohol Health & Research World. Quarterly. $12.00/yr. domestic, $15.00/yr. foreign.

Reports current research findings. Order from: Superintendent of Documents, U.S. Government Printing Office, Washington, DC 20402.

Selected List of Books and Pamphlets

"Alcohol Abuse and Women: A Guide to Getting Help." n.d. 25p. free. PH73.

Provides information for the woman with an alcohol problem.

"Alcohol Resources: National Prevention Network Directory." 1985. 6p. free.

Lists names, titles, addresses, and telephone numbers of representatives in each state of the National Prevention Network.

"Alcohol Topics Fact Sheet: Fetal Alcohol Syndrome." 1985. 2p. free.

Gives statistics and facts about fetal alcohol syndrome. References.

"An Introduction to the National Clearinghouse for Alcohol Information." 1985. 4p. free. DHHS Publication No. (ADM) 85-971.

Tells what the clearinghouse does and has to offer.

"Getting Drunk." 14"x17" color poster. free. AV88.7.

Illustrates that there really are no good reasons for getting drunk.

"Is Beer a Four-Letter Word?" 1980. 58p. free. PH95.

Gives ideas for alcohol education from across the country. Encourages young people to begin alcohol abuse prevention projects. Gives addresses and information about teaching materials. "On the Sidelines: An Adult Leader Guide for Youth Alcohol Programs" (free. PH183) is a 32-page companion guide.

"Preventing Alcohol Problems through a Student Assistance Program." 1984. 47p. free. DHHS Publication No. (ADM) 84-1344.

Model program developed by the New York State Division of Alcoholism and Alcohol Abuse in Westchester County, New York.

Audiovisuals:

Filmographies, Sales Lists, etc.

"Resource List for Information on Alcohol-Related Audiovisuals." 1985. 21p. free. MS 264.

Lists films that have been previewed at the clearinghouse to determine content and audience. Audience categories are: children up to 13, youth 14-21, and adults. For rent, purchase, or free loan. Some on videocassette.

Individual Audiovisuals

"Alcohol, Drugs, and You: A Losing Combination." Barr Films. 1982. 24½ minutes. 16mm. for sale.

Covers many of the problems experienced by teenagers. Includes suggestions for positive confrontations. Order from: Barr Films, P.O. Box 5667, Pasadena, CA 91107. (213) 793-6153.

"But If You Live." 1982. 15 minutes. film and videocassette. for sale or free loan.

Geared toward high school age. Shows consequences of drinking and driving. Order from: Kemper Group, Kemper Television Center, F-6 Long Grove, IL 60049. (312) 540-2819.

"Choice: Your Own Best Friend/Your Own Worst Enemy?" 1982. 30 minutes. film and videocassette. for sale or rent.

Talks about smoking, exercise, alcohol, drugs, nutrition, stress. Order from: Cally Curtis, 111 N. Las Palmas Ave., Hollywood, CA 90038. (213) 467-1101.

"Get the Message." 1984. 25 minutes. 16mm. free loan.

Shows reasons people give for using drugs. Interviews. For children. Order from: Modern Talking Picture Service, Inc., 711 Fourth St., NW, Washington, DC 20001. (202) 659-9234.

"Too High a Price." 1984. 25 minutes. 16mm. free loan.

Shows actual interviews with family members of innocent victims of drunk drivers. Order from: South Carolina Commission on Alcohol and Drug Abuse, 3700 Forest Dr. Columbia, SC 29204. (803) 758-3866.

Library: Library and reading room are open from 8:30 A.M. to 5:30 P.M., Monday through Friday. It is located at 1776 E. Jefferson St., Fourth Floor, Rockville, MD. (301) 468-2600.

Special Services: Mailing list service. Receive information about new clearinghouse materials, grant announcements, and clearinghouse happenings. Request information. Mailings are geared to your specified needs.

Inquire about the alcohol resources update materials that provide recent information on various topics.

Clearinghouse analysts perform database searches. When requesting a search, define it as specifically as possible and include a daytime telephone number if you need to be reached.

A group or individual may find out about tours by calling the clearinghouse: (301) 468-2600.

NATIONAL CLEARINGHOUSE FOR BILINGUAL EDUCATION
1555 Wilson Blvd.
Suite 605
Rosslyn, VA 22209
VA: (703) 522-0710
(800) 336-4560

Date Established: 1977

Objectives of the Agency: Collect, analyze, and disseminate information about bilingual education and related programs.

Curriculum: English

Subjects: Bilingualism
Languages, modern—study and teaching

Publications: Fact sheets. Newsletter. Lists on activities. Services.

Bibliographies, Sales Catalogs, Publications Lists, etc.

"MICRO Search Service." 2p. free.
Explains Microcomputer Courseware Resources Online. MICRO contains information about available microcomputer courseware that may be used in bilingual education and related settings.

"NCBE Products List." Updated quarterly. 20p. free.
Divides publications into such categories as *curriculum and instruction, directories,* and *microfiche collections.* Most are for sale. Title index. Order form. Ordering information.

"NCBE Searches-on-File: Bilingual Education Policy." n.d. 1p. free.
Lists topics created to address the needs of those interested in bilingual education policy. Includes such topics as *administration, court decision,* and *history.* Also includes length and number of records, search number, and price.

"NCBE Search-on-File Collection." n.d. 2p. free.
Prints collection of annotated bibliographies on such areas as teacher and administrator education. Includes number of citations, selection of databases, an NCBE code/order number, month/year of search update, and price.

Serials, Subscription Publications, etc.

"Forum." Bimonthly. 8p. free.
Provides current information in the field of bilingual education. Includes information on new publications from various sources.

Selected List of Books and Pamphlets

"BEBA." Current. 2p. free.
Describes Bilingual Education Bibliographic Abstracts. Database contains citations to print and nonprint materials about bilingual/bicultural education. Includes how to obtain documents and sample record.

"BROL." Current. 1p. free.
Bilingual Research On-Line is a computerized database containing information about current research studies relevant to bilingual education. Contains information about what information BROL provides, who has access, and how to submit information.

"Educational Technology Information Services." Current. 1p. free.
Gives information about Educational Technology Reference and Referral Services.

"National Clearinghouse for Bilingual Education: Information on Minority Language Education." n.d. 5-fold. free.
Explains services, publications, resources available.

"MCBE Custom Search Service." Current. 2p. free.
Provides a fast, efficient means of locating current, relevant bibliographic information on a desired topic. Includes information on what kind of information can be searched in databases. Gives an example, how to request a search, and search cost.

Special Services: Photocopy service offers inexpensive reproductions of various unpublished manuscripts or limited-distribution materials.

NATIONAL CLEARINGHOUSE FOR DRUG ABUSE INFORMATION
P.O. Box 416
Kensington, MD 20795
(301) 443-6487

Date Established: 1970

Objectives of the Agency: Serve as the focal point within the federal government for the collection, dissemination, and exchange of drug abuse information.

Curriculum: Guidance, health

Subjects: Drug abuse

Publications: Pamphlets. Posters. Reports. Monographs. Guides. Workbooks. Flyers. Curriculum Materials.

Bibliographies, Sales Catalogs, Publications Lists, etc.

"Publications Listing." Current. 8p. free.

Lists prevention/education materials, prevention resources, posters, report series, special reports, and technical materials. Single copies are available at no cost. The listing may be used as an order form.

Selected List of Books and Pamphlets

Adolescent Peer Pressure. 1984. 115p. free. DHHS Publication No. (ADM) 84-1152.

Provides a better understanding of the pressures of adolescence, problem behavior, peer program approaches, and ways in which peer programs can be implemented. The last chapter is devoted to books, articles, and curricular materials.

"Channel One a Government/Private Sector Partnership for Drug Abuse Prevention." 1985. 46p. free. DHHS Publication No. (ADM) 851174.

Attempts to replicate a process in communities across the country leading to the development of an effective alternative program. Channel One is a drug abuse prevention program now in most states that was developed by youth for youth, making the total environment a factor for learning.

"Drug Abuse Flyers Set." 1983-84. 3-4 fold. free.

A set of six pamphlets on: *Marijuana, Hallucinogens and PCP, Sedative-Hypnotics, Opiates, Inhalants,* and *Stimulants and Cocaine.* Explains what they are, their effects, and the dangers.

"For Kids Only: What You Should Know about Marijuana." 1985. 12p. free. DHHS Publication No. (ADM) 85-986.

Describes what marijuana is, what dependence is, and its effects on the body.

"Heroin-Addicted Parents and Their Children." 1980. 40p. free. DHHS Publication No. (ADM) 81-1028.

Compares children of heroin-addicted and non-addicted mothers in attitudes, beliefs, parenting experiences, and a comparative investigation in five urban sites. Two reports.

"Just Say No!" 1984. 19p. free. DHHS Publication No. (ADM) 85-1271.

Gives some suggestions for youth on what to say if offered drugs.

National Directory of Drug Abuse and Alcoholism Treatment and Prevention Programs. Current. 429p. free. DHHS Publication No. (ADM) 85-231.

Comprises thousands of names, addresses, telephone numbers, and services of alcoholism and drug abuse programs.

A Needs Assessment Workbook for Prevention Planning. 1981. 190p. free. DHHS Publication No. (ADM) 81-1061.

Goes with "Prevention Planning Workbook" described next. Designed to help structure a needs assessment, choose appropriate data gathering techniques, and use the data in prevention program planning and implementation.

"Prevention Planning Workbook." 1981. 56p. free. DHHS Publication No. (ADM) 81-1062.

Gives eight steps of a systematic prevention program planning process beginning with assessing needs and ending in evaluation. To be used with *A Needs Workbook for Prevention Planning* described above.

"Teens in Action." 1985. 47p. free. DHHS Publication No. (ADM) 85-1376.

Shows challenges and successes that 15 young people experienced in taking action against drug abuse in their homes, schools, and communities.

"Treatment Research Report: Drug Taking among the Elderly." 1982. 25p. free. DHHS Publication No. (ADM) 84-1229.

Makes a case for a responsible and cautious approach to psychoactive drug taking by the elderly.

"Use of Licit and Illicit Drugs by America's High School Students." Annual. 159p. free. DHHS Publication No. (ADM) 85-1394.

Annual series reporting the drug use and related attitudes of America's high school seniors conducted by the University of Michigan's Institute for Social Research. Each year's sample is drawn from seniors in private and public high schools in the coterminous United States.

"You're a Drug Quiz Whiz!" 1984. 8p. free. DHHS Publication No. (ADM) 84-1082.

Gives 20 questions (and answers) to test your knowledge about drugs and drug abuse.

Audiovisuals:

Filmographies, Sales Lists, etc.

"Films from the National Institute on Drug Abuse Free-Loan Collection." 1985. 26p. free.

Describes the free-loan collection of 16mm films and videocassettes. Topics include: *Drug Abuse Prevention, Pharmacology, Individual Drugs, International Efforts against Drug Use, Treatment and Rehabilitation,* and *Nature of Drug Dependence.* For a variety of audiences. Most are commercially produced. Includes recommended audience, grade levels, and age levels. Includes borrowing instructions and the Modern Talking Picture Service scheduling center address.

170 / National Clearinghouse for Drug Abuse Information

Special Services: The clearinghouse maintains six mailing lists by subject area: epidemiology, laws/policy documents, prevention/education, research papers/reports, training, and treatment. These automatically provide the addressees with copies or annotated announcements of new publications. To request placement on the mailing lists, write: NCDAI, Dept. ML, Room 10A-43, Parklawn Bldg., 5600 Fishers Lane, Rockville, MD 20857.

The clearinghouse supports a nation-wide Drug Abuse Communications Network (DRACON) of satellite information centers affiliated with federal, state and local government agencies and universities.

NATIONAL COMMISSION ON LIBRARIES AND INFORMATION SCIENCE
General Services Administration Bldg.
Seventh and D Sts., SW
Suite 3122
Washington, DC 20024
(202) 382-0840

Date Established: 1970

Objectives of the Agency: Provide advice and aid to the executive and legislative branches on national library and information-related policies and plans; and work with libraries, the information industry and others.

Curriculum: Library

Subjects: Library science

Publications: Books. Papers. Hearings. Pamphlets. Reports.

Bibliographies, Sales Catalogs, Publications Lists, etc.
"Library and Information Services in a Learning Society." Current. 87p. free.
Supplies information (8p.) about free and for sale publications in appendix 3. Includes addresses where materials may be obtained.

Selected List of Books and Pamphlets
"Library and Information Services in a Learning Society." Annual report. 87p. free.
Explains the role of library and information services in lifelong learning, furthering access to information and related topics. Includes personnel and administration and future planning. Fiscal statement. Projects.

NATIONAL COUNCIL ON THE HANDICAPPED
800 Independence Avenue, SW
Suite 814
Washington, DC 20591
(202) 453-3846

Date Established: 1978

Objectives of the Agency: Evaluate all federal programs related to disability concerns and to report its findings directly to Congress and the President.

Curriculum: Special education

Subjects: Handicapped

Publications: Newsletters. Reports. On council activities.

Serials, Subscription Publications, etc.
"NCH Reporter." Current. 4p. free.
Gives news about meetings, policies, and progress of the handicapped.

Selected List of Books and Pamphlets
"Annual Report." Current. 31p. free.
Relates activities and accomplishments of the previous fiscal year. Recommendations. Summary. Appendices: *Members of the Council, Resumes and Committees; Description of Specialist Roles;* and *Council Fellowship Program.*

NATIONAL DIGESTIVE DISEASES EDUCATION AND INFORMATION CLEARINGHOUSE
1555 Wilson Blvd.
Suite 600
Rosslyn, VA 22209-2461
(301) 496-9707

Date Established: 1980

Objectives of the Agency: Educate the public, patients, and their families, as well as physicians and health care providers in a wider understanding of digestive health and disease. It is a service of the National Institute of Arthritis, Diabetes, and Digestive and Kidney Diseases and the National Institutes of Health.

Curriculum: Health

Subjects: Digestion

Publications: Fact sheets. Pamphlets. Bibliographies. Directories. Guidelines.

Bibliographies, Sales Catalogs, Publications Lists, etc.
"Patient Education Materials." Current. 4p. free.
Lists free publications. Order form.

Selected List of Books and Pamphlets
"Are You the One American in Ten Who Suffers from a Chronic Digestive Disease?." n.d. folded poster. free.
Explains what the Digestive Clearinghouse is, how the clearinghouse can help you, and what are digestive diseases. One side illustrates the digestive system.

"Digestive Diseases Directory." n.d. 2p. free.
Provides a guide to lay organizations. Includes title, address, telephone number, and contact name.

"Glossary of DD Terms." 1982. 6p. free.

Defines terms, beginning with *abdomino-perineal resection* and ending with *Wilson's disease*.

"Happenings along the GI Tract." 1982. 4p. free.

Describes the digestive process and common problems such as gallstones and ulcerative colitis.

Special Services: A series of free, one-page, question-and-answer sheets on topics such as ulcers that are suitable for newsletter fillers.

NATIONAL ENDOWMENT FOR THE ARTS
Office of Public Information
Nancy Hanks Center
1100 Pennsylvania Ave., NW
Washington, DC 20506
(202) 682-5400

Date Established: 1965

Objectives of the Agency: Encourage and support American arts and artists by awarding grants and through its leadership and advocacy activities.

Curriculum: Art, English, humanities

Subjects: Art
Education—curricula
Reading materials

Locations:

CT, DC, DE, MA, MD, ME, NH, NJ, NY, PA, PR, RI, VI, VT

National Endowment for the Arts
Regional Representative
2 Columbus Circle
New York, NY 10019
(212) 957-9760

AK, AS, CA, GU, HI, Northern Marianas, OR, WA

Contact the regional representative coordinator in Washington, DC, for more information: (202) 682-5759.

AR, KS, MO, NE, OK, TX

National Endowment for the Arts
Regional Representative
P.O. Box 22489
Kansas City, MO 64113
(816) 523-0001

AL, FL, GA, KY, LA, MS, NC, SC, TN, VA, WV

National Endowment for the Arts
Regional Representative
310 N. Hull St.
Montgomery, AL 36104
(205) 264-3797

IA, IL, IN, MI, MN, ND, OH, SD, WI

National Endowment for the Arts
Regional Representative
4200 Marine Dr.
Chicago, IL 60613
(312) 935-9530

AZ, CO, ID, MT, NM, NV, UT, WY

National Endowment for the Arts
Regional Representative
General Delivery
Millcreek Post Office
Salt Lake City, UT 84108

State Arts Agencies

Alabama State Council on the Arts and Humanities
323 Adams Ave.
Montgomery, AL 36130
(205) 261-4076

Alaska State Council on the Arts
619 Warehouse Ave.
Suite 220
Anchorage, AK 99501
(907) 279-1558

American Samoa Council on Culture, Arts and Humanities
Office of the Governor
P.O. Box 1540
Pago Pago, American Samoa 96799
(011) 684-633-5613

Arizona Commission on the Arts
417 W. Roosevelt
Phoenix, AZ 85003
(602) 255-5884
(602) 255-5882

Arkansas Arts Council
The Heritage Center
225 E. Markham St.
Suite 200
Little Rock, AR 72201
(501) 371-2539

California Arts Council
1901 Broadway
Suite A
Sacramento, CA 95818
(916) 445-1530

Colorado Council on the Arts and Humanities
Grant-Humphries Mansion
770 Pennsylvania St.
Denver, CO 80203
(303) 866-2617

Connecticut Commission on the Arts
190 Trumbell St.
Hartford, CT 06103
(203) 566-4770

Delaware State Arts Council
State Office Bldg.
820 N. French St.
Wilmington, DE 19801
(302) 571-3540

District of Columbia
Commission on the Arts and Humanities
420 Seventh St., NW
Second Floor
Washington, DC 20004
(202) 724-5613
(202) 727-9332

Arts Council of Florida
Division of Cultural Affairs
Department of State
The Capitol
Tallahassee, FL 32301
(904) 487-2980

Georgia Council for the Arts and Humanities
2082 E. Exchange Place
Suite 100
Tucker, GA 30084
(404) 493-5780

Guam Council on the Arts and Humanities
Office of the Governor
P.O. Box 2950
Agana, GU 96910
(011) 671-477-9845
(011) 671-477-7413

Hawaii State Foundation on Culture and the Arts
335 Merchant St.
Room 202
Honolulu, HI 96813
(808) 548-4145

Idaho Commission on the Arts
304 W. State St.
C/O Statehouse Mail
Boise, ID 83720
(208) 334-2119

Illinois Arts Council
State of Illinois Center
100 W. Randolph St.
Suite 10-500
Chicago, IL 60601
(312) 793-6750

Indiana Arts Commission
32 E. Washington St.
Sixth Floor
Indianapolis, IN 46204
(317) 232-1268

Iowa State Arts Council
State Capitol Complex
Des Moines, IA 50319
(515) 281-4451

Kansas Arts Commission
112 W. Sixth St.
Suite 401
Topeka, KS 66603
(913) 296-3335

Kentucky Arts Council
Berry Hill
Louisville Rd.
Frankfort, KY 40601
(502) 564-3757

Louisiana Department of Culture, Recreation and Tourism
Division of the Arts
P.O. Box 44247
Baton Rouge, LA 70804
(504) 925-3930
(504) 925-3934

Maine State Commission on the Arts and Humanities
55 Capitol St.
State House Station 25
Augusta, ME 04333
(207) 289-2724

Maryland State Arts Council
15 W. Mulberry St.
Baltimore, MD 21201
(301) 685-6740

Massachusetts Council on the Arts and Humanities
80 Boylston St.
Tenth Floor
Boston, MA 02116
(617) 727-3668

Michigan Council for the Arts
1200 Sixth Ave.
Detroit, MI 48226
(313) 256-3735

Minnesota State Arts Board
432 Summit Ave.
St. Paul, MN 55102
(800) 652-9745 (toll free within Minnesota)

Mississippi Arts Commission
P.O. Box 1341
Jackson, MS 39215-1341
(601) 354-7336

Missouri State Council on the Arts
Wainwright State Office Complex
111 N. Seventh St.
Suite 105
St. Louis, MO 63101-2188
(314) 444-6845

Montana Arts Council
35 S. Last Chance Gulch
Helena, MT 59620
(406) 444-6430

Nebraska Arts Council
1313 Farnham-on-the-Mall
Omaha, NE 68102-1873
(402) 554-2122

Nevada State Council on the Arts
329 Flint St.
Reno, NV 89501
(702) 789-0225

New Hampshire Commission on the Arts
Phoenix Hall
40 N. Main St.
Concord, NH 03301
(603) 271-2789

New Jersey State Council on the Arts
109 W. State St.
Trenton, NJ 08625
(609) 292-6130

New Mexico Arts Division
224 E. Palace Ave.
Santa Fe, NM 87501
(505) 827-6490

New York State Council on the Arts
915 Broadway
Eighth Floor
New York, NY 10010
(212) 614-2900

North Carolina Arts Council
Department of Cultural Resources
Raleigh, NC 27611
(919) 733-2821

North Dakota Council on the Arts
Black Bldg.
Suite 606
Fargo, ND 58102
(701) 237-8962

Northern Mariana Islands
Commonwealth Council for Arts and Culture
Convention Center
Capitol Hill
P.O. Box 553, CHRB
Saipan, Mariana Islands 96950
(011) 670-9982-83
District Office
2121 R St., NW
Washington, DC 20008
(202) 328-3847

Ohio Arts Council
727 E. Main St.
Columbus, OH 43205
(614) 466-2613

State Arts Council of Oklahoma
Jim Thorpe Bldg.
2101 N. Lincoln Blvd.
Room 640
Oklahoma City, OK 73105
(405) 521-2931

Oregon Arts Commission
835 Summer St., NE
Salem, OR 97301
(503) 378-3625

Pennsylvania Council on the Arts
Room 216
Finance Bldg.
Harrisburg, PA 17120
(717) 787-6883

Institute of Puerto Rican Culture
Apartado Postal 4184
San Juan, PR 00905
(809) 723-2115

Rhode Island State Council on the Arts
312 Wickenden St.
Providence, RI 02903
(401) 277-3880

South Carolina Arts Commission
1800 Gervais St.
Columbia, SC 29201
(803) 758-3442

South Dakota Arts Council
108 W. Eleventh St.
Sioux Falls, SD 57102
(605) 339-6646

Tennessee Arts Commission
320 Sixth Ave., North
Suite 100
Nashville, TN 37219
(615) 741-1701
(615) 741-6395

Texas Commission on the Arts
Capitol Station
P.O. Box 13406
Austin, TX 78711
(512) 475-6593

Utah Arts Council
617 E. South Temple St.
Salt Lake City, UT 84102
(801) 533-5895

Vermont Council on the Arts, Inc.
136 State St.
Montpelier, VT 05602
(802) 828-3291

Virgin Islands Council on the Arts
P.O. Box 6732
St. Thomas, VI 00801
(809) 774-5984

Virginia Commission for the Arts
James Monroe Bldg.
101 N. Fourteenth St.
Seventeenth Floor
Richmond, VA 23219
(804) 225-3132

Washington State Arts Commission
Ninth and Columbia Bldg.
Mail Stop GH-11
Olympia, WA 98504
(206) 753-3860

West Virginia Department of Culture and History
Arts and Humanities Division
Science and Culture Center
Capitol Complex
Charleston, WV 25305
(304) 348-0240

Wisconsin Arts Board
107 S. Butler St.
Madison, WI 53703
(608) 266-0190

Wyoming Council on the Arts
2320 Capitol Ave.
Cheyenne, WY 82002
(307) 777-7742

Publications: Reports. Reviews. Calendar. Guides. Lists. Guidelines. Handbooks. Workbooks.

Serials, Subscription Publications, etc.

"Arts Review." Quarterly.
Contains feature articles and news about new programs, application deadlines, and other features. Order from: Superintendent of Documents, Government Printing Office, Washington, DC 20402. Subscription forms are available from the Endowment.

Selected List of Books and Pamphlets

"Guide to the National Endowment for the Arts." Current. 50p. free.
Helps individuals and organizations determine whether their artistic projects might be eligible for grants from the National Endowment for the Arts. Includes the purpose of the programs and outlines the types of projects supported in funding categories.

NATIONAL ENDOWMENT FOR THE HUMANITIES
Public Affairs Office
1100 Pennsylvania Ave., NW
Room 409
Washington, DC 20506
(202) 786-0438

Date Established: 1965

Objectives of the Agency: Support scholarship, research, education, and public programs in literature, philosophy, history, and other humanistic disciplines.

Curriculum: Education

Subjects: Humanities

Locations:

AK

Alaska Humanities Forum
943 W. Sixth Ave.
Room 10
Anchorage, AK 99501
(907) 272-5341

AL

The Committee for the Humanities in Alabama
Birmingham-Southern College
Box A-40
Birmingham, AL 35254
(205) 324-1314

AR

Arkansas Endowment for the Humanities
The Remmel Bldg.
1010 W. Third St.
Suite 102
Little Rock, AR 72201
(501) 372-2672

AZ

Arizona Humanities Council
First Interstate Bank Plaza
100 W. Washington
Suite 1290
Phoenix, AZ 85003
(602) 257-0335

CA

California Council for the Humanities
312 Sutter St.
Suite 601
San Francisco, CA 94108
(415) 391-1474

CO

Colorado Endowment for the Humanities
1836 Blake St.
#100
Denver, CO 80202
(303) 292-4458

CT

Connecticut Humanities Council
41 Lawn Ave.
Wesleyan Station
Middletown, CT 06457
(203) 347-6888

DC

D.C. Community Humanities Council
1341 G St., NW
Suite 620
Washington, DC 20005
(202) 347-1732

DE

Delaware Humanities Forum
2600 Pennslvania Ave.
Wilmington, DE 19806
(302) 573-4410

FL

Florida Endowment for the Humanities
University of South Florida
LET 468
Tampa, FL 33620
(813) 974-4094

GA

Georgia Endowment for the Humanities
Emory University
1589 Clifton Rd., NE
Atlanta, GA 30322
(404) 329-7500

HI

Hawaii Committee for the Humanities
2615 S. King St.
Suite 211
Honolulu, HI 96826
(808) 947-5891

IA

Iowa Humanities Board
University of Iowa
Oakdale Campus
Iowa City, IA 52242
(319) 353-6754

ID

The Association for the Humanities in Idaho
Len B. Jordon Bldg.
650 W. State St.
Room 300
Boise, ID 83720
(208) 345-5346

IL

Illinois Humanities Council
618 S. Michigan Ave.
Chicago, IL 60605
(312) 939-5212

IN

Indiana Committee for the Humanities
3135 N. Meridian St.
Indianapolis, IN 46208
(317) 925-5316

KS

Kansas Committee for the Humanities
112 W. Sixth St.
Suite 509
Topeka, KS 66603
(913) 357-0359

KY

Kentucky Humanities Council, Inc.
University of Kentucky
Ligon House
Lexington, KY 40508
(606) 257-5932

LA

Louisiana Committee for the Humanities
1001 Howard Ave.
Suite 4407
New Orleans, LA 70113
(504) 523-4352

MA

Massachusetts Foundation for the Humanities and Public Policy
155 Woodside Ave.
Amherst, MA 01002
(413) 545-1936

MD

Maryland Humanities Council
516 N. Charles St.
#304-305
Baltimore, MD 21201
(301) 837-1938

ME

Maine Humanities Council
P.O. Box 7202
Portland, ME 04112
(207) 773-5051

MI

Michigan Council for the Humanities
Nisbet Bldg.
1407 S. Harrison Rd.
Suite 30
East Lansing, MI 48824
(517) 355-0160

MN

Minnesota Humanities Commission
580 Park Square Court
Sixth and Sibley Sts.
St. Paul, MN 55101
(612) 224-5739

MO

The Missouri Committee for the Humanities, Inc.
Loberg Bldg.
11425 Dorsett Rd.
Suite 204
Maryland Heights, MO 63043
(314) 739-7368

MS

Mississippi Committee for the Humanities
3825 Ridgewood Rd.
Room 111
Jackson, MS 39211
(601) 982-6752

MT

Montana Committee for the Humanities
P.O. Box 8036
Hellgate Station
Missoula, MT 59807
(406) 243-6022

NC

North Carolina Humanities Committee
UNC—Greensboro
112 Foust Bldg.
Greensboro, NC 27412
(919) 379-5325

ND

North Dakota Humanities Council
Box 2191
Bismarck, ND 58502
(701) 663-1948

NE

Nebraska Committee for the Humanities
Cooper Plaza
211 N. Twelfth St.
Suite 405
Lincoln, NE 68508
(402) 474-2131

NH

New Hampshire Council for the Humanities
112 S. State St.
Concord, NH 03301
(603) 224-4071

NJ

New Jersey Committee for the Humanities
73 Easton Ave.
New Brunswick, NJ 08903
(201) 932-7726

NM

New Mexico Humanities Council
University of New Mexico
Albuquerque, NM 87131
(505) 277-3705

NV

Nevada Humanities Committee
P.O. Box 8065
Reno, NV 89507
(702) 784-6587

NY

New York Council for the Humanities
33 W. Forty-Second St.
New York, NY 10036
(212) 354-3040

OH

The Ohio Humanities Council
760 Pleasant Ridge Ave.
Columbus, OH 43209
(614) 231-6879

OK

Oklahoma Foundation for the Humanities
Executive Terrace Bldg.
2809 Northwest Expressway
Suite 500
Oklahoma City, OK 73112
(405) 840-1721

OR

Oregon Committee for the Humanities
418 S.W. Washington
Room 410
Portland, OR 97204
(503) 241-0543

PA

Pennsylvania Humanities Council
401 N. Broad St.
Philadelphia, PA 19108
(215) 925-1005

PR

Fundacion Puertorriquena de las Humanidades
Box S-4307
Old San Juan, PR 00904
(809) 721-2087

RI

Rhode Island Committee for the Humanities
463 Broadway
Providence, RI 02909
(401) 273-2250

SC

South Carolina Committee for the Humanities
P.O. Box 6925
Columbia, SC 29260
(803) 738-1850

SD

South Dakota Committee on the Humanities
University Station
Box 7050
Brookings, SD 57007
(605) 688-6113

TN

Tennessee Committee for the Humanities
1001 Eighteenth Ave. South
Nashville, TN 37212
(615) 320-7001

TX

Texas Committee for the Humanities
1604 Nueces
Austin, TX 78701
(512) 473-8585

UT

Utah Endowment for the Humanities
Broadway Bldg.
10 W. Broadway
Suite 900
Salt Lake City, UT 84101
(801) 531-7868

VA

Virginia Foundation for the Humanities and Public Policy
1939 Ivy Rd.
Charlottesville, VA 22903
(804) 924-3296

VI

Virgin Islands Humanities Council
Market Square
Conrad Bldg.
#6 Torvet Straede
Fourth Floor, Suite 6
St. Thomas, VI 00801
(809) 774-4044

VT

Vermont Council on the Humanities and Public Issues
Grant House
P.O. Box 58
Hyde Park, VT 05655
(802) 888-3183

WA

Washington Commission for the Humanities
Olympia, WA 98505
(206) 866-6510

WI

Wisconsin Humanities Committee
716 Langdon St.
Madison, WI 53706
(608) 262-0706

WV

The Humanities Foundation of West Virginia
Box 204
Institute, WV 25112
(304) 768-8869

WY

Wyoming Council for the Humanities
University Station
Box 3972
Laramie, WY 82071-3972
(307) 766-6496

Publications: Pamphlets. Guidelines. Serials. Catalogs. Lists.

Bibliographies, Sales Catalogs, Publication Lists, etc.

"In Response." n.d. 1p. free.
Summarizes publications and services and where to obtain various publications of other sources.

Serials, Subscription Publications, etc.

Humanities. Bimonthly. $14.00/yr. domestic, $17.25/yr. foreign.
Reviews current work and thought in the humanities. Describes grants. Calendar of application deadlines.

Selected List of Books and Pamphlets

Medialog. n.d. 106p. free.
Describes more than 315 programs developed with endowment support. Sections include: *U.S. History; Archaeology and Anthropology; Folk Traditions and Local History; World Culture and History; History, Theory and Criticism of the Arts; The Humanities in Literature;* and *Philosophy, Religion and Ethics.* Includes addresses of distributors and prices of rental or purchase.

"Overview of Endowment Programs." Current. 32p. free.

Gives overview of the National Endowment, its programs, the members of the National Council on the Humanities, and addresses and phone numbers of other sources of information.

NATIONAL EYE INSTITUTE
Office of Scientific Reporting
National Institutes of Health
Building 31
Room 6A32
Bethesda, MD 20205
(301) 496-5248

Date Established: 1968

Objectives of the Agency: Conduct, foster, and support basic and applied research related to the cause, natural history, prevention, diagnosis, and treatment of disorders of the eye and visual system and related fields.

Curriculum: Health

Subjects: Eye

Publications: Fact sheets. Lists. Brochures.

Bibliographies, Sales Catalogs, Publications Lists, etc.

"List of Fact Sheets and Brochures." n.d. 1p. free.

Names of fact sheets and brochures that are available in single copies without charge.

Selected List of Books and Pamphlets

"Age Page." 1983. 3p. free.

Gives suggestions for maintaining good vision as you age. Describes common eye complaints and common eye diseases in the elderly. Includes addresses of organizations that can send information on eye care and eye disorders.

"Age-Related Macular Degeneration." n.d. 4-fold. free. NIH Publication No. 85-2294.

Describes what age-related macular degeneration is, and the methods of treatment, prevention, and getting help.

"Cataracts." 1983. 24p. free. NIH Publication No. 83-201.

Explains what cataracts are, and what causes them. Includes types, symptoms, treatments, and surgery. Gives addresses from which to obtain more information, bibliography.

"Diagram of the Eye." n.d. 1p. free.

Labels the basic parts of the eye in a black-and-white illustration.

NATIONAL GALLERY OF ART
Department of Extension Programs
Washington, DC 20565
(202) 842-6353

Date Established: 1944

Objectives of the Agency: Provide free loan of art slide programs, films, videocassettes, and other materials.

Curriculum: Art

Subjects: Art—galleries and museums

Audiovisuals:

Filmographies, Sales Lists, etc.

"Extension Programs." Current. 36p. free.

Describes audiovisual material on such topics as art histories, American crafts, and folk arts. Includes curriculum guides, videocassettes, slides and cassettes, and films.

Individual Audiovisuals

"African Art." n.d. 86 minutes. 77 slides, cassette, and text. free loan. Cat. No. 015.

Reviews African works of art in terms of their ritual usage and regional or tribal characteristics.

"Blake." n.d. 5 minutes. 16mm. color. free loan. Cat. No. 120.

Contains watercolors and excerpts of his verse.

"The Eye of Thomas Jefferson: Art and Reason." n.d. 29 minutes. 18 slides, cassette, and text. free loan. Cat. No. 045.

Shows aspects of the Enlightenment as a background to Jefferson's contributions.

"Famous Men and Women in Portraits." n.d. 46 minutes. 50 slides, cassette, and text. free loan. Cat. No. 006.

Shows the development of portraiture in Western art. Includes famous personalities since the Renaissance such as the Medici, Voltaire, and Lincoln.

"Introduction to Understanding Art." n.d. 40 minutes. 40 slides, cassette, and text. free loan. Cat. No. 007.

Gives a basis for art appreciation. Shows simple examples of paintings, ceramics, sculpture, and tapestry.

"Of Time, Tombs, and Treasure: The Treasures of Tutankhamun." n.d. 29 minutes. 16mm. color. free loan. Cat. No. 132. videocassette. color. Cat. No. VC132.

Includes the tomb's discovery and examples of the works of art.

"Pennsylvania German Folk Art." n.d. 27 minutes. cassette and text. free loan. Cat. No. 022

Surveys crafts, decoration, and design motifs.

"700 Years of Art." n.d. 40 minutes. 60 slides, cassette, and text. free loan. Cat. No. 001.
   Shows paintings from the Middle Ages to the present which are in the National Gallery.

"The Quiet Collector: Andrew W. Mellon Remembered." n.d. 28 minutes. 16mm. color. free loan. Cat. No. 142; 28 minutes. videocassette. color. free loan. Cat. No. VC142.
   Describes Mellon's life as a collector and his gift of an art gallery to the American people.

NATIONAL HEALTH INFORMATION CLEARINGHOUSE
P.O. Box 1133
Washington, DC 20013-1133
VA: (703) 522-2590
   (800) 336-1133

Date Established: 1979

Objectives of the Agency: Identify health information resources; channel requests for information to these resources; provide direct information to the inquirer; and develop publications providing information on health-related topics.

Curriculum: Health, library

Subjects: Health education
Library science

Publications: Pamphlets. Directories. Summaries. Bibliographies. Fact sheets. Microfiche. Proceedings.

Bibliographies, Sales Catalogs, Publications Lists, etc.

"Health Promotion Software." 1984. 14p. free.
   Lists microcomputer software on health topics with ordering information.

"Healthfinders Publications List." Current. 1p. free.
   Describes guides to sources of health-related materials. Order form.

"Locating Audiovisual Materials." 1984. 5p. free.
   Gives names of directories and databases for finding health-related audiovisuals for loan, rent, or purchase.

"Publications List." 1985. 4p. free.
   Lists materials for the general public, reports, papers for health professionals, proceedings of conferences and others that the Office of Disease Prevention and Health Promotion has sponsored or co-sponsored.

"Staying Healthy." 1984. 42p. free.
   Gives a bibliography of health promotion materials: booklets, fact sheets, films, posters, program guides, and reports.

"Stress Information Resources." 1984. 2p. free.
   Lists organizations and publication providing information on stress.

Selected List of Books and Pamphlets

"Fact Sheet." 1985. 2p. free.
   Explains functions of the Office of Disease Prevention and Health Promotion. Lists selected publications.

"National Health Information Clearinghouse." Current. 5p. free.
   Tells what the clearinghouse is and what it has to offer.

"NICODARD." n.d. 4p. free.
   Explains what the National Information Center for Orphan Drugs and Rare Diseases does.

"Selected Federal Health Information Clearinghouses and Information Centers." Current. 2p. free.
   Lists clearinghouses that provide publications, referrals, or answers to inquiries.

Library: Open to the public. Provides medical and health reference books, directories and books on health promotion, and files on over 800 health topics.

Special Services: Database is publicly accessible through DIRLINE, part of the National Library of Medicine's MEDLARS system. Contains descriptions of diverse health-related groups, federal and state agencies, voluntary associations, self-help and support groups, and information centers, all of which share health information with the public or health professionals.

NATIONAL HEART, LUNG, AND BLOOD INSTITUTE
Office of Information
Bethesda, MD 20205
(301) 496-4236

Date Established: 1976

Objectives of the Agency: Promote a national program in the diseases of the heart, blood vessels, and blood and lungs and in the use of blood.

Curriculum: Health

Subjects: Blood
Heart
Lungs

Publications: Pamphlets. Fact sheets. Handbooks.

Selected List of Books and Pamphlets

"Blacks and High Blood Pressure." 1982. 8p. free. NIH Publication No. 83-2024.
   Tells what high blood pressure is, how many people have it, how to find out if you have it. Includes information on medicine, weight, salt, and health tips.

"Do I Have a Chronic Cough?" 1982. 24p. free. NIH Publication No. 83-559

Explains what a chronic cough is, what coughs do, chronic lung diseases, other symptoms, and where to obtain more information.

"Exercise and Your Heart." 1983. 44p. free. NIH Publication No. 1677.

Explains the benefits of exercise, calories burned in various activities, risks in exercising, and warm-up exercises. Includes a sample 13-week walking program and a sample 16-week jogging program. Lists exercises that help condition the heart and lungs.

"Fact Sheet: Hyperlipoproteinemia." 1981. 10p. free. NIH Publication No. 81-734.

Tells what it is, what cholesterol and triglycerides are, the types of hyperlipoproteinemia, how it is diagnosed, its treatment, diets, drugs, and current research programs.

"Facts about: Blood Cholesterol." 1985. 4p. free. NIH Publication No. 85-2696.

Tells what it is, how it is measured, what determines the level, why it should be reduced, and how to lower it. Includes tables of oils and fats and cholesterol found in animal foods.

"A Handbook of Heart Terms." 1984. 59p. free. DHEW Publication No. (NIH) 84-131.

Defines technical terms in nontechnical language. Includes selection of words and phrases commonly used in the heart field with accent marks and pronunciation aids. Arranged alphabetically. Illustrations.

"High Blood Pressure Facts and Fiction." 1984. 4p. free. NIH Publication No. 84-1218.

Examines various ideas and discusses what is true about high blood pressure.

"How Doctors Diagnose Heart Disease." 1981. 18p. free. NIH Publication No. 81-753.

Explains the office visit, special tests, risk factors, warning signals of a heart attack, and what to do if someone has a heart attack.

"State and Local Programs on Smoking and Health." 88p. free. PHS-82-50190.

Describes programs being conducted nationwide to reduce smoking. Lists them alphabetically by organization by state. Includes for each organization the name and address, title of the program, the name and telephone number of a contact person(s), a brief description of the objectives of the program, methods and materials used, and evaluation mechanisms used.

NATIONAL HIGHWAY TRAFFIC SAFETY ADMINISTRATION

U.S. Department of Transportation
400 Seventh St., SW
Washington, DC 20590
(202) 426-9550

Date Established: 1970

Objectives of the Agency: Carry out programs relating to the safety performance of motor vehicles and related equipment, motor vehicle drivers and pedestrians, and a uniform speed limit; carry out programs and studies aimed at reducing economic losses in motor vehicle crashes and repairs; administer the federal odometer law; and promulgate average fuel economy standards.

Curriculum: Driver education, safety

Subjects: Automobile drivers—education

Locations:

Regional Offices

CT, MA, ME, NH, RI, VT

National Highway Traffic Safety Administration
Regional Office
Kendall Square
Code 903
Cambridge, MA 02142

NJ, NY, PR, VI

National Highway Traffic Safety Administration
Regional Office
222 Mamaroneck Ave.
White Plains, NY 10605

DC, DE, MD, PA, VA, WV

National Highway Traffic Safety Administration
Regional Office
793 Elkridge Landing Rd.
Linthicum, MD 21090

AL, FL, GA, KY, MS, NC, SC, TN

National Highway Traffic Safety Administration
Regional Office
1720 Peachtree Rd., NW
Atlanta, GA 30309

IL, IN, MI, MN, OH, WI

National Highway Traffic Safety Administration
Regional Office
18209 Dixie Hwy.
Homewood Heights, IL 60430

AR, LA, NM, OK, TX

National Highway Traffic Safety Administration
Regional Office
819 Taylor St.
Fort Worth, TX 76102

IA, KS, MO, NE

National Highway Traffic Safety Administration
Regional Office
P.O. Box 19515
Kansas City, MO 64141

CO, MT, ND, SD, UT, WY

National Highway Traffic Safety Administration
Regional Office
555 Zang St.
First Floor
Denver, CO 80228

AS, AZ, CA, GU, HI, NV

National Highway Traffic Safety Administration
Regional Office
211 Main St.
Suite 1000
San Francisco, CA 94105

AK, ID, OR, WA

National Highway Traffic Safety Administration
Regional Office
915 Second Ave.
Seattle, WA 98174

State Offices

AK

Highway Safety Planning Agency
Pouch N
Juneau, AK 99801
(907) 465-4371

AL

Highway and Traffic Safety Division
P.O. Box 2939
Montgomery, AL 36105-0939
(205) 284-8790

AR

Arkansas Highway Safety Program
#1 Capitol Mall
Level 4B
Suite 215
Little Rock, AR 72201
(501) 371-1101

AZ

Governor's Highway Safety Representative
Office of Highway Safety
1801 W. Jefferson
Room 465
Phoenix, AZ 85078
(602) 255-3216

CA

Office of Traffic Safety
Business and Transportation Agency
State of California
7000 Franklin Blvd.
Suite 330
Sacramento, CA 95823
(916) 445-5373

CO

Division of Highway Safety
4201 E. Arkansas Ave.
Denver, CO 80222
(303) 757-9381

CT

Department of Transportation
Bureau of Highways
24 Wolcott Hill Rd.
Wethersfield, CT 06109
(203) 566-4248

DC

Highway Safety Program Coordinator
DPW, Transportation Safety Branch
Presidential Bldg.
415 Twelfth St., NW
Suite 314
Washington, DC 20004
(202) 727-5777

DE

Office of Highway Safety
Thomas Collins Bldg.
540 S. Dupont Hwy.
Dover, DE 19901
(302) 736-4475

FL

Chief, Bureau of Public Safety Management
Department of Community Affairs
2571 Executive Center Circle East
Tallahassee, FL 32301
(904) 488-5455

GA

Office of Highway Safety
959 Confederate Ave., SE
P.O. Box 1497
Atlanta, GA 30301
(404) 656-6996

HI

Motor Vehicle Safety Office
State Department of Transportation
79 South Nimitz Hwy.
Honolulu, HI 96813
(808) 548-5755

IA

Governor's Highway Safety Office
Capitol Hill Annex
523 E. Twelfth St.
Des Moines, IA 50319
(515) 281-3868

ID

Office of Highway Safety
Idaho Department of Transportation
P.O. Box 7129
Boise, ID 83707
(208) 334-3533

IL

Bureau of Safety Programs
Department of Transportation
2300 S. Dirksen Pkwy.
Springfield, IL 62764
(217) 782-4974

IN

Division of Traffic Safety
801 State Office Bldg.
Room 801
Indianapolis, IN 46204
(317) 232-1287

KS

Transportation Safety Administration
K-DOT
State Office Bldg.
Tenth Floor
Topeka, KS 66612
(913) 296-3756

KY

Highway Safety Standards Branch
Kentucky State Police Hq.
919 Versailles Rd.
Frankfort, KY 40601-9980
(502) 695-6356

LA

Louisiana Highway Safety Commission
P.O. Box 66336
Baton Rouge, LA 70896
(504) 925-6991

MA

Governor's Highway Safety Bureau
Saltonstall State Office Bldg.
100 Cambridge St.
Room 2104
Boston, MA 02202
(617) 727-5074

MD

Division of Transportation Safety
Department of Transportation
P.O. Box 8755
Baltimore-Washington International Airport
Baltimore, MD 21240-0755
(301) 859-7157

ME

Highway Safety Representative
Department of Public Safety
36 Hospital St.
Augusta, ME 04330
(207) 289-2581

MI

Office of Highway Safety Planning
111 S. Capitol Ave.
Lower Level
Lansing, MI 48913
(517) 373-8011

MN

Department of Traffic Safety
Transportation Bldg.
St. Paul, MN 55155
(612) 296-6953

MO

Division of Highway Safety
P.O. Box 749
Jefferson City, MO 65102
(314) 751-4161

MS

Governor's Representative for Highway Safety
Governor's Highway Safety Program
510 George St.
Suite 246
Jackson, MS 39201
(601) 354-6892

MT

Highway Traffic Safety Division
Department of Justice
303 N. Roberts
Helena, MT 59620
(406) 444-3412

NC

Governor's Highway Safety Representative
215 E. Lane St.
Raleigh, NC 27601
(919) 733-3083

ND

North Dakota Highway Dept.
600 E. Boulevard Ave.
Bismarck, ND 58505-0178
(701) 224-4397

NE
Nebraska Highway Safety Program Office
State House Station 94612
Lincoln, NE 68509
(402) 471-2515

NH
New Hampshire Highway Safety Agency
117 Manchester St.
Concord, NH 03301
(603) 271-2131

NJ
New Jersey Highway Safety Office
CN−048
Trenton, NJ 08625
(609) 292-3900

NM
Traffic Safety Bureau
P.E.R.A. Bldg.
Room 224
P.O. Box 1028
Santa Fe, NM 87503
(505) 827-4776

NV
Traffic Safety Division
Department of Motor Vehicles
555 Wright Way
Room 258
Carson City, NV 89711
(702) 885-5720

NY
Traffic Safety Committee
Empire State Plaza
Swan St. Bldg.
Albany, NY 12228
(518) 474-5777

OH
Office of Governor's Highway Safety Representative
P.O. Box 7167
Columbus, OH 43205
(614) 466-3250

OK
Oklahoma Highway Safety Office
200 N.E. Twenty-First St.
D-4
Oklahoma City, OK 73105
(405) 521-3314

OR
Oregon Traffic Safety Commission
State Library Bldg.
Fourth Floor
Salem, OR 97310
(503) 378-3670

PA
Bureau of Safety Programming and Analysis
215 Transportation Safety Bldg.
Harrisburg, PA 17120
(717) 787-7350

PR
Traffic Safety Commission
P.O. Box 41289
Santurce, PR 00940
(809) 726-5290
(809) 726-5150, ext. 3550

RI
Governor's Office of Highway Safety
345 Harris Ave.
Providence, RI 02909
(401) 277-3024

SC
Division of Public Safety Programs
Edgar A. Brown State Office Bldg.
1205 Pendleton St.
Room 453
Columbia, SC 29201
(803) 758-2237

SD
State and Community Programs
Department of Public Safety
118 W. Capitol Ave.
Pierre, SD 57501
(605) 773-3675

TN
Governor's Highway Safety Program
James K. Polk State Office Bldg.
505 Deaderick St.
Suite 600
Nashville, TN 37219
(615) 741-2589

TX
Traffic Safety Section (D-18-TS)
State Department of Highways and Public Transportation
Eleventh and Brazos
Austin, TX 78701
(512) 465-6360

UT
Highway Safety Division
Department of Public Safety
4501 South, 2700 West
Salt Lake City, UT 84109
(801) 965-4410

184 / *National Highway Traffic Safety Administration*

VA

Deputy Commissioner for Transportation Safety
P.O. Box 27412
Richmond, VA 23269
(804) 257-6620

VT

Vermont Highway Safety Program
Agency of Transportation
133 State St.
Montpelier, VT 05602
(802) 828-2706

WA

Washington Traffic Safety Commission
1000 Cherry St.
Olympia, WA 98504
(206) 753-6197

WI

Wisconsin Highway Safety Coordinator
P.O. Box 7910
4802 Sheboygan Ave.
Madison, WI 53707
(608) 266-0402

WV

Governor's Office of Economic and Community Development
5790-A MacCorkle Ave.
Charleston, WV 25304
(304) 348-8814

WY

Wyoming Highway Safety Dept.
Highway Safety Branch
P.O. Box 1708
Cheyenne, WY 82002-9019
(307) 777-7296

Publications: Reports. Pamphlets. Curriculum materials. Guides.

Bibliographies, Sales Catalogs, Publications Lists, etc.

"A Guide to Audiovisual and Print Materials' on Safety Belts and Child Car Safety Seats." 1983. 48p. free. DOT HS 806 418.
Describes print materials on safety belts, child car safety seats, and posters (pages PM-1 and PM-2).

"Subject Bibliography Series." Current. 1p. free.
Lists bibliographies available for purchase from National Technical Information Service, 5285 Port Royal Rd., Springfield, VA 22161. (703) 487-4650.

Selected List of Books and Pamphlets

Highway Safety. Current. 196p. free.
Reports on activities for the year. Tables. Figures. Appendices.

Motor Vehicle Safety. Current. 138p. free.
Reports on activities for the year. Tables. Figures. Appendices.

"Restrain Yourself." n.d. kit. free.
Provides teacher's guide and learning activities designed to help students get the facts, analyze the issues, and understand the implications of the decision to use or not use safety restraints.

Audiovisuals:

Filmographies, Sales Lists, etc.

"A Guide to Audiovisual and Print Materials on Safety Belts and Child Car Safety Seats." 1983. 48p. free. DOT HS 806 418.
Contains a film and slide guide designed to help in selecting materials most appropriate for various audiences and situations. Provides suggested presentation questions and answers.

Special Services: For online search of highway safety literature, write:
Transportation Research Board
2101 Constitution Avenue, NW
Washington, DC 20418

NATIONAL HISTORICAL PUBLICATIONS AND RECORDS COMMISSION
National Archives Bldg.
Washington, DC 20408
(202) 523-3092

Date Established: 1934

Objectives of the Agency: Make plans, estimates, and recommendations for the publication of vital historical documents; work with public and private institutions in gathering, annotating, and publishing papers and records of national historical significance; and provide grants to state and local governments, historical societies, archives, libraries, and associations.

Curriculum: History, library

Subjects: Archives
Library science

Locations of State Historical Records Coordinators:

AK

State Archivist
Department of Administration
Pouch C, MS 0207
Juneau, AK 99811
(907) 465-2275

AL

Department of Archives and History
624 Washington Ave.
Montgomery, AL 36130
(205) 261-4361

AR

Director and State Historian
Arkansas History Commission
1 Capitol Mall
Little Rock, AR 72201
(501) 371-2141

AS

Assistant to the Governor
Government House
Pago Pago, AS 96799

AZ

State Librarian
State Capitol
1700 W. Washington
Third Floor
Phoenix, AZ 85007
(602) 255-4035

CA

California State Archives
Office of the Secretary
1020 Q St.
Sacramento, CA 95814
(916) 445-4293

CO

Colorado Historical Society
1300 Broadway
Denver, CO 80203
(303) 839-2136

CT

State Archivist
Connecticut State Library
231 Capitol Ave.
Hartford, CT 06106
(203) 566-3690

DC

Acting Vice President for University Affairs
University of the District of Columbia
4200 Connecticut Ave., NW
Building 39
Room 301
Washington, DC 20008
(202) 282-7568

DE

State Archivist
Division of Historical and Cultural Affairs
Hall of Records
Dover, DE 19901
(302) 736-5318

FL

State Archivist
Department of State
The Capitol
Tallahassee, FL 32304
(904) 487-2073

GA

Department of Archives and History
330 Capitol Ave.
Atlanta, GA 30334
(404) 656-2358

GU

Territorial Librarian
P.O. Box 652
Agana, GU 96910

HI

State Archivist
Hawaii State Archives
Iolani Palace Grounds
Honolulu, HI 96813
(808) 548-2355

IA

Iowa State Historical Department
E. Seventh and Court Ave.
Des Moines, IA 50319
(515) 281-6974

ID

State Archivist
Idaho State Archives
610 N. Julia Davis Dr.
Boise, ID 83706
(208) 334-2120

IL

Director of Archives
Office of the Secretary of State
Archives Bldg.
Springfield, IL 62756
(217) 782-4682

IN

State Archivist
Indiana State Library
140 Senate Ave.
Indianapolis, IN 46204
(317) 232-3737

KS

Kansas State Historical Society
120 W. Tenth St.
Topeka, KS 66612
(913) 296-3251

KY
Department for Libraries and Archives
300 Coffeetree Rd.
Frankfort, KY 40601
(502) 875-7000

LA
State Archivist
Capitol Station
Box 44125
Baton Rouge, LA 70804
(504) 342-5440

MA
Archives of the Commonwealth
Office of the Secretary
State House
Boston, MA 02133
(617) 727-2816

MD
State Archivist
Maryland Hall of Records
Box 828
Annapolis, MD 21404
(301) 269-3915

ME
Inquire at Washington, D.C. office.

MI
Michigan History Division
3500 N. Logan St.
Lansing, MI 48906
(517) 373-0512

MN
State Archivist
Minnesota Historical Society
1500 Mississippi
St. Paul, MN 55101
(612) 296-6980

MO
State Archivist
1001 Industrial Dr.
Jefferson City, MO 65102
(314) 751-3280

MS
Mississippi Department of Archives and History
P.O. Box 571
Jackson, MS 39205
(601) 354-6218

MT
Archivist
Montana Historical Society
225 N. Roberts St.
Helena, MT 59601
(406) 449-2681

NC
Division of Archives and History
Department of Cultural Resources
109 E. Jones St.
Raleigh, NC 27611
(919) 733-7305

ND
State Archivist
North Dakota Historical Society
Bismarck, ND 58505
(701) 224-2668

NE
Nebraska Historical Society
1500 R St.
Lincoln, NE 68508
(402) 432-2793

NH
Division of Records Management and Archives
71 S. Fruit St.
Concord, NH 03301
(603) 271-2236

NJ
Division of Archives and Records Management
Department of State
CN-307
2300 Stuyvesant Ave.
Trenton, NJ 08625
(609) 633-7273

NM
State Records Center and Archives
404 Montezuma St.
Santa Fe, NM 87501
(505) 827-8860

Northern Mariana Islands
Division of Historic Preservation
Department of Community and Cultural Affairs
Saipan, Mariana Islands 96950

NV
Director of Archives
101 S. Fall St.
Carson City, NV 89701
(702) 885-5210

NY
State Archivist
Cultural Education Center
Empire State Plaza
Room 10A46
Albany, NY 12234
(518) 474-1195

OH

Archives and Manuscripts Division
Ohio Historical Society
Interstate 71 and Seventeenth Ave.
Columbus, OH 43211
(614) 466-1500

OK

Archivist
Oklahoma Department of Libraries
200 N.E. Eighteenth St.
Oklahoma City, OK 73105
(405) 521-2502

OR

Oregon Historical Society
1230 S.W. Park Ave.
Portland, OR 97205
(503) 222-1741

PA

Pennsylvania Historical and Museum Commission
P.O. Box 1026
Harrisburg, PA 17120
(717) 787-2891

PR

Institute of Puerto Rican Culture
Box 4184
San Juan, PR 00905

RI

Rhode Island State Archives
State House
Room 43
Providence, RI 02903
(401) 277-2353

SC

South Carolina Department of Archives and History
Capitol Station
P.O. Box 11669
Columbia, SC 29211
(803) 758-5816

SD

Archives Resource Center
State Library Bldg.
800 N. Illinois
Pierre, SD 57501
(605) 773-3173

TN

Tennessee State Library and Archives
403 Seventh Ave. North
Nashville, TN 37219
(615) 741-2561

TX

State Archivist
Capitol Station
Box 12927
Austin, TX 78711
(512) 475-2445

UT

Division of State History
300 Rio Grande
Salt Lake City, UT 84101
(801) 533-5755

VA

State Archivist
Virginia State Library
Twelfth and Capitol Sts.
Richmond, VA 23219
(804) 786-5579

VI

Bureau of Libraries and Museums
49-50 King St.
Christiansted
St. Croix, VI 00830

VT

State Papers Division
Pavillion Bldg.
Montpelier, VT 05602
(802) 828-2363

WA

State Archivist
Legislative Bldg.
Olympia, WA 98504
(206) 753-5485

WI

Historical Society of Wisconsin
816 State St.
Madison, WI 53706
(608) 262-3266

WV

Department of Archives and History
Science and Culture Center
Charleston, WV 25305
(304) 348-0230

WY

Archives and Historical Department
Barrett Bldg.
Cheyenne, WY 82002
(307) 777-7826

Publications: Pamphlets. Newsletters. Guidelines. Reports on activities and programs.

188 / National Historical Publications and Records Commission

Serials, Subscription Publications, etc.

"Annotation." Current. 12p. free.

Provides a newsletter of events, new publications, and projects. Photographs.

Selected List of Books and Pamphlets

"The National Historical Publications and Records Commission and Its Work Fact Sheet." n.d. 2p. free.

Gives the history, development, and activities of the commission.

"National Historical Publications and Records Commission Annual Report." Current. 38p. free.

Reports progress in the records program, publications program, statistics, and chronology. Lists publications and grants. Prints scholarly reviews. Photographs.

"National Historical Publications and Records Commission Microfilm Guidelines." 1985. 15p. free.

Explains the introduction and development of the program, eligible types of microfilm proposals, and how grant proposals are processed. Selected bibliography.

"National Historical Publications and Records Commission Publications Program Guidelines and Procedures: Applications and Grants." 1985. 9p. free.

Gives general information, and information about grant applications and the National Historical Publications program.

"National Historical Publications and Records Commission Records Program Guidelines and Procedures: Applications and Grants." n.d. 52p. free.

Explains grants, types of projects, and grant support. Includes administration, application and procedures, and suggestions to follow. Appendices.

NATIONAL INFORMATION CENTER FOR HANDICAPPED CHILDREN AND YOUTH
Box 1492
Washington, DC 20013
(703) 522-3332

Date Established: 1982

Objectives of the Agency: Help parents, educators, care-givers, advocates, and others to improve the lives of children and youth with handicaps; answer questions; develop and share new information through publications; work with groups; and connect people who have similar problems.

Curriculum: Special education

Subjects: Handicapped children

Publications: Pamphlets. Directories. Papers. Kits. Lists. Fact sheets. Newsletters. Curriculum materials. On handicaps, special education careers, and legal information.

Bibliographies, Sales Catalogs, Publications Lists, etc.

"NICHCY Publication List." n.d. 6p. free.

Lists available materials, stating title, date, pages, and contents.

Serials, Subscription Publications, etc.

"News Digest." Monthly. approx. 10p. free.

Provides a newsletter of events and happenings, bibliographies.

Selected List of Books and Pamphlets

"General Information about Handicaps and People with Handicaps." n.d. 2p. free.

Defines 11 types of handicaps such as *speech impaired* or *orthopedically impaired*. Bibliography. List of resources.

"National Information Center for Handicapped Children and Youth." n.d. 3-fold. free.

Tells what the center is and how it works. Includes a form to get on the mailing list for free subscriptions to materials.

"National Toll-Free Numbers." Rev. 1985. 2p. free.

Toll-free numbers for such concerns as Alzheimer's disease & related disorders and tripod-service for the hearing impaired.

"Protect Your Disabled Child." n.d. 4-fold. free.

Provides information from the child safety program on safety rules that you can teach disabled children.

"Public Agencies." 2p. free.

Describes agencies that are responsible for providing certain kinds of assistance to people with handicaps and their families.

"Sources of Help and Information." n.d. 2p. free.

Gives addresses of magazines, directories, newspapers, and other resources such as the Council for Exceptional Children.

"State Resource Sheet." n.d. current. approx. 2p. free.

Lists names, addresses, and telephone numbers of such organizations as the State Mental Retardation Program, and the Protection and Advocacy Agency. Request one for your particular state.

NATIONAL INJURY INFORMATION CLEARINGHOUSE
U.S. Consumer Product Safety Commission
5401 Westbard Ave.
Room 625
Washington, DC 20207
(301) 492-6424

Date Established: 1972

Objectives of the Agency: Collect, investigate, analyze, and disseminate injury data and information relating to the causes and prevention of death, injury, and illness associated with consumer products.

Curriculum: Child care, consumer education, safety

Subjects: Accidents—prevention
Children—care and hygiene
Consumer protection
Fire prevention
Safety education

Publications: Pamphlets. Curriculum materials. Reports. Lists. Handbooks. Guides. Fact sheets.

Bibliographies, Sales Catalogs, Publications Lists, etc.

"A Look at the Playground Safety Education Materials." n.d. 8p. free.

Describes materials that provide guidance in how to select, install, maintain, and use playground equipment more safely. Includes basic safety tips for swings, slides, seesaws, and climbing apparatus. Provides order form for free materials.

"Publications List." n.d. 6p. free.

Lists available publications, some of which are also in Spanish.

Selected List of Books and Pamphlets

"Bumps Activity Guide." n.d. 17p. free.

Gives activity suggestions about safety for children between 9 and 12 years of age.

"Buyer's Guide: The Safe Nursery." 1985. 17p. free.

Includes such hazards as cribs, gates, toy chests, rattles, and other products used in infant care. Nursery equipment checklist.

"A Guide to Flammable Products and Ignition Sources for Secondary Schools." 1977. 32p. free.

Provides activities for the liberal arts teacher, industrial arts teacher, physical and social science teachers. Includes information for the school librarian.

"A Handbook for Public Playground Safety." Vol. 1. 1981. 19p. free.

Gives general guidelines for new and existing playgrounds. Includes information on playground injuries, planning a new playground, making existing playgrounds safer, and playground safety checklists. Selected bibliography.

"A Handbook for Public Playground Safety." Vol. 2. 1982. 27p. free.

Gives technical guidelines for equipment and surfacing. Covers such topics as: assembly, installation and maintenance, moving impact of swings, entrapment, and surfaces. Drawings. Tables.

It's No Accident. n.d. 121p. free.

Provides a consumer product safety curriculum resource guide for teachers of grades 3-6. Designs activities to teach students safety habits and practices that can reduce product-related accidents and injuries. Loose-leaf format.

"The National Electronic Injury Surveillance System (NEISS)." Rev. 1984. 6p. free.

Explains what NEISS is, what work it does, and the cost of services and products.

"The National Injury Information Clearinghouse." Rev. 1984. 6p. free.

Tells what the clearinghouse does, who uses injury data, cost of services, and products available.

"Play Happy, Play Safely." 1979. 13p. free.

Provides a playground equipment guide for teachers, park and recreation directors, parents, youth leaders and other concerned adults. Includes a checklist.

"Preliminary NEISS Estimates." Current. 18p. free.

Gives compilation of information derived from product-associated injuries treated in hospital emergency rooms participating in the National Electronic Injury Surveillance System (NEISS).

"A Toy & Sports Equipment Safety Guide." 1980. 24p. free.

Tells what safety problems can arise when using toys and a variety of wheeled and sports equipment, and how to avoid the hazards.

Special Services: "How To Use CPSC's Hotline 800-638-CPSC" is a free, eight-page information survey about hotline hours, when to use it, and services.

NATIONAL INSTITUTE OF ALLERGY AND INFECTIOUS DISEASES
Information Office, ORRPR
National Institutes of Health
Building 31
Room 7A32
Bethesda, MD 20205
(301) 496-5717

Date Established: 1955

Objectives of the Agency: Conduct and support research to better understand the causes of allergic, immunologic, and infectious diseases; and develop better means of preventing, diagnosing, and treating illnesses.

Curriculum: Health

Subjects: Allergy
Communicable diseases
Diseases

Publications: Pamphlets. Essays. Speeches. Reports.

190 / National Institute of Allergy and Infectious Diseases

Bibliographies, Sales Catalogs, Publications Lists, etc.

NIH Publications List. 1985. 118p. free. NIH Publication No. 85-7.

Groups free publications into those for the general public and those for health professionals (pages 34-37).

Selected List of Books and Pamphlets

"Profile." Current. 81p. free.

Explains directory of personnel, important events in the institute's history, disease statistics, research grants, and other programs. Graphs. Tables. Organization structure.

Audiovisuals:

Filmographies, Sales Lists, etc.

"Jennifer: A Revealing Story of Genital Herpes." 1p. free. #12766.

Describes the free loan, 28-minute film about a young woman striving to cope with this disease. Available from: Modern Talking Picture Service, Film Scheduling Center, 5000 Park St. North, St. Petersburg, FL 33709. (813) 541-6661.

"NIAID Slide Shows on Asthma and Allergies." n.d. 1p. free.

Describes shows available, order number, price, length of audio cassette, script, and number of slides.

NATIONAL INSTITUTE OF DENTAL RESEARCH
Department of Health and Human Services
Public Health Service
National Institutes of Health
9000 Rockville Pike
Building 31
Room 2C36
Bethesda, MD 20205
(301) 496-2883

Date Established: 1976

Objectives of the Agency: Support and conduct clinical and laboratory research directed toward ending tooth decay and other oral-facial disorders.

Curriculum: Health

Subjects: Teeth

Publications: Posters. Guides. Fact sheets. Pamphlets.

Bibliographies, Sales Catalogs, Publications Lists, etc.

"Oral Health Education and Promotion Materials." 1980. 2p. free. NIH Publication No. 81-2133.

Describes available materials and how to order them.

Selected List of Books and Pamphlets

"Fluoride To Protect the Teeth of Adults." 1983. 8p. free. NIH Publication No. 83-2329.

Explains how fluoride acts. Includes using it in the dental office and at home.

"A Healthy Start . . . Fluoride Tablets for Children in Preschool Programs." 1982. 4p. free. NIH Publication No. 82-1838.

Shows desirability of fluoride tablets in preschool settings.

"NIDR Fact Sheet: Periodontal (Gum) Disease." n.d. 3p. free.

Explains what it is, who is affected, what causes it, the different types of periodontal disease, and how to protect yourself.

"Preventing Tooth Decay: A Guide for Implementing Self-Applied Fluorides in School Settings." 1981. kit of assorted materials. free. NIH Publication No. 82-1196.

Provides a guide for implementing self-applied fluorides in school settings.

"RX for Sound Teeth." 1984. 8p. free. NIH Publication No. 84-793.

Explains what plaque is, how to tell if you have it, and how to fight it and prevent diseases. Includes illustrations on how to floss, rinse, and brush.

"Snack Facts." 1983. 12p. free. NIH Publication No. 83-1680.

Tells what makes snacks harmful and how to choose those in non-sugar groups.

"Tooth Decay." 1982. 6p. free. NIH Publication No. 82-1146.

Explains what causes decay and how to prevent it.

Special Services: Free loan exhibit designed to emphasize the importance of fluorides: a table-top exhibit of four panels, 60 inches on the side and 26 inches high. To reserve write:
Health Promotion and Science Transfer Section
National Institute of Dental Research, NIH
Building 31
Room 2031
Bethesda, MD 20205
(301) 496-2883

NATIONAL INSTITUTE OF EDUCATION
Dissemination and Improvement of Practice Program
Washington, DC 20208
(202) 254-5500

Date Established: 1966

Objectives of the Agency: Provide users with ready access primarily to the English-language literature dealing with education.

Curriculum: Education, library
Subjects: Education
Library Science
Locations:

Adult, Career, and Vocational Education
Ohio State University
1960 Kenny Rd.
Columbus, OH 43210
(614) 486-3655

Counseling and Personnel Services
University of Michigan
2108 School of Education Bldg.
Ann Arbor, MI 48109
(313) 764-9492

Educational Management
University of Oregon
Eugene, OR 97403
(503) 686-5043

Elementary and Early Childhood
University of Illinois
805 W. Pennsylvania Ave.
Urbana, IL 61601
(217) 333-1386

Handicapped and Gifted Children
Council for Exceptional Children
1920 Association Dr.
Reston, VA 22091
(703) 620-3660

Higher Education
George Washington University
1 Dupont Circle, NW
Suite 630
Washington, DC 20036
(202) 296-2597

Information Resources
Syracuse University
School of Education
130 Huntington Hall
Syracuse, NY 13210
(315) 423-3640

Junior Colleges
University of California
96 Powell Library Bldg.
Los Angeles, CA 90024
(213) 825-3931

Languages and Linguistics
Center for Applied Linguistics
3520 Prospect St., NW
Washington, DC 20007
(202) 298-9292

Reading and Communication Skills
National Council of Teachers of English
1111 Kenyon Rd.
Urbana, IL 61801
(217) 328-3870

Rural Education and Small Schools
New Mexico State University
Box 3AP
Las Cruces, NM 88003
(505) 646-2623

Science, Mathematics, and Environmental Education
Ohio State University
1200 Chambers Rd.
Third Floor
Columbus, OH 43212
(614) 422-6717

Social Studies/Social Science Education
855 Broadway
Boulder, CO 80302
(303) 492-8434

Teacher Education
American Association of Colleges for Teacher
 Education
1 Dupont Circle NW
Suite 610
Washington, DC 20036
(202) 293-2450

Tests, Measurement, and Evaluation
Educational Testing Service
Rosedale Rd.
Princeton, NJ 08540
(609) 921-9000, ext. 2176

Urban Education
Teachers College
Columbia University
525 W. One Hundred Twentieth St.
Box 40
New York, NY 10027
(212) 678-3437

Support Organizations:

ERIC Document Reproduction Service
Computer Microfilm International Corporation
3030 N. Fairfax Dr.
Suite 200
Arlington, VA 22201
(703) 841-1212

ERIC Processing and Reference Facility
Information Systems Division
4833 Rugby Ave.
Suite 301
Bethesda, MD 20814
(301) 656-9723

Oryx Press
2214 N. Central Ave. at Encanto
Phoenix, AZ 85004
(602) 254-6156

Publications: Databases. Serials. Microfiche. Document reproductions. Indexes. Pamphlets. Lists. Newsletters. Bibliographies. Fact sheets. Digests.

Bibliographies, Sales Catalogs, Publications Lists, etc.

Materials described below are available from:
ERIC Clearinghouse on Information Resources
130 Huntington Hall
Syracuse University
Syracuse, NY 13210
Because of space considerations, only selections from one clearinghouse were used.

"Computer Searches at ERIC/IR." Current. 6p. free.
   Explains what a computer search provides, how it works, how to request a search, and the cost. Order form.

"In Brief . . . Online Public Access Catalogs." 1982. 2p. free.
   Considers the online catalog, sometimes called OPAC, or Public Online Catalog, a computer-based and supported library catalog. Bibliography.

"Information Resources Publications." Current. 8p. free.
   Lists what is available and for sale in books.

"Information Resources on . . . Courseware Evaluation for CAI." 1985. 2p. free.
   Gives a selected ERIC bibliography and information on where to obtain materials from coded sources.

"Information Resources on . . . Media Specialists and the Curriculum." 1985. 2p. free.
   Gives a selected ERIC bibliography from the Educational Resources Information Center.

"Information Resources on . . . Online at the Reference Desk." 1984. 2p. free.
   Prints a selected ERIC bibliography taken from *Current Index to Journals in Education* and *Resources in Education.*

"Information Resources on . . . Teaching Methods for Bibliographic Instruction." 1985. 2p. free.
   Prints a selected ERIC bibliography prepared for ACRL continuing education course 202.

"User Services Products." Current. 1p. free.
   Examines free ERIC digests and mini-bibliographies on various topics. Order form provides a space to mark. Return form with a stamped, self-addressed envelope.

Serials, Subscription Publications, etc.

ERIC/IR Update." Semiannual bulletin. 6p. free.
   Includes new items available from ERIC in an information bulletin.

Selected List of Books and Pamphlets

"Accessing ERIC with Your Microcomputer." 1984. 2p. free.
   Explains what is needed to make a microcomputer act as a terminal. Includes configuring the software and hardware.

"Computer Literacy for Teachers." 1984. 2p. free.
   Prints a discussion of needs and references to studies. Bibliography.

"Directory of ERIC Microfiche Collections." 1983. 69p. free.
   Lists name of facility, address, telephone, contact, collection status, equipment, and access hours. Arranged by country, state and city. Statistical tables.

"Managing Computer Software Collections." 1984. 2p. free.
   Includes problems, using AACR2, procedures, bibliography.

"Networking and Microcomputers." 1984. 2p. free.
   Explains what networking is, types of networks, getting started, services available, and trouble shooting.

"A Pocket Guide to ERIC." n.d. 12p. free.
   Describes ERIC, major ERIC products, document delivery, microfiche collections, online retrieval, search services, etc.

"Software Copyright Interpretation." 1985. 2p. free.
   Discusses such topics as back-up copies, and multiple-loading. Reprints articles from *The Computing Teacher.* Reading list.

"Teleconferencing in Education." 1983. 2p. free.
   Explains what it is, why use it, audio teleconferencing, audio graphic teleconferencing, video teleconferencing, and computer conferencing. Bibliography.

Special Services: The ERIC database can be searched online by computer by DIALOG, System Development Corporation, and Bibliographic Retrieval Services.

Addresses and telephone numbers as well as other information on online retrieval is available in "A Pocket Guide to ERIC," described above in *Selected List of Books and Pamphlets.*

NATIONAL INSTITUTE OF GENERAL MEDICAL SCIENCES
Office of Research Reports
National Institutes of Health
Bethesda, MD 20205
(301) 496-7301

Date Established: 1962

Objectives of the Agency: Support non-disease-targeted research and research training in the basic biomedical sciences such as cellular and molecular biology, genetics, pharmacology, biophysics and physiological sciences, and minority access to research careers.

Curriculum: Science

Subjects: Biology
Genetics
Science—study and teaching

Publications: Pamphlets. Bibliographies. On the functions of the National Institute of General Medical Sciences.

Bibliographies, Sales Catalogs, Publications Lists, etc.

"Readings and Resources on Genetics." 1983. 1p. free.
Includes author, title, place of publication, publishing company, and date of publication of books; author, title, magazine, date of publication, and pages of articles.

Selected List of Books and Pamphlets

"The National Institute of General Medical Sciences." 1984. 31p. free.
Surveys the National Institute of General Medical Sciences. Includes important events in its history and programs. Photographs. Appendices include information about grant applications.

"Welcome to the National Institute of General Medical Sciences." 1985. 8-fold. free.
Gives titles, names, building, room, telephone number, and program of the staff. Map.

NATIONAL INSTITUTE OF JUSTICE
U.S. Department of Justice
Box 6000
Rockville, MD 20850
(301) 251-5500

Date Established: 1972

Objectives of the Agency: Meet the technical information needs of the nation's law enforcement, criminal justice, juvenile justice, and investigative communities.

Curriculum: Government

Subjects: Crime—U.S.

Publications: Reports. Microfiche. Summaries. Documents. Reviews. User packets. Pamphlets. Bulletins. Bibliographies. Topical searches. Statistics. Technical, reference, and general material.

Bibliographies, Sales Catalogs, Publications Lists, etc.

"Books in Brief." Current. 2p. free.
Provides an explanation and order form of a book service that summarizes recent documents relevant to policy.

"National Institute of Justice Publications." Current. 4p. free.
Includes topical bibliographies, reviews, summaries, and case studies.

Serials, Subscription Publications, etc.

NIJ Reports. Bimonthly. 30p. free.
Provides a bulletin about current criminal justice research, publications, and events.

Selected List of Books and Pamphlets

"Crime of Rape." n.d. 28p. free. NCJ 96777 No. 40.
National crime survey covers the decade from 1973 through 1982. Includes information on rape and its impact on victims.

"Expand Your Research Ability with 19,500 Full-Text Criminal Justice Documents." Current. 8p. free.
Gives microfiche collection description and order form.

"Risk of Violent Crime." n.d. 28p. free. NCJ 97119. No. 41.
Crime risk index gives information about the 3 percent of Americans that were victims of violent crimes.

"Toll-Free Telephone Number Announcement." Current. 1p. free.
Gives numbers of services and clearinghouse.

"Registration Form." Current. 4p. free.
Tells what products and services are available. Includes registration form. Material is geared to your interests and needs.

NATIONAL INSTITUTE OF MENTAL HEALTH
Public Inquiries Section
Division of Communications and Education
Science Communication Branch
Room 15C-05
5600 Fishers Lane
Rockville, MD 20857
(301) 443-3877

Date Established: 1974

Objectives of the Agency: Provide a national focus to increase knowledge and advance the means of dealing with issues; and promote mental health and the prevention and treatment of mental illness.

Curriculum: Guidance, psychology

Subjects: Mental health
Psychology

Publications: Lists. Pamphlets. Books. General and technical publications free and for sale.

Bibliographies, Sales Catalogs, Publications Lists, etc.

Coping and Adaptation. 1981. 480p. free DHHS Publication No. (ADM) 81-863.

Provides an annotated bibliography and study guide to literature concerned with the wide range of human responses to catastrophic events, injury, and crises. Includes an author index to the 988 abstracts.

"Publications of the National Institute of Mental Health." Current. 10p. free.

Lists publications by subject areas. Will provide single copies of 10 titles per request. Order multiple copies or bulk quantities directly from: Superintendent of Documents, U.S. Government Printing Office, Washington, DC 20402. Order form provided.

Selected List of Books and Pamphlets

"Adolescence and Depression." Packet. $1.00. S/N 017-024-01237-8. DHHS Publication No. (ADM) 84-1337.

Covers in 11 nontechnical summaries subjects like: *Adolescent Loneliness, Depression and Low Self-Esteem,* and *Identity Formation.* Order from: Superintendent of Documents, U.S. Government Printing Office, Washington, DC 20402.

"Careers in Mental Health." 1984. 2p. free.

Tells what occupational therapists, psychiatric nurses, psychiatrists, and other mental health professionals do. Gives addresses of associations and councils to obtain more information.

"The Consumer's Guide to Mental Health and Related Federal Programs." 1979. 204p. free. DHEW Publication No. (ADM) 79-760.

Helps in understanding and applying for participation in federal programs. Besides mental health services, it describes federal programs and benefits in employment, housing, social security, welfare, food, and transportation.

"A Consumer's Guide to Mental Health Services." 1980. 22p. free. DHHS Publication No. (ADM) 80-214.

Relates warning signals of mental disturbance, what to do in emergency situations, types of help available, and questions and answers about seeking help. Includes addresses to obtain more information.

"Depression: What We Know." 1985. 65p. free. DHHS Publication No. (ADM) 85-1318.

Explains what clinical depression is, how to recognize it, and what to do about it. Examines the origins of depression, different age groups, suicide, and treatment alternatives.

Handbook of Federal Resources on Domestic Violence. 1980. 261p. free.

Helps users identify pertinent federal government funding for domestic violence programs. Organized alphabetically by government agency. Detailed table of contents. Subject index.

"He Told Me Not To Tell." 1979. 28p. free.

Provides a guide for talking about sexual assault. Defines child sexual abuse. Shows how to help children protect themselves.

National Directory: Rape Prevention and Treatment Resources. 1981. 150p. free. DHHS Publication No. (ADM) 81-1008.

Lists nationwide inventory of prevention and treatment services and related resources. Arranged by state. Also includes Canada. Includes name, address, telephone number, hours, and services provided by various centers.

"Plain Talk about Adolescence." 1981. 2p. free.

Examines how parents can keep communications open. Includes how to deal with confused feelings teenagers experience.

"Plain Talk about Aging." 1983. 4p. free.

Discusses changing roles, challenges of growing older, and changes in mind and body as well as in economics and family patterns.

Television and Behavior: Ten Years of Scientific Progress and Implications for the Eighties. 1982. 362p. free. DHHS Publication No. (ADM) 82-1196.

Includes list of contributors, cognitive and affective aspects of television, violence and aggression, social beliefs and social behavior, television and social relations, television and health, and television in American society. Technical reviews have references and tables.

"You Are Not Alone: Facts about Mental Health and Mental Illness." 1981. 12p. free. DHHS Publication No. (ADM) 81-1178.

Explains what mental health is, what to watch for, what some of the major mental illnesses are, and how to find help.

NATIONAL INSTITUTE OF NEUROLOGICAL AND COMMUNICATIVE DISORDERS AND STROKE
Office of Scientific and Health Reports
Department of Health and Human Services
Public Health Service
National Institutes of Health
Bethesda, MD 20205
(301) 496-5751

Date Established: 1975

Objectives of the Agency: Be the principal federal agency supporting research on the causes of hearing loss, as well as on prevention, treatment and rehabilitation; promote the development of better hearing aids and other ways to aid hearing; and sponsor research on speech, head injuries, stroke, and other neurological matters.

Curriculum: Health

Subjects: Health education

Publications: Pamphlets. Surveys. On research of stroke, head injury, stuttering, hearing loss, headache, and dementia. Of interest to those in the health field.

Selected List of Books and Pamphlets

"The Dementias." 1983. 32p. free NIH Publication No. 83-2252.
  Explains what dementia is, diagnostic and research programs, voluntary health organizations.

"Head Injury." 1984. 37p. free. NIH Publication No. 84-2478.
  Explains how head injuries occur, two major types of injuries, coma, and rehabilitation.

"Headache." 1984. 37p. free. NIH Publication No. 84-158.
  Describes types of headache and methods of treatment.

"Hearing Loss." 1982. 36p. free. NIH Publication No. 82-157.
  Explains fundamentals of sound, conductive problems, and detecting hearing loss. Includes addresses of associations.

"National Survey of Stroke." 1983. 14p. free. NIH Publication No. 83-2069.
  Gives highlights of a survey. Charts. Graphs.

NATIONAL INSTITUTE ON AGING
Information Office
9000 Rockville Pike
Building 31
Room 5C35
Bethesda, MD 20205
(301) 496-1752

Date Established: 1974

Objectives of the Agency: Conduct and support biomedical, social, and behavioral research and training related to aging and the diseases, problems, and needs of the aged.

Curriculum: Health

Subjects: Aging

Publications: White House Conference on Aging summaries. Fact sheets. Pamphlets. Reports. General and technical material on subjects related to aging.

Bibliographies, Sales Catalogs, Publications Lists, etc.

"Publications List." n.d. 1p. free.
  Provides a check list of publications available in single copies.

Selected List of Books and Pamphlets

"High Blood Pressure: A Common but Controllable Disorder." 1981. 2p. free.
  Explains blood pressure readings and how high blood pressure is controlled.

"National Institute on Aging." 1983. 38p. free. NIH Publication No. 83-1129.
  Gives mission, history, programs, and grant and training mechanisms.

"National Institute on Aging Special Report on Aging." 1983. 32p. free. NIH Publication No. 83-2489.
  Reports highlights and progress in knowledge of the aging process.

Special Services: Your name may be placed on the mailing list upon request.

NATIONAL INSTITUTES OF HEALTH
Department of Health and Human Services
Public Health Service
Building 31
9000 Rockville Pike
Room 213-10
Bethesda, MD 20205
(301) 496-4000

Date Established: 1930

Objectives of the Agency: Conduct and support biomedical research into the causes, prevention, and cure of diseases; support research training and research resources; and communicate biomedical information.

Curriculum: Health

Subjects: Health education

Publications: Catalog.

Bibliographies, Sales Catalogs, Publications Lists, etc.

NIH Publications List. Current. 117p. free. NIH Publication No. 85-7.
  Lists what publications are available for sale and free from the various departments such as the National Cancer Institute and National Eye Institute. Publications are arranged by department, title, and number. Includes a wide variety of materials aimed at the general public, program planners, communicators, and health professionals.

NATIONAL LABOR RELATIONS BOARD
1717 Pennsylvania Ave., NW
Washington, DC 20570
(202) 655-4000

Date Established: 1935

Objectives of the Agency: Administer the nation's laws relating to labor relations; protect employees' rights to organize, to determine through elections whether workers want unions; and give aid in unfair labor practices.

Curriculum: Government

Subjects: Labor contract

Locations (arranged alphabetically by city):

National Labor Relations Board
Field Office
Clinton Ave. at N. Pearl St.
Albany, NY 12207
(518) 472-2215

National Labor Relations Board
Field Office
5000 Marble Ave., NE
Albuquerque, NM 87110
(505) 766-2508

National Labor Relations Board
Field Office
701 C St.
Anchorage, AK 99513
(907) 271-5015

National Labor Relations Board
Field Office
101 Marietta St.
Atlanta, GA 30323
(404) 221-2896

National Labor Relations Board
Field Office
109 Market Pl.
Baltimore, MD 21202
(301) 962-2822

National Labor Relations Board
Field Office
2026 Second Ave. North
Birmingham, AL 35203
(205) 254-1492

National Labor Relations Board
Field Office
120 Boylston St.
Boston, MA 02116
(617) 223-3300

National Labor Relations Board
Field Office
16 Court St.
Brooklyn, NY 11241
(212) 330-7713

National Labor Relations Board
Field Office
111 W. Huron St.
Buffalo, NY 14202
(716) 846-4931

National Labor Relations Board
Field Office
219 S. Dearborn St.
Chicago, IL 60604
(312) 353-7570

National Labor Relations Board
Field Office
550 Main St.
Cincinnati, OH 45202
(513) 684-3686

National Labor Relations Board
Field Office
1240 E. Ninth St.
Cleveland, OH 44199
(216) 522-3715

National Labor Relations Board
Field Office
721 Nineteenth St.
Denver, CO 80202
(303) 837-3555

National Labor Relations Board
Field Office
907 Walnut St.
Des Moines, IA 50309
(515) 284-4391

National Labor Relations Board
Field Office
477 Michigan Ave.
Detroit, MI 48226
(313) 226-3200

National Labor Relations Board
Field Office
109 N. Oregon St.
El Paso, TX 79901
(915) 541-7737

National Labor Relations Board
Field Office
819 Taylor St.
Fort Worth, TX 76102
(817) 334-2921

National Labor Relations Board
Field Office
82 Ionia, NW
Grand Rapids, MI 49503
(616) 456-2679

National Labor Relations Board
Field Office
750 Main St.
Hartford, CT 06103
(203) 722-2540

National Labor Relations Board
Field Office
Carlos E. Chardon Ave.
Hato Rey, PR 00918
(809) 753-4347

National Labor Relations Board
Field Office
300 Ala Moana Blvd.
Honolulu, HI 96850
(808) 546-5100

National Labor Relations Board
Field Office
515 Rusk St.
Houston, TX 77002
(713) 229-3748

National Labor Relations Board
Field Office
575 N. Pennsylvania Ave.
Indianapolis, IN 46204
(317) 269-7430

National Labor Relations Board
Field Office
400 W. Bay St.
Jacksonville, FL 32202
(904) 791-3768

National Labor Relations Board
Field Office
Fourth at State
Kansas City, KS 66101
(913) 236-3846

National Labor Relations Board
Field Office
720 S. Seventh St.
Las Vegas, NV 89101
(702) 385-6416

National Labor Relations Board
Field Office
1 Union National Plaza
Little Rock, AR 72210
(501) 378-6311

National Labor Relations Board
Field Office
11000 Wilshire Blvd.
Los Angeles, CA 90024
(213) 824-7351

National Labor Relations Board
Field Office
606 S. Olive St.
Los Angeles, CA 90014
(213) 688-5200

National Labor Relations Board
Field Office
1407 Union Ave.
Memphis, TN 38174
(901) 521-2725

National Labor Relations Board
Field Office
51 S.W. First Ave.
Miami, FL 33130
(305) 350-5391

National Labor Relations Board
Field Office
310 W. Wisconsin Ave.
Milwaukee, WI 53203
(414) 291-3861

National Labor Relations Board
Field Office
110 S. Fourth St.
Minneapolis, MN 55401
(612) 725-2611

National Labor Relations Board
Field Office
801 Broadway
Nashville, TN 37203
(615) 251-5921

National Labor Relations Board
Field Office
970 Broad St.
Newark, NJ 07102
(201) 645-2100

National Labor Relations Board
Field Office
600 South St.
New Orleans, LA 70130
(504) 589-6361

National Labor Relations Board
Field Office
26 Federal Plaza
New York, NY 10278
(212) 264-0300

National Labor Relations Board
Field Office
2201 Broadway
Oakland, CA 94604
(415) 273-7200

National Labor Relations Board
Field Office
411 Hamilton Blvd.
Peoria, IL 61602
(309) 671-7080

National Labor Relations Board
Field Office
615 Chestnut St.
Philadelphia, PA 19106
(215) 597-7601

National Labor Relations Board
Field Office
3030 N. Central Ave.
Phoenix, AZ 85012
(602) 241-2350

National Labor Relations Board
Field Office
1000 Liberty Ave.
Pittsburgh, PA 15222
(412) 644-2977

National Labor Relations Board
Field Office
921 S.W. Washington St.
Portland, OR 97205
(503) 221-3085

National Labor Relations Board
Field Office
210 Tucker Blvd. North
St. Louis, MO 63101
(314) 425-4167

National Labor Relations Board
Field Office
727 E. Durango Blvd.
San Antonio, TX 78206
(512) 229-6140

National Labor Relations Board
Field Office
940 Front St.
San Diego, CA 92189
(619) 293-6184

National Labor Relations Board
Field Office
450 Golden Gate Ave.
San Francisco, CA 94102
(415) 556-3197

National Labor Relations Board
Field Office
915 Second Ave.
Seattle, WA 98174
(206) 442-4532

National Labor Relations Board
Field Office
700 Twiggs St.
Tampa, FL 33601
(813) 228-2641

National Labor Relations Board
Field Office
440 S. Houston Ave.
Tulsa, OK 74127
(918) 581-7951

National Labor Relations Board
Field Office
2120 L St., NW
Washington, DC 20037
(202) 254-7612

National Labor Relations Board
Field Office
251 N. Main St.
Winston-Salem, NC 27101
(919) 761-3201

Publications: Pamphlets.

Selected List of Books and Pamphlets

"A Guide to Basic Law and Procedures under the National Labor Relations Act." Rev. ed. 59p. free.
Summarizes the act (the rights of employees, collective bargaining and representation of employees, unfair labor practices of employers, unfair labor practices of labor organizations, and enforcement) in a nontechnical way. Chart. Directory.

"The National Labor Relations Board and You: Representation Cases." 1983. 4-fold. free.
Explains what the National Labor Relations Board is and what it does in processing of representation petitions. Includes types of petitions, what a bargaining unit is, when a petition can be filed, and what you can expect if you file a petition.

"The National Labor Relations Board and You: Unfair Labor Practices." 1983. 4-fold. free.
Explains what the board is, what your rights are as an employee, what the board does not do.

"The NLRB . . . What It Is, What It Does." 1979. 3-fold. free.
Tells what the board is, and what its aim, structure, and procedures are. Gives history of the law the board administers, lists field offices.

"To Protect the Rights of the Public." n.d. 4-fold free.
Describes what the National Labor Relations Act provides, what the rights of employees are, and what the rights of employers are. Lists field offices.

"Your Government Conducts an Election for You—On the Job." 1985. 3-fold. free.

Explains the voting place, voting procedure, challenged ballots, rights of employees, protection of your rights and other information about voting.

NATIONAL LIBRARY OF MEDICINE
Office of Inquiries and Publications Management
8600 Rockville Pike
Bethesda, MD 20209
(301) 496-6491

Date Established: 1836

Objectives of the Agency: Serve as the nation's chief medical information source, the world's largest research library in a single scientific and professional field. The regional medical library program provides health science practitioners, investigators, educators, and administrators with convenient access to health care and biomedical information resources.

Curriculum: Health, library

Subjects: Medicine—research

Locations:

CT, DE, MA, ME, NH, NJ, NY, PA, PR, RI, VT

Greater Northeastern Regional Medical Library Program
The New York Academy of Medicine
2 E. One Hundred Third St.
New York, NY 10029
(212) 876-8763

AL, DC, FL, GA, MD, MS, NC, SC, TN, VA, WV

Southeastern/Atlantic Regional Medical Library Services
University of Maryland
Health Sciences Library
111 S. Greene St.
Baltimore, MD 21201
(301) 528-2855
(800) 638-6093

IA, IL, IN, KY, MI, MN, ND, OH, SD, WI

Regional Medical Library
University of Illinois at Chicago
Library of the Health Sciences
Health Sciences Center
P.O. Box 7509
Chicago, IL 60680
(312) 996-2464

CO, KS, MO, NE, UT, WY

Midcontinental Regional Medical Library Program
University of Nebraska
Medical Center Library
Forty-Second and Dewey Ave.
Omaha, NE 68105
(402) 559-4326

AR, LA, NM, OK, TX

South Central Regional Medical Library Program
University of Texas
Health Science Center at Dallas
5323 Harry Hines Blvd.
Dallas, TX 75235
(214) 688-2095

AK, ID, MT, OR, WA

Pacific Northwest Regional Health Sciences Library Service
Health Sciences Library
University of Washington
Seattle, WA 98195
(206) 543-8262

AZ, CA, HI, NV

Pacific Southwest Regional Medical Library Service
UCLS Biomedical Library
Center for the Health Sciences
Los Angeles, CA 90024
(213) 825-1200

Publications: Fact sheets. Pamphlets.

Bibliographies, Sales Catalogs, Publications Lists, etc.

"Health Sciences Serials." Quarterly. $15.00/yr. domestic, $18.75/yr. foreign; $4.75/single copy domestic, $5.95/single copy foreign. GPO Code HSS.

Designed to help health science librarians identify serial titles and locate the nearest library to fill interlibrary loans. Includes about 38,000 records, location information for about 6,700 titles, and bibliographic and acquisitions information to help librarians in the management of their own serials collection. Microfiche only.

"National Library of Medicine Literature Searches." Current. 4p. free.

Gives titles of bibliographies available without charge and directions on requesting the searches.

"National Library of Medicine Publications." Current. 36p. free.

Tells how to order and what is available. Includes Government Printing Office and National Technical Information Service order forms. A publication is issued each year to provide current ordering information for the library's publications.

Serials, Subscription Publications, etc.

Abridged Index Medicus. Monthly. $43.00/yr. domestic, $53.75/yr. foreign; $5.50/single copy domestic, $6.88/single copy foreign. GPO Code ABIM.

Provides bibliography of articles from 117 English-language journals. Each issue represents a subset of one month's input into the National Library of

Medicine's computer-based MEDLARS system. Arranged in subject and author sections. Also available in microform. Order from: Superintendent of Documents, U.S. Government Printing Office, Washington, DC 20402.

Index Medicus. $161.00/yr. domestic, $201.25/yr. foreign; $23.00/single copy domestic, $28.75/single copy foreign. GPO Code IM.

Lists bibliographic references to current articles from about 2,700 of the world's biomedical journals published in 36 languages. Subject and author sections. Includes a separate "Bibliography of Medical Reviews." Order from: Superintendent of Documents, U.S. Government Printing Office, Washington, DC 20402.

National Library of Medicine Current Catalog. Quarterly. $26.00/yr. domestic, $32.50/yr. foreign; $9.50/single copy domestic, $11.88/single copy foreign.

Lists bibliography of monographs and serials cataloged by the library. Lists by subject and name. Includes "Notes for Medical Catalogers." Order from: Superintendent of Documents, U.S. Government Printing Office, Washington, DC 20402.

"The National Library of Medicine News." Monthly. free publication.

For those interested in health sciences communications. To be placed on the mailing list, write: Editor, NLM News, Office of Inquiries and Publications Management, National Library of Medicine, 8600 Rockville Pike, Bethesda, MD 20209.

Selected List of Books and Pamphlets

"Fact Sheet: Bibliographic Services Division." 1985. 2p. free.

Gives bibliographic access to biomedical journal literature.

"Fact Sheet: DIRLINE." 1984. 2p. free.

What DIRLINE (Directory of Information Resource Online) is, and how it can be accessed and searched. Includes availability and user services.

"Fact Sheet: National Library of Medicine." 1985. 2p. free.

Describes its function, its computer-based medical literature analysis and retrieval system (MEDLARS), research and development, statistical profile, and information for visitors.

"Fact Sheet: NLM Online Services Program Policy Statement." 1985. 1p. free.

Gives network objectives, service policies, and user information.

"Fact Sheet: References Services Division." 1984. 1p. free.

Includes the mission, the Reference Section, the Circulation and Control Section, and the Audiovisual Resources Section.

"Fact Sheet: Regional Medical Libraries." 1983. 1p. free.

Explains what the regional medical library program is. Gives name, address, and telephone number of the seven libraries.

Medical Subject Headings. 1985. $17.00/yr. domestic, $21.25/yr. foreign. S/N 017-052-722278-6.

Prints the alphabetical and categorized list of subject descriptors used to analyze the biomedical literature in the National Library of Medicine. Order from: Superintendent of Documents, U.S. Government Printing Office, Washington, DC 20402.

"MEDLARS." 1983. 16p. free.

Describes the library's computer-based literature retrieval services for potential users. Includes description of various databases available on the online network and addresses of online centers with access to NLM databases.

"National Library of Medicine." n.d. 6p. free.

Gives directions and maps for arrival by car, airport limousine, mass transit, or taxi. Includes information about library hours, parking, and tours.

"The Prints and Photographs Collection of the National Library of Medicine." n.d. 12p. free.

Gives descriptions and photographs of the prints and photographs collection that includes: woodcuts, engravings, etchings, mezzotints, lithographs, photographs, halftones, and others.

Audiovisuals:

Filmographies, Sales Lists, etc.

"Audiovisual Sales Program." Current. 1p. free.

Explains what services are available from the National Audiovisual Center and information about these services.

Health Sciences Audiovisuals. Quarterly. $34.00/yr. domestic, $42.50/yr. foreign; $23.00/single copy domestic, $16.25/single copy foreign. GPO Code HSA.

Gives citations to all audiovisuals cataloged by the National Library of Medicine since 1975, except CIP titles and titles which have been withdrawn. Microfiche only. Order from: Superintendent of Documents, U.S. Government Printing Office, Washington, DC 20402.

National Library of Medicine Audiovisuals Catalog. Quarterly with annual cumulation. $24.00/yr. domestic, $30.00/yr. foreign; not available in single issues. GPO code MAC.

Lists audiovisuals cataloged by NLM from new additions to AVLINE, the library's computerized database of information on audiovisual items used in health sciences education. Cites distributor for materials listed. Order from: Superintendent of Documents, U.S. Government Printing Office, Washington, DC 20402.

Special Services: Photocopies and slides of pictorial material in the library's collections will be prepared for a fee upon request. For more information and help contact:
History of Medicine Division
National Library of Medicine
8600 Rockville Pike
Bethesda, MD 20014

Organizational chart of the National Library of Mecicine shows structure, names of offices, and people in charge. This one-page chart is free.

Further information on bibliographic services may be obtained from:
Chief
Bibliographic Services Division
National Library of Medicine
Bethesda, MD 20209

NATIONAL LIBRARY SERVICE FOR THE BLIND AND PHYSICALLY HANDICAPPED
The Library of Congress
1291 Taylor St., NW
Washington, DC 20542
(202) 287-5100

Date Established: 1931

Objectives of the Agency: Distribute talking and Braille books and magazines through regional and subregional libraries to the blind and physically handicapped.

Curriculum: Library, special education

Subjects: Handicapped
Library Science

Locations:

Regional and Subregional Libraries

(The regional library is the first one listed in each state; the ones following are subregional libraries)

AK

Services for the Blind and Physically Handicapped
Alaska State Library
650 W. International Airport Rd.
Anchorage, AK 99502
(907) 561-1003

AL

Alabama Regional Library for the Blind and Physically Handicapped
Alabama Public Library Service
State of Alabama
Montgomery, AL 36130
(205) 277-7330

Library for the Blind and Handicapped
Public Library of Anniston and Calhoun County
P.O. Box 308
Anniston, AL 36201
(205) 237-8501

Department for the Blind and Physically Handicapped
Houston-Love Memorial Library
P.O. Box 1369
Dothan, AL 36301
(205) 793-9767

Huntsville Subregional Library for the Blind and Physically Handicapped
P.O. Box 443
Huntsville, AL 35804
(205) 536-0022

Library for the Blind and Physically Handicapped
Alabama Institute for Deaf and Blind
525 N. Court St.
Talladega, AL 35160
(205) 362-1054, ext. 401
(205) 362-1054, ext. 402

Tuscaloosa Subregional Library for the Blind and Physically Handicapped
Tuscaloosa Public Library
1801 River Rd.
Tuscaloosa, AL 35401
(205) 345-5820

AR

Library for the Blind and Physically Handicapped
1 Capitol Mall
Little Rock, AR 72201
(501) 371-1155

Library for the Blind and Handicapped, NW
Ozarks Regional Library
217 E. Dickson St.
Fayetteville, AR 72701
(501) 442-6253

Fort Smith Public Library for the Blind and Handicapped
61 S. Eighth
Fort Smith, AR 72901
(501) 783-0229

Library for the Blind and Physically Handicapped, NE
Crowley Ridge Regional Library
315 W. Oak
Jonesboro, AR 72401
(501) 935-5133

Library for the Blind and Handicapped, Southwest
CLOC Regional Library
P.O. Box 668
Magnolia, AR 71753
(501) 234-1991

AZ

Arizona State Library for the Blind and Physically
  Handicapped
1030 N. Thirty-Second St.
Phoenix, AZ 85008
(602) 255-5578

Flagstaff City-Coconino County
Library Special Services
324 W. Aspen
Flagstaff, AZ 86001
(602) 774-0270

Prescott Talking Book Library
215 E. Goodwin
Prescott, AZ 86301
(602) 445-8110

CA (Southern)

Braille Institute of America, Inc.
Library
741 N. Vermont Ave.
Los Angeles, CA 90029
(213) 663-1111

CA (Northern)

Braille and Talking Book Library
California State Library
600 Broadway
Sacramento, CA 95818
(916) 322-4090

Fresno County Free Library
Blind and Physically Handicapped Services
770 N. San Pablo
Fresno, CA 93728
(209) 488-3217

San Francisco Public Library for the Blind and Print
  Handicapped
3150 Sacramento St.
San Francisco, CA 94115
(415) 558-5035

CO

Colorado State Library
Services for the Blind and Physically Handicapped
1313 Sherman St.
Denver, CO 80203
(303) 866-2081

CT

Connecticut State Library
Library for the Blind and Physically Handicapped
198 West St.
Rocky Hill, CT 06067
(203) 566-2151

DC

District of Columbia Regional Library for the Blind
  and Physically Handicapped
901 G St., NW
Room 215
Washington, DC 20001
(202) 727-2142

DE

Delaware Division of Libraries
Special Services
43 S. Dupont Hwy.
P.O. Box 639
Dover, DE 19901
(302) 736-4748

FL

Florida Division of Blind Services
Library for the Blind and Physically Handicapped
P.O. Box 2299
Daytona Beach, FL 32015
(904) 252-4722

Talking Book Service
Manatee County Central Library
1301 Barcarrota Blvd., West
Bradenton, FL 33505
(813) 748-5555

Broward County Talking Book Library
100 S. Andrews Ave.
Ft. Lauderdale, FL 33301
(305) 765-5999

Talking Book Library
Jacksonville Public Libraries
2809 Commonwealth Ave.
Jacksonville, FL 32205
(904) 388-6135

Dade County Talking Book Library
Miami-Dade Public Library System
150 N.E. Seventy-Ninth St.
Miami, FL 33138
(305) 751-8687

Orlando Public Library
Talking Book Section
10 N. Rosalind Ave.
Orlando, FL 32801
(305) 425-4694

Tampa Subregional Library
Tampa-Hillsborough County Public Library System
900 N. Ashley St.
Tampa, FL 33602
(813) 223-8349

Talking Books—Palm Beach County
Public Library System
3650 Summit Blvd.
West Palm Beach, FL 33406
(305) 686-0895

GA

Library for the Blind and Physically Handicapped
1050 Murphy Ave., SW
Atlanta, GA 30310
(404) 656-2465

Albany Talking Book Center
Dougherty County Public Library
2040 Newton Rd.
Albany, GA 31701
(912) 439-1685

Talking Book Center
Athens Regional Library
435 N. Lumpkin St.
Athens, GA 30601
(404) 354-2625

Talking Book Center
Augusta-Richmond County Public Library
425 Ninth St.
Augusta, GA 30901
(404) 724-8255

Talking Book Center
Southwest Georgia Regional Library
Shotwell and Monroe Sts.
Bainbridge, GA 31717
(912) 246-3895

Talking Book Center
Brunswick-Glynn County Regional Library
208 Gloucester St.
Brunswick, GA 31523
(912) 264-7360

Talking Book Center
Chattahoochee Valley Regional Library
Bradley Dr.
Columbus, GA 31995
(404) 327-0211

Talking Book Center
Oconee Regional Library
806 Highland Ave.
Dublin, GA 31021
(912) 275-3322

Talking Book Center
Chestatee Regional Library
322 Oak St.
#5
Gainesville, GA 30501
(404) 535-5738

Talking Book Center
Cherokee Regional Library
305 S. Duke St.
Lafayette, GA 30728
(404) 638-2992

Talking Book Center
Washington Memorial Library
1180 Washington Ave.
Macon, GA 31201
(912) 744-0877

Sara Highower Regional Library
Talking Book Center
606 Broad St.
Rome, GA 30161
(404) 291-6030

Talking Book Center
CEL Regional Library
2002 Bull St.
Savannah, GA 31499
(912) 234-5127

Talking Book Center
South Georgia Regional Library
110 W. Central Ave.
Valdosta, GA 31601
(912) 333-5210

GU

Guam Public Library for the Blind and Physically
    Handicapped
Nieves M. Flores Memorial Library
254 Martyr St.
Agana, GU 96910
(671) 472-6417

HI

Library for the Blind and Physically Handicapped
402 Kapahulu Ave.
Honolulu, HI 96815
(808) 732-7767

IA

Library
Iowa Commission for the Blind
Fourth and Keosauqua
Des Moines, IA 50309
(515) 283-2601

ID

Idaho State Library
325 W. State St.
Boise, ID 83702
(208) 334-2117

IL

Illinois Regional Library for the Blind and Physically
  Handicapped
1055 W. Roosevelt Rd.
Chicago, IL 60608
(312) 738-9210

Shawnee Library System
Greenbriar Rd.
Carterville, IL 62918
(618) 985-3713

Chicago Library Service for the Blind and Physically
  Handicapped
1055 W. Roosevelt Rd.
Chicago, IL 60608
(312) 738-9200

Talking Books Program
River Bend Library System
P.O. Box 125
Coal Valley, IL 61240
(309) 799-3155

Lewis and Clark Library System
P.O. Box 368
R.R. 4
Edwardsville, IL 62025
(618) 656-3216

Cumberland Trail Library System
Twelfth and McCawley
Flora, IL 62839
(618) 662-2679

Western Illinois Library System
1518 South Henderson
Galesburg, IL 61401
(309) 343-2380

Dupage Library System
Subregional Library for the Blind and Physically
  Handicapped
127 S. First St.
Geneva, IL 60134
(312) 232-8457

Suburban Audiovisual Service
B.P.H.
920 Barnsdale Rd.
La Grange Park, IL 60525
(312) 352-7671

Corn Belt, Lincoln Trail, and Rolling Prairie Library
  System
Service to the Blind and Physically Handicapped
1809 W. Hovey Ave.
Normal, IL 61761
(309) 454-2711

Subregional Library for the Blind and
  Physically Handicapped
Starved Rock Library System
900 Hitt St.
Ottawa, IL 61350
(815) 434-7537

Illinois Valley Library System
845 Brenkman Dr.
Pekin, IL 61554
(309) 353-4115

Talking Book Library
Great River Library System
515 York St.
Quincy, IL 62301
(217) 223-2560

Northern Illinois Library System
4034 E. State St.
Rockford, IL 61108
(815) 229-0330

Services for the Blind and Physically Handicapped
Bur Oak Library System
405 Earl Rd.
Shorewood, IL 60436
(815) 729-2039

Kakaskia Library System
P.O. Box 325
Smithton, IL 62285
(618) 235-4220

IN

Indiana State Library
Division for the Blind and Physically Handicapped
140 N. Senate Ave.
Indianapolis, IN 46204
(317) 232-3684

Bartholomew County Library
Fifth at Lafayette
Columbus, IN 47201
(812) 379-1277

Blind and Physically Handicapped Services
Elkhart Public Library
300 S. Second
Elkhart, IN 46516
(219) 522-2665, ext. 46

Talking Books Service
Evansville-Vanderburgh County Public Library
22 S.E. Fifth
Evansville, IN 47708
(812) 428-8235

Readers' Services Department
Allen County Public Library
Box 2270
Fort Wayne, IN 46801
(219) 424-7241, ext. 215

Talking Book Service
Lake County Public Library
1919 W. Eighty-First Ave.
Merrillville, IN 46410
(219) 769-3541

KS

Kansas State Library
Division for the Blind and Physically Handicapped
ESU Memorial Union
1200 Commercial
Emporia, KS 66801
(316) 343-7124

Talking Book Service
CKLS Headquarters
1409 Williams
Great Bend, KS 67530
(316) 792-2393

South Central Kansas Library System
Talking Book Subregional
910 N. Main
Hutchinson, KS 67501
(316) 663-5441

Manhattan Public Library
Juliette and Poyntz
Manhattan, KS 66502
(913) 776-4741

Talking Books
Northwest Kansas Library System
408 N. Norton
Norton, KS 67654
(913) 877-5148

Talking Books
Topeka Public Library
1515 W. Tenth St.
Topeka, KS 66604
(913) 233-2040

Wichita Public Library
Talking Books Department
223 S. Main
Wichita, KS 67202
(316) 262-0611

KY

Kentucky Library for the Blind and Physically
  Handicapped
300 Coffee Tree Rd.
P.O. Box 818
Frankfort, KY 40602
(502) 875-7000

Northern Kentucky Talking Book Library
502 Scott St.
Covington, KY 41011
(606) 491-7610

Talking Book Library
Louisville Free Public Library
301 W. York St.
Louisville, KY 40203
(502) 587-1069

LA

Louisiana State Library
Section for the Blind and Physically Handicapped
760 Riverside North
Baton Rouge, LA 70802
(504) 342-4944

MA

Regional Library for the Blind and Physically
  Handicapped
Perkins School for the Blind
175 N. Beacon St.
Watertown, MA 02172
(617) 924-3434

Talking Book Library
Worcester Public Library
Salem Square
Worcester, MA 01608
(617) 799-1730

MD

Maryland State Library for the Blind and Physically
  Handicapped
1715 N. Charles St.
Baltimore, MD 21201
(301) 659-2668

Talking Book Center
Prince George's County Memorial Library
6530 Adelphi Rd.
Hyattsville, MD 20782
(301) 779-9330, ext. 28

Service for the Physically Handicapped
Montgomery County Department of Public Libraries
99 Maryland Ave.
Rockville, MD 20850
(301) 279-1679

ME

Library Services for the Blind and Physically
  Handicapped
Maine State Library
State House Station 64
Augusta, ME 04333
(207) 289-3959

Bangor Public Library
145 Harlow St.
Bangor, ME 04401
(207) 947-8336

Cary Library
107 Main St.
Houlton, ME 04730
(207) 532-3967

Lewiston Public Library
105 Park St.
Lewiston, ME 04240
(207) 783-2331

Talking Books Department
Portland Public Library
5 Monument Square
Portland, ME 04101
(207) 773-4761

Waterville Public Library
73 Elm St.
Waterville, ME 04901
(207) 872-5433

MI (except Wayne County)

Library for the Blind and Physically Handicapped
Library of Michigan
Box 30007
Lansing, MI 48909
(517) 373-1593

Northland Library Cooperative
316 E. Chisholm
Alpena, MI 49707
(517) 356-4444

Washtenaw County Library
Library for the Blind and Physically Handicapped
P.O. Box 8645
Ann Arbor, MI 48107
(313) 971-6059

Willard Subregional Library
7 W. Van Buren
Battle Creek, MI 49016
(616) 968-8166, ext. 21

Oakland County Subregional Library
Farmington Community Library
32737 W. Twelve Mile Road
Farmington Hills, MI 48018
(313) 553-0300

Mideastern Michigan Library Co-Op
Library for the Blind and Physically Handicapped
G-4195 W. Pasadena Ave.
Flint, MI 48504
(313) 732-1120

Kent County Library for the Blind and Physically Handicapped
775 Ball, NE
Grand Rapids, MI 49503
(616) 774-3262

Upper Peninsula Library for the Blind and Physically Handicapped
217 N. Front St.
Marquette, MI 49855
(906) 228-7697

Macomb Library for the Blind and Physically Handicapped
16480 Hall Rd.
Mount Clemens, MI 48044
(313) 286-6660, ext. 34

Muskegon County Library for the Blind and Physically Handicapped
635 Ottawa St.
Muskegon, MI 49442
(616) 724-6257

Blue Water Library Federation
Blind and Physically Handicapped Library
210 McMorran Blvd.
Port Huron, MI 48060
(313) 982-3600

Southwest Michigan Library for the Blind and Physically Handicapped
300 Library Lane
Portage, MI 49002
(616) 323-3714

Grand Traverse Area Library for the Blind and Physically Handicapped
322 Sixth St.
Traverse City, MI 49684
(616) 941-2311

MI (Wayne County only)

Wayne County Regional Library for the Blind and Physically Handicapped
33030 Van Born Rd.
Wayne, MI 48184
(313) 274-2600

Downtown Detroit Subregional Library for the Blind and Physically Handicapped
121 Gratiot Ave.
Detroit, MI 48226
(313) 224-0580

MN

Minnesota Library for the Blind and Physically Handicapped
Braille and Sight Saving School
Faribault, MN 55021
(507) 332-3279

MO

Wolfner Memorial Library for the Blind and
 Physically Handicapped
Truman State Office Bldg.
Second Floor
P.O. Box 387
Jefferson City, MO 65102
(314) 751-3615

MS

Mississippi Library Commission
Service for the Handicapped
5455 Executive Place
Jackson, MS 39206
(601) 354-7208

MT

Montana State Library
Division for the Blind and Physically Handicapped
1515 E. Sixth Ave.
Helena, MT 59620
(406) 444-2064

NC

North Carolina Library for the Blind and Physically
 Handicapped
Department of Cultural Resources
1811 North Blvd.
Raleigh, NC 27635
(919) 733-4376

ND

See SD.

NE

Nebraska Library Commission
Library for the Blind and Physically Handicapped
1420 P St.
Lincoln, NE 68508
(402) 471-2045

North Platte Public Library
Blind and Physically Handicapped Program
120 W. Fourth St.
North Platte, NE 69101
(308) 532-6424

NH

New Hampshire State Library
Division of Library Services to the Handicapped
17 S. Fruit St.
Concord, NH 03301
(603) 271-3429

NJ

New Jersey Library for the Blind and Handicapped
2300 Stuyvesant Ave.
Trenton, NJ 08618
(609) 292-6450

NM

New Mexico State Library for the Blind and
 Physically Handicapped
325 Don Gaspar
Santa Fe, NM 87503
(505) 827-3829

NV

Nevada State Library
Talking Book Program
Capitol Complex
Carson City, NV 89710
(702) 885-5160

Clark County Library District
Special Services
1401 E. Flamingo Rd.
Las Vegas, NV 89109
(702) 733-7810

NY (except New York City and Long Island)

New York State Library for the Blind and Visually
 Handicapped
Cultural Education Center
Empire State Plaza
Albany, NY 12230
(518) 474-5935

New York City and Long Island

Library for the Blind and Physically Handicapped
The New York Public Library
166 Avenue of the Americas
New York, NY 10013
(212) 925-1011

Reading for the Handicapped
Suffolk Cooperative Library System
627 N. Sunrise Service Rd.
Bellport, NY 11713
(516) 286-1600

Talking Books
Nassau Library System
900 Jerusalem Ave.
Uniondale, NY 11553
(516) 292-8920

OH (southern)

Library for the Blind and Physically Handicapped
Library Square
800 Vine St.
Cincinnati, OH 45202
(513) 369-6074

OH (northern)

Library for the Blind and Physically Handicapped
Cleveland Public Library
325 Superior Ave.
Cleveland, OH 44114
(216) 623-2911

OK

Oklahoma Library for the Blind and Physically
  Handicapped
1108 N.E. Thirty-Sixth
Oklahoma City, OK 73111
(405) 521-3514

Tulsa City-County Library System
Special Services
400 Civic Center
Tulsa, OK 74103
(918) 592-7920

OR

Oregon State Library
Services for the Blind and Physically Handicapped
555 Thirteenth St., NE
Salem, OR 97301
(503) 378-3849

PA (eastern)

Library for the Blind and Physically Handicapped
Free Library of Philadelphia
919 Walnut St.
Philadelphia, PA 19107
(215) 925-3213

PA (western)

Library for the Blind and Physically Handicapped
Carnegie Library of Pittsburgh
4724 Baum Blvd.
Pittsburgh, PA 15213
(412) 687-2440

PR

Puerto Rico Regional Library for the Blind and
  Physically Handicapped
520 Ponce de Leon Ave.
Stop 8½
Puerto de Tierra
San Juan, PR 00901
(809) 723-2519

RI

Regional Library for the Blind and Physically
  Handicapped
Rhode Island Department of State
Library Services
95 Davis St.
Providence, RI 02908
(401) 277-2726

SC

South Carolina State Library
Division for the Blind and Physically Handicapped
700 Knox Abbott Dr.
Cayce, SC 29033
(803) 758-2726

SD

South Dakota State Library for the Handicapped
State Library Bldg.
800 N. Illinois
Pierre, SD 57501
SD: (605) 773-3514
ND: (701) 781-2604

TN

Tennessee Regional Library for the Blind and
  Physically Handicapped
Tennessee State Library and Archives
403 Seventh Ave. North
Nashville, TN 37219
(615) 741-3915

TX

Division for the Blind and Physically Handicapped
Texas State Library
Capitol Station
P.O. Box 12927
Austin, TX 78711
(512) 475-4758

UT

Utah State Library Commission
Division for the Blind and Physically Handicapped
2150 South, 300 West
Suite 16
Salt Lake City, UT 84115
(801) 533-5855

VA

Virginia State Library for the Visually and Physically
  Handicapped
1901 Roane St.
Richmond, VA 23222
(804) 786-8016

Special Services
Fairfax County Public Library
6209 Rose Hill Dr.
Alexandria, VA 22310
(703) 971-6612

Alexandria Library
Talking Book Service
John Adams Center
5651 Rayburn Ave.
Alexandria, VA 22311
(703) 998-5463

Talking Book Service
Arlington County Department of Libraries
1015 N. Quincy St.
Arlington, VA 22201
(703) 527-4777

Hampton Subregional Library for the Visually and
  Physically Handicapped
107 E. Howard St.
Hampton, VA 23663
(804) 727-6630

Library for the Blind and Physically Handicapped
Newport News Public Library System
112 Main St.
Newport News, VA 23601
(804) 599-6475

Roanoke City Public Library System
706 S. Jefferson St.
Roanoke, VA 24011
(703) 981-2921

Talking Book Center
Staunton Public Library
19 S. Market St.
Staunton, VA 24401
(703) 885-6215

Special Services Division
Virginia Beach Public Library
936 Independence Blvd.
Virginia Beach, VA 23455
(804) 464-9175

VI

Virgin Islands Regional Library for the Blind and
  Physically Handicapped
Lagoon Complex #3
Fredericksted
St. Croix, VI 00840
(809) 772-2250

VT

State of Vermont Department of Libraries
Special Services Unit
Montpelier, VT 05602
(802) 828-3273

WA

Washington Library for the Blind and Physically
  Handicapped
821 Lenora St.
Seattle, WA 98129
(206) 464-6930

WI

Wisconsin Regional Library for the Blind and
  Physically Handicapped
813 W. Wells St.
Milwaukee, WI 53233
(414) 278-3045

Special Services Division
Brown County Library
515 Pine St.
Green Bay, WI 54301
(414) 497-3473

WV

West Virginia Library Commission
Services for the Blind and Physically Handicapped
Science and Culture Center
Greenbrier and Washington Sts.
Charleston, WV 25305
(304) 348-4061

Services for the Blind and Physically Handicapped
Kanawha County Public Library
123 Capitol St.
Charleston, WV 25301
(304) 343-4646, ext. 24

Services for the Blind and Physically Handicapped
Cabell County Public Library
455 Ninth St. Plaza
Huntington, WV 25701
(304) 523-9451

Parkersburg and Wood County Public Library
Services for the Blind and Physically Handicapped
3100 Emerson Ave.
Parkersburg, WV 26101
(304) 485-6564

West Virginia School for the Blind
Romney, WV 26757
(304) 822-3521, ext. 217

Ohio County Public Library
52 Sixteenth St.
Wheeling, WV 26003
(304) 232-0244

WY

See UT.

***American Citizens Residing in Foreign
Countries Receive Library Service from:***

Consumer Relations Section
Library of Congress
1291 Taylor St., NW
Washington, DC 20542
(202) 287-9226

Publications: Newsletters. Bibliographies. Pamphlets. Fact sheets. Applications. Bookmarks. Catalogs.

Bibliographies, Sales Catalogs, Publications Lists, etc.

"Bibles and Other Scriptures in Special Media." 1983. 43p. free. No. 84-1.

Represents works from many religions and denominations. Grouped by medium such as braille, large type, etc.

"Books for Blind and Physically Handicapped Individuals." 1984. 4p. free.
  Surveys services. Provides check list to order materials. Publications are grouped by type, such as reprints of articles, reference circulars, etc.

"Building a Library Collection on Blindness and Physical Handicaps: Basic Materials and Resources." 1985. 53p. free. No. 85-2.
  Lists materials recommended to libraries and organizations as basic resources for providing a current information service on visual and physical handicaps.

"Guide to Spoken-Word Recordings: Educational, Professional, and Self-Development Materials." 1983. 39p. free. No. 84-3.
  Lists sources of spoken-word recordings pertaining to preschool and early childhood development, adult basic education, and supplemental teaching materials.

"Guide to Spoken-Word Recordings: General Nonfiction." Current. 43p. free. No. 84-4.
  Lists sources of spoken-word recordings compiled from catalogs and brochures submitted by producers and distributors. Includes address, media, subject, and price.

"Guide to Spoken-Word Recordings: Literature." 1982. 19p. free. No. 83-1.
  Lists sources of spoken-word recordings of novels, short stories, drama, etc.

"Magazines in Special Media: Subscription Sources." 1985. 75p. free. No. 85-1.
  Gives information about the availability of magazines in formats such as braille, cassette, disc, large type, and moon type. Entries are direct or loan, or must be ordered from the source indicated.

"National Organizations Concerned with Visually and Physically Handicapped Persons." 1983. 27p. free. No. 84-2.
  Lists representative national-level organizations providing a variety of direct services to handicapped persons.

"Reading Materials in Large Type." 1983. 61p. free. No. 83-4.
  Lists sources, producers, and distributors of large-type materials.

"Reference Books in Special Media." 1982. 75p. free. No. 82-4. Groups reference books under broad subject categories and then by medium such as braille, cassette, disc, large type, etc. Includes complete addresses of all sources cited.

Romances. 1984. 170p. free.
  Bibliography to selected romances available on disc, cassette, or braille in the network library collections provided by the National Library Service for the Blind and Physically Handicapped. Describes each book briefly. Order form.

"Talking Book Topics." Bimonthly. 90p. free.
  Covers news of the developments and activities in library services. Lists recorded books and magazines available through a national network of cooperating libraries. Subscription information is located on the inside back cover. Free to individuals participating in the reading program.

Serials, Subscription Publications, etc.

"The Musical Mainstream." Bimonthly. 47p. free.
  Selected articles from national magazines about classical music, criticism, music education, etc. Available in braille, cassette, and large print.

"News." Quarterly. 12p. free.
  Covers recent events, domestic and international, in library services for the blind and physically handicapped.

Selected List of Books and Pamphlets

"Application for Free Library Service." 1981. 4p. free.
  Provides a check list for books and equipment, reading preferences. Eligibility rules, and lending of materials.

"Becoming a Volunteer: Resources for Individuals, Libraries, and Organizations." 1981. 18p. free.
  Lists activities to consider and resources to contact. Lists national volunteer organizations and publications that provide guidance in volunteer programs.

"Books Talk—Library Path Well Trodden by the Blind." 1981. 4p. free.
  Reprints feature article and editorial from the *Los Angeles Times.*

"R Is for Reading." 1985. 193p. free.
  Provides articles by users to characterize the handicapped juvenile library user and nonuser. Groups interviews: *Children and Mothers, Special Education Teachers, Child Development Counselors, Reading Specialists,* and *Librarians.*

"Reading Is for Everyone." n.d. 8p. free.
  Surveys services, materials, and equipment. Includes an application for free library service.

"Reference and Information Services." kit.
  Contains four summaries of how to make contact for service and what services are available.

Special Services: Readers may order catalogs and subject bibliographies from cooperating libraries to learn more about the wide range of books.

NATIONAL MARINE FISHERIES SERVICE
U.S. Department of Commerce
National Oceanic and Atmospheric Administration
Washington, DC 20235
(202) 377-4190

Date Established: 1972

Objectives of the Agency: Discover, describe, develop, and conserve the living resources of the global sea, especially as these affect the American economy and diet; and help enforcement and surveillance operations on the high seas and in territorial waters.

Curriculum: Social studies

Subjects: Fisheries
Fishes

Locations:

National Marine Fisheries Service
Northeast Region
14 Elm St.
Gloucester, MA 01930

National Marine Fisheries Service
Southeast Region
9450 Koger Blvd.
St. Petersburg, FL 33702

National Marine Fisheries Service
Northwest and Alaska Region
7600 Sand Point Way
Seattle, WA 98115

National Marine Fisheries Service
Southwest Region
300 S. Ferry St.
Terminal Island, CA 90731

National Marine Fisheries Service
Alaska Region
P.O. Box 1668
Juneau, AK 99802

Publications: Briefs. Reprints. Lists.

Selected List of Books and Pamphlets

"Clamshell Commerce: How Seafood Started the States." 1976. 7p. free. NOAA reprint.

Explains the importance of various kinds of fish to American colonists and the settlement attempts by the Pilgrims. Includes various uses made of fish. Illustrations.

"Fish: The Most-Asked Questions." 1973. 8p. free. NOAA reprint.

Questions and answers on marine finfish and how they live, shellfish and other invertebrates. Illustrations.

"Fisheries Scientists." 1982. 4p. free. Chronicle Occupational Brief 190.

Describes what work fisheries scientists engage in, working conditions, hours and earnings, education and training, personal qualifications, where employed, employment outlook, entry and advancement, and related occupations. Includes addresses and titles of materials for further information.

"NOAA." 1976. 6p. free.

Explains what the National Oceanic and Atmospheric Administration does. Includes a survey of various services. Photographs.

Audiovisuals:

Filmographies, Sales Lists, etc.

"Films from NOAA." 1981. 11p. free.

Gives title, date, color, running time, and description of contents of free loan films. Includes various kinds of fish. Order from: Modern Talking Pictures, 5000 Park St. North, St. Petersburg, FL 33709.

NATIONAL MEDIATION BOARD
1425 K St., NW
Washington, DC 20572
(202) 523-5920

Date Established: 1934

Objectives of the Agency: Help maintain a free flow of commerce in the railroad and airline industries by resolving disputes; and provide financial supervision of the National Railroad Adjustment Board which handles rail grievances.

Curriculum: Social studies

Subjects: Labor disputes

Publications: Lists. Serials. Reports. Manuals.

Bibliographies, Sales Catalogs, Publications Lists, etc.

"NMB Publication—Price Listing." Current. 2p. free.

Describes materials and different subscription mailing lists available, prices, and ordering information.

NATIONAL MUSEUM OF AMERICAN ART
Smithsonian Institution
Eighth and G Sts., NW
Washington, DC 20560
(202) 357-2627

Date Established: 1829

Objectives of the Agency: Oversee collections of over 30,000 paintings, sculptures, prints, dawings, and photographs representing 250 years of American work; and sponsor public programs, library, database projects, conservation, and research.

Curriculum: Art

Subjects: Art—galleries and museums

Publications: Pamphlets. News Releases. Lists. Calendars.

Bibliographies, Sales Catalogs, Publications Lists, etc.

"Publications Available from the National Museum of American Art." n.d. 11p. free.

Tells what is available free and for sale. Includes paper and hardback books, and pamphlets published by the museum unless otherwise noted.

Selected List of Books and Pamphlets

"Barney Studio House." 1985. 6p. free.

Gives history of Studio House and its founder, Alice Pike Barney. Includes museum hours and visitor information.

"Calendar of Events." Monthly. 12p. free.

Lists events, recent publications, and visitor information on the National Museum of American Art. Photographs of exhibits.

"History of the National Museum of American Art." n.d. 3p. free.

Chronicles the development since 1829, name changes, and building restoration.

"National Museum of American Art: General Information." 1984. 10p. free.

Describes collections, programs, tours, access, research, and other services offered by the museum. Floor plans. Photographs.

"Renwick Gallery." 1984. 6p. free.

Describes exhibits of designers and craftsmen, past and present. Includes programs and visitor information. Photographs.

Sharing Traditions: Five Black Artists in Nineteenth-Century America. 1985. 116p. $14.95.

Written by Lynda Roscoe Hartigan, with a foreword by Charles C. Eldredge and essay by James Oliver Horton. 75 B&W and 12 color illustrations.

"Throne of the Third Heaven by James Hampton." n.d. 2p. free.

Gives description and background of "The Throne of the Third Heaven of the Nations' Millennium General Assembly," a piece of visionary religious art.

Library: Shared with the National Portrait Gallery. Open to students and researchers. The Smithsonian's Archives of American Art and the National Museum of American Art's inventory of American paintings executed before 1914 is also located here.

Special Services: The Office of Research Support administers six automated database projects and study collections of photographic materials related to American art and artists and to the National Museum of American Art's collections. For information or to order photographs of works in the permanent collections, write:
Office of Research Support
National Museum of American Art
Washington, DC 20560
(202) 357-1626

To be placed on the mailing list to receive the monthly National Museum of American Art's calendar of events, contact:
Office of Public Affairs
National Museum of American Art
G Street between Seventh and Ninth Sts., NW
Washington, DC 20560
(202) 357-2273

The Conservation Department offers consultation on the care and handling of works of art. For more information, call: (202) 357-2685.

The Scholars' Research Program encourages resident research through seminars and lectures and using the museum's resources. Through the Intern Program, selected undergraduate and graduate students can take workshops and seminars or gain professional experience at the museum.

For information and reservations for tours at the National Museum of American Art, Renwick Gallery, and Barney Studio, call: (202) 357-3111.

NATIONAL OCEAN SERVICE
National Oceanic and Atmospheric Administration
External Affairs Staff (N/EA)
Herbert C. Hoover Bldg.
Washington, DC 20230
(202) 377-4190

Date Established: 1807

Objectives of the Agency: Be the nation's nautical (U.S. coastal, estuarine waters, Great Lakes) chart maker; provide a wide range of geodetic data and services; and establish and maintain the National Networks of Geodetic Control.

Curriculum: Geography, guidance, library

Subjects: Charts
Navigation
Occupations

Locations:

National Ocean Service Field Office
Atlantic Marine Center
439 W. York St.
Norfolk, VA 23510
(804) 441-6616

National Ocean Service Field Office
Pacific Marine Center
1801 Fairview Ave. East
Seattle, WA 96102
(206) 442-7657

National Ocean Service
Chart Sales and Geodetic Control
Federal Bldg. and U.S. Courthouse
701 C St.
Box 38
Anchorage, AK 99513
(907) 271-5040

National Ocean Service (N/CG33)
Distribution Branch
Riverdale, MD 20737
(301) 436-6990

Publications: Catalogs. Pamphlets. Reprints. Charts.

Bibliographies, Sales Catalogs, Publications Lists, etc.

"Chart Editions." Quarterly. 27p. free.
 Gives dates of latest editions and nautical charts. Includes chart number, scale, price, edition number, edition date, and latest revised date.

"Nautical Chart Catalog 4: United States Great Lakes and Adjacent Waterways." 1985. 14-fold. free.
 Lists charts for sale for Great Lakes, connecting channels, Minnesota-Ontario, border lakes, Lake Winnebago, Michigan's inland route, New York canals, and Lake Champlain. Includes map of the Great Lakes, data on the Great Lakes system, and length of outflow of rivers. Lists publications with prices relating to nautical charts published and issued by the National Ocean Service such as tide tables and U.S. coast pilots. Lists nautical chart agents for the sale of nautical charts and related publications of the National Ocean Service grouped by state and foreign country.

The following catalogs are also available:
"Nautical Chart Catalog 1: Atlantic and Gulf Coasts Including Puerto Rico and the Virgin Islands." 1985. free.
"Nautical Chart Catalog 2: Pacific Coast Including Hawaii, Guam and Samoa Islands." 1985. free.
"Nautical Chart Catalog 3: Alaska." 1985. free.
"Nautical Chart Catalog 5: Bathymetric Maps and Special Purpose Charts." 1985. folded chart. free.

Selected List of Books and Pamphlets

"The Answers to Ten Questions about the NOAA Corps." 1981. 4p. free.
 Gives answers to questions about the corps as an employer. Includes information about requirements, what types of jobs are done at sea, and how to apply.

"Hassler's Legacy." Reprinted 1984. 8p. free.
 Reports the accomplishments of Rudolph Hassler, the first superintendent of the National Ocean Service. Photographs.

"Institutions Offering Degrees in Ocean and Marine Sciences." 1983. 6p. free.
 Arranged by state. Includes name, address of institution, degrees offered, and other facilities available at the institution.

"National Ocean Service Products and Services." 1984. 36p. free.
 Describes charting and geodetic services, ocean and coastal resource management, oceanography and marine assessments, and marine operations. Photographs. Three—page index.

"The NOAA Corps: Careers in Science and Service." Rev. 1983. 12p. free.
 Explains the purpose of the corps, NOAA organization, assignments and career sequence for officers, types of shore duty, qualifications required, and application procedures. Includes addresses and telephone numbers of recruiting offices.

"Office of Charting and Geodetic Services." 1984. 14p. free.
 Describes history, development, charting services, aeronautical charting, and geodesy.

"Seafarers and Scientists: The Nation's Chartmaker." Reprinted 1984. 8p. free.
 Chronicles the beginnings of American maritime scientific tradition, early heads of the survey, and its development under such men as Ferdinand Rudolph Hassler, Alexander Dallas Bache, and E. Lester Jones.

Special Services: Over-the-counter sales of charts and related publications from: 6501 Lafayette Ave., Riverdale, MD.; Building 1, 6001 Executive Blvd., Room 715, Rockville, MD.; 439 W. York St., Norfolk, VA.

For free information about current Great Lakes levels, request "Bulletin of Lake Levels" from:
Detroit District
U.S. Army Corps of Engineers
P.O. Box 1027
Detroit, MI 48231

NATIONAL OCEANIC AND ATMOSPHERIC ADMINISTRATION
Office of Public Affairs
U.S. Department of Commerce
NESDIS/NODC OC21
Room 6013
Rockville, MD 20235
(202) 377-4190

Date Established: 1970

Objectives of the Agency: Explore and map the oceans and their resources; manage these resources; describe, monitor, and predict conditions in the atmosphere, the ocean, and in space and issue warnings; and develop beneficial ways of environmental change and assess the consequences.

Curriculum: Environmental studies, geography

Subjects: Atmosphere
Environment
Oceanography—research

Locations:

National Weather Service
Eastern Region
585 Stewart Ave.
Garden City, Long Island, NY 11530

National Weather Service
Central Region
601 E. Twelfth St.
Kansas City, MO 64106

National Weather Service
Southern Region
819 Taylor St.
Fort Worth, TX 76102

National Weather Service
Western Region
125 S. State St.
Salt Lake City, UT 84147

National Weather Service
Alaska Region
Box 23
701 C. St.
Anchorage, AK 99513

National Weather Service
Pacific Region
Room 4110
300 Ala Moana Blvd.
Honolulu, HI 96850

National Meteorological Center
5200 Auth Rd.
Camp Springs, MD 20233

National Hurricane Center
1320 S. Dixie Hwy.
Coral Gables, FL 33146

National Severe Storms Forecast Center
601 E. Twelfth St.
Kansas City, MO 64106

National Ocean Service
Atlantic Marine Center
439 W. York St.
Norfolk, VA 23510

National Ocean Service
Pacific Marine Center
1801 Fairview Ave. East
Seattle, WA 98102

National Marine Fisheries Service
Northeast Region
14 Elm St.
Gloucester, MA 01930

National Marine Fisheries Service
Southeast Region
9450 Koger Blvd.
St. Petersburg, FL 33702

National Marine Fisheries Service
Northwest and Alaska Region
7600 Sand Point Way
Seattle, WA 98115

National Marine Fisheries Service
Southwest Region
300 S. Ferry St.
Terminal Island, CA 90731

National Marine Fisheries Service
Alaska Region
P.O. Box 1668
Juneau, AK 99802

National Environmental Satellite, Data and
Information Service
National Climatic Data Center
Federal Bldg.
Asheville, NC 28801

National Environmental Satellite, Data and
Information Service
National Oceanographic Data Center
2001 Wisconsin Ave., NW
Washington, DC 20235

National Environmental Satellite, Data and
Information Service
National Geophysical Data Center
3100 Marine Ave.
Boulder, CO 80302

Office of Oceanic and Atmospheric Research
Environmental Research Laboratories
3100 Marine Ave.
Boulder, CO 80302

Western Administrative Support Center
7600 Sand Point Way
Seattle, WA 98115

Mountain Administrative Support Center
3100 Marine Ave.
Boulder, CO 80302

Central Administrative Support Center
601 E. Twelfth St.
Kansas City, MO 64106

Eastern Administrative Support Center
253 Monticello Ave.
Norfolk, VA 23510

Publications: Pamphlets. Guides. Tapes. Microforms. Bulletins. Data. Reports. Periodicals. Maps. Charts. On what the various centers do in climate research, geophysical data, oceanography, glaciology, meterology, and related activities. General and technical material.

Bibliographies, Sales Catalogs, Publications Lists, etc.

"Publications." Current. 9p. free.
Describes what is available from the National Oceanographic Data Center, World Data Center, National Oceanographic Data Center, and others. Free and for sale.

Serials, Subscription Publications, etc.

Coastal Ocean Pollution Assessment News. Quarterly. free.
Provides a newsletter about pollution in U.S. coastal waters. Supported by the National Marine Fisheries Service, Ocean Assessment Division, and others. Order from: Marine Sciences Research Center, State University of New York at Stony Brook, Long Island, NY 11794.

Mariners Weather Log. Quarterly. $13.00/yr. domestic, $16.75/yr. foreign.
Prints articles on marine environment, weather over the North Atlantic and North Pacific oceans. Describes tropical cyclones worldwide.

Selected List of Books and Pamphlets

"The National Climatic Data Center." 1983. 8p. free.
Tells what information, services, and functions are performed at the center.

"NESDIS." 1983. 8p. free.
Explains what the National Environmental Satellite, Data and Information Service does.

"National Geophysical Data Center." n.d. 8p. free.
Describes products and services in solid earth geophysics, marine geology and geophysics, solar-terrestrial physics, and glaciology.

"National Oceanic and Atmospheric Administration." 1984. 28p. free.
Summarizes what the administration does. Includes available user services and organizational chart. Illustrations.

"National Oceanographic Data Center Annual Report." Annual. 18p. free.
Describes highlights and accomplishments of the year.

"NODC." 1984. 8p. free.
Tells what the National Oceanographic Data Center does and what data is available.

"WDC.A." 1978. 16p. free.
What the various centers (Rockets and Satellites, Rotation of the Earth, Meteorology, etc.) do.

Audiovisuals:

Filmographies, Sales Lists, etc.

"Films from NOAA." 1981. 11p. free.
Lists films with annotations that are free loan. Films cover the atmosphere, coasts, oceans, ocean life, and National Oceanic and Atmospheric Administration. Order from: Modern Talking Pictures, 5000 Park St. North, St. Petersburg, FL 33709.

Individual Audiovisuals

"Down to the Monitor." 1980. 22 minutes. 16mm. color. free loan.
The ship, famed for its Civil War battle with the "Merrimack," became the nation's first designated underwater marine sanctuary.

"Global Weather Experiment." 1980. 28 minutes. 16mm. color. free loan.
Describes how most of the nations of the world joined together to obtain an understanding of how the earth's oceans and atmosphere interact.

"Ocean World." 1980. 29 minutes. 16mm. color. free loan.
Describes animals and resources of the sea and coastal zone. Includes segments on commercial fishery management aquaculture research, seafloor mineral mining, and scientific measurements to improve weather forecasting.

Special Services: Information about tours of NOS headquarters in Rockville, MD, may be addressed to:
Visitors Liaison Officer
National Ocean Survey
C513
Rockville, MD 20852

Inquire about the available sea grant publications for your state.

Visitors are welcome at the National Climatic Data Center. Advance notice is desirable, especially if the visitor wishes to confer with staff. If unable to visit, assistance with specific weather-related information can be obtained from:
National Climatic Data Center
NOAA, NESDIA
Federal Building
Asheville, NC 28801
(704) 259-0682

216 / National Oceanic and Atmospheric Administration

Satellite data available from:
Satellite Data Services Division
World Weather Building
5200 Auth Rd.
Room 100
Camp Springs, MD
(301) 763-8111

NATIONAL PARK SERVICE
U.S. Department of the Interior
P.O. Box 37127
Washington, DC 20013-7127
(202) 343-7394

Date Established: 1916

Objectives of the Agency: Administer national parks, monuments, historic sites, scenic parkways, riverways, seashores, lakeshores, reservoirs, and recreation areas.

Curriculum: Geography

Subjects: National parks and reserves—U.S.

Locations:

CT, MA, ME, NH, NJ, NY, RI, VT

National Park Service
Regional Office
15 State St.
Boston, MA 02109

DE, MD (except near DC), PA, VA (except near DC), WV

National Park Service
Regional Office
143 S. Third St.
Philadelphia, PA 19106

AL, FL, GA, KY, MS, NC, PR, SC, TN, VI

National Park Service
Regional Office
75 Spring St., SW
Atlanta, GA 30303

IA, IL, IN, KS, MI, MN, MO, NE, OH, WI

National Park Service
Regional Office
1709 Jackson St.
Omaha, NE 68102

CO, MT, ND, SD, UT, WY

National Park Service
Regional Office
P.O. Box 25287
Denver, CO 80225

AR, LA, NM, OK, TX

National Park Service
Regional Office
Box 728
Santa Fe, NM 87501

AZ, CA, GU, HI, NV, Northern Mariana Islands

National Park Service
Regional Office
450 Golden Gate Ave.
San Francisco, CA 94102

ID, OR, WA

National Park Service
Regional Office
2001 Sixth Ave.
Seattle, WA 98121

AK

National Park Service
Regional Office
2525 Gambell St.
Anchorage, AK 99503

DC and nearby MD and VA

National Park Service
Regional Office
1100 Ohio Dr., SW
Washington, DC 20242

Publications: National park subjects. Historical highlights of people and events. Service handbooks. Indexes.

Bibliographies, Sales Catalogs, Publications Lists, etc.

"How To Buy National Park Publications." Current. 2p. free.
 Gives information about pricing, unit of issue, and ordering prodecures.

"National Park Service Handbooks." Current. 8p. free.
 Gives ordering information on handbooks and general publications.

Selected List of Books and Pamphlets

"Guide and Map." 1984. folded map. $1.25. 024-005-00852-7.
 Gives map and information of national park facilities. Order from: Consumer Information Center, Pueblo, CO 81009.

"Index of the National Park System and Related Areas." Current. 96p. $4.75. 024-005-00829-2.
 Covers more than 330 units within the system. Arranged by state. Includes addresses, acreage, and description. Order from: Superintendent of Documents, U.S. Government Printing Office, Washington, DC 20402.

Audiovisuals:

"National Park Service Films." n.d. 2p. free.

Describes most recent releases, where to obtain, and cost. Order all films from: Harpers Ferry Historical Association, P.O. Box 197, Harpers Ferry, WV 25425.

Individual Audiovisuals

"Antietam Visit." n.d. 26:51 minutes. 16mm. $15.00 rental.

Shows historical impact of the Battle of Antietam. Reenacts President Lincoln's visit. Includes quotations from period diaries and letters, battle re-enactments, photographs, and music of the period. Inquire about current sale price.

"Booker T. Washington—The Life and the Legacy." n.d. 31:30 minutes. 16mm. $15.00 rental.

Recreates the life of Booker T. Washington. Reveals the turning points of his educational and political career. Historical photographs give background of the Reconstruction. Inquire about current sale price.

"Lava Beds National Monument." n.d. 28 minutes. 16mm. $15.00 rental.

Reveals through animation and contemporary volcanic footage how natural forces devastated this area long ago. Describes shield volcanoes, types of lava, splatter cones. Traces the slow return of life. Inquire about current sale price.

"Night of the Sun." n.d. 20 minutes. 16mm. $15.00 rental.

Explores the last, great Ice Age, land formations, and legacies such as rich farm lands, recreational lakes, etc. Inquire about current sale price.

"Sleeping Bear." n.d. 9 minutes. 16mm. $15.00 rental.

Shows lakeshore features and formation in Sleeping Bear Dunes National Lakeshore. Explains factors that determine which plants will grow in a given environment.

Special Services: Check with your regional office about film lists and other publications relating to your region. The midwest office, for example, has a 15-page film list and other lists on safety and information dealing with the midwest service areas.

**NATIONAL PARK SERVICE SCIENCE
PUBLICATIONS OFFICE**
75 Spring Street, SW
Room 1058
Atlanta, GA 30303

Date Established: 1983

Objectives of the Agency: Publish and distribute scientific national park publications.

Curriculum: Science, geography

Subjects: Ecology
National parks and reserves—U.S.

Publications: Monographs. Reports. Papers. Transactions and proceedings.

Bibliographies, Sales Catalogs, Publications Lists, etc.

"Isle Royale Biosphere Reserve: A Bibliography of Scientific Studies." 1985. 55p. U.S. Man and the Biosphere Program U.S. MAB Report No. 11, vol. 11.

Prepared as part of the science assessment for Isle Royale National Park and Biosphere Reserve. Arranged alphabetically by author.

"Publications List." Current. 7p. free.

Groups publications by type and includes title, author, date, stock number and price (if available from the U.S. Government Printing Office); those available from the Science Publications Office are free.

Selected List of Books and Pamphlets

"The Geologic History of Fossil Butte National Monument and Fossil Basin." n.d. 37p. free. National Park Service Occasional Paper No. 3. Publication No. NPS 147.

Relates the history of Fossil Lake and its now fossilized inhabitants. Maps. Drawings. Glossary. References. Bibliography.

"Tree Repair." 1975. 5p. free. Publication No. NPS 138.

Explains pruning and taking care of the injuries of trees through wind, lightning, and other causes.

NATIONAL PORTRAIT GALLERY
F St. at Eighth, NW
Washington, DC 20560
(202) 357-2920

Date Established: 1962

Objectives of the Agency: Exhibit and study the portraiture of men and women who have made significant contributions to the history, development, and culture of the United States.

Curriculum: Art

Subjects: Art, American
Art—galleries and museums

Publications: Pamphlets. Calendars. Lists. Post cards. Books. On famous Americans and art.

Bibliographies, Sales Catalogs, Publications Lists, etc.

"National Portrait Gallery Museum Shop Catalogue List." n.d. 6p. free.

Lists what is available with prices of hardback and softback books.

"Post Card List." Current. 1p. free.

Lists portraits, prices, and ordering information.

Serials, Subscription Publications, etc.

"The National Portrait Gallery Calendar of Events." Current. 3-fold. free.

Prints recent events, publications, and tour information.

Selected List of Books and Pamphlets

"The National Portrait Gallery." 1982. 16p. free.

Describes history, progress, collections, services, and publications. Includes visitor information and telephone numbers.

"School Services." n.d. 10p. free.

Tells what the gallery offers in educational services. Gives various programs and what grades they cover. Includes information on teacher workshops and special topic tours.

Audiovisuals:

Filmographies, Sales Lists, etc.

"Slide List." Current. 3p. free.

Tells what is available, with price and ordering information.

NATIONAL PRESERVATION PROGRAM OFFICE
LM G07
The Library of Congress
Washington, DC 20540
(202) 287-5213

Date Established: 1977

Objectives of the Agency: Provide technical information about the preservation and restoration of library and archival material.

Curriculum: Library

Subjects: Library science

Publications: Leaflets. Bibliographies. Newsletters.

Bibliographies, Sales Catalogs, Publications Lists, etc.

"Library of Congress Publications on Conservation." 1985. 2p. free.

Gives title, author, date, pages, call number, SUDOCS number, price, and other information. Includes slide/tape and hardcover books. Provides addresses from which to obtain materials.

"Preservation of Library Materials: First Sources." Rev. 1982. 6p. free. Preservation Leaflet No. 1.

Lists references with annotations providing basic information about preserving library and archival materials. Covers bibliographies, monographs, serials, and other formats.

Serials, Subscription Publications, etc.

"National Preservation News." Current. 16p. free.

Newsletter highlights cooperative efforts to preserve our documentary heritage and reports on preservation activities, publication of the National Preservation Program Office.

Selected List of Books and Pamphlets

"Marking Paper Manuscripts." 1983. 4p. free. Preservation Leaflet No. 4.

Addresses the problems associated with marking paper manuscripts. Discusses embossing, punching and perforating, visible inks, and invisible inks.

"Newsprint and Its Preservation." Rev. 1981. 4p. free. Preservation Leaflet No. 5.

Explains what newsprint is, its preservation through storage, other means of preservation, and preserving clippings.

"Paper and Its Preservation: Environmental Controls." Rev. 1983. 6p. free. Preservation Leaflet No. 2.

Discusses the composition of paper, causes of paper deterioration, temperature and humidity, light, mold, and other threats. Includes list of recommended reading and sources of supplies.

Audiovisuals:

Filmographies, Sales Lists, etc.

"Audiovisual Resources for Preserving Library and Archival Materials." 1983. 7p. free. Preservation Leaflet No. 6.

Covers free loan films, videotapes, 35mm slides, magnetic tapes as an aid in familiarizing people with problems encountered in preserving material that is a record of civilization. Each entry includes title, producer, place and date of publication, format, running time, and a description of the contents.

NATIONAL REHABILITATION INFORMATION CENTER
4407 Eighth St., NE
The Catholic University of America
Washington, DC 20017
(202) 635-5826
(800) 34-NARIC

Date Established: 1977

Objectives of the Agency: Provide a rehabilitation information service and research library funded by the Department of Education, National Institute of Handicapped Research to help gain access to National Institute of Handicapped Research and Rehabilitation Services Administration's funded research reports; make available information on assistive devices; and disseminate other rehabilitation-related information resources.

Curriculum: Special education

Subjects: Handicapped

Publications: Pamphlets. Newsletters. Reviews. Books. Fact sheets.

Bibliographies, Sales Catalogs, Publications Lists, etc.

"NARIC Services." n.d. 4p. free.

Lists research, documents, publications, and database tools available. Includes prices.

"Organizational Resources." Current. 4p. free.

Lists a sampling of organizations, agencies, and programs that may be contacted for additional information. Includes federal agencies and federally funded programs.

The Periodical List: A Guide to Disability-Related Journals and Newsletters. 1985. 164p. $15.00.

Lists over 320 listings ranging from professional research journals to consumer-oriented newsletters. Each listing includes title, publisher name and address, indexing/abstracting sources, frequency of publication, and content summary. Includes a subject index and a publisher's index.

"Rehabilitation Research Review." Current. 2p. free.

Lists titles and authors of reviews which may be ordered for $9.00 each.

Serials, Subscription Publications, etc.

"Rehabilitation Information Service." n.d. 6p. free.

Describes resources available from the National Rehabilitation Information Center.

"Updatable." Quarterly. 4p. $35.00/yr.

Reports developments with online ABLEDATA and ERIC databases. Available with membership in ABLEDATA Users' Group, D:ATA Institute, 4407 Eighth St., NE, Washington, DC 20017.

Selected List of Books and Pamphlets

"ABLEDATA: How Can ABLEDATA Help Disabled Persons and Their Families?" 1985. 1p. free.

Gives online rehabilitation product information about what ABLEDATA does and how it can be accessed.

ABLEDATA Thesaurus. 3d ed. 102p. $25.00.

Indexes the terms listed in ABLEDATA to aid in retrieval. Has 15 categories arranged by product type bound in a 3-ring binder. Quarterly thesaurus updates will inform of any changes or additions made in the database.

"ABLEDATA Sample Search." Current. 5p. free.

Gives an idea of the kinds of information available from ABLEDATA, the institute's computerized listing of commercially available products to meet the needs of a person with a physical limitation.

"Current D:ATA." Current. 4p. free.

Gives information about technology advances of the National Institute of Handicapped Research.

"Rehab Brief." Current. 4p. free.

Gives information using research findings.

"REHABDATA Sample Search." 1985. 4p. free.

Provides an idea of the kinds of information available from REHABDATA, the institute's computerized listing of rehabilitation research and related literature.

"Resource Directory: A State Guide to Disability-Related Information." Current. 56p. $7.00.

Provides a state-by-state list of disability resources.

Special Services: REHABDATA and ABLEDATA are available for public access through Bibliographic Retrieval Services (BRS). For information, write:
BRS
Route 7
Latham, NY 12110
(800) 833-4707
New York Residents: (518) 783-1161

NATIONAL SCIENCE FOUNDATION
1800 G St.
Washington, DC 20550
(202) 357-9498

Date Established: 1950

Objectives of the Agency: Promote the progress of science and engineering through research and educational programs.

Curriculum: Science

Subjects: Science—study and teaching

Publications: Research. Programs. Announcements. Bulletins.

Serials, Subscription Publications, etc.

"NSF Bulletin." Monthly. 12p. free.

Prints news about NSF programs, deadline dates, publications, meetings, and sources for more information. Lists publications in each bulletin.

Selected List of Books and Pamphlets

"Ethics and Values in Science and Technology." n.d. 7p. free.

Describes the program which supports research to improve professional and public consideration of the ethical and value aspects of contemporary issues involving science and technology. Explains submission of proposals, evaluation, information about grants.

220 / National Science Foundation

"Teacher Enhancement and Informal Science Education." 1985. 28p. free.

Discusses projects wanted for strengthening science and mathematics education for middle/junior high and elementary level.

Audiovisuals:

Filmographies, Sales Lists, etc.

"Films." Current. 19p. free.

Describes films and where to obtain. Rent, purchase and free loan. Subjects include: general science, astronomy, earth science, ecology and environment, education and learning, energy, engineering, ocean sciences, physics, polar research, research applications, weather, and climate.

Individual Audiovisuals

"Antarctica: Laboratory for Science." 1978. 27 minutes. 16mm. color. rent or purchase.

Describes U.S. research into terrestrial and marine ecosystems, weather and climate, surface and subsurface geology, and changes in the size of the ice sheet of Antarctica.

"Monex: The Monsoon Experiment." 1980. 20 minutes. 16mm. color. rent or purchase.

Shows an experiment on the mechanism of monsoons for the purpose of predicting monsoon rainfall, cyclones, and related events and determining the interactions of monsoons with the global atmospheric circulation.

"The New Industrial Revolution." 1979. 12 minutes. 16mm. color. rent or purchase.

Shows research that will help create change by transferring intelligence, strength, and skill to machines.

"The Observatories." 1982. 27 minutes. 16mm. color. rent, purchase, or free loan.

Explains in lay terms and with animated visuals such phenomena as black holes and quasars. Demonstrates work at six astronomy centers in North and South America.

"Science: Woman's Work." 1982. 27 minutes. 16mm. color. rent, purchase, or free loan.

Encourages girls to take math and science in high school for satisfying, well-paying careers.

Library: A reading room is available during regular business hours. Indexes and documents are available.
NSF Library
1800 G St., NW
Room 1242
Washington, DC 20550
(202) 357-7811

NATIONAL SUDDEN INFANT DEATH SYNDROME CLEARINGHOUSE
3520 Prospect St., NW
Ground Floor
Suite 1
Washington, DC 20057
(202) 625-8410

Date Established: 1980

Objectives of the Agency: Provide information on Sudden Infant Death Syndrome to health care professionals, community service personnel, parents, and general public.

Curriculum: Child care

Subjects: Child Development
Infants

Publications: Fact sheets. Pamphlets.

Bibliographies, Sales Catalogs, Publications Lists, etc.

"Resource List." n.d. 2p. free.

Provides annotated list of limited materials. Order blank.

Selected List of Books and Pamphlets

"Fact Sheet: SIDS Information for the EMT." 2p. free.

Gives statistics, facts, how to distinguish between Sudden Infant Death Syndrome and child abuse and neglect.

"Fact Sheet: What Is SIDS?" n.d. 2p. free.

Explains what Sudden Infant Death Syndrome is. Includes coping with grief by parents and other children.

"Facts about Sudden Infant Death Syndrome." Rev. 12p. free.

Gives basic facts, frequently asked questions and information about where to obtain help and more information.

Special Services: Provides database of current literature.

NATIONAL TECHNICAL INFORMATION SERVICE
U.S. Department of Commerce
5285 Port Royal Rd.
Springfield, VA 22161
(703) 487-4600

Date Established: 1945 (under the name Publications Board)

Objectives of the Agency: Be a permanent central source of specialized business, economic, scientific, and social information, mostly originated by federal agencies.

Curriculum: Library

Subjects: Library science
Publications: Catalogs. Guides. Flyers.

Bibliographies, Sales Catalogs, Publications Lists, etc.

"Catalog of Government Patents Flyer." Current. 3-fold. free. PR-735-A.

Lists government patents. Includes samples of subject index, inventor index, and summaries.

"Data Base Services and Federal Technology in Machine-Readable Formats." Current. 44p. free. PR-595.

Describes NTIS database services such as DATAPLOT, LABSTATA, FCC, and Water Resources Database. Tells how to order and pay. Includes key telephone numbers.

"Directory of Technology Resources Flyer." Current. 4-fold. free. PR-746

Lists the 30 technical areas available with sample main entries. Order form.

"Federal Information Processing Standards Publications." Current. rev. 1985. 39p. free. PR-357.

Details standards relating to federal information processing grouped by: *General Publications, Hardware Standards and Guidelines, Software Standards and Guidelines, Data Standards and Guidelines,* and *ADP Operations Standards and Guidelines.* Lists Federal Information Processing Standards publications by FIPS number with price, ordering information, and order form. Includes form to request that your name be added to the announcement list of new publications and changes.

"Federal Patent Licensing Flyer." Current. 4-fold. free. PR-751

Gives information developed to help clarify the licensing processes of the Office of Federal Patent Licensing. Order form for publications.

"The Federal Software Exchange Catalog Flyer." Current. 3-fold. free. PR-383.

Includes what the catalog has to offer, a list of subject categories, and an order form.

"The Federal Technology Catalog Flyer." Current. 3-fold. free. PR-732-A.

Describes the catalog. Gives an example of a typical summary. Order form.

"Government Reports Announcements and Index Flyer." n.d. 4p. free. PR-195-B.

Tells what the guide covers in current federal technical information. Sample abstract page. Sample index page.

"A Guide to Selected Research in Microfiche." n.d. 28p. free. PR-271.

Aids in selecting current federal research reports. Lists selection subject areas. Provides a guide to alphabetical subject areas. Sample entry. Order form.

"NTIS Abstract Newsletters." Current. 4-fold. free. PR-733-A.

Reports what the newsletters cover. Includes titles and annual subscription rates of the 27 newsletters available. Order form.

NTIS Published Searches. Current. 152p. free. PR-186.

Lists searches available in softcover publications. Each search gives current bibliographic citations indicating the information available on a specific subject from a database. Citations include researcher's or author's name, sponsor, accession number, and in most instances a summary of the project.

"The NTIS Title Index Flyer." Current. 4p. free. PR-567-C.

Gives description, cost, and order form of current cumulative index, retrospective index package, and retrospective indexes.

"Tech Notes Flyer." 1984. 4p. free. PR-365-G.

Provides special fact sheets that alert you to federal technology selected for commercial or practical application. Subscription can be to a single area or several of the available ten categories: computers, electrotechnology, energy, engineering, life sciences, physical sciences, machinery and tools, manufacturing, materials, testing & instrumentation. Order form includes prices.

Selected List of Books and Pamphlets

Directory of Computer Software from NTIS. Current. $40.00/yr. domestic, $70.00/yr. foreign (plus a $3.00 shipping and handling charge). Available in paper copy or microfiche. PB85-162121/BAL.

Describes machine-readable software of over 100 federal agencies. Lists over 1,300 computer programs. Covers 21 subject categories such as chemistry, health care, library and information sciences, communications, etc.

Government Reports Annual Index. Annual. $420.00/yr. domestic, $565.00/yr. outside of North America.

Consists of six hardbound volumes of approximately 7,000 pages. Lists about 70,000 report titles. Indexed by keyword, personal and corporate author, contract number, and report or accession number. Cross references.

"National Technical Information Service." Current. 40p. free. PR-154.

Discusses what NTIS is, principal products,

economic data, published searches, abstract newsletters, tech notes, computer products, selected research in microfiche, and other products. Includes maps showing NTIS locations and key telephone numbers. Order forms.

"NTIS: 40 Years a Brief History." 1985. 6p. free. PR-796.

Gives history and development, major services currently offered, statistics, and names of directors and their terms.

"1980 Census Data Report 3: Social Indicators for Planning and Evaluation." Current. Approx. 30p. $25.00/paper copy, $10.00/microfiche.

Includes various reports containing tabular and graphic information. Request flyer for specific ordering information.

"A Reference Guide to the NTIS Bibliographical Data Base." 2d ed. 1980. 23p. free. NTIS-PR 253.

Gives information about the database which will be helpful to users working with the NTIS files on their own computer service, on a publicly available online service, or in the printed format. Index.

NATIONAL TECHNICAL INSTITUTE FOR THE DEAF
Rochester Institute of Technology
Division of Public Affairs
1 Lomb Memorial Dr.
P.O. Box 9887
Rochester, NY 14623-9979
(716) 475-6400

Date Established: 1968

Objectives of the Agency: Represent the first effort to educate large numbers of deaf students within a college campus planned primarily for hearing students; serve the deaf throughout the world through educational outreach, publications, and related service; and conduct research.

Curriculum: Education, handicapped

Subjects: Deaf
Deaf—education
Physically handicapped

Publications: Pamphlets. Catalogs. Reprints of journal articles. Manuals. Books. On opportunities, concerns, and education of the deaf.

Bibliographies, Sales Catalogs, Publications Lists, etc.

"A Catalog of Educational Resources." Current. 45p. free.

Describes material. Includes ordering information and forms. Free and for sale materials. Products are available from various distributors and order forms and addresses are provided for each distributor.

Audiovisuals:

Filmographies, Sales Lists, etc.

"A Catalog of Educational Resources." Current. 45p. free.

Describes (pages 17-22) free loan and/or purchase videotapes from Modern Talking Picture Service, Inc., Captioned Films for the Deaf, 5000 Park St. North, St. Petersburg, FL 33709. 1-800-237-6213. Order form.

NATIONAL TRANSPORTATION SAFETY BOARD
800 Independence Ave., SW
Washington, DC 20594
(202) 382-6600

Date Established: 1975

Objectives of the Agency: Assure that all types of transportation in the United States are conducted safely; investigate accidents; conduct studies; and make recommendations to the government and transportation industry.

Curriculum: Driver education

Subjects: Automobile drivers
Transportation

Locations:

National Transportation Safety Board
Field Office
701 C St.
Suite C-145
Box 11
Anchorage, AK 99513

National Transportation Safety Board
Field Office
15000 Aviation Blvd.
P.O. Box 6117
Lawndale, CA 90261

National Transportation Safety Board
Field Office
10255 E. Twenty-Fifth Ave.
Suite 14
Aurora, CO 80010

National Transportation Safety Board
Field Office
8375 N.W. Fifty-Third St.
Suite 210
Miami Springs, FL 33166

National Transportation Safety Board
Field Office
120 Peachtree St., NW
Atlanta, GA 30309

National Transportation Safety Board
Field Office
2300 E. Devon Ave.
Suite 140
Des Plaines, IL 60018

National Transportation Safety Board
Field Office
601 E. Twelfth St.
Room 1748
Kansas City, MO 64106

National Transportation Safety Board
Field Office
Federal Bldg.
JFK International Airport
Room 102
Jamaica, NY 11430

National Transportation Safety Board
Field Office
819 Taylor St.
Room 7A07
Fort Worth, TX 76102

National Transportation Safety Board
Field Office
19414 Pacific Hwy. South
Room 303
Seattle, WA 98188

Publications: Accident briefs and reports. Annual reports and reviews. Computer tapes. Initial decisions. News digest. Directives. Opinions and orders. Pamphlets. Public records and files. Regulations. Recommendations. Studies. Investigations. Speeches. Spill maps. Microfiche. Photographs. Books. Serials. Press releases. Indexes. General and technical safety investigative materials in many formats. Free and for sale.

Bibliographies, Sales Catalogs, Publications Lists, etc.

"NTSB Documents and Information." 1984. 13p. free.
Describes what types of materials are available and how to obtain them. Order from: National Transportation Safety Board, Public Inquiries Section, 800 Independence Ave., SW, Room 805F, Washington, DC 20594.

"NTSB News Digest." Bimonthly. 4p. free.
Describes activities. Summarizes some publications. To be placed on the mailing list to receive "NTSB News Digest" regularly, write: National Transportation Safety Board, Public Inquiries Section, 800 Independence Ave., SW, Room 805F, Washington, DC 20594.

"National Transportation Safety Board Fee Schedule." 1984. 2p. free.
Lists fees for various kinds of materials. Also lists free materials. Order from: National Transportation Safety Board, Public Inquiries Section, 800 Independence Ave., SW, Room 805F, Washington, DC 20594.

"Special Order Form for National Transportation Safety Publications." n.d. 2p. free.
Gives list and ordering information of available serials.

Serials, Subscription Publications, etc.

Highway Accident Reports. Annual. $50.00/yr. in United States, Canada, Mexico. PB82-916200.
Order from: National Technical Information Service, 5285 Port Royal Rd., Springfield, VA 22161. (703) 487-4630.

Library: Documents and information in public files may be examined without charge:
National Transportation Safety Board
Public Reference Room
Public Inquiries Section
800 Independence Ave., SW
Washington, DC 20594
(202) 382-6735

Special Services: Individual members of the board respond to speaking invitations. Direct inquiries to:
Office of Government and Public Affairs
National Transportation Safety Board
Washington, DC 20594
(202) 382-6600

NATIONAL WEATHER SERVICE
Office of Public Affairs (PAW)
National Oceanic and Atmospheric Administration
U.S. Department of Commerce
8060 Thirteenth St.
Silver Spring, MD 20910
(301) 427-7622

Date Established: 1890

Objectives of the Agency: Provide forecasts and weather warnings to the general public and specialized users; give meteorological support for the aviation industry; issue river state forecasts; provide oceanographic, overseas, and space operation support services; and acquire meteorological data.

Curriculum: Geography

Subjects: Weather forecasting

Locations:

National Weather Service
Eastern Region Field Organization
585 Stewart Ave.
Garden City, Long Island, NY 11530

National Weather Service
Central Region Field Organization
601 E. Twelfth St.
Kansas City, MO 64106

National Weather Service
Southern Region Field Organization
819 Taylor St.
Fort Worth, TX 76102

National Weather Service
Western Region Field Organization
125 S. State St.
Salt Lake City, UT 84147

National Weather Service
Alaska Region Field Organization
701 C St.
Box 23
Anchorage, AK 99513

National Weather Service
Pacific Region Field Organization
300 Ala Moana Blvd.
Room 4110
Honolulu, HI 96850

National Weather Service
National Meteorological Center
5200 Auth Rd.
Camp Springs, MD 20233

National Weather Service
National Hurricane Center
1320 S. Dixie Hwy.
Coral Gables, FL 33146

National Weather Service
National Severe Storms Forecast Center
601 E. Twelfth St.
Kansas City, MO 64106

National Weather Service
Office of Public Affairs (PAW)
National Oceanic and Atmospheric Administration
8060 Thirteenth St.
Silver Springs, MD 20910
(301) 427-7622

Publications: Fact sheets. Directories.

Selected List of Books and Pamphlets

"A Brief History of the National Weather Service." 1979. 5p. free.
Describes early efforts at weather diaries, government observations during the War of 1812, first systematized synchronous meteoritic reports, local forecasts, and other developments.

"National Weather Service Offices and Stations." Current. 51p. free.
Lists all first and second order offices and stations operated by or under the supervision of the national service. Shows the type and location of each station. Indicates briefly the nature of the observation program provided by each station.

Audiovisuals:

Filmographies, Sales Lists, etc.

"Films from NOAA." Rev. 9p. free.
Lists free loan films grouped under such subjects as weather, the oceans, NOAA, etc. Order from: Modern Talking Pictures, 5000 Park St. North, St. Petersburg, FL 33709.

NATIONAL WILDLIFE REFUGES
United States Department of the Interior
United States Fish and Wildlife Service
Eighteenth and C Sts., NW
Washington, DC 20240
(202) 343-4311

Date Established: 1966

Objectives of the Agency: Oversee a network of over 400 refuges in 49 states and five trust territories. Lands and waters provide feeding and resting areas for migrations of birds and sanctuaries for endangered and unusual species.

Curriculum: Social studies

Subjects: Wildlife — conservation

Locations:

CA, HI, ID, NV, OR, WA
National Wildlife Refuges
U.S. Fish and Wildlife Service
Lloyd 500 Bldg.
500 N.E. Multnomah St.
Suite 1692
Portland, OR 97232

AZ, NM, OK, TX
National Wildlife Refuges
U.S. Fish and Wildlife Service
Box 1306
Albuquerque, NM 87103

IA, IL, IN, MI, MN, MO, OH, WI
National Wildlife Refuges
U.S. Fish and Wildlife Service
Federal Bldg.
Fort Snelling
St. Paul, MN 55111

AL, AR, FL, GA, KY, LA, MS, NC, SC, TN, PR
National Wildlife Refuges
U.S. Fish and Wildlife Service
75 Spring St., SW
Atlanta, GA 30303

CT, DE, MA, MD, ME, NH, NJ, NY, PA, VA, VT, WV

National Wildlife Refuges
U.S. Fish and Wildlife Service
1 Gateway Center
Suite 700
Newton Corner, MA 02158

CO, KS, MT, NE, ND, SD, UT, WY

National Wildlife Refuges
U.S. Fish and Wildlife Service
Denver Federal Center
Box 25486
Denver, CO 80225

AK

National Wildlife Refuges
U.S. Fish and Wildlife Service
1011 E. Tudor Rd.
Anchorage, AK 99503

Publications: Pamphlets. Lists. Guides. On the refuge system and management.

Selected List of Books and Pamphlets

"National Wildlife Refuge System." n.d. 8p. free.
Includes an introduction, functions, and locations. Map shows locations and regional divisions.

"National Wildlife Refuges." Current. folded map. free.
Provides a visitor's guide. Includes names, addresses, and facilities of refuges. Map. Photographs.

"Refuge Managers' Address List." Current. 13p. free.
Lists refuges' names, their addresses, manager's names, and telephone numbers. Arranged by states.

NUCLEAR REGULATORY COMMISSION
Office of Public Affairs
1717 H St., NW
Washington, DC 20555
(301) 492-7000

Date Established: 1974

Objectives of the Agency: Regulate the civilian uses of nuclear materials in the United States to protect the public health, safety, and environment.

Curriculum: Environmental studies

Subjects: Atomic energy

Publications: Summary of functions. Reports. Directories. Bulletins. Guides.

Selected List of Books and Pamphlets

"Citizen's Guide to U.S. Nuclear Regulatory Commission Information." n.s. 20p. free. NUREG/BR-0010.

Explains types of documents and ways each may be obtained; special audience groups and how each is served. Includes a section on ways of obtaining information. Lists various reference tools to help in identifying nuclear regulatory documents that may be of interest.

"The Nuclear Regulatory Commission." 1985. 4p. free.
Describes what the commission does, its history, functions, organization, offices, investigations, and the independent organizations that serve the commission.

Special Services: A public document room makes publicly available over 300 new documents daily. Documents may be examined at no charge. Computer searches can be requested and documents can be reproduced.
Public Document Room
1717 H St., NW
Washington, DC 20555
(202) 634-3273

A variety of publications are available. It is also possible to be put on mailing lists. Inquire about those currently available.

The Nuclear Safety Information Center provides service as a focal point for the collection, analysis, and dissemination of information related to the safety of nuclear facilities. For further information, write:
Nuclear Safety Information Center
Oak Ridge National Laboratory
P.O. Box Y
Oak Ridge, TN 37830

The Technical Information Clearinghouse answers inquiries and provides contacts.
Maryland residents: (800) 492-8106
Others: (800) 638-8282

OCCUPATIONAL SAFETY AND HEALTH ADMINISTRATION
U.S. Department of Labor
Division of Communications Production
200 Constitution Ave., NW
Washington, DC 20210
(202) 523-8017

Date Established: 1970

Objectives of the Agency: Promote and regulate safety and health standards.

Curriculum: Health, safety

Subjects: Labor and laboring classes—accidents

Locations:

CT, MA, ME, NH, RI, VT
U.S. Department of Labor
OSHA Region 1 Office
16-18 North St.
1 Dock Square Bldg.
Fourth Floor
Boston, MA 02109
(617) 223-6710

NJ, NY, PR, VI
U.S. Department of Labor
OSHA Region 2 Office
1 Astor Plaza
1515 Broadway
Room 3445
New York, NY 10036
(212) 944-3426

DC, DE, MD, PA, VA, WV
U.S. Department of Labor
OSHA Region 3 Office
3535 Market St.
Philadelphia, PA 19104
(215) 596-1201

AL, FL, GA, KY, MS, NC, SC, TN
U.S. Department of Labor
OSHA Region 4 Office
1375 Peachtree St., NW
Suite 587
Atlanta, GA 30367
(404) 881-3573

IL, IN, MI, MN, OH, WI
U.S. Department of Labor
OSHA Region 5 Office
230 S. Dearborn St.
Thirty-Second Floor
Room 3244
Chicago, IL 60604
(312) 353-2220

AR, LA, NM, OK, TX
U.S. Department of Labor
OSHA Region 6 Office
555 Griffin Square Bldg.
Room 602
Dallas, TX 75202
(214) 767-4731

IA, KS, MO, NE
U.S. Department of Labor
OSHA Region 7 Office
911 Walnut St.
Room 406
Kansas City, MO 64106
(816) 374-5861

CO, MT, ND, SD, UT, WY
U.S. Department of Labor
OSHA Region 8 Office
1961 Stout St.
Denver, CO 80294
(303) 837-3061

AS, AZ, CA, GU, HI, NV, Pacific Trust Territories
U.S. Department of Labor
OSHA Region 9 Office
450 Golden Gate Ave.
Box 36017
San Francisco, CA 94102
(415) 556-7260

AK, ID, OR, WA
U.S. Department of Labor
OSHA Region 10 Office
Federal Office Bldg.
909 First Ave.
Room 6003
Seattle, WA 98174
(206) 442-5930

Publications: Bibliographies. Pamphlets. Guides. Catalogs. Reports. Manuals. On job safety, regulation, and health concerns. Technical and general material.

Bibliographies, Sales Catalogs, Publications Lists, etc.

"Occupational Safety and Health—A Bibliography." 1978. $46.00; microfiche $4.50.
Lists an annotated bibliography of published sources dealing with both general and specific aspects of occupational safety and health.

"OSHA Publications and Audiovisual Programs." 1983. 22p. free. OSHA 2019.
Describes printed materials and audiovisual programs.

Selected List of Books and Pamphlets

"All about OSHA." 1982. free. OSHA 2056.
Describes general provisions of the Occupational Safety and Health Act of 1970 and the policies of OSHA.

"Consumer Information Leaflets." n.d.
Highlights OSHA programs on a variety of job safety subjects in a series of leaflets available from national, regional, and area offices.

"General Industry Safety and Health Regulations: Part 1910." 1983. $12.00. 029-015-00063-5.
Prints job safety and health rules and regulations issued by OSHA about industry in general.

"The Occupational Safety and Health Act of 1970, P.L. 91-596." 1970. free. OSHA 2001.
Prints full text of the act.

Audiovisuals:

Filmographies, Sales Lists, etc.

"OSHA Publications and Audiovisual Programs." n.d. 1983. 22p. free. OSHA 2019.
Describes audiovisual programs.

Individual Films

"Asbestos Abatement in Schools." n.d. four sound slide sets. color. $130.00. Film Order No. A05806/NK.
Reports information for anyone coming in contact with asbestos in buildings. Includes guides. Order from: National Audiovisual Center, Washington, DC 20409.

"More Than a Paycheck." n.d. 28 minutes. 16mm. rental $25.00, purchase $265.00. Film Order No. A00278/CF. Video Cassette No. A02575/CF.
Illustrates how workers in some industries can bring home contamination and cancer. Order from: National Audiovisual Center, Washington, DC 20409.

Library:
Department of Labor Library
Frances Perkins Bldg.
200 Constitution Ave., NW
Room N2439
Washington, DC 20210
(202) 523-6992

Special Services: For information on OSHA speakers, call: (202) 523-8615. Tell what your potential audience is, preferred topic, location, and scheduled date. For information on grants, write:
OSHA Training Institute
1555 Times Dr.
Des Plaines, IL 60018
(312) 297-2810

If you have a specific job safety and health question or research problem, contact:
Data Center
Frances Perkins Bldg.
200 Constitution Ave., NW
Room N2439
Washington, DC 20210
(202) 523-6992

OCCUPATIONAL SAFETY AND HEALTH REVIEW COMMISSION
1825 K St., NW
Fourth Floor
Washington, DC 20006
(202) 634-7943

Date Established: 1971

Objectives of the Agency: Rule on cases forwarded to it by the Department of Labor when there is disagreement over the results of safety and health inspections performed by the department's Occupational Safety and Health Administration.

Curriculum: Health, industrial education, safety, social studies

Subjects: Labor and laboring classes—accidents

Locations:

Occupational Safety Review Commission
Review Commission Judges
1365 Peachtree St., NE
Atlanta, GA 30309
(404) 861-4086

Occupational Safety Review Commission
Review Commission Judges
John W. McCormack Post Office
Boston, MA 02110
(617) 223-3757

Occupational Safety Review Commission
Review Commission Judges
55 E. Monroe St.
Chicago, IL 60603
(312) 353-2564

Occupational Safety Review Commission
Review Commission Judges
1100 Commerce St.
Dallas, TX 75242
(214) 767-5271

Occupational Safety Review Commission
Review Commission Judges
1050 Seventeenth St.
Denver, CO 80265
(303) 837-2281

Occupational Safety Review Commission
Review Commission Judges
1515 Broadway
New York, NY 10036
(212) 944-3455

Occupational Safety Review Commission
Review Commission Judges
1114 Market St.
St. Louis, MO 63101
(314) 425-5071

Publications: Guides. Acts. Reports. Proceedings on procedures.

Selected List of Books and Pamphlets

"A Guide to Procedures of the Occupational Safety and Health Review Commission." Rev. 28p. free. OSHRC Form 6.
Explains how conventional proceedings are conducted.

228 / *Occupational Safety and Health Review Commission*

"The Occupational Safety and Health Act of 1970." n.d. 1p. free. OSHRC Form OEXD 330.

Explains purpose, standards, enforcement, penalties, administration of the act. Includes addresses for further information.

"The President's Report on Occupational Safety and Health." Current. 19p. free.

Describes case highlights and commission members.

"Public Law 91-596." n.d. 31p. free.

Reprints the Occupational Safety and Health Act of 1970.

"Rules of Procedure." 1983. 37p. free.

Reprints the Rules of Procedure as codified in Title 29 of the Code of Federal Regulations.

Special Services: Inquire about speakers at the address given above.

Decisions of the commission are available on the WESTLAW system.

Free individual copies of OSHRC decisions are available. An index to decisions is sold for $14.00. Subscriptions to microfiche copies of OSHRC decisions (OSHRC Reports) are available for sale from:
Superintendent of Documents
Government Printing Office
Washington, DC 20401

OFFICE OF CLINICAL REPORTS AND INQUIRIES
9000 Rockville Pike
Building 10
Room 1C255
Bethesda, MD 20205
(301) 496-4625

Date Established: 1953

Objectives of the Agency: Provide primary medical research to the federal government.

Curriculum: Health

Subjects: Health education

Publications: Pamphlets. Lists.

Bibliographies, Sales Catalogs, Publications Lists, etc.

"Medicine for the Layman Series." n.d. 1p. free.

Lists title and NIH Publication No. of publications available in single copies.

Selected List of Books and Pamphlets

"Blood Transfusions: Benefits and Risks." 1981. 32p. free. NIH Publication No. 81-1949.

Describes what blood is, blood groups, benefits and risks of transfusions. Includes blood transfusion checklist and five pages of questions and answers.

"The Brain." 1981. 20p. free. NIH Publication No. 81-1813.

Describes what the brain does, how it works. Includes problems and diagnosis.

"Brain in Aging and Dementia." 1983. 33p. free. NIH Publication No. 83-2625.

Discusses brain anatomy and physiology; the brain in aging; characteristics, types, and causes of dementia. Includes six pages of questions and answers.

"Clinical Center." 1982. 8p. free.

Describes the research program, medical services, design and layout, admission procedures and patient care, and mission of the clinical center.

"Depression and Manic-Depressive Illness." 1982. 29p. free. NIH Publication No. 82-1940.

Discusses depression, biological factors, amine neurotransmitter systems, biological rhythms, antidepressants, preventing recurrences. Includes five pages of questions and answers.

"Environment and Disease." 1982. 29p. free. NIH Publication No. 82-2368.

Discusses environment and life expectancy, chemicals and human disease, cancer and chemicals, epidemiology, studies, and tests. Includes five pages of questions and answers.

"Lung Cancer." 1984. 29p. free. NIH Publication No. 84-2626.

Describes symptoms, diagnosis, treatment, response to surgery, radiotherapy, chemotherapy treatment, and research goals. Includes one page of questions and answers.

"Radiation Risks and Radiation Therapy." 1982. 27p. free. NIH Publication No. 83-2367.

Describes what radiation is, types of radiation, medical applications of radiation, measuring radiation doses, and assessing risk. Includes two pages of questions and answers.

Audiovisuals:

Filmographies, Sales Lists, etc.

"Films from National Audiovisual Center and Modern Talking Picture Service." n.d. 1p. free.

Lists available films. Gives addresses and telephone numbers of the two sources.

OFFICE OF CONSUMER AFFAIRS
U.S. Department of Commerce
Room H5725
Washington, DC 20230
(202) 377-5001

Date Established: 1976

Objectives of the Agency: Advise the President on all matters relating to consumer interest; and help business and consumers with advertising, servicing, complaints, credit, and product safety.

Curriculum: Consumer education

Subjects: Consumer protection

Publications: Handbook. Fact sheet. Guides. Manuals. Bulletin. Directory on consumerism.

Bibliographies, Sales Catalogs, Publications Lists, etc.

"Office of Consumer Affairs." n.d. 2p. free.
Lists publications available for business managers, workshop coordinators and others interested in consumer issues. Materials include a directory, plain English materials, guides about good business practices, and study manuals.

Serials, Subscription Publications, etc.

"Simply Stated." Monthly. 4p. free.
A newsletter of the Document Design Center, American Institutes for Research Advocating Plain English in the Business World.

Selected List of Books and Pamphlets

"Advertising, Packaging, & Labeling." Rev. 35p. free.
Discusses responsive business approaches to consumer needs. Gives recommendations in advertising, packaging, and labeling to promote consumer loyalty and goodwill. Key-word index.

"Consumer Product Safety." 1981. 24p. free.
Gives recommendations for responsible business practices in consumer product safety. The recommendations are applicable to the entire business community. Appendices include sources of information and assistance. Key-word index.

Consumer's Resource Handbook. Current. 111p. free.
Explains sources of help for the consumer, how to write a complaint letter, handling your own complaint, consumer assistance directory, selected federal agencies. Includes a sample complaint letter. Subject and organization index.

"Credit and Financial Issues." 1981. 19p. free.
Discusses recommendations for responsible business practices in credit and financial issues to define and encourage exemplary standards of business conduct and to heighten business sensitivity.

"Inventory of U.S. Department of Commerce Consumer Services." 1985. 30p. free.
Describes consumer-related activities and services of commerce department agencies. Lists publications and audiovisuals.

"Managing Consumer Complaints." 1984. 16p. free.
Gives recommendations for responsible business practices in managing consumer complaints. Includes complaint management checklist and additional sources of help. Key-word index.

"Office of Consumer Affairs." n.d. 2p. free.
Explains functions and aims of the office, and what it has to offer business and consumers.

"Product Warranties & Servicing." 1981. 30p. free.
Explains types of warranties and recommendations for good warranties and product servicing. Key-word index.

OFFICE OF ELEMENTARY AND SECONDARY EDUCATION
Office of the Assistant Secretary
United States Department of Education
400 Maryland Ave., SW
Washington, DC 20202
(202) 245-3081

Date Established: 1981

Objectives of the Agency: Administer programs that assist state and local educational agencies to maintain and improve preschool, elementary, and secondary education.

Curriculum: Education

Subjects: Education—U.S.

Locations:

Region 1 Secretary's Regional Representative
U.S. Department of Education
John W. McCormack Post Office and Courthouse
Room 526
Post Office Square
Boston, MA 02109
(617) 223-7500

Region 2 Secretary's Regional Representative
U.S. Department of Education
26 Federal Plaza
Room 3954
New York, NY 10278
(212) 264-7005

Region 3 Secretary's Regional Representative
U.S. Department of Education
3535 Market St.
Room 16350
Philadelphia, PA 19104
(215) 596-1001

Region 4 Secretary's Regional Representative
U.S. Department of Education
101 Marietta Tower Bldg.
Suite 2221
Atlanta, GA 30323
(404) 221-2502

Region 5 Secretary's Regional Representative
U.S. Department of Education
300 S. Wacker Dr.
Sixteenth Floor
Chicago, IL 60606
(312) 353-5215

Region 6 Secretary's Regional Representative
U.S. Department of Education
1200 Main Tower Bldg.
Room 1460
Dallas, TX 75202
(214) 767-3626

Region 7 Secretary's Regional Representative
U.S. Department of Education
324 E. Eleventh St.
Ninth Floor
Kansas City, MO 64106
(816) 374-2276

Region 8 Secretary's Regional Representative
U.S. Department of Education
1961 Stout St.
Room 380
Denver, CO 80294
(303) 837-3544

Region 9 Secretary's Regional Representative
U.S. Department of Education
50 United Nations Plaza
Room 205
San Francisco, CA 94102
(415) 556-4920

Region 10 Secretary's Regional Representative
U.S. Department of Education
Third and Broad Bldg.
2910 Third Ave.
Seattle, WA 98121
(206) 399-0460

Publications: Guides about the functions and services of the office.

Selected List of Books and Pamphlets

"Guide to Department of Education Programs." Annual. 27p. free.
Provides information to begin the process of applying for funding under individual federal education programs.

"Office of the Assistant Secretary for Elementary and Secondary Education Overview." Current. 21p. free.
Gives purpose, background, authorizing legislation, appropriation, and other information about: compensatory education programs, state and local educational programs, and Indian educational programs. Organization chart.

OFFICE OF FEDERAL PROCUREMENT POLICY
Office of the Administrator
New Executive Office Bldg.
726 Jackson Place, NW
Washington, DC 20503
(202) 395-5802

Date Established: 1974

Objectives of the Agency: Improve the economy, efficiency, and effectiveness of the procurement processes by giving direction to procurement policies, regulations, forms, and procedures. Its authority applies to procurement by executive agencies and recipients of federal grants or assistance of: property, other than real property in being; services, including research and development; and construction, alteration, repair, or maintenance of real property.

Curriculum: Government

Subjects: Public administration

Publications: Reports. Proposals. Policies about procurement.

Bibliographies, Sales Catalogs, Publications Lists, etc.

"Report to the Congress." Current. 86p. free.
Appendix includes a section listing publications of the Office of Federal Procurement Policy.

Selected List of Books and Pamphlets

Procurement Policy Letters. 1984. 163p. free. OFPP Pamphlet No. 6.
Compiles policy letters arranged by year of issue illustrating the nature and scope of activities. Copies of the volume and individual policy letters are available from: Publications Office, Executive Office of the President, 726 Jackson Place, NW, Room 2200, Washington, DC 20503.

Proposal for a Uniform Federal Procurement System. 1982. 148p. free.
Describes desirable reforms in federal procurement and management systems as well as the substance of changes in legislation to accomplish these reforms. Appendix section includes acronyms. Graphics.

"Report to Congress." Current. 86p. free.
Relates activities of the current year of the Office of Federal Procurement Policy. Examines programs, plans and objectives, conclusions, and recommendations.

OFFICE OF HUMAN DEVELOPMENT SERVICES
Department of Health and Human Services
Office of Public Affairs
200 Independence Ave., SW
Washington, DC 20201
(202) 245-7246

Date Established: 1973

Objectives of the Agency: Provide leadership and direction to human services programs for the elderly, children and youth, families, Native Americans, persons living in rural areas, handicapped persons, and public assistance recipients.

Curriculum: Government

Subjects: Public welfare

Locations:

CT, MA, ME, NH, RI, VT

Department of Health and Human Services
Region 1 Office
John F. Kennedy Federal Bldg.
Boston, MA 02203
(617) 223-6830

NJ, NY, PR, VI

Department of Health and Human Services
Region 2 Office
26 Federal Plaza
New York, NY 10278
(212) 264-4600

DC, DE, MD, PA, VA, WV

Department of Health and Human Services
Region 3 Office
3535 Market St.
Philadelphia, PA 19101
(215) 596-6492

AL, FL, GA, KY, MS, NC, SC, TN

Department of Health and Human Services
Region 4 Office
101 Marietta Towers, NE
Atlanta, GA 30323
(404) 221-2442

IL, IN, MI, MN, OH, WI

Department of Health and Human Services
Region 5 Office
300 S. Wacker Dr.
Chicago, IL 60606
(312) 353-5160

AR, LA, NM, OK, TX

Department of Health and Human Services
Region 6 Office
1200 Main Tower Bldg.
Dallas, TX 75202
(214) 767-3301

IA, KS, MO, NE

Department of Health and Human Services
Region 7 Office
601 E. Twelfth St.
Kansas City, MO 64106
(616) 374-2821

CO, MT, ND, SD, UT, WY

Department of Health and Human Services
Region 8 Office
1961 Stout St.
Denver, CO 80294
(303) 844-3373

AZ, CA, HI, NV, Pacific Trust Territories

Department of Health and Human Services
Region 9 Office
50 United Nations Plaza
San Francisco, CA 94102
(415) 556-6746

AK, ID, OR, WA

Department of Health and Human Services
Region 10 Office
2901 Third Ave.
Seattle, WA 98101
(206) 442-0420

Publications: Fact sheets. Pamphlets.

Selected List of Books and Pamphlets

"Media Information." n.d. 31p. free.
Surveys the Office of Human Development and its various administrations and bureau.

"Private Sector Initiatives: Challenges and Opportunities." n.d. 6p. free.
Explores public and private partnerships, nonprofit help, corporate and business help as sources of providing assistance to those in need.

OFFICE OF OCEAN AND COASTAL RESOURCE MANAGEMENT
CZIC NOAA N/ORM4 RM357
2001 Wisconsin Ave., NW
Washington, DC 20235
(202) 634-4255

Date Established: 1972

Objectives of the Agency: Administer the National Coastal Zone Management Program, the Coastal Energy Impact Program, and the National Estuarine Sanctuary Program, all mandated by the Coastal Zone Management Act. The Coastal Zone Management Act encourages and helps states and territories in dealing with the increasing demands for the use of the nation's coastal areas.

Curriculum: Environmental studies, geography

Subjects: Environment
Ocean

Locations:

AK

Office of the Governor
Policy Development and Planning Division
Pouch AP
Juneau, AK 99801
(907) 465-3474

AL
Coastal Area Board
General Delivery
Daphne, AL 36526
(205) 626-1880

CA
California Coastal Commission
631 Howard St.
Fourth Floor
San Francisco, CA 94105
(415) 391-6800

CT
Coastal Area Management Program
Department of Environmental Protection
71 Capitol Ave.
Hartford, CT 06115
(203) 566-7404

DE
Coastal Management Program
Office of Management, Budget, and Planning
James Townsend Bldg.
Dover, DE 19901
(302) 678-4271

FL
Bureau of Coastal Zone Planning
Department of Environmental Regulation
Twin Towers Office Bldg.
2600 Blair Stone Rd.
Tallahassee, FL 32301
(904) 488-8614

GA
Coastal Resources Program
Department of Natural Resources
1200 Glynn Ave.
Brunswick, GA 31520
(912) 264-4771

GU
Bureau of Planning
Government of Guam
P.O. Box 2950
Agana, GU 96910
Via Overseas Operator: 477-9502

HI
Department of Planning and Economic Development
P.O. Box 2359
Honolulu, HI 96804
Via San Francisco Operator: 8-556-0220
(808) 548-4609

IL
Illinois Coastal Zone Management Program
300 N. State St.
Room 1010
Chicago, IL 60610
(312) 793-3126

LA
Coastal Resources Program
Department of Transportation and Development
Capitol Station
P.O. Box 44245
Baton Rouge, LA 70804
(504) 923-0765

MA
Executive Office of Environmental Affairs
100 Cambridge St.
Boston, MA 02202
(617) 727-9530

MD
Department of Natural Resources
Energy and Coastal Zone Administration
Tawes State Office Bldg.
Annapolis, MD 21401
(301) 269-3382

ME
State Planning Office
Resource Planning Division
189 State St.
Augusta, ME 04333
(207) 289-3155

MI
Coastal Zone Management Program
Department of Natural Resources
Division of Land Use Programs
Stephens T. Mason Bldg.
Lansing, MI 48926
(517) 373-1950

MN
State Planning Agency
Capitol Square Bldg.
550 Cedar St.
Room 100
St. Paul, MN 55155
(612) 296-2633

MS
Mississippi Marine Resources Council
P.O. Drawer 959
Long Beach, MS 39560
(601) 864-4602

NC
Department of Natural and Economic Resources
Box 27687
Raleigh, NC 27611
(919) 733-2293

NH

Division of Regional Planning
Office of Comprehensive Planning
26 Pleasant St.
Concord, NH 03301
(603) 271-2155

NJ

Office of Coastal Zone Management
Department of Environmental Protection
P.O. Box 1889
Trenton, NJ 08625
(609) 292-8262

Northern Mariana Islands

Office of Planning and Budget Affairs
Executive Office of the Governor
Saipan, Mariana Islands 96950
Via Overseas Operator: 9457

NY

Coastal Management Unit
Department of State
162 Washington Ave.
Albany, NY 12231
(518) 474-8834

OH

Dept. of Natural Resources
Division of Water
Fountain Square
1930 Belcher Dr.
Columbus, OH 43224
(614) 466-6557

OR

Land Conservation and Development Commission
1175 Court St., NE
Salem, OR 97310
(503) 378-4928

PA

Division of Outdoor Recreation
Department of Environmental Resources
Third and Reilly Sts.
P.O. Box 1467
Harrisburg, PA 17120
(717) 787-6674

PR

Department of Natural Resources
P.O. Box 5887
Puerto de Tierra, PR 00906
(809) 724-8774

RI

Statewide Planning Program
Department of Administration
265 Melrose St.
Providence, RI 02907
(401) 277-2656

SC

Wildlife and Marine Resources Department
1116 Bankers Trust Tower
Columbia, SC 29201
(803) 758-8442

TX

Texas Coastal Management Program
General Land Office
1700 N. Congress Ave.
Austin, TX 79711
(512) 472-7765

VA

Office of Commerce and Resources
Ninth St. Office Bldg.
Fifth Floor
Richmond, VA 23219
(804) 786-7652

VI

Virgin Islands Planning Office
P.O. Box 2606
Charlotte Amalie
St. Thomas, VI 00801
(809) 774-7859

WA

Department of Ecology
State of Washington
Olympia, WA 98504
(206) 753-6879

WI

Office of State Planning and Energy
1 West Wilson St.
B-130
Madison, WI 53702
(608) 266-3687

Publications: Pamphlets. Curriculum material. Lists. Papers.

Selected List of Books and Pamphlets

"Coastal Awareness: A Resource Guide for Teachers in Elementary Science." 1978. 83p. free.

For teachers interested in the ecological value of the coast. Could be used in a week-long unit. Illustrated. Last section has reading suggestions, list of suggested films, games, where to obtain data and information, and a glossary.

234 / Office of Ocean and Coastal Resource Management

"Coastal Awareness: A Resource Guide for Teachers in Junior High Science." 1978. 92p. free.
   Discusses characteristics of the coast such as the shore, currents, dunes, waves, etc. Activities. Resources. Glossary.

"Coastal Awareness: A Resource Guide for Teachers in Senior High Science." 1978. 72p. free.
   Discusses currents, tides, waves, shores, estuaries, marshes of the coast. Includes addresses for further resources. Activities. Glossary.

"Coastal Zone Management Act of 1972." n.d. 18p. free.
   Reprints original act of 1972, as well as amendments.

Improving Your Waterfront: A Practical Guide. 1980. 108p. free.
   Examines waterfronts today, management structures, zoning and districting, and land acquisition. Includes addresses, summaries of federal grant-in-aid programs. Bibliography. Appendices.

"Reviving the Urban Waterfront." n.d. 48p. free.
   Describes seven projects to demonstrate changes that can occur through imaginative reuses of urban waterfronts. Foreword by the National Endowment for the Arts, Office of Coastal Management and Partners for Livable Places.

"Where Land and Water Meet." 1979. 60p. free.
   Discusses marine sanctuaries and offshore industries such as drilling, marine salvors, and deep-sea mining. Includes questions and answers on coastal zone management. Written by the National Ocean Industries Association.

Audiovisuals:

Filmographies, Sales Lists, etc.

"Films from NOAA." 11p. free.
   Describes films produced by the National Oceanic and Atmospheric Administration that are available on free loan from a distributor.

Individual Audiovisuals

"It's Your Coast." 1976. 28 minutes. 16mm. color. free loan.
   Shows scenes of various places highlighting coastal zone problems. Discusses land development, oil pollution and beach erosion. Order from: Modern Talking Pictures, 5000 Park St. North, St. Petersburg, FL 33709.

OFFICE OF PRESIDENTIAL LIBRARIES
General Services Administration (NL)
Washington, DC 20408
(202) 523-3212

Date Established: 1955

Objectives of the Agency: Provide archival and museum complexes dedicated to a recent American President located in an area associated with his life; and preserve and make available materials relating to the history of the contemporary American presidency.

Curriculum: History, library

Subjects: Library science
            Presidents—U.S.

Locations:

Herbert Hoover Library
Parkside Drive
P.O. Box 488
West Branch, IA 52358
(319) 643-5301

Franklin D. Roosevelt Library
259 Albany Post Rd.
Hyde Park, NY 12538
(914) 229-8114

Harry S. Truman Library
Independence, MO 64050
(816) 833-1400

Dwight D. Eisenhower Library
Abilene, KS 67410
(913) 263-4751

John F. Kennedy Library
Columbia Point
Boston, MA 02125
(617) 929-4500

Lyndon Baines Johnson Library
2313 Red River St.
Austin, TX 78705
(512) 482-5137

Gerald R. Ford Library
1000 Beal Ave.
Ann Arbor, MI 48109
(313) 668-2218

Gerald R. Ford Museum
303 Pearl St., NW
Grand Rapids, MI 49504
(616) 456-2675

Nixon Presidential Materials Project
Office of Presidential Libraries
National Archives (NLN)
Washington, DC 20408
(703) 756-6498

Carter Presidential Materials Project
77 Forsyth St., SW
Atlanta, GA 30303
(404) 221-3942

Publications: Pamphlets on the various presidential libraries.

Selected List of Books and Pamphlets

"Draft of a Brochure on Presidential Libraries." 1985. 13p. free.

Discusses history, administration, holdings, uses, archival research programs, and the future of the presidential libraries.

"The Dwight D. Eisenhower Library." n.d. 8p. free.

Explains the history, development, attractions, hours, and fees of the library. Map.

"The Franklin D. Roosevelt Library and Museum." n.d. 4p. free.

Describes the library and museum, the first of the presidential libraries and museums. Includes photographs of exhibits and information about hours and admission charges.

"The Gerald R. Ford Library and Museum. n.d. 8p. free.

Describes the only presidential library and museum that is in two separate sites, Ann Arbor and Grand Rapids, Michigan. Illustrations.

"The Harry S. Truman Library and Museum." n.d. 4p. free.

Includes map, admission information, photographs, and summary of attractions.

"The Herbert Hoover Presidential Library and Museum." n.d. 16p. free.

Includes photographs, map, a description of Hoover's life, holdings of the library, and museum hours.

"John Fitzgerald Kennedy Library." n.d. 6p. free.

Gives floor plans of entrance level and exhibit level and attractions. Includes directions and map for reaching the library.

"Lyndon Baines Johnson Library and Museum." n.d. 12p. free.

Includes photographs, attractions, map, and the location of the LBJ Library on the University of Texas campus in Austin.

Special Services: Each library publishes a free list of its archival holdings for the use of researchers. It is not a detailed finding aid, but it does give a general idea of the types of historical materials available. If you want a list of holdings, write to the appropriate library.

OFFICE OF SCIENTIFIC AND TECHNICAL INFORMATION
U.S. Department of Energy
P.O. Box 62
Oak Ridge, TN 37831
(615) 576-1305

Date Established: 1977

Objectives of the Agency: Provide information on energy.

Curriculum: Consumer education

Subjects: Energy conservation

Publications: Pamphlets. Curriculum aids. Serials. Manuals. Books. Monographs.

Bibliographies, Sales Catalogs, Publications Lists, etc.

"Selected Publications Published by the Technical Information Center." Current. 8p. free.

Lists current awareness publications, energy-grams, technical progress reviews, books and monographs, DOE critical review and symposium series, technology transfer publications. Includes order form to the National Technical Information Service, U.S. Department of Commerce, Springfield, VA 22161.

Serials, Subscription Publications, etc.

Energy Research Abstracts. Semimonthly. $165.00/yr. domestic, $206.25/yr. foreign. $9.50/single copy domestic, $11.90/single copy foreign.

A comprehensive abstract journal devoted to energy-related information produced by the Department of Energy and State, federal government organizations, and foreign governments.

Selected List of Books and Pamphlets

"Guide for the Submission of Unsolicited Proposals." 1983. 29p. free. DOE/MA-0095.

Describes the policies and procedures for the preparation and submission of proposals for prospective contractors/grantees.

"How To Understand Your Utility Bill." 1980. 12p. free. DOE/PA-0010.

Gives definitions. Explains reading electric and gas meters, how to understand bills, and energy costs of home appliances.

"Ocean Energy." 1980. 4p. free. DOE/CS-0203.

Explains history, technology, current programs, future outlook of using the oceans as sources of energy.

"Solar/Renewable Energy." n.d. 19¾"x24" color poster. free.

Shows a picture of the sun and a landscape with the title and address of the technical information center to obtain more information.

236 / *Office of Scientific and Technical Information*

Audiovisuals:

Filmographies

"Film List." n.d. 1p. free.
  Gives titles and rental prices of films. Also gives address and telephone number of the National Audiovisual Center where the films may be rented.

OFFICE OF STUDENT FINANCIAL ASSISTANCE
U.S. Department of Education
Federal Student Aid Programs
Public Document Distribution Center
Pueblo, CO 81009

Date Established: 1979

Objectives of the Agency: Distribute information about student aid.

Curriculum: Guidance

Subjects: Education—finance

Locations:

CT, MA, ME, NH, RI, VT

Office of Student Financial Assistance
U.S. Department of Education
J. W. McCormack Post Office and Court House
Room 510
Boston, MA 02109
(617) 223-6895

CZ, NJ, NY, PR, VI

Office of Student Financial Assistance
U.S. Department of Education
26 Federal Plaza
Room 3954
New York, NY 10278
(212) 264-4426

DC, DE, MD, PA, VA, WV

Office of Student Financial Assistance
U.S. Department of Education
3535 Market St.
P.O. Box 13716
Philadelphia, PA 19101
(215) 596-0247

AL, FL, GA, KY, MS, NC, SC, TN

Office of Student Financial Assistance
U.S. Department of Education
101 Marietta Tower
Room 42223
Atlanta, GA 30323
(404) 221-4171

IL, IN, MI, MN, OH, WI

Office of Student Financial Assistance
U.S. Department of Education
300 S. Wacker Dr.
Chicago, IL 60606
(312) 353-8942

AR, LA, NM, OK, TX

Office of Student Financial Assistance
U.S. Department of Education
1200 Main Tower Bldg.
Room 1645
Dallas, TX 75202
(214) 767-3811

IA, KS, MO, NE

Office of Student Financial Assistance
U.S. Department of Education
324 E. Eleventh St.
Ninth Floor
Kansas City, MO 64106
(816) 374-3136

CO, MT, ND, SD, UT, WY

Office of Student Financial Assistance
U.S. Department of Education
Federal Office Bldg.
1961 Stout St.
Third Floor
Denver, CO 80294
(303) 844-3676

AS, AZ, CA, GU, HI, NV, Trust Territory of the Pacific Islands, Wake Island

Office of Student Financial Assistance
U.S. Department of Education
50 United Nations Plaza
San Francisco, CA 94102
(415) 556-0137

AK, ID, OR, WA

Office of Student Financial Assistance
U.S. Department of Education
Third and Broad Bldg.
2901 Third Ave.
Mail Stop 102
Seattle, WA 98121
(206) 442-4027

Publications: Guides to federal student aid programs.

Selected List of Books and Pamphlets

"The Student Guide." Current. 44p. free.
  Gives information about Pell Grants, loans, and other financial aid programs. Includes addresses of state sources on guaranteed student loans and state student aid.

OFFICE OF TECHNOLOGY ASSESSMENT
Congress of the United States
600 Pennsylvania Ave., SE
Washington, DC 20510
(202) 224-8996

Date Established: 1972

Objectives of the Agency: Help Congress anticipate and plan for the consequences of technology.

Curriculum: Government

Subjects: Current events
Technology

Publications: Catalogs. Reports. Technical memoranda. Background papers. Case studies. Workshop proceedings. On such topics as the technological aspects of energy, food, oceans, etc.

Bibliographies, Sales Catalogs, Publications Lists, etc.

"Assessment Activities." Current. 43p. free. OTA-PC-105.

Lists recent publications, publications in press, current projects, and selected publications of interest.

"List of Publications." 1985. 53p. free. OTA-P-58.

Lists what is available in publications. Arranged by subjects: *Energy & Materials; Industry, Technology & Employment; International Security & Commerce; Biological Applications; Food & Renewable Resources; Health; Communication & Information Technologies; Oceans & Environment;* and *Science, Transportation & Innovation.* Most publications for sale from the Government Printing Office and/or the National Technical Information Service. Provides order blanks. Index.

Selected List of Books and Pamphlets

"What OTA Is What OTA Does How OTA Works." 1985. 15p. free. OTA-PC 104.

Provides organization chart, functions, selected publications of interest.

OFFICE OF TERRITORIAL AND INTERNATIONAL AFFAIRS
Department of the Interior
Washington, DC 20240
(202) 343-4822

Date Established: 1980

Objectives of the Agency: Promote the economic, social, political development of the U.S. territories.

Curriculum: Social studies

Subjects: U.S. — colonies

Publications: Pamphlets about history, government, geography and related information about U.S. territories.

Selected List of Books and Pamphlets

"Territorial Areas Administered by the United States." n.d. 21p. free.

Describes territories briefly. Glossary of political terms and oceanographic terms. Includes addresses of sources of more information. Maps.

OFFICE OF THE FEDERAL REGISTER
National Archives and Record Service
Washington, DC 20408
(202) 523-5240

Date Established: 1935

Objectives of the Agency: Place documents on public inspection; publish agency documents in the daily *Federal Register;* and codify general and permanent regulations in *Code of Federal Regulations,* and other publications.

Curriculum: Library

Subjects: Government publications

Publications: Indexes. Serials. Microfiche. Microfilm. Papers. Books. On government regulations, acts of Congress, presidential proclamations and executive orders as well as speeches and other messages and other government publications.

Bibliographies, Sales Catalogs, Publications Lists, etc.

"Code of Federal Regulations." Current. 6p. free.

Tells what the code is, purpose of the code, and how it is organized. Includes ordering information.

"Federal Register." Current. 6p. free.

Explains what the register is and its organization of information. Includes order form.

"Office of the Federal Register Publications." Current. 8p. free.

Describes available publications and ordering information.

"Public Papers of the Presidents." Current. 4p. free.

Explains what the papers are and what volumes are currently available (beginning with 1929). Provides order form.

"The United States Government Manual." Current. 2p. free.

Tells what the manual contains and how to order.

"The Weekly Compilation of Presidential Documents." Current. 2p. free.

Tells what the documents contain and how it is organized. Includes order form.

"Would You Like To Know . . ." Current. 2p. free.

Gives information about "LSA" (List of CFR Sections Affected), and "Federal Register Index." "LSA" is designed to direct users of the *Code of Federal Regulations* to amendatory actions published in the *Federal Register.* It is issued monthly in cumulative form. The "Index" covering the contents of the daily *Federal Register,* is issued monthly in cumulative form.

Selected List of Books and Pamphlets

"The Federal Register: What It Is and How To Use It." n.d. 4p. free.
Gives background information beginning with its history.

OFFICE OF THE LAW LIBRARIAN
Library of Congress
James Madison Memorial Bldg.
Law Library
Room 240
Washington, DC 20540
(202) 287-9838

Date Established: 1832

Objectives of the Agency: Be the foreign law research arm of Congress; and provide American law reference and foreign law research and reference to other branches of government and to the public.

Curriculum: Library

Subjects: Library science

Publications: Bibliographies. Pamphlets.

Bibliographies, Sales Catalogs, Publications Lists, etc.

"Law Library Publications." Current. 6p. free.
Lists foreign and American publications for sale and free. Provides order form for publications and order form for photoduplication to the Library of Congress.

"U.S. Consumer Protection Articles." Current. 45p. free.
Provides CRS bibliographic citation file.

"U.S. Consumer Protection Books." Current. 10p. free.
Prints the Library of Congress computerized catalog on the subject.

Selected List of Books and Pamphlets

"How To Prepare a Legislative History." 1978. 45p. free.
Explains the activity before legislation is introduced, how proposals may originate, forms of legislation, and reference materials.

"Services of the Law Library of the Library of Congress." 1981. 8p. free.
Explains location, collections, reading room services, public reference service, interlibrary loan, photoduplication, and other services.

Special Services: Office of the Law Librarian, Room LM240, (202) 287-5065; Processing Section, Room LM233, (202) 287-5067; American-British Law Division, Room LM235, (202) 287-5077; European Law Division, Room LM240, (202) 287-5088; Hispanic Law Division, Room LM235, (202) 287-5070; Far Eastern Law Division, Room LM235, (202) 287-5085; Near Eastern and African Law Division, Room LM240, (202) 287-5073.

OFFICE OF WOMEN IN DEVELOPMENT
Agency for International Development
320 Twenty-First St., NW
Room 3243 New State
Washington, DC 20523
(202) 632-1772

Date Established: 1974

Objectives of the Agency: Promote and support policies and activities which would integrate women into the main economies of developing nations; and raise their income, status, productivity, and self-sufficiency.

Curriculum: Women's studies

Subjects: Women

Publications: Pamphlets. Policy papers. Policy determinations. Chartbooks. Serials. Reports.

Serials, Subscription Publications, etc.

"Horizons." Current. 44p. free.
Reports news in the field of international development for women.

Selected List of Books and Pamphlets

"A.I.D. Policy Paper: Women in Development." 1982. 12p. free.
Provides policy summary, resources, work, and productivity of women in developing countries. Includes implementation of policy.

"An Introduction to the Office of Women in Development." n.d. 8p. free.
Explains services and functions performed by the Office of Women in Development.

"Women in Development: The First Decade 1975-1984." 1985. 59p. free.
Reprints a report to the Committee on Foreign Relations U.S. Senate and the Committee on Foreign Affairs U.S. House of Representatives: Progress in Agriculture, Employment, Education, Energy, and Water. Includes conclusion, recommendations, and statistical data.

"Women of the World: A Chartbook for Developing Regions." 1985. 70p. free.
Charts represent data for Latin America, Caribbean, Sub-Saharan Africa, Near East, North Africa, and Asia.

Special Services: Briefings, specialized mailings, project information, and recommendations about sources of materials and information.

OFFICE ON SMOKING AND HEALTH
Park Bldg.
5600 Fishers Lane
Room 1-58
Rockville, MD 20857
(301) 443-1575

Date Established: 1978

Objectives of the Agency: Plan, coordinate, and develop activities in public information on smoking and health; maintain a technical information center to collect, organize, and disseminate information; be a liaison with other government and nongovernment agencies; and prepare an annual Surgeon General's report.

Curriculum: Health

Subjects: Smoking

Publications: Posters. Bibliographies. Pamphlets. Bulletins. Lists. On health consequences, reasons for smoking, quitting. Some materials aimed at such groups as teenagers or pregnant women. Some available in Spanish.

Bibliographies, Sales Catalogs, Publications Lists, etc.

"Publications List." Current. 2p. free.
Lists what is available. Single copies are available free of charge. Arranged alphabetically by title.

Selected List of Books and Pamphlets

"If Your Kids Think Everybody Smokes, They Don't Know Everybody." n.d. 8p. free. (PHS) 83-50201.
Discusses why teenagers start smoking and continue to smoke, and what a parent can do.

"Now You're Smoking for Two." n.d. 8p. free. (PHS) 83-50198.
A guide to smoking and pregnancy. Discusses health concerns for the unborn child.

"Office on Smoking and Health." Current. 2p. free.
Describes functions and responsibilities of the office and its public information program.

"Smoking, Tobacco & Health." 1981. 36p. free. (PHS) 80-50150.
Gives facts, charts, and tables on the economic, social, and medical consequences of smoking.

"Why People Smoke Cigarettes." n.d. 5p. free. (PHS) 83-50195.
Discusses characteristics of dependence, role of nicotine, smoking patterns, and quitting.

PANAMA CANAL COMMISSION
2000 L St., NW
Fifth Floor
Washington, DC 20036
(202) 724-0104

Date Established: 1979

Objectives of the Agency: Manage, operate, and maintain the Canal, its complementary works, installations, and equipment to provide for smooth transit of vessels.

Curriculum: Social studies

Subjects: Panama canal
Waterways

Publications: Pamphlets. Fact sheets.

Selected List of Books and Pamphlets

"The Panama Canal." 1984. 8-fold. free.
Discusses history, physical features of the waterway, statistics, points of interest, special information, and the Panama railroad. Map. Photographs.

"Panama Canal Fact Sheet." Current. 2p. free.
Lists toll rates, booking system, maximum allowable dimensions for regular transits, traffic statistics, distances to the Panama Canal, principal commodities, and other vital facts.

"Panama Canal: The Vital Link for World Trade." n.d. 6p. free.
Shows ships going through the canal. Includes addresses for obtaining more information. Graphs. Map. Photographs.

PASSPORT SERVICES
Bureau of Consular Affairs
1425 K St., NW
Room G-62
Washington, DC 20524
(202) 783-8170

Date Established: 1856

Objectives of the Agency: Provide information on the issuance of U.S. Passports.

Curriculum: Government

Subjects: Travel

Locations:

(Twenty-four hour recordings provide general passport information, passport agency location, and hours of operation; for other questions, call public inquiries numbers.)

Boston Passport Agency
John F. Kennedy Bldg.
Government Center
Room E123
Boston, MA 02203
Recording: (617) 223-3831
Public Inquiries: (617) 223-2946

240 / Passport Services

Chicago Passport Agency
Kluczynski Federal Bldg.
230 S. Dearborn St.
Suite 380
Chicago, IL 60604
Recording: (312) 353-5426
Public Inquiries: (312) 353-7155

Honolulu Passport Agency
New Federal Bldg.
Room C-106
300 Ala Moana Blvd.
P.O. Box 50185
Honolulu, HI 96850
Recording: (808) 546-2131
Public Inquiries: (808) 546-2130

Houston Passport Agency
1 Allen Center
500 Dallas St.
Houston, TX 77002
Recording: (713) 229-3607
Public Inquiries: (713) 229-3600

Los Angeles Passport Agency
Federal Bldg.
11000 Wilshire Blvd.
Thirteenth Floor
Los Angeles, CA 90024
Recording: (213) 209-7070
Public Inquiries: (213) 209-7075

Miami Passport Agency
Federal Office Bldg.
51 S.W. First Ave.
Sixteenth Floor
Miami, FL 33130
Recording: (305) 350-5395
Public Inquiries: (305) 350-4681

New Orleans Passport Agency
International Trade Mart
2 Canal St.
Room 400
New Orleans, LA 70130
Recording: (504) 589-6728
Public Inquiries: (504) 589-6161

New York Passport Agency
Rockefeller Center
630 Fifth Ave.
Room 270
New York, NY 10111
Recording: (212) 541-7700
Public Inquiries: (212) 541-7710

Philadelphia Passport Agency
Federal Bldg.
600 Arch St.
Room 4426
Philadelphia, PA 19106
Recording: (215) 597-7482
Public Inquiries: (215) 597-7480

San Francisco Passport Agency
525 Market St.
Suite 200
San Francisco, CA 94105
Recording: (415) 974-7972
Public Inquiries: (415) 974-9941

Seattle Passport Agency
Federal Bldg.
915 Second Ave.
Room 992
Seattle, WA 98174
Recording: (206) 442-7941
Public Inquiries: (206) 442-7945

Stamford Passport Agency
1 Landmark Square
Street Level
Stamford, CT 06901
Recording: (203) 325-4401
Public Inquiries: (203) 325-3538

Washington Passport Agency
1425 K St., NW
Washington, DC 20524
Recording: (202) 783-8200
Public Inquiries: (202) 783-8170

Publications: Passport applications. Notices. Pamphlets.

Selected List of Books and Pamphlets

"Passport Application." Current. 2p. free.
Gives form and instructions.

"Your Trip Abroad." Rev. 32p. free. Department of State Publication 8872, Department and Foreign Series 155.
Gives tips for before leaving on your trip, while you are overseas, and when you return. Includes sources of additional information. Designed to help prepare for a trouble-free trip.

PATENT AND TRADEMARK OFFICE
U.S. Department of Commerce
Washington, DC 20231
(703) 557-3428

Date Established: 1949

Objectives of the Agency: Examine applications for design patents, plant patents, and utility patents; process international applications for patents under the provisions of the Patent Cooperation Treaty. Besides the examination of patent and trademark applications, issuance of patents and registration of trademarks, the agency sells documents, records and indexes documents transferring ownership, and participates in legal proceedings involving the issue of patents or trademark registrations.

Curriculum: Business

Subjects: Patents
Trademarks

Publications: Indexes. Guides. Manuals. Pamphlets. Serials. Codes.

Bibliographies, Sales Catalogs, Publications Lists, etc.

"Patent and Trademark Publications." 1983. 2p. free.

Gives description and ordering information for publications available from the Superintendent of Documents and the Patent and Trademark Office.

Serials, Subscription Publications, Etc.

Patent Official Gazette. Weekly. $250.00/yr. domestic, $312.00/yr. foreign; $7.50/single copy domestic.

The official journal of the Patent and Trademark Office relating to patents. Contains a selected figure of the drawings and an abstract of patents granted, indexes of patents, and related information.

Trademark Official Gazette. Weekly. $205.00/yr. domestic, $256.25/yr. foreign; $5.00/single copy domestic, $6.25/single copy foreign.

The official journal of the Patent and Trademark Office relating to trademarks. Contains an illustration of trademarks published for opposition, a list of those registered, and related information.

Selected List of Books and Pamphlets

"Q & A about Patents." n.d. free.

Gives general information to answer commonly asked questions about patents.

"Q & A about Plant Patents." n.d. free.

Gives general information to answer commonly asked questions about plant patents.

"Q & A about Trademarks." n.d. free.

Gives general information to answer questions commonly asked about trademarks.

Library: Scientific library and search files of over 25 million documents. Provides search rooms for the public to research their applications.

THE PRESIDENT'S COMMITTEE ON EMPLOYMENT OF THE HANDICAPPED
1111 Twentieth St., NW
Washington, DC 20036
(202) 653-5044

Date Established: 1947

Objectives of the Agency: Promote a positive climate of opinion in America leading to full acceptance of physically and mentally handicapped people in the world of work; and strive to eliminate environmental and attitudinal barriers against their chances and progress.

Curriculum: Special education

Subjects: Handicapped

Locations:

AK
Governor's Committee on Employment of the Handicapped
P.O. Box 346
Bethel, AK 99559

AL
Governor's Committee on Employment of the Handicapped
2129 E. South Blvd.
P.O. Box 11586
Montgomery, AL 36111

AR
Governor's Committee on Employment of the Handicapped
P.O. Box 2981
Little Rock, AR 72203

AZ
Governor's Committee on Employment of the Handicapped
1400 W. Washington St.
Room 229
P.O. Box 6123
Phoenix, AZ 85007

CA
Governor's Committee on Employment of the Handicapped
800 Capitol Mall
Room 5054
Sacramento, CA 95814

CO
Governor's Committee on Employment of the Handicapped
1313 Sherman St.
Room 420
Denver, CO 80203

CT
Governor's Committee on Employment of the Handicapped
Department of Labor Bldg.
Wethersfield, CT 06109

DC
Governor's Committee on Employment of the Handicapped
122 C. St., NW
Room 205-A
Washington, DC 20001

DE
Governor's Committee on Employment of the Handicapped
State Office Bldg.
820 French St.
Seventh Floor
Wilmington, DE 19801

FL
Governor's Committee on Employment of the Handicapped
Madison St.
204 Caldwell Bldg.
Tallahassee, FL 32304

GA
Governor's Committee on Employment of the Handicapped
1599 Memorial Dr., SE
Atlanta, GA 30317

HI
Governor's Committee on Employment of the Handicapped
250 S. King St.
Room 602
Honolulu, HI 96813

IA
Governor's Committee on Employment of the Handicapped
Grimes State Office Bldg.
Des Moines, IA 50319

ID
Governor's Committee on Employment of the Handicapped
P.O. Box 35
Boise, ID 83735

IL
Governor's Committee on Employment of the Handicapped
623 E. Adams St.
Springfield, IL 62706

IN
Governor's Committee on Employment of the Handicapped
1330 W. Michigan St.
Indianapolis, IN 46206

KS
Governor's Committee on Employment of the Handicapped
126 South, State Office Bldg.
Topeka, KS 66612

KY
Governor's Committee on Employment of the Handicapped
600 W. Cedar St.
Louisville, KY 40203

LA
Governor's Committee on Employment of the Handicapped
530 Lakeland Dr.
Baton Rouge, LA 70802

MA
Governor's Committee on Employment of the Handicapped
Government Center
Staniford and Cambridge Sts.
Boston, MA 02114

MD
Governor's Committee on Employment of the Handicapped
2100 Guilford Ave.
Baltimore, MD 21218

ME
Governor's Committee on Employment of the Handicapped
32 Winthrop St.
Augusta, ME 04330

MI
Governor's Committee on Employment of the Handicapped
Box 30015
309 Washington Ave.
Lansing, MI 48909

MN
Governor's Committee on Employment of the Handicapped
Seventh and Roberts Sts.
St. Paul, MN 55101

MO
Governor's Committee on Employment of the Handicapped
1411 Main St.
Kansas City, MO 64105

MS
Governor's Committee on Employment of the Handicapped
416 N. State St.
Suite 5
Jackson, MS 39201

MT
Governor's Committee on Employment of the Handicapped
Capitol Bldg.
35 S. Last Chance Gulch
P.O. Box 169
Helena, MT 59601

NC
Governor's Committee on Employment of the Handicapped
116 W. Jones St.
Raleigh, NC 27611

ND
Governor's Committee on Employment of the Handicapped
State Capitol
Thirteenth Floor
Bismarck, ND 58505

NE
Governor's Committee on Employment of the Handicapped
301 Centennial Mall
S. Sixth Floor
Lincoln, NE 68509

NH
Governor's Committee on Employment of the Handicapped
6 Loudon Rd.
Concord, NH 03301

NJ
Governor's Committee on Employment of the Handicapped
P.O. Box 208
Trenton, NJ 08625

NM
Governor's Committee on Employment of the Handicapped
P.O. Box 1830
Santa Fe, NM 87503

NV
Governor's Committee on Employment of the Handicapped
505 King St.
Room 502
Carson City, NV 89710

NY
Governor's Committee on Employment of the Handicapped
2 World Trade Center
Room 3712
New York, NY 10047

OH
Governor's Committee on Employment of the Handicapped
4656 Heaton Rd.
Columbus, OH 43214

OK
Governor's Committee on Employment of the Handicapped
301 Will Rogers Bldg.
Oklahoma City, OK 73105

OR
Governor's Committee on Employment of the Handicapped
875 Union, NE
Salem, OR 97311

PA
Governor's Committee on Employment of the Handicapped
1306 Labor and Industry Bldg.
Seventh and Forster Sts.
Harrisburg, PA 17120

PR
Governor's Committee on Employment of the Handicapped
G.P.O. Box 2554
San Juan, PR 00936

RI
Governor's Committee on Employment of the Handicapped
150 Washington St.
Providence, RI 02903

SC
Governor's Committee on Employment of the Handicapped
1550 Gadsen St.
P.O. Box 1406
Columbia, SC 29202

SD
Governor's Committee on Employment of the Handicapped
Richard F. Kneip Bldg.
Illinois St.
Second Floor
Pierre, SD 57401

TN
Governor's Committee on Employment of the Handicapped
1808 West End Ave.
Room 424
Nashville, TN 37203

TX

Governor's Committee on Employment of the Handicapped
118 E. Riverside Dr.
Austin, TX 78704

UT

Governor's Committee on Employment of the Handicapped
250 East, 500 South
Salt Lake City, UT 84111

VA

State Vocational Rehabilitation Office
4615 W. Broad St.
P.O. Box 11045
Richmond, VA 23230

VI

Governor's Committee on Employment of the Handicapped
P.O. Box 539
St. Thomas, VI 00801

VT

Governor's Committee on Employment of the Handicapped
P.O. Box 504
Waterbury, VT 05676

WA

Governor's Committee on Employment of the Handicapped
Employment Security Bldg.
Olympia, WA 98504

WI

Governor's Committee on Employment of the Handicapped
1 S. Park St.
Fifth Floor
Madison, WI 53715

WV

Governor's Committee on Employment of the Handicapped
4407 MacCorkle Ave., SE
Charleston, WV 25304

WY

Governor's Committee on Employment of the Handicapped
Hathaway Bldg.
Room 317
Cheyenne, WY 82002

Publications: Pamphlets. Fact sheets. Directories. On affirmative action for disabled, mentally retarded, physically handicapped, and mentally restored in the work world.

Selected List of Books and Pamphlets

"Affirmative Action for Disabled People." 1983. 12p. free.
  Gives suggestions for employers and handicapped persons to make affirmative action and non-discrimination programs effective.

"Affirmative Action To Employ Mentally Retarded People." n.d. 20p. free.
  A pocket guide on Sections 503 and 504 of the Rehabilitation Act of 1973. Includes addresses of state contacts for: Association for Retarded Citizens, State Vocational Rehabilitation Office and the Governor's Committee on Employment of the Handicapped.

"Fact Sheet: The President's Committee on Employment of the Handicapped." 1981. 2p. free.
  Describes background, standing committees, major activities, trends, and achievements.

Membership Directory. 1984. 105p. free.
  Lists names and addresses of executive committee members, associate members, advisory council, president's committee, and other members.

THE PRESIDENT'S COUNCIL ON PHYSICAL FITNESS AND SPORTS

Judiciary Plaza Bldg.
450 Fifth St.
Room 7103
Washington, DC 20001
(202) 272-3421

Date Established: 1968

Objectives of the Agency: Promote physical fitness through exercise.

Curriculum: Health, physical education

Subjects: Physical fitness

Publications: Pamphlets. Lists.

Bibliographies, Sales Catalogs, Publications Lists, etc.

"American Alliance Publications and Audiovisuals Catalog." Current. 24p. free.
  Describes materials for health, physical education, recreation, and dance for sale from the American Alliance. Includes materials such as manuals, awards, caps, directories, and patches, for youth fitness programs. Audiovisuals (16mm films, video cassettes, slides-cassettes) for purchase or rental.

"Publications List." n.d. 4p. free.
Gives description and ordering information for various publications. Some prices are given per 100 copies.

Selected List of Books and Pamphlets

"Exercise and Weight Control." 1979. 5-fold. $2.25/single copy, $13.00/hundred copies. S/N 040-000-00371-1.
Gives tips on exercise, weight control fallacies, advantages of exercise, and importance of diet. Includes chart of activities and gross energy cost in calories per hour.

"An Introduction to Running: One Step at a Time." n.d. 20p. $2.75. S/N 017-001-00425-1.
A handbook for beginning runners. Includes tips on pace, form, clothing with illustrated stretching exercises. Running log.

SAINT LAWRENCE SEAWAY DEVELOPMENT CORPORATION
Operations Headquarters
180 Andrews St.
P.O. Box 520
Massena, NY 13662
(315) 764-3233

Date Established: 1954

Objectives of the Agency: Operate and maintain that part of the seaway between Montreal and Lake Erie, within the territorial limits of the United States, and develop the full seaway system from the western tip of Lake Superior to the Atlantic Ocean.

Curriculum: Geography

Subjects: Waterways

Locations:
Saint Lawrence Seaway Development Corporation
Policy Headquarters
400 Seventh St., SW
Room 5424
Washington, DC 20590
(202) 426-3574

Publications: Fact sheets. Reports. Pamphlets.

Selected List of Books and Pamphlets

"Annual Report." Current. 20p. free.
Relates activities, progress, statistics, and a financial review. Tables. Graph. Photographs.

"Chronology of Selected Significant Dates." Current. 10p. free.
Begins with 1798 with the establishment of the first Great Lakes lighthouse and includes such dates as 1855 when the first lock at Sault Ste. Marie was built. Includes 2-page summary.

"Geography of the Great Lakes." n.d. 1p. free.
A fact sheet about the statistics of various Great Lakes and the lakes as a group.

"The St. Lawrence Seaway." n.d. 16p. free.
Surveys seaway shipping, statistics, and history. Tables. Map. Photographs.

"Seaway Distances: Atlantic to Lake Ontario." n.d. 4p. free.
Gives statistics about the seaway. Maps. Table.

SALEM MARITIME NATIONAL HISTORIC SITE
National Park Service
Custom House
Derby St.
Salem, MA 01970

Date Established: 1938

Objectives of the Agency: Preserve the site of the wharves of Salem, the waterfront area buildings vital in the commercial shipping in early U.S. economy.

Curriculum: History

Subjects: Shipping—U.S.

Publications: Flyers about the historic site.

Selected List of Books and Pamphlets

"Customs and Salem." n.d. 2p. free.
Examines the U.S. Customs Service, Customs Service employees, clearing a ship, the Salem Custom House.

"Salem Maritime." 1984. 12-fold. free.
Discusses Salem's trade empire, shipping routes, cargo, ship owners, and related information. Photographs. Illustrations.

SECURITIES AND EXCHANGE COMMISSION
Office of Public Affairs
450 Fifth St., NW
Washington, DC 20549
(202) 272-2650

Date Established: 1934

Objectives of the Agency: Provide disclosure to the investing public; and protect the interests of the public and investors against malpractices in the securities and financial markets.

Curriculum: Consumer education

Subjects: Finance—U.S.
Securities

Locations:

NJ, NY

U.S. Securities and Exchange Commission
New York Regional Office
26 Federal Plaza
New York, NY 10278
(212) 264-1636

CT, MA, ME, NH, RI, VT

U.S. Securities and Exchange Commission
Boston Regional Office
150 Causeway St.
Boston, MA 02144
(617) 223-2721

AL, FL, GA, LA (east of the Atchafalaya River), MS, NC, PR, SC, TN, VI

U.S. Securities and Exchange Commission
Atlanta Regional Office
1375 Peachtree St., NE
Suite 788
Atlanta, GA 30367
(404) 881-4768

U.S. Securities and Exchange Commission
Miami Branch Office
Dupont Plaza Center
300 Biscayne Blvd.
Suite 1114
Miami, FL 33131
(305) 350-5765

IA, IL, IN, KY, MI, MN, MO, OH, WI

U.S. Securities and Exchange Commission
Chicago Regional Office
Everett McKinley Dirksen Bldg.
219 S. Dearborn St.
Room 1204
Chicago, IL 60604
(312) 353-7390

U.S. Securities and Exchange Commission
Detroit and Branch Office
1044 Federal Bldg.
Detroit, MI 48226
(313) 226-6070

AR, KS, LA (west of the Atchafalaya River), OK, TX

U.S. Securities and Exchange Commission
Fort Worth Regional Office
411 W. Seventh St.
Fort Worth, TX 76102
(817) 334-3821

U.S. Securities and Exchange Commission
Houston Branch Office
Scanlon Bldg.
405 Main St.
Houston, TX 77002
(713) 226-2775

CO, ND, NE, NM, SD, UT, WY

U.S. Securities and Exchange Commission
Denver Regional Office
410 Seventeenth St.
Suite 700
Denver, CO 80202
(303) 837-2071

U.S. Securities and Exchange Commission
Salt Lake Branch Office
Boston Bldg.
1 Exchange Place
Suite 810
Salt Lake City, UT 84111

AZ, CA, HI, GU, NV

U.S. Securities and Exchange Commission
Los Angeles Regional Office
10960 Wilshire Blvd.
Suite 1710
Los Angeles, CA 90024
(213) 473-4511

U.S. Securities and Exchange Commission
San Francisco Branch Office
450 Golden Gate Ave.
Box 36042
San Francisco, CA 94102

AK, ID, MT, OR, WA

U.S. Securities and Exchange Commission
Seattle Regional Office
3040 Federal Bldg.
915 Second Ave.
Seattle, WA 98174
(206) 442-7990

DC, DE, MD, PA, VA, WV

U.S. Securities and Exchange Commission
Washington Regional Office
Ballston Center Tower 3
4015 Wilson Blvd.
Arlington, VA 22203
(703) 557-8201

U.S. Securities and Exchange Commission
Philadelphia Branch Office
William J. Green, Jr. Federal Bldg.
600 Arch St.
Room 2204
Philadelphia, PA 19106
(215) 597-3100

Publications: Serials. Books. Reports. Directories. Pamphlets. Statutes.

Bibliographies, Sales Catalogs, Publications Lists, etc.

"SEC Publications." Current. 8p. free.

Lists materials for sale or free from the Exchange or the Superintendent of Documents. Provides order form.

Serials, Subscription Publications, etc.

Official Summary. Monthly. $59.00/yr. domestic, $73.75/yr. foreign; $6.00/single copy domestic, $7.50/single copy foreign.

Summarizes security transactions and holdings by those associated with the SEC.

Selected List of Books and Pamphlets

"Consumers Should Know." n.d. 8p. free.

Explains how investors may obtain consumer aid. Includes addresses of sources of other financial information.

"Investigate Before You Invest." n.d. 11p. free.

Provides brief information for the possible investor about the intricacies of investing.

"What Every Investor Should Know." 1982. 44p. free.

Discusses the securities markets, how investors are protected, types of investments, how to choose an investment, trading stocks and bonds, and other consumer information. Glossary.

"The Work of the SEC." 1984. 32p. free.

Examines the Securities Act of 1933, Securities Exchange Act of 1934, Public Utility Holding Company Act of 1935, and other acts. Includes information about the workings of the SEC.

Individual Audiovisuals

"Eagle on the Street." 22 minutes. videotape or 16mm. $235.00 purchase of film; $30.00 3 days rental; $90.00 for a video cassette made from the film. A03778.

Gives an overview of the securities markets, the history of the SEC, and how the commission functions today. Order from: National Audiovisual Center (GSA), Attn: Order Section, 8700 Edgeworth Dr., Capital Heights, MD 20743-3702. (202) 763-1896. Specify the desired audiovisual format.

Special Services: Registration statements, reports, applications, and other similar documents filed with the commission are available for inspection in the Public Reference Room of the commission's office headquarters in Washington, DC. For cost estimates of copies, write:
Public Reference Room
Securities and Exchange Commission
450 Fifth Avenue, NW
Washington, DC 20549
(202) 272-7460

SMALL BUSINESS ADMINISTRATION
1441 L St., NW
Washington, DC 20416
(202) 653-6565

Date Established: 1953

Objectives of the Agency: Aid, counsel, and protect the interests of small business.

Curriculum: Business

Subjects: Business

Locations:

AK

Small Business Administration Field Office
101 Twelfth Ave.
Box 14
Fairbanks, AK
(907) 456-0211

AL

Small Business Administration Field Office
908 S. Twentieth St.
Birmingham, AL 35256
(205) 254-1344

AR

Small Business Administration Field Office
320 W. Capitol Ave.
Suite 601
Little Rock, AR 72201
(501) 378-5871

AZ

Small Business Administration Field Office
3030 N. Central Ave.
Suite 1201
Phoenix, AZ 85012
(602) 241-2206

Small Business Administration Field Office
Federal Bldg.
301 W. Congress St.
Box 33
Tucson, AZ 85701
(602) 792-6715

CA

Small Business Administration Field Office
2202 Monterey St.
Fresno, CA 93721
(209) 487-5791

Small Business Administration Field Office
660 J St.
Suite 215
Sacramento, CA 95814
(916) 440-2956

Small Business Administration Field Office
880 Front St.
Room 4-S-29
San Diego, CA 92188
(714) 293-5444

Small Business Administration Regional Office
450 Golden Gate Ave.
Box 36044
San Francisco, CA 94102
(415) 556-7487

Small Business Administration Field Office
211 Main St.
Fourth Floor
San Francisco, CA 94105
(415) 974-0594

Small Business Administration Field Office
350 S. Figueroa St.
Sixth Floor
Los Angeles, CA 90071
(213) 688-2956

Small Business Administration Field Office
Fidelity Federal Bldg.
Suite 400
Santa Ana, CA 92701
(714) 836-2494

Small Business Administration Field Office
111 W. St. John St.
Room 424
San Jose, CA 95113
(408) 291-7584

CO

Small Business Administration Regional Office
Executive Tower Bldg.
1405 Curtis St.
Twenty-Second Floor
Denver, CO 80202-2395
(303) 844-5441

Small Business Administration Field Office
721 Nineteenth St.
Room 420
Denver, CO 80202-2599
(303) 844-3984

CT

Small Business Administration Field Office
1 Hartford Square West
Hartford, CT 06106
(203) 722-4041

DC

Small Business Administration Field Office
1111 Eighteenth St., NW
Sixth Floor
Washington, DC 20036
(202) 634-1818

DE

Small Business Administration Field Office
844 King St.
Lockbox 16
Room 5207
Wilmington, DE 19801
(302) 573-6294

FL

Small Business Administration Field Office
400 W. Bay St.
Room 261
P.O. Box 35067
Jacksonville, FL 32202
(904) 791-3782

Small Business Administration Field Office
2222 Ponce de Leon Blvd.
Fifth Floor
Coral Gables, FL 33134
(305) 350-5521

Small Business Administration Field Office
700 Twiggs St.
Suite 607
Tampa, FL 33602
(813) 228-2594

Small Business Administration Field Office
3500 Forty-Fifth St.
Suite 6
West Palm Beach, FL 33407
(305) 689-2223

GA

Small Business Administration Field Office
Federal Bldg.
52 N. Main St.
Room 225
Statesboro, GA 30458
(912) 489-8719

Small Business Administration Regional Office
1375 Peachtree St., NE
Fifth Floor
Atlanta, GA 30367
(404) 881-4948

Small Business Administration Field Office
1720 Peachtree St., NW
Sixth Floor
Atlanta, GA 30309
(404) 881-4325

GU

Small Business Administration Field Office
Pacific News Bldg.
238 O'Hara St.
Room 508
Agana, GU 96910
(671) 472-7277

HI

Small Business Administration Field Office
300 Ala Moana Blvd.
Room 2213
P.O. Box 50207
Honolulu, HI 96850
(808) 546-8950

IA

Small Business Administration Field Office
210 Walnut St.
Des Moines, IA 50309
(515) 284-4567

Small Business Administration Field Office
373 Collins Rd., NE
Cedar Rapids, IA 52402
(319) 399-2571

ID

Small Business Administration Field Office
1020 Main St.
Second Floor
Boise, ID 83702
(208) 334-1096

IL

Small Business Administration Regional Office
230 S. Dearborn St.
Room 510
Chicago, IL 60604
(312) 353-4542

Small Business Administration Field Office
219 S. Dearborn St.
Room 437
Chicago, IL 60604
(312) 353-4528

Small Business Administration Field Office
Washington, Bldg.
4 N. Old State
Capitol Plaza
Springfield, IL 62701
(217) 492-4416

IN

Small Business Administration Field Office
River Glen Office Plaza
Suite 160
South Bend, IN 46601
(219) 236-8361

Small Business Administration Field Office
New Federal Bldg.
575 N. Pennsylvania St.
Fifth Floor
Indianapolis, IN 46204-1584
(317) 269-7278

KS

Small Business Administration Field Office
Main Place Bldg.
110 E. Waterman St.
Wichita, KS 67202
(316) 269-6273

KY

Small Business Administration Field Office
Federal Office Bldg.
Room 188
P.O. Box 3517
Louisville, KY 40201
(502) 582-5971

LA

Small Business Administration Field Office
Ford-Fisk Bldg.
1661 Canal St.
Second Floor
New Orleans, LA 70112
(504) 589-6685

Small Business Administration Field Office
500 Fannin St.
Federal Bldg. and Courthouse
Room 5 B04
Shreveport, LA 71101
(318) 226-5196

MA

Small Business Administration Regional Office
60 Batterymarch St.
Tenth Floor
Boston, MA 02110
(617) 223-1005

Small Business Administration Field Office
150 Causeway St.
Tenth Floor
Boston, MA 02114
(617) 223-7991

Small Business Administration Field Office
Federal Bldg. and Courthouse
1550 Main St.
Room 212
Springfield, MA 01103
(413) 785-0268

MD

Small Business Administration Field Office
8600 LaSalle Rd.
Room 630
Towson, MD 21204
(301) 962-2233

ME

Small Business Administration Field Office
40 Western Ave.
Room 512
Augusta, ME 04330
(207) 622-8378

MI

Small Business Administration Field Office
McNamara Bldg.
477 Michigan Ave.
Room 515
Detroit, MI 48226
(313) 226-6075

Small Business Administration Field Office
220 W. Washington St.
Suite 310
Marquette, MI 49885
(906) 225-1108

MN

Small Business Administration Field Office
610-C Butler Square
100 N. Sixth St.
Minneapolis, MN 55403
(612) 349-3574

MO

Small Business Administration Regional Office
911 Walnut St.
Thirteenth Floor
Kansas City, MO 64106
(816) 374-3316

Small Business Administration Field Office
1103 Grand Ave.
Sixth Floor
Kansas City, MO 64106
(816) 374-5557

Small Business Administration Field Office
815 Olive St.
Room 242
St. Louis, MO 63101
(314) 425-6600

Small Business Administration Field Office
339 Broadway
Room 140
Cape Giradeau, MO 63701
(314) 335-6039

Small Business Administration Field Office
309 N. Jefferson
Springfield, MO 65806
(417) 864-7670

MS

Small Business Administration Field Office
Gulf National Life Insurance Bldg.
111 Fred Haise Blvd.
Second Floor
Biloxi, MS 39530
(601) 435-3676

Small Business Administration Field Office
Federal Bldg.
100 W. Capitol St.
Suite 322
Jackson, MS 39269
(601) 960-4371
(601) 960-4372

MT

Small Business Administration Field Office
301 S. Park Ave.
Room 528
Drawer 10054
Helena, MT 59626
(406) 449-5381

Small Business Administration Field Office
Billings Post-of-Duty
Post Office Bldg.
2601 First Ave. North
Room 216
Billings, MT 59101
(406) 657-6047

NC

Small Business Administration Field Office
230 S. Tryon St.
Suite 700
Charlotte, NC 28202
(704) 371-6561

Small Business Administration Field Office
215 S. Evans St.
Room 102-E
Greenville, NC 27834
(919) 752-3798

ND

Small Business Administration Field Office
657 Second Ave., North
P.O. Box 3086
Fargo, ND 58102
(701) 237-5131

NE

Small Business Administration Field Office
Empire State Bldg.
Nineteenth and Farnam Sts.
Omaha, NE 68102
(402) 221-4691

NH

Small Business Administration Field Office
55 Pleasant St.
Concord, NH 03301
(603) 224-4724

NJ

Small Business Administration Field Office
1800 E. Davis St.
Camden, NJ 08104
(609) 757-5183

Small Business Administration Field Office
60 Park Place
Fourth Floor
Newark, NJ 07102
(201) 645-3683

NM

Small Business Administration Field Office
Patio Plaza Bldg.
5000 Marble Ave., NE
Albuquerque, NM 87110
(505) 766-3430

NV

Small Business Administration Field Office
Downtown Station
301 E. Stewart
Box 7527
Las Vegas, NV 89101
(702) 385-6611

Small Business Administration Field Office
50 S. Virginia St.
Room 308
P.O. Box 3216
Reno, NV 89505
(702) 784-5268

NY

Small Business Administration Regional Office
26 Federal Plaza
Room 29-118
New York, NY 10278
(212) 264-7755

Small Business Administration Field Office
445 Broadway
Room 236-A
Albany, NY 12207
(518) 472-6300

Small Business Administration Field Office
111 W. Huron St.
Room 1311
Buffalo, NY 14202
(716) 846-4301

Small Business Administration Field Office
333 E. Water St.
Room 412
Elmira, NY 14901
(607) 733-4686

Small Business Administration Field Office
35 Pinelaw Rd.
Room 102E
Melville, NY 11747
(516) 454-0764

Small Business Administration Field Office
26 Federal Plaza
Room 3100
New York, NY 10278
(212) 264-1766

Small Business Administration Field Office
100 State St.
Room 601
Rochester, NY 14614
(716) 263-6700

Small Business Administration Field Office
Federal Bldg.
100 S. Clinton St.
Room 1071
Syracuse, NY 13260
(315) 423-5382

OH

Small Business Administration Field Office
AJC Federal Bldg.
1240 E. Ninth St.
Room 317
Cleveland, OH 44199
(216) 522-4194

Small Business Administration Field Office
85 Marconi Blvd.
Room 512
Columbus, OH 43215
(614) 469-6860

Small Business Administration Field Office
550 Main St.
Room 5028
Cincinnati, OH 45202
(513) 684-2814

OK

Small Business Administration Field Office
200 N.W. Fifth St.
Suite 670
Oklahoma City, OK 73102
(405) 231-5239

Small Business Administration Field Office
333 W. Fourth St.
Room 3104
Tulsa, OK 74103
(918) 581-7495

OR

Small Business Administration Field Office
Federal Bldg.
1220 S.W. Third Ave.
Room 676
Portland, OR 97204-2882
(503) 423-5221

PA

Small Business Administration Regional Office
One Bala Cynwyd Plaza
231 St. Asaphs Rd.
Suite 640
West Lobby
Bala Cynwyd, PA 19004
(215) 596-5889

Small Business Administration Field Office
One Bala Cynwyd Plaza
Suite 400
East Lobby
Bala Cynwyd, PA 19004
(215) 596-3311

Small Business Administration Field Office
100 Chestnut St.
Room 309
Harrisburg, PA 17101
(717) 782-3840

Small Business Administration Field Office
Convention Tower
960 Penn Ave.
Fifth Floor
Pittsburgh, PA 15222
(412) 644-5441

Small Business Administration Field Office
Penn Place
20 N. Pennsylvania Ave.
Wilkes-Barre, PA 18702
(717) 826-6497

PR

Small Business Administration Field Office
Federal Bldg.
Carlos Chardon Ave.
Sixth Floor
Hato Rey, PR 00919
(809) 753-4422

RI

Small Business Administration Field Office
380 Westminster Mall
Providence, RI 02903
(401) 528-4586

SC

Small Business Administration Field Office
1835 Assembly St.
Third Floor
P.O. Box 2786
Columbia, SC 29201
(803) 765-5376

SD

Small Business Administration Field Office
101 S. Main Ave.
Suite 101
Sioux Falls, SD 57102-0577
(605) 336-2980

TN

Small Business Administration Field Office
404 James Robertson Pkwy.
Suite 1012
Nashville, TN 37219
(615) 251-5881

TX

Small Business Administration Field Office
Federal Bldg.
300 E. Eighth St.
Room 780
Austin, TX 78701
(512) 482-7811

Small Business Administration Field Office
400 Mann St.
Suite 403
P.O. Box 9253
Corpus Christi, TX 78401
(512) 888-3331

Small Business Administration Regional Office
Building C
8625 King George Dr.
Dallas, TX 75235-3391
(214) 767-7643

Small Business Administration Field Office
1100 Commerce St.
Room 3C36
Dallas, TX 75242
(214) 767-0495

Small Business Administration Field Office
10737 Gateway West
Suite 320
El Paso, TX 79902
(915) 541-7560

Small Business Administration Field Office
222 E. Van Buren St.
Suite 500
Harlingen, TX 78550
(512) 423-4533

Small Business Administration Field Office
2525 Murthworth
Houston, TX 77054
(713) 660-4409

Small Business Administration Field Office
1611 Tenth St.
Suite 200
Lubbock, TX 79401
(806) 743-7466

Small Business Administration Field Office
100 S. Washington St.
Room G-12
Marshall, TX 75670
(214) 935-5257

Small Business Administration Field Office
Federal Bldg.
727 E. Durango St.
Room A-513
San Antonio, TX 78206
(512) 229-6272

UT

Small Business Administration Field Office
125 S. State St.
Room 2237
Salt Lake City, UT 84138-1195
(801) 524-3209

VA

Small Business Administration Field Office
400 N. Eighth St.
Room 3015
P.O. Box 10126
Richmond, VA 23240
(804) 771-2765

VI

Small Business Administration Field Office
Veterans Dr.
Room 283
St. Thomas, VI 00801
(809) 774-8530

Small Business Administration Field Office
P.O. Box 4010
Christiansted, VI 00820
(809) 773-3480

VT

Small Business Administration Field Office
87 State St.
Room 205
Montpelier, VT 05602
(802) 229-0538

WA

Small Business Administration Regional Office
Fourth and Vine Bldg.
2615 Fourth Ave.
Room 440
Seattle, WA 98121
(206) 442-5677

Small Business Administration Field Office
915 Second Ave.
Room 1792
Seattle, WA 98174
(206) 442-8405

Small Business Administration Field Office
651 U.S. Courthouse
P.O. Box 2167
Spokane, WA 99210
(509) 456-3781

WI

Small Business Administration Field Office
500 S. Barstow St.
Room 17
Eau Claire, WI 54701
(715) 834-9012

Small Business Administration Field Office
212 E. Washington Ave.
Room 213
Madison, WI 53703
(608) 264-5205

Small Business Administration Field Office
310 W. Wisconsin Ave.
Room 420
Milwaukee, WI 53203
(414) 291-3942

WV

Small Business Administration Field Office
168 W. Main St.
Sixth Floor
Clarksburg, WV 26301
(304) 623-5631

Small Business Administration Field Office
Charleston National Plaza
Suite 628
Charleston, WV 25301
(304) 347-5220

WY

Small Business Administration Field Office
P.O. Box 2839
100 E. B St.
Casper, WY 82602-2839
(307) 261-5761

Publications: Management aids and concerns of the small-business person. Many for sale and free booklets. Booklets revised regularly.

Bibliographies, Sales Catalogs, Publications Lists, etc.

"For Sale Management Assistance Publications." 1984. 6p. free. SBA 115B.
　　Lists and explains ordering of business management booklets.

"Free Management Assistance Publications." 1984. 6p. free. SBA 115A.
　　Lists booklets available without charge. Limit of 50 titles, one copy per title.

Selected List of Books and Pamphlets

The ABC's of Borrowing." n.d. free. MA 1.001.
　　Covers basics of borrowing for business financial management.

"Checklist for Developing a Training Program." n.d. free. MA 5.001.
　　A booklet on personnel.

"Consumer Credit." n.d. $4.50. No. 1013. 045-000-00179-2.
　　Explains the basics of handling credit.

"Delegating Work and Responsibility." n.d. free. MA 3.001.
　　A booklet on business management.

"An Employee Suggestion System for Small Companies." n.d. $3.50. No. 1. 045-000-00020-6.
　　Aids managers to establish accounting procedures that help control production and business costs.

"Guides for Profit Planning." n.d. $4.50. No. 25. 045-000-00137-7.
　　Gives guides for computing and using the break-even point, the level of gross profit, and rate of return on investment.

"Small Business and Government Research and Development." n.d. $4.25. No. 28. 045-000-00130-0.
　　Explains procedures necessary to locate and sell to government agencies.

"Understanding Your Customer." n.d. free. MA 4.001.
　　A booklet on marketing.

"U.S. Government Purchasing and Sales Directory." n.d. $7.00. 045-000-00153-9.
　　A directory for businesses interested in selling to the U.S. government. Lists the purchasing needs of various agencies.

"Your Business and the SBA." 1985. 24p. free. OPC 2.
　　Outlines what the Small Business Administration does: duties, types of available financial and managerial assistance, etc.

Special Services: Small business development centers have been organized as a pilot program on some college campuses to provide a variety of small business managerial and financial information and aid. A district office can furnish a list of these centers. Retired business executives provide managerial assistance. These volunteers work in each district office and provide free services.

SMITHSONIAN ENVIRONMENTAL RESEARCH CENTER
Box 28
Edgewater, MD 21037-0028

Date Established: 1983

Objectives of the Agency: Do scientific research aimed at understanding the processes occurring in the environment and their influence on biological systems and organisms. The research is long-term and emphasizes both laboratory and field-oriented studies in regulatory biology, environmental biology, and radiocarbon dating.

Curriculum: Environmental studies

Subjects: Environment

Publications: Reports. Pamphlets. Bibliographies.

Bibliographies, Sales Catalogs, Publications Lists, etc.

"Site Bibliography." 1984. 13p. free.
　　Includes author, date, title, type of publication, pages, and place of publication.

Selected List of Books and Pamphlets

"Report of the Smithsonian Environmental Research Center." Current. 28p. free.
　　Relates the activities, studies, student appointments, publications, and staff of the fiscal year.

"Work-Learn Opportunities in Environmental Studies." n.d. 14p. free.
　　Explains application procedures and instructions for work/learn program.

SMITHSONIAN INSTITUTION OFFICE OF ELEMENTARY AND SECONDARY EDUCATION
Arts and Industries Bldg.
900 Jefferson Dr., SW
Room 1163
Washington, DC 20560
(202) 357-3049

Date Established: 1974

Objectives of the Agency: Be the Smithsonian Institution's central education office; serve teachers directly through programs and publications; and serve the education offices located in each of the Smithsonian museums.

Curriculum: Education

Subjects: Education—curricula

Publications: Newsletter. Calendar.

Serials, Subscription Publications, etc.

"Art to Zoo." Quarterly. 6p. free.
    Encourages teachers to promote the use of community resources, based on the belief that objects stimulate. Each issue has a pull-out page that may be reproduced for students. Includes bibliographies, resources, notices of contests. Covers such topics as trains, fossils, stamps. For teachers of grades 3-8.

Selected List of Books and Pamphlets

"Museum Adventures." Current. 32p. free.
    A picture calendar of the National Portrait Gallery, Natural Museum of Natural History and other Smithsonian attractions. Includes names, addresses, and telephone numbers of the various museums, galleries, etc.

"The Office of Elementary and Secondary Education." n.d. 2p. free.
    Tells what the office is, what it does, and what it has to offer.

Audiovisuals:

Filmographies, Sales Lists, etc.

"The Office of Elementary and Secondary Education." n.d. 2p. free.
    Describes slide-tape kit, film, and other audiovisuals on museums. Free-loan, rental, or purchase. For teachers and elementary students.

Special Services: Inquire about regional workshop programs held in various locations across the country, summer internship programs, in-service programs, the Career Awareness Program, and summer courses and seminars.

SMITHSONIAN INSTITUTION PRESS
1111 N. Capitol St.
Washington, DC 20002
(202) 357-1793

Date Established: 1848

Objectives of the Agency: Issue publications related to the sciences, technology, history, air and space, and the arts.

Curriculum: Library

Subjects: Library science

Publications: Books. Reports. Studies. Catalogs. Subjects include air and space, military history, anthropology, archaeology, folklife, Native American studies, art, architecture, decorative arts, history, museology, natural history, Washingtonia, etc.

Bibliographies, Sales Catalogs, Publications Lists, etc.

"Complete Catalog." Current. 65p. free.
    Lists what is available. Includes ordering information and order blank.

Selected List of Books and Pamphlets

Hoage, R.J., ed. *Animal Extinctions: What Everyone Should Know.* 1985. 160p. $9.95. HOAEP.
    First in the series. Written by leading authorities. Contains information for the general reader and the scientist. Examines ways to combat species extinctions and the destruction of habitat locally and globally.

Lapham, Lewis H., ed. *High Technology and Human Freedom.* 1985. 176p. cloth. $19.95. 598-5, LAHT.
    Uses George Orwell's vision to begin probing issues in the ethics and potentialities of technology. Written by scholars, writers, media representatives, and others. Also available in paper ($9.95. 599-3, LAHTP.).

Whipple, Fred L. *The Mystery of Comets.* 1985. 208p. cloth. $24.95. 968-9, WHMC.
    Explores from the earliest speculations on comets to the author's own pioneering research into the nature of comets and the mysteries of our solar system. Written for the general reader. Also available in paper ($12.50. 971-9, WHMCP.).

SMITHSONIAN INSTITUTION TRAVELING EXHIBITION SERVICE
Washington, DC 20560
(202) 357-3168

Date Established: 1952

256 / Smithsonian Institution Traveling Exhibition Service

Objectives of the Agency: Organize and circulate exhibitions on art, history and science, and other social themes.

Curriculum: Art, history

Subjects: Art—exhibitions

Publications: Catalogs. Newsletter. Books. Pamphlets. Posters. Promotional materials.

Bibliographies, Sales Catalogs, Publications Lists, etc.

"Publications from Sites." n.d. 4p. free.
  Lists books and pamphlets for sale in decorative arts, painting, sculpture, graphics, photography, history, and other topics. Photographs. Order blank.

Update. Current. 151p. free.
  Gives information about services, exhibitions by subject, requirements and rules, and photographs and background of the exhibitions. Includes such information as number of pieces, exhibition period, security requirements, and loan fee. Paper panel exhibitions are also available for purchase and come with interpretive materials.

Serials, Subscription Publications, etc.

"Sideline." Quarterly. 6p. free.
  A newsletter about Smithsonian traveling exhibitions and exhibitors. Provides response cards.

SMITHSONIAN INSTITUTION VISITOR INFORMATION AND ASSOCIATES' RECEPTION CENTER
Washington, DC 20560
(202) 357-2700

Objectives of the Agency: Provide information about services and visitor information.

Curriculum: History, library

Subjects: Library science

Publications: Pamphlets. Catalogs. On publications, attractions, and services.

Bibliographies, Sales Catalogs, Publications Lists, etc.

"Catalog of Smithsonian Books." Current. 12p. free.
  Lists publications with annotations, prices, and ordering information.

"Teaching Materials." Current. 3p. free.
  Gives information on materials and programs helpful to teachers outside the Washington, DC, area from the Office of Elementary and Secondary Education, Anacostria Neighborhood Museum, and other Smithsonian sources.

Serials, Subscription Publications, etc.

"Quarterly Sampler of Upcoming Exhibitions." Quarterly 2p. free.
  Gives dates and other information about exhibitions.

Selected List of Books and Pamphlets

"Planning Your Smithsonian Visit." 1985. 19p. free.
  Provides information on where to eat, where to stay, the transportation, the layout of Washington, DC, and other aids.

"The Smithsonian." 1985. 12p. free.
  Contains information, visitor information, telephone numbers, highlights, and the location of the various museums of the Smithsonian such as the National Museum of American History and the National Air and Space Museum.

Audiovisuals:

Filmographies, Sales Lists, etc.

"Catalog of the Smithsonian Collection of Recordings." Current. 20p. free.
  Describes records, cassettes, prices, and ordering information.

"Slide List." Current. 1p. free.
  Lists 35mm color slides, filmstrips, prices, and ordering information.

Special Services: Membership in the Smithsonian Institution entitles members to receive *Smithsonian,* a monthly magazine, discounts on books, records,

NY
State Conservationist
James M. Hanley Federal Bldg.
Room 771
100 S. Clinton St.
Syracuse, NY 13260
(315) 423-5521

OH
State Conservationist
200 N. High St.
Room 522
Columbus, OH 43215
(614) 469-6962

OK
State Conservationist
Agriculture Center Bldg.
Farm Rd. and Brumley St.
Stillwater, OK 74074
(405) 624-4360

OR
State Conservationist
Federal Bldg.
1220 S.W. Third Ave.
Sixteenth Floor
Portland, OR 97204
(503) 221-2751

PA
State Conservationist
Federal Sq. Station
228 Walnut St.
Room 850
Box 985
Harrisburg, PA 17108
(717) 782-2202

PR
State Conservationist
Federal Bldg.
Room 639
Chardon Ave.
GPO Box 4868
Hato Rey, PR 00918
(809) 753-4206

RI
State Conservationist
45 Quaker Lane
West Warwick, RI 02893
(401) 828-1300

SC
State Conservationist
Strom Thurmond Federal Bldg.
1835 Assembly St.
Room 950
Columbia, SC 29201
(803) 765-5681

SD
State Conservationist
Federal Bldg.
200 Fourth St., SW
Huron, SD 57350
(605) 352-8651, ext. 333

TN
State Conservationist
U.S. Courthouse
801 Broadway St.
Room 675
Nashville, TN 37203
(615) 251-5471

TX
State Conservationist
W.R. Poage Federal Bldg.
101 S. Main St.
Temple, TX 76501-7682
(817) 774-1214

UT
State Conservationist
125 S. State St.
Room 4012
Salt Lake City, UT 84138
(801) 524-5050

VA
State Conservationist
Federal Bldg.
400 N. Eighth St.
Room 9201
Richmond, VA 23240
(804) 771-2455

VT
State Conservationist
69 Union St.
Winooski, VT 05404
(802) 951-6795

WA
State Conservationist
360 U.S. Courthouse
West 920 Riverside Ave.
Spokane, WA 99201
(509) 456-3711

WI
State Conservationist
4601 Hammersley Rd.
Madison, WI 53711
(608) 264-5577

WV

State Conservationist
75 High St.
Room 301
Morgantown, WV 26505
(304) 291-4151

WY

State Conservationist
Federal Office Bldg.
100 E. B St.
Room 3124
Casper, WY 82601
(307) 261-5201

National Technical Centers

Midwest National Technical Center
Federal Bldg.
100 Centennial Mall North
Room 345
Lincoln, NE 68508-3866
(402) 471-5345

West National Technical Center
Federal Bldg.
511 N.W. Broadway
Room 547
Portland, OR 97209-3489
(503) 221-2824

Northeast National Technical Center
160 E. Seventh St.
Chester, PA 19013
(215) 499-3904

South National Technical Center
Fort Worth Federal Center
Building 23
Felix and Hemphill Sts.
Room 60
P.O. Box 6567
Fort Worth, TX 76115
(817) 334-5253

Publications: Pamphlets on conservation plantings and services.

Selected List of Books and Pamphlets

"Assistance Available from the Soil Conservation Service." 1984. 30p. free. Program Aid No. 1352.

Explains the mission of the service and what it does in such areas as: soil and water conservation, community resource protection and development, environmental education, and fish and wildlife.

"Conservation Highlights." Current. 4p. free.

Summarizes activities of the Soil Conservation Service for the past year in such areas as: *Conservation Tillage, Soil Survey, Water Quality, Windbreaks, Rural Abandoned Mine Program, Soil Erosion Research, Fish and Wildlife,* and many other projects.

"The Importance of the Civilian Conservation Corps to the Soil Conservation Service." 1983. 26p. free. National Bulletin No. 260-3-26.

Describes accomplishments of the Civilian Conservation Corps begun in the 1930s. Includes statistics of certain phases of the program from 1933 to 1942.

"Invite Birds to Your Home." n.d. 8-fold. free.

Discusses plants to grow for attracting birds, landscaping tips, and ways of attracting birds. Photographs.

"Soil Conservation Service: What It Is and What It Does." Rev. 21p. free. SCS-CA-9.

Gives summary of soil survey work, international assistance, plant materials work, wildlife conservation work, snow surveys, watershed program activities, far woodland work, and other activities.

Statutory Authorities for the Activities of the Soil Conservation Service. 1981. 126p. free. Agriculture Handbook No. 588.

Compiles the most frequently used legislation administered by or used by the Soil Conservation Service. Divided into such sections as: "Water Resources," "Surface Mining," "Water Quality," and "Technical Assistance to Other Agencies." Refers the reader to other sources for those laws that are not included.

"Where To Get Information about Soil & Water Conservation." 1983. 16p. free.

Lists name, area of expertise, and telephone number of various conservation specialists.

TENNESSEE VALLEY AUTHORITY
400 W. Summit Hill Dr.
Knoxville, TN 37902
TN: (800) 362-9250
Other Tennessee Valley states: (800) 251-9242

Date Established: 1933

Curriculum: Environmental studies, geography

Subjects: Energy Conservation
Geography

Locations:

*District Administrators
(Liaisons between local citizens and the
TVA Board)*

Western District Administrator
Commerce Center
P.O. Box 1788
Jackson, TN 38302
(901) 668-6088

Central District Administrator
444 Metroplex Dr.
Suite 240
Nashville, TN 37203
(615) 360-1540

Appalachian District Administrator
207 Heritage Federal Bldg.
4105 Fort Henry Dr.
Kingsport, TN 37663
(615) 239-5981

Southeastern District Administrator
68 Mouse Creek Rd.
Cleveland, TN 37311
(615) 476-9131

Alabama District Administrator
529 First Federal Bldg.
Florence, AL 35631
(205) 767-4620

Mississippi District Administrator
1014 N. Gloster
P.O. Box 1623
Tupelo, MS 38802
(601) 842-5825

Kentucky District Administrator
115 Hammond Plaza
Hopkinsville, KY 42240
(502) 885-3398

*Power District Offices
(Coordinate activities between TVA and local power distributors and oversee consumer energy conservation programs)*

Western Power District Office
P.O. Box 999
Jackson, TN 38302
(901) 668-0915

Central Power District Office
444 Metroplex Dr.
Suite 260
Nashville, TN 37203
(615) 360-1560

Appalachian Power District Office
200 Brookvale Bldg.
Knoxville, TN 37902
(615) 632-6750

Southeastern Power District
1709 S. Lee Hwy.
Cleveland, TN 37311
(615) 478-1141

Alabama Power District Office
501 First Federal Bldg.
Florence, AL 35631
(205) 386-2051

Mississippi Power District Office
P.O. Box 470
Tupelo, MS 38802
(601) 842-5825

Kentucky Power District Office
P.O. Box 1088
Hopkinsville, KY 42240
(502) 885-4357

Publications: Pamphlets. Maps. Catalogs. Guides. Reports. On TVA functions, energy conservation, maps, consumer education, etc.

Bibliographies, Sales Catalogs, Publications Lists, etc.

"Catalog of Conservation & Solar Publications." Current. 14p. free. TVA/OP/ECR-84/5.
   Lists publications on general conservation, do-it-yourself projects, wood heaters, and other topics. Materials are free.

"TVA Maps." 1985. 24p. free.
   Lists maps covering the Tennessee Valley region as well as other areas. Also sells historical maps of the United States. Price catalog. Archaeological reports.

"TVA Publications Order Form." Current. 1p. free.
   Provides a check list to obtain information on agriculture, energy, general topics, etc. Free materials.

Selected List of Books and Pamphlets

"Answers to the Most Frequently Asked Questions about TVA." 1984, 16p. free. TVA/OGM/10-83/11.
   Groups questions and answers under such topics as *Flood Control, Power, Environmental Protection, Valley Forest Resources,* etc.

"Citizen's Guide to TVA." n.d. 9p. free. TVA/OGM/10-84/12.
   Helps reach the information sources and obtain answers to questions about TVA.

"Fact about TVA Dams and Steam Plants." 1984. 6p. free. TVA/OGM/10-84/7.
   Gives statistics, map, and information about TVA dams and steam plants. Photographs.

"How Topographic Maps Are Made." 5th ed. 22p. free.
   Gives a better understanding of procedures involved in making topographic maps of the Mapping Services Branch. Includes steps in map making beginning with the actual aerial photo.

"How To Save on Your Electric Bills." n.d. 14p. free. TVA/OP/ECR-84/53.

Examines low-cost and no-cost ideas for various rooms in the home, appliance energy use, and labeling.

"Introduction to Solar Energy." n.d. 12p. free.

Tells what solar energy is, how to use it, and how it works.

"A Student History of TVA." 20p. free. TVA/OGM/10-84/5.

Chronicles how TVA began, its development, progress, and priorities.

"Wind Energy Information." 20p. free. TVA/OP/ECR-82/29.

Describes types of wind machines, uses, and where to obtain information for wind monitoring devices and wind systems.

Audiovisuals:

Filmographies, Sales Lists, etc.

"Motion Pictures Available from the Tennessee Valley Authority." n.d. 5p. free. TVA/OGM/10-82/22.

Lists free loan films with annotations.

U.S. ARMS CONTROL AND DISARMAMENT AGENCY
320 Twenty-First St., NW
Washington, DC 20451
(202) 655-4000

Date Established: 1961

Objectives of the Agency: Formulate and implement arms control and disarmament policies to promote national security; and prepare and participate in discussions and negotiations with countries.

Curriculum: Current issues

Subjects: Disarmament
U.S.—national security

Publications: Pamphlets. Reports. Books. On activities, treaties, statements about arms control and disarmament.

Selected List of Books and Pamphlets

Arms Control and Disarmament Agreements. 5th ed. 290p. free.

Prints texts and histories of negotiations. Includes such treaties as the Limited Test Ban Treaty, Outer Space Treaty, SALT II. Includes the texts of the Geneva Protocol of 1925 and, in chronological order, all major arms control agreements concluded after World War II in which the United States has been a participant.

Fiscal Year Arms Control Impact Statements. Annual. 350p. free.

Reprints statements submitted to the Congress by the President.

"The Non-Proliferation Treaty 1970-1985." 1985. 21p. free.

Describes origins, objectives, and treaty articles. Map of signatory countries. List of treaty signatories.

"The President's Strategic Defense Initiative." 1985. 10p. free.

Prints a foreword by the President. Explains the initiative (sometimes referred to as "Star Wars"), with questions and answers.

"Soviet Strategic Defense Programs." 1985. 27p. free.

Explains the soviet approach: ballistic missile defense, laser weapons, radio frequency weapons, computer technololgy, etc. Charts. Illustrations.

U.S. Arms Control and Disarmament Agency Annual Report. Annual. 140p. free.

Covers the past calendar year. Covers such information as research and publications, multilateral negotiations, and strategic programs. List of abbreviations and acronyms. Organization chart. Appendices.

U.S. ARMY CORPS OF ENGINEERS
Office of the Chief of Engineers
20 Massachusetts Ave., NW
Washington, DC 20314
(202) 272-6001

Date Established: 1775

Objectives of the Agency: Serve as the Army's real property manager; manage and execute engineering, construction and real estate programs for the Army and Air Force; research and develop support of those programs; and manage and execute civil works programs.

Curriculum: Geography

Subjects: Geography

Locations:

U.S. Army Engineer Division
Lower Mississippi Valley
P.O. Box 80
Vicksburg, MS 39180

U.S. Army Engineer District
Memphis
668 Clifford Davis Federal Bldg.
Memphis, TN 38103

U.S. Army Engineer District
New Orleans
P.O. Box 60267
New Orleans, LA 70160

U.S. Army Engineer District
St. Louis
210 N. Twelfth St.
St. Louis, MO 63101

U.S. Army Engineer District
Vicksburg
P.O. Box 60
Vicksburg, MS 39180

U.S. Army Engineer Division
Missouri River
Downtown Station
P.O. Box 103
Omaha, NE 68101

U.S. Army Engineer District
Kansas City
700 Federal Bldg.
Kansas City, MO 64106

U.S. Army Engineer District
Omaha
6014 U.S. Post Office and Court House
Omaha, NE 68102

U.S. Army Engineer Division
New England
424 Trapelo Rd.
Waltham, MA 02154

U.S. Army Engineer Division
North Atlantic
90 Church St.
New York, NY 10007

U.S. Army Engineer District
Baltimore
P.O. Box 1715
Baltimore, MD 21203

U.S. Army Engineer District
New York
26 Federal Plaza
New York, NY 10278

U.S. Army Engineer District
Norfolk
803 Front St.
Norfolk, VA 23510

U.S. Army Engineer District
Philadelphia
U.S. Custom House
Second and Chestnut Sts.
Philadelphia, PA 19106

U.S. Army Engineer Division
North Central
536 Clark St.
Chicago, IL 60605

U.S. Army Engineer District
Buffalo
1776 Niagara St.
Buffalo, NY 14207

U.S. Army Engineer District
Detroit
P.O. Box 1027
Detroit, MI 48231

U.S. Army Engineer District
St. Paul
1135 USPO and Customhouse
St. Paul, MN 55101

U.S. Army Engineer Division
North Pacific
P.O. Box 2870
Portland, OR 97208

U.S. Army Engineer District
Alaska
P.O. Box 7002
Anchorage, AK 99510

U.S. Army Engineer District
Portland
P.O. Box 2946
Portland, OR 97208

U.S. Army Engineer District
Seattle
P.O. Box C-3755
Seattle, WA 98124

U.S. Army Engineer District
Walla Walla
Building 602
City-County Airport
Walla Walla, WA 99362

U.S. Army Engineer Division
Ohio River
P.O. Box 1159
Cincinnati, OH 45201

U.S. Army Engineer Division
Huntington
P.O. Box 2127
Huntington, WV 25721

U.S. Army Engineer District
Louisville
P.O. Box 59
Louisville, KY 40201

U.S. Army Engineer District
Nashville
P.O. Box 1070
Nashville, TN 37202

266 / U.S. Army Corps of Engineers

U.S. Army Engineer District
Pittsburgh
Federal Bldg.
1000 Liberty Ave.
Pittsburgh, PA 15222

U.S. Army Engineer Division
South Atlantic
510 Title Bldg.
30 Pryor St., SW
Atlanta, GA 30303

U.S. Army Engineer District
Charleston
P.O. Box 919
Charleston, SC 29402

U.S. Army Engineer District
Jacksonville
P.O. Box 4970
Jacksonville, FL 32201

U.S. Army Engineer District
Mobile
P.O. Box 2288
Mobile, AL 36628

U.S. Army Engineer District
Savannah
P.O. Box 889
Savannah, GA 31402

U.S. Army Engineer District
Wilmington
P.O. Box 1890
Wilmington, NC 28401

U.S. Army Engineer Division
South Pacific
630 Sansome St.
Room 1216
San Francisco, CA 94111

U.S. Army Engineer District
Los Angeles
P.O. Box 2711
Los Angeles, CA 90053

U.S. Army Engineer District
Sacramento
650 Capital Mall
Sacramento, CA 95914

U.S. Army Engineer District
San Francisco
211 Main St.
San Francisco, CA 94105

U.S. Army Engineer District
Southwestern
1114 Commerce St.
Dallas, TX 75242

U.S. Army Engineer District
Albuquerque
P.O. Box 1580
Albuquerque, NM 87103

U.S. Army Engineer District
Fort Worth
P.O. Box 17300
Fort Worth, TX 76102

U.S. Army Engineer District
Galveston
P.O. Box 1229
Galveston, TX 77553

U.S. Army Engineer District
Little Rock
Little Rock, AR 72203

U.S. Army Engineer District
Tulsa
P.O. Box 61
Tulsa, OK 74102

Selected List of Books and Pamphlets

"Historical Highlights of the United States Army Corps of Engineers." 1978. 28p. free. EP 360-1-13.
    Relates the contributions of the corps from the Battle of Bunker Hill to modern times.

"Lakeside Recreation in New England." 1980. 28p. free. EP-1130-2-411.
    Describes corps projects in New England. A directory of recreation opportunities. Map. Chart. Addresses.

"Lakeside Recreation in the Midwest." 1980. 28p. free. EP-1130-2-414.
    Describes corps projects in the Midwest. A directory of recreation opportunities. Map. Chart. Addresses.

"Lakeside Recreation in the Northeast." 1979. 28p. free. EP 1130-2-412.
    Describes corps projects in the Northeast. Directory of recreation opportunities. Map. Chart. Addresses.

"Lakeside Recreation in the Southeast." 1979. 28p. free. EP 1130-2-413.
    Describes corps projects in the Southeast. A directory of recreation opportunities. Map. Chart. Addresses.

"Lakeside Recreation in the Southwest." 1980. 28p. free. EP 1130-2-416.
    Describes corps projects in the Southwest. Directory of recreation opportunities. Map. Chart. Addresses.

"Lakeside Recreation in the West." 1980. 28p. free. EP 1130-2-415.

Describes corps projects in the West. Directory of recreation opportunities. Map. Chart. Addresses.

"Statistics Volume 1." Current. 93p. free. EP 1130-2-401.
Gives data for Lower Mississippi, Missouri, New England, North Atlantic, North Central, North Pacific, Ohio River, South Atlantic, South Pacific, and Southwestern Division.

Audiovisuals:

Filmographies, Sales Lists, etc.

"Films." Current. 13p. free. EP 360-1-16.
Free loan or for purchase, what films are available, and where to obtain them.

Individual Audiovisuals

"Blue Rock." n.d. 25 minutes. 16mm. free loan or purchase.
Illustrates the need for wise management of water. Shows how water is used in many ways and the people who manage those supplies. Order from: Modern Talking Picture Service. 5000 Park St. North, St. Petersburg, FL 33709.

"The Great Lakes." n.d. 28½ minutes. 16mm. free loan or purchase.
Shows the geography, use, history, environment of the Great Lakes. Order from: Modern Talking Picture Service, 5000 Park St. North, St. Petersburg, FL 33709.

"The Great Lakes Connection." n.d. 25 minutes. 16mm. free loan.
Shows the operation of the locks at Sault Ste. Marie. Order from: Modern Talking Picture Service, 5000 Park St. North, St. Petersburg, FL 33709.

"Survival of the Pacific Salmon." n.d. 22 minutes. 16mm. free loan or purchase.
Shows the work of the corps in creating safe passage of adult salmon and steelhead upstream to spawning grounds and back again in the upper Columbia River and tributaries. Order from: Modern Talking Picture Service, 5000 Park St. North, St. Petersburg, FL 33709.

U.S. COAST GUARD
Department of Transportation
2100 Second St., SW
Washington, DC 20593
(202) 426-2158

Date Established: 1915

Objectives of the Agency: Maintain a system of rescue vessels, aircraft, and communications facilities for saving life and property in and over the high seas and navigable waters of the United States; provide flood relief; and remove navigation hazards.

Curriculum: Safety, social studies
Subjects: U.S. Coast Guard
Locations:

MA, ME, NH, RI, VT
U.S. Coast Guard
District 1 Atlantic Area
150 Causeway St.
Boston, MA 02114
(617) 223-3601

CO, IA, IL, IN, KS, KY, MN, MO, ND, NE, OH, OK, PA (western), SD, TN, WI, WV, WY
U.S. Coast Guard
District 2 Atlantic Area
1430 Olive St.
St. Louis, MO 63103
(314) 425-4601

CT, DE, NJ, NY (eastern), PA (eastern)
U.S. Coast Guard
District 3 Atlantic Area
Governors Island
New York, NY 10004
(212) 668-7196

DC, MD, NC, VA
U.S. Coast Guard
District 5 Atlantic Area
431 Crawford St.
Portsmouth, VA 23705
(804) 398-6000

FL, GA, PR, SC, VI
U.S. Coast Guard
District 7 Atlantic Area
51 S.W. First Ave.
Miami, FL 33130
(305) 350-5654

AL, LA, MS, NM, TX
U.S. Coast Guard
District 8 Atlantic Area
500 Camp St.
New Orleans, LA 70130
(504) 589-6298

Great Lakes Area
U.S. Coast Guard
District 9 Atlantic Area
1240 E. Ninth St.
Cleveland, OH 44199
(216) 522-3910

AZ, CA (southern)
U.S. Coast Guard
District 11 Pacific Area
400 Oceangate Blvd.
Long Beach, CA 90822
(213) 590-2211

268 / U.S. Coast Guard

CA (northern), NV, UT

U.S. Coast Guard
District 12 Pacific Area
2 Government Island
Alameda, CA 94501
(415) 536-6150

ID, MT, OR, WA

U.S. Coast Guard
District 13 Pacific Area
915 Second Ave.
Seattle, WA 98174
(206) 442-5078

AS, GU, HI, Pacific Islands

U.S. Coast Guard
District 14 Pacific Area
300 Ala Moana Blvd.
Ninth Floor
Honolulu, HI 96850
(808) 546-7109

AK

U.S. Coast Guard
District 17 Pacific Area
P.O. Box 3-5000
Juneau, AK 99802
(907) 586-7347

Publications: Pamphlets. Bibliographies. On recreational boating and Coast Guard information.

Bibliographies, Sales Catalogs, Publications Lists, etc.

"Federal Requirements for Recreation Boats." 1983. 20p. free.

Explains numbering requirements, law enforcement, fire extinguishers, minimum required equipment by length of boat, lights, boating accident reports, visual distress signals, and other helpful hints for boating safety.

United States Coast Guard Annotated Bibliography. 1982. 148p. free.

Grouped by such topics as: *Biographies, Icebreaking, Bibliographies and Research Aids, Search and Rescue,* and *World War II.* Includes a book's author, title, place of publication, publisher, date, number of pages, and contents. Includes a magazine article's author, title, name of magazine, date, pages, graphics, and contents. Author and editor index. Intended as a reasearch tool for those interested in the Coast Guard and its predecessors.

U.S. CUSTOMS SERVICE
Department of the Treasury
1301 Constitution Ave., NW
Washington, DC 20229
(202) 566-5286

Date Established: 1973

Objectives of the Agency: Collect revenue from imports and enforce customs and related laws.

Curriculum: Social Studies

Subjects: Travelers, American

Locations (arranged alphabetically by city):

U.S. Customs District Office
620 E. Tenth Ave.
Anchorage, AK 99501
(907) 271-4043

U.S. Customs District Office
40 S. Gay St.
Baltimore, MD 21202
(301) 962-2666

U.S. Customs District Office
2 India St.
Boston, MA 02109
(617) 223-6598

U.S. Customs District Office
120 Middle St.
Bridgeport, CT 06601
(203) 579-5606

U.S. Customs District Office
111 W. Huron St.
Buffalo, NY 14202
(716) 846-4373

U.S. Customs District Office
200 E. Bay St.
Charleston, SC 29402
(803) 724-4312

U.S. Customs District Office
P.O. Box 510
Charlotte Amalie
St. Thomas, VI 00801
(809) 774-2530

U.S. Customs District Office
610 Canal St.
Chicago, IL 60607
(312) 353-6100

U.S. Customs District Office
55 Erieview Plaza
Cleveland, OH 44114
(216) 522-4284

U.S. Customs District Office
700 Parkway Plaza
P.O. Box 61050
Dallas/Fort Worth, TX 75261
(214) 574-2170

U.S. Customs District Office
477 Michigan Ave.
Detroit, MI 48226
(313) 226-3177

U.S. Customs District Office
209 Federal Bldg.
515 W. First St.
Duluth, MN 55802
(218) 727-6692

U.S. Customs District Office
Building B
Bridge of the Americas
Room 134
P.O. Box 9516
El Paso, TX 79985
(925) 541-7435

U.S. Customs District Office
215 First Ave. North
Great Falls, MT 59401
(406) 453-7631

U.S. Customs District Office
335 Merchant St.
P.O. Box 1641
Honolulu, HI 98606
(808) 546-3115

U.S. Customs District Office
701 San Jacinto St.
Houston/Galveston, TX 77052
(713) 226-4316

U.S. Customs Area Office
Kennedy Airport Area
Cargo Building 80
Room 2E
Jamaica, NY 11430
(718) 917-1542

U.S. Customs District Office
P.O. Box 3130
Mann Rd. and Santa Maria
Laredo, TX 78041
(512) 723-2956

U.S. Customs District Office
Terminal Island
San Pedro
300 Ferry St.
Los Angeles/Long Beach, CA 90731
(213) 548-2441

U.S. Customs District Office
77 S.E. Fifth St.
Miami, FL 33131
(305) 350-4101

U.S. Customs District Office
628 E. Michigan St.
Milwaukee, WI 53202
(414) 291-3924

U.S. Customs District Office
110 S. Fourth St.
Minneapolis, MN 55401
(612) 725-2317

U.S. Customs District Office
250 N. Water St.
Mobile, AL 36601
(205) 690-2106

U.S. Customs District Office
423 Canal St.
New Orleans, LA 70130
(504) 589-6353

U.S. Customs Area Office
New York Seaport Area
Customhouse 6
World Trade Center
New York, NY 10048
(212) 466-5817

U.S. Customs Area Office
Airport International Plaza
Newark Area
Newark, NJ 07114
(201) 645-3760

U.S. Customs District Office
International and Terrace Sts.
Nogales, AZ 85621
(602) 287-4955

U.S. Customs District Office
101 E. Maine St.
Norfolk, VA 23510
(804) 441-6546

U.S. Customs District Office
1327 N. Water St.
Ogdensburg, NY 13669
(315) 393-0660

U.S. Customs District Office
Post Office Bldg.
Pembina, ND 58271
(701) 825-6201

U.S. Customs District Office
Second and Chestnut Sts.
Philadelphia, PA 19106
(215) 597-4605

U.S. Customs District Office
Fifth and Austin Ave.
Port Arthur, TX 77640
(409) 724-0087

U.S. Customs District Office
312 Fore St.
Portland, ME 04111
(207) 780-3326

270 / U.S. Customs Service

U.S. Customs District Office
511 N.W. Broadway
Portland, OR 97209
(503) 221-2865

U.S. Customs District Office
24 Weybosset St.
Providence, RI 09203
(401) 528-5081

U.S. Customs District Office
Main and Stebbins St.
P.O. Box 111
St. Albans, VT 05478
(802) 524-6527

U.S. Customs District Office
120 S. Central Ave.
St. Louis, MO 63105
(314) 425-3134

U.S. Customs District Office
880 Front St.
San Diego, CA 92189
(619) 293-5360

U.S. Customs District Office
555 Battery St.
P.O. Box 2450
San Francisco, CA 94126
(415) 556-4340

U.S. Customs District Office
P.O. Box 2112
San Juan, PR 00903
(809) 723-2091

U.S. Customs District Office
1 E. Bay St.
Savannah, GA 31401
(912) 944-4256

U.S. Customs District Office
909 First Ave.
Seattle, WA 98174
(206) 442-0554

U.S. Customs District Office
301 S. Ashley Dr.
Tampa, FL 33602
(813) 228-2381

U.S. Customs District Office
POB 17423
Gateway 1 Bldg.
International Airport
Washington, DC 20041
(202) 566-8511

U.S. Customs District Office
1 Virginia Ave.
Wilmington, NC 28401
(919) 343-4601

Publications: Pamphlets on custom information.

Selected List of Books and Publications

"Foreign Trade Zones." 1979. 8p. free. Customs Information Series C:79-2.

Explains U.S. Customs procedures and requirements. Describes what foreign trade zones are, advantages of using them, how they are established, customs involvement, etc.

"GSP and the Traveler." Rev. 8p. free. Publication No. 515.

Explains information on bringing articles from developing countries under the Generalized System of Preferences. GSP is a way to help developing nations improve themselves through exports, becoming effective 1976.

"Import Quotas." 1981. 8p. free. Customs Publication No. 519.

Explains absolute quotas, tariff-rate quotas, commodities subject to import quotas, and quotas administered by other agencies.

"Information for Travelers: State Laws on Importing Alcoholic Beverages." 1981. 4p. free. Publication No. 523.

Tells how much, if any, alcohol may be imported into a state for personal use without liability for state tax, or having to obtain a permit. Limitations on such importation.

"Know Before You Go." Rev. 14p. free. Publication No. 512.

Gives consumer information about declarations, exemptions, residency, duty, and gifts.

"Pets, Wildlife." 1980. 8p. free. Customs Publication No. 509.

Explains regulations of the U.S. Customs regarding pets and wildlife.

"This Is Customs." 1976. 9p. free.

Explains various customs activities. Photographs.

"Travelers' Tips on Bringing Food, Plant, and Animal Products into the United States." Rev. 18p. free. Program Aid No. 1083.

Explains agricultural inspection, smuggling, what you can bring home, entry status lists, commercial shipments, and other federal requirements.

"U.S. Customs: Importing a Car." Rev. 8p. free. Customs Publication No. 520.

Describes making prior arrangements, documentation, dutiable entry, and other considerations when importing a car.

"U.S. Customs Service Trademark Information for Travelers." 1984. 22p. free. Customs Publication No. 508.

Discusses trademark laws and their application to various products such as musical instruments and watches.

"Worth Repeating Special Rules for Bringing Pet Birds into the United States." 1980. 2p. free.

Reprints rules regarding birds, their reasons, and special exceptions.

U.S. GEOLOGICAL SURVEY
Publications Division
National Center
Mail Stop #582
Reston, VA 22092
(703) 860-7444

Date Established: 1879

Objectives of the Agency: Identify the nation's land, water, energy, minerals; classify federally owned lands for power potential; investigate natural hazards like landslides; prepare maps; collect data; perform research; and make reports.

Curriculum: Geography, science

Subjects: Geography
Science

Locations:

(Public Inquiries Offices serve walk-in customers and also answer inquiries by mail or telephone. These offices aid in the selection and ordering of materials and provide counter service for topographic, geologic, and water-resources maps and reports. They also distribute catalogs, circulars, indexes, and leaflets.)

AK

Public Inquiries Office
U.S. Geological Survey
Room 101
4230 University Dr.
Anchorage, AK 99508-4664
(907) 561-5555

Public Inquiries Office
Earth Science Information and Sales
U.S. Geological Survey
E-146 Federal Bldg.
701 C St.
Box 53
Anchorage, AK 99508-4664
(907) 271-4307

AR, LA, NM, OK, TX

Public Inquiries Office
U.S. Geological Survey
1-C-45 Federal Bldg.
1100 Commerce St.
Dallas, TX 75242
(214) 767-0198

AK, AZ, CO, KS, MT, NE, NM, ND, SD, UT, WY

Public Inquiries Office
U.S. Geological Survey
169 Federal Bldg.
1961 Stout St.
Denver, CO 80294
(303) 844-4169

AK, AZ, CA, HI, NV, OR, WA

Public Inquiries Office
U.S. Geological Survey
7638 Federal Bldg.
300 N. Los Angeles St.
Los Angeles, CA 90012
(213) 894-2850

AK, AZ, CA, HI, ID, NV, OR, UT, WA

Public Inquiries Office
U.S. Geological Survey
Building 3
Mail Stop 533
345 Middlefield Rd.
Room 122
Menlo Park, CA 94025
(415) 323-8111, ext. 2817

All States

Public Inquiries Office
U.S. Geological Survey
503 National Center
12201 Sunrise Valley Dr.
Room 1-C-402
Reston, VA 22092
(703) 860-6167

AZ, CO, ID, NM, NV, UT, WY

Public Inquiries Office
U.S. Geological Survey
8105 Federal Bldg.
125 S. State St.
Salt Lake City, UT 84138
(801) 524-5652

AK, AZ, CA, HI, ID, NV, OR, WA

Public Inquiries Office
U.S. Geological Survey
504 Custom House
555 Battery St.
San Francisco, CA 94111
(415) 556-5627

AK, ID, MT, OR, WA

Public Inquiries Office
U.S. Geological Survey
678 U.S. Courthouse
West 920 Riverside Ave.
Spokane, WA 99201
(509) 456-2524

All States

Public Inquiries Office
U.S. Geological Survey
1028 GSA Bldg.
Nineteenth and F Sts., NW
Washington, DC 20244

Eastern Distribution Branch

The Eastern Distrubition Branch sells over-the-counter and by mail the geologic, hydrologic, topographic, and land use and land cover maps of areas east of the Mississippi River, including Minnesota, Puerto Rico, and the Virgin Islands. It distributes map indexes, "List of Geological Survey Geologic and Water-Supply Reports and Maps for State," and "Water Resources Investigations of the U.S. Geological Survey for State," as well as general interest publications. Contact:
Eastern Distribution Branch
U.S. Geological Survey
1200 S. Eads St.
Arlington, VA 22202
(703) 557-2751

Western Distribution Branch

The Western Distribution Branch sells over-the-counter and by mail the geologic, hydrologic, topographic, and land use and land cover maps of areas west of the Mississippi River, including Alaska, Hawaii, Louisiana, Guam, and American Samoa. It distributes map indexes, "List of Geological Survey Geologic and Water Supply Reports and Maps for State," and "Water-Resources Investigations of the U.S. Geological Survey in State" for the states in its region and copies of annual supplements to survey catalogs and general interest publications. It accepts orders for those reports held by the Open-File Services Section. Contact:
Western Distribution Branch
U.S. Geological Survey
Box 25286
Federal Center
Denver, CO 80225
(303) 236-7477

Alaska Distribution Section

The Alaska Distribution Section sells over-the-counter and by mail the geologic, hydrologic, and topographic maps of Alaska to Alaska residents. It distributes topographic and geologic map indexes of Alaska, "List of Geologic Survey Geologic and Water-Supply Reports and Maps for Alaska," and "Water-Resources Investigations of the U.S. Geological Survey in Alaska," as well as other general interest publications. Contact:
Alaska Distribution Section
U.S. Geological Survey
New Federal Bldg.
101 Twelfth Ave.
Box 12
Fairbanks, AK 99701
(907) 456-7535

Cartographic Information Centers

The National Cartographic Information Center is the main center for the National Mapping Division. It answers general and technical questions on cartography, geography, geodesy, and remote sensing. It gathers, organizes, and distributes descriptions of maps, charts, aerial photographs, digital map data, geodetic control data, geographic data, and satellite products. The Mid-Continent Mapping Center sells topographic maps of its region.

National Cartographic Information Center
U.S. Geological Survey
507 National Center
12201 Sunrise Valley Dr.
Room 1-C-107
Reston, VA 22092
(703) 860-6045

Rocky Mountain Mapping Center—NCIC
U.S. Geological Survey
Federal Center
Mail Stop 504
Box 25046
Denver, CO 80225
(303) 236-5829

Eastern Mapping Center—NCIC
U.S. Geological Survey
536 National Center
12201 Sunrise Valley Dr.
Room 2-B-200
Reston, VA 22091
(703) 860-6336

Mid-Continent Mapping Center—NCIC
U.S. Geological Survey
1400 Independence Rd.
Rolla, MO 65401
(314) 341-0851

Western Mapping Center—NCIC
U.S. Geological Survey
345 Middlefield Rd.
Menlo Park, CA 94025
(415) 323-8111, ext. 2427

National Space Technology Laboratories
National Cartographic Information Center
U.S. Geological Survey
Building 3101
NSTL Station, MS 39529
(601) 688-3544

Alaska Office—NCIC
U.S. Geological Survey
4230 University Dr.
Room 110
Anchorage, AK 99508-4664
(907) 271-4148

TVA Region

This federal affiliate NCIC office has access to NCIC information aids in ordering, and sells map products of the TVA region:
Tennessee Valley Authority
National Cartographic Information Center
200 Haney Bldg.
311 Broad St.
Chattanooga, TN 37401
(615) 751-6277

Water Resources Division District

Water Resources Division District offices provide information on water data and answer questions on the water resources of their specific regions.

AK

Water Resources Division District Office
U.S. Geological Survey
1515 E. Thirteenth Ave.
Anchorage, AK 99501
(907) 271-4138

AL

Water Resources Division District Office
U.S. Geological Survey
520 Nineteenth Ave.
Tuscaloosa, AL 35401
(205) 752-8104

AR

Water Resources Division District Office
U.S. Geological Survey
2301 Federal Office Bldg.
700 W. Capitol Ave.
Little Rock, AR 72201
(501) 378-6391

AZ

Water Resources Division District Office
U.S. Geological Survey
Federal Building, FB 44
301 W. Congress St.
Tucson, AZ 85701-1393
(602) 629-6671

CA

Water Resources Division District Office
U.S. Geological Survey
Federal Bldg.
2800 Cottage Way
Room W-2235
Sacramento, CA 95825
(916) 484-4606

CO

Water Resources Division District Office
U.S. Geological Survey
Federal Center
Box 25046
Mail Stop 415
Denver, CO 80225
(303) 236-4882

CT

Water Resources Division
Connecticut Office
U.S. Geological Survey
525 Ribicoff Federal Bldg.
450 Main St.
Hartford, CT 06103
(203) 244-2528

DC, DE

See MD.

FL

Water Resources Division District Office
U.S. Geological Survey
Hobbs Federal Bldg.
Suite 3015
Tallahassee, FL 32301
(904) 681-7620

GA

Water Resources Division District Office
U.S. Geological Survey
6481 Peachtree Industrial Blvd.
Suite B
Doraville, GA 30360
(404) 221-4858

HI

Water Resources Division District Office
U.S. Geological Survey
P.O. Box 50166
300 Ala Moana Blvd.
Room 6110
Honolulu, HI 96850
(808) 546-8331

IA

Water Resources Division District Office
U.S. Geological Survey
269 Federal Bldg.
400 S. Clinton St.
P.O. Box 1230
Iowa City, IA 52244
(319) 337-4191

ID

Water Resources Division District Office
U.S. Geological Survey
230 Collins Rd.
Boise, ID 83702
(208) 334-1750

IL

Water Resources Division District Office
U.S. Geological Survey
Champaign County Bank Plaza
102 E. Main
Fourth Floor
Urbana, IL 61801
(217) 398-5353

IN

Water Resources Division District Office
U.S. Geological Survey
6023 Guion Rd.
Suite 201
Indianapolis, IN 46254
(317) 927-8640

KS

Water Resources Division District Office
U.S. Geological Survey
University of Kansas
1950 Constant Ave., Campus West
Lawrence, KS 66044
(913) 864-4321

KY

Water Resources Division District Office
U.S. Geological Survey
572 Federal Bldg.
600 Federal Place
Louisville, KY 40202
(502) 582-5241

LA

Water Resources Division District Office
U.S. Geological Survey
P.O. Box 66492
6554 Florida Blvd.
Baton Rouge, LA 70896
(504) 389-0281

MA

Water Resources Division District Office
U.S. Geological Survey
150 Causeway St.
Suite 1309
Boston, MA 02114
(617) 223-2822

MD

Water Resources Division District Office
U.S. Geological Survey
208 Carroll Bldg.
8600 LaSalle Rd.
Towson, MD 21204
(301) 828-1535

ME

See MA.

MI

Water Resources Division District Office
U.S. Geological Survey
6520 Mercantile Way
Suite 5
Lansing, MI 48910
(517) 377-1608

MN

Water Resources Division District Office
U.S. Geological Survey
702 Post Office Bldg.
St. Paul, MN 55101
(612) 725-7841

MO

Water Resources Division District Office
U.S. Geological Survey
Mail Stop 200
1400 Independence Rd.
Rolla, MO 65401
(314) 341-0824

MS

Water Resources Division District Office
U.S. Geological Survey
Federal Bldg.
100 W. Capitol St.
Suite 710
Jackson, MS 39269
(601) 960-4600

MT

Water Resources Division District Office
U.S. Geological Survey
428 Federal Bldg.
301 S. Park Ave.
Drawer 10076
Helena, MT 59626
(406) 449-5302

NC

Water Resources Division District Office
U.S. Geological Survey
436 Century Station
300 Fayetteville St. Mall
P.O. Box 2857
Raleigh, NC 27602
(919) 755-4510

ND
Water Resources Division District Office
U.S. Geological Survey
821 E. Interstate Ave.
Bismarck, ND 58501
(701) 255-4011, ext. 601

NE
Water Resources Division District Office
U.S. Geological Survey
406 Federal Building and U.S. Courthouse
100 Centennial Mall North
Lincoln, NE 68508
(402) 471-5082

NH
See MA.

NJ
Water Resources Division District Office
U.S. Geological Survey
430 Federal Bldg.
402 E. State St.
Trenton, NJ 08608
(609) 989-2162

NM
Water Resources Division District Office
U.S. Geological Survey
720 Western Bank Bldg.
505 Marquette, NW
Albuquerque, NM 87102
(505) 766-2246

NV
Water Resources Division
Nevada Office
U.S. Geological Survey
229 Federal Bldg.
705 N. Plaza St.
Carson City, NV 89701
(702) 882-1388

NY
Water Resources Division District Office
U.S. Geological Survey
P.O. Box 1669
343 U.S. Post Office and Courthouse Bldg.
Albany, NY 12201
(518) 472-3107

OH
Water Resources Division District Office
U.S. Geological Survey
975 W. Third Ave.
Columbus, OH 43212
(614) 469-5553

OK
Water Resources Division District Office
U.S. Geological Survey
215 Dean A. McGee Ave.
Room 621
Oklahoma City, OK 73102
(405) 231-4256

OR
Water Resources Division District Office
U.S. Geological Survey
847 N.E. Nineteenth Ave.
Suite 300
Portland, OR 97232
(503) 231-2009

PA
Water Resources Division District Office
U.S. Geological Survey
Federal Bldg.
228 Walnut St.
Fourth Floor
P.O. Box 1107
Harrisburg, PA 17108
(717) 782-4514

PR
Water Resources Division District Office
U.S. Geological Survey
GPO Box 4424
GSA Center, Building 652
Highway 28, Pueblo Viejo
San Juan, PR 00936
(809) 783-4660

RI
See MA.

SC
Water Resources Division District Office
U.S. Geological Survey
1835 Assembly St.
Suite 658
Columbia, SC 29201
(803) 765-5966

SD
Water Resources Division District Office
U.S. Geological Survey
317 Federal Bldg.
200 Fourth St., SW
Huron, SD 57350
(605) 352-8651, ext. 258

TN
Water Resources Division District Office
U.S. Geological Survey
A-413 Federal Bldg. and U.S. Courthouse
Nashville, TN 37203
(615) 251-5424

276 / U.S. Geological Survey

TX

Water Resources Division District Office
U.S. Geological Survey
649 Federal Bldg.
300 E. Eighth St.
Austin, TX 78701
(512) 482-5766

UT

Water Resources Division District Office
U.S. Geological Survey
Administration Bldg.
1745 West, 1700 South
Room 1016
Salt Lake City, UT 84104
(801) 524-5663

VA

Water Resources Division
Virginia Office
U.S. Geological Survey
200 W. Grace St.
Room 304
Richmond, VA 23220
(804) 771-2427

VT

See MA.

WA

Water Resources Division District Office
U.S. Geological Survey
1201 Pacific Ave.
Suite 600
Tacoma, WA 98402
(206) 593-5410

WI

Water Resources Division District Office
U.S. Geological Survey
1815 University Ave.
Madison, WI 53705
(608) 262-2488

WV

Water Resources Division District Office
U.S. Geological Survey
3416 Federal Building and U.S. Courthouse
500 Quarrier St. East
Charleston, WV 25301
(304) 347-5130

WY

Water Resources Division District Office
U.S. Geological Survey
4007 J.C. O'Mahoney Federal Center
2120 Capitol Ave.
Cheyenne, WY 82003
(307) 772-2153

State Agencies

Many state agencies sell materials that pertain to their state or area. Many have reference collections that include survey materials. Some are depositories of specific survey open-file reports. The survey cooperates with state agencies in various projects and publications are available.

AK

Division of Geological and Geophysical Survey
3001 Porcupine Dr.
Anchorage, AK 99701
(907) 786-2179

AL

Geological Survey of Alabama
P.O. Drawer O
University, AL 35486
(205) 349-2886

AR

Arkansas Geological Commission
3815 W. Roosevelt Rd.
Little Rock, AR 72201
(501) 371-1488

AZ

Bureau of Geology and Mineral Technology
845 N. Park Ave.
Tucson, AZ 85719
(602) 621-7906

CA

California Division of Mines and Geology
1416 Ninth St.
Room 1341
Sacramento, CA 95814
(916) 445-1923

CO

Colorado Geological Survey
1313 Sherman St.
Room 715
Denver, CO 80203
(303) 866-2611

CT

Department of Environmental Protection
Natural Resource Center
165 Capitol Ave.
Room 553
Hartford, CT 06106
(203) 556-3540

DE

Delaware Geological Survey
University of Delaware
101 Penny Hall
Newark, DE 19711
(302) 738-2833

FL

Bureau of Geology
903 W. Tennessee St.
Tallahassee, FL 32304
(904) 488-4191

GA

Georgia Geologic Survey
19 Martin Luther King Dr., SW
Room 400
Atlanta, GA 30334
(404) 656-3214

HI

Department of Land and Natural Resources
Division of Water and Land Development
P.O. Box 373
Honolulu, HI 96809
(808) 548-7533

IA

Iowa Geological Survey
123 N. Capitol
Iowa City, IA 52242
(319) 338-1173

ID

Idaho Geological Survey
University of Idaho Campus
Moscow, ID 83843
(208) 885-7991

IL

Illinois State Geological Survey
615 E. Peabody Dr.
Room 121
Champaign, IL 61820
(217) 344-1481

IN

Indiana Geological Survey
Department of Natural Resources
611 N. Walnut Grove
Bloomington, IN 47401
(812) 335-2862

KS

Kansas Geological Survey
The University of Kansas
1930 Avenue A, Campus West
Lawrence, KS 66044
(913) 864-3965

KY

Kentucky Geological Survey
University of Kentucky
311 Breckenridge Hall
Lexington, KY 40506
(606) 257-5863

LA

Louisiana Geological Survey
Department of Natural Resources
University Station
Box G
Baton Rouge, LA 70813
(504) 342-6754

MA

Department of Environmental Quality Engineering
Division of Water Ways
1 Winter St.
Seventh Floor
Boston, MA 02108
(617) 292-5690

MD

Maryland Geological Survey
The Rotunda
711 W. Fortieth St.
Suite 440
Baltimore, MD 21211
(301) 338-7084

ME

Maine Geological Survey
Department of Conservation
State House
Station 22
Augusta, ME 04330
(207) 289-2801

MI

Geologic Survey Division
Michigan Department of Natural Resources
Stevens T. Mason Bldg.
P.O. Box 30028
Lansing, MI 48909
(517) 373-1256

MN

Minnesota Geological Survey
2642 University Ave.
St. Paul, MN 55114
(612) 373-3372

MO

Department of Natural Resources
Division of Geology and Land Survey
P.O. Box 250
Rolla, MO 65401
(314) 364-1752

MS

Mississippi Geological, Economic and
   Topographical Survey
P.O. Box 5348
Jackson, MS 39216
(601) 354-6228

MT

Montana Bureau of Mines and Geology
Montana College of Mineral Science and Technology
Butte, MT 59701
(406) 496-4181

NC

North Carolina Geological Survey Section
P.O. Box 27687
Raleigh, NC 27611
(919) 733-2423

ND

North Dakota Geological Survey
University Station
Box 8156-58202
Grand Forks, ND 58201
(701) 777-2231

NE

Conservation and Survey Division
The University of Nebraska
Lincoln, NE 68588
(402) 472-3471

NH

Department of Resources and Economic
   Development
University of New Hampshire
117 James Hall
Durham, NH 03824
(603) 862-1216

NJ

New Jersey Geological Survey
CN-029
Trenton, NJ 08625
(609) 292-2576

NM

New Mexico Bureau of Mines and Mineral Resources
Campus Station
Socorro, NM 87801
(505) 835-5420

NV

Nevada Bureau of Mines and Geology
University of Nevada
Reno, NV 89557-0088
(702) 784-6691

NY

New York State Geological Survey
State Science Service
Cultural Education Center
Room 3140
Albany, NY 12230
(518) 474-5816

OH

Ohio Division of Geological Survey
Fountain Square
Building B
Columbus, OH 43224
(614) 265-6605

OK

Oklahoma Geological Survey
The University of Oklahoma
830 Van Vleet Oval
Room 163
Norman, OK 73019
(405) 325-3031

OR

Department of Geology and Mineral Industries
1005 State Office Bldg.
Portland, OR 97201
(503) 229-5580

PA

Bureau of Topographic and Geological Survey
Department of Environmental Resources
P.O. Box 2357
Harrisburg, PA 17120
(717) 787-2169

PR

Servicio Geologico de Puerto Rico
Departmento de Recursos Naturales
Apartado 5887
Puerta de Tierra
San Juan, PR 00906
(809) 723-2716

RI

Statewide Planning Program
265 Melrose St.
Providence, RI 02907
(401) 277-2656

SC

South Carolina Geological Survey
Harbison Forest Rd.
Columbia, SC 29210
(803) 758-6431

SD

South Dakota Geological Survey
University of South Dakota
Science Center
Vermillion, SD 57069
(605) 624-4471

TN
Department of Conservation
Division of Geology
701 Broadway
Nashville, TN 37203
(615) 742-6691

TX
Bureau of Economic Geology
The University of Texas at Austin
University Station
Box X
Austin, TX 78712
(512) 471-1534

UT
Utah Geological and Mineral Survey
606 Black Hawk Way
Salt Lake City, UT 84108
(801) 581-6831

VA
Virginia Division of Mineral Resources
P.O. Box 3667
Charlottesville, VA 22903
(804) 293-5121

WA
Division of Geology and Earth Resources
Department of Natural Resources
Olympia, WA 98504
(206) 459-6372

WI
Wisconsin Geological and Natural History Survey
University of Wisconsin Extension
1815 University Ave.
Madison, WI 53705
(608) 262-1705

WV
West Virginia Geological and Economic Survey
P.O. Box 879
Morgantown, WV 26507
(304) 594-2331

WY
Geological Survey of Wyoming
P.O. Box 3008
University Station
Laramie, WY 82071
(307) 742-2054
(307) 766-2286

Publications: Books. Maps, Photographs. Catalogs. Bulletins. Circulars. Indexes. Periodicals. Reports. News releases. Teachers' packets. Leaflets. Audiovisuals. Landsat images. Exhibit displays. Various data formats. On geology, hydrology, cartography, geography, remote sensing, land use, energy, and mineral and water resources.

Bibliographies, Sales Catalogs, Publications Lists, etc.

"New Publications of the U.S. Geological Survey." Monthly. 46p. free.

Prints annotated list of recent publications. Ordering information. To be placed on the mailing list, apply to: U.S. Geological Survey, 582 National Center, Reston, VA 22092.

"Publications of the Geological Survey, 1879-1961."
"Publications of the Geological Survey, 1962-1970." $2.00/copy.

Indexed by author, subject, and area. Beginning with 1971, annual supplements are available without charge from: Eastern Distribution Branch, Text Products Section, 604 S. Pickett St., Alexandria, VA 22304.

Various other catalogs and lists are available from those offices serving your state and region. Check the addresses that have been included.

Selected List of Books and Pamphlets

"Guide to Obtaining USGS Information." n.d. 35p. free. Circular 900.

Explains how to obtain materials, offices and their functions, and reference collections. Includes maps, books, and services. Order from: U.S. Department of the Interior, Geological Survey, 503 National Center, Reston, VA 22092.

"Postdoctoral Research Associateships." 1985. 106p. free.

Describes opportunities for research at the Geological Survey. Includes addresses of research facilities and index of research advisers.

"Scientific and Technical, Spatial, and Bibliographic Data Bases and Systems of the U.S. Geological Survey, 1983." rev. ed. 413p. free. Circular 817.

Compiled by the Office of the Data Administrator and prepared with the cooperation of the Bureau of Land Management and Minerals Management service. Includes databases, systems, and indexes.

Audiovisuals:

Filmographies, Sales Lists, etc.

"Motion Picture Film Services of the U.S. Geological Survey." 1981. 20p. free.

Provides annotations and information on how to borrow free loan films. More information on films may be obtained from the Visual Information Services Office for potential viewers. Categories include: *Geology, Topographic Mapping, Water Resources,*

Astrogeology, Aerial Photo Interpretation, etc. Order from: Visual Information Services Office, U.S. Geological Survey, 790 National Center, Reston, VA 22092. (703) 860-6171.

Individual Audiovisuals

"The Alaskan Earthquake, 1964." 1966. 20 minutes. 16mm. color. free loan.

Shows the effects of the earthquake. Looks at engineering problems. Animated sequences explain nature and cause of earthquakes.

"Geology of the Belize Reef." 1977. 16 minutes. 16mm. color. free loan.

How survey scientists determine the composition of the Belize barrier reef off the coast of Central America through a diver-operated coring device.

"In the Beginning." 1954. 28 minutes. 16mm. color. free loan.

Shows fundamental geologic principles illustrated by the natural features exposed in the Grand Canyon.

"National Petroleum Reserve in Alaska." 1980. 16 minutes. 16mm. color. free loan.

Shows the role of the survey in finding new sources of oil and gas. Explains the need for providing new energy resources while preserving ecology.

"Water Below." 1964. 30 minutes. 16mm. B&W. free loan.

Illustrates the importance of water found below the crust of the earth. Includes water supply problems and ways to conserve.

Library: The library system is one of the largest earth science library systems in the world. The main library is in Reston, with branches in Denver, Flagstaff, and Menlo Park. A separate field records collection and a photographic library are in Denver. The following list includes other facilities providing services. The main purpose is to support the survey but libraries also serve other federal agencies, state agencies, universities, and research organizations. The libraries are open to the public. Most materials may be borrowed through interlibrary loan.

Library
U.S. Geological Survey
950 National Center
12201 Sunrise Valley Dr.
Room 4-A-100
Reston, VA 22092
(703) 860-6671

Library
U.S. Geological Survey
345 Middlefield Rd.
Mail Stop 55
Menlo Park, CA 94025
(415) 323-8111, ext. 2207

Library
U.S. Geological Survey
Federal Center
Box 25046
Mail Stop 914
Denver, CO 80225
  Street address:
Denver West Office Park
Building 3
1526 Cole Blvd.
Golden, CO 80401
(303) 236-1000

Library
U.S. Geological Survey
2255 N. Gemini Dr.
Flagstaff, AZ 86001
(602) 779-3322, ext. 1386

Photographic Library
U.S. Geological Survey
Federal Center
Box 25046
Mail Stop 914
Denver, CO 80225
  Street address:
Denver West Office Park
Building 3
1526 Cole Blvd.
Golden, CO 80401
(303) 236-1010

Field Records
U.S. Geological Survey
Federal Center
Box 25046
Mail Stop 914
Denver, CO 80225
  Street address:
Denver West Office Park
Building 3
1526 Cole Blvd.
Golden, CO 80401
(303) 236-1005

Don Lee Kulow Memorial Library
EROS Data Center
Sioux Falls, SD 57198
(605) 594-6500

Core Library
U.S. Geological Survey
Federal Center
Box 25046
Mail Stop 975
Denver, CO 80225
  Street address:
Building A
5293 Ward Rd.
Arvada, CO 80002
(303) 236-1931

Special Services: The Branch of Geographic Names answers questions about geographic names, compiles name information, manages a names data depository, publishes materials, and coordinates name usage between the federal and state governments. Questions may be directed to:
Branch of Geographic Names
U.S. Geological Survey
523 National Center
Reston, VA 22092
(703) 860-6262

The EROS Data Center receives, processes and distributes earth-image data obtained by satellite and aircraft. Includes high and low altitude photographs as well as photographs from NASA's manned spacecraft, LANDSAT digital and photographic data of the National Oceanic and Atmospheric Administration's national environmental satellite, data, and information service.

Aerial Photographs

U.S. Geological Survey
EROS Data Center
Sioux Falls, SD 57198
(605) 594-6151

LANDSAT Data

NOAA/NESDIS
LANDSAT Customer Service
Mundt Federal Bldg.
Sioux Falls, SD 57198
(605) 594-6151

The National Earthquake Information Service provides information about recent earthquakes, computes, and publishes epicenter locations for earthquakes. Tours are available by appointment.
National Earthquake Information Service
U.S. Geological Survey
Federal Center
Mail Stop 967
Box 25046
Denver, CO 80225
(303) 236-1500

The Hydrologic Information Unit answers questions on hydrology, water as a resource, hydrologic mapping, as well as questions on the products, projects, and services of the Water Resources Division and other services. It offers free subscriptions to "National Water Conditions," a monthly summary of water resource conditions in the United States and southern Canada.
Hydrologic Information Unit
U.S. Geological Survey
419 National Center
Reston, VA 22092
(703) 860-7531

The Branch of Computer Information Services provides information on the federal software exchange program and on survey reports.
Branch of Computer Information Services
Information Systems Division
U.S. Geological Survey
802 National Center
Reston, VA 22092
(703) 860-7103

Certain survey reports, most water resources investigations released before 1982, and data compilations can only be purchased from:
National Technical Information Service
U.S. Department of Commerce
5285 Port Royal Rd.
Springfield, VA 22161
(703) 487-4650

The National Geophysical Data Center is a data management center. Data file holdings include solid earth geophysics and solar-terrestrial physics.
NOAA/NGDC
Mail Code E/GC
325 Broadway
Boulder, CO 80303
Marine data: (303) 497-6338
Seismological data: (303) 497-6472

U.S. HOUSE OF REPRESENTATIVES
Office of the Clerk
Washington, DC 20515
(202) 225-7000

Date Established: 1789 (first meeting of Congress)

Objectives of the Agency: Be legislative, administrative, and budgetary officer; keep the journal; take votes; certify passage of bills; process legislation; prepare the House budget; disburse funds; and be the contracting officer, purchaser, and provider of furnishings and supplies.

Curriculum: Government

Subjects: U.S.—Congress, House

Publications: Lists of members.

Selected List of Books and Pamphlets

"List of Standing Committees and Select Committees and Their Subcommittees of the House of Representatives of the United States together with Joint Committees of Congress." Current. 50p. free.

Lists committee members, indicating political party. Groups committees by type, arranged alphabetically.

"Official Alphabetical List of the House of Representatives of the United States." Current. 18p. free.

Lists name, political party, representative district, state, and committee(s).

"Official List of Members of the House of Representatives of the United States and their Places of Residence." Current. 16p. free.

Provides names arranged alphabetically by state, with political party, service in the previous Congress, predecessors, and city.

"United States House of Representatives." Current. 14p. free.

Indicates political party, state, telephone number, and room number. Alphabetical arrangement. Includes information on room locations and telephoning. Also includes senators, committees, and miscellaneous House numbers.

U.S. INFORMATION AGENCY
Office of Public Liaison
Room 602
301 Fourth St., SW
Washington, DC 20547
(202) 485-2355

Date Established: 1978

Objectives of the Agency: Be responsible for this country's overseas information and cultural programs; and report and advise on worldwide public opinion.

Curriculum: Education

Subjects: International education

Publications: Newsletters. Pamphlets. Magazines. Fact sheets.

Serials, Subscription Publications, etc.

"USIA Update." Current. 4p. free.

Summarizes news about agency appointments, accomplishments, and services.

Selected List of Books and Pamphlets

"Artistic Ambassador Program." Current. 6p. free.

Explains how the program uses American musical talent for cross-cultural understanding.

"Arts America." Current. 12p. free.

Explains the purpose and presentations of the Arts America program that was created in 1979.

"Fulbright Program." n.d. 8p. free.

Gives information about the Fulbright Program, established in 1946 to increase mutual understanding between our country and others by scholarships given to Americans to study, teach, and do research abroad and have foreign nationals come to this country and engage in similar pursuits.

"U.S. Information Agency Fact Sheet." 1985. 10p. free.

Describes the purposes, publications, organization, and current programs of the agency.

"Work-Study-Travel-Abroad Guidelines." Current. 6p. free.

Discusses what to ask in evaluating organizations sponsoring work, study, or travel abroad. Addresses and telephone numbers.

U.S. INTERNATIONAL TRADE COMMISSION
Secretary
701 E St., NW
Washington, DC 20436
(202) 523-0161

Date Established: 1916

Objectives of the Agency: Furnish reports, recommendations, and studies about international trade and tariffs to the President, the Congress, and other government agencies; and conduct investigations, public hearings, and research projects.

Curriculum: Government

Subjects: U.S.—commerce

Publications: Catalogs. Reports. Surveys. Summaries.

Bibliographies, Sales Catalogs, Publications Lists, etc.

"Selected Publications of the United States International Trade Commission." Current. 42p. free. USITC Publication 1714.

Lists cumulative, periodic, miscellaneous general reports, publications by countries and geographic areas, and reports by commodities. For sale or free.

U.S. MISSION TO THE UNITED NATIONS
799 United Nations Plaza
New York, NY 10017

Date Established: 1947

Objectives of the Agency: Assist the President and the Department of State in conducting U.S. policy at the United Nations.

Curriculum: Government

Subjects: United Nations—officials and employees

Publications: Fact sheets.

Selected List of Books and Pamphlets

"Fact Sheet." n.d. 2p. free.

Explains what the U.S. Mission to the United Nations does and where it is located. Includes functions, sections, staff, and chronology of U.S. representatives to the United Nations from 1945 to the present.

"Vernon A. Walters." 1985. 1p. free.

Provides a biographical sketch of the current U.S. Permanent Representative to the United Nations.

U.S. POSTAL SERVICE
Public and Employee Communications Department
475 L'Enfant Plaza, SW
Washington, DC 20260-3100
(202) 245-5145

Date Established: 1775

Objectives of the Agency: Provide mail delivery; and protect the mail.

Curriculum: Social studies

Subjects: Postage stamps

Locations:

IA, IL, IN, KS, KY, MI, MN, MO, ND, NE, OH, SD, WI

U.S. Postal Service Regional Office
433 W. Van Buren St.
Chicago, IL 60699-0100
(312) 886-3550

AL, AR, FL, GA, LA, MS, NC, OK, SC, TN, TX

U.S. Postal Service Regional Office
1407 Union Ave.
Memphis, TN 38166
(901) 722-7532

DC, DE, MD, NJ (ZIP 080-087), NY (ZIP 130-149), PA, VA, WV

U.S. Postal Service Regional Office
P.O. Box 8601
Philadelphia, PA 19197
(215) 496-6001

AK, AZ, CA, CO, HI, ID, MT, NM, NV, OR, UT, WA, WY, Pacific Possessions and Trust Territories

U.S. Postal Service Regional Office
850 Cherry Ave.
San Bruno, CA 94099-0100
(415) 470-9000

CT, MA, ME, NH, NJ (ZIP 070-079, 088-089), NY (ZIP 090-129), PR, RI, VI, VT

U.S. Postal Service Regional Office
1633 Broadway
New York, NY 10098-0100
(212) 974-8200

Publications: History. Regulations. Postage stamps. Concerns of U.S. mail delivery as related in booklets, bulletins, guides, transmittal letters, and manuals.

Bibliographies, Sales Catalogs, Publications Lists, etc.

"History of the U.S. Postal Service." 1985. 38p. free. Publication 100.
 Begins with 1775 and ends with 1984. Includes postal bibliography and recent statistics.

"Subject Bibliography." 1984. 4p. free. SB-169.
 What is available regarding the Postal Service. Annotation includes price ordering information. Order from: Superintendent of Documents, U.S. Government Printing Office, Washington, DC 20402.

Serials, Subscription Publications, etc.

Postal Bulletin. Weekly. $71.00/yr. domestic, $88.75/yr. foreign. S/N 039-000-80001-2.
 Gives current information relating to the Postal Service and commemorative stamp posters. Order from: Superintendent of Documents, U.S. Government Printing Office, Washington, DC 20402.

Selected List of Books and Pamphlets

"The Saga of the Pony Express." 1983. 19p. free. Publication 290.
 Describes pony relays through 2,000 miles of frontier America between St. Joseph, MO, and Sacramento, CA. The trips were made from April, 1860 to October, 1861.

United States Postage Stamps: Transmittal Letters 1-7. n.d. 570p. $21.00. S/N 039-000-00267-1.
 Gives information on U.S. postage stamps issued from July 1, 1847 through 1980. Looseleaf. Order from: Superintendent of Documents, U.S. Government Printing Office, Washington, DC 20402.

Audiovisuals:

Filmographies, Sales Lists, etc.

"A Reference List of Audiovisual Materials." 1984. 6p. free.
 Annotates films available. Includes distributor and intended primary audience.

If you enclose a self-addressed, stamped envelope and request postal film information, you should receive a catalog listing other postal-related films, available free for limited use from:
Audience Players, Inc.
5107 Douglas Fir Rd.
Calabasis, CA 91302-1472

Individual Films

"America the Beautiful (in Stamps)." 4½ minutes. 16mm. loan.
 Visualizes the popular American patriotic hymn with a montage of historical and cultural U.S. postage stamps and scenic footage.

"The Gift of Letters." 28 minutes. 16mm. loan.
 James Whitmore is the host for a series of dramatizations of letters representative of periods in U.S. history. Portrays letters in comic and dramatic styles. Reflection on the meaning of letters.

"Timbromania." n.d. 29 minutes. 16mm. loan.
 Features Ernest Borgnine. Takes a look at stamp collecting from its beginning as a fad in England and France to the present time. The title is a French word for *stamp craze.*

Library: Reading rooms located at:
U.S. Postal Service
475 L'Enfant Plaza, SW
Washington, DC 20260-3100
Eleventh Floor North
Library Division
(202) 245-4023

Special Services: To request speakers, contact your local postmaster. Availability depends largely upon the type of presentation you wish and your audience. The local post office usually provides tours and presentations for schools.

U.S. SECRET SERVICE
Office of Public Affairs
Department of the Treasury
1800 G St., NW
Washington, DC 20223
(202) 535-5708

Date Established: 1865

Objectives of the Agency: Detect and arrest any person committing any offense against the laws of the United States relating to coins, currency, and other obligations, and securities of the country and of foreign governments; execute warrants issued under U.S. authority; protect the President of the United States and members of his immediate family as well as others in the order of succession to the presidential office; and execute other duties as authorized by the law.

Curriculum: Government, guidance

Subjects: Secret Service

Locations (arranged alphabetically by city):

U.S. Secret Service District Office
235 Roosevelt Ave.
Albany, GA 31701
(912) 436-0323

U.S. Secret Service District Office
Federal Blvd.
Room 244
Albany, NY 12207
(518) 472-2884

U.S. Secret Service District Office
Western Bank Bldg.
Albuquerque, NM 87102
(505) 766-3336

U.S. Secret Service District Office
701 C St.
Anchorage, AK 99513
(907) 271-5148

U.S. Secret Service District Office
Equitable Bldg.
Atlanta, GA 30303
(404) 221-6111

U.S. Secret Service District Office
Atlantic City Post Office
Atlantic City, NJ 08401
(609) 347-0772

U.S. Secret Service District Office
Federal Office Bldg.
Austin, TX 78701
(512) 482-5103

U.S. Secret Service District Office
U.S. Courthouse
Baltimore, MD 21201
(301) 962-2200

U.S. Secret Service District Office
500 Bldg.
Birmingham, AL 35233
(205) 254-1144

U.S. Secret Service District Office
Federal Bldg.
Bismarck, ND 58501
(701) 255-3294

U.S. Secret Service District Office
550 Fort St.
Boise, ID 83702
(208) 334-1403

U.S. Secret Service District Office
470 Atlantic Ave.
Boston, MA 02110
(617) 223-2827

U.S. Secret Service District Office
Federal Bldg.
Room 1208
Buffalo, NY 14202
(716) 846-4401

U.S. Secret Service District Office
Frank T. Bow Federal Bldg.
Canton, OH 44701
(216) 489-4400

U.S. Secret Service District Office
1 Valley Square
Charleston, WV 25301
(304) 347-5188

U.S. Secret Service District Office
226 Skeens Bldg.
Charlotte, NC 28209
(704) 523-9583

U.S. Secret Service District Office
Post Office Bldg.
Chattanooga, TN 37401
(615) 266-4014

U.S. Secret Service District Office
2120 Capitol Ave.
Cheyenne, WY 82001
(307) 772-2380

U.S. Secret Service District Office
219 S. Dearborn St.
Chicago, IL 60604
(312) 353-5431

U.S. Secret Service District Office
Federal Office Bldg.
Cincinnati, OH 45202
(513) 684-3585

U.S. Secret Service District Office
550 Investment Bldg.
Cleveland, OH 44114
(216) 522-4365

U.S. Secret Service District Office
Strom Thurmond Federal Bldg.
Columbia, SC 29201
(803) 765-5446

U.S. Secret Service District Office
411 Federal Office Bldg.
Columbus, OH 43215
(614) 469-7370

U.S. Secret Service District Office
545 N. Upper Broadway
Corpus Christi, TX 78476
(512) 888-3401

U.S. Secret Service District Office
1100 Commerce St.
Dallas, TX 75242
(214) 767-8021

U.S. Secret Service District Office
Federal Bldg.
Room 704
Dayton, OH 45402
(513) 222-2013

U.S. Secret Service District Office
1660 Lincoln St.
Denver, CO 80264
(303) 837-3027

U.S. Secret Service District Office
Federal Office Bldg.
Des Moines, IA 50309
(515) 284-4565

U.S. Secret Service District Office
231 Lafayette Blvd.
Detroit, MI 48226
(313) 226-6400

U.S. Secret Service District Office
Pershing Blvd. West
El Paso, TX 79902
(915) 541-7546

U.S. Secret Service District Office
Tenth and Lamar Sts.
Fort Worth, TX 76102
(817) 334-2015

U.S. Secret Service District Office
1130 O St.
Fresno, CA 93721
(209) 487-5204

U.S. Secret Service District Office
110 Michigan Ave., NW
Grand Rapids, MI 49503
(616) 456-2276

U.S. Secret Service District Office
Post Office Bldg.
Great Falls, MT 59401
(406) 452-8515

U.S. Secret Service District Office
228 Walnut St.
Harrisburg, PA 17108
(717) 782-4811

U.S. Secret Service District Office
300 Ala Moana Blvd.
Honolulu, HI 96850
(808) 546-5637

U.S. Secret Service District Office
515 Rust St.
Houston, TX 77002
(713) 229-2755

U.S. Secret Service District Office
Federal Bldg.
Indianapolis, IN 46204
(317) 269-6444

U.S. Secret Service District Office
Depositors Savings Bldg.
Jackson, MS 39201
(601) 960-4436

U.S. Secret Service District Office
7820 Arlington Expressway
Jacksonville, FL 32211
(904) 724-4530

U.S. Secret Service District Office
U.S. Courthouse Bldg.
Kansas City, MO 64142
(816) 374-5022

U.S. Secret Service District Office
U.S. Courthouse Bldg.
Knoxville, TN 37901
(615) 673-4527

U.S. Secret Service District Office
300 Las Vegas Blvd. South
Las Vegas, NV 89101
(702) 385-6446

U.S. Secret Service District Office
Savers Federal Bldg.
Little Rock, AR 72201
(501) 378-6241

U.S. Secret Service District Office
300 N. Los Angeles St.
Los Angeles, CA 90012
(213) 688-4830

U.S. Secret Service District Office
U.S. Post Office and Courthouse
Louisville, KY 40201
(502) 582-5171

U.S. Secret Service District Office
Federal Office Bldg.
Lubbock, TX 79401
(806) 743-7347

U.S. Secret Service District Office
131 W. Wilson St.
Madison, WI 53703
(608) 264-5191

U.S. Secret Service District Office
560 Broad Hollow Rd.
Melville, NY 11747
(516) 249-0404

U.S. Secret Service District Office
Federal Bldg.
Memphis, TN 38103
(901) 521-3568

U.S. Secret Service District Office
8375 N.W. Fifty-Third St.
Miami, FL 33166
(305) 350-5961

U.S. Secret Service District Office
517 E. Wisconsin Ave.
Milwaukee, WI 53202
(414) 291-3587

U.S. Secret Service District Office
218 U.S. Courthouse
Minneapolis, MN 55401
(612) 725-2801

U.S. Secret Service District Office
107 St. Francis St.
Mobile, AL 36602
(205) 690-2851

U.S. Secret Service District Office
15 Lee St.
Montgomery, AL 36104
(205) 832-7601

U.S. Secret Service District Office
801 Broadway St.
Nashville, TN 37203
(615) 251-5841

U.S. Secret Service District Office
150 Court St.
New Haven, CT 06510
(203) 865-2449

U.S. Secret Service District Office
500 Camp St.
New Orleans, LA 70130
(504) 589-4041

U.S. Secret Service District Office
6 World Trade Center
New York, NY 10048-0953
(212) 466-4400

U.S. Secret Service District Office
60 Evergreen Pl.
Newark, NJ 07018
(201) 645-2334

U.S. Secret Service District Office
Federal Bldg.
Norfolk, VA 23510
(804) 441-3200

U.S. Secret Service District Office
Federal Bldg.
Oklahoma City, OK 73102
(405) 231-4476

U.S. Secret Service District Office
Union Pacific Bldg.
Omaha, NE 68102
(402) 221-4671

U.S. Secret Service District Office
80 N. Hughey Ave.
Orlando, FL 32801
(305) 420-6333

U.S. Secret Service District Office
600 Arch St.
Philadelphia, PA 19106
(215) 597-0600

U.S. Secret Service District Office
230 N. First Ave.
Phoenix, AZ 85025
(602) 261-3556

U.S. Secret Service District Office
1000 Liberty Ave.
Pittsburgh, PA 15222
(412) 644-3384

U.S. Secret Service District Office
151 Forest Ave.
Portland, ME 04105
(207) 780-3493

U.S. Secret Service District Office
121 S.W. Salmon St.
Portland, OR 97204
(503) 221-2162

U.S. Secret Service District Office
44 Washington St.
Providence, RI 02903
(401) 331-6456

U.S. Secret Service District Office
Post Office and Federal Bldg.
Raleigh, NC 27601
(919) 755-4335

U.S. Secret Service District Office
Federal Office Bldg.
Reno, NV 89509
(702) 784-5354

U.S. Secret Service District Office
400 N. Eighth St.
Richmond, VA 23240
(804) 771-2274

U.S. Secret Service District Office
3890 Orange St.
Riverside, CA 92502
(714) 351-6781

U.S. Secret Service District Office
210 Franklin Rd.
Roanoke, VA 24001
(703) 982-6208

U.S. Secret Service District Office
Federal Bldg.
Rochester, NY 14614
(716) 263-6830

U.S. Secret Service District Office
U.S. Courthouse
Sacramento, CA 95814
(916) 440-2413

U.S. Secret Service District Office
1114 Market St.
St. Louis, MO 63101
(314) 425-4238

U.S. Secret Service District Office
350 S. Main St.
Salt Lake City, UT 84101
(801) 524-5910

U.S. Secret Service District Office
Federal Bldg.
San Antonio, TX 78206
(512) 271-0120

U.S. Secret Service District Office
88 Front St.
San Diego, CA 92188
(619) 293-5640

U.S. Secret Service District Office
450 Golden Gate Ave.
San Francisco, CA 94102
(415) 566-8771

U.S. Secret Service District Office
Crocker Bank Bldg.
San Jose, CA 95113
(408) 275-7233

U.S. Secret Service District Office
U.S. Courthouse
San Juan, PR 00918
(809) 753-4539

U.S. Secret Service District Office
222 E. Corrillo St.
Santa Barbara, CA 93111
(805) 963-9391

U.S. Secret Service District Office
Federal Bldg., Courthouse
Savannah, GA 31402
(912) 944-4401

U.S. Secret Service District Office
Post Office Bldg.
Scranton, PA 18501
(717) 346-5781

U.S. Secret Service District Office
Federal Bldg.
Seattle, WA 98174
(206) 442-5495

U.S. Secret Service District Office
Federal Bldg.
Shreveport, LA 71101
(318) 226-5299

U.S. Secret Service District Office
208 E. Thirteenth St.
Sioux Falls, SD 57102
(605) 331-4565

U.S. Secret Service District Office
920 W. Riverside Ave.
Spokane, WA 99201
(509) 456-2532

U.S. Secret Service District Office
Federal Bldg.
Springfield, IL 62701
(217) 492-4033

U.S. Secret Service District Office
300 S. Jefferson
Springfield, MO 65806
(417) 864-8340

U.S. Secret Service District Office
100 S. Clinton St.
Syracuse, NY 13202
(315) 423-5338

U.S. Secret Service District Office
700 Twiggs St.
Tampa, FL 33602
(813) 228-2636

U.S. Secret Service District Office
Federal Bldg.
Toledo, OH 43604
(419) 259-6434

U.S. Secret Service District Office
Federal Bldg.
Tucson, AZ 85701
(602) 629-6819

U.S. Secret Service District Office
Federal Bldg.
Tulsa, OK 74101
(918) 581-7272

U.S. Secret Service District Office
221 W. Ferguson St.
Tyler, TX 75710
(214) 595-6611

U.S. Secret Service District Office
1800 G St., NW
Washington, DC 20223
(202) 535-5100

U.S. Secret Service District Office
701 Clematis St.
West Palm Beach, FL 33401
(305) 659-0184

U.S. Secret Service District Office
300 Hamilton Ave.
White Plains, NY 10601
(914) 682-8181

U.S. Secret Service District Office
220 W. Douglas
Wichita, KS 67202
(316) 267-1452

U.S. Secret Service District Office
844 King St.
Wilmington, DE 19801
(302) 573-6188

Publications: Pamphlets about functions of the Secret Service and career opportunities.

Selected List of Books and Pamphlets

"Counterfeiting and Forgery." n.d. 5-fold. free.
   Gives history of counterfeiting and facts about U.S. paper currency. Includes recognizing a counterfeit bill and what to do if you receive a counterfeit bill. Tips on counterfeit coins. Forgery of U.S. government checks. Tips about U.S. savings bonds. Photographs.

"The Secret Service and Its Protective Responsibilities." n.d. 14p. free.
   Explains what the Secret Service is authorized to protect. Includes attempts and assassinations of various presidents.

"The Secret Service Story." n.d. 4-fold. free.
   Explains the history, missions, divisions, duties of the Secret Service. Photographs.

"Special Agent." n.d. 3-fold. free.
   Describes what types of protective and investigative work are done by special agents. Includes employment opportunities, educational and physical requirements, promotional opportunities, and benefits.

"United States Secret Service Uniformed Division." n.d. 3-fold. free.
   Describes the history, protective responsibilities, requirements, appointments, training, and benefits of the U.S. Secret Service Uniformed Division.

URBAN MASS TRANSPORTATION ADMINISTRATION
U.S. Department of Transportation
Office of Technical Assistance
400 Seventh St., SW
Washington, DC 20590
(202) 426-4043

Date Established: 1964

Objectives of the Agency: Assist in the development of improved mass transportation facilities, equipment, techniques, methods; encourage the planning and establishment of areawide urban mass transportation systems where they are cost-effective; aid state and local governments in financing such systems; and encourage private sector involvement.

Curriculum: Government

Subjects: Transportation

Locations:

Urban Mass Transportation Administration
  Region 1 Office
C/O Transportation System Center
55 Broadway
Cambridge, MA 02142
(617) 494-2055

Urban Mass Transportation Administration
  Region 2 Office
26 Federal Plaza
New York, NY 10278
(212) 263-8162

Urban Mass Transportation Administration
  Region 3 Office
434 Walnut St.
Philadelphia, PA 19106
(215) 597-8098

Urban Mass Transportation Administration
  Region 4 Office
1720 Peachtree Rd., NW
Atlanta, GA 30309
(404) 881-3948

Urban Mass Transportation Administration
  Region 5 Office
200 S. Wacker Dr.
Chicago, IL 60606
(312) 353-2789

Urban Mass Transportation Administration
  Region 6 Office
819 Taylor St.
Fort Worth, TX 76102
(817) 334-3787

Urban Mass Transportation Administration
  Region 7 Office
6301 Rockhill Rd.
Kansas City, MO 64131
(816) 926-5053

Urban Mass Transportation Administration
  Region 8 Office
1050 Seventeenth St.
Denver, CO 80265
(303) 837-3242

Urban Mass Transportation Administration
  Region 9 Office
211 Main St.
San Francisco, CA 94105
(415) 974-7313

Urban Mass Transportation Administration
  Region 10 Office
915 Second Ave.
Seattle, WA 98174
(206) 442-4210

Publications: Pamphlets. Directories.

Selected List of Books and Pamphlets

"Finding Your Way in DOT." 1984. 11p. free.
  Explains what agencies belong to the Department of Transportation, how they can help, and how to reach them.

"Innovation in Public Transportation." Current. 149p. free.
  Describes technical assistance projects sponsored by the Urban Mass Transportation Administration to inform the public about the work which is underway to improve services and reduce the cost of public transportation.

"Urban Mass Transportation Research Information Service." n.d. 6p. free.
  Tells what the service is and what kinds of information it offers. Includes information about online and literature searches.

WATER RESOURCES SCIENTIFIC INFORMATION CENTER
U.S. Department of the Interior
Geological Survey
Mail Stop 425
Reston, VA 22092

Date Established: 1982

Objectives of the Agency: Be the national center for the collection and dissemination of scientific and technical information on water resources.

Curriculum: Environmental studies, geography

Subjects: Water resources development

Publications: Monthly abstract journal.

Serials, Subscription Publications, etc.

Selected Water Resources Abstracts. Monthly. approx. 201p. for the North American Continent: $50.00/yr. indexes only; $100.00/yr. journal only; $125.00/yr. journal and annual indexes.
  Includes abstracts of current and earlier pertinent monographs, journal articles, reports, and other publication formats covering water resources as treated in the life, physical, and social sciences. Also covers the related engineering and legal aspects of the

characteristics and supply conditions. The Center does not provide copies of documents abstracted in the journal.

Selected List of Books and Pamphlets

"Water Resources Scientific Information Center." 1985. 1p. free.

Tells what the center is and what services it provides.

THE WHITE HOUSE OFFICE
1600 Pennsylvania Ave., NW
Washington, DC 20500
(202) 456-1414

Date Established: 1800

Objectives of the Agency: Be the home and office of the President, and also a national museum.

Curriculum: Government, history

Subjects: U.S. history

Publications: Pamphlets. Bibliographies.

Bibliographies, Sales Catalogs, Publications Lists, etc.

"Publications." n.d. 1p. free.

Tells where to obtain such materials as "The United States Constitution," and portraits of the chief justices.

Selected List of Books and Pamphlets

"The President's House." n.d. 28p. free.

Contains descriptions and photographs of various rooms of the White House and the life of a president. Includes portraits and terms of the presidents.

WOMEN'S BUREAU
Office of the Secretary
U.S. Department of Labor
Washington, DC 20210
(202) 523-6611

Date Established: 1920

Objectives of the Agency: Improve the economic status of all women through participating in the development of policy and programs which have an impact on women's employment and their employability and through working with target groups of women with special employment-related needs to develop programs to meet those needs.

Curriculum: Women's studies

Subjects: Women—employment

Locations:
(write to the nearest office)

Womens Bureau Region 1 Office
U.S. Department of Labor
Office of the Secretary
JFK Bldg.
Room 1600
Boston, MA 02203

Women's Bureau Region 2 Office
U.S. Department of Labor
Office of the Secretary
1515 Broadway
Room 3575
New York, NY 10036

Women's Bureau Region 3 Office
U.S. Department of Labor
Office of the Secretary
Gateway Bldg.
3535 Market St.
Room 13280
Philadelphia, PA 19104

Women's Bureau Region 4 Office
U.S. Department of Labor
Office of the Secretary
1371 Peachtree St., NE
Room 323
Atlanta, GA 30367

Women's Bureau Region 5 Office
U.S. Department of Labor
Office of the Secretary
230 S. Dearborn St.
Tenth Floor
Chicago, IL 60604

Women's Bureau Region 6 Office
U.S. Department of Labor
Office of the Secretary
555 Griffin Square Bldg.
Griffin and Young Sts.
Room 863
Dallas, TX 75202

Women's Bureau Region 7 Office
U.S. Department of Labor
Office of the Secretary
Federal Bldg.
911 Walnut St.
Room 2511
Kansas City, MO 64106

Women's Bureau Region 8 Office
U.S. Department of Labor
Office of the Secretary
Federal Bldg.
1961 Stout St.
Room 1456
Denver, CO 80202

Women's Bureau Region 9 Office
U.S. Department of Labor
Office of the Secretary
Federal Bldg.
450 Golden Gate Ave.
Room 9301
San Francisco, CA 94102

Women's Bureau Region 10 Office
U.S. Department of Labor
Office of the Secretary
Federal Office Bldg.
909 First Ave.
Room 3094
Seattle, WA 98174

Publications: Fact sheets. Pamphlets. Handbooks. On activities of the Women's Bureau, concerns in employment practices for women, and statistics and employment trends.

Bibliographies, Sales Catalogs, Publications Lists, etc.

"Publications of the Women's Bureau." Current. 4p. free.

Lists what is available. Tells how to order the free and for sale materials.

Selected List of Books and Pamphlets

"Brief Highlights of Major Federal Laws on Sex Discrimination in Employment." 1980. 6p. free.

Discusses how laws, such as the Equal Pay Act, provide protection and how women can assert their job rights.

"History of the Women's Bureau 1920-1965." 1985. 2p. free.

Traces the development of the Women's Bureau, beginning with the passage of a law creating the bureau in 1920.

"Job Options for Women in the 80's." 1980. 22p. free.

Contains types of jobs, employment resources, and work patterns.

"Maternity Leave." 1980. 1p. free. Consumer Information Leaflet No. USDL-35(WB-1).

Explains Title VII prohibiting discrimination in employment on the basis of sex, race, religion, color, or national origin.

"Protection against Sex Discrimination in Employment." 1980. 2p. free. Consumer Information Leaflet No. USDL-27(WB-3).

Explains Title VII, amendment, and executive order. Includes things you can complain about and to whom.

"A Working Woman's Guide to Her Job Rights." 1984. 56p. free. Leaflet 55.

Discusses getting the job and being on the job. Includes federal protection for jobseekers, retirement benefits, and how women can assert their job rights.

Special Services: If you are interested in receiving notices of future Women's Bureau publications, write the bureau at the Washington address given above and state the specific subject in which you are interested.

Check with your regional office for films that may be available.

WOMEN'S RIGHTS NATIONAL HISTORICAL PARK
National Park Service
P.O. Box 70
Seneca Falls, NY 13148
(315) 568-2991

Date Established: 1980

Objectives of the Agency: Preserve and interpret the significant sites associated with the first women's rights convention, held in Seneca Falls in 1848.

Curriculum: History, women's studies

Subjects: America—history
Feminism
Women—civil rights
Women—U.S.
Women's liberation movement

Publications: Fact sheets. Flyers. On the park and personalities connected with the women's rights movement.

Selected List of Books and Pamphlets

"Answers to Frequently Asked Questions about the Park." n.d. 3p. free.

Answers to such questions as what the park is, and who organized the first women's rights convention.

"The Bloomer Costume and Dress Reform." n.d. 6p. free.

Describes the introduction of knee-length skirts worn over baggy pantaloons as a convenient form of dress. Includes public reaction, use, and arguments.

"Declaration of Sentiments." n.d. 2p. free.

Modeled on the Declaration of Independence, the Declaration of Sentiments of 1848, asserted the rights of women. Includes the names of the men and women who signed the declaration.

"Frederick Douglass and the Women's Rights Movement." n.d. 6p. free.

Describes what the connection between Douglass and the movement was, his friendship with Elizabeth Cady Stanton, and his contributions to fighting injustice.

"Lucretia Mott." n.d. 8p. free.

Gives biographical sketch of Mott and her contributions to the women's rights movement.

"Women's Rights National Historical Park." n.d. 6p. free.

Discusses the history of Seneca Falls and the development of the women's rights movement. Map. Visitor information.

"Women's Rights National Historical Park Authorizing Legislation." n.d. 2p. free.

Reprints Public Law 96-607, Title XVI signed December 28, 1980 for the establishment of the park.

Acronyms and Abbreviations

Federal agencies often use or are referred to by the following acronyms or abbreviations. They have been included for convenient reference. Arrangement is alphabetical by abbreviation or acronym.

ABMC	American Battle Monuments Commission
ACDA	U.S. Arms Control and Disarmament Agency
ACP	Agricultural Conservation Program
ACUS	Administrative Conference of the United States
ACYF	Administration for Children, Youth, and Families
ADAMHA	Alcohol, Drug Abuse, and Mental Health Administration
ADB	Asian Development Bank
ADD	Administration on Developmental Disabilities
ADEA	Age Discrimination in Employment Act
ADP	Automatic Data Processing
AEDS	Atomic Energy Detection System
AFDC	Aid to Families with Dependent Children
AFIDA	Agricultural Foreign Investment Disclosure Act
AFIS	American Forces Information Service
AFPC	Armed Forces Policy Council
AFR	Air Force Reserve
AFRRI	Armed Forces Radiobiology Research Institute
AFSC	Armed Forces Staff College
AGRICOLA	Agricultural Online Access
AID	Agency for International Development
AIS	Automated Information Systems
ALJ	Administrative Law Judge
AMS	Agricultural Marketing Service
AMTRAK	National Railroad Passenger Corporation
ANA	Administration for Native Americans
AOA	Administration on Aging
APHIS	Animal and Plant Health Inspection Service
ARC	Appalachian Regional Commission
ARS	Agricultural Research Service
ASCS	Agricultural Stabilization and Conservation Service
ATSDR	Agency for Toxic Substances and Disease Registry
BCP	Blended Credit Program
BEA	Bureau of Economic Analysis
BIA	Bureau of Indian Affairs
BIB	Board for International Broadcasting
BJS	Bureau of Justice Statistics

294 / Acronyms and Abbreviations

BLM	Bureau of Land Management	CSRS	Cooperative State Research Service
BLS	Bureau of Labor Statistics	DA	Department of the Army
BPA	Bonneville Power Administration	DARPA	Defense Advanced Research Projects Agency
CALS	Current Awareness Literature Service	DAVA	Defense Audiovisual Agency
CBO	Congressional Budget Office	DCA	Defense Communications Agency
CCA	Crop Condition Assessment	DCAA	Defense Contract Audit Agency
CCC	Commodity Credit Corporation	DCAR'S	Defense Contract Administration Services Regions
CCEA	Cabinet Council on Economic Affairs	DCII	Defense Central Index of Investigations
CCR	Commission on Civil Rights	DCS	Defense Communications System
CDBG	Community Development Block Grant	DEA	Drug Enforcement Administration
CDC	Centers for Disease Control	DEERS	Defense Enrollment Eligibility Reporting System
CEA	Council of Economic Advisers	DIA	Defense Intelligence Agency
CEQ	Council on Environmental Quality	DIPEC	Defense Industrial Plant Equipment Center
CFA	Commission of Fine Arts	DIS	Defense Investigative Service
CFC	Cooperative Finance Corporation	DISAM	Defense Institute of Security Assistance Management
CFR	Code of Federal Regulations	DLA	Defense Logistics Agency
CFTC	Commodity Futures Trading Commission	DLSA	Defense Legal Services Agency
CG	Commanding General	DMA	Defense Mapping Agency
CHAMPVA	Civilian Health and Medical Program of the Veterans Administration	DMS	Defense Mapping School
CIA	Central Intelligence Agency	DNA	Defense Nuclear Agency
CIC	Consumer Information Center	DOD	Department of Defense
CID'S	Commercial Item Descriptions	DODCI	Department of Defense Computer Institute
CNO	Chief of Naval Operations	DODDS	Department of Defense Dependents Schools
COGP	Commission on Government Procurement	DOE	Department of Energy
COMARC	Cooperative Machine-Readable Cataloging Program	DOT	Department of Transportation
CONRAIL	Consolidated Rail Corporation	DSAA	Defense Security Assistance Agency
COTP'S	Captains of the Port	DSN	Deep Space Network
CPSC	Consumer Product Safety Commission		
CRS	Community Relations Service		

DVOP	Disabled Veterans' Outreach Program	FCS	Foreign Commercial Service
EDA	Economic Development Administration	FCU	Federal Credit Union
		FDA	Food and Drug Administration
EEO	Equal Employment Opportunity	FDIC	Federal Deposit Insurance Corporation
EEOC	Equal Employment Opportunity Commission	FEB'S	Federal Executive Boards
EIA	Energy Information Administration	FEC	Federal Election Commission
EO	Executive Order	FEMA	Federal Emergency Management Agency
EOUSA	Executive Office for United States Attorneys	FFB	Federal Financing Bank
EPA	Environmental Protection Agency	FGIS	Federal Grain Inspection Service
EPIC	Energy Conservation Program Guide for Industry and Commerce	FGP	Foster Grandparent Program
ERA	Economic Regulatory Administration	FHA	Federal Housing Administration
ERISA	Employee Retirement Income Security Act	FHLBB	Federal Home Loan Bank Board
		FHWA	Federal Highway Administration
ERS	Economic Research Service	FIA	Federal Insurance Administration
ESA	Employment Standards Administration	FIC	Federal Information Center
ESF	Economic Support Fund	FICC	Fixed Income Consumer Counseling
ETA	Employment and Training Administration	FIP	Forestry Incentive Program
		FLETC	Federal Law Enforcement Training Center
EXIMBANK	Export-Import Bank of the United States	FLITE	Federal Legal Information through Electronics
FAA	Federal Aviation Administration	FLRA	Federal Labor Relations Authority
FAIR	Fair Access to Insurance Requirements	FMC	Federal Maritime Commission
FAO	Food and Agriculture Organization of the United Nations	FMCS	Federal Mediation and Conciliation Service
FAR	Federal Acquisition Regulations	FMHA	Farmers Home Administration
FAS	Foreign Agricultural Service	FNMA	Federal National Mortgage Association
FBI	Federal Bureau of Investigation		
FCA	Farm Credit Administration	FNS	Food and Nutrition Service
FCC	Federal Communications Commission	FOIA	Freedom of Information Act
FCIA	Foreign Credit Insurance Association	FOMC	Federal Open Market Committee
FCIC	Federal Crop Insurance Corporation	FPM	Federal Personnel Manual

FPRS	Federal Property Resources Service	ICAF	Industrial College of the Armed Forces
FRA	Federal Railroad Administration	ICAO	International Civil Aviation Organization
FRS	Federal Reserve System	ICC	Interstate Commerce Commission
FSIS	Food Safety and Inspection Service	ICM	Intergovernmental Committee for Migration
FSLIC	Federal Savings and Loan Insurance Corporation	IDA	International Development Association; Institute for Defense Analyses
FSS	Office of Federal Supply and Services	IDCA	United States International Development Cooperation Agency
FSTS	Federal Secure Telephone Service	IFC	International Finance Corporation
FTC	Federal Trade Commission	IHS	Indian Health Service
FTS	Federal Telecommunications System	IMF	International Monetary Fund
FWS	Fish and Wildlife Service	IMS	Institute of Museum Services
GAO	General Accounting Office	INF	Intermediate-Nuclear Forces
GATT	General Agreement of Tariffs and Trade	INS	Immigration and Naturalization Service
GNMA	Government National Mortgage Association	INTERPOL	International Criminal Police Organization
GNP	Gross National Product	IRA	Individual Retirement Account
GPO	Government Printing Office	IRS	Internal Revenue Service
GSA	General Services Administration	ISSN	International Standard Serial Numbers
HCFA	Health Care Financing Administration	ITA	International Trade Administration
HDS	Office of Human Development Services	ITU	International Telecommunication Union
HHS	Department of Health and Human Services	IYC	Individual Yield Coverage Program
HMO'S	Health Maintenance Organizations	JAG	Judge Advocate General
HNIS	Human Nutrition Information Service	JCS	Joint Chiefs of Staff
HRA	Health Resources Administration	JSIA	Justice System Improvement Act
HRSA	Health Resources and Services Administration	JTPA	Job Training Partnership
HUD	Department of Housing and Urban Development	LC	Library of Congress
IADB	Inter-American Defense Board; Inter-American Development Bank	LMRDA	Labor Management Reporting and Disclosure Act
IAEA	International Atomic Energy Agency	LMSA	Labor-Management Services Administration
IAF	Inter-American Foundation		

LSC	Legal Services Corporation	NCPC	National Capital Planning Commission
LVER	Local Veterans' Employment Representative	NCSL	National Center for Service Learning
MA	Maritime Administration	NCUA	National Credit Union Administration
MAC	Military Airlift Command	NDU	National Defense University
MARC	Machine Readable Cataloging	NFIP	National Flood Insurance Program
MBDA	Minority Business Development Agency	NHTSA	National Highway Traffic Safety Administration
MBFR	Mutual and Balanced Force Reduction	NIC	National Institute of Corrections
MDB'S	Multilateral Development Banks	NIE	National Institute of Education
MEECN	Minimum Essential Emergency Communications Network	NIH	National Institutes of Health
MILSATCOM	Military Satellite Communications Systems	NIJ	National Institutes of Justice
		NIS	Naval Investigative Service
MMS	Minerals Management Service	NLETS	National Law Enforcement Telecommunications System
MSB-COD	Minority Small Business Capital Ownership Development Program	NLM	National Library of Medicine
MSC	Military Sealift Command	NLRB	National Labor Relations Board
MSHA	Mine Safety and Health Administration	NMB	National Mediation Board
MSPB	Merit Systems Protection Board	NMCS	National Military Command System
MSSD	Model Secondary School for the Deaf	NOAA	National Oceanic and Atmospheric Administration
MTB	Materials Transportation Bureau	NOS	National Ocean Survey
MTN	Multilateral Trade Negotiations	NRC	Nuclear Regulatory Commission
NARA	National Archives and Records Administration	NSA	National Security Agency
NASA	National Aeronautics and Space Administration	NSC	National Security Council
NATO	North Atlantic Treaty Organization	NSF	National Science Foundation
NBS	National Bureau of Standards	NSTL	National Space Technology Laboratories
NCA	National Command Authorities	NTIA	National Telecommunications and Information Administration
NCCB	National Consumer Cooperative Bank		
NCI	National Cancer Institute	NTID	National Technical Institute for the Deaf
NCIC	National Cartographic Information Center	NTIS	National Technical Information Service
NCJRS	National Criminal Justice Reference Service	NTS	Naval Telecommunications System

NTSB	National Transportation Safety Board	ORR	Office of Refugee Relief
NWC	National War College	OSHA	Occupational Safety and Health Administration
OA	Office of Administration		
OAS	Organization of American States	OSHRC	Occupational Safety and Health Review Commission
OASDI	Old Age Survivors and Disability Insurance Program	OSTP	Office of Science and Technology Policy
OCA	Office of Consumer Advisor	OT	Office of Transportation
OCHAMPUS	Office of Civilian Health and Medical Program of the Uniformed Services	OTA	Office of Technology Assessment
		OTAA	Office of Trade Adjustment Assistance
OCS	Office of Community Services; Officer Candidate School; Outer Continental Shelf	OVRR	Office of Veterans' Reemployment Rights
OCSE	Office of Child Support Enforcement	OWBO	Office of Women's Business Ownership
OECD	Organization for Economic Cooperation and Development	PADC	Pennsylvania Avenue Development Corporation
OES	Office of Employment Security		
OFCC	Office of Federal Contract Compliance	PAHO	Pan American Health Organization
OFPP	Office of Federal Procurement Policy	PASS	Procurement Automated Source System
OFR	Office of the Federal Register	PBGC	Pension Benefit Guaranty Corporation
OGPS	Office of Grants and Program Systems	PBS	Public Buildings Service
OICD	Office of International Cooperation and Development	PCC	Panama Canal Commission
		PHA'S	Public Housing Agencies
OIRM	Office of Information Resources Management	PHS	Public Health Service
OJARS	Office of Justice Assistance, Research, and Statistics	PIH	Public and Indian Housing Programs
		PIK	Payment-in-Kind Program
OJJDP	Office of Juvenile Justice and Delinquency Prevention	PRC	Postal Rate Commission
OMB	Office of Management and Budget	PSI	Personnel Security Investigation
OPD	Office of Policy Development	PTO	Patent and Trademark Office
OPFI	Office of Program and Fiscal Integrity	RCWP	Rural Clean Water Program
OPIC	Overseas Private Investment Corporation	REA	Rural Electrification Administration
		RETRF	Rural Electrification and Telephone Revolving Fund
OPM	Office of Personnel Management		
ORDP	Office of Rural Development Policy		
ORM	Office of Regional Management	RFE	Radio Free Europe

RIT	Rochester Institute of Technology	SSI	Supplemental Security Income Program
RL	Radio Liberty	SSS	Selective Service System
RRB	Railroad Retirement Board	START	Strategic Arms Reduction Talks
RSA	Rehabilitation Services Administration	STAT	United States Statutes at Large
RSPA	Research and Special Programs Administration	STDN	Spaceflight Tracking and Data Network
RSVP	Retired Senior Volunteer Program	TAC	Tactical Air Command
RTB	Rural Telephone Bank	TCE	Tax Counseling for the Elderly Program
SAC	Strategic Air Command	TDP	Trade and Development Program
SADBU	Small and Disadvantaged Business Utilization	TDRS	Tracking and Data Relay Satellite System
SAO	Smithsonian Astrophysical Observatory	TEA	Treasury Enforcement Agent
SBA	Small Business Administration	TFCS	Treasury Financial Communication System
SBIC'S	Small Business Investment Companies	TRIMIS	Tri-Service Medical Information System
SCP	Senior Companion Program	TRI-TAC	Joint Tactical Communications Program
SCS	Soil Conservation Service	TSC	Transportation Systems Center
SCSEP	Senior Community Service Employment Program	TVA	Tennessee Valley Authority
SEAN	Scientific Event Alert Program	UCPP	Urban Crime Prevention Program
SEC	Securities and Exchange Commission	UDAG	Urban Development Action Grant
SERC	Smithsonian Environmental Research Center	UIS	Unemployment Insurance Service
SGLI	Servicemen's Group Life Insurance	UMTA	Urban Mass Transportation Administration
SIL	Smithsonian Institution Libraries	UN	United Nations
SITES	Smithsonian Institution Traveling Exhibition Service	UNESCO	United Nations Educational, Scientific and Cultural Organization
SLS	Saint Lawrence Seaway Development Corporation	UNICEF	United Nations International Children's Emergency Fund (*now* United Nations Children's Fund)
SMIDA	Small Business Innovation Development Act	UNICOR	Federal Prison Industries, Inc.
SPC	South Pacific Commission	UPU	Universal Postal Union
SRIM	Standing Order Microfiche Service	USA	United States Army
SRS	Statistical Reporting Service		
SSA	Social Security Administration		

USACE	United States Army Corps of Engineers	VGLI	Veterans Group Life Insurance
USAF	United States Air Force	VISTA	Volunteers in Service to America
U.S.C.	United States Code	VITA	Volunteer Income Tax Assistance Program
USCG	United States Coast Guard	VMLI	Veterans Mortgage Life Insurance
USCS	United States Commercial Service	VMSP	Volunteer Management Support Program
USDA	United States Department of Agriculture	VOA	Voice of America
USES	United States Employment Service	VVLP	Vietnam Veterans Leadership Program
USIA	United States Information Agency	WAPA	Western Area Power Administration
USITC	United States International Trade Commission	WBP	Water Bank Program
		WHO	World Health Organization
USMC	United States Marine Corps	WHS	Washington Headquarters Services
USN	United States Navy	WIC	Special Supplemental Food Program for Women, Infants, and Children
USNCB	United States National Central Bureau		
USPS	United States Postal Service	WIN	Work Incentive Program
USRA	United States Railway Association	WMO	World Meteorological Organization
USTTA	United States Travel and Tourism Administration	WWMCCS	Worldwide Military Command and Control System
VA	Veterans Administration	YCC	Youth Conservation Corps
VETS	Veterans' Employment and Training Service	YVA	Young Volunteers in Action

Federal Information Centers

Federal Information Centers help with questions about government. They have access to information from over 125 agencies and departments of the federal government, and they are clearinghouses for information about the federal government. If you are unsure of what agency to contact, check with the center nearest you. Either your question will be answered or you will be given a referral. Persons living in key cities have direct access by local telephone service.

AK

Federal Information Center
701 C St.
Box 33
Anchorage, AK 99513
(907) 271-3650

CA

Federal Information Center
300 N. Los Angeles St.
Los Angeles, CA 90012
(213) 688-3800

Federal Information Center
650 Capitol Mall
Sacramento, CA 95814
(916) 440-3344

Federal Information Center
Government Information Center
880 Front St.
San Diego, CA 92188
(619) 293-6030

Federal Information Center
450 Golden Gate Ave.
Box 36082
San Francisco, CA 94102
(415) 556-6600

CO

Federal Information Center
Federal Center
P.O. Box 25006
Denver, CO 80225
(303) 236-7181

FL

Federal Information Center
144 First Ave. South
Room 105
St. Petersburg, FL 33701
(813) 893-3495

GA

Federal Information Center
75 Spring St., SW
Atlanta, GA 30303
(404) 221-6891

HI

Federal Information Center
300 Ala Moana Blvd.
Box 50091
Honolulu, HI 96850
(808) 546-8620

IL

Federal Information Center
230 S. Dearborn St.
Thirty-Third Floor
Chicago, IL 60604
(312) 353-4242

MA

Federal Information Center
McCormack P.O.C.H. Bldg.
Room 812
Boston, MA 02109
(617) 223-7121

MI

Federal Information Center
477 Michigan Ave.
Room M-25
Detroit, MI 48226
(313) 226-7016

MO

Federal Information Center
1520 Market St.
Room 2616
St. Louis, MO 63103
(314) 425-4106

NE

Federal Information Center
215 N. Seventeenth St.
Omaha, NE 68102
(402) 221-3353

NY

Federal Information Center
111 W. Huron
Buffalo, NY 14202
(716) 846-4010

Federal Information Center
26 Federal Plaza
Room 2-110
New York, NY 10278
(212) 264-4464

OH

Federal Information Center
550 Main St.
Room 7411
Cincinnati, OH 45202
(513) 684-2801

OR

Federal Information Center
1220 S.W. Third Ave.
Room 318
Portland, OR 97204
(503) 221-2222

PA

Federal Information Center
600 Arch St.
Room 1232
Philadelphia, PA 19106
(215) 597-7042

TX

Federal Information Center
819 Taylor St.
Fort Worth, TX 76102
(817) 334-3624

Federal Information Center
515 Rusk Ave.
Houston, TX 77002
(713) 229-2552

Land Grant University Film Libraries

U.S. Department of Agriculture films are available from these institutions. The films cover such topics as trees, foods, animals, soils, agriculture, fire prevention, and water resources. In Michigan, for example, films are available for a three-day rental period at a fee of $7.00 plus round-trip shipping and insurance. Orders must be confirmed in writing.

Division of Libraries
Pouch G
Juneau, AK 99801

Cooperative Extension Film Library
Auburn University
Auburn, AL 36830

Cooperative Extension Film Library
University of Arkansas
P.O. Box 391
Little Rock, AR 72203

Film Library
University of Arizona
Media and Instructional Services Bldg.
Tucson, AZ 85721

Visual Aids
University of California
Cooperative Extension Bldg. Lobby
Riverside, CA 92521

Film Library
Office of Educational Media
Colorado State University
Fort Collins, CO 80521

Audiovisual Center
University of Connecticut
Storrs, CT 06268

Cooperative Extension Film Library
University of Delaware
Agricultural Hall
Newark, DE 19711

Motion Picture Service
Florida Cooperative Extension Service
University of Florida
Editorial Department
Gainesville, FL 32601

Film Library
Cooperative Extension Service
University of Georgia
Athens, GA 30601

Film Library
Cooperative Extension Service
College of Tropical Agriculture
University of Hawaii
2500 Dole St.
Room 108
Honolulu, HI 96822

Media Resources Center
Iowa State University
Pearson Hall
Ames, IA 50010

Audiovisual Center
University of Idaho
Moscow, ID 83843

Visual Aids Service
University of Illinois
Division of University Extension
1325 S. Oak
Champaign, IL 61820

Audiovisual Center
Purdue University
Stewart Center
West Lafayette, IN 47907

Cooperative Extension Service
Film Library
Kansas State University
Umberger Hall
Manhattan, KS 66502

Audiovisual Services
University of Kentucky
Scott Street Bldg.
Lexington, KY 40506

Cooperative Extension Service
Film Library
Louisiana State University
Knapp Hall
University Hall
University Station
Baton Rouge, LA 70803

Krasker Film Library
School of Education
Boston University
765 Commonwealth Ave.
Boston, MA 02215

MD and DC borrowers, please inquire of the nearest library or: National Audiovisual Center, GSA-Archives, Washington, DC 20409. (301) 763-1896.

Instructional Systems Center
University of Maine
Orono, ME 04473

Instructional Media Center
Michigan State University
East Lansing, MI 48823

Agricultural Extension Service
Film Library
University of Minnesota
St. Paul, MN 55101

Audiovisual and Communication Services
University of Missouri
203 Whitten Hall
Columbia, MO 65201

Cooperative Extension Service
Film Library
Mississippi State University
Mississippi State, MS 39762

Campus Film Library for Cooperative Extension Service
Montana State University
Bozeman, MT 59715

Department of Agricultural Information
North Carolina State University
P.O. Box 5037
Raleigh, NC 27607

Cooperative Extension Service
Film Library
North Dakota State University
State University Station
Fargo, ND 58102

University of Nebraska
Instructional Media Center
901 N. Seventeenth
Room 421
Lincoln, NE 68508

Audio Visual Center
University of New Hampshire
Hewitt Hall
Durham, NH 03824

Communications Center
College of Agriculture and Environmental Science
Rutgers University
New Brunswick, NJ 08903

Cooperative Extension Service
Film Library
New Mexico State University
Drawer 3AI
Las Cruces, NM 88003

Audio Visual Center
University of Nevada
Reno, NV 89507

Audio-Visual Resource Center
Cornell University
8 Research Park
Ithaca, NY 14850

Extension Service Film Library
Ohio State University
2021 Coffey Rd.
Columbus, OH 43210

Audiovisual Center
Oklahoma State University
Stillwater, OK 74074

Audiovisual Instruction
DCE Bldg.
P.O Box 1383
Portland, OR 97207

Agricultural Extension Service
Pennsylvania State University
104 Agricultural Administration Bldg.
University Park, PA 16802

Agricultural Extension Service
University of Puerto Rico
Mayaguez Campus
Rio Piedras, PR 00928

Audiovisual Center
University of Rhode Island
Kingston, RI 02881

Agricultural Communications Dept.
Clemson University Extension Service
Plant and Animal Science Bldg.
Room 92
Clemson, SC 29631

Cooperative Extension Service
Film Library
South Dakota State University
Brookings, SD 57006

Teaching Materials Center
Division of Continuing Education
University of Tennessee
Knoxville, TN 37916

Agricultural Communications
Texas A&M University
Services Building
Room 201
College Station, TX 77843

Audio Visual Services
Utah State University
Logan, UT 84321

Media Services
Virginia Polytechnic Institute
Patton Hall
Blacksburg, VA 24061

The Audio Visual Center
University of Vermont
Ira Allen Chapel
Burlington, VT 05401

Audio Visual Center
Washington State University
Pullman, WA 99163

University of Wisconsin — Extension
Bureau of Audio Visual Instruction
P.O. Box 2093
Madison, WI 53701

Cooperative Extension Service
West Virginia University
215 Coloseum
Morgantown, WV 26506

Audio Visual Services
The University of Wyoming
Laramie, WY 82070

Sea Grant Programs

The National Oceanic and Atmospheric Administration administers and directs the National Sea Grant Program by providing grants to institutions for marine research, education, and advisory services. It also develops a system of data buoys for obtaining and disseminating marine environmental data and promotes the development of technology to meet future marine needs.

Sea Grant Programs provide information on the use of the Great Lakes and oceans. Their publications cover topics like pollution, tourism, marinas, fish, wetlands, and shipping. Request a listing of what is available. In Michigan, for example, free and for sale materials are available on subjects like shore erosion, underwater cultural resources, the role of the federal government in managing Lake Michigan, fishes, and many other subjects. Materials include a middle school teaching guide on the sea lamprey in the Great Lakes for sale. There is a 5-page list/order form of publications.

AK
Alaska Sea Grant Program
University of Alaska
590 University of Alaska
Suite 102
Fairbanks, AK 99701

AL
See MS.

CA
California Sea Grant College Program
University of California, A-032
La Jolla, CA 92093

California USC Sea Grant Program
University Park
Los Angeles, CA 90089-0341

CT
University of Connecticut Marine Advisory Service
Avery Point
Building 24
Groton, CT 06340

DE
Delaware Sea Grant College Program
College of Marine Studies
University of Delaware
Newark, DE 19711

FL
Florida Sea Grant College Program
University of Florida
G022 McCarty Hall
Gainesville, FL 32611

GA
Sea Grant College Program
Ecology Bldg.
University of Georgia
Athens, GA 30602

HI
Publications Production Specialist
University of Hawaii
Sea Grant College Program
1000 Pope Rd.
Room 200
Honolulu, HI 96822

IL, IN
Illinois and Indiana Marine Extension Project
University of Illinois at Urbana-Champaign
1206 S. Fourth St.
Huff Gym
Room 104
Champaign, IL 68210

LA

Publications and Distribution
Louisiana Sea Grant College Program
Center for Wetland Resources
Louisiana State University
Baton Rouge, LA 70803-7507

MA

Sea Grant College Program
Massachusetts Institute of Technology
Building E38, 329
77 Massachusetts Ave.
Cambridge, MA 02139

MD

Production Coordinator
Sea Grant Program
University of Maryland
H. J. Patterson Hall
College Park, MD 20742

ME

Marine Advisory Program
University of Maine
30 Coburn Hall
Orono, ME 04469

MI

Michigan Sea Grant College Program
The University of Michigan
2200 Bonisteel Blvd.
Ann Arbor, MI 48109-2099

MN

Minnesota Sea Grant Program
University of Minnesota
116 Classroom-Office Bldg.
1994 Buford Ave.
St. Paul, MN 55108

MS, AL

Mississippi-Alabama Sea Grant Consortium
Caylor Bldg.
Gulf Coast Research Lab.
Ocean Springs, MS 39564

NC

UNC Sea Grant College Program
North Carolina State University
Box 8605
Raleigh, NC 27695-8605

NH

UNH Marine Program and Sea Grant College
    Program
UNH Marine Program Bldg.
University of New Hampshire
Durham, NH 03824

NY

New York Sea Grant Institute
37 Elk St.
Albany, NY 12246

Sea Grant Extension Program
Cornell University
10 Fernow Hall
Ithaca, NY 14853

OH

Ohio Sea Grant Program
College of Biological Sciences
Ohio State University
484 W. Twelfth Ave.
Columbus, OH 43210

OR

Sea Grant Communications
Oregon State University
AdS A418
Corvallis, OR 97331

PR

U.P.R. Sea Grant Program
Department of Marine Sciences
University of Puerto Rico
Mayaguez, PR 00708

RI

Publications Coordinator
URI Marine Advisory Services
Marine Resources Bldg.
University of Rhode Island
Narragansett, RI 02882

SC

South Carolina Sea Grant Consortium
221 Fort Johnson Rd.
Charleston, SC 29412

TX

Sea Grant College Program
Texas A&M University
College Station, TX 77843

VA

Sea Grant Program
Department of Food Science and Technology
VPI and SU
Blacksburg, VA 24061

WA

Washington Sea Grant College Program
3716 Brooklyn, NE
Seattle, WA 98105

WI

University of Wisconsin
Sea Grant Institute
1800 University Ave.
Madison, WI 53705

Subject Bibliographies

The subject bibliographies available from the Superintendent of Documents cover topics in books, pamphlets, posters, periodicals, subscription services, and other government publications available for purchase. Their length varies. "Motion Pictures, Films and Audiovisual Information," for example, is 3 pages, while "Statistical Publications" is 22 pages. An order form and publication dates are included. These subject bibliographies are free from: Superintendent of Documents, United States Government Printing Office, Washington, DC 20402. The order number follows the title in the list below.

"Accidents and Accident Prevention" SB229

"Accounting and Auditing" SB42

"Adult Education" SB214

"Aircraft, Airport, and Airways" SB13

"Africa" SB284

"Aging" SB39

"Agricultural Research, Statistics, and Economic Reports" SB162

"Agriculture Yearbooks" (Department of) SB31

"Air Force Manuals" SB182

"Air Pollution" SB46

"Aircraft, Airports, and Airways" SB13

"Airman's Information Manual" SB14

"Alcohol, Tobacco and Firearms" SB246

"Alcoholism" SB175

"American Revolution" SB144

"Annual Reports" SB188

"Anthropology and Archeolgy" SB205

"Architecture" SB215

"Armed Forces" SB131

"Army Technical and Field Manuals" SB158

"Art and Artists" SB107

"Asia and Oceania" SB288

"Astronomy and Astrophysics" SB115

"Atomic Energy and Nuclear Power" SB200

"Aviation Information and Training Materials" SB18

"Background Notes" SB93

"Banks and Banking" SB128

"Birds" SB177

"Board of Tax Appeals and Tax Court Reports" SB67

"Budget of the United States Government and Economic Report of the President" SB204

"Building Science Series" SB138

"Bureau of Land Management Publications" SB256

"Bureau of Reclamation Publications" SB249

"Business and Business Management" SB4

"Canada" SB278

"Canning, Freezing, and Storage of Foods" SB5

310 / Subject Bibliographies

"Care and Disorders of the Eyes" SB28

"Census of Agriculture" SB277

"Census of Business" SB152

"Census of Construction" SB157

"Census of Governments" SB156

"Census of Housing, Metropolitan Housing Characteristics" SB313

"Census of Manufactures" SB146

"Census of Mineral Industries" SB310

"Census of Population and Housing" SB181

"Census of Population and Housing, Block Statistics" SB311

"Census of Population and Housing, Census Tracts" SB312

"Census of Transportation" SB149

"Child Abuse and Neglect" SB309

"Children and Youth" SB35

"China" SB299

"Civil Aeronautics Board Publications" SB186

"Civil and Structural Engineering" SB308

"Civil Rights and Equal Opportunity" SB207

"Civil War" SB192

"Coast Guard Publications" (U.S.) SB263

"Coins and Medals" SB198

"College Debate Topic" SB176

"Computers and Data Processing" SB51

"Congress" SB201

"Congressional Budget Office Publications" SB282

"Congressional Directory" SB228

"Conservation" SB238

"Construction Industry" SB216

"Consumer Information" SB2

"Cookbooks and Recipes" SB65

"Copyrights" SB126

"Court of Customs and Patent Appeals Reports and U.S. Court of International Trade" SB52

"Courts and Correctional Institutions" SB91

"Crime and Criminal Justice" SB36

"Customs, Immunization, and Passport Publications" SB27

"Day Care" SB92

"Dentistry" SB22

"Digest of U.S. Practice in International Law and Digest of International Law" SB185

"Directories and Lists of Persons and Organizations" SB114

"Disarmament and Arms Control" SB127

"Disaster Preparedness and Civil Defense" SB241

"Diseases in Humans" SB8

"Drug Education" SB163

"Earth Sciences" SB160

"Educational Statistics" SB83

"Electricity and Electronics" SB53

"Elementary Education" SB196

"Employment and Occupations" SB44

"Energy Conservation and Research Technology" SB306

"Energy Management for Consumers and Businesses" SB303

"Energy Policy, Issues and Programs" SB305

"Energy Supplies, Prices and Consumption" SB304

"Engineering Other than Civil" SB132

"Environmental Education and Protection" SB88

"Europe (Including the United Kingdom)" SB289

"Family Planning" SB292

"Farms and Farming" SB161

"Federal Aviation Regulations" SB12

"Federal Communications Commission Publications" SB281

"Federal Government" SB141

"Federal Government Forms" SB90

"Federal Trade Commission Decisions and Publications" SB100

"Financial Aid to Students" SB85

"Firefighting, Prevention and Forest Fires" SB76

"Fish and Marine Life" SB209

"Food, Diet and Nutrition" SB291

"Foreign Affairs of the U.S." SB75

"Foreign Area Studies" SB166

"Foreign Education" SB235

"Foreign Investments" SB275

"Foreign Languages" SB82

"Foreign Relations of the U.S." SB210

"Foreign Trade and Tariff" SB123

"Fossils" SB143

"Gardening" SB301

"General Accounting Office Publications" SB250

"General Services Administration Publications" SB247

"Government Printing Office (U.S.) Publications" SB244

"Government Specifications and Standards" SB231

"Grants and Awards" SB258

"The Handicapped" SB37

"Hearing and Hearing Disability" SB23

"Higher Education" SB217

"Highway Construction, Safety, and Traffic" SB3

"Historical Handbook Series" SB16

"The Home" SB41

"Home Economics" SB276

"Hospitals" SB119

"Housing, Urban and Rural Development" SB280

"How To Sell to Government Agencies" SB171

"Immigration, Naturalization and Citizenship" SB69

"Insects" SB34

"Insurance" SB294

"Intergovernmental Relations" SB211

"Internal Revenue Cumulative Bulletins" SB66

"Interstate Commerce Commission Decisions and Reports" SB187

"Irrigation and Drainage" SB94

"Juvenile Delinquency" SB74

"Labor-Management Relations" SB64

"Latin America and the Caribbean" SB287

"Law Enforcement" SB117

"Libraries and Library Collections" SB150

"Livestock and Poultry" SB10

"Mammals and Reptiles" SB70

"Maps and Atlases (U.S. and Foreign)" SB102

"Marine Corps Publications" SB237

"Marketing Research" SB125

"Mass Transit" SB55

"Mathematics" SB24

"Medicine and Medical Science" SB154

"Mental Health" SB167

"Middle East" SB286

"Military History" SB98

"Minerals and Mining" SB151

"Minerals Yearbooks" SB99

"Minorities" SB6

312 / Subject Bibliographies

"Motion Pictures, Films, and Audiovisual Information" SB73

"Motor Vehicles" SB49

'Music" SB221

"NASA Educational Publications" SB222

"NASA Scientific and Technical Publications" SB257

"National and World Economy" SB97

"National Bureau of Standards Handbooks and Monographs" SB133

"National Bureau of Standards Special Publications" SB271

"National Bureau of Standards Technical Notes" SB148

"National Credit Union Administration Publications" SB267

"National Defense and Security" SB153

"National Ocean Survey Publications" SB260

"National Park Service Folders" SB170

"National Science Foundation Publications" SB220

"National Standard Reference Data Series" SB139

"Naval Facilities Engineering Command Publications" SB219

"Naval History (U.S.)" SB236

"Naval Personnel Bureau and Naval Education and Training Command Publications" SB173

"Navigation" SB29

"Noise Abatement" SB63

"Nurses and Nursing Care" SB19

"Occupational Outlook Handbook" SB270

"Occupational Safety and Health" SB213

"Oceanography" SB32

"Office of Personnel Management Publications" SB300

"Patents and Trademarks" SB21

"Personnel Management, Guidance, and Counseling" SB202

"Pesticides, Insecticides, Fungicides, and Rodenticides" SB227

"Photography" SB72

"Physical Fitness" SB239

"Poetry and Literature" SB142

"Postal Service" SB169

"Posters, Charts, Picture Sets, and Decals" SB57

"Presidents of the United States" SB106

"Prices, Wages, and the Cost of Living" SB226

"Procurement, Supply Cataloging, and Classification" SB129

"Public and Private Utilities" SB298

"Public Buildings, Landmarks, and Historic Sites of the United States" SB140

"Public Health" SB122

"Publications Relating to the College Debate Topic" SB176

"Publications Relating to the National High School Debate Topic" SB43

"Radiation and Radioactivity" SB48

"Railroads" SB218

"Reading" SB164

"Recreational and Outdoor Activities" SB17

"Retirement" SB285

"Revenue Sharing" SB59

"Rural Electrification Administration (REA) Forms and Bulletins" SB168

"School Administration, Buildings, and Equipment" SB223

"Secondary Education" SB68

"Securities and Investments" SB295

"Shipping and Transportation" SB40

"Ships, Shipping, and Shipbuilding" SB225

"Small Business" SB307

"Smithsonian Institution Popular Publications" SB252

"Smoking" SB15

"Social Security" SB165

"Social Welfare and Services" SB30

"Soil and Soil Management" SB7

"Solar Energy" SB9

"Soviet Union" SB279

"Space, Rockets, and Satellites" SB297

"Spanish Publications" SB130

"Stenography, Typing and Writing" SB87

"Subversive Activities" SB259

"Surveying and Mapping" SB183

"Taxes and Taxation" SB195

"Teachers and Teaching Methods" SB137

"Telecommunications" SB296

"Travel and Tourism" SB302

"Treaties and Other International Agreements of the United States" SB191

"Trees, Forest Products and Forest Management" SB86

"United States Air Force Manuals" SB182

"United States Corps of Engineers" SB261

"United States Code" SB197

"United States Court of Claims Reports" SB174

"United States Intelligence Activities" SB272

"United States Postage Stamps" SB11

"United States Reports" SB025

"Veterans Affairs and Benefits" SB80

"Vital and Health Statistics" SB121

"Vocational and Career Education" SB110

"Voting and Elections" SB245

"Waste Management" SB95

"Water Pollution and Water Resources" SB50

"Weather" SB234

"Weights and Measures" SB109

"Wildlife Management" SB116

"Women" SB111

"Worker's Compensation" SB108

Subject Index

Accidents and injury, 188-89, 225-28
Acronyms and abbreviations list, 293-300
Administrative Conference of the United States, 1
Administrative Office of the United States Courts, 1
Aeronautics and Space Administration, National, 138-42
Aerospace, 49, 73-75, 138-42, 211, 255
Aged, 195
Agency. *See other part of title*
Aging, National Institute on, 195
Agricultural Cooperative Service, 2
Agricultural Library, National, 142-43
Agricultural Research Service, 2-3
Agricultural Stabilization and Conservation Service, 3
Agriculture, 2-5, 12-14, 33-36, 56-59, 68-72, 81-82, 107-8, 142-43, 258-62
Agriculture, Department of, 36
Air Force, Department of the, 49
Alcohol Information, National Clearinghouse for, 162-68
Alcohol, Tobacco and Firearms, Bureau of, 7-9
Alcoholic beverages and alcoholism, 7-9, 162-68
Allergy and Infectious Diseases, National Institute of, 189-90
American Folklife Center, 3-4
American Indians, 9-10, 49, 117, 137-38
American Red Cross, 25-26
Anacostia Neighborhood Museums, 4
Animal and Plant Health Inspection Service, 4-5
Animal husbandry, 2, 4-5, 33-35
Antietam National Battlefield, 5
Appalachian Regional Commission, 5
Architect of the Capitol, 6
Architectural and Transportation Barriers Compliance Board, 6-7
Architecture
  accessibility for disabled, 6-7
  Washington, DC, 6, 27, 290
Archives, 143-45, 184-88, 217. *See also* Library science; Special libraries
Archives and Records Service, National, 143-45
Archives Trust Fund Board, National, 145

Arms Control and Disarmament Agency, U.S., 264
Army Corps of Engineers, U.S., 264-67
Art, 3, 27, 171-74, 211-12. *See also* Architecture
  cultural activities, 178-79, 255-56
  portraits, 217-18
Art, National Gallery of, 178-79
Art, National Museum of American, 211-12
Arts, National Endowment for the, 171-74
Astronomy, 138-42, 213-16
Atmospheric research, 213-16, 223-24, 307-8
Audiovisual Center, National, 145-47
Authors, 19, 59, 117, 135, 174-78
Aviation. *See* Aerospace
Aviation Administration, Federal, 73-75

Banks and banking, 29-30, 82-83, 98-100
Battlefields. *See under* Historic sites
Bibliographies by subject area, 309-13
Bilingual Education, National Clearinghouse for, 168
Biology, 19-20, 153-54, 193, 254. *See also* Agriculture
Biomedicine, 193-95
Birth Defects and Developmental Disabilities, Division of, 55-56
Black studies, 4, 109, 137-38
Blind and Physically Handicapped, National Library Service for the, 201-11
Blood pressure, 117-18, 179-80
Book, Center for the, 20
Botanic Gardens, United States, 6
Braille, 201-11
Buildings and grounds of Washington, DC, 6, 27, 152-53, 290
Bureau. *See other part of title*
Business education, 247-54. *See also* Commerce; Economics; Labor and labor relations
  banking and investment, 29-30, 82-83, 98-100, 128-31, 245-74
  minority groups, 137-38

316 / Subject Index

Business education (*continued*)
   patents and trademarks, 240-41
   taxes, 123-28
   women, 238, 290-91

Cancer Institute, National, 152
Capital Parks, National, 152-53
Capitalism, 100-102
Cardiovascular system, 117-18, 179-80
Career guidance, 11-12, 51, 67, 73-75
Carl Sandburg Home, 19
Census, Bureau of the, 16-18
Center. *See other part of title*
Central Intelligence Agency, 25
Child Abuse and Neglect Information, Clearinghouse on, 26-27
Child development, 26-27, 68-72, 114-15, 155-61
   disabilities and diseases, 55-56, 188-89, 220
Children's Literature Center, 25
Citizenship, 119-23
Civics. *See* Government
Civil defense, 84-93
Civil rights, 28-29, 67, 93-94, 109, 291
Civil Rights, Commission on, 28-29
Civil War (U.S.), 5
Clara Barton National Historic Site, 25-26
Clearinghouse. *See other part of title*
Clinical Reports and Inquiries, Office of, 228
Coast Guard, U.S., 267-68
Coin collecting, 18-19, 51
Commerce, 36, 100-102. *See also* Business education
   agriculture, 107-8
   international relations, 107-8, 128-31, 282
   interstate, 94, 131-32
Commerce, Department of, 36
Commission. *See other part of title*
Communicable diseases, 20-24, 189-90
Communications Commission, Federal, 80-81
Community development, 36, 41-42, 118-19, 288-89
Comptroller of the Currency, 29-30
Congress, House of Representatives, 281-82
Congressional Budget Office, 30
Conservation, 3, 30, 36-41, 60-65, 235-36, 262-64. *See also* Environment
Conservation and Renewable Energy Inquiry and Referral Service, 30
Consumer Affairs, Office of, 228-29
Consumer education, 11-12, 228-29
   banking and investment, 82-83, 98-100, 245-47
   commerce, 100-102, 131-32
   employment, 59-60
   energy conservation, 37-41, 235-36
   insurance, 82-83
   mortgages, 94-95
   safety, 31-32, 188-89
   social security, 257-58
   taxes, 123-28
Consumer Product Safety Commission, 31-32
Copyright Office, 32-33
Correctional institutions, 79-80

Council. *See other part of title*
Counseling, 26-27, 230-31
   alcoholism, 162-68
   drug abuse, 168-70
   mental health, 193-94
   rape, 161-62
   volunteer training, 162
Courts, 1, 42-46, 193, 238. *See also* Crime; Law enforcement
Crime, 7-9, 42-46, 75-79, 161-62, 193
Crop Insurance Corporation, Federal, 81-82
Crop Reporting Board, 33-35
Cultural activities and exhibitions, 178-79, 211-12, 255-56, 282. *See also* Art; Humanities
Current events
   disarmament, 264
   international relations, 1, 48-49, 108, 282
   technology, 236-37
Customs Service, U.S., 268-71

Deafness. *See* Hearing impairments
Death Valley National Monument, 36
Dental Research, National Institute of, 190
Department. *See other part of title*
Depository Administration Branch, 52-55
Deposit Insurance Corporation, Federal, 82-83
Deserts, 36
Devices and Radiological Health, National Center for, 153-54
Digestive Diseases Education and Information Clearinghouse, National, 170-71
Disabled. *See* Handicapped
Disaster readiness. *See* Civil defense
Discrimination. *See* Social discrimination
Disease Control, Centers for, 20-24
Diseases and disease control, 19-24, 195
   allergy, 189-90
   cardiovascular system, 179-80
   communicable, 189-90
   digestive system, 170-71
   from injury, 188-89
   sudden infant death syndrome, 220
Division. *See other part of title*
Driver education, 94, 179-84, 222-23
Drug Abuse Information, National Clearinghouse for, 168-70
Drug education, 103-5, 168-70

Early childhood education, 114-15. *See also* Elementary education
Earth sciences, 271-81. *See also* Natural resources; Oceanography
   meteorology, 213-16, 223-24, 307-8
   physical geography, 36, 133, 258-62
Earthquakes, 281
Economic Analysis, Bureau of, 9
Economic Development Administration, 56
Economic Research Service, 56-59

Economics, 5, 9, 16-19. *See also* Business education; Commerce
  agriculture, 2, 56-59
  banking and investment, 29-30, 82-83, 98-100, 128-31, 245-47
  fiscal policy, 51
  international relations, 1-2
  monetary system, 98-100
Edgar Allan Poe National Historic Site, 59
Education courses, 36-37, 67-68, 161, 190-92, 229-30, 254-55. *See also* Consumer education; Special education
  bilingualism, 168
  child development, 114-15
  humanities, 174-78
  volunteer training, 162
Education, Department of, 36-37
Education in Maternal and Child Health, National Center for, 155-61
Education, National Institute of, 190-92
Education Statistics, National Center for, 161
Educational Resources Information Center (ERIC), 190-92. *See also* ERIC Processing and Reference Facility
Election Commission, Federal, 84
Elementary and Secondary Education, Office of, 229-30
Elementary education, 229-30, 254-55. *See also* Early childhood education
Emergency Management Agency, Federal, 84-93
Employment, 47-48, 59-60, 67, 241-44, 290-91
Employment of the Handicapped, The President's Committee on, 241-44
Employment Standards Administration, 59-60
Endowment for the Arts, National, 171-74
Endowment for the Humanities, National, 174-78
Energy and energy conservation, 30, 37-41, 60-65, 235-36, 262-64
  nuclear, 225
Energy, Department of, 37-41
Energy Information Administration, 60-65
English (second language), 168
English language arts, 171-74
  literature, 19, 25, 59, 117, 135, 174-78
Engraving. *See* Printing and engraving
Engraving and Printing, Bureau of, 9
Environment, 33, 49, 65-67, 94, 108-9, 254. *See also* Conservation; Earth sciences
  hazardous substances, 136-37
  nuclear energy, 225
Environmental Protection Agency, 65-67
Environmental Quality, Council on, 33
Equal Employment Opportunity Commission, 67
ERIC Processing and Reference Facility, 67-68. *See also* Educational Resources Information Center
Export/import trade. *See* Commerce: international relations
Extension Service, 68-72
Eye Institute, National, 178

Federal. *See also other part of title*
  information centers, 301-2
Federal Register, Office of the, 237-38
Films, 133-34, 303-5
Financial support for education, 236
Fine Arts, Commission of, 27
Firearms, 7-9
Fiscal policy. *See under* Economics
Fish and Wildlife Service, 102
Fisheries, 211
Folk culture, 3, 133-34
Food and Drug Administration, 103-5
Food and nutrition, 19-20, 68-72, 103-7, 119
Food and Nutrition Information Center, 105-6
Food and Nutrition Service, 106-7
Foreign affairs assistance. *See* International relations
Foreign Agricultural Service, 107-8
Foreign Claims Settlement Commission of the United States, 108
Forest Service, 108-9
Frederick Douglass Home, 109
Freedom of speech, 93-94

Gallery of Art, National, 178-79
General Accounting Office, 109-10
General Services Administration, 110-12
Genetics, 193
Geography and Map Division, Library of Congress, 133
Geography, 12-14, 49, 84-93, 108-9, 264-67. *See also* Earth sciences: physical geography
  maps, 133, 271-81
  Panama Canal, 239
  parks, 36, 152-53, 216-17
  St. Lawrence Seaway, 245
  Tennessee Valley Authority, 262-64
  U.S. territories, 237
Geological Survey, U.S., 271-81
Geology. *See* Earth sciences
Government, 97, 236-37. *See also* Buildings and grounds of Washington, DC; Civil rights; Courts; Current events; International relations; Law enforcement; Military science; Public administration; Welfare services
  citizenship, 119-23
  congress, 281-82
  elections, 84
  labor relations, 47-48, 95-98, 196-99, 211
  passports, 239-40
  patents and trademarks, 240-41
  social security, 257-58
  transportation, 288-89
Government Printing Office, 112-14
Government publications, 9, 52-54, 109-14, 134-35, 143-45, 237-38
  subject bibliographies, 309-13
Grants
  arts and humanities, 171-78
  sea programs, 306-8

Grounds. *See* Buildings and grounds of Washington, DC
Guidance. *See* Career guidance; Counseling

Hall National Memorial, Federal, 93-94
Handicapped, 6-7, 170, 188, 218-19, 222
   education and employment, 115-17, 241-44
Handicapped Children and Youth, National Information Center, 188
Handicapped, Clearinghouse on the, 27
Handicapped, National Council on the, 170
Handicapped, The President's Committee on Employment of the, 241-44
Hazardous substances, 136-37
Head Start Bureau, 114-15
Health, 19-20, 65-67, 189-90. *See also* Food and nutrition; Medical research
   aged, 195
   alcoholism, 162-68
   allergy, 189-90
   birth defects, 55-56
   cancer, 152
   cardiovascular system, 117-18, 179-80
   dental care, 190
   digestion, 170-71
   drug abuse, 103-5, 168-70
   eyes, 178
   infectious diseases, 189-90
   neurological impairments, 194-95
   physical fitness, 244-45
   radiation biology, 153-54
   smoking, 239
Health Information Clearinghouse, National, 179
Health, National Institutes of, 195
Health Promotion and Education, Center for, 19-20
Health Resource Center, 115-17
Health Resources and Services Administration, 117
Hearing impairments, 194-95, 222
Heart disorders, 117-18, 179-80
Heart, Lung, and Blood Institute, The National, 179-80
Hemingway Museum, 117
High Blood Pressure Information Center, 117-18
Highway Administration, Federal, 94
Highway Traffic Safety Administration, National, 179-84
Hispanic Americans, 137-38
Historic sites, 25-26, 59, 93-94, 109, 216-17
   administration of, 49
   battlefields, 5
Historical Publications and Records Commission, National, 184-88
History, 25-26, 174-78, 255-57, 291
   Appalachian region, 5
   archives, 143-45, 184-88, 217
   art, 3
   Civil War (U.S.), 5
   freedom of speech, 93-94
   minority groups, 109
   popular media, 133-34
   Presidents, 234-35
   shipping, 245
Home economics, 36, 68-72. *See also* Child development; Food and nutrition
Home finance, 41-42, 94-95, 118-19
Home Loan Bank Board, Federal, 94-95
House of Representatives, U.S., 281-82
Housing and Urban Development, Department of, 41-42. *See also* HUD User
HUD User, 118-19. *See also* Housing and Urban Development, Department of
Human Development Services, Office of, 230-31
Human Nutrition Information Service, 119
Humanities, 132-33, 171-78
Humanities, National Endowment for the, 174-78

Immigration and Naturalization Service, 119-23
Immunization programs, 20
Indian Affairs, Bureau of, 9-10
Industrial education, 41-42, 118-19, 225-27
Information Agency, U.S., 282
Injury. *See* Accidents and injury
Injury Information Clearinghouse, The National, 188-89
Institute. *See other part of title*
Insurance, 81-83, 94-95
Interior, Department of the, 49
Interlibrary loan, 133
Internal Revenue Service, 123-28
International Development, Agency for, 1-2
International relations, 1-2, 48-49, 237. *See also* Commerce: international relations
   war claims, 108
International trade. *See* Commerce: international relations
International Trade Administration, 128-31
International Trade Commission, U.S., 282
Interstate Commerce Commission, 131-32
Investment, 128-31, 245-47

John F. Kennedy Center for the Performing Arts, 132-33
Judicial system. *See* Courts
Justice, Department of, 42-46
Justice, National Institute of, 193

Kennedy, John F. *See* John F. Kennedy Center for the Performing Arts

Labor and labor relations, 11-12, 47-48, 95-98, 196-99, 211
Labor Relations Authority, Federal, 95-97
Labor Relations Board, National, 196-99
Labor Statistics, Bureau of, 11-12
Land grant university film libraries, 303-5
Land Management, Bureau of, 12-14
Land use, 3, 12-14, 258-62
Languages, bilingualism, 168
Law enforcement, 7-9, 42-46, 75-79, 161-62, 193. *See also* Legal education

Law Librarian, Office of the, 238
Legal education, 1, 42-46, 193, 238
Libraries and Information Science, National Commission on, 170
Library of Congress Geography and Map Division, 133
Library of Congress Information Office, 133
Library of Congress Loan Division, 133
Library of Congress Motion Picture, Broadcasting and Recorded Sound Division, 133-34
Library of Congress Science Reference Section, 134
Library of Congress Serial and Government Publications Division, 134-35
Library of Congress Tour Office, 135
Library of Medicine, National, 199-201
Library science, 20, 25, 32-33, 51, 67-68, 109-14, 170, 179, 184-88, 190-92, 212-13, 218, 255-57. *See also* Research; Special libraries; and *entries beginning* Library of Congress
Library Service for the Blind and Physically Handicapped, National, 201-11
Literature, 19, 59, 117, 135, 174-78
Longfellow National Historic Site, 135
Lungs, 179-80

Maps, 133, 271-81
Marine Fisheries Service, National, 211
Maritime Administration, 135-36
Maritime Commission, Federal, 97
Materials and Transportation Bureau, 136-37
Mathematics instruction, 147-52
Measurement, 147-52
Mediation and Conciliation Service, Federal, 98
Mediation Board, National, 211
Medical research, 193, 195, 199-201, 228
Medical Sciences, National Institute of General, 193
Medicine, National Library of, 199-201
Mental Health, National Institute of, 193-94
Merchant Marine, 135
Meteorology. *See under* Earth sciences
Military science, 25, 49-51, 264-68, 284-88
Minerals Management Service, 137
Mines and mining, 14-15, 49, 137, 271-81
Mines, Bureau of, 14-15
Minority Business Development Agency Information Clearinghouse, 137-38
Minority groups, 109, 137-38
Mint, Bureau of the, 18-19
Mission to the United Nations, U.S., 282
Money and the monetary system, 18-19, 29-30, 98-100
Monuments, 36, 216-17
Mortgages. *See* Home finance
Motion Picture, Broadcasting and Recorded Sound Division, Library of Congress, 133-34
Motion pictures. *See* Films
Museum of American Art, National, 211-12
Museums, 4, 117, 211-12, 290
Music, 132-34

National. *See other part of title*
National defense and security, 25, 75-79, 264, 284-88
Native Americans. *See* American Indians
Natural resources, 12-15, 36, 49, 137, 211, 216-17, 271-81. *See also* Water resources
Navigation, 49-51, 135, 212-16, 307-8
Navy, Department of the, 49-51
Neurological and Communicative Disorders and Stroke, National Institute of, 194-95
Nuclear Regulatory Commission, 225
Nutrition. *See* Food and nutrition

Occupational Safety and Health Administration, 225-27
Occupational Safety and Health Review Commission, 227-28
Ocean and Coastal Resource Management, Office of, 231-34
Ocean Service, National, 212-13
Oceanic and Atmospheric Administration, National, 213-16
  sea grant program, 307-8
Oceanography, 49-51, 212-16, 231-34, 307-8
Office. *See other part of title*
Outdoor recreation, 12-14, 49, 216-17, 244-45, 267-68
  Washington, DC, 152-53

Panama Canal Commission, 239
Park Service, National, 216-17
Park Service Science Publications Office, National, 217
Parks, 36, 152-53, 216-17
  Washington, DC, 6, 152-53
Passport Services, 239-40
Patent and Trademark Office, 240-41
Patents, 36, 240-41
Performing arts. *See* Theater arts
Pesticides, 65-67
Petroleum, 137
Philosophy, 174-78
Physical education, 244-45
Physical Fitness and Sports, The President's Council on, 244-45
Plant pathology, 4-5
Poe. *See* Edgar Allan Poe National Historic Site
Poets, U.S., 19
Political science. *See* Government
Pollution, 65-67
Popular culture. *See* Folk culture
Population trends, 16-18
Portrait Gallery, National, 217-18
Postage stamps, 9, 282-84
Postal Service, U.S., 282-84
Postsecondary education for the disabled, 115-17
Pregnancy and prenatal influences, 19-20, 55-56, 155-61
Preservation Program Office, National, 218
Presidential Libraries, Office of, 234-35

320 / Subject Index

Presidents, 234-35, 290
Prevention and Control of Rape, National Center, for, 161-62
Prevention Services, Center for, 20
Preventive medicine. *See entries beginning* Disease control
Printing and engraving, 9, 20
Prisons, Federal Bureau of, 79-80
Procurement Policy, Office of Federal, 230
Psychology, 193-94
Public administration, 1, 16-18, 20, 41-42, 109-12, 230

Radiation biology, 153-54
Radio, 80-81, 133-34
Radiological Health, National Center for Devices and, 153-54
Railroad labor relations, 211
Rape, 161-62
Reclamation, Bureau of, 15-16
Rehabilitation Information Center, National, 218-19
Reproduction (biology), 19-20
Research, 2, 9, 56-59, 134, 195, 199-201, 236-37, 254. *See also* Library science
Reserve System, Federal, 98-100
Rural development, 36. *See also* Agriculture

Safety education, 31-32
   accidents and injury, 188-89, 225-28
   driver training, 180-84, 222-23
   emergency programs, 84-93
   hazardous substances, 136-37
   water recreation, 267-68
Saint Lawrence Seaway Development Corporation, 245
Salem Maritime National Historic Site, 245
Science and technology, 134, 217, 219-20, 255. *See also* Biology; Earth sciences; Environment; Health
   aerospace, 138-42
   measurement, 147-52
   research, 220-22, 235-37
Science Foundation, National, 219-20
Science Reference Section, Library of Congress, 134
Scientific and Technical Information, Office of, 235-36
Sea grant programs, 307-8
Secondary education, 229-30, 254-55
Secret Service, U.S., 284-88
Securities and Exchange Commission, 245-47
Serial and Government Publications Division, Library of Congress, 134-35
Service Learning, National Center for, 162
Shipping, 97, 135-36, 245
Slavery, 109
Small Business Administration, 247-54
Smithsonian Environmental Research Center, 254
Smithsonian Institution Office of Elementary and Secondary Education, 254-55

Smithsonian Institution Press, 255
Smithsonian Institution Traveling Exhibition Service, 255-56
Smithsonian Institution Visitor Information and Associates' Reception Center, 256-57
Smoking and Health, Office on, 239
Social discrimination, 28-29, 37, 67
Social Security Administration, 257-58
Social studies, 5, 18-19, 51-52, 73-75, 131-32, 135-36, 269-71, 282-84. *See also* American Indians; Black studies; Current events; Economics; Environment; Geography; Government; History; International relations
   census figures, 16-18
   community development, 36, 41-42, 118-19, 288-89
   cultural activities and exhibitions, 255-56
   labor relations, 11-12, 47-48, 95-98, 196-99, 211
   military science, 49-51, 267-68
   Washington, DC, 6, 152-53
Social work education, 26-27, 114-15, 161-62, 230-31
Sociology, 16-18
Soil Conservation Service, 258-62
Space sciences. *See* Aerospace
Special education, 27, 115-17, 170, 188, 201-11, 217-18, 222, 241-44
Special libraries. *See also* Archives; *entries beginning* Library of Congress
   aerospace, 142
   agriculture, 142-43
   alcohol, 167
   audiovisual, 133-34, 145-47, 303-6
   civil rights, 29
   for the disabled, 201-11
   earth sciences, 280
   elections, 84
   government publications, 52-54
   interlibrary loan, 133
   labor and labor relations, 12, 227
   law, 238
   map, 133
   medicine, 199-201
   presidential, 234-35
   science and technology, 134, 220
   transportation, 75, 132
Speech handicaps, 194-95
Sportsmanship, 244-45
Stamps. *See* Postage stamps
Standards, National Bureau of, 147-52
State, Department of, 48-49
Statistics, 16-18, 33-36, 161
Stroke, 194-95
Student Financial Assistance, Office of, 236
Sudden Infant Death Syndrome Clearinghouse, National, 220

Talking books, 201-11
Taxes, 123-28
Technical Information Service, National, 220-22
Technical Institute for the Deaf, National, 222

Technology. *See* Science and technology
Technology Assessment, Office of, 236-37
Teeth, 190
Telephone communications systems, 80-81
Television, 80-81, 133-34
Tennessee Valley Authority, 262-64
Territorial and International Affairs, Office of, 237
Territories (U.S.), 237
Theater arts, 132-33
Tobacco, 7-9, 239
Trade Commission, Federal, 100-102
Trademarks, 36, 240-41
Traffic safety, 94, 179-84, 222-23
Transportation, 51-52, 94, 131-32, 222-23, 288-89
   accessibility for the disabled, 6-7
   of hazardous substances, 136-37
Transportation, Department of, 51-52
Transportation Safety Board, National, 222-23
Travel abroad, 239-40, 268-71, 282
Treasury, Department of the, 51
Treaties, 48-49

U.S. *See other part of title*
Unions. *See* Labor and labor relations
United Nations, 48-49, 282
Urban development, 41-42, 288-89
Urban Mass Transportation Administration, 288-89

Vaccinations. *See* Immunization programs
Veterinary medicine, 4-5

Washington, DC, 6, 27, 132-33, 152-53
Water resources, 15-16, 49, 213-16, 239, 245, 271-81, 289-90, 307-8
Water Resources Scientific Information Center, 289-90
Weather forecasting, 213-16, 223-24, 307-8
Weather Service, National, 223-24
Welfare services, 230-31
White House Office, The, 290
Wildlife management, 102, 224-25
Wildlife Refuges, National, 224-25
Women in Development, Office of, 238
Women's Bureau, 290-91
Women's Rights National Historic Park, 291
Women's studies, 25-26, 109
   business and economics, 238, 290-91
   history, 291
   rape, 161-62

X-rays. *See* Radiation biology